GAME
AI PRO

COLLECTED WISDOM
OF GAME AI
PROFESSIONALS

GAME AI PRO

COLLECTED WISDOM OF GAME AI PROFESSIONALS

EDITED BY
STEVEN RABIN

CRC Press
Taylor & Francis Group
Boca Raton London New York

CRC Press is an imprint of the
Taylor & Francis Group, an **informa** business

AN A K PETERS BOOK

CRC Press
Taylor & Francis Group
6000 Broken Sound Parkway NW, Suite 300
Boca Raton, FL 33487-2742

First issued in hardback 2019
First issued in paperback 2022

© 2014 by Taylor & Francis Group, LLC
CRC Press is an imprint of Taylor & Francis Group, an Informa business

No claim to original U.S. Government works

ISBN 13: 978-1-03-247745-9 (pbk)
ISBN 13: 978-1-4665-6596-8 (hbk)

DOI: 10.1201/b16725

Visit the Taylor & Francis Web site at
http://www.taylorandfrancis.com

and the CRC Press Web site at
http://www.crcpress.com

Contents

Part I   General Wisdom

Part II Architecture

Part III   Movement and Pathfinding

Part IV   Strategy and Tactics

Part V   Agent Awareness and Knowledge Representation

Part VI   Racing

Part VII   Odds and Ends

Preface

It has been 5 years since a book similar to this one has been released, and it is long overdue. After the end of the *AI Game Programming Wisdom* series in 2008, many of us who worked on these books refocused our effort toward building a community of game AI programmers by forming the AI Game Programmers Guild (www.gameai.com) and organizing the AI Summit at the annual Game Developers Conference. While these continue to be extremely worthwhile endeavors, it became obvious that something was just missing.

Although it appears that technical books might be on the decline with the exponential rise of information on the Internet, I think you'll agree that it's difficult to find high quality, detailed expert knowledge for a niche field such as game AI. The truth is that there are just not that many game AI experts in the world, relative to people in other fields. The AI Game Programmers Guild has a membership of over 350 professional game AI developers that it's been building over the last 5 years, so perhaps the number of total professional game AI developers in the world is double or triple that number. The reality is that it's a small world and to be able to get 54 of them to share their expertise with you within this one book is quite a gift that I'm extremely grateful for.

What I personally love about creating a book like this one is that it is a force multiplier. The knowledge and wisdom gained from one game can be shared with hundreds or thousands of other game developers by simply distilling the techniques and concepts onto the printed page. Knowledge and wisdom that might otherwise disappear or have to be reinvented is instead allowed to spread and pollinate within dozens or hundreds of other development studios and minds. We aren't forced to reinvent techniques and instead can stand on the shoulders of our peers.

Fortunately, the field is finally maturing and building up some solid institutional knowledge. Gone are the days of inventing everything from scratch. Nowadays, we build architectures based on well documented ideas like behavior trees and utility theory. We can leverage pathfinding knowledge and know-how that took dozens of years to figure out. Yet, there is still much to invent and many directions to explore. Hopefully, the contributions in this book will give you the leg up you need and the inspiration you crave.

Steve Rabin

Web Materials

Example programs and source code to accompany some of the chapters are available at http://www.gameaipro.com.

General System Requirements

The following is required to compile and execute the example programs:

- The DirectX August 2009 SDK
- DirectX 9.0 compatible or newer graphics card
- Windows 7 or newer
- Visual C++ .NET 2008 or newer

Updates

Updates of the example programs and source code will be updated as needed.

Comments and Suggestions

Please send any comments or suggestions to steve.rabin@gmail.com.

Web Materials

Acknowledgments

The *Game AI Pro: Collected Wisdom of Game AI Professionals* book series covers practical techniques and wisdom that can be applied to commercial game development.

This first book in the series required a huge team effort to make happen. First, I would like to humbly thank the six section editors for the excellent job they did in selecting, guiding, and editing the contributions in this book. The section editors were

- Neil Kirby—General Wisdom
- Dave Mark—Architecture
- Nathan Sturtevant—Movement and Pathfinding
- Kevin Dill—Strategy and Tactics, Odds and Ends
- Damián Isla—Agent Awareness and Knowledge Representation
- Simon Tomlinson—Racing

Additionally, I'd like to thank the assistant section editors that helped review and edit the contributions. Specifically, I'm extremely thankful to Luke Dicken, Paul Elliot, John Manslow, Bill Merrill, Ian Millington, Fernando Silva, and Vicky Smalley, who helped ensure the quality and integrity of this new book series.

The wonderful cover artwork has been provided courtesy of Square Enix and Gas Powered Games from the game *Supreme Commander 2*. Two chapters covering techniques from this game appear in this book: *Crowd Pathfinding and Steering Using Flow Field Tiles* and *Using Neural Networks to Control Agent Threat Response*.

The team at CRC Press and A K Peters have done an excellent job making this whole project happen. I want to thank Rick Adams, Kari Budyk, and the entire production team who took the contributions and carefully turned them into this book.

Special thanks go out to our families and friends, who have supported us and endured the intense production cycle that required long hours, evenings, and weekends.

The Editors

Kevin Dill is a member of the Group Technical Staff at Lockheed Martin Global Training and Logistics, and chief architect of the Game AI Architecture. He is a veteran of the game industry, with seven published titles under his belt, including *Red Dead Redemption, Iron Man, Zoo Tycoon 2: Marine Mania, Zoo Tycoon 2: Endangered Species, Axis & Allies, Kohan 2: Kings of War,* and *Master of Orion 3.* Kevin was the technical editor for *Introduction to Game AI* and *Behavioral Mathematics for Game AI,* and a section editor for *AI Game Programming Wisdom 4* and the book you hold in your hands. He is a frequent speaker at conferences such as I/ITSEC and GDC, and has taught classes on game development and game AI at Harvard University, Boston University, Worcester Polytechnic Institute, and Northeastern University.

Damián Isla has been working on and writing about game technology for over a decade. He is president and cofounder of Moonshot Games, a studio dedicated to the creation of downloadable and mobile games with triple-A production values and technology. Before Moonshot, Damián was AI and Gameplay engineering lead at Bungie Studios, where he was responsible for the AI for the mega-hit first-person shooters *Halo 2* and *Halo 3.* A leading expert in the field of AI for Games, Damián has spoken on games, AI, and character technology at the International Joint Conference on Artificial Intelligence (IJCAI), at the AI and Interactive Digital Entertainment Conference (AIIDE), and at Siggraph, and is a frequent speaker at the Game Developers Conference (GDC). Before joining the industry, Damián earned a master's degree at the Massachusetts Institute of Technology Media Lab, where he did research on learning and behavior for synthetic characters. He holds a BS in computer science, also from MIT.

Neil Kirby is a member of the technical staff at Bell Laboratories, the R&D arm of Alcatel-Lucent. He is the author of *An Introduction to Game AI,* and his other publications include articles in volumes I, II, and IV of *AI Game Programming Wisdom.* His 1991 paper "Artificial Intelligence Without AI: An Evolutionary Approach" may well show the first use of what is now known as "circle strafing" in a game. His other papers and presentations can be found in the proceedings of the Computer Game Developers Conference from 1991 to present as well as the 2003 Australian Game Developers Conference. Neil holds a master's degree in computer science from Ohio State University. He was a driving force behind the creation of the IGDA Foundation and serves on its board.

Dave Mark is the president and lead designer of Intrinsic Algorithm, LLC, an independent game development studio and AI consulting company in Omaha, Nebraska. He is the author of the book *Behavioral Mathematics for Game AI* and is a contributor to the *AI Game Programming Wisdom* and *Game Programming Gems* book series. Dave is also a founding member of the AI Game Programmers Guild and coadvisor of the annual GDC AI Summit. Dave continues to further his education by attending the University of Life. He has no plans to graduate any time soon.

Steve Rabin is a principal software engineer at Nintendo of America, where he researches new techniques for Nintendo's current and future platforms, architects development tools such as the Wii U CPU Profiler, and supports Nintendo developers. Before Nintendo, Steve worked primarily as an AI engineer at several Seattle start-ups including Gas Powered Games, WizBang Software Productions, and Surreal Software. He organized and edited the *AI Game Programming Wisdom* series of books, the book *Introduction to Game Development*, and has over two dozen articles published in the *Game Programming Gems* series. He's been an invited keynote speaker at several academic AI conferences, spoken at the Game Developers Conference, and spoken at numerous Nintendo development conferences in North America and Europe. He organizes the 2-day AI Summit at GDC and has moderated the AI roundtables. Steve founded and manages the professional group known as the AI Game Programmers Guild, with over 350 members worldwide. He has also taught game AI at the DigiPen Institute of Technology for the last 8 years and has earned a BS in computer engineering and an MS in computer science, both from the University of Washington.

Nathan Sturtevant is a professor of computer science at the University of Denver, working on AI and games. He began his games career working on shareware games as a college student, writing the popular Mac tank game *Dome Wars* in the mid-90s, and returned to the games industry to write the pathfinding engine for *Dragon Age: Origins*. Nathan continues to develop games in his free time, and is currently porting *Dome Wars* to iOS.

Simon Tomlinson, PhD, studied physics at Manchester University in England and went on to gain a PhD in electrical engineering and to work as a research fellow in electronic applications and computational physics. In 1997 he joined the games industry as an AI programmer. He has worked on a variety of platforms and projects including billiard games, flight and space combat, racing games, FPS combat, and card games, including Poker. He has also worked as project lead on mobile Java platforms and had occasional forays into production and R&D. He has retained his academic interests with several game related publications and presentations in the UK and has assisted local academia in starting and running game programming courses. In 2008 he formed his own consultancy company, S1m On Ltd, and has most recently contributed to the highly acclaimed *Need for Speed Shift* series under a contract for Slightly Mad Studios.

The Contributors

Bobby Anguelov works as an AI/animation programmer at Io Interactive, where he focuses on low-level locomotion and behavior frameworks. He earned an MSc in computer science from the University of Pretoria, South Africa, and spent the first part of his career working in enterprise software. This was followed by a 2-year stint teaching graphics programming at a university before moving to Denmark to pursue his lifelong dream of working in games. He's currently working on building a new behavior-authoring framework for the *Glacier 2* game engine while trying to catch up on the latest animation techniques in his spare time. In his less busy past, he used to regularly update his tech blog at www.takinginitiative.net.

Tomasz Bednarz is a computational research scientist and project leader at CSIRO's Division of Mathematics, Informatics, and Statistics (www.csiro.au/cmis). He is active in the computational simulation sciences where heterogeneous architectures play an essential role in speeding up computationally expensive scientific code. He coorganizes the Sydney GPU Meetup (http://www.meetup.com/Sydney-GPU-Users/) and also the OzViz workshops (https://sites.google.com/site/ozvizworkshop/).

Doug Binks makes games at Enkisoftware Limited, having recently left his position as technical lead of Games Architecture Initiative at Intel. Prior to joining Intel in 2008 he worked in the games industry in roles ranging from lead programmer, head of studio at Strangelite, and R&D development manager at Crytek. Despite an early interest in games development, Doug careered sideways into a doctorate in physics at Oxford University, and undertook two postdoctoral posts as an academic researcher in experimental nonlinear pattern formation, specializing in fluid mechanics. His earliest memories are of programming games in assembly on the ZX81.

Stephen Bjore graduated from Washington State University with a bachelor's degree in computer science, and later acquired a BS in real-time interactive simulation from DigiPen

Institute of Technology. After graduating, he spent 2 years working at Wizards of the Coast, initially on various video game prototypes and later on the server side for *Magic the Gathering Online*. In 2008, he moved to Nintendo of America, where he became a part of its Software Development Support Group. After several years with SDSG, he switched over to an internal development group which has been working on 3DS and Wii-U projects.

Conan Bourke is a senior programming lecturer at the Academy of Interactive Entertainment's Sydney campus in Australia. His main role is teaching software engineering for all aspects of interactive media with his passions lying in graphics and AI programming. Prior to teaching he worked for Blue Tongue Entertainment Pty Ltd, an in-house studio for THQ, as a gameplay programmer on multiple systems and numerous cross-platform titles.

Daniel Brewer graduated from the University of Natal–Durban, South Africa, in 2000 with a BScEng in electronic engineering focusing on artificial intelligence, control systems, and data communications. He worked at Cathexis Technologies for 6 years, as a software engineer writing software for digital surveillance systems, responsible for operating system drivers for PCI video capture cards, image capture scheduling, video compression, and image processing algorithms such as motion detection, people counting, and visual camera tamper detection. He moved to Digital Extremes in 2007 where he is the lead AI programmer and has worked on several titles including *Dark Sector* (March 2008), *BioShock 2* multiplayer (February 2010), and *The Darkness II* (February 2012).

Phil Carlisle is an independent game developer at MindFlock Ltd and a senior lecturer in videogame design and development at the University of Bolton in England. Prior to setting up MindFlock, Phil was responsible for game programming duties on numerous titles in the "Worms" franchise for Team17 Ltd. Phil is a great believer in iterative prototype game development and a rabid observer of human behaviors.

Alex Champandard is the founder of AiGameDev.com, the largest online hub for artificial intelligence in games. He has worked in industry as a senior AI programmer for many years, most notably for Rockstar Games where he also worked on the animation technology of *Max Payne 3*. He regularly consults with leading studios in Europe, most notably at Guerrilla Games on the multiplayer bots for *KillZone 2 & 3*. Alex is also the event director for the Game/AI Conference, the largest independent event dedicated to AI in games.

Jarosław Ciupiński knew what he wanted to do with his life when he turned 9 years old. While he was coding since then, he started to work professionally in game development in 2007 as an animation programmer. In 2012 he still sees many things that can be improved in the field of animation in game development.

Carle Côté has been a senior AI programmer at Eidos Montreal since 2009 and currently leads the AI development on the next *Thief* game. In 2012, he received his PhD in electrical engineering applied to AI and robotics from Sherbrooke University in Canada. His focus is mainly on decision-making systems and cognitive AI.

Michael Dawe has been programming AI in the games industry since 2007 and worked at Big Huge Games on NPC behavior for *Kingdoms of Amalur: Reckoning*. He has spoken numerous times at the AI Summit at the Game Developer's Conference, is a founding member of the AI Game Programmer's Guild, and has previously written for the *Game Programming Gems* series. Michael holds an MS in computer science from DigiPen Institute of Technology, as well as bachelor of science degrees in computer science and philosophy from Rensselaer Polytechnic Institute.

Luke Dicken is the founder of Robot Overlord Games, and a researcher with the Strathclyde Artificial Intelligence and Games group at the University of Strathclyde in the United Kingdom. He contributes to AltDevBlogADay and is a principal organizer for the AltDev Conference family. Luke has been passionate about artificial intelligence since playing *Creatures* as a teenager, and pursued it in college, first through several degrees in traditional AI before specializing in AI for games as part of a PhD he is still (occasionally) pursuing. Luke is a member of the AI Game Programmers Guild, on the board of directors for IGDA Scotland, and recently took over as chair of the IGDA's Special Interest Group on AI.

Kevin Dill is a member of the Group Technical Staff at Lockheed Martin Global Training and Logistics, and the chief architect of the Game AI Architecture. He is a veteran of the game industry, with seven published titles under his belt, including *Red Dead Redemption*, *Iron Man*, *Zoo Tycoon 2: Marine Mania*, *Zoo Tycoon 2: Endangered Species*, *Axis & Allies*, *Kohan 2: Kings of War*, and *Master of Orion 3*. Kevin was the technical editor for *Introduction to Game AI* and *Behavioral Mathematics for Game AI*, and a section editor for *AI Game Programming Wisdom 4* and the book you hold in your hands. He is a frequent speaker at conferences such as I/ITSEC and GDC, and has taught classes on game development and game AI at Harvard University, Boston University, Worcester Polytechnic Institute, and Northeastern University.

Philip Dunstan, as a senior AI R&D engineer at AiGameDev.com, prototypes cutting-edge solutions to the artificial intelligence challenges found in today's games. In addition, Philip has 6 years of development experience within Electronic Arts' EATech Central Technology Group. As a specialist in physics simulation, core technology, and console performance, he worked on several of EA's biggest franchises including *FIFA*, *Need for Speed*, *Battlefield*, and *Harry Potter*.

Elijah Emerson started his lifelong dream of creating video games in his childhood, creating games on paper for friends and family to play. Since then, every step in his life was toward that singular goal of creating new and creative game experiences for others to enjoy. After obtaining a BS in real-time interactive simulation from Digipen Institute of Technology, he began work as a game programming teacher for Digipen. A year later he went to Amaze Entertainment to work on *Harry Potter 2*. After that he moved to Gas Powered Games to work on *Dungeon Siege 2*, *Supreme Commander 1* and *2*, *Age of Empires Online*, and other unannounced titles over the last 12 years. He currently works at Gas Powered Games as the lead engineer on an unannounced project.

Simon Franco started programming on the Commodore Amiga by writing a *Pong* clone in AMOS and has been coding ever since. He joined the games industry in 2000, after completing a degree in computer science. He started at The Creative Assembly in 2004, where he has been to this day. When he's not keeping his daughter entertained, he'll be playing the latest game or writing games in assembly code for the ZX Spectrum.

Steve Gargolinski has been working on games professionally since 2003, spending time at Blue Fang Games, Rockstar New England, and 38 Studios. Steve has a strong technical background, and enjoys thinking, writing, and speaking about game AI, programming, and the development process. He has presented at conferences such as the Game Developers Conference (GDC) and the AI and Interactive Digital Entertainment Conference (AIIDE), and has been interviewed by *The Independent* and *Gamasutra* for his work in gaming AI. While not programming computers Steve enjoys nonfiction, cooking, hockey, and walking in the woods.

Jay Goldblatt is a programmer at Nintendo Technology Development and contributed to the hardware launch of the Wii U. He earned an MS in computer science from the DigiPen Institute of Technology, where he helped TA the artificial intelligence class for over a year. Jay also earned a BS in computer science from Lawrence University.

David "Rez" Graham is an AI programmer at Electronic Arts, working at Maxis on *The Sims* team. His most recent game was *The Sims Medieval* and the *Pirates & Nobles* expansion. Rez is currently the lead AI programmer on an upcoming *Sims* title. He has worked in the games industry as an engineer since 2005 spending most of that time working on various kinds of AI, from platformer enemy AI to full simulation games. He is the coauthor of *Game Coding Complete, 4th Edition,* and regularly speaks at the Game Developers Conference, as well as various colleges and high schools. Rez spends his free time performing improv, running tabletop RPGs, and dyeing his hair shades of blue.

Fabien Gravot made his debut in the game industry in 2011 as AI researcher with SQUARE ENIX. Previously, he had been working on robot AI and autonomous driving. He thought that games were less risky than moving one ton of metal with his program. He received his PhD in computer science from the University Paul Sabatier in France in 2004.

D. Hunter Hale, PhD, completed his doctoral work at the University of North Carolina at Charlotte in 2011. He has been a research assistant in the Game Intelligence Group in the Games + Learning Lab for the last 4 years; prior to that he was a research assistant in the Visualization Lab at UNC–Charlotte while completing his master's degree. He received his bachelor's degree with honors from Western Carolina University in 2005.

Daniel Hilburn has been making video games since 2007. He has worked on several console games including *Kinect Star Wars*™, *Ghostbusters: The Video Game*™, and *DefJam's Rapstar*™. He currently works in Irving, Texas, at Terminal Reality, Inc.

Troy Humphreys has been involved in game mechanics and AI since 2005. Since then, he has worked on the games *The Bourne Conspiracy*, *Transformers: War for Cybertron*, and *Transformers: Fall of Cybertron*. He currently works as a senior programmer at High Moon Studios, where he helps lead the studio's AI development. Prior to working on games, he taught game development as an Associate Course Director at Full Sail, where he still serves as an adviser.

Matthew Jack founded Moon Collider (www.mooncollider.com) in 2010, where he consults on AI for companies in the US and Europe and builds bespoke AI systems. He specializes in *CryEngine 3* and *Recast/Detour*. He developed AI at Crytek for many years in a senior R&D role, including work on *Crysis* and *Crysis 2*. He has since worked for Microsoft and AiGameDev.com, and consulted for games and serious games companies. Clients include Xaviant LLC and Enodo, with products delivered to companies such as BMW. He has written for *Games Programming Gems* and presented at the GDC, Paris Game AI Conference, Develop and at Google.

Hylke Kleve (hylke.kleve@guerrilla-games.com) is principal AI programmer at Guerrilla Games, where he has worked on *Killzone 2* and *Killzone 3*. He developed planning and pathfinding technology. Hylke Kleve holds an MS in computer science (2003) from the University of Groningen, the Netherlands.

Brett Laming has now been in the industry for more years than anyone should care to remember. He currently finds himself in the enviable role of leading the full range of technical teams at Rockstar Leeds. Critical-thinking skills matured by years of AI, gameplay, and engine programming now drive much wider development, production, and management arenas—skills that see *LA Noire* join a portfolio of titles that span Rockstar Games, Criterion, Argonaut, and Particle Systems. His long-suffering partner Katherine continues to be exasperated by a heavy bias towards game development over that of DIY.

Mike Lewis broke into the game industry as an AI and gameplay programmer in early 2002. He has since shipped three successful titles with Egosoft GmbH in the "*X Series*," and designed AI systems instrumental to a fourth, as-yet unreleased title. Today, he calls ArenaNet, Inc., home, where he plots incessantly to unleash bigger, better, and more entertaining AI upon the realm of massively multiplayer online gaming.

Dave Mark is the president and lead designer of Intrinsic Algorithm, LLC, an independent game development studio and AI consulting company in Omaha, Nebraska. He is the author of the book *Behavioral Mathematics for Game AI* and is a contributor to the *AI Game Programming Wisdom* and *Game Programming Gems* book series. Dave is also a founding member of the AI Game Programmers Guild and coadvisor of the annual GDC AI Summit. Dave continues to further his education by attending the University of Life. He has no plans to graduate any time soon.

Eric Martel began his career in the games industry in 2001 when he joined Microids to work on the acclaimed adventure games series *Syberia*. In 2004 he joined Ubisoft Montreal where he had the opportunity to work on *FarCry: Instincts* and *Assassin's Creed*. He then joined GRIP Entertainment (now Autodesk) in 2007 to shape the development of its *Digital Extra System* and finally moved to Eidos Montreal in 2008 to work on *Thief 4*.

He also had the pleasure to be the technical reviewer for Mat Buckland's book *Game AI by Example* and wrote an article for *AI Game Programming Wisdom 3* on the anchor system in *FarCry: Instinct*.

Michael Mateas is the codirector of Expressive Intelligence Studio and director of the Center for Games and Playable Media at the University of California–Santa Cruz. His research in game AI focuses on enabling new forms of gameplay through innovative AI solutions. The Expressive Intelligence Studio has ongoing projects in autonomous characters, interactive storytelling, game design support systems, AI models of creativity, and automated game generation. With Andrew Stern, Michael created *Façade*, which uses AI techniques to combine rich autonomous characters with interactive plot control to create the world's first, fully-produced, real-time, interactive drama. Michael received his PhD in computer science from Carnegie Mellon University.

Josh McCoy recently completed his PhD in Computer Science in the Expressive Intelligence Studio at the University of California–Santa Cruz. Coming to UC–Santa Cruz with a dual background in computer science and sociology, his PhD dissertation was on social simulation. He was the lead developer of the CiF architecture, and a core team member in the creation of *Prom Week*. Josh is currently a postdoc at UC–Santa Cruz in the Center for Games and Playable Media, where he is working on extending CiF to support real-time first-person character performance.

Dr. Nic Melder, prior to attending university, worked for a global bank designing and implementing their payment and query systems. Upon graduating with a BSc in cybernetics and control engineering, instead of doing the sensible thing and getting a "real" job, he entered the games industry as an AI programmer. After working on some predator–prey simulations and a third-person action title, he returned to academia for 5 years to conduct research in multifingered haptics before taking up a position as an AI programmer at Codemasters. Over 6 years later, Nic has worked on the hugely successful *DiRT*, *GRID*, and *F1* titles and is now lead AI programmer within the racing studio. However, even after spending over 6 years making racing games, Nic is still regarded as the worst driver in the studio!

Bill Merrill is the AI lead at Turtle Rock Studios working hard on an unannounced project, having previously worked as AI lead and senior generalist at Double Helix Games, shipping cross-platform game projects including *Dirty Harry*, *Silent Hill: Homecoming*, *Front Mission: Evolved*, and various tools and demos. He currently splits his time between technology and toddlers.

Brook Miles was inspired by games like *SimCity 2000* and the *King's Quest* series, and began teaching himself C++ while in high school. Shortly after graduating he was interviewed and hired on an EFNet IRC channel to work remotely for a Silicon Valley startup during the rise of the dot-com bubble. After the bubble burst, he dabbled in enterprise software before finally getting his break into game development at EA Black Box in 2006 where he worked on *Skate* and *Need For Speed: Undercover*. Brook joined Klei Entertainment in early 2011 to work on *Mark of the Ninja*, because … you know … Ninjas.

Youichiro Miyake is the lead AI researcher at SQUARE ENIX, working as leader of the AI unit for the next-generation game engine, Luminous Studio. He is chairman of IGDA JAPAN SIG-AI and a member of the committee of DiGRA JAPAN. He has been developing and researching game AI since 2004. He developed the technical design of AI for the following game titles: *CHROME HOUNDS* (2006, Xbox360), *Demon's Souls* (2009, PlayStation3), and *Armored Core V* (2012, Xbox360, PlayStation3) developed by FROM SOFTWARE. He has published several papers and books about game AI technologies as well as given many lectures at universities and conferences. He was a keynote speaker of GAMEON ASIA 2012.

Robert Morcus is a senior AI developer at Guerrilla Games. There, he has helped build the tools and technology for most titles released by Guerrilla Games: *ShellShock:Nam'67*, *Killzone, Killzone 2*, and *Killzone 3*. His field of interest before starting game development was in electronics and audio synthesis / signal processing.

Graham Pentheny leads AI development at Subatomic Studios in Cambridge, Massachusetts, where he recently worked on the iOS games *Fieldrunners* and *Fieldrunners 2*. He received a BS in computer science and a BS in interactive media and game development from Worcester Polytechnic Institute. In his spare time he reads an unhealthy number of books on AI and programming language theory and is an avid musician.

Steve Rabin is a principal software engineer at Nintendo of America, where he researches new techniques for Nintendo's current and future platforms, architects development tools such as the Wii U CPU Profiler, and supports Nintendo developers. Before Nintendo, Steve worked primarily as an AI engineer at several Seattle start-ups including Gas Powered Games, WizBang Software Productions, and Surreal Software. He organized and edited the *AI Game Programming Wisdom* series of books, the book *Introduction to Game Development*, and has over two dozen articles published in the *Game Programming Gems* series. He's been an invited keynote speaker at several academic AI conferences, presented at the Game Developers Conference, and spoken at numerous Nintendo development conferences in North America and Europe. He organizes the 2-day AI Summit at GDC and has moderated the AI roundtables. Steve founded and manages the professional group known as the AI Game Programmers Guild, with over 350 members worldwide. He has also taught game AI at the DigiPen Institute of Technology for the last 8 years and has earned a BS in computer engineering and a MS in computer science, both from the University of Washington.

Mike Ramsey is the principle programmer on the *Noumena AI Engine*. Mike has developed core technologies for the Xbox 360, PC, and Wii at various companies, including a handful of shipped games: *World of Zoo* (PC and Wii), *Men of Valor* (Xbox and PC), *Master of the Empire, Second Life*, and several *Zoo Tycoon 2* products. Mike has contributed multiple articles to the *Game Programming Gems, AI Game Programming Wisdom*, and the *Game Engine Gems* series, as well as presented at the AIIDE conference at Stanford on uniform spatial representations for dynamic environments. Mike has a BS in computer science from MSCD and his forthcoming book is titled *A Practical Cognitive Engine for AI*.

When Mike isn't working he enjoys long walks in the Massachusetts countryside with his wife, daughter, and their dog, Rose!

Michael Robbins is a gameplay engineer with Gas Powered Games working on everything from UI to AI. He has been working in the industry since 2009, after being a long time member of the Gas Powered Games modeling community. His most notable work is featured in the AI of *Supreme Commander 2*, released in March 2010.

Fernando Silva is a software engineer at Nintendo of America, providing engineering support to licensed game developers and internal groups, specializing on the Nintendo Wii U platform. He completed an undergraduate degree in computer science in real-time interactive simulation at DigiPen Institute of Technology, where he minored in mathematics. He also develops tools for current and next-gen Nintendo platforms. In his free time, Fernando enjoys working on electronic projects with a focus on the Arduino platform, reverse engineering processes or devices, studying biological processes that can be applied to computer science, and most importantly, dining.

Remco Straatman for 10 years led the AI coding team at Guerrilla, and developed AI for *ShellShock:Nam67, Killzone, Killzone:Liberation, Killzone 2*, and *Killzone 3*. Currently, Remco is feature architect and leads a game code team at Guerrilla. Before joining Guerrilla, Remco worked as a researcher in the field of expert systems and machine learning, and as developer of multimedia software. He holds an MS in computer science (1991) from the University of Amsterdam.

William van der Sterren is an AI consultant for games and simulations at CGF-AI. He worked on the AI of Guerrilla Games' *Killzone* and *Shellshock Nam'67* games. William has spoken at the Game Developer Conference and AIGameDev conference, and has contributed chapters to both the *Game Programming Gems* and *AI Game Programming Wisdom* series. His interest is in creating tactical behaviors, from tactical path-finding and terrain analysis to squad behaviors and company level maneuver planning. William holds an MSc in computer science from University of Twente and a PDEng Software Technology from Eindhoven University of Technology.

Nathan Sturtevant is a professor of computer science at the University of Denver, working on AI and games. He began his games career working on shareware games as a college student, writing the popular Mac tank game *Dome Wars* in the mid-90s, and returned to the games industry to write the pathfinding engine for *Dragon Age: Origins*. Nathan continues to develop games in his free time, and is currently porting *Dome Wars* to iOS.

Ben Sunshine-Hill received a PhD in computer science from the University of Pennsylvania for his work in video game-focused computational techniques. Since then, he has been a software developer at Havok.

Simon Tomlinson, PhD, studied physics at Manchester University in the United Kingdom and went on to gain a PhD in electrical engineering and to work as a research fellow in electronic applications and computational physics. In 1997 he joined the games industry as an AI programmer. He has worked on a variety of platforms and projects including billiard games, flight and space combat, racing games, FPS combat, and card games, including poker. He has also worked as project lead on mobile Java platforms and had occasional forays into production and R&D. He has retained his academic interests with several game-related publications and presentations in the UK and has assisted local academia in starting and running game programming courses. In 2008 he formed his own consultancy company, S1m On Ltd., and has most recently contributed to the highly acclaimed *Need for Speed Shift* series under a contract for Slightly Mad Studios.

Joseph Vasquez II provides engineering support to third party developers and internal groups at Nintendo, specializing in the Nintendo 3DS platform. He completed an under-graduate degree in real-time interactive simulation at DigiPen Institute of Technology, where he minored in computer engineering and codeveloped the Augger: a handheld game system with augmented reality features. He also wrote the AI for all of his game projects. He is currently finishing a master's of computer science at DigiPen. When he is not doing homework or hiking with his wife and dog in the beautiful Northwest, he enjoys going to work.

Tim Johan Verweij is a senior AI programmer at Guerrilla, Amsterdam, The Netherlands. The past six years he has worked on AI technology and AI behaviors for *Killzone 2* and *Killzone 3*, both first-person shooters for the Playstation 3. He studied AI at VU University, Amsterdam. For his master's thesis he did a research project on multiplayer bot AI at Guerrilla.

Rich Welsh, after graduating from Durham University and moving abroad to teach games development in a Californian summer camp, returned back to his hometown of Newcastle to work on PC games at Virtual Playground. While the team there taught him a lot about both programming and the games industry, he eventually left in order to pursue the chance of working on AAA titles. Rich has been programming professionally for the games industry for over 5 years with a focus on AI, and has worked on the following titles to date: *Crackdown 2, Crysis* for Console, *Crysis 2, Crysis 3*, and *Homefront 2*.

Will Wilson recently founded Indefiant Ltd. in order to focus on developing software and consulting for improving the iteration times and reducing costs in game develop-ment and testing. His 10 years in the games industry includes being lead programmer at Firefly Studios and senior programmer at Crytek, where he worked on *Crysis 2* and the *Crysis* console conversion. At Crytek he developed the SoftCoding implementation for the CryENGINE 3 for use in *Ryse* and *Crysis 3*.

Takanori Yokoyama has worked as a game programmer in the game industry since 2004. He has been especially interested in game AI and implemented it for many game titles: *ENCHANT ARMS* (2006, Xbox360), *CHROME HOUNDS* (2006, Xbox360), and *Demon's Souls* (2009, PlayStation3) developed by FROM SOFTWARE. Now he is working as an AI engineer at SQUARE ENIX.

G. Michael Youngblood, PhD, is an associate professor of computer science at the University of North Carolina at Charlotte. He is codirector of the Games + Learning Lab and head of the Game Intelligence Group, which conducts research on and builds systems involving interactive artificial intelligence in the games and simulation domains, focusing on character behaviors, creation, and analysis. He has published over 60 scholarly papers on topics of interactive artificial intelligence and support technologies. More information about him can be seen on his website at gmichaelyoungblood.com.

Mieszko Zielinski, People Can Fly Senior AI programmer, has been developing games for nearly a decade. He found his game industry calling in 2003, when he joined a little known studio, Aidem Media, to get his foot in the door. Since then, Zielinski has worked at CD Projekt Red, Crytek, and People Can Fly, where he developed the AI system for *Bulletstorm* almost from scratch, with a team of great programmers. He is currently developing AI system elements for Epic Games' *Unreal Engine 4*. Also, he's a retired Polish national kickboxing champion, so don't mess with him!

PART I
General Wisdom

1

What Is Game AI?

Kevin Dill

1.1 Introduction

Game AI should be about one thing and one thing only: enabling the developers to create a compelling experience for the player. Every technique we use, every trick we play, every algorithm we encode, all should be in support of that single goal.

Wikipedia gives the following as a definition for artificial intelligence (or AI): "the study and design of intelligent agents," where an intelligent agent is "a system that perceives its environment and takes actions that maximize its chances of success" [Wikipedia 12-A]. This is certainly not the only definition for the term—"artificial intelligence" is a term that is notoriously difficult to define—but it does accurately describe much of AI as it is researched and taught in our universities. We will use the term *academic AI* to describe AI as it is commonly taught today.

Film animators often describe the artificial life which they create as the *illusion of life*—a phrase which is believed to have originated with Walt Disney. This is a very different goal. The characters in a cartoon don't necessarily "take actions that maximize their chances of success"; Wile E. Coyote, for example, does just the opposite much of the time. Instead, they seek to engender in the viewer a gut-level belief in their reality (despite the fact that they are obviously artificial), and to create a compelling experience, which is what movies are all about.

Every game is different, and the AI needs for games vary widely. With that said, the goals for a game's AI generally have much more in common with Disney's view of artificial life than with a classic academic view of AI. Like cartoons, games are created for entertainment. Like cartoons, games are not about success maximization, cognitive modeling, or real intelligence, but rather about telling a story, creating an experience, creating the *illusion of intelligence* [Adams 99]. In some cases, the techniques that we need in order to create this illusion can be drawn from academic AI, but in many cases they differ. We use the term *game AI* to describe AI, which is focused on creating the appearance of intelligence, and on creating a particular experience for the viewer, rather than being focused on creating true intelligence as it exists in human beings.

1.2 Creating an Experience

It is often said that rather than maximizing the chances of success, the goal of game AI is to maximize the player's fun. This certainly *can* be the goal of AI, but it probably isn't the best definition. For one thing, much like the term AI, "fun" is a word that is notoriously hard to define. For another, not all games are about fun. Some games are about telling a story, or about the really cool characters that they contain. Others are about creating a sense of excitement, adventure, suspense, or even fear (like a horror movie). Still others are about giving the player a sense of empowerment, making him (or her) feel like "The Man."

The one thing that is universally true is that games are about creating a particular experience for the player—whatever that experience may be. The purpose of Game AI (and every other part of a game, for that matter) is to support that experience. As a consequence, the techniques that are appropriate for use are simply those that best bring about the desired experience—nothing more, nothing less.

1.2.1 Suspension of Disbelief

Players are willing participants in the experience that we are creating for them. They want to buy in to our illusion, and so willingly suspend the natural disbelief they would normally feel for such obviously artificial characters and events. With that said, it is our responsibility to provide an illusion that is sufficiently compelling to enable them to do this—that is, to maintain the player's *suspension of disbelief*. We succeed any time that the user thinks about and responds to the AI as if it were real, even if the underlying algorithm is actually quite simple. We fail any time that some action (or inaction) on the part of the AI reminds the user that the AI is only a machine program, not real. ELIZA—an AI psychologist developed by Joseph Weizenbaum in 1964 [Wikipedia 12-B]—exemplifies both how easy it can be to capture the player's belief with a simple algorithm, and how quickly you can lose that belief when the algorithm misbehaves.

Because they are willing participants in the experience, and because of the way the human mind works, players are actually quite forgiving. As long as the AI produces behavior that is basically reasonable, the player's mind will come up with explanations for the AI's decisions, that are often quite complex—much more complex than what is really going on inside of the AI—but also fundamentally compelling and believable. In fact, to some extent it can be a mistake to build an AI that thinks too hard. Not only can it be a waste of precious developer hours to overengineer your AI, but it can also result in a character that will perform actions that, while sensible to the AI, don't match the player's mental model of what the AI is doing. In other words, the actions make sense if you know what the AI is thinking—but, of course, the player can't know that. As a result, those carefully chosen decisions end up looking random or just plain wrong.

The one thing that we absolutely must avoid at all costs is *artificial stupidity*—that is, selecting an action that looks obviously wrong or just doesn't make any sense. Common examples are things like walking into walls, getting stuck in the geometry, or ignoring a player that is shooting at you. Even some behaviors that actual humans would display should be avoided, because those behaviors *appear* inhuman when performed by an AI-controlled character. For example, humans quite frequently change their minds—but when an AI does so, it often gives the impression of a faulty algorithm rather than a reevaluation of the situation.

One solution to the problem of artificial stupidity is simply to make the AI better—but player expectations can be so diverse that it is hard to meet all of them all of the time. As a result, a variety of other approaches have been used. In some games—zombie games are a good example of this—the characters are deliberately made to be a little bit stupid or wonky, so that their strangeness will be more acceptable. In others, the characters use short spoken lines, sometimes called "barks," to clue the player in to what's going on. For example, they might yell "Grenade!" or "I'm hit!" These aren't really used to communicate with other AI characters (we do that by passing messages in the code), but rather to explain their actions to the player. Some games (such as *The Sims* or *Zoo Tycoon*) go so far as to put icons over the characters' heads, signaling what's going on internally. *Creatures*, a game still known 15 years after its release for its ground-breaking AI, even used a "puzzled" icon when a creature changed its mind, to show that the resulting change in behavior was deliberate.

1.2.2 Reactivity, Nondeterminism, and Authorial Control

Much discussion has been given to the various architectures and which is the best for game AI. Indeed, an entire section of this book is dedicated to that purpose. The first thought that one might draw from Academic AI is to build an AI with a heuristic definition of the desired experience, and then use machine learning to optimize for that experience. There are several problems with this approach, but the most obvious is that the experience is typically something defined by a game designer—who may or may not be a programmer—using squishy human language terms. How do you write a heuristic function to maximize "fun" or "excitement" or "cool attitude?"

That isn't to say that heuristic functions are useless—in fact, utility-based approaches to AI are one of the more common approaches, particularly for games with more complex decision making (e.g., strategy games, and simulation games like *The Sims* or *Zoo Tycoon*). It is critical, however, to retain *authorial control*—which is, to say, to ensure that the AI's author can tune and tweak the AI so as to ensure that the desired experience is achieved. If we relinquish that control to a machine learning algorithm, it becomes much more difficult to ensure that we get the results we want.

There is a competing need, however, which is that we want our characters to be *reactive*—that is, able to sense the environment and select actions that are appropriate to the subtle, moment-to-moment nuance of the in-game situation. Reactivity and authorial control are not mutually exclusive. You can build a system that is reactive, but because you control the way that it evaluates the situation when making its decisions it still provides authorial control. Controlling a reactive AI is more complex, however, because you as the developer have to think through how your changes will alter the AI's decision making, rather than simply changing what the character does directly

There isn't a single right answer here. Some games (such as strategy games or games like *The Sims*) require more reactivity, while other games (such as *World of Warcraft*) make a deliberate design decision to have a more heavily scripted AI that delivers a carefully

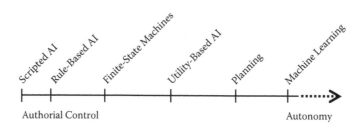

Figure 1.1

The tradeoff between authorial control and reactivity for certain popular AI architectures.

crafted—but highly predictable—experience to the player. Neither is wrong—there are excellent games of each type—but the experience being delivered is different, and that's something that you need to think about when choosing your approach to AI.

There are a variety of architectures that are popular for game AI, many of which are discussed later in this book. Some provide better reactivity, while others allow more direct authorial control. Figure 1.1 shows a rough graph that gives some indication of this tradeoff for several of the most popular game AI architectures. Bear in mind, however, that each architecture has its own advantages, disadvantages, and idiosyncrasies. This is intended as a rough guideline only.

Of note, machine learning is placed on the graph merely due to its popularity in academic circles. Very few games have used machine learning for their core AI. Also, behavior trees have been deliberately omitted from this graph. This is because the performance of a behavior tree depends greatly on the types of decision-making components that are used. If these components are all simple, such as those originally envisioned by Damian Isla [Isla 05], then behavior trees fall in much the same space as finite-state machines. One of the great strengths of a behavior tree, however, is that each node can contain whatever decision-making logic best fits, allowing you to use the most appropriate architecture for each individual decision.

Another complicating factor when selecting an AI architecture is nondeterminism. For many games, we want to add a certain amount of randomness to our characters, so that they won't be predictable (and quite possible exploitable) by the player. At the same time, we don't want the AI to pick an action that is obviously wrong, so we need to ensure that our random choices are all still reasonable. Some architectures are more conducive to adding a bit of randomness into the mix (in particular, behavior trees and utility-based architectures handle this well), so that is another factor that you may need to take into account when designing your game.

1.2.3 Simplicity and Scalability

Both the need for authorial control and the avoidance of artificial stupidity require that the configuration of game AI be an iterative process. Configuring an AI so that it will handle every possible situation—or at least every likely one—while delivering the author's intent and compelling, believably realistic behavior is far too difficult to get right on the first try. Instead, it is necessary to repeatedly test the AI, find the worst problems, correct them, and then test again.

Brian Kernighan, codeveloper of Unix and the C programming language, is believed to have said, "Debugging is twice as hard as writing the code in the first place. Therefore, if you write the code as cleverly as possible, you are, by definition, not smart enough to debug it" [Kernighan]. This goes double for game AI. Any change to the code could have unintended side effects. That is, you may fix a bug or a balance issue in one place, only to cause a more subtle issue somewhere else. A simpler underlying algorithm means that you can hold more of the AI in your head. As a result, you will be able to more fully envision all of the side effects of a change, your development will be safer and more rapid, and the final result will be more highly polished (and, for lack of a better term, more "fun" to play).

If you look at the sorts of decision-making algorithms commonly used in games—finite-state machines, scripting, behavior trees, weight-based random, even goal-oriented action planning—the algorithms themselves are quite simple. The configurations built on top of those frameworks may be complex indeed, but the underlying code is simple, easy to understand, and easy to trace through and debug.

There is a caveat, however. Many simple algorithms (finite-state machines being the archetypical example) scale poorly as the AI grows. In the case of finite-state machines, the number of transitions grows exponentially with the number of states. Clearly, this becomes unmanageable quickly. Thus, a truly elegant architecture is one that is not only simple to understand, but also simple to use—which, among other things, means that it must scale well.

1.2.4 Tricks and Cheats

Much has been said about cheating with respect to game AI, but it often seems that we can't even agree on what "cheating" is. Is it cheating to make the AI character a little bit more powerful than the player? What if I give them an item to justify that bonus? Is it cheating to give the AI character in a strategy game an economic bonus, so that they can buy units more cheaply? What if I allow the player to pick the size of the bonus, and call it "difficulty level?"

There is a great story, which I recently confirmed in conversation with Bob Fitch, the AI lead for Blizzard's strategy game titles [Fitch 11]. Apparently the scenario AI for the original *Warcraft* would simply wait a fixed amount of time, and then start spawning a wave of units to attack you. It would spawn these units at the edge of the gray fog—which is to say, just outside of the visibility range of your units. It would continue spawning units until your defenses were nearly overwhelmed—and then it would stop, leaving you to mop up those units that remained and allowing you to win the fight.

This approach seems to cross the line fairly cleanly into the realm of "cheating." The AI doesn't have to worry about building buildings, or saving money, or recruiting units—it just spawns whatever it needs. On the other hand, think about the experience that results. No matter how good or bad you are at the game, it will create an epic battle for you—one which pushes you to the absolute limit of your ability, but one in which you will ultimately, against all odds, be victorious.

Of course, there's a dark side to that sort of cheating, which is that it only works if the player remains ignorant. If the player figures out what you're up to, then the experience they have is entirely different—and nobody likes being patronized. Unfortunately, these days, particularly with the advent of the Internet, players are quite a bit harder to fool (and quite a bit less forgiving) than they were in 1994.

Another type of cheating is purely informational. That is, does the AI have to sense a unit in order to know that it exists and where it is located? The problem is that, while doing line-of-sight checks for visibility is fairly straightforward, remembering what you saw and using that to predict future events is quite a bit harder. In other words, if I see a unit but then it goes out of sight, how do I remember that it exists? How do I guess its location? If I see a unit of the same type later on, how do I know whether it is the same unit or a different one? Humans are fairly good at this sort of thing, but doing it well requires a combination of opponent modeling, intuition, and sheer guesswork. These are things that computers are notoriously bad at.

Unfortunately, for many types of games it is critically important that the AI have a reasonably good ability to predict things like the locations of resources, and enemy strengths and positions. If the player gets this wrong then they will lose—but that is an acceptable sort of a loss to most players. "I just never found anything I could work with," or "You tricked me this time—but next time I'll get you!" They start another game, or reload from a save, and if anything the challenge pulls them right back into the game. If the AI gets it wrong, on the other hand, then the player will win easily, never experiencing any significant challenge at all. They won't be thinking, "Well, the AI probably just had bad luck." They'll be thinking, "Man, that is one stupid AI." Once they start thinking about the AI as "stupid," the experience you were chasing is almost certainly lost.

At the end of the day, the decision of whether or not to write an AI that cheats is a relatively simple one. You should make the AI cheat if and only if it will improve the player's experience—but bear in mind that if you cheat and get caught, that in itself will change the player's experience, and typically not for the best. In *Kohan 2*, an RTS that received accolades for its AI, we had two subtle cheats. First, when exploring, we gave the AI a random chance every 30 seconds or so to cheat and explore an area where we knew there was something good to find. This helped us to avoid games where the AI just didn't happen to find any of the nearby resources early enough in the game. The second was to keep track of the approximate amount of enemy strength in an area (but not the specific locations of units). This allowed us to assign reasonable amounts of strength to our attack and defend goals, and to avoid sending units off on a wild goose chase. None of the reviewers caught on to either cheat, and in fact many of the intelligent behaviors they ascribed to the AI were, as suggested earlier, really just side effects of the ways in which we cheated.

1.3 Conclusion

Academic AI can be about a great many things. It can be about solving hard problems, recreating human intelligence, modeling human cognition in order to learn more about how our brain works, optimizing performance in complex operational environments (for instance, for an autonomous robot), or any of a host of other extremely challenging and worthwhile pursuits. All of these things are hard and worth doing—but the solutions that apply to them don't necessarily apply to games.

Game AI should be about one thing and one thing only: enabling the developers to create a compelling experience for the player—an experience that will make the player want to spend time with the game, and want to buy the expansion packs and sequels, that will inevitably result if you succeed.

The rest of this book is packed with tips, tricks, techniques, and solutions that have been proven to work for our industry. Game schedules are tight, with little margin for error and few opportunities for extensions if the AI isn't working right when it is time to ship. Furthermore, simply building a compelling AI for a game is challenge enough. We have neither the time nor the inclination to tackle the hard problems where we don't need to, or to reinvent solutions that have already been found. With those challenges in mind, hopefully some of the approaches found within will work for you as well.

References

[Adams 99] E. Adams. "Putting the Ghost in the Machine." Lecture, 1999 American Association for Artificial Intelligence Symposium on Computer Games and AI, 1999.

[Fitch 11] B. Fitch. "Evolution of RTS AI." Lecture, *2011 AI and Interactive Digital Entertainment Conference*, 2011.

[Isla 05] D. Isla. "Handling complexity in the Halo 2 AI." *2005 Game Developer's Conference*, 2005. Available online (http://www.gamasutra.com/view/feature/130663/gdc_2005_proceeding_handling_.php).

[Kernighan] B. Kernighan. Original source unknown. Available online (http://www.software-quotes.com/printableshowquotes.aspx?id = 575).

[Wikipedia 12-A] Wikipedia. "Artificial Intelligence." Available online (http://en.wikipedia.org/wiki/Artificial_intelligence, 2012).

[Wikipedia 12-B] Wikipedia. "ELIZA." Available online (http://en.wikipedia.org/wiki/ELIZA, 2012).

2

Informing Game AI through the Study of Neurology

Brett Laming

2.1 Introduction

Human beings are fascinating machines, and the world of science is an amazing place. But as AI programmers we usually end up closeted in computer science and conditionals, rather than taking inspiration from the worlds we are trying to emulate. Math, psychology, biology, engineering, and the physical sciences all have a part to play in the inspiration and mechanisms we use in our daily jobs.

Focusing on neurology, this article aims to inspire you to think further afield, giving you a detailed understanding of the neuron while illustrating aspects that have contributed to the author's programming tool kit and critical thinking. It is not intended as a full course in the field but aims to inspire further reading. With that and brevity in mind, much will be simple illustration at the potential cost of over-simplification.

2.2 Critical Thinking

AI often involves mimicking higher cognizant behavior. Faced with hypothetical situations most people correctly start with *introspection*, answering the question, "What would I do?"

As a programmer, this then becomes, "How do I code that?" followed by, "How do I code that efficiently?" But if we remove deadlines and programming from the equation for a minute and take some time to reflect on our thoughts, then maybe better questions are, "How would I do that?" and "Why?" Think a bit more and you realize that these questions are the primary drive of the psychological and biological sciences, a point that has not gone unnoticed before [Kirby 02].

If we invest the time to answer those questions we might be more likely to arrive at physically grounded behavior. But in this high pressure world, is it really that necessary? After all, we as AI programmers have survived quite well already.

And herein lies the most dangerous assumption of all, because with advances in loco-motion fidelity, emotional content, and facial expressiveness, even the slightest nuance may immeasurably affect immersion. Without trying, we will never know, and with the Internet at our ready disposal, is there really an excuse for not doing some research, even if we just take the low hanging fruit?

2.3 Neurology

We are in the business of writing AI, the predominant output of which is *behavior*. Whether this output is represented as animation, speech, or thought, it is none the less analogous to the role of the brain and wider nervous system. From robotics to cognitive science, disciplines have taken their cues from their biological counterparts.

As such, considering its involvement in everything from the senses, through higher thought, to motor output, the study of neurology is one of our best foundations in the AI world. While our understanding of this huge and complex subject is very incomplete, it has one key redeeming feature. Almost the entire nervous system, brain, or nerves, is made out of one very fundamental cell—the *neuron*—and this single building block arms us with more information than you would at first expect. As AI programmers, it is wise at first to understand as much as possible about the cognitive mechanisms and build-ing blocks of the creatures we are trying to represent. Hopefully, this section will serve as both a primer and provide keyword hooks to help further understanding. Commonly misrepresented as a purely electrical process, this section will introduce the biophysical side that has been gaining popularity in the field of computational neuroscience. It will take you through the full signaling properties and mechanisms of the neuron in sections, interspersed with the inspiration and history of some useful AI techniques before culmi-nating in derivation of the perceptron as the basic building block of the neural network and why it is still useful by itself. Should you wish to delve into a little more detail on the neuroscience side, *The Computational Brain* [Churchland 99] and *From Neuron to Brain* [Nicholls 92] are both excellent resources.

2.3.1 Primer: The Electrical Processing Myth

Before we begin, it is important to clarify a dangerous preconception. We often assume the nervous system communicates by electrical signals. It unfortunately does not; we have merely adopted this metaphor as a handy way of generalizing the actual process. For now, we need to temporarily forget the visualization of electrical signals running down wires from the brain because it comes with preconceptions.

In fact, our notion of this electrical signal is really just a view of the voltage (*membrane potential*) at a single point on the neuron's *cell membrane*. Obtained by a pair of electrodes seated on either side of the membrane, it can give the impression of a spatial nature when really it is just a point voltage changing over time. The notion of voltage arises because the semipermeable cell membrane separates different concentrations of ions, and being thin, exhibits capacitance that eventually gives rise to membrane potential. Drawn in graph form then, over time, it would appear as a flat line situated around –70 mV or the *resting potential*.

2.3.2 Takeaway: Don't Neglect the Temporal Aspects

A different view of the same data immediately transforms our perception. What is traditionally considered an electric signal racing around the body, when clamped to one location, merely becomes a meter registering activity. But as we shall shortly see, drawn over time this once again provides the signal with a shape. Being reminded to think about problems in both time, as well as the current state, definitely has its merits, especially in utility theory [Mark et al. 10], and if you are ever overwhelmed by AI state—for example, AI steering signals given to vehicles—try graphing sections of it over time; the patterns and problems often become very much more obvious in the time domain.

2.3.3 Primer: The Neuron at Rest

For the neuron to remain balanced at rest, a number of conditions need to be met. Two of the most important are, first, that the net charge on either side of the cell membrane must be zero and, second, the concentrations of solute particles inside (*intracellular*) and outside (*extracellular*) must balance. A common misconception then is that if this were so, there would be no difference in charge (both sides zero) and the membrane potential would be 0 mV also. So where did that –70 mV come from? The key here is the difference in *individual* ion concentrations and the clue that the membrane is semipermeable.

Two primary forces act on charged ions. *Diffusion* seeks to push ions towards areas of lower concentration, and *electrical attraction* seeks to pull them towards areas of opposite charge. So looking at Figure 2.1, we can see that overall concentrations on either side are indeed balanced, and the overall charge on either side is zero. However, there are still vastly different concentrations of all relevant ions. At rest, the cell membrane is essentially closed to sodium ions (Na^+), and proteins are too big to go through. So while diffusion might want to alter the balance, proteins and Na^+ have nowhere to go. However, the cell membrane is permeable to chlorine ions (Cl^-) and very permeable to potassium ions (K^+). As such K^+ tries to flow out of the cell by diffusion. In doing so, its exit causes a charge imbalance that sees the now more negative inside attracting the positive ions. Cl^- similarly gets pulled back to the outside because traveling inside would make the outside even more positive. When the system eventually settles and overall ions are at rest, this more negative inside, with respect to the outside, gives us our resting potential.

Before we move on you might be wondering, what if K^+ and Cl^- were left long enough that ions on either side normalized, and concentrations became neutral across the membrane? Two things spoil the plan. First, the permeability to K^+ is very much higher than to Cl^-, so K^+ is far more effective in creating an electrical pull that affects both types of ions. As such K^+ is the dominant partner, and Cl^- can be thought as just reshuffling to match. Second, a number of *active transport* mechanisms, including *membrane pumps*, work as necessary to return ions to their relevant sides.

2.3.4 Takeaway: Diffusion

Diffusion is a nice technique, and if you have used influence maps you will no doubt work out why. Most of the general tweaks for making influence maps work [Champandard 11]

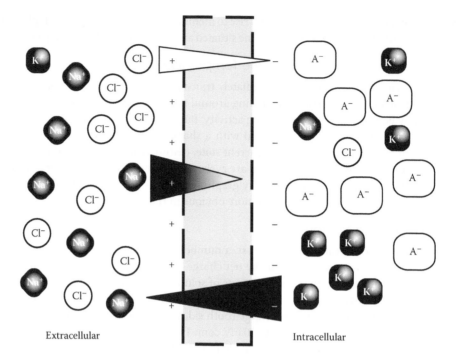

K⁺ ... (image labels as shown)

Extracellular   Intracellular

Figure 2.1

Diagrammatic representation of a neuron at rest. Four ions are represented, potassium (K⁺), sodium (Na⁺), chlorine (Cl⁻), and an electrically charged anion (A⁻) representing intracellular proteins. Notice here that total charge on either side of the cell is net zero and that the number of counted ions is balanced at 16 on each side.

can be, in actual fact, worked into the *diffusion equation*. In textbooks, the equation has a tendency to look formidable:

$$\frac{\partial c(r,t)}{\partial t} = \nabla . \left[D(c,r) \nabla c(r,t) \right]$$

But ignoring the math for a minute, it really just states that rate of change $\frac{\partial c}{\partial t}$ of concentration c at a distance r and time t depends on neighboring concentrations $\nabla c(r,t)$ and the ease of diffusion $D(c,r)$, as defined by the *diffusion coefficient* D. If the diffusion coefficient remains constant in space and time, then we obtain a simpler form, which is the heat equation:

$$\frac{\partial c(r,t)}{\partial t} = D \nabla^2 c(r,t)$$

∇^2 is known as the Laplacian operator, and it turns out that it can be computed by finite methods. If we create a grid of a variable α, for example ion concentration or influence, with constant grid cell width r, then the change in α after a time dt by diffusion is simply the sum of α for any connected neighbors minus any relatively scaled contribution before being averaged by grid cell area. If over time we then add on anything that might change this value of α, like a drip feed of ions or an increase of influence k, we obtain the following for a 2D grid of cell location i,j at time t:

$$\alpha(i,j,t+dt)=$$

$$\alpha(i,j,t)+\left(dt\times\left(k+\frac{D(\alpha(i_{-1},j,t)+\alpha(i_{+1},j,t)+\alpha(i,j_{-1},t)+\alpha(i,j_{+1},t)-4(\alpha(i,j,t))}{r^2}\right)\right)$$

Here, k could model anything from a decay rate to suppression by a different influence map. The beauty of this system is that it is both compensated for in time and space, which means it allows us to work with rate of change. Imagine its use in a real-time strategy domain, where production rates could be factored in, in place of production spikes!

But the best news is that this technique has already been adopted by the graphics community for many similar things due to its easy visualization in texture space. This also means it would be quite possible to get AI based simulations to work by just following similar GPU diffusion or gas examples—where the code is significantly easier to visualize than the math [Pharr 05].

2.3.5 Primer: Perturbation from Equilibrium

We have stated that the cell must always remain in equilibrium. But if it did so then the resting membrane potential would stay at ~–70 mV, and nothing would happen. As such, much processing of the neuron comes about by either electrical charge or concentration changes. Consider what happens if we increase the concentration of K^+ outside the cell. A decrease in K^+ concentration gradient now means K^+ has less inclination to leave the cell, and so less charge is required to pull it back. The relative membrane potential therefore becomes more positive, which also means less resistance to Cl^- moving in. Postperturbation, extracellular diffusion, and an increase in active transport work hard to return the neuron to equilibrium and standard resting concentrations. This results in a decay of membrane potential to resting values as illustrated in Figure 2.2. This common response-decay curve is a characteristic of most changes in local concentration.

2.3.6 Primer: The Spike or Action Potential

While a small change in membrane potential like the above is at least a signal, its effects are local and will dissipate quickly. To facilitate neuronal transmission we are going to need something of a very different magnitude.

Recall that we said that K^+ was permeable at rest and Na^+ was not. This is made possible because a number of K^+ specific *membrane channels* situated in the cell wall are in the *open state* allowing K^+ ions to be free to move if they want to. Similar Na^+ specific *membrane channels* in the cell membrane remain closed at the specified membrane potential. It turns out that there are many different *ion channels* found in neurons, sensitive to a wide range of factors, including membrane potential range.

Now consider the case where we temporarily push the membrane potential above the opening point of the Na^+ channels as seen in Figure 2.3. This opens Na^+ channels which,

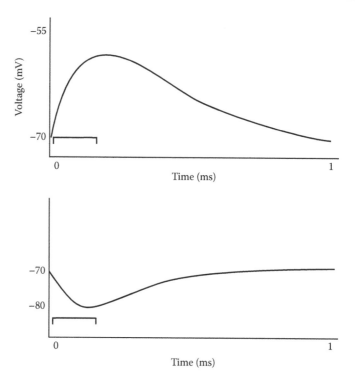

Figure 2.2

An illustrative representation of the membrane potential response curve due to a localized change in extracellular K⁺ concentration (top). Notice that after an initial sharp change from the delivery, a slow decay to rest represents active processes returning concentrations to normal resting levels. (bottom) Increasing intracellular K⁺ leads to a reverse effect.

combined with a massive concentration gradient into the cell and the accelerant of negative charge inside as shown in Figure 2.1, cause a massive influx of Na⁺ ions. This pushes a huge swing in membrane potential towards the positive (*depolarization*). All things being equal, we might then expect the top response of Figure 2.2 albeit with much greater magnitude and duration. But as the voltage swings positive, high voltage potassium channels open and K⁺ flows out of the cell also at great speed, driven by both a concentration gradient and repulsion from a more positive inside. This causes a rapid swing back the other way (*repolarization*). Because channels represent a rearrangement of lipids in the cell membrane, there is both a delay in closing and a period before which they will reopen again. In the case of the rapid efflux of K⁺, this delay means the membrane potential dips below rest (*hyperpolarization*) before active processes, now working very hard in the form of a combined K⁺/Na⁺ pump, attempt to return the concentrations to rest. The resulting climb is called the *refractory period,* and at this stage it is performing as in the bottom case of Figure 2.2. Once channels are ready to reopen again, it will be possible for a second action potential to be generated. If the concentrations get the chance to return to rest, then this process is lossless and will result in a similar action potential if activated again. If ion concentrations haven't returned to rest, it is still possible to activate further action

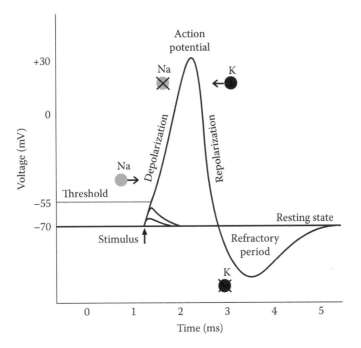

Figure 2.3

The action potential profile. Phases are marked alongside key ion changes that help produce the characteristic shape. Notice that failure to produce an action potential elicits a similar response to Figure 2.2.

potentials. However, the ion concentrations will become more and more imbalanced, with each action potential starting at a higher membrane potential, until the system will fail to respond, at which point it will have to decay to operating conditions again. This over-excitation results in a *burst* of spike activity, followed by periods where the neuron simply cannot fire.

2.3.7 Primer: Signal Transmission

So if the change in membrane potential is local to a specific location, how do signals travel? Recall that we said that the imbalance of ions causes a charge on the membrane, the same charge that gives us the membrane potential. Just like lightning, if an area of higher charge is different from its surroundings, it spreads outwards. Likewise if a change in ion concentration occurs at a particular site, then inside or outside the cell, diffusion will try to normalize the overall concentration on either side of the membrane.

If these changes are enough to push the neighboring membrane potential above the threshold for Na^+ channels to open, a similar action potential will be generated on a neighboring site on the cell membrane, causing a ripple effect as action potential generation spreads outwards. It is this "The Wave" style of propagation that gives us our notion of the electrical signals traveling around the nervous system. Because activated channels need time to recover and the refractory period helps keep the local membrane potential negative, neighboring sites cannot retrigger an action potential again in the same region

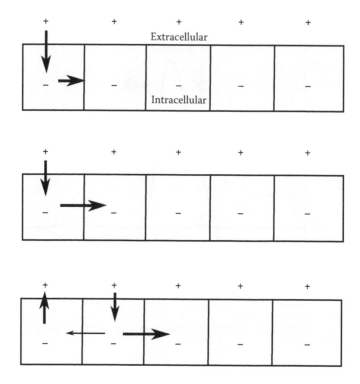

Figure 2.4

An illustration of action potential propagation through nerve fibers over time. The resulting swing in repolarization and the delay in membrane channels reopening prevent previously excited sites from firing again.

so signal transmission carries lossless in an outwards direction as illustrated in Figure 2.4. This is true of both single signal and bursting neurons.

2.3.8 Takeaway: The Schmitt Trigger and Hysteresis

At a similar time that action potential and nerve fiber transmission was being discovered, Otto Schmitt was taking inspiration from its workings. In his 1937 dissertation he introduced the thermionic trigger later to be known as the Schmitt trigger [Schmitt 38].

While it has many other uses in electronics, the Schmitt trigger has the interesting property that the switch between two states, say on or off, is based on an overlap of different activation conditions between them, in essence covering the dead zone from one to the other. Hence, in systems that might vary around a key trigger value, this system ensures that a period of change must occur before the state will switch. We call this dual threshold approach *hysteresis*. It is often a key to keeping clean control in AI systems, especially where switches in animations are concerned as best illustrated by Listing 2.1.

A key point to remember about Schmitt triggers is that they rely on a physically changing property, such as voltage or concentration, incorporated in the system. The most common mistake is to believe you can add hysteresis with a timer. It is not hysteresis and it is not protecting you; it is just changing the frequency of oscillation. Proper hysteresis might not

Listing 2.1. An example of hysteresis. If we were just to base our approach distance around a single value (5m), then every slight move outside that radius would cause us to follow. With hysteresis, once we start to follow we will continue until we are inside 2.5 m, and won't start again until we are further away than 5 m. This noise reduction means the player has some maneuvering room before we decide we need to be closer.

```
const float SEPARATION_DISTANCE = 2.5f;
const float APPROACH_DISTANCE = 5.0f;
if (approach_player = = false)
{
    if (distance > APPROACH_DISTANCE)
    {
        approach_player = true;
    }
}
else
{
    if (distance < SEPARATION_DISTANCE)
    {
        approach_player = false;
    }
}
```

be as clean as a single variable either; it might be a complicated series of conditionals that separate logic space. Yet the principle will still hold, provided there is the relevant overlap.

2.3.9 Takeaway: Compartmentalize to Solve Hard Spatial Problems

Notice how a potentially hard problem, the transmission of action potentials, can be better conceptualized by compartmentalizing the space (Figure 2.4). At this stage, each compartment represents just a local area, and the comprehension is immediately simplified. Now consider a tactical warfare simulation with a realistic AI communication system. Rather than working out a route for each agent "A" to get a message to another agent "B," it is easier to imagine all such agents on a compartmentalized grid, posting messages to neighboring agents who then carry the transmission that way. In doing so, we get some nice extras for free: the potential for spies, utterance signaling, realistic transmission delays, and bigger signaling distances covered by nonverbal gestures or field phones. In either case, by thinking about the problem as a different representation, we have instantly simplified the procedure and got some realistic wins as well!

2.3.10 Primer: Morphology

If neurons were just a wire, comprising the same action potential generating membrane channels, then life would be a lot easier. Unfortunately, most neurons have a complex shape or *morphology*, and very different ion channels along the membrane. This means that the neuron itself is responsible for a lot of implicit processing.

The morphology of a typical neuron consists of four parts: the *dendrites*, the *soma*, the *axon*, and the *axon terminals* (as illustrated in Figure 2.5).

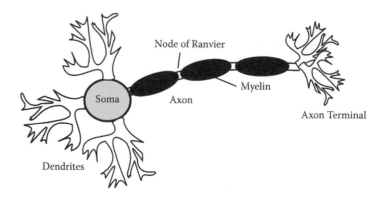

Figure 2.5

A diagrammatic representation of the key components forming the morphology of the neuron.

For the time being we can think of signals in the neuron starting as a change in membrane potential at dendritic sites that generates one of two different types of responses similar in nature to Figure 2.2. With a distinct absence of Na^+ gated channels, the voltage profile of the first response is very similar, albeit reaching higher magnitudes and therefore a longer decay. The second response is inhibitory and inverted, with its changes actively making the membrane potential more negative, but otherwise following a similar path. The near lack of action potential generation in the dendrites means transmission is generally *passive*, spreading merely by change of charge in neighboring regions. While a single signal might die out, the frequency at which dendrites are activated means that there is generally constant stimulation, be that excitation or inhibition that sums in both distance and time. If this summation of charge reaches the soma and creates a high enough potential difference, then traditional spike generation channels at the axon head carry a new signal down the *axon* to the *axon terminals*. While the distance between dendrites and soma is usually small, axons are generally much longer. To facilitate quicker conduction velocity, the axon is usually insulated by a *myelin sheath* that focus charge build-up from strong action potentials at the nodes of Ranvier. This charge is strong enough to cause excitation in a neighboring node faster than it could be carried there normally.

2.3.11 Primer: Synaptic Transmission and Plasticity

The last section mentioned that when dendrites are excited or inhibited there is a strong change in membrane potential, the general cause of which is attributed to *synaptic transmission*. As illustrated in Figure 2.6, when a conducted signal reaches the axon terminals, a change in membrane potential triggers *vesicles* (think seed pods) in the *presynaptic* cell membrane that shoot a packet of complex chemicals (*neurotransmitters*) into the medium between cells. Pointedly projected at other neurons, neurotransmitters travel a short distance through this medium to be picked up by receptors on the dendrites of neighboring *postsynaptic* neurons. This in turn triggers the opening of a number of ion channels, resulting in either an excitatory (positive) or inhibitory (negative) change in membrane potential. These changes are called EPSP (excitatory postsynaptic membrane

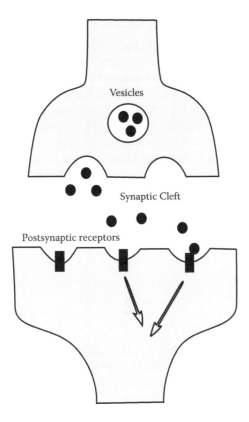

Figure 2.6

A diagrammatic representation of the synapse. In response to stimuli, vesicles in the presynaptic neuron expel their contents into the synaptic cleft. These cross the cleft to the postsynaptic neuron where receptors trigger changes in postsynaptic potential.

potential) and IPSP (inhibitory postsynaptic membrane potential), respectively, and can be thought of as high magnitude variants of Figure 2.2.

2.3.12 Primer: Plasticity and Learning

We know that the brain can learn and adapt. Dendritic excitation is generally a short term byproduct of postsynaptic potentials and action potential generation is for the most part fire-and-forget; so where is the mechanism for learning? Again the purely electrical viewpoint doesn't suffice. Only by understanding the chemical processes are we able to hypothesize on the mechanisms that might do so.

Recall that in synaptic transmission, synapses expel neurotransmitters across to other neurons. If we were to change the sensitivity of these postsynaptic neurons or the amount of neurotransmitters expelled, then obviously the resulting effect will be an increase or reduction in the postsynaptic potential. Both mechanisms could therefore be used by pre- and postsynaptic neurons to control the strength of that connection. We call this *synaptic plasticity*, and it is here that the principles of learning and adaptation are believed to lie.

2.3.13 Primer: The Hebb Rule and Rosenblatt's Perceptron

In 1949, Donald Hebb, in an effort to understand learning, made the assumption that if the axon terminals of one neuron regularly excited the dendrites of another, such that they regularly took part in firing it, then some growth or metabolic process would increase both their efficiencies in doing so [Hebb 49]. In other words, for each synapse i of a total number j contacting the neuron, the change in their strength w_i would be a proportion of how much their contributory input x correlated with the output y. Here Hebb defined output as the summation of all the input to synapses x_i times their individual strength w_i. In other words, he attempted to mimic primitive synaptic sensitivity and interaction in the dendritic tree. In line with real neurons, he hypothesized that this change would happen slowly over time (using a learning rate μ). Put into mathematics we say:

$$\omega_i = \mu x_i y$$

where

$$y = \sum_{i=0}^{j} \omega_i x_i$$

In 1957, Frank Rosenblatt took Hebb's rule of learning and applied it in algorithmic form as the perceptron algorithm, making a number of improvements at the same time [Rosenblatt 57]. First, the synaptic strength in Hebb's rule can quickly grow unstable if all inputs continue to contribute. So Rosenblatt favored learning only if the result was unexpected. He also constrained output, mimicking the firing of the axon only if a summation threshold is reached and applied a bias term to keep things moving if all other inputs were 0.

Hence the Rosenblatt perceptron can be specified as follows:

For a vector of potential inputs $v_i = \left[-1, i_1, \ldots, i_j \right]$ and a vector of weights $v_w = \left[\omega_0, \omega_{1, \ldots}, \omega_j \right]$ where ω_0 represents the bias weight, but always for a constant input ($i_0 = -1$):

$$y = v_i . v_w > 0 \ then \ 1 \ else \ 0$$

Rosenblatt's perceptron has two phases, a learning pass and a prediction pass. In the learning pass, a definition of v_i is passed in as well as a desired output, y_{ideal}, normalized to a range of 0 ... 1. On each presentation of v_i and y_{ideal} a learning rule is applied in a similar form to Hebb's.

Here, each weight is affected by the difference in overall output and expected output y_{ideal} multiplied up by contributory input and learning rate.

$$\omega_{i,t+1} = \omega_i + \mu \left(y_{ideal} - y \right) i_i$$

So by presenting a series of these vectors and desired output, it is possible to train this artificial neuron to start trying to give new output in the absence of untrained conditions by just applying the output calculation without training.

2.3.14 Takeaway: The Hebb Rule and Rosenblatt's Perceptron

There are a number of key points here. First, unlike neural networks that commonly consist of many of these units, at this simple level the meaning of the parameters is understandable. In AI terms, this gives us both the glamorous, a potential prediction of player behavior, and the less so, in the tuning of parameter unknowns.

The perceptron is essentially a Boolean classifier. For n changeable variables in an input vector, it tries to train the weights to correctly classify an nD point as being on one side (1) or another (0) of an imaginary separator through that space. Hence, if $n = 1$, the separator is a value that splits i_1. At $n = 2$, it represents a line that divides $[i_1, i_2]$. At $n = 3$, it is a plane dividing $[i_1, i_2, i_3]$ and so on.

Provided the inputs can be logically separated—the XOR function is an example that can't be linearly ($n = 2$) separated—then with enough training, weights should settle and $(y_{ideal} - y) \to 0$. If this does not eventually happen, then this tells us that either the problem is not Boolean classifiable, or we have not used the correct input. However, with some common-sense guesses on dependent variables, results are generally obtainable.

Moreover, its synaptic strength w_i is potentially understandable. Removing bias, which just seeks to modify the threshold as $w_i \to 0$, then we know that particular input we are passing in doesn't factor much on our decision. Just like at synapses, if it is less than 0 it inhibits the 1 result, and if greater than 0, it adds towards it. Now combine this with a notion of utility [Mark 09] essentially heuristic in form, and you can test what factors are critical in influencing a decision and whether you have got them right.

The key here is the training on input. For example, here is a utility equation from a recent talk [Mark 10]:

$$cover\ chance = 0.2 + reload\ need \times 1.0 + heal\ need \times 1.5 + threat\ rating \times 1.3$$

Now, these values probably took some degree of trial and error to arrive at and probably had to be normalized into sensible ranges. But consider this:

$$cover\ chance = -1 \times w_0 + reload\ need \times w_1 + heal\ need \times w_2 + threat\ rating \times w_3$$

If we present the player with a number of scenarios and ask them whether they would take cover, we can easily get values that, after enough questions, are still easily accessible in meaning and therefore can make better initial guesses at the equation that might want to drive our AI.

A final nice property is that we don't necessarily need to answer the false side of the equation if we don't want to; we could just supply random values to represent false. Imagine each time the player goes into cover we measure these values and return true, following it by random values that return false. Even if we happen to get a lucky random true cover condition, over time it will just represent noise. If we then clamp all weights to sensible ranges, potentially found by training in test circumstances, we now have a quick to compute run-time predictor of what determines when the player may think of going into cover!

Figure 2.7

Diagrammatic view of the reflex arc. Sensory input (1) gets carried by neuron (A) to an intermediate neuron (B) and onto the muscle (2) through neuron (C).

Table 2.1 The time for various stimuli to reach the brain

Stimulus	Time to brain (ms)
Auditory	8–20 ms
Visual	20–40 ms
Touch	155 ms

2.3.15 Primer: Pathways

Our final foray into the world of the nervous system involves what happens when neurons combine at synapses and networks are formed. When we talk about these series of identifiable connections we talk about *pathways*.

The shortest and least complicated pathway, the *reflex arc* in Figure 2.7, connects a sensory neuron through a synapse to an intermediate neuron, through another synapse to a motor neuron. Other pathways, on the other hand, pass through many more neurons. Considering what we know about the signal transmission process, it seems reasonable, then, that transmission times should scale based on neuron count and travel distance.

Recall that we said one of the key dangers with neurology was thinking of signaling as electrical impulses traveling through wires. Electrical current approaches the speed of light at 3×10^8 m/s. The fastest myelinated axons can only achieve speeds of 120 m/s. To put this in perspective, Table 2.1 shows the time taken for different sensory signals to reach the brain. This is before considering any further processing or motor output. It is hardly surprising then that the senses we rely on the most are the ones located closest to our brains.

Once you start bringing in motor control, however, even for simple tasks, the times just continue to rise. Ask a friend to hold a ruler, with your thumb and finger ready to grasp it at the bottom. Let them drop the ruler unannounced and as soon as you see it move, close your fingers to grasp the ruler.

Now because $s = ut + \frac{1}{2}at^2$, where a is gravity and u is 0, reaction time can be worked out from the equation

$$t = \sqrt{\frac{2*s}{9.8}}$$

where s is the distance traveled on the ruler where you grasped it (in meters). Do the math and the value should come out around 0.2 seconds.

The point here is, even at 30 frames per second, your reaction time to a reasonably simple coordination task is actually already 6 frames.

Compare this with receiving a burn. Your natural reaction is to pretty instantaneously pull away. Yet by our calculations, assuming touch speed, if the signal was traveling from hand to brain to hand again, this travel time would be in the range of 300 ms. So here, the answer almost certainly lies in a reflex arc transferring pain signals, through a really small pathway, to a motor neuron and therefore producing an uncontrolled involuntary reflex.

In a lot of precise or fast-acting systems, any uncompensated latency is going to have a serious detrimental effect on accuracy. Imagine the hard task of trying to grasp a moving feather in a drafty room. Here, our visual cues need to be processed into some spatial representation and transformed into motor commands to coordinate a large number of muscles that allow us to finally grasp it. Yet, remarkably, we can do this with some ease.

Trying to reduce this error in a traditional closed loop way, with the latency we have discussed, would mean we would consistently fail to react to the near-random changes in direction. Instead, the nervous system uses a different technique to cope. We call this *open-loop ballistics*.

As a simple example, saccades are the fast movement of the eyes that swing focus to different points in the visual field. Given that visual feedback to the brain takes between 20–40 ms to return and measured eye travel velocities can reach 900 deg/sec, any attempt at error correction by a closed loop is going to lead to overshoots of ~3 degrees and therefore be untenable. It turns out that in order to cope, saccades make use of a ballistic open loop. Put simply, the journey is preplanned prior to onset. Experiments show that eye muscles respond to bursts of spikes, the frequency of which roughly maps linearly to eye velocity. We also know that to move the eye, a series of spikes come in that force the eye to travel very fast to a new position, before the frequency scales down, so that it applies only enough velocity to counteract the elasticity of the muscles wanting to return.

Something then is controlling the output of these spikes. If the brain was only predicting a velocity with no feedback on error, then chances are the elastic forces trying to return muscles would mean we could not hold the position.

So it turns out that a number of things happen. First, there is a clear proof that we do not need to rely on visual stimulus to perform this operation. Just think about a point in space to the top left of your view, and you will find you can intentionally direct your gaze there by saccade. This ability to make voluntary saccades without the usual sensory input means we must maintain a mental image of the calculations involved. We call this mental image the *efference copy*. It means we can make an initial guess at velocity and start eye movement as soon as possible using the ballistic open loop. When we do receive visual information about our progress, it arrives late. However, because we know about our journey or where we should be at any time, the discrepancy between the two can be applied as a change in *gain*, strengthening or weakening a few synapses based on previous error. With a mostly linear velocity response, this change can scale the remaining journey sensibly helping tune mid-flight. With a 100 ms delay before onset and a total travel time of about 200 ms, this journey preplanning makes sense with respect to the timings.

It turns out that you get the same notion of a separate mental representation when you try to grasp something. Again, an internal representation is definitely at play. If you close your eyes and then go to pick something up, even blind and moving your head, you will still have reasonable success. You are once more running off a mental representation, open loop feedback only coming late from muscle sensors (*proprioceptors*) providing a notion of yourself in space.

2.3.16 Takeaway: Constrain to the Nervous System

We know that with the exception of reflexes, most response is comparatively slow. We should always bear in mind that some of the quickest processing at 200 ms or so is still 6 frames at 30 frames per second. This means that distributing AI planning over frames is not only viable, it may be more biologically plausible.

We know that neural latency almost always prohibits direct feedback and indeed various systems have worked around this with open loop feedback. This tells us a few things.

First, the flow of information at a single frame level is one-way, because there is no natural system for returning information. Hence, sensory input passes to the brain and then onto motor control. This leads to the notion of one-way information flow in the frame, through sense, think, and act stages [Laming 09].

By much the same reasoning, we should probably get out of the habit of requesting more information, such as a spatial query, midway through AI processing. If we need that info, it's probably better precached with other sensory info for all to use. Considering our brain is comparatively sluggish anyway, we can easily spread this vast information gathering over separate frames and threads.

We also know that in the majority of control cases, such as animation, movement by the nervous system involves initial planning, setting off, and then refining mid process. Consider a long-jumper trying to hit a launch board. They may do their best to plan for hitting the board upfront, but they are constantly reacting to change and error on the way up, which is why it is never an exact launch position. Preplanning exact paths by animations then, while it might give excellent results, may not be the most realistic. Some planning is clearly good, but continuous adaptation by techniques such as steering and velocity avoidance has its part to play [Laming 09].

Finally, we know that, although some information is stored in memory, signals to muscles (essentially our animation cues) are just the output of neurons being fired each frame. Hence, it should be possible to model these signals in AI without necessarily storing them. It is this that lies behind the reasoning for stack-based control signals [Laming 09].

There are obviously plenty more gems out there hidden inside the recommended reading. For example, in the high definition, facially close-up world of our AI character's eye gaze, pupillary response will not only sell emotion [Mark 12] but will provide a more subtle alternative to the traditional notion of head tracking. With the addition of accurate latency, this should start to give anticipation for free!

2.4 Conclusion

Ultimately this chapter is a *primer* in neurology. Its purpose is to introduce a world of neuroscience, neurons, and neural nets to those that may never have learned about them in detail before. By looking at the beauty encapsulated by the neuron, nervous system, and its signal processing potential by shape, make-up, and connections, it hopefully inspires you to think about the biophysical and psychological nature of other AI topics you may encounter.

In doing so it occasionally interrupted with a *takeaway* section, providing the history, background, and concepts behind some gems the author has used and written about before, illustrating the relevant reasoning and critical thinking that drove those decisions.

In this article we discussed potential uses for diffusion and the importance and proper use of hysteresis. We also explored the *perceptron*, the base unit of neural networks, what it actually represents, and how we might make sensible use of it without going overboard. Finally, we looked at some AI architecture design considerations which can be extrapolated from the nervous system as a whole.

You should now have a simple overview that allows you to make sense of the various references and surrounding literature and realize the benefit of exploring outside the computer science box.

References

[Champandard 11] Champandard, A. J. "The Mechanics of Influence Mapping: Representation, Algorithm & Parameters." http://aigamedev.com/open/tutorial/influence-map-mechanics/

[Churchland et al. 99] Churchland, P. S. and Sejnowski, T. J. *The Computational Brain*. Cambridge, MA: MIT Press, 1999.

[Hebb 49] Hebb, D. O., *The Organization of Behavior*. New York: John Wiley & Sons, 1949.

[Kirby 02] Kirby, N. "Solving the right problem." In *A.I. Game Programming Wisdom*, edited by Steve Rabin, pp. 21–28. Hingham, MA: Charles River Media, 2002.

[Laming 09] Laming, B., "AI Architecture and Design Patterns" Session, AI Summit, Game Developers Conference, 2009. Slides available online http://www.gdcvault.com/play/1460/(307)-from-the-ground-up.pdf.

[Mark 09] Mark, D. *Behavioral Mathematics for Game AI*. Course Technology PTR, 2009.

[Mark et al. 10] Mark, D. and Dill, K. "Improved AI Decision Modeling through Utility Theory" Session, AI Summit, Game Developers Conference, 2010.

[Mark et al. 12] Mark, D. and Schwab, B. "Less A More I: Using Psychology in Game AI." Session, AI Summit, Game Developers Conference, 2012.

[Nicholls et al. 92] Nicholls, J. G., Martin, A. R., and Wallace, B. G. *From Neuron to Brain*. Sunderland, MA: Sinauer Associates, 1992.

[Pharr et al. 05] Pharr, M. and Fernando, R. *Programming Techniques for High Performance Graphics and General Purpose Computation*. Chapter 31. Reading, MA: Addison-Wesley, 2005. Available online (http://http.developer.nvidia.com/GPUGems2/gpugems2_chapter31.html).

[Rosenblatt 57] Rosenblatt, F. "The Perceptron—A Perceiving and Recognizing Automaton." Report 85-460-1, Cornell Aeronautical Laboratory, 1957.

[Schmitt 38] Scmitt, O. H. "A thermionic trigger." *J. Sci. Instrum.* 15, 24, 1938.

3

Advanced Randomness Techniques for Game AI
Gaussian Randomness, Filtered Randomness, and Perlin Noise

Steve Rabin, Jay Goldblatt, and Fernando Silva

3.1 Introduction

Game programmers have a special relationship with the rand() function. We depend on it for variation in our games, using it to keep our gameplay fresh and our NPCs from becoming predictable. Whether it's decision making, gameplay events, or animation selection, the last thing we want are repetitive characters or predictable gameplay; therefore randomness has become an essential tool.

However, randomness is a fickle beast, and humans are particularly bad at accessing or reasoning about it. This makes it easy to misuse or misunderstand what randomness actually provides. This chapter will introduce three advanced techniques that our trusty old friend rand() simply isn't capable of delivering.

The first technique involves discarding uniform randomness and embracing *Gaussian randomness* for variation in agent characteristics and behavior. Whether it's the speed of a unit, the reaction time of an enemy, or the aim of a gun, in real life these biological and physical phenomena display *normal* (Gaussian) distributions, not uniform distributions. Once the difference is understood, you will find dozens of uses for Gaussian randomness in the games you make.

The second technique is to manipulate randomness to appear more random to players over short time frames. Randomness notoriously *does not look random* when looking at small isolated runs, so we will aim to fix this with *filtered randomness*.

The final technique is to use a special type of randomness that isn't uniform or Gaussian, but rather generates a wandering characteristic, where consecutive random numbers are related to each other. Often used in graphics, *Perlin noise* can be leveraged for situations where behavior varies randomly over time in a smooth manner. Whether it is movement, accuracy, anger, attention, or just being in the groove, there are dozens of behavior characteristics that could be varied over time using *one-dimensional* Perlin noise.

With each of the three techniques, there are demos and C++ libraries available on the book's website (http://www.gameaipro.com) that you can drop right into your game.

3.2 Techinique 1: Gaussian Randomness

Normal distributions (also known as *Gaussian distributions* or *bell curves*) are all around us, hiding in the statistics of everyday life. We see these distributions in the height of trees, the height of buildings, and the height of people. We see these distributions in the speed of shoppers strolling in a mall, the speed of runners in a marathon, and the speed of cars on the highway. Anywhere we have a large population of creatures or things, we have characteristics about that population that display a normal distribution.

There is randomness in these distributions, but they are not *uniformly* random. For example, the chance of a man growing to be 6 feet tall is not the same as the chance of him growing to a final height of 5 feet tall or 7 feet tall. If the chance were the same, then the distribution would be uniformly random. Instead, we see a normal distribution with the height of men centered around 5 feet 10 inches and dropping off progressively in the shape of a bell curve in either direction. In fact, almost every physical and mental characteristic has some kind of average, with individuals varying from the average with a normal distribution. Whether it's height, reaction time, visual acuity, or mental ability, these characteristics will follow a normal distribution among a given population.

Some random things in life do show a uniform distribution, such as the chance of giving birth to a boy or a girl. However, the large majority of distributions in life are closer to a normal distribution than a uniform distribution. But why?

The answer is quite simple and is explained by the *central limit theorem*. Basically, when many random variables are added together, the resulting sum will follow a normal distribution. This can be seen when you roll three 6-sided dice. While there is a uniform chance of a single die landing on any face, the chance of rolling three dice and their sum equaling the maximum of 18 is not uniform with regard to other outcomes. For example, the odds of three dice adding up to 18 is 0.5% while the odds of three dice adding up to 10 is 12.5%. Figure 3.1 shows that the sum of rolling three dice actually follows a normal distribution.

So now that we've shown that the addition of random variables results in a normal distribution, the question still exists: Why do most distributions in life follow a normal distribution? The answer is that almost everything in the universe has more than one contributing factor, and those contributing factors have random aspects to them.

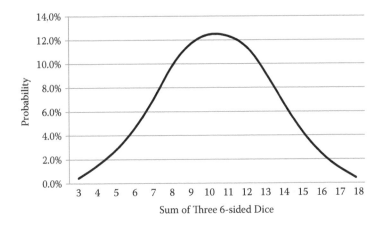

Figure 3.1

The probability of the sum of rolling three six-sided dice will follow a normal distribution, even though the outcomes of any single die have a uniform distribution. This is due to the central limit theorem.

For example, let's take the distribution of mature tree heights in a forest. What determines how tall a tree will grow? Mature tree height is influenced by its genes, precipitation, soil quality, air quality, amount of sunlight, temperature, and exposure to insects or fungi. For an entire forest, each tree experiences varying aspects of each quality, depending on where the tree is located (on the side of a hill versus in a valley, for example). Even two trees right next to each other will experience subtle differences in contributing factors. The final height of the tree is, in essence, the sum of the effects of each individual factor. In other words, the effect of the qualities that influence the tree's height are additive, so they result in a normal distribution of height among all trees. As you might imagine, it is possible to construct a similar argument for almost any other property of a biological system or physical system. Normal distributions are all around us.

3.2.1 Generating Gaussian Randomness

Now that we've shown how common normal distributions are in real life, it makes sense to include them in our games. With that in mind, you might be wondering how Gaussian randomness is generated. The previous dice example gives us a clue. If we take three uniform random numbers (generated from `rand()`, for example) and add them together, we can generate random numbers with a normal distribution.

To be more precise, the central limit theorem states that the addition of uniform random numbers in the range of [–1, 1] will approach a normal distribution with a mean of zero and a standard deviation of $\sqrt{K/3}$, where K is how many numbers are summed. If we choose K to be 3, then the standard deviation is equal to 1, and we will get nearly a *standard normal distribution*. The code in Listing 3.1 shows how easy it is to create Gaussian randomness.

The code in Listing 3.1 is sufficient for generating Gaussian randomness in games. However, there are some hidden nuances that need to be explained. A true normal distribution will produce values far into the tails, beyond the range of [–3, 3] provided by Listing 3.1. While certain financial or medical simulations might want an accurate normal

Listing 3.1 Gaussian randomness can be generated by adding three uniformly random numbers. In this example, the uniform random numbers are created with an XOR-shift pseudo-random number generator. The function returns numbers in the range of [-3.0, 3.0] with 66.7% of them falling within one standard deviation, 95.8% falling within two standard deviations, and 100% falling within three standard deviations.

```
unsigned long seed = 61829450;
double GaussianRand()
{
    double sum = 0;
    for (int i = 0; i < 3; i++)
    {
        unsigned long holdseed = seed;
        seed ^ = seed << 13;
        seed ^ = seed >> 17;
        seed ^ = seed << 5;
        long r = (Int64)(holdseed + seed);
        sum + = (double)r * (1.0/0x7FFFFFFFFFFFFFFF);
    }
    return sum; //returns [-3.0, 3.0] at (66.7%, 95.8%, 100%)
}
```

distribution (with a 1 in a million chance of a −4 value), games do not, so it is good to have a guarantee that the generated values will lie within the [−3, 3] range.

3.2.2 Applications of Gaussian Randomness

There are many uses for Gaussian randomness in AI [Mark 09], but one that is very visible within games is the aiming of projectiles [Rabin 08]. While many games probably don't perturb projectiles at all or perturb them using uniform randomness, the correct method is to apply Gaussian randomness.

Figure 3.2 shows both uniform and Gaussian bullet spreads on a target (generated from the sample demo on the book's website). It should be evident that the Gaussian one on the right looks much more realistic, but how is it generated? The trick is to use polar coordinates and a mix of both uniform and Gaussian randomness. First, a random uniform angle is generated from 0 to 360°. This value is used as a polar coordinate to determine an angle around the center of the target. It is important for this value to be uniform because there should be an equal chance of any angle. Second, a random Gaussian number is generated to determine the distance from the center of the target. By combining the random uniform angle and the random Gaussian distance from the center, you can recreate a very realistic bullet spread.

Other applications for Gaussian randomness in games include any aspect of an NPC that should vary within a population. These might include:

- Average or max speed
- Average or max acceleration
- Size, width, height, or mass

- Visual or physical reaction time
- Fire or reload rate for firing
- Refresh rate or cool-down rate for healing or special abilities
- Chance of missing or striking a critical hit

One thing to think about is whether you want to vary a characteristic between members of a population, vary that characteristic each time it is used, or both. For example, an individual soldier might have a slower innate rate of fire than average for the population (determined at unit creation time using Gaussian randomness), but any one instance of that unit firing can then also vary within a normal distribution around the unit's innate rate (sometimes the unit is a little faster at firing and sometimes a little slower).

Now imagine a group of 30 units all firing at the enemy. If each unit has an innate fire rate (normally distributed) and each unit varies around that rate (also normally distributed), then the emergent behavior of the group should be extremely natural, with no units firing in lock-step with each other.

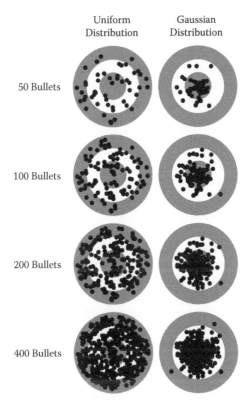

Figure 3.2

Uniform and Gaussian distributions for bullet spreads on a target. Note that each ring in the target represents a standard deviation, with 66.7% of the Gaussian bullets hitting within the innermost ring and 95.8% of the bullets hitting within the two innermost rings. This demo can be found on the book's website.

3.3 Technique 2: Filtered Randomness

Let's just say it: Randomness is too random (for many uses in games). At first, this seems like a ridiculous statement, but there is a mountain of evidence that humans don't see small runs of randomness as being random [Diener et al. 85, Wagenaar et al. 91]. However, this brings up an interesting follow-up question: If humans don't think small runs of randomness look random, then what do they actually think? Perhaps they think that the thing creating the sequence is either broken, rigged, or cheating—all of which are terrible qualities to attribute to a game or an AI.

3.3.1 Small Runs of Randomness Don't Look Random

Now that we have the outrageous statement out there, let's back it up. First, let's establish that small runs of randomness don't look random. Grab a piece of scrap paper and start writing down 0's and 1's in a random sequence with a 50% chance of each—do it until you have a list of 100 numbers. Go ahead and *really* try this. No really, it'll make you a better person. We'll wait ….

Now to make this truly fair, take out a coin and start flipping it, recording the sequence of heads and tails as 0s and 1s. Flip it 100 times to make a comparable list to the one you created with your mind. Again, we'll wait. You must actually do this if you want the big payoff….

Now we can also compare the two lists you made to a list created by a pseudo-random number generator (PRNG) such as rand(), with the same 50% chance of either a 0 or a 1. The following is a random generated sequence of 100 coin flips.

```
0110110000110000101000000100101111001100111000110
1010101101111101001011110011111101011111101000011
```

Notice anything different between your hand-generated list, the coin flip list, and the PNRG generated one? It's very likely that the coin flip and PRNG list are a lot more "clumpy" containing many more long runs of 0's or 1's compared to your hand-generated list. What most people don't realize is that real randomness almost always contains these long runs and that these are very typical and to be expected. However, most people simply don't believe a fair coin or real randomness will produce those long runs of heads or tails. In fact, until you've actually flipped a coin yourself and seen it happen, it is extremely difficult to internalize this lesson (which is why we wanted you to actually do it).

So how does this apply to games? Many games include situations where a uniformly distributed random number determines something that will affect the player, either positively or negatively. If the player has the expectation of certain odds and the game appears to negatively defy those odds in the short term (especially with an outcome that harms the player), then the player thinks the game is broken or cheating [Meier 10]. Remember that we've now entered the realm of psychology, and we have temporarily left mathematics [Mark 09]. If the player thinks the game is cheating, then the game effectively *is* cheating despite what is really happening; perception is far more important than reality when it comes to the player's enjoyment of the game.

For example, imagine that the game designer determined that enemies should strike with a critical hit 10% of the time. Unfortunately, after many battles during the course of a 30 hour game, the player has a very high probability of being hit three times in a row with a critical hit! Did the game designer ever want this to happen? No! But this is the reality of random numbers. In many situations, *randomness is too random* for what the game designer actually wanted.

3.3.2 Randomness Doesn't Look Random: The Fix

How can random numbers be forced to look more random to humans? The truthful, but nonhelpful, answer is to make the numbers slightly less random in a very special way. What we will do is trade a very tiny bit of randomness integrity to achieve a sequence that looks more random to humans.

The strategy is very simple: When generating a random sequence of numbers, if the next number will hurt the appearance of randomness, pretend that you never saw it and generate a new number [Rabin 04]. It really is that simple. With that said, since we're dealing with psychology here, the actual implementation of this strategy is subjective. Also, if the elimination of numbers is too overzealous, it can hurt the integrity of the randomness, so the actual implementation must be carefully considered.

3.3.3 Identifying Anomalies

Keeping the core strategy in mind, the first task is to identify the kinds of things that make a sequence look less random. As it turns out, there are really only two main causes:

1. The sequence has a pattern that stands out, like in the coin flip sequence 11001100 or 111000.
2. The sequence has a long run of the same number, as in the coin flip sequence 01011111110.

We can classify both of these causes as "anomalies" that look nonrandom (weird or unusual) to humans. The goal is then to write some kind of rules that will identify these anomalies. Once we have the rules, we can throw out the last number that triggers a rule (completes the offending pattern). As an implementation detail, our code will have to track the last 10 to 20 generated numbers, *per decision*, for our rules to examine. We will explore this more in a later section.

So what does a rule look like? That depends on the type of randomness being generated. Rules for a coin flip will be different from rules for a random range or Gaussian randomness. Unfortunately, there is no simple way around this since we are dealing with subjective human feelings.

3.3.3.1 Filtering Binary Randomness

If a 50% chance is desired, like a coin flip, then the following rules will filter randomness in a way that will look more random to humans. Note that this is an ordered list of rules to check every time a new random number is generated. Additionally, only one rule should be allowed to trigger per new generated number.

1. If the newest value will produce a run of 4 or more, then there is a 75% chance to flip the newest value. This doesn't make runs of 4 or more impossible, but progressively much less likely (the probability of a run of 4 occurring goes from 1/8 to 1/128). Runs of a particular length can be prohibited altogether, but this will more negatively affect the integrity of the randomness.

2. If the newest value causes a repeating pattern of four values, like 11001100, then flip the last value (so that the sequence becomes 11001101).
3. If the newest value causes a repeating pattern of 111000 or 000111, then flip the last value.

Taking the binary generated random sequence from earlier in the article, here it is before and after filtering:

Before filtering:

```
011011000011000010100000010010111100111001110000110
101010110111111010010111100111111010111111101000011
```

After filtering (underlined numbers were toggled from the original sequence):

```
01101100011100010101000100100101111001110011100110
1010111001110110100101110011100110101110110100010110
```

3.3.3.2 Filtering Integer Ranges

Similar to binary randomness, rules can be constructed to filter out anomalies that occur with ranges of numbers. The following is a list of fairly aggressive rules that could be implemented. For this set of rules, any violation of a rule results in rerolling the value and then validating against the rules again:

1. Repeating numbers, like "7, 7" or "3, 3"
2. Repeating numbers separated by one digit, like "8, 3, 8" or "6, 2, 6"
3. A counting sequence of 4 that ascends or descends, like "3, 4, 5, 6"
4. Too many values at the top or bottom of a range within the last N values, like "6, 8, 7, 9, 8, 6, 9"
5. Patterns of two numbers that appear in the last 10 values, like "5, 7, 3, 1, 5, 7"
6. Too many of a particular number in the last 10 values, like "9, 4, 5, 9, 7, 8, 9, 0, 2, 9".

Before filtering:

```
2231255222257775067756406144848210243550098938 8459
5960788996495778075328157460548213844623510374 5368
```

After filtering (highlighted numbers are thrown out since they violated a rule):

```
2231255222257775067756406144848210243550098938 8459
5960788996495778075328157460548213844623510374 5368
```

3.3.3.3 Filtering Floating-Point Ranges

To filter floating-point in the range of [0, 1], we'll have to design rules that tend to avoid clumps of similar numbers and avoid increasing or decreasing runs. If any of these rules are violated, we'll simply throw out the value and ask for a new random number that must pass all of the rules.

1. Reroll if two consecutive numbers differ by less than 0.02, like 0.875 and 0.856.
2. Reroll if three consecutive numbers differ by less than 0.1, like 0.345, 0.421, and 0.387.
3. Reroll if there is an increasing or decreasing run of 5 values, such as 0.342, 0.572, 0.619, 0.783, and 0.868.
4. Reroll if too many numbers at the top or bottom of the range within the last N values, such as 0.325, 0.198, 0.056, 0.432, and 0.216.

3.3.3.4 Filtering Gaussian Ranges

Since Gaussian numbers are very similar to floating-point numbers, the same rules would apply. However, you might introduce the following rules to avoid particular anomalies that are unique to Gaussian numbers.

5. Reroll if there are four consecutive numbers that are all above or below zero.
6. Reroll if there are four consecutive numbers that lie within the second or third deviations.
7. Reroll if there are two consecutive numbers that lie within the third deviation.

3.3.3.5 Randomness Integrity

The rules outlined in the last four sections are arbitrary and can be changed to be more or less strict. However, the stricter the rules, the less random the resulting values become. In the extreme case, very strict rules will overconstrain the sequence to the point where it might be possible to predict the next number, which would defeat the purpose of using random numbers in the first place.

At this point you should be asking yourself if *any* number of rules for filtering random numbers might significantly hurt the mathematical integrity of the randomness. The only way to categorically answer this is to run benchmarks on the filtered random numbers to measure the quality of the randomness. The open source program ENT will run a variety of metrics to evaluate the randomness, so it would be advisable to run these benchmarks if you design your own rules [Walker 08]. In general, as long as the rules don't overconstrain or predetermine the next number, as in the examples given, then the randomness will be suitable for almost all uses in game AI [Rabin 04].

3.3.4 Implementation Details for Filtered Randomness

When implementing filtered randomness, care must be taken to apply the algorithm to each particular *use* of randomness. Each unique random decision using filtered randomness needs to keep its own history from which to filter subsequent random numbers. Otherwise, since the sequence of numbers for a particular use is not consecutive in the overall sequence, pure randomness can creep back in despite your filtering. For example, if you need a random chance for a critical hit from the player, that sequence must be filtered separately from the random chance of a critical hit from an enemy. The two uses are independent, so a critical hit from one should not influence the subsequent chance of a critical hit from the other. One advantage of this is that you can (if you desire) alter your filter characteristics for different uses. For example, you might want to allow more sequences to appear when your character plays poker, or does some smithing, where the sensation of being "on a lucky streak" could benefit the player's experience, but still strongly constrain sequences of critical hits.

3.4 Technique 3: Perlin Noise for Game AI

If you are familiar with computer graphics, you have probably heard of *Perlin noise* [Perlin 85, Perlin 02]. This computer-generated visual effect was developed by Ken Perlin in 1983, who incidentally won an Academy Award for the technique due to its widespread use in digital effects for movies. Perlin noise is typically used as a component to generate organic textures and geometry. Figure 3.3 shows typical examples of Perlin noise textures.

While Perlin noise can be used to help provide an organic feel to visual effects (for example, procedural generation of smoke, fire, or clouds), it's not immediately obvious how you could use such a technique for game AI. The key realization is that Perlin noise generates a form of randomness that is not uniform or normal, but rather can be described as coherent randomness, where consecutive random numbers are related to each other. This "smooth" nature of randomness means that we don't get wild jumps from one random number to another, which can be a very desirable trait. But how could this be useful for game AI?

The first step is to visualize Perlin noise in one-dimension, as shown in Figure 3.4. This can be thought of as a random wandering signal (a series of related random numbers). We can use this signal to control the movement or variation of particular behavior traits of our AI characters over time. The following is a list of possibilities for game AI.

- Movement (direction, speed, acceleration)
- Layered onto animation (adding noise to facial movement or gaze [Perlin 97])
- Accuracy (winning or losing streaks, being in the groove, luck, or success)
- Attention (guard alertness, response time)
- Play style (defensive, offensive)
- Mood (calm, angry, happy, sad, depressed, manic, bored, engaged)

So while uniform or Gaussian randomness can be used to vary an individual's physical or behavioral characteristics within a population, Perlin noise can be used to vary those characteristics *over time*. When you have a large population of characters, this can make

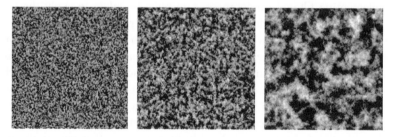

Figure 3.3

Three examples of Perlin noise generated textures with different levels of detail.

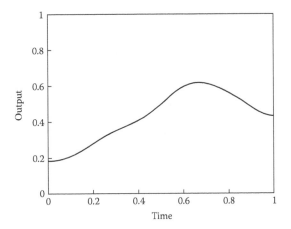

Figure 3.4

Perlin noise in one-dimension. This is a series of random numbers that smoothly wander over time (coherent randomness). We can control the look and feel by manipulating the algorithm that produces the numbers.

the simulation much more interesting, since each particular character can vary their behavior characteristics over durations spanning seconds, minutes, or hours.

Let's explore some of the examples from the previous list of possible game AI uses in more depth. Simple wandering can be achieved by varying the steering direction and speed over time. For arbitrary wandering, Perlin noise is a better alternative to the ad hoc coherent randomness for steering behaviors proposed by Craig Reynolds, because Perlin noise is far more configurable than Reynold's solution [Reynolds 99].

Hot and cold streaks can be purposely simulated, instead of accidentally occurring in retrospect. This is particularly useful since you can anticipate the streak and optionally make the player aware of it midway through, perhaps with an utterance such as, "Boys, I'm feeling lucky tonight!" While uniform randomness will have natural streaks, Perlin noise can be configured to control the behavior of the streaks and predict when you'll be moving into one.

Another possible use is to vary a character's mood in some way, for example, along the calm versus angry scale. While you could come up with an underlying simulation to generate any of these characteristics or mood shifts, it might be overkill and much simpler (development time-wise and computationally) to have them randomly generated using Perlin noise, especially in a large population when no one individual is being scrutinized by the player. However, the players might direct their focus on a character, in which case this apparent lack of rationale behind the deviations in behavior can pose a problem. One solution to this problem is to shift the simulation from Perlin noise to something more robust when it is determined that the character is being noticed. In this sense, Perlin noise can be an LOD level that can be supplanted when it is deemed that it might cause a break in reality [Sunshine-Hill 13a]. Additionally, if the character is now being watched by the player, it might be time to create an *alibi*, or backstory, for the AI, as described in another article in this book [Sunshine-Hill 13b].

3.4.1 Generating One-Dimensional Perlin Noise

Now that we know why we need one-dimensional Perlin noise, let's look at how we can generate it and craft the output to fit our needs. As we describe the algorithm, take note of the knobs and controls that will allow you to customize the randomness to your own preferences. These will be crucial to getting the most out of the algorithm. As you explore the generation part, you might want to get the demo on this book's website to follow along and try different settings.

While Perlin noise generation is difficult to explain due to the nuances of the math, we'll focus on giving you a more intuitive visual explanation through the use of figures. Note that the exact details can be seen in the example code within the demo.

In one-dimension, Perlin noise is constructed by first deciding how many *octaves* to use. Each octave contributes to the signal detail at a particular scale, with higher octaves adding more fine-grained detail. Each octave is computed individually and then they are added to each other to produce the final signal. Figure 3.5 shows one-dimensional Perlin noise, constructed with four octaves.

In order to explain how each octave signal is produced, let's start with the first one. The first octave is computed by starting and ending the interval with two different uniform random numbers, in the range [0, 1]. The signal in the middle is computed by applying a mathematical function that interpolates between the two. The ideal function to use is the S-curve function $6t^5 - 15t^4 + 10t^3$, because it has many nice mathematical properties, such as being smooth in the first and second derivatives [Perlin 02]. This is desirable so that the signal contained within higher octaves is smooth.

For the second octave, we choose three uniform random numbers, place them equidistant from each other, and then interpolate between them using our sigmoid function. Similarly, for the third octave, we choose five uniform random numbers, place them equidistant from each other, and then interpolate between them. The number of uniform random numbers for a given octave is equal to $2^{n-1} + 1$. Figure 3.5 shows four octaves with randomly chosen numbers within each octave.

Once we have the octaves, the next step is to scale each octave with an *amplitude*. This will cause the higher octaves to progressively contribute to the fine-grained variance in the final signal. Starting with the first octave, we multiply the signal by an amplitude of 0.5, as shown in Figure 3.5. The second octave is multiplied by an amplitude of 0.25, and the third octave is multiplied by an amplitude of 0.125, and so on. The formula for the amplitude at a given octave is p^i, where p is the *persistence* value and i is the octave (our example used a persistence value of 0.5). The persistence value will control how much influence higher octaves have, with high values of persistence giving more weight to higher octaves (producing more high-frequency noise in the final signal).

Now that the octaves have been appropriately scaled, we can add them together to get our final one-dimensional Perlin noise signal, as shown at the bottom right of Figure 3.5. While this is all fine and good, it is important to realize that for the purposes of game AI, you are not going to compute and store the entire final signal, since there is no need to have the whole thing at once. Instead, given a particular *time* along the signal, in the range [0, 1] along the x-axis, you'll just compute that particular point as needed for your simulation. So if you want the point in the middle of the final signal, you would compute the individual signal in each octave at time 0.5, scale each octave value with their correct

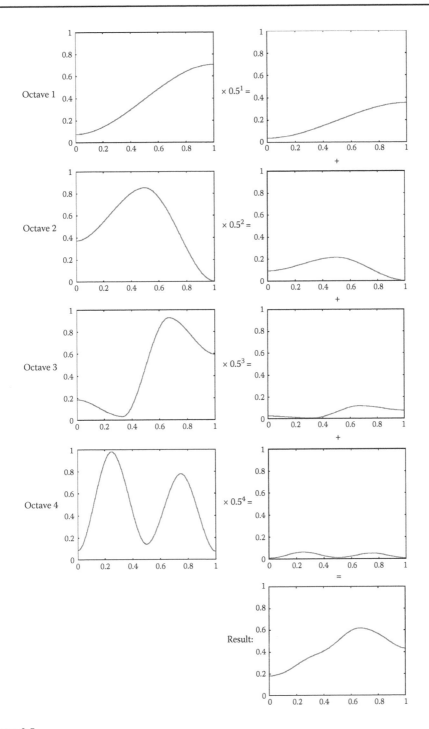

Octave 1 $\times\ 0.5^1 =$

+

Octave 2 $\times\ 0.5^2 =$

+

Octave 3 $\times\ 0.5^3 =$

+

Octave 4 $\times\ 0.5^4 =$

=

Result:

Figure 3.5

Generation of one-dimensional Perlin noise with four octaves.

amplitude, and add them together to get a single value. You can then run your simulation at any rate by requesting the next point at 0.500001, 0.51, or 0.6, for example.

3.4.1.1 Controlling Perlin Noise

As alluded to in the previous section, there are several controls that will allow you to customize the randomness of the noise. The following list is a summary.

- *Number of octaves*: Lower octaves offer larger swings in the signal while higher octaves offer more fine-grained noise. This can be randomized within a population as well, so that some individuals have more octaves than others when generating a particular behavior trait.
- *Range of octaves*: You can have any range, for example octaves 4 through 8. You do not have to start with octave 1. Again, the ranges can be randomized within a population.
- *Amplitude at each octave*: The choice of amplitude at each octave can be used to control the final signal. The higher the amplitude, the more that octave will influence the final signal. Simply ensure that the sum of amplitudes across all octaves does not exceed 1.0 if you don't want the final signal to exceed 1.0.
- *Choice of interpolation*: The S-curve function is commonly used in Perlin noise, with original Perlin noise using $3t^2 - 2t^3$ [Perlin 85] and improved Perlin noise using $6t^5 - 15t^4 + 10t^3$ (smooth in the second derivative) [Perlin 02]. However, you might be able to get other interesting effects by choosing a different formula [Komppa 10].

3.4.1.2 Sampling Perlin Noise Beyond the Interval

When looking at Figure 3.5, it might have occurred to you that there is a problem once we get to the end of the interval (the very right edge of the signal). Once we have sampled at time 1.0, there is no place to go since the signal abruptly stops. One solution is to just start over again at time 0.0, but that would cause a huge discontinuity and repetitive behavior. Fortunately, there is a more elegant solution.

When we need to sample beyond time 1.0, we can generate a completely new Perlin noise signal that attaches to the end of our current signal. If we simply copy all of the uniform random numbers at the right edge of each octave into the far left edge of each new octave, then our signal will seamlessly migrate into a new Perlin noise signal (with the smoothness of the transition dependent on the particular interpolation function used). Of course, we'll need newly generated uniform random numbers for the remaining slots within each new octave, but this is desirable so that we begin generating a completely new signal.

3.4.2 Game AI Perlin Noise Demo

On the book's website (http://www.gameaipro.com), you'll find the Perlin noise demo that accompanies this section. In the demo you can play with the various knobs to control the noise generation. Perlin noise is used to vary individual agent wandering, speed, and aggressiveness. In addition, look at the source code to discover the exact details of how Perlin noise is generated.

3.5 Conclusion

This article presented three advanced randomness techniques that help augment our old friend the `rand()` function. While uniform randomness is the backbone of variation in games, techniques such as Gaussian randomness, filtered randomness, and Perlin noise can offer cool tricks that plain old `rand()` just can't deliver on its own.

In the quest for realism, Gaussian randomness gives us normal distributions that help mimic the actual variation that surrounds us in real life, whether it's natural variations in physical traits, cognitive ability, reaction time, or bullet spread. In order to keep the player content, we can leverage filtered randomness to ensure that influential random decisions that impact the player either positively or negatively appear fair and unbiased. Finally, Perlin noise isn't just for graphics anymore. The one-dimensional coherent randomness of Perlin noise can be used to smoothly vary movement, animation, and dozens of other behavioral characteristics over time.

As a final note, all of the three techniques have accompanying code and demos that can be found on the book's website (http://www.gameaipro.com).

References

[Diener et al. 85] D. Diener and W. Burt Thompson. "Recognizing randomness." *American Journal of Psychology*. 98: 433–447, 1985.

[Komppa 10] J. Komppa. "Interpolation Tricks." http://sol.gfxile.net/interpolation/, 2010.

[Mark 09] D. Mark. *Behavioral Mathematics for Game AI*. Boston, MA: Course Technology, 2009.

[Meier 10] S. Meier. "GDC 2010 Keynote address: Sid Meier." *Game Developers Conference, 2010*. Available online (http://www.gamespot.com/sid-meiers-civilization-v/videos/gdc-2010-keynote-address-sid-meier-6253529/).

[Perlin 85] K. Perlin. "An image synthesizer." *Computer Graphics* 19(3). 1985.

[Perlin 97] K. Perlin. "Layered compositing of facial expression." *SIGGRAPH 97*, Technical Sketch, 1997. Demo available at (http://mrl.nyu.edu/~perlin/experiments/facedemo/).

[Perlin 02] K. Perlin. "Improving noise." *Computer Graphics* 35(3). 2002.

[Rabin 04] S. Rabin. "Filtered randomness for AI decisions and logic." In *AI Game Programming Wisdom 2*, edited by Steve Rabin. Hingham, MA: Charles River Media, 2004, pp. 71–82.

[Rabin 08] S. Rabin. "Using Gaussian randomness to realistically vary projectile paths." In *Game Programming Gems 7*, edited by Scott Jacobs. Hingham, MA: Charles River Media, 2008, pp. 199–204.

[Reynolds 99] C. Reynolds. "Steering behaviors for autonomous characters." *Game Developers Conference, 1999*. Available online (http://www.red3d.com/cwr/steer/).

[Sunshine-Hill 13a] B. Sunshine-Hill. "Phenomenal AI level-of-detail control with the LOD trader." In *Game AI Pro*, edited by Steve Rabin. Boca Raton, FL: CRC Press, 2013.

[Sunshine-Hill 13b] B. Sunshine-Hill. "Alibi generation: fooling all of the players all of the time." In *Game AI Pro*, edited by Steve Rabin. Boca Raton, FL: CRC Press, 2013.

[Wagenaar et al. 91] W. A. Wagenaar and M. Bar-Hille. "The perception of randomness." *Advances in Applied Mathematics*. 12: 428–454, 1991.

[Walker 08] J. Walker. ENT: A Pseudorandom Number Sequence Test Program. https://www.fourmilab.ch/random/, 2008.

PART II
Architecture

4

Behavior Selection Algorithms
An Overview

Michael Dawe, Steve Gargolinski, Luke Dicken,
Troy Humphreys, and Dave Mark

4.1 Introduction

Writing artificial intelligence systems for games has become increasingly complicated as console gamers demand more from their purchases. At the same time, smaller games for mobile platforms have burst onto the scene, making it important for an AI programmer to know how to get the best behavior out of a short frame time.

Even on complicated games running on powerful machines, NPCs can range from simple animals the player might run past or hunt to full-fledged companion characters that need to stand up to hours of player interaction. While each of these example AIs may follow the Sense–Think–Act cycle, the "think" part of that cycle is ill-defined. There are a variety of algorithms to choose from, and each is appropriate for different uses. What might be the best choice to implement a human character on the latest consoles might not be suitable for creating an adversarial player for a web-based board game.

This article will present some of the most popular and proven decision-making algorithms in the industry, providing an overview of these choices and showing when each might be the best selection to use. While it is not a comprehensive resource, hopefully it will prove a good introduction to the variety of algorithmic choices available to the AI programmer.

4.2 Finite-State Machines

Finite-state machines (FSMs) are the most common behavioral modeling algorithm used in game AI programming today. FSMs are conceptually simple and quick to code, resulting in a powerful and flexible AI structure with little overhead. They are intuitive and easy to visualize, which facilitates communication with less-technical team members. Every game AI programmer should be comfortable working with FSMs and be aware of their strengths and weaknesses.

An FSM breaks down an NPC's overall AI into smaller, discrete pieces known as *states*. Each state represents a specific behavior or internal configuration, and only one state is considered "active" at a time. States are connected by *transitions*, directed links responsible for switching to a new active state whenever certain conditions are met.

One compelling feature of FSMs is that they are easy to sketch out and visualize. A rounded box represents each state, and an arrow connecting two boxes signifies a transition between states. The labels on the transition arrows are the conditions necessary for that transition to fire. The solid circle indicates the initial state, the state to be entered when the FSM is first run. As an example, suppose we are designing an FSM for an NPC to guard a castle, as in Figure 4.1.

Our guard NPC starts out in the *Patrol* state, where he follows his route and keeps an eye on his part of the castle. If he hears a noise, then he leaves *Patrol* and moves to *Investigate* the noise for a bit before returning to *Patrol*. If at any point he sees an enemy, he will move into *Attack* to confront the threat. While attacking, if his health drops too low, he'll *Flee* to hopefully live another day. If he defeats the enemy, he'll return to *Patrol*.

While there are many possible FSM implementations, it is helpful to look at an example implementation of the algorithm. First is the `FSMState` class, which each of our concrete states (*Attack*, *Patrol*, etc.) will extend:

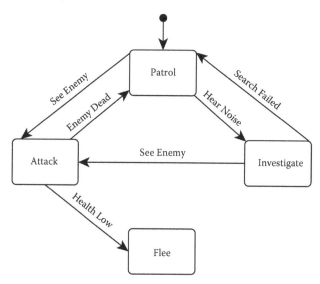

Figure 4.1

This FSM diagram represents the behavior of a guard NPC.

```
class FSMState
{
    virtual void onEnter();
    virtual void onUpdate();
    virtual void onExit();
    list<FSMTransition> transitions;
};
```

Each `FSMState` has the opportunity to execute logic at three different times: when the state is entered, when it is exited, and on each tick when the state is active and no transitions are firing. Each state is also responsible for storing a list of `FSMTransition` objects, which represent all potential transitions out of that state.

```
class FSMTransition
{
    virtual bool isValid();
    virtual FSMState* getNextState();
    virtual void onTransition();
}
```

Each transition in our graph extends from `FSMTransition`. The `isValid()` function evaluates to true when this transition's conditions are met, and `getNextState()` returns which state to transition to when valid. The `onTransition()` function is an opportunity to execute any necessary behavioral logic when a transition fires, similar to `onEnter()` in `FSMState`.

Finally, the `FiniteStateMachine` class:

```
class FiniteStateMachine
{
    void update();
    list<FSMState> states;
    FSMState* initialState;
    FSMState* activeState;
}
```

The `FiniteStateMachine` class contains a list of all states in our FSM, as well as the initial state and the current active state. It also contains the central `update()` function, which is called each tick and is responsible for running our behavioral algorithm as follows:

- Call `isValid()` on each transition in `activeState.transtitions` until `isValid()` returns true or there are no more transitions.
- If a valid transition is found, then:
  - Call `activeState.onExit()`
  - Set `activeState` to `validTransition.getNextState()`
  - Call `activeState.onEnter()`
- If a valid transition is not found, then call `activeState.onUpdate()`

With this structure in place, it's a matter of setting up transitions and filling out the `onEnter()`, `onUpdate()`, `onExit()`, and `onTransition()` functions to produce the desired AI behavior. These specific implementations are entirely design dependent. For example, say our Attack state triggers some dialogue, "There he is, get him!" in onEnter() and uses onUpdate() to periodically choose tactical positions, move to cover, fire on the enemy, and so on. The transition between *Attack* and *Patrol* can trigger some additional dialogue: "Threat eliminated!" in onTransition().

Before starting to code your FSM, it can be helpful to sketch a few diagrams like the one in Figure 4.1 to help define the logic of the behaviors and how they interconnect. Start writing the code once the different states and transitions are understood. FSMs are flexible and powerful, but they only work as well as the thought that goes into developing the underlying logic.

4.3 Hierarchical Finite-State Machines

FSMs are a useful tool, but they do have weaknesses. Adding the second, third, or fourth state to an NPC's FSM is usually structurally trivial, as all that's needed is to hook up transitions to the few existing required states. However, if you're nearing the end of development and your FSM is already complicated with 10, 20, or 30 existing states, then fitting your new state into the existing structure can be extremely difficult and error-prone.

There are also some common patterns that FSMs are not well-equipped to handle, such as situational behavior reuse. To show an example of this, Figure 4.2 shows a night watchman NPC responsible for guarding a safe in a building.

This NPC will simply patrol between the front door and the safe forever. Suppose a new state called *Conversation* is to be added that allows our night watchman to respond to a cell phone call, pause to have a brief conversation, and return to his patrol. If the watchman is in *Patrol to Door* when the call comes in, then we want him to resume patrolling to the door when the conversation is complete. Likewise, if he is in *Patrol to Safe* when the phone rings, he should return to *Patrol to Safe* when transitioning out of *Conversation*.

Since we need to know which state to transition back to after the call, we're forced to create a new *Conversation* state each time we want to reuse the behavior, as shown in Figure 4.3.

In this simple example we require two *Conversation* behaviors to achieve the desired result, and in a more complicated FSM we might require many more. Adding additional states in this manner every time we want to reuse a behavior is not ideal or elegant. It leads to an explosion of states and graph complexity, making the existing FSM harder to understand and new states ever more difficult and error-prone to add.

Thankfully, there is a technique that will alleviate some of these structural issues: the Hierarchical Finite-State Machine (HFSM). In an HFSM, each individual state can be an entire state machine itself. This technique effectively separates one state machine into multiple state machines arranged in a hierarchy.

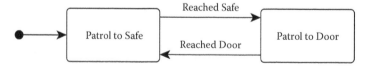

Figure 4.2

This FSM diagram represents the behavior of a night watchman NPC.

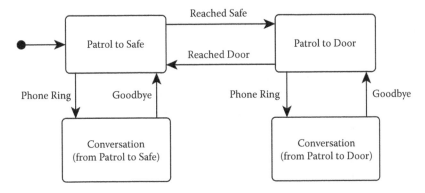

Figure 4.3

Our night watchman FSM requires multiple instances of the Conversation state.

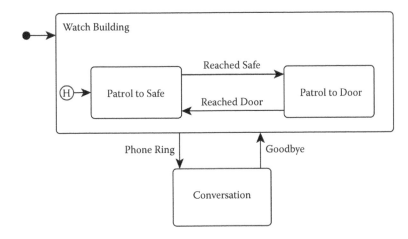

Figure 4.4

An HFSM solves the problem of duplicate Conversation states.

Returning to the night watchman example, if we nest our two *Patrol* states into a state machine called *Watch Building*, then we can get by with just one *Conversation* state, as shown in Figure 4.4.

The reason this works is that the HFSM structure adds additional hysteresis that isn't present in an FSM. With a standard FSM, we can always assume that the state machine starts off in its initial state, but this is not the case with a nested state machine in an HFSM. Note the circled "H" in Figure 4.4, which points to the "history state." The first time we enter the nested *Watch Building* state machine, the history state indicates the initial state, but from then on it indicates the most recent active state of that state machine.

Our example HFSM starts out in *Watch Building* (indicated by the solid circle and arrow as before), which chooses *Patrol to Safe* as the initial state. If our NPC reaches the safe and transitions into *Patrol to Door*, then the history state switches to *Patrol to Door*. If the NPC's phone rings at this point, then our HFSM exits *Patrol to Door* and *Watch*

Building, transitioning to the *Conversation* state. After *Conversation* ends, the HFSM will transition back to *Watch Building* which resumes in *Patrol to Door* (the history state), not *Patrol to Safe* (the initial state).

As you can see, this setup achieves our design goal without requiring duplication of any states. Generally, HFSMs provide much more structural control over the layout of states, allowing larger, complex behaviors to be broken down into smaller, simpler pieces.

The algorithm for updating an HFSM is similar to updating an FSM, with added recursive complexity due to the nested state machines. Pseudocode implementation is fairly complicated, and beyond the scope of this overview article. For a solid detailed implementation, check out Section 5.3.9 in the book *Artificial Intelligence for Games* by Ian Millington and John Funge [Millington and Funge 09].

FSMs and HFSMs are incredibly useful algorithms for solving a wide variety of problems that game AI programmers typically face. As discussed there are many pros to using an FSM, but there are also some cons. One of the major potential downsides of FSMs is that your desired behavior might not fit into the structure elegantly. HFSMs can help alleviate this pressure in some cases, but not all. For example, if an FSM suffers from "transition overload" and hooks up every state to every other state, and if an HFSM isn't helping, other algorithms may be a better choice. Review the techniques in this article, think about your problem, and choose the best tool for the job.

4.4 Behavior Trees

A *behavior tree* describes a data structure starting from some root node and made up of *behaviors*, which are individual actions an NPC can perform. Each behavior can in turn have child behaviors, which gives the algorithm its tree-like qualities.

Every behavior defines a *precondition*, which specifies the conditions where the agent will execute this behavior, and an *action*, specifying the actual things the agent should do when performing the behavior. The algorithm starts at the root of the tree and examines the preconditions of the behaviors, deciding on each behavior in turn. At each level of the tree, only one behavior can be selected, so if a behavior executes, none of its siblings will be checked, though its children will still be examined. Conversely, if a behavior's precondition does not return true, the algorithm skips checking any of that behavior's children and instead moves onto the next sibling. Once the end of the tree is reached, the algorithm has decided on the highest-priority behaviors to run, and the actions of each are executed in turn.

The algorithm to execute a behavior tree is as follows:

- Make root node the current node
- While current node exists,
  - Run current node's precondition
  - If precondition returns true,
    - Add node to execute list
    - Make node's child current node
  - Else,
    - Make node's sibling current node
- Run all behaviors on the execute list

The real strength of a behavior tree comes from its simplicity. The base algorithm can be implemented quickly due to its straightforward nature. Since trees are stateless, the algorithm doesn't need to remember what behaviors were previously running in order to determine what behaviors should execute on a given frame. Further, behaviors can (and should) be written to be completely unaware of each other, so adding or removing behaviors from a character's behavior tree do not affect the running of the rest of the tree. This alleviates the problem common with FSMs, where every state must know the transition criteria for every other state.

Extensibility is also an advantage with behavior trees. It is easy to start from the base algorithm as described and start adding extra functionality. Common additions are behavior `on_start`/`on_finish` functions that are run the first time a behavior begins and when it completes. Different behavior selectors can be implemented as well. For example, a parent behavior could specify that instead of choosing one of its children to run, each of its children should be run once in turn, or that one of its children should be chosen randomly to run. Indeed, a child behavior could be run based on a utility system-type selector (see below) if desired. Preconditions can be written to fire in response to events as well, giving the tree flexibility to respond to agent stimuli. Another popular extension is to specify individual behaviors as nonexclusive, meaning that if their precondition is run, the behavior tree should keep checking siblings at that level.

A behavior tree, though simple and powerful, is not always the best choice for a selection algorithm. Since the tree must run from the root every time behaviors are selected, the running time is generally greater than that of a finite-state machine. Additionally, the naïve implementation can have a large number of conditional statements, which can be very slow, depending on your target platform. On the other hand, evaluating every possible behavior in the tree may be slow on others where processing power is the limiting factor. Either approach can be a valid implementation of the algorithm; so the programmer would have to decide what is best.

Since behaviors themselves are stateless, care must be taken when creating behaviors that appear to apply memory. For example, imagine a citizen running away from a battle. Once well away from the area, the "run away" behavior may stop executing, and the highest-priority behavior that takes over could take the citizen back into the combat area, making the citizen continually loop between two behaviors. While steps can be taken to prevent this sort of problem, traditional planners can tend to deal with the situation more easily.

4.5 Utility Systems

Much of AI logic—and, for that matter, computer logic—is based on simple Boolean questions. For example, an agent may ask "Can I see the enemy?" or "Am I out of ammunition?" These are purely "yes or no" questions. The decisions that come out of Boolean questions are often just as polarized. As we saw in the prior architectures, the results of these questions are often mapped directly to a single action. For instance,

```
if (CanSeeEnemy())
{
    AttackEnemy();
}
```

```
if (OutOfAmmo())
{
    Reload();
}
```

Even when multiple criteria are combined, Boolean equations tend to lead to a very discrete result set.

```
if (OutOfAmmo() && CanSeeEnemy())
{
    Hide();
}
```

Many aspects of decision making aren't quite as tidy, however. There are numerous questions that can be asked where a "yes or no" answer is not appropriate. For example, we may want to consider how far away the enemy is, how many bullets I have left, how hungry I am, how wounded I am, or any number of continuous values. Correspondingly, these continuous values can be mapped over into *how much* I want to take an action rather than simply whether to take the action or not. A utility-based system measures, weighs, combines, rates, ranks, and sorts out many considerations in order to decide the *preferability* of potential actions. Using the above example as a guide, we could assess how *strongly* we want (or need!) to attack, reload, hide, etc.

While utility techniques can be used to supplement the transition logic of other architectures, it is very possible to build an entire decision engine based on utility. In fact, there are times when building a utility-based AI is far preferable to other methods. These might include games where there are many possible actions, and either there isn't a single "right" answer or the selection of a preferable action might be based on a large number of competing inputs. In these cases, we are going beyond simply using utility to measure or rate something. Instead, we are using it to drive the actual decision mechanism as well. Another way of stating it is that, rather than saying "This is the one action you will do," the utility-based system *suggests*, "Here are some possible options that you might want to do."

One well-documented example of this is the use of utility in *The Sims*. In these games, the agents (i.e., the actual "Sims") take information from their environment and combine it with their own internal state to arrive at a preferability score for each potential action. For example, the fact that I am "very hungry" combined with the availability of "poor food" would certainly be more attractive than if I was only "a little hungry." Additionally, the proximity of "spectacular" food might still make for a high priority even if I was only "a little hungry." Note that the descriptors "spectacular," "rather," "poor," and "a little" would actually be numbers between some set minimum and a maximum. (A typical method to use is a floating point number between 0 and 1.)

When it is time to select a new action (either because the current one is finished or through some sort of interrupt system), some method is used to select from among the candidates. For example, the scores for the potential actions could be sorted so that we can simply select the "most appropriate" action—that is, the one with the highest score. An alternate way is to use the scores to seed a weighted random selection. By casting a random number against these weighted probabilities, the most preferable actions have a higher chance of being selected. As an action's suitability goes up, its score goes up, as does its chance of being selected.

Another example of where utility-based architectures might be preferable to other architectures is RPGs. Often in these games, the options that an agent has are varied and possibly only subtly better or worse, given the situation. For instance, selecting what weapon, spell, item, or action should be taken given the type of enemy, the agent's status, the status of the player, etc., can be a complicated balancing act.

Another wheelhouse of utility architectures is any game system with an economic decision layer. The question of units or buildings to construct in a real-time strategy game, for example, is a juggling act of costs, times, and often many axes of priority (e.g., "offense" or "defense"). An architecture based on utility can often be more adaptable to changing game situations. As such, it can recover better from being disrupted than can more scripted models, which can suffer from either being hopelessly confused or can simply trundle along as if nothing ever happened.

The primary reason for this adaptability is that preferability scores are highly dynamic. As the game situation changes—either through a change in the environment or a change in state of the agent—the scores for most (if not all) of the actions will change. As the action scores change, so does their likelihood of being selected as a "reasonable" action. The resulting ebb and flow of action scores—especially when combined with a weighted random selection—often leads to very dynamic emergent behavior.

On the other hand, unlike the architectures that use Boolean-transitioned decision logic, utility systems are often somewhat unpredictable. Because the selections are based on how much the actions "make sense" in a given situation and context, however, the actions should tend to look *reasonable*. This unpredictability has benefits and drawbacks. It can improve believability because the variety of actions that could occur in a given situation can make for far more natural-looking agents rather than the predictably robotic if/then-based models. While this is desirable in many situations, if your design calls for specific behaviors at very certain moments, you must make a point to override the utility calculations with more scripted actions.

Another caveat to using utility-based architecture is that all the subtlety and responsiveness that you gain often comes at a price. While the core architecture is often relatively simple to set up, and new behaviors can be added simply, they can be somewhat challenging to tune. Rarely does a behavior sit in isolation in a utility-based system. Instead, it is added to the pile of all the other potential behaviors with the idea that the associated mathematical models will encourage the appropriate behaviors to "bubble to the top." The trick is to juggle all the models to encourage the most reasonable behaviors to shine when it is most appropriate. This is often more art than science. As with art, however, the results that are produced are often far more engaging than those generated by using simple science alone.

For more on utility-based systems, see the article in this book, *An Introduction to Utility Theory* [Graham 13] and the book *Behavioral Mathematics for Game AI* [Mark 09].

4.6 Goal-Oriented Action Planners

Goal-Oriented Action Planning (GOAP) is a technique pioneered by Monolith's Jeff Orkin for the game *F.E.A.R.* in 2005, and has been used in a number of games since, most recently for titles such as *Just Cause 2* and *Deus Ex: Human Revolution*. GOAP is derived from the Stanford Research Institute Problem Solver (STRIPS) approach to AI which was first developed in the early 1970s. In general terms, STRIPS (and GOAP) allows an AI system to create its own approaches to solving problems by being provided with a description of how the game world works—that is, a list of the actions that are possible, the requirements before each action can be used (called "preconditions"), and the effects of the action. The system then takes a symbolic representation of the initial state of the world and some set of objective facts that need to be achieved. In GOAP these objectives are typically chosen from a predetermined set of goals that an NPC may want to achieve, chosen by some method such as priority or state transition. The planning system can then determine a sequence of actions that will allow the agent that it is controlling to change the world from the original state into a state that contains the facts that need to be true to satisfy its current goals. In classical planning this would ideally be the critical path to the target state, and that target would be the most easily reachable state that contained all of the objective facts.

GOAP works by "*backwards chaining search*," which is a fancy phrase which means starting with the goals you want to achieve, working out what actions are required for those to happen, then working out what needs to happen in order to achieve the preconditions of the actions you just identified and so on. You continue to work backwards in this fashion until you arrive at the state you started from. It's a fairly traditional approach, which has fallen out of favor in the scientific world, replaced by "*forwards chaining search*" which relies on heuristic search, pruning, and other tricks. Backwards search is a solid workhorse, however, and although it's less elegant, it's far easier to understand and implement than more modern techniques.

Backwards chaining search works in the following manner:

- Add the goal to the outstanding facts list
- For each outstanding fact
  - Remove this outstanding fact
  - Find the actions that have the fact as an effect
  - If the precondition of the action is satisfied,
    - Add the action to the plan,
    - Work backwards to add the now-supported action chain to the plan
  - Otherwise,
    - Add the preconditions of the action as outstanding facts

One final interesting aspect of GOAP is that it allows "context preconditions" that are ignored by the planning system, but must be satisfied at run-time in order for an action to be executed. This allows for reasoning to bypass certain aspects of the world that cannot be easily represented symbolically—such as ensuring line of sight to a target before beginning to fire—while ensuring that by accessing information not made available during planning (to ensure the search remains tractable), these constraints can be met. This allows the plan GOAP generates to be somewhat flexible, and the actions it calls for apply more at a tactical level than at the most basic level of execution. That is, the plan tells you *what* to do, but not necessarily *how* to do it. For example, detailed instructions such as how to establish a line of sight to begin shooting are omitted and can be handled more reactively.

Let's suppose we have a typical NPC soldier character, whose goal is to kill another character. We can represent this goal as `Target.Dead`. In order for the target to die, the character needs to shoot him (in a basic system). A precondition of shooting is having a weapon equipped. Assuming our character doesn't have one, we now need an action that can give the character a weapon, perhaps by drawing one from a holster. This, of course, has its own precondition—that there is a weapon available in the character's inventory. If this is the case, we have just created a simple plan of drawing the weapon and then shooting. What if the character doesn't have a weapon? Then our search would have to find a way to get one. If that isn't possible the search can backtrack and look for alternatives to the shoot action. Perhaps there is a mounted weapon nearby that could be used to provide the `Target.Dead` effect, or even a vehicle that we can use for running over the target. In either case, it's clear that by providing a comprehensive set of action choices of what *can* be done in the world, we can leave it up to the character to decide what *should* be done, letting dynamic and interesting behaviors emerge naturally, rather than having to envisage and create them during development.

Finally, consider a game in which weapons have a maximum range. As a context precondition, we can say that the target must be within that range. The planner won't spend time in its search trying to make this true—it can't, as it would involve reasoning about how the target might move and so on—but it either won't fire its weapon until the condition is true, or it will instead use an alternative tactic such as a different weapon with a longer range.

There's a lot to like about an approach to NPC control based on automated planning. It streamlines the development process by allowing designers to focus on creating simple components that will self-assemble into behaviors, and it also allows for "novel" solutions, which may never have been anticipated by the team, often making for excellent anecdotes that players will re-tell. GOAP itself remains the lowest hanging fruit of what automated planning can provide and, from a purely scientific point of view, the state of the art has progressed significantly since it was developed. With that said, it can still be a very powerful technique when used correctly, and provides a good, adaptable starting point for specific customization.

It is worth noting that these kinds of approaches that adopt a character-centric view of intelligence remove a lot of the authorial and directorial control from the development team. Characters that can "think" for themselves can become loose cannons within the game world, creating plans that, while valid for achieving the character's goals, do not achieve the broader goals of creating immersive and engaging experiences, and this can then potentially disrupt cinematic set-pieces if, for example, a soldier's plan doesn't take him past the conveniently placed Big Red Barrel.

While it's possible to avoid these kinds of issues by using knowledge engineering techniques and representational tricks, it isn't as straightforward as with architectures such as behavior trees, which would allow the desired behavior to be injected directly into the character's decision logic. At the same time, a GOAP approach is significantly easier to design than one based around hierarchical task networks, since in GOAP you just need to describe the mechanics of the objects within a world.

GOAP and similar techniques are not silver bullet solutions, but in the right circumstances they can prove to be very powerful in creating realistic behaviors and immersive-feeling characters that players can fully engage with.

4.7 Hierarchical Task Networks

Though GOAP is perhaps the best-known game planner, other types of planners have gained popularity as well. One such system, *hierarchical task networks* (HTN), has been used in titles such as Guerrilla Games' *KillZone 2* and High Moon Studios' *Transformers:*

Fall of Cybertron. Like other planners, HTN aims to find a plan for the NPC to execute. Where it differs is how it goes about finding that plan.

HTN works by starting with the initial world state and a root task representing the problem we are looking to solve. This high-level task is then decomposed into smaller and smaller tasks until we end up with a plan of tasks we can execute to solve our problem. Each high-level task can have multiple ways of being accomplished, so the current world state will be used to decide which set of smaller tasks the high-level task should be decomposed into. This allows for decision making at multiple levels of abstraction.

As opposed to *backward* planners like GOAP, which start with a desired world state and move backwards until it reaches the current state world state, HTN is a *forward* planner, meaning that it will start with the current world state and work towards a desired solution. The planner works with several types of primitives, starting with the *world state*. The world state represents the state of the problem space. An example in game terms might be an NPC's view of the world and him in it. This world state is broken up into multiple properties such as his health, his stamina, enemy's health, enemy's range, and the like. This knowledge representation would allow the planner to reason about what to do.

Next, we have two different types of tasks: *primitive tasks* and *compound tasks*. A primitive task is an actionable thing that can be done to solve a problem. In game terms, this could be *FireWeapon*, *Reload*, and *MoveToCover*. These tasks are able to affect the world state, such as how the *FireWeapon* task would use ammo and the *Reload* task would refill the weapon. *Compound tasks* are higher level tasks that can be accomplished in different ways, described as *methods*. A method is a set of tasks that can accomplish the compound task, along with preconditions determining when a method may be used. Compound tasks allow HTN to reason about the world and decide which course of action to take.

Using compound tasks, we can now build an HTN domain. The domain is a large hierarchy of tasks that represent all the ways of solving our problem, such as how to behave as an NPC of some type. The following pseudocode shows how a plan is built.

- Add the root compound task to our decomposing list
- For each task in our decomposing list
  - Remove task
  - If task is compound
    - Find method in compound task that is satisfied by the current world state
    - If a method is found, add method's tasks to the decomposing list
    - If not, restore planner to the state before the last decomposed task
  - If task is primitive
    - Apply task's effects to the current world state
    - Add task to the final plan list

As mentioned, HTN planners start with a very high-level root task and continuously decompose it into smaller and smaller tasks. This decomposition is steered with each compound task's set of methods by comparing each method's conditions with the current world state. When we finally come across a primitive task, we add it to our final plan. Since each primitive task is an actionable step, we can apply its effects to the world state, essentially moving forward in time. Once the decomposing list is empty we will either have a valid plan or have backed out entirely leaving us with no plan.

To demonstrate how an HTN works, suppose a game has a Soldier NPC that needs its AI written. The root compound task might be named *BeSoldierTask*. Next, the soldier should behave differently if he had an enemy to attack or not. Therefore, two methods are needed to describe what to do in these cases. In the case where an enemy is present, the *BeSoldierTask* would decompose using the method that required that condition. The method's task in this case would be *AttackEnemyTask*. This task's methods define the different ways that the soldier could attack. For example, the soldier could shoot from a cover position if he has ammunition for his rifle. If he didn't have ammo for his firearm, he could charge the enemy and attack him with his combat knife. Writing these give *AttackEnemyTask* two methods to complete the task.

The more we drill down on a soldier's behavior, the more the hierarchy forms and refines. The structure of the domain fits naturally in how one might describe the behavior to another person.

Since HTNs describe behavior using a hierarchical structure, building and reasoning about characters is done in a natural way, allowing designers to more easily read through HTN domains, assisting with collaboration between programming and design. Like other planners, the work that is actually done by the AI is kept in nice modular primitive tasks, allowing a lot of reuse across different AI characters.

Since HTN is a search through a graph, the size of your graph will affect search times, but there are two ways to control search size. First, the method's conditions can be used to cull entire branches of the hierarchy. This happens naturally as behaviors are built. Second, having partial plans can defer complex calculations until plan execution. For example, consider the compound task *AttackEnemy*. One method might have the subtasks *NavigateToEnemy* followed by *MeleeEnemy*. *NavigateToEnemy* requires pathing calculations, which can not only be costly, but could be affected by the state of the world, which might change between planning and execution. To utilize partial plans, split these two tasks into two methods, rather than one method with subtasks: *NavigateToEnemy*, if the enemy is out of range, and *MeleeEnemy* when in range. This allows us to only form a partial plan of *NavigateToEnemy* when the enemy is out of range, shortening our search time.

One other note is that the user needs to build the network for HTN to work. This is a double-edged sword when comparing it to GOAP-style planners. While this allows the designer to be very expressive in the behavior they are trying to achieve, it removes the NPC's ability to build plans that the designer might not have thought of. Depending on the game you are building, this can be considered either a strength or a weakness.

4.8 Conclusion

With such a wide variety of behavior selection algorithms available, it is imperative that the AI programmer have knowledge of each tool in the toolbox in order to best apply each to a given situation. Which algorithm is best for a given NPC can depend on the game, the knowledge state of the NPC, the target platform, or more. While this is not a comprehensive treatment on every available option, knowing a bit about where to start with the options can be invaluable. By taking time to think carefully about the needs of the game, an AI system can be crafted to give the best player experience while maintaining the balance between development time and ease of creation.

References

[Graham 13] R. Graham. "An Introduction to Utility Systems." In *Game AI Pro*, edited by Steve Rabin. Boca Raton, FL: CRC Press, 2013.

[Mark 09] D. Mark. *Behavioral Mathematics for Game AI*. Boston, MA: Cengage Learning, 2009.

[Millington and Funge 09] I. Millington and J. Funge. *Artificial Intelligence for Games*. Burlington, MA: Morgan Kaufmann, 2009, pp. 318–331.

5

Structural Architecture— Common Tricks of the Trade

Kevin Dill

5.1 Introduction

When discussing game AI, developers often get hyper-focused on advocating for a particular approach or a particular architecture, but many of the problems that make AI programming so hard appear regardless of the architecture you use, and many of the most common solutions have been reinvented time after time in architecture after architecture. For example, we can use *hierarchy* to divide up the AI logic, simplifying both configuration and execution. We can use *option stacks* to allow one option to temporarily suspend another, without changing the overall plan of attack. We can use a *blackboard* to share information and ideas between AI components or between characters. We can *move the intelligence* into the objects, the terrain, the abilities, or the events in order to more logically divide the code and data, and to improve our ability to extend the game. (Some games, such as *The Sims* franchise, have used this approach to ship downloadable content or even entire expansion packs without a change to the executable.) Finally, we can use modularity to extract reusable pieces of AI logic, thus simultaneously eliminating duplicate code and enabling the AI's author to think at a coarser level of granularity.

In the remainder of this chapter we describe each of these ideas. The intent is to provide enough information to paint the big picture, to spark new ideas and solutions to problems that you, the reader, might face, but not to dig deeply into the technical details of any given solution. For that, we refer you to the bibliography and the references contained therein.

5.2 Definitions

The ideas that we will address in this paper are fairly universal, but there aren't necessarily universal terms to describe them—and in some cases, terms mean one thing to one person and something different to another. As a result, this section will define terms that might not be clear, so that we can have a common vocabulary to work with as we forge ahead.

The *AI architecture* is the underlying code—typically in C++—that controls the process by which the AI evaluates the situation and makes a decision. Several examples of architectures will be given below, and the other articles in this section describe many of them in detail.

A *configuration* is the behavioral specification that maps from specific sensory data (i.e., specific inputs) to specific decisions or actions (i.e., specific outputs). For example, the configuration for a First-Person Shooter (FPS) character would contain all of the logic necessary to decide what that character should do at each point in the game—e.g., should it attack, should it run away, should it reload its weapon, and so on. The configuration is built on top of the architecture and usually specified in data (i.e., XML or similar).

We will often refer to the thing that an AI controls as the *character*. Not all AIs control single characters—for example, you might be working on the AI for an opposing player in a strategy game (which controls many characters), or the AI for a missile in a flying game, or even an AI that controls some aspect of the user interface. You will also hear AI-controlled entities referred to as *agents*, *enemies*, or simply as *AIs*. The generic term *character*, however, is a convenient term, and most AI does apply to characters, so we will stick with it in this chapter.

It is often the case that a character will contain more than one decision-maker. For example, a character might have one algorithm that selects which weapon to use, another that selects the target to shoot at, and a third that decides what emotion he should display. We refer to these decision makers as *reasoners*. Reasoners may have clear cut responsibilities (such as those described above), or they may be organized in a more ad hoc fashion (such as the selectors in a behavior tree [Isla 05]).

Similarly, we will refer to the things that reasoners choose as *options*. A reasoner functions by first evaluating the situation, and then selecting one or more options to execute. When a reasoner picks a new option and starts executing it, we say that it has *selected* the option, and when it stops executing an option we say that the option is *deselected*. These options might be *actions* (that is, physical things that the AI does), but they might also be more abstract. For example, a character's emotional reasoner might simply change the AI's internal state (perhaps by setting an enumerated value to the appropriate state—eHappy, eSad, eAngry, etc.—or by assigning an intensity value to each emotion) so that other reasoners can then select appropriate actions (smiling, frowning, attacking the player, etc.) based on that state.

5.3 Common Architectures

Although the techniques described here are intended to be architecture-agnostic, it is often useful to discuss a specific architecture when describing them. All of these architectures are described in detail elsewhere, so we give just a very high level definition of each one.

Scripting is perhaps the most basic architecture possible. In it, the designer or AI programmer specifies the sequence of options that the AI will select and when they will be selected (e.g., wait 48 seconds, and then spawn three units and attack the player). Scripts may include very simple sensory input, such as trigger zones, but in general the idea is that every decision is fully specified by the AI's author [Berger et al. 02].

Finite-state machines (FSMs) were once the most popular game AI architecture, but have been largely replaced by behavior trees in recent years. An FSM is a collection of states and transitions. The states represent the options that the reasoner can select, whereas the transitions represent the conditions under which the AI will change from one state to another. For example, a very simple first-person shooter (FPS) character might have four states: *Attack, Flee, Reload,* and *Search for Enemy.* The *Attack* state would contain transitions to *Flee* (which fires if the character is nearly dead), *Reload* (which fires when the character is out of ammo), and *Search for Enemy* (which fires when the character loses sight of the enemy) [Buckland 05, Rabin 00].

A *rule-based AI* is one that consists of a sequence of predicate-option pairs. The AI evaluates the predicate for each rule in order. When it gets to a rule whose predicate is true, it executes the option for that rule and stops evaluating additional rules. Thus, a rule-based AI for our simple FPS character would have four rules. The first would make it flee if its health is low. The second would make it reload if it is out of ammo. The third would make it attack the player if the player is in sight. Finally, the fourth would search for the player [Millington et al. 09a, Nilson 94].

A *utility-based AI* uses a *heuristic function* to assign a floating-point value (typically called a *weight, priority,* or *utility*) to each option. It then selects the option to execute based on those values—for example, by taking the option with the highest utility, or by assigning a weight to each option and using that to guide the probability of random selection. Our simple FPS character would still have the same four possible options, but now it would decide which one to do by evaluating the heuristic function for each option and using the resulting values to guide its final selection [Mark 09, Dill 06, Dill et al. 12a, Dill 12c].

Planners such as *goal-oriented action planners (GOAP)* or *hierarchical task-network (HTN) planners* build a sequence of options that will get them to some goal state. For example, our FPS character might have the goal *Enemy Dead.* It would search through its possible options and the ways in which they can change the state of the world in order to find a sequence of options which will get it into the goal state. That plan might be something like *Search for Enemy–Attack–Reload–Attack* (if it expects two magazines of ammo to be enough to get the job done). Planners typically have the ability to replan if the situation changes. So if our character finds itself nearly dead then it might replan with a new goal, such as *Don't Die.* This new plan might have only a single option: *Flee* [Orkin 04, Gorniak et al. 07].

The *behavior tree (BT)* architecture is a bit of a special case, because it is an architecture that can contain other architectures. A BT is a tree of *selectors,* each of which makes a single piece of the overall decision. In their original formulation [Isla 05], the selectors were all exceedingly simple and not really architectures in their own right. However, more recent work has discussed the ability to use nearly any architecture in a selector [Dill 11a], making the behavior tree more of a framework (or meta-architecture) than an architecture in its own right.

5.4 Hierarchical Reasoning

The difficulty of building an AI configuration generally scales worse than linearly with the size of the configuration. In other words, the more situations your AI can handle, the more things it takes into account, the more options it contains, etc., the more complex it is to add yet another of one of those things. The reason for this should be fairly intuitive. Whenever you add something new to your AI you need to put at least some effort into considering how that new thing interacts with each thing already in existence. Thus, the cost of adding a new thing increases the more things you have.

The severity of that increase depends in large part on the architecture you are using. FSMs, for example, scale exponentially because the number of transitions that is exponential on the number of states. This becomes unmanageable very quickly. This is one of the principal reasons that FSMs have largely passed out of use for complex problems. Utility-based AI, on the other hand, only requires you to balance the heuristic functions appropriately, while rule-based AI typically just requires you to place your new rule at the proper place in the list. With that said, even a rule-based AI will become brittle when it contains hundreds or thousands of rules (which is not an unreasonable size for many games).

One common way to address this challenge—an approach that has been applied to nearly every architecture, both in games and in academia—is to break the decision making up hierarchically. That is, have a high-level reasoner that makes the big, overarching decisions, and then one or more lower-level reasoners that handle implementation of the higher-level reasoners' decisions. For example, a high-level reasoner might decide whether to execute a daily schedule of ambient tasks (e.g., get up, get breakfast, go to work, etc.), start a conversation with the player, go into combat, and so forth. Each of those options would contain another reasoner, which decides how to go about accomplishing the goal.

The advantage here is that the complexity of AI configuration scales worse than linearly on the number of options *in a particular reasoner*. To give a sense of the relevance, imagine that the cost of configuring the AI is $O(n^2)$ on the number of options (as it is for FSMs). If we have 25 options, then the cost of configuring the AI is on the order of $25^2 = 625$. On the other hand, if we have five reasoners, each with five options, then the cost of configuring the AI is only $5 \times (5^2) = 125$. Conceptually, this makes sense. When we add a new option, we only need to consider how it relates to other options within the same reasoner—which is much simpler than comparing it to every other option anywhere in the AI.

Examples of this approach abound, from hierarchical FSMs [Millington et al. 09b] to HTN planners [Gorniak et al. 07] and GOAP implementations [Cerpa et al. 08] to strategy game AIs that break the opposing player AI into command hierarchies [Pittman 08]. Behavior trees are perhaps the archetypical example—a BT is really nothing more than a hierarchical infrastructure in which you can place whatever sorts of reasoning architectures best encapsulate the decisions to be made.

5.5 Option Stacks

Most reactive AIs function by evaluating the situation very frequently (often every frame), and deciding what is the best thing to do right at that particular moment. They may have a history of past decisions that guides their choices, they may even have some greater plan that they're following, but decisions are made moment-to-moment. This is what allows the AI to respond if the situation changes.

Of course, we do want options to be persistent. That is, we don't want the AI to be constantly flip-flopping between different decisions—attacking on one frame, fleeing on the next, and then attacking again on the frame after. Or, for another example, attacking with a shotgun, and then a flamethrower, and then right back to the shotgun after only a frame or two, switching weapons too fast to even get a shot off. That sort of indecisiveness makes the AI look stupid, even if there is a good reason *at that moment* for the decision being made. As we discussed in an earlier chapter [Dill 13], looking stupid is the single worst thing that an AI can do. It breaks the player's suspension of disbelief—that is, their immersion in the experience. As a result, most architectures have some form of *inertia* built in, which keeps the AI doing the same thing unless there is a good reason for the change.

When the AI does change options, one of two possible situations pertains. In most cases, the AI's decision is lasting—that is, it has decided to stop the old option and start a new one, and it's not expecting to go back to what it was doing before. For example, if the AI is in a fight and it kills one enemy, now it can pick a new enemy to attack (or pick something else to do if the fight is over). The decision can be lasting even if the AI wasn't done with the previous option. For example, when an AI decides to flee, that's a lasting decision, even though it typically happens *before* the AI finishes its attack. Regardless, the AI has made a deliberate decision to stop doing what it was doing and do something else instead. In this case, we should stop applying inertia to the deselected option, and in fact may even want to apply a *cooldown* which will prevent us from returning to it for a short period of time.

There are situations, however, when the AI needs to react to an immediate need or opportunity, but once that reaction is complete it should return to its previous option. For example, if an AI needs to reload, it should return to the same action (presumably firing a particular weapon) when it finishes reloading. It wouldn't make sense to reload your shotgun, only to then immediately switch weapons to a flamethrower (or decide to flee). That's not to say that the AI can't change its mind, but it should have to overcome the option's inertia to do so, just as if that option were still executing. Thus, we might switch to the flamethrower immediately after reloading the shotgun—but only if we suddenly spotted some new enemy who is highly vulnerable to fire.

One common trick which has been applied to a great many architectures is to have a stack of currently executing options. This stack is sometimes referred to as a *state stack* [Tozour 04], or a *goal stack* [Cerpa 08], or *subsumption* [Heckel et al. 09], depending on the underlying architecture, but we will simply call it an *option stack*, since that is an architecture-agnostic term. Option stacks allow us to push a new, high priority option on top of the stack, *suspending* the currently executing option but retaining its internal state. When the high priority option completes execution, it will pop itself back off of the stack, and the previously executing option will *resume* as if nothing had ever happened.

There are a myriad of uses for option stacks, and they can often be several levels deep. For example, a high-level strategic reasoner might have decided to send a unit to attack a distant enemy outpost. Along the way, that unit could be ambushed—in which case, it might push a *React to Ambush* option on top of its option stack. While responding to the ambush, one of the characters in the unit might notice that a live grenade has just been thrown at its feet. That character might then push an *Avoid Grenade* option on top of

React to Ambush. Once the grenade has gone off (assuming the character lives) it can pop *Avoid Grenade* off the stack, and *React to Ambush* will resume. Once the enemy ambush is over, it will be popped as well, and the original *Attack* option will resume.

One handy trick is to use option stacks to handle your hit reaction. If a character is hit by an enemy attack (e.g., a bullet), we typically want them to play a visible reaction. We also want the character to stop whatever it was doing while it reacts. For instance, if an enemy is firing their weapon when we hit them, they should not fire any shots while the hit reaction plays. It just looks wrong if they do. Thus, we push an *Is Hit* option onto the option stack, which suspends all previously running options while the reaction plays, and then pop it back off when the reaction is done.

We mentioned this above, but it's worth reemphasizing that the option stack is not meant to *prevent* the AI from changing what it's doing, but simply to preserve its previous state so that can be figured into the decision appropriately. To extend the previous example, imagine that the character was hit in the arm and as a result lost the use of that arm—and therefore could no longer fire its weapon. In that case, it should certainly pick a different option. The option stack simply ensures that the AI has the context of the previous actions available to it so that it can make an informed decision.

Option stacks are surprisingly simple to implement for most architectures. In the AI configuration, each option can specify whether it should suspend the previous option (i.e., push the new option on the stack) or deselect it (i.e., this is a lasting decision). When an option that suspended its predecessor finishes execution, it automatically pops the stack and resumes the previous option. There are a few edge cases to handle (e.g., What to do if another option is selected while there are options on the stack?), but they're not difficult to manage. An example of the interfaces to support this can be found in our GAIA architecture [Dill 12c].

5.6 Knowledge Management

Knowledge is the key to good decision making. This is true in the real world, and it is doubly true in the realm of game AI, where most decisions boil down to relatively simple checks against the current situation. Of course, there are two different kinds of knowledge implied in that statement—knowledge of the situation itself, and knowledge of how to evaluate the situation in order to make a decision. Looked at that way, there isn't much to an AI beyond knowledge.

Given knowledge's central role in game AI, it's worth putting effort into thinking about how to best store and access our knowledge.

5.6.1 Blackboards

In the academic AI community, blackboard architectures typically refer to a specific approach in which multiple reasoners propose potential solutions (or partial solutions) to a problem, and then share that information on a *blackboard* [Wikipedia 12, Isla et al. 02]. Within the game community, however, the term is often used simply to refer to a shared memory space which various AI components can use to store knowledge that may be of use to more than one of them, or may be needed multiple times. In our architecture, for example, every character has access to two blackboards. The *character blackboard* stores information specific to the character, and is only accessible by that character's AI. The *global blackboard* is accessible by all characters, and is used to store general information.

There are many types of information that can be stored on a blackboard. One common use is to store expensive checks on the blackboard, so as to avoid the cost of running them more than once. Line of sight (LOS) checks are a common example. Quite often, more than one component in the AI (or more than one character's AI) will want to check for visibility between the same two objects. These checks can be extremely expensive. To lessen the impact of this problem, we can run the check once and then cache it on the blackboard. Path-planning checks are similar.

Another common use is to store information used to coordinate AI components. This could include partial solutions such as those found in classic blackboard systems, but it could also simply be information used to coordinate between multiple characters or between different AI components within a character. For example, if you want your characters to focus their attacks on a single enemy or to ensure that every enemy is attacked, you can store target assignments on the blackboard. If you want to coordinate spatial motion—perhaps flanking, or placing the tanks in front and the DPS and healers in back, then you can store movement plans on the blackboard. If you want to ensure that two characters don't try to use the same cover spot, then you can have them reserve it on the blackboard. If you have one reasoner whose output is the input for another—for example, the emotional reasoner that we discussed earlier in this paper—then that output can be placed on the blackboard.

There is an interview with Damián Isla on AIGameDev.com, which gives an excellent introduction to blackboard architectures as they are commonly used in games [Isla 10].

5.6.2 Intelligent Everything

When we think about the AI for a character, it seems intuitive to put all of the knowledge needed in the character. This can result in a monolithic, difficult to extend AI, however. It can also result in considerable duplication between similar (but not identical) characters.

One trick is to put the intelligence in the world, rather than in the character. This technique was popularized by *The Sims*, though earlier examples exist. In *The Sims* (and its sequels), objects in the world not only advertise the benefits that they offer (for example, a TV might advertise that it's entertaining, or a bed might advertise that you can rest there), they also contain information about how to go about performing the associated actions [Forbus et al. 01].

Another advantage of this approach is that it greatly decreases the cost of expansion packs. In the *Zoo Tycoon 2* franchise, for example, every other expansion pack was "content only." Because much of the intelligence was built into the objects, we could create new objects that would be used by existing animals, and even entirely new animals, without having to make any changes to the source code. This greatly reduced the cost of developing those expansions, allowing us to focus our efforts on the larger expansions and put out two expansions a year instead of just one.

Intelligence can also be placed in the world itself. For example, in *Red Dead Redemption* the people who populate the towns have very little intelligence of their own—but the town has hundreds of hotspots. Each hotspot has information about who can use it, what time of day the hotspots is valid, and the behavior tree for characters who are on that hotspot. Some hotspots can even require multiple characters. So, for example, a chair in a tavern might have a hotspot for sitting and drinking and another hotspot for playing poker—but the latter is only valid if there are four people at the table (and includes a mechanism for coordinating their actions). The piano bench has a hotspot that only the piano player can use, and the bar has multiple hotspots for the bartender (some that require other characters to join him, some not). Even the conversation AI works by creating a dynamic hotspot for the two characters that are going to have a conversation.

Of course, intelligence can go anywhere, not just in physical objects or locations. For example, games that have a wide range of special abilities can put the intelligence into those abilities. *Darkspore*, a game that had hundreds of abilities—many of them quite unique—took this approach [McHugh et al. 11]. Similarly, events can carry information about appropriate responses. For example, a fire in a school could carry information about how different categories of people (e.g., teachers, children, firemen, parents, etc.) should react [Stocker et al. 10].

5.7 Modularity

Component systems for characters have become commonplace in the games community. For example, a character might have a *Movement* component, an *Animation* component, an *AI* component, a *Weapon* component, and so forth. Each component encapsulates one aspect of the character's functionality behind a shared interface. This sort of modularity—breaking a large piece of code into small, reusable pieces with a consistent interface—can be tremendously powerful [Dill et al. 12b]. It can allow us to greatly reduce code duplication and to reuse more of our code both within a project and across projects. In addition, we can more rapidly implement our characters, because we simply have to plug in the appropriate module, rather than reimplement the functionality in code. It is tremendously liberating to be able to think at the level of broad concepts (i.e., entire modules), rather than having to concentrate on individual lines of code.

One extremely powerful use of modules is to create *considerations*, which are modules that can be combined to evaluate the validity of an option [Dill 11b, Dill 12c]. Hearkening back to our simple FPS character, the *Reload* option would have only a single consideration, which checks how much ammo is left in the current weapon. The *Flee* option, on the other hand, might have considerations to evaluate the current health, the number of allies left, how much health the enemy has left, what weapons are available, and so forth. The AI would combine the output of these considerations into a final evaluation of how important it is to flee, given the current situation. The output of these considerations sets might be Boolean (for example, to drive a rule-based reasoner or the transition in an FSM), or it might be continuous (for example, to drive a utility-based AI). The big advantage of considerations is that those exact same considerations can be used for other decisions—such as whether to attack aggressively, whether to use a health pack, etc. What's more, the considerations themselves can be reused across projects. Even a very different game (say, a real-time strategy game or a role-playing game) might require health checks, counts of surviving allies, distance checks, and so forth. Furthermore, many meta-concepts such as option inertia and cooldowns (described in a previous section) can be expressed easily as considerations.

Once you embrace modularity, you will find that it can be applied throughout your code base. For example, we often have an action that needs a target. The target could be a particular character (perhaps the player), or the camera, or a specific (x, y, z) position. It could even be the output of another reasoner—perhaps one which evaluates all enemies and selects the best one to attack. By having a modular *target* class, we can decouple the logic for specifying and updating the target from the actions that use it [Dill 12c]. Furthermore, targets can also be used elsewhere, such as in considerations—for example, a distance consideration might measure the distance between two targets without knowing or caring what types of targets they are. Targets can even be stored on the blackboard, allowing characters to communicate about them (as described in a previous section).

Another example of modularity is a weight function. When we are using considerations to drive utility-based AI, we have found that there are a great many considerations that need to map from a floating-point value (such as a distance, the amount of health remaining, the amount of ammo remaining, the number of enemies remaining, the time since some action was taken, the character's current hunger, bathroom need, opinion of the player, etc.) to a utility value. Although there might be dozens or even hundreds of considerations like that, there are actually only a few ways to handle the mapping from input value (i.e., the value the consideration computes) to return value (i.e., the consideration's output). For example, we might simply return the input value directly, apply a mathematical function to the input value and return the result, or divide the input value into ranges and return a specific output value for each range. *Weight functions* are modular components that use one of those three techniques to do the mapping for us [Dill et al. 12b]. They allow us to decouple the mapping from the consideration, ensure that we have a consistent data specification for each type of mapping, and enable us to move massive amounts of duplicate code, some of it quite complex, into a few relatively simple classes. In addition, they allow us to add advanced features, such as hysteresis, in a consistent, well-tested way.

These are just a few of the many ways in which AI concepts can be abstracted into reusable modules. Other ideas for the widespread use of modularity can be found in our previous papers [Dill 11b, Dill et al. 12b, Dill 12c]. Our experience has been that finding ways to think about our AI in terms of reusable, pluggable modules (rather than in terms of C++ code) provides a tremendous boost in productivity, even on extremely fast-paced projects.

5.8 Conclusion

In this paper we have discussed a number of common techniques that have been used across many AI architectures, which can facilitate the creation of your game. Hierarchy can be used to divide up the decision making into reasonably-sized pieces, greatly easing the process of configuration. Option stacks can enable the AI to respond to a temporary situation or opportunity, and then return to what it was previously doing. Knowledge can be shared on a blackboard, or placed in an object, in the terrain, in an action, or in an event. Finally, modularity can be used when implementing your AI to eliminate massive amounts of duplicate code, and to allow you to think in terms of broad concepts, rather than individual lines of code, when performing configuration.

References

[Berger et al. 02] L. Berger, F. Poiker, J. Barnes, J. Hutchens, P. Tozour, M. Brockington, and M. Darrah. "Section 10: Scripting." In *AI Game Programming Wisdom*, edited by Steve Rabin. Hingham, MA: Charles River Media, 2002, pp. 503–554.

[Buckland 05] M. Buckland. *Programming Game AI by Example*. Plano, TX: Wordware Publishing 2005, pp. 43–84.

[Cerpa 08] D. H. Cerpa. "A goal stack-based architecture for RTS AI." In *AI Game Programming Wisdom 4*, edited by Steve Rabin. Boston, MA: Course Technology, 2008, pp. 457–466.

[Cerpa et al. 08] D. H. Cerpa and J. Obelleiro. "An advanced motivation-driven planning architecture." In *AI Game Programming Wisdom 4*, edited by Steve Rabin. Boston, MA: Course Technology, 2008, pp. 373–382.

[Dill 06] K. Dill. "Prioritizing actions in a goal-based RTS AI." In *AI Game Programming Wisdom 3*, edited by Steve Rabin. Boston, MA: Charles River Media, 2006, pp. 321–330.

[Dill 11a] K. Dill. "A game AI approach to autonomous control of virtual characters." In *Proceedings of the 2011 Intraservice/Industry Training, Simulation, and Education Conference*. Available online (http://www.iitsec.org/about/PublicationsProceedings/Documents/11136_Paper.pdf).

[Dill 11b] K. Dill. "A pattern-based approach to modular AI for Games." In *Game Programming Gems 8*, edited by Adam Lake. Boston, MA: Course Technology, 2011, pp. 232–243.

[Dill et al. 12a] K. Dill, E. R. Pursel, P. Garrity, and G. Fragomeni. "Design patterns for the configuration of utility-based AI." In *Proceedings of the 2012 Intraservice/Industry Training, Simulation, and Education Conference*, 2012.

[Dill et al. 12b] K. Dill, E. R. Pursel, P. Garrity, and G. Fragomeni. "Achieving modular AI through conceptual abstractions." In *Proceedings of the 2012 Intraservice/Industry Training, Simulation, and Education Conference*, 2012.

[Dill 12c] K. Dill. "Introducing GAIA: A Reusable, Extensible architecture for AI behavior." In *Proceedings of the 2012 Spring Simulation Interoperability Workshop*. Available online (http://www.sisostds.org/conference/download.cfm?Phase_ID=2&FileName=12S-SIW-046.docx).

[Dill 13] K. Dill. "What is game AI?" In *Game AI Pro*, edited by Steve Rabin. Boca Raton, FL: CRC Press, 2013.

[Forbus et al. 01] K. Forbus and W. Wright. "Some Notes on Programming Objects in the Sims." Available online (http://www.qrg.northwestern.edu/papers/files/programming_objects_in_the_sims.pdf).

[Gorniak et al. 07] P. Gorniak and I. Davis. "SquadSmart: Hierarchical planning and coordinated plan execution for squads of characters." In *Proceedings, The Third Artificial Intelligence and Interactive Digital Entertainment Conference*, pp 14–19. Available online (http://petergorniak.org/papers/gorniak_aiide07.pdf).

[Heckel et al. 09] F. W. P. Heckel, G. M. Youngblood, and D. H. Hale. "BehaviorShop: An intuitive interface for interactive character design." In *Proceedings, The Fifth AAAI Artificial Intelligence and Interactive Digital Entertainment Conference*, pp. 46–51. Available online (http://www.aaai.org/ocs/index.php/AIIDE/AIIDE09/paper/viewFile/811/1074).

[Isla 05] D. Isla. "Handling complexity in the *Halo 2* AI." *2005 Game Developer's Conference*, 2005. Available online (http://www.gamasutra.com/view/feature/130663/gdc_2005_proceeding_handling_.php).

[Isla 10] D. Isla. "HALO Inspired Blackboard Architectures and Knowledge Representation." On AIGameDev.com, interview with Alex Champandard, 2002. Available online (http://aigamedev.com/premium/masterclass/blackboard-architecture/).

[Isla et al. 02] D. Isla and B. Blumberg. "Blackboard architectures." In *AI Game Programming Wisdom*, edited by Steve Rabin, pp. 333–342. Hingham, MA: Charles River Media, 2002.

[Mark 09] D. Mark. *Behavioral Mathematics for Game AI*. Boston, MA: Course Technology, 2009.

[McHugh et al. 11] L. McHugh, D. Kline, and R. Graham. "AI Development Postmortems: Inside Darkspore and The Sims: Medieval." Lecture, *Game Developer's Conference 2011 AI Summit*, 2011. Available online (http://twvideo01.ubm-us.net/o1/vault/gdc2011/slides/Lauren_McHugh_AI_Development_Postmortems.ppt).

[Millington et al. 09a] I. Millington and J. Funge. *Artificial Intelligence for Games*, Second Edition. Burlington, MA: Morgan Kaufmann, 2009, pp. 427–457.

[Millington et al. 09b] I. Millington and J. Funge. *Artificial Intelligence for Games*, Second Edition. Burlington, MA: Morgan Kaufmann, 2009, pp. 318–330.

[Nilson 94] N. Nilson. "Teleo-reactive programs for agent control." In *Journal of Artificial Intelligence Research* 1: 139–158, 1994. Available online (http://www.jair.org/media/30/live-30-1374-jair.pdf).

[Orkin 04] J. Orkin. "Applying goal oriented action planning to games." In *AI Game Programming Wisdom 2*, edited by Steve Rabin. Hingham, MA: Charles River Media, 2004, pp. 217–228.

[Pittman 08] D. Pittman. "Command hierarchies using goal-oriented action planning." In *AI Game Programming Wisdom 4*, edited by Steve Rabin. Boston, MA: Course Technology, 2008, pp. 383–392.

[Rabin 00] S. Rabin. "Designing a general robust AI engine." In *Game Programming Gems 8*, edited by Mark DeLoura. Rockland, MA: Charles River Media, 2000, pp. 221–236.

[Stocker et al. 10] C. Stocker, L. Sun, P. Huang, W. Qin, J. Allbeck, and N. Badler. "Smart events and primed agents." In *Proceedings of the 10th International Conference on Intelligent Virtual Agents*, pp. 15–27, 2010.

[Tozour 04] P. Tozour. "Stack-based finite-state machines." In *AI Game Programming Wisdom 2*, edited by Steve Rabin. Hingham, MA: Charles River Media, 2004, pp. 303–306.

[Wikipedia 12] Wikipedia. "Blackboard System." http://en.wikipedia.org/wiki/Blackboard_system, 2012.

6

The Behavior Tree Starter Kit

Alex J. Champandard and Philip Dunstan

6.1 Introduction

You've done your homework and found that behavior trees (BTs) are a proven and established technique that game developers regularly use to build their AI [Isla 05, Champandard 07]. Not only does a BT give you a solid foundation to build upon, but it also gives you a lot of flexibility to include other techniques in a way that gives you full control over behavior and performance. Now you're ready to start coding!

This article introduces the simplest piece of code that you can call a behavior tree, and builds it up incrementally. The associated source code is called the Behavior Tree Starter Kit [BTSK 12], and is intended to serve as an example of a working BT for you to learn from. Since it's under an open-source license, you can use this as a starting point for your own projects. This is not a reusable middleware library, however, and it's important that you understand the core concepts and take ownership of the code.

The first section of this article paints the big picture for behavior trees, introducing a simple example tree, and explaining how to build BTs and how to use them for making AI decisions. The second section dives into the implementation of a first-generation BT, along with all its building blocks (e.g., sequences and selectors) and a discussion of the API. Finally, the third section explains the principles of second-generation BTs, and the improvements they offer. You'll learn about memory optimizations and event-driven implementations that scale up significantly better on modern hardware.

Throughout this article, source code examples are provided to demonstrate the concepts. Note, that the code listings in this article are edited for print, in particular using C++11 syntax, and some shortcuts have been taken for the sake of brevity. For the original implementations see the source code at http://github.com/aigamedev.

6.2 The Big Picture

To assist in the demonstration of the components that comprise a behavior tree it is first useful to see how such a tree might be structured. Following is an example of how a simple behavior tree might be designed for a robot guard that is hunting the Player.

6.2.1 A Simple Example

This AI is split into three main behaviors. First, if the robot guard can see the Player then it will either shoot three times at the Player if it is close enough, or move closer to the Player. Second, if the robot has recently seen the Player but can no longer see them then it will move to the Player's last known position and look around. Third, in case the robot has not seen the Player for some time, the fallback behavior is to move to some random location and look around.

```
BehaviorTree* bt = BehaviorTreeBuilder()
    .activeSelector()
    .sequence()      //Attack the player if seen!
        .condition(IsPlayerVisible)
        .activeSelector()
            .sequence()
                .condition(IsPlayerInRange)
                .filter(Repeat, 3)
                    .action(FireAtPlayer)
            .action(MoveTowardsPlayer)
    .sequence()      //Search near last known position.
        .condition(HaveWeGotASuspectedLocation)
        .action(MoveToPlayersLastKnownPosition)
        .action(LookAround)
    .sequence()      //Randomly scanning nearby.
        .action(MoveToRandomPosition)
        .action(LookAround)
    .end();
```

The example above demonstrates the use of the Tree Builder Pattern to separate the construction of the behavior tree from the behavior tree nodes. (This example has been edited for print.) The full source code for the tree builder and its examples can be found with the rest of the Behavior Tree Starter Kit source code as described in Section 6.1.

6.2.2 Updating the Behavior Tree

Given a behavior tree, how does the game logic update it? How often is this done and does it involve traversing the tree from the root every time? These are common questions about BTs.

To assist in the updating of a behavior tree it is useful to introduce a `BehaviorTree` object, which will serve as the central point for storing and updating the tree. The BehaviorTree object is most often created by a `BehaviorTreeBuilder` as shown in the example in Section 6.2.1, or using another builder that loads a tree from a file.

```
class BehaviorTree {
protected:
    Behavior* m_pRoot;
public:
    void tick();
};
```

This is a first-generation BT, and as such, the `BehaviorTree` class remains simple. It contains a single pointer to the root of the behavior tree, and a `tick()` function which performs the traversal of the tree. This is the entry point of the BT, and is called anytime an update is needed. It is often not necessary to update the behavior tree every game frame, with many games deciding to update each behavior tree every other frame or at 5Hz so that the load for updating the behavior trees of all characters can be spread across multiple game frames.

While this example seems straightforward and the implementation simply delegates the `tick()` to the root node, Section 6.4 of this article shows the advantages of such a centralized `BehaviorTree` class. It enables several advanced features such as improving runtime performance by controlling the memory allocation of BT nodes (Section 6.4.3), and an event-driven traversal that modifies the functionality of the `tick()` function to reduce node accesses.

6.3 Building Blocks

Moving on from the big picture, this section jumps to the lowest level of the implementation, progressing bottom-up and building up complexity incrementally with new features.

6.3.1 Behaviors

The concept of a *behavior* is the most essential part of a BT. The easiest way to think of a behavior from a programming perspective is an abstract interface that can be activated, run, and deactivated. At the leaf nodes of the tree, *actions* (e.g., "open door," "move to cover," "reload weapon") and *conditions* (e.g., "do I have ammunition?" "am I under attack?") provide specific implementations of this interface. Branches in the tree can be thought of as high-level behaviors, hierarchically combining smaller behaviors to provide more complex and interesting behaviors.

Here is how such an interface is implemented in the BTSK:

```
class Behavior {
public:
    virtual void onInitialize()          {}
    virtual Status update()              = 0;
    virtual void onTerminate(Status)     {}
    /*... */
};
```

This API is the core of any BT, and it's critical that you establish a clear specification for these operations. For example, the code expects the following contracts to be respected:

- The `onInitialize()` method is called once, immediately before the first call to the behavior's update method.
- The `update()` method is called exactly once each time the behavior tree is updated, until it signals it has terminated thanks to its return status.
- The `onTerminate()` method is called once, immediately after the previous update signals it's no longer running.

When building behaviors that rely on other behaviors (such as the sequence and selector behaviors described later in this section), it's important to keep these API contracts in mind. To help make sure you don't break these assumptions, it can help to wrap these functions into a single entry point.

```
class Behavior {
protected:
    /* API identical to previous code listing. */
private:
    Status m_eStatus;
public:
    Behavior() : m_eStatus(BH_INVALID) {}
    virtual ~Behavior() {}
    Status tick() {
        if (m_eStatus != BH_RUNNING) onInitialize();
        m_eStatus = update();
        if (m_eStatus != BH_RUNNING) onTerminate(m_eStatus);
        return m_eStatus;
    }
};
```

This approach is a bit slower, since you must use conditional branches every `tick()`. Most composite behaviors could handle this more efficiently since they process the return statuses anyway. However, having such a wrapper function avoids many beginner mistakes.

6.3.2 Return Statuses

Each behavior, when executed, passes back a return status. The return status is a critical part of any behavior tree, without which it simply wouldn't work. In practice, return statuses plays two roles:

- **Completion Status**—If the behavior has terminated, the return status indicates whether it achieved its purpose. There are two completion statuses most commonly used: SUCCESS (indicates that everything went as expected) and FAILURE (specifies that something apparently went wrong).
- **Execution Hints**—While the behavior is running, each update of the behavior also returns a status code. Most of the time, this is RUNNING, but modern BTs can leverage this status code to provide much more efficient implementations. For example, the SUSPENDED status code is an essential part of an event-driven BT, as you will see in Section 6.4.4.

In certain special cases, you might be tempted to add additional return statuses to the list. For example, there are some implementations that distinguish between expected issues (FAILURE) and unforeseen problems (ERROR). However, this quickly makes the code in the rest of the tree much more complex, and does not make the BT any more powerful. A more convenient approach to deal with failures is to let behaviors check for specific types of failure they expect, and deal with those cases outside of the tree's return statuses.

6.3.3 Actions

In a behavior tree, the leaf nodes have the responsibility of accessing information from the world and making changes to the world. Leaf behaviors that make such changes are called `Actions`.

When an action succeeds in making a change in the world it returns SUCCESS; otherwise it's simply a FAILURE. A status code of RUNNING indicates processing is underway. Actions are little more than a `Behavior`, except for initialization and shutdown that require extra care.

- **Initialization**—All but the simplest of actions will need to interface with other systems and objects to do the work. For example, a particular action may need to fetch data from a blackboard, or make a request of the animation systems. In a well-defined modular architecture getting access to these other games systems can be problematic. Extra work is required during the setup of behavior tree actions to provide the systems that those actions will use. This is often solved by passing extra parameters during node instantiation or through the use of the Visitor software design pattern.
- **Shutdown**—Like initialization, the shutdown of actions can be problematic due to the dependencies on external systems. Special care must be taken when shutting down an action to ensure that freeing resources does not interfere with other behaviors. For example, you cannot simply reset the animation system once an action shuts down as another instance of that action may have recently been activated elsewhere.

Helper functions can be set up to facilitate initialization and shutdown of actions if needed. In most cases, actions will simply inherit the functionality from the base `Behavior` class.

An example action used in the robot guard example of Section 6.2.1 is the action to move to the Player's last known location if the robot can no longer see the Player. This action will likely instruct the navigation system to move the robot to that location and return a SUCCESS status code. If for some reason the navigation system is unable to perform the request—for instance, a door has closed and the navigation system is unable to find a path to the target location—the action will return a FAILURE status code.

6.3.4 Conditions

Conditions are also leaf nodes in the tree and are the tree's primary way of checking for information in the world. For example, conditions would be used to check if there's cover nearby, if an enemy is in range, or if an object is visible. All conditions are effectively Boolean, since they rely on the return statuses of behaviors (success and failure) to express True and False.

In practice, conditions are used in two particular cases:

- **Instant Check Mode**—See if the condition is true given the current state of the world at this point in time. The check is run once immediately and the condition terminates.
- **Monitoring Mode**—Keep checking a condition over time, and keep running every frame as long as it is True. If it becomes False, then exit with a FAILURE code.

As well as being able to specify the mode of execution of a Condition, it's also useful to provide a negation parameter that effectively tells the code to do the exact opposite. This allows for the simpler reuse of existing code, such as checking to see if an enemy is in range, to create a condition to test for the opposite, i.e., that the enemy is not within range. In *Check* mode, this is Boolean negation, but in *Monitoring* mode the condition would keep running as long as it is False.

6.3.5 Decorators

The next step to building up an interesting BT is to wrap behaviors with other behaviors, adding detail, subtlety, and nuance to its logic. Decorator behaviors, named after the object-oriented design pattern, allow you to do this. Think of them as a branch in the tree with only a single child, for example, a behavior that repeats its child behavior *n* times, a behavior that hides the failure of its child node, or a behavior that keeps going forever even if its child behavior exits. All of these are decorators, and are very useful for technically minded developers using BTs.

```
class Decorator : public Behavior {
protected:
    Behavior* m_pChild;
public:
    Decorator(Behavior* child) : m_pChild(child) {}
};
```

The base `Decorator` class provides all the common functionality for implementing a decorator efficiently, only storing a single child for instance. Specific types of decorators are implemented as derived classes; for instance the update method on the `Repeat` decorator might be implemented as follows.

```
Status Repeat::update() {
    while (true) {
        m_pChild->tick();
        if (m_pChild->getStatus() == BH_RUNNING) break;
        if (m_pChild->getStatus() == BH_FAILURE) return BH_FAILURE;
            if (++m_iCounter == m_iLimit) return BH_SUCCESS;
    }
}
```

In this example, the repeating behavior keeps executing its child behavior until a limit is reached. If the child fails, the decorator also fails. When the child behavior succeeds, its next execution happens immediately in the same update once it has been reset.

The robot guard example introduced in Section 6.2.1 uses a *Repeat* condition to fire three times if the player is within firing range. Decorators like this provide a simple way to introduce subtle behavior patterns to the behavior tree without duplicating nodes in the tree.

6.3.6 Composites

Branches with multiple children in a behavior tree are called *composite behaviors*. This follows the composite pattern in software engineering, which specifies how objects can be assembled together into collections to build complexity. In this case, we're making more interesting, intelligent behaviors by combining simpler behaviors together.

It's often a good idea to have a base class for composite behaviors to avoid redundant code in the subclasses. The helper functions to add, remove, and clear children can be implemented just once in this base class.

```
class Composite : public Behavior {
public:
    void addChild(Behavior*);
    void removeChild(Behavior*);
    void clearChildren();
protected:
    typedef vector<Behavior*> Behaviors;
    Behaviors m_Children;
};
```

Common composite behaviors, like sequences and selectors, derive from this base class.

6.3.7 Sequences

Sequences are one of the two most common branch types. Sequences allow the BT to purposefully follow "plans" that are hand-specified by the designers. Sequences execute each of their child behaviors in sequence until all of the children have executed successfully or until one of the child behaviors fail.

The example behavior tree introduced in Section 6.2.1 for the robot guard uses sequences at several points to group together behaviors into larger behaviors. An example is the branch that the guard uses to search near the player's last known position when the player is not visible. In this branch the first behavior node is a condition node to check whether the robot has a suspected location for the player. If this condition succeeds the action to move to the suspected location and search around that location will be run. Otherwise, if the condition fails the sequence node will fail and the behavior tree will continue on to the next branch outside the sequence—searching a random location.

In the code shown below, a sequence is a composite behavior, which just happens to chain together its child behaviors one by one.

```
class Sequence : public Composite {
protected:
    Behaviors::iterator m_CurrentChild;
    virtual void onInitialize() override {
        m_CurrentChild = m_Children.begin();
    }
    virtual Status update() override {
        //Keep going until a child behavior says it's running.
        while (true) {
            Status s = (*m_CurrentChild)->tick();
            //If child fails or keeps running, do the same.
            if (s != BH_SUCCESS) return s;
            //Move on until we hit the end of the array!
            if (++m_CurrentChild == m_Children.end())
                return BH_SUCCESS;
        }
        return BH_INVALID;//Unexpected loop exit.
    }
};
```

The initialization code for the sequence starts at the beginning of the array of children. The update processes each child behavior in the list one by one, bailing out if any of them fail. The sequence returns a SUCCESS status if all of the children execute successfully.

There's one important thing to note about this implementation; the next child behavior is processed immediately after the previous one succeeds. This is critical to make sure the BT does not miss an entire frame before having found a low-level action to run.

6.3.8 Filters and Preconditions

A filter is a branch in the tree that will not execute its child behavior under specific conditions. For instance, if an attack has a cooldown timer to prevent it from executing too often, or a behavior that is only valid at a specific distance away from a target, etc. Designers can easily use filters to customize the execution of common behaviors—for instance, customizing them for a specific character or situation.

Using the modular approach of the BTSK, it's trivial to implement a filter as a type of sequence. Assuming the filter has a single condition, you can attach it to the start of the sequence—ensuring that it gets executed (and therefore, checked) first. If the filter has a single branch (or action), it comes next in the sequence. Of course, it's equally easy to set up a sequence with multiple preconditions and multiple action branches afterwards.

```
class Filter : public Sequence {
public:
    void addCondition(Behavior* condition) {
        //Use insert() if you store children in std::vector
        m_Children.push_front(condition);
    }
    void addAction(Behavior* action) {
        m_Children.push_back(action);
    }
};
```

You can also easily create Boolean combinations of conditions to add to the filter, as a testimony to the power of core BT nodes like sequences (AND) and selectors (OR).

6.3.9 Selectors

Selectors are the other most common branch type. Selectors let the BT react to impediments in the world, and effectively trigger transitions between different fallback behaviors. A selector executes each of its child behaviors in order until it finds a child that either succeeds or that returns a RUNNING status.

In the robot guard behavior tree example described in Section 6.2.1 a selector is used to decide which of the three main behavior branches should be picked. The first branch—attacking the player—is first executed. If this branch fails—if the player is not visible, for instance—the sequence node will execute the second branch, searching near the player's last known position. If that behavior also fails the sequence will execute the final behavior—searching a random location.

From the code perspective, a selector is the counterpart of a sequence; the code not only derives from a composite, but looks very similar as well. Only the two lines dealing with the specific return statuses are different.

```
virtual Status update() {
    //Keep going until a child behavior says it's running.
    while (true) {
        Status s = (*m_Current)->tick();
        //If child succeeds or keeps running, do the same.
        if (s != BH_FAILURE) return s;
        //Continue search for fallback until the last child.
        if (++m_Current == m_Children.end())
            return BH_FAILURE;
    }
    return BH_INVALID;//"Unexpected loop exit."
}
```

The rest of the selector is identical to the sequence implementation. Similarly, note that the selector keeps searching for fallback behaviors in the same update() until a suitable behavior is found or the selector fails. This allows the whole BT to deal with failures within a single frame without pausing.

6.3.10 Parallels

A parallel node is another type of composite branch in the tree that allows you to do more advanced control structures, such as monitoring if assumptions have been invalidated while you are executing a behavior. Like other composites, it's made up of multiple behaviors; however, these are all executed at the same time! This allows multiple behaviors (including conditions) to be executed in parallel and for those behaviors to be aborted if some or all of them fail.

A parallel node is not about multithreading or optimizations, though. Logically speaking, all child behaviors are run at the same time. If you trace the code, their update functions would be called sequentially one after another in the same frame.

```
class Parallel : public Composite {
public:
    enum Policy {
        RequireOne,
        RequireAll,
    };
    Parallel(Policy success, Policy failure);
protected:
    Policy m_eSuccessPolicy;
    Policy m_eFailurePolicy;
    virtual Status update() override;
};
```

It's important for the parallel to be extremely precisely specified, so that it can be understood intuitively and relied upon without trying to second-guess the implementation. In this case, there are two parameters; one specifies the conditions under which the parallel succeeds and the other for failure. Does it require all child nodes to fail/succeed or just one before failing/succeeding? Instead of enumerations, you could also add counters to allow a specific number of behaviors to terminate the parallel, but that complicates the everyday use of the parallel without any additional power. Most useful BT structures can be expressed with these parameters, using decorators on child nodes if necessary to modify their return statuses.

```
virtual Status update() {
    size_t iSuccessCount = 0, iFailureCount = 0;
    for (auto it: m_Children) {
        Behavior& b = **it;
        if (!b.isTerminated()) b.tick();
        if (b.getStatus() == BH_SUCCESS) {
            ++iSuccessCount;
            if (m_eSuccessPolicy == RequireOne)
                return BH_SUCCESS;
        }
        if (b.getStatus() == BH_FAILURE) {
            ++iFailureCount;
            if (m_eFailurePolicy == RequireOne)
                return BH_FAILURE;
        }
    }
    if (m_eFailurePolicy == RequireAll && iFailureCount == size)
        return BH_FAILURE;
    if (m_eSuccessPolicy == RequireAll && iSuccessCount == size)
        return BH_SUCCESS;
    return BH_RUNNING;
}
```

The implementation of the parallel iterates through each child behavior, and updates it. Counters are kept for all terminated behaviors, so the failure policy and success policy can be checked afterwards. Note that failure takes priority over success since the BT itself should assume the worst case and deal with it rather than proceed regardless. Also, in this implementation the parallel terminates as soon as any policy is satisfied, even if there are behaviors not yet run.

When a parallel terminates early because its termination criteria are fulfilled, all other running behaviors must be terminated. This is done during the onTerminate() function that iterates through all the child nodes and handles their termination.

```
void Parallel::onTerminate(Status) {
    for (auto it: m_Children) {
        Behavior& b = **it;
        if (b.isRunning()) b.abort();
    }
}
```

Parallels are the foundation of more advanced BT control structures and therefore tend to uncover a wide variety of little issues, like how to cleanly shutdown (see Section 6.3.3) and how to handle interrupting behaviors. There are two schools of thought on how to handle behaviors that need to be interrupted before they terminate on their own, for example, when they are run together in a parallel node.

- All behaviors should have the option to keep running if they want to, effectively having a noninterruptible flag that will cause the parent behavior to wait for termination. In this case, the abort() function becomes a request that is taken into account during the next update() if appropriate. Low-level BTs, in particular those dealing with animation control directly, tend to benefit from this option.

- All behaviors should support immediate termination, though they are given the option to clean-up after themselves using `onTerminate()`, which can optionally be given a special `ABORTED` status code. High-level BTs work best this way, since they don't want to micro-manage low-level states; the noninterruptible animation can be handled elsewhere in supporting systems.

The BTSK takes this second approach. When the behavior tree switches from a branch to another, this is done instantly, and any transitions (e.g., audio, animation) must be set up during the switch and managed by external systems. Then, in the next branch, if the same system is requested, it will simply delay the BTs request until the transition is over (e.g., play sound, play animation).

6.3.11 Monitors

Arguably, continuously checking if assumptions are valid (i.e., monitoring conditions) is the most useful pattern that involves running behaviors in parallel. Many behaviors tend to have assumptions that should be maintained while a behavior is active, and if those assumptions are found invalid the whole sub-tree should exit. Some examples of this include using an object (assumes the object exists) or melee attacks (assumes the enemy is in range), and many others.

The easiest way to set this up is to reuse the parallel node implementation, as a Monitor node can be thought of as a parallel behavior with two sub-trees; one containing conditions which express the assumptions to be monitored (read-only), and the other tree of behaviors (read–write). Separating the conditions in one branch from the behaviors in the other prevents synchronization and contention problems, since only one sub-tree will be running actions that make changes in the world.

```
struct Monitor : public Parallel {
    //Implementation is identical to the Filter sequence.
    void addCondition(Behavior* condition);
    void addAction(Behavior* action);
};
```

In the exact same way as a `Filter`, the monitor provides simple helper functions to ensure the conditions are set up first in the parallel. These conditions will be checked first before the actions are executed, bailing out early if there are any problems. This API is useful only if you create your BTs in C++, but most likely you'll impose these orderings in your BT editing tool.

6.3.12 Active Selectors

One final building block you'll most likely need in a production BT is an "active" selector, which actively rechecks its decisions on a regular basis after having made them. This differs from the traditional "passive" selectors by using another form of parallelism to retry higher-priority behaviors than the one that was previously chosen. You can use this feature to dynamically check for risks or opportunities in select parts of the tree, for example, interrupting a patrol with a search behavior if a disturbance is reported.

Active selectors appear twice during the short behavior tree example in Section 6.2.1. At the top level of the behavior tree an active selector is used to allow the high priority behavior of attacking a visible enemy to interrupt lower-priority behaviors such as searching for the player or randomly patrolling. A second instance of an active selector is during the evaluation of behaviors when the player is visible to the guard robot. Here, an active selector is used so that the higher-priority behavior of shooting at the player if the player is within range preempts the lower-priority behavior of moving towards the player if they are not in range.

One simple way to implement this is to reuse a Monitoring node within a passive selector from Section 6.3.9 that terminates the low-priority node if the higher-priority behavior's preconditions are met. This type of implementation can be easier for straightforward cases with one condition, and works efficiently for event-driven implementations discussed in Section 6.4.4. However, you'll most likely require a specialized implementation to deal with more complex situations.

```
Status ActiveSelector::update() {
    Behaviors::iterator prev = m_Current;
    Selector::onInitialize();
    Status result = Selector::update();
    if (prev != m_Children.end() && m_Current != prev)
        (*previous)->abort();
    return result;
}
```

This active selector implementation reuses the bulk of the underlying Selector code, and forces it to run every tick by calling onInitialize(). Then, if a different child node is selected the previous one is shutdown afterwards. Separately, the m_Current iterator is initialized to the end of the children vector. Keep in mind that forcefully aborting lower-priority behaviors can have unwanted side effects if you're not careful; see Section 6.3.3.

6.4 Advanced Behavior Tree Implementations

As BTs have grown in popularity in the games industry the forms of implementation have become increasingly diverse, from the original implementation in *Halo 2* [Isla 05] to *Bulletstorm*'s event-driven version [PSS 11]. Despite the diversity there have been some common changes over the past couple of years in the ways that behavior trees have been implemented. These changes led to our coining of the terms first- and second-generation behavior trees at the Paris Shooter Symposium 2011 [PSS 11].

6.4.1 First- versus Second-Generation Trees

While there are no hard rules for classifying a behavior tree implementation, there are some common patterns behind original implementations and more modern ones. In general, first-generation BTs have the following characteristics:

- Small and shallow trees with relatively few nodes in them.
- Large behaviors written in C++ with "complex" responsibilities.
- No (or little) sharing of data between multiple behavior tree instances.
- Simple implementations with no worry about performance.
- Often written in one .h and .cpp file, not necessarily reusable outside of AI.
- The behavior tree concept is mostly used as a pattern for writing C++.

In contrast, second-generation trees have had to deal with a console hardware transition and designs with additional complexity and scale. They are defined as follows:

- Larger and deeper trees with many more nodes.
- Smaller powerful nodes that better combine together.
- BT data that is shared between multiple instances wherever possible.
- A heavily optimized implementation to improve scalability.
- Written as a reusable library that can be applied to any game logic.
- The behavior tree becomes a DSL with efficient interpreter.

It's important to point out that first-generation implementations are not necessarily worse than their successor, they just fulfill different requirements. If you can use a simpler implementation that avoids the complexity of the second-generation, then don't hesitate to do so!

6.4.2 Sharing Behavior Trees Between Entities

A powerful extension to first-generation behavior trees is the ability to share data between multiple instances, in particular, the structure of the tree or common parameters. This can significantly reduce the memory requirements for BT-based systems, especially in scenes with large numbers of complex characters.

The most important requirement for sharing data is the separation of two concepts:

- **Nodes**—Express the static data of the BT nodes, for instance the pointers to children of a composite node, or common parameters.
- **Tasks**—The transient node data required to execute each BT node. For example, sequences need a current behavior pointer and actions often require context.

In practice, the Task is a base class for runtime instance data and managing execution.

```
class Task {
protected:
    Node* m_pNode;
public:
    Task(Node& node);
    //onInitialize(), update() and onTerminate() as 3.3.1
};
```

The Task refers to a tree node which stores the shared data, including tree structure and parameters. Then, the Node implementation effectively becomes a factory for creating these tasks at runtime, when the node is executed by the tree.

```
class Node {
public:
    virtual Task* create() = 0;
    virtual void destroy(Task*) = 0;
};
```

To make these two classes compatible with the Behavior of Section 6.3.1, all that's required is to keep a Node and a Task together as member variables, and track their

Status. The node's factory functions `create()` must be called before the behavior's `tick()` function can be run the first time, and `destroy()` after the task has terminated.

While separating these two forms of BT data is relatively simple mechanically, it has a profound impact on the rest of the code. All composite nodes, for instance, must be able to "convert" nodes into tasks before execution. This can be done locally in all composites, or the `Task` instances can be managed centrally in a `BehaviorTree` class similar to Section 6.2.2. Then, the decision remains whether to allocate these instances on-the-fly or pre-allocate them—which will often depend on the size and complexity of the tree. The next section discusses similar memory issues relating to the allocation of `Node` objects forming the tree structure.

6.4.3 Improving Memory Access Performance

One of the significant drawbacks of first-generation behavior trees on modern hardware is the memory access patterns exhibited when executing the BTs. This is especially an issue on current generation console hardware with small cache sizes and limited hardware memory prefetching.

The primary cause of the poor memory access patterns is the dynamic memory allocation of the behavior tree nodes. Without careful management, the BT node storage may be scattered throughout memory, resulting in frequent cache misses as the BT execution moves from one node to the next. By changing the layout of the BT nodes in memory, it is possible to significantly improve the memory performance of behavior trees.

6.4.3.1 Node Allocation

The core mechanism for changing the memory layout of the behavior tree nodes is the introduction of centralized memory allocation API to the central `BehaviorTree` object that was introduced in Section 6.2.2. These additional allocate functions will be responsible for all node allocations.

When this object is constructed it allocates a block of memory into which all of the BT nodes will be allocated. To instantiate a BT node, the templated `allocate` function is used rather than the normal allocation functions. This function uses in-place new to allocate the new node within the block of memory owned by the `BehaviorTree` object.

```
class BehaviorTree {
public:
    BehaviorTree()
    : m_pBuffer(new uint8_t[k_MaxBehaviorTreeMemory])
    , m_iOffset(0)
    {}
    ~BehaviorTree() {
        delete [] m_pBuffer;
    }
    void tick();
    template <typename T>
    T& allocate() {
        T* node = new ((void*)((uintptr_t)m_pBuffer+m_iOffset)) T;
        m_iOffset += sizeof(T);
        return *node;
    }
```

```
protected:
    uint8_t* m_pBuffer;
    size_t m_iOffset;
};
```

By allocating all of the BT nodes via the custom allocate function it is possible to ensure that all of the nodes for a tree are allocated in the same localized area of memory. Furthermore, by controlling the order in which nodes are allocated (depth- or breadth-first), it is possible to optimize the layout so that it reduces cache misses during traversal. Improving the memory usage patterns as a BT is traversed can have significant impacts on the runtime performance.

6.4.3.2 Composite Node Implementations

As this change only affects the node memory allocations, the internal implementations of many of the behavior tree nodes described in Section 6.3 are completely unaffected. There are, however, additional optimizations that can be made to some of these implementations to further improve the resultant memory layout.

The primary candidates for further optimizations are the Composite nodes: Sequences, Selectors, and Parallels. In the simple implementation described in Section 6.3.6 each of these node types stored their children in a vector<Behavior*> in the Composite base class, resulting in additional heap allocations by the vector class for the data storage. This can be prevented by replacing the vector storage by an internal static array as shown in the code below.

```
class Composite : public Behavior
{
public:
    Composite() : m_ChildCount(0) {}
    void addChild(Behavior& child) {
        ptrdiff_t p = (uintptr_t)&child - (uintptr_t)this;
        m_Children[m_ChildCount++] = static_cast<uint32_t>(p);
    }
protected:
    uint32_t m_Children[k_MaxChildrenPerComposite];
    uint32_t m_ChildCount;
};
```

In this example, the child nodes store the child node address information as part of the primary node data. Each composite node contains static storage for n child nodes. In most trees, a limit of 7 on the maximum number of child nodes is more than sufficient. In cases where there are more children than this, then it is typically possible to use additional composite nodes to split apart the larger composite nodes (e.g., multiple nested sequences or selectors).

Rather than storing pointers to each of the child nodes, it is also possible to take advantage of the spatial locality of the nodes in memory and store only the offset of each child node from the composite node. As compiling software with support for 64-bit pointers becomes more common, this can result in significant memory savings. The Composite node example shown here requires 32 bytes of memory, whereas a naïve implementation storing pointers would require 64 bytes, occupying half of a cache line on current generation consoles.

6.4.3.3 Transient Data Allocation

The same transformations that were applied to the memory layout of the BT nodes in Section 6.4.3.2 can equally by applied to the transient data that is stored when each node is executed.

It is useful to think of this transient data as a stack. As a node is executed, its transient data is pushed onto the top of the stack. When a node execution is terminated, the transient data is popped back off the stack. This stack-like data structure is perfect for the depth-first iteration used in behavior trees. It allows for very simple management of transient data and results in very cache-friendly memory access patterns.

6.4.4 Event-Driven Behavior Trees

A final approach for optimizing BT traversal involves event-driven techniques. Instead of traversing the tree from the root every frame, simply to find previously active behaviors, why not maintain them in a list (of size one or more) for fast access? You can think of this list as a *scheduler* that keeps active behaviors and ticks the ones that need updating.

This is the essence of an event-based approach, and there are two ways to maintain it:

- Traverse the whole tree from scratch if the currently executing behaviors terminate, or there are changes in the world (or its blackboard). This effectively repopulates the task list from scratch when necessary, in a similar way than a planner would.
- Update the list of active behaviors incrementally as they succeed or fail. The parent of behaviors that terminate can be requested to decide what to do next, rather than traversing the whole tree for the root.

The first approach is a simple optimization to a traditional first-generation BT, but the second requires a much more careful implementation of the scheduler, which we'll dig into in the following sections.

6.4.4.1 Behavior Observers

The most important part of an event-driven BT is the concept of an observer. When a behavior terminates, the scheduler that was updating it also fires a notification to the parent, which can deal with the information as appropriate.

```
typedef Delegate<void (Status)> BehaviorObserver;
```

In the BTSK, the observer is implemented using a template-based fast delegate implementation, but this could be replaced with any functor implementation.

6.4.4.2 Behavior Scheduler

The central piece of code responsible for managing the execution of an event-driven BT is called a *scheduler*. This can be a stand-alone class, or left for the `BehaviorTree` class to implement such as in the BTSK. Essentially, the class is responsible for updating behaviors in one central place rather than letting each composite manage and run its own children. The example object below expands on the `BehaviorTree` class API that was first introduced in Section 6.2.2 to provide the management of BT tasks.

```
class BehaviorTree {
protected:
    deque<Behavior*> m_Behaviors;
public:
    void tick();
    bool step();
    void start(Behavior& bh, BehaviorObserver* observer);
    void stop(Behavior& bh, Status result);
};
```

The scheduler stores a list of active behaviors, in this case in a `deque` that has behaviors taken from the front and pushed to the back as they are updated. The main entry point is the `tick()` function, which processes all behaviors until an end-of-update marker is found.

```
void tick() {
    //Insert an end-of-update marker into the list of tasks.
    m_Behaviors.push_back(NULL);
    //Keep going updating tasks until we encounter the marker.
    while (step()) {}
}
```

One of the many benefits of this type of implementation is support for single-stepping of behaviors. This can be done directly via the `step()` function if necessary.

```
bool step() {
    Behavior* current = m_Behaviors.front();
    m_Behaviors.pop_front();
    //If this is the end-of-update marker, stop processing.
    if (current == NULL) return false;
    //Perform the update on this individual behavior.
    current->tick();
    //Process the observer if the task terminated.
    if (current->isTerminated() && current->m_Observer)
        current->m_Observer(current->m_eStatus);
    else//Otherwise drop it into the queue for the next tick()
        m_Behaviors.push_back(current);
    return true;
}
```

As for managing the execution of behaviors, the implementations of `start()` simply pushes a behavior on the front of the queue, and `stop()` sets its status and fires the observer manually.

6.4.4.3 Event-Driven Composites

The event-driven paradigm is most obvious in the composite nodes in the tree. Every composite has to make a request to the scheduler to update its child nodes rather than execute them directly.

For example, let's take a look at how a `Sequence` would be implemented.

```
class Sequence : public Composite {
protected:
    BehaviorTree* m_pBehaviorTree;
    Behaviors::iterator m_Current;
```

```
public:
    Sequence(BehaviorTree& bt);
    virtual void onInitialize() override;
    void onChildComplete(Status);
}
```

Since the composites rely on the scheduler to update the child nodes, there's no need for an update() function. The setup of the first child in the sequence is done by the onInitialize() function.

```
void Sequence::onInitialize() {
    m_Current = m_Children.begin();
    auto observer = BehaviorObserver::                      \
        FROM_METHOD(Sequence, onChildComplete, this);
    m_pBehaviorTree->insert(**m_Current, &observer);
}
```

Every subsequent child in the sequence is set up in the onChildComplete() callback.

```
void onChildComplete() {
    Behavior& child = **m_Current;
    //The current child behavior failed, sequence must fail.
    if (child.m_eStatus == BH_FAILURE) {
        m_pBehaviorTree->terminate(*this, BH_FAILURE);
        return;
    }
    //The current child succeeded, is this the end of array?
    if (++m_Current == m_Children.end()) {
        m_pBehaviorTree->terminate(*this, BH_SUCCESS);
    }
    //Move on and schedule the next child behavior in array.
    else {
        BehaviorObserver observer = BehaviorObserver::          \
            FROM_METHOD(Sequence, onChildComplete, this);
        m_pBehaviorTree->insert(**m_Current, &observer);
    }
}
```

Event-driven code has a reputation for being more complex, but this composite code remains very easy to understand at a glance. However, it is a little harder to trace the tree of behaviors by simply looking at a callstack, unlike first-generation BT implementations.

6.4.4.4 Event-Driven Leaf Behaviors

Many actions and conditions remain unaffected by an event-driven implementation, though some could be optimized to use an event-driven approach rather than polling. For instance, a monitoring condition that's waiting for a callback from the navigation system to terminate does not need to be updated every frame. Instead, this condition can be rewritten to return the SUSPENDED status, in which case the scheduler would ignore the behavior during its tick.

Upon receiving an external notification (e.g., from the navigation system), an event-driven condition could then tell the scheduler to reactivate it and process it during the next step of the update. This kind of logic requires special care and ordering of behaviors during the update, but can save a lot of unnecessary function calls.

6.5 Conclusion

In this article, you saw multiple variations of BTs, including a simple first-generation implementation to learn from, as well as a second-generation version that you can use as a starting point in your own project. A few principles recur throughout the code:

- Modular behaviors with simple (unique) responsibilities, to be combined together to form more complex ones.
- Behaviors that are very well specified (even unit tested) and easy to understand, even by nontechnical designers.

While there are always exceptions to these rules in practice, this approach works reliably for creating in-game behaviors. If you're having trouble with code duplication, explaining a bug to a designer, or not being able to understand interactions between your behaviors, then it's best to break down the code into simpler behaviors.

The original un-edited source code for this article can be found online under an open-source license [BTSK 12]. If you'd like to see the details, especially the stuff that couldn't be covered in this article, you're highly encouraged to check out the code!

References

[BTSK 12] A. Champandard and P. Dunstan. The Behavior Tree Starter Kit. http://github.com/aigamedev, 2012.

[Champandard 07] A. Champandard. "Behavior trees for Next-Gen AI." *Game Developers Conference Europe*, 2007.

[Isla 05] D. Isla. "Handling complexity in the Halo 2 AI." *Game Developers Conference*, 2005.

[PSS 11] M. Martins, G. Robert, M. Vehkala, M. Zielinski, and A. Champandard (editor). "Part 3 on Behavior Trees." Paris Shooter Symposium, 2011. http://gameaiconf.com/.

7

Real-World Behavior Trees in Script

Michael Dawe

7.1 Introduction

While there are many different architectures for an AI programmer to pick from, behavior trees are one of the most popular algorithms for implementing NPC action selection in games due to their simplicity to code and use. They are quick to implement from scratch and can be extended to add additional features or provide game-specific functionality as needed. While not as simple as a finite-state machine, they are still simple enough to be easily debugged and designed by other team members as well, making them appropriate to use on games with a large team implementing the behaviors.

On *Kingdoms of Amalur: Reckoning*, we wrote a behavior tree system that used behaviors written in script, while the algorithm itself was processed within the C++ engine. This allowed the design team to have rapid iteration on the behaviors while the programming team retained control over the algorithm features and how the engine processed the behavior tree. Here, we present a functional implementation of a simplified version of the algorithm (available on the book's website http://www.gameaipro.com). It can be used "as is" or extended for a more demanding application. Additionally, we discuss some of the pros and cons we found using such a system in the development of *Reckoning*.

7.2 Architecture Overview

The behavior tree algorithm implemented in the sample code is straightforward and assumes only the knowledge of a tree data structure. Each node in the tree is a *behavior*,

Listing 7.1. Pseudocode for running the behavior tree. Called with the root node to start, this recursively determines the correct branch behaviors to run.

```
process_behavior_node(node)
    if (node.precondition returns true) {
        node.action()
        if (node.child exists)
            process_behavior_node(node.child)
    } else {
        if (node.sibling exists)
            process_behavior_node(node.sibling)
    }
```

with some *precondition* defining when that behavior should run and an *action* defining what the agent should do to perform that behavior. A root behavior is defined to start at, with child behaviors listed in order. Starting from the root, the precondition of the behavior is examined, and if it determines that the behavior should run, the action is performed. The algorithm would continue with any children of that behavior. If a precondition determines that a behavior should not be run, the next sibling at that behavior is examined in turn. In this manner, the algorithm recurses down the tree until the last leaf behavior is run. The pseudocode for the algorithm is shown in Listing 7.1. This process on the behavior tree can be run as often as needed to provide behavior fidelity, either every frame or considerably less often for lower level-of-detail.

In the code sample, we define classes for each `Behavior`, as well as a `BehaviorMgr` to keep track of each `Behavior` loaded. The `BehaviorTree` is its own class as well, so that we can define multiple trees that use the same behaviors and process them separately. Since each `BehaviorTree` is made up of a list of `Behaviors`, multiple characters running the same behavior tree can run separate instances of the `BehaviorTree` class.

7.3 Defining Script Behaviors

There are several compelling reasons to define behaviors in script. First, when developing intelligent agents, quick iteration is often a key factor in determining final behavior quality. Having an environment where behaviors can be written, changed, and reloaded without restarting the game is highly desirable. Another reason to use a scripting language might be to take advantage of your team. On *Reckoning*, a large percentage of the design team had a programming background, making it feasible for them to implement behaviors in script without much programming input or oversight. While some programming time was needed to support the creation of new ways to pass information back and forth between the C++ engine and script, overall the time spent by engineers on the behavior creation process was much less than it would have been otherwise.

In order to write our behavior tree to take advantage of behaviors written in script, we first need to integrate a scripting language to a C++ engine. For *Reckoning*, we chose Lua, a popular scripting language within the games industry. Since Lua is written in C, it can easily be plugged into an existing engine, and since its source is distributed for free, it can even be modified as necessary and compiled into the game.

Lua defines a native data structure—a *table*—which is analogous to a *dictionary* or *map* in other languages. For each behavior, we defined a table with that behavior's name (to avoid name collisions). The members of the table were functions named "precondition" and "behavior." With known names, the C++ algorithm could look for and call the appropriate functions at the correct times.

7.4 Code Example

Besides the behavior classes, the code sample used in this article also defines a `LuaWrapper` class to manage the Lua integration, and an `NTreeNode` class as a generic tree class. In `main()`, a `LuaWrapper` is created and used to load all *.lua files in the Scripts directory, where every *.lua file is a well-defined behavior. While the `LuaWrapper::load_all_scripts()` function is written for Windows systems, all operating-system specific calls are in that function, so porting to a different system should be confined to that function.

From there, a test behavior tree is created based on the script files loaded. Using the `add_behavior_as_child_of()` function, an entire behavior tree can be created from scratch. Finally, the tree is run using `process()`, which simply starts the recursive function at the root of the behavior tree and tests each behavior in turn.

7.5 Integration into a Game Engine

While functional, the sample provided holds more power if plugged into a full game engine. The `Behavior` and `BehaviorTree` classes can be taken "as is" and extended as needed. The `LuaWrapper` could also be taken as written, but ideally an engine would include functionality for reloading the Lua state at runtime, in order to take advantage of being able to rewrite behaviors and test them without restarting or recompiling the game.

Each agent can define its own `BehaviorTree`, either in code or as some sort of data file. For *Reckoning*, behavior trees were assets just as behaviors were, so trees had their own manager and data definition for ease of sharing among multiple different types of NPCs. If the behaviors are written generically enough, many different agents could share not only the behaviors, but even whole trees.

7.6 Script Concerns

While the benefits of having script-defined behaviors are manifest, there are particular concerns that should be kept in mind if using the approach.

Perhaps the first thing to come to mind for game programmers is performance. While written in C, Lua is still a garbage-collected language, and has a floating-point representation for all numbers within the Lua environment. With this in mind, *Reckoning* took a few precautions to safeguard the framerate of the game from poor script performance.

First, since Lua can be compiled directly into the game engine, all Lua allocations can be routed through whatever allocation scheme the engine implements, which means it's possible to take advantage of small-block allocators to avoid general fragmentation issues. By preemptively garbage collecting at known times, it's possible to prevent the Lua garbage collector from running anytime it would be disadvantageous. In particular, *Reckoning* ran the garbage collector every frame at a predetermined time to avoid mid-frame collection that can occur when left up to Lua.

To further increase performance when in Lua, the source was changed to make Lua's internal number system use traditional integers instead of floating-point numbers. This had a few consequences for scripters, the most obvious of which was dealing with integers for percentages, i.e., the number "56" instead of "0.56" for 56%. Once this was well communicated, it was merely a matter of scripting style.

Trigonometry and geometry became impossible to complete within Lua, though, and while this is precisely the outcome planned for, it was a larger workflow change. Since the point was to avoid any complex math in script, it was planned that anytime a behavior or other script needed a trigonometric or geometric problem solved, it would ask the C++ engine for an answer. This meant that while most of the mathematical calculation was kept out of script, more programmer time was required to write and test the necessary functions for script any time a new result was needed.

In general, though it was still a positive time gain to have designers writing more script behaviors, programmers could not be entirely hands-off during behavior development. After *Reckoning* completed, both the designers and programmers agreed that more formal engineering oversight was needed in the scripting process; so while a majority of behaviors in the game were written by designers, the team thought more collaboration would be warranted. A suggested workflow was to have members of the engineering team code review script check-ins, though periodic reviews would also work.

7.7 Enhancements

While the sample can be used "as is," part of the appeal of a behavior tree is implementing extensions as needed for your own project. There are a wide variety of additional features that can be added to this base tree. Here are some examples used on *Reckoning*.

7.7.1 Behavior Asset Management

Although this example just loads files in a given directory, if the behavior tree system needs to interact with a large number of behaviors, it will become easier to have some sort of behavior asset manager to load and track each behavior. While initially this simply shifts the responsibility of loading the behaviors to the new asset manager, the manager can add new functionality by creating a unique ID for each behavior. Trees can reference behaviors by this ID, while the manager can enforce uniqueness of names among behaviors. By having a centralized place to do error-checking on the scripts, finding and recovering from data errors can be handled more easily.

Having an asset manager for your behaviors has other advantages, as well. While this sample creates the trees as part of the program, ideally trees are defined by some data file that's read in when the game starts. This allows the development of external tools to create trees or even define trees containing other trees.

7.7.2 Behavior Definition Extras

As noted, our behavior definitions are simply tables in Lua, which are analogous to dictionaries or maps. Tables can hold arbitrary data, a fact this implementation takes advantage of by storing functions within our behavior table. Since there's no limit on the data, though, we can also store any data with the behavior we want besides just the precondition and behavior functions themselves. For example, a behavior could store a separate table of parameterized data for use within the behavior, or data for use by the behavior tree. In *Reckoning*, behaviors specified a hint to the behavior-level-of-detail system based on how important it was that they run again soon. For example, creatures running combat behaviors had a higher probability of getting to process their tree than creatures merely walking to a destination.

7.7.3 Behavior Class Improvements

The `Behavior` class itself can be improved to allow for faster processing of the tree. In this example, behaviors must define a precondition function and a behavior function, or else the tree will fail to process correctly. It is possible to use the `lua_isfunction()` family of functions to determine if the behavior or precondition functions exist before calling them. While the behavior tree could push the known function location onto the Lua stack to determine its existence every frame, a better solution is one where the behavior itself checks and tracks what functions are defined when it first loads. Then the behavior tree can call or skip a behavior function call based on a flag within the behavior itself without incurring a significant performance cost while processing the tree.

7.7.4 Previously Running Behaviors

Often it is useful when debugging a behavior tree to know which behaviors were running on a given frame. The behavior tree can keep track of which behaviors were running on the last frame or on an arbitrary number of frames prior. The smallest way to do this is by using a bit field. By taking advantage of the fact that a behavior tree is laid out in the same way every run, we can assign the first position in the bit field to the root, then the next its first child, followed by any children that child behavior has before moving on similarly. Algorithmically, we can then simply mark the behaviors to be run while checking behavior preconditions, then save that bit field off when we are finished processing.

In fact, a behavior tree can be compressed considerably using this technique. For example, instead of storing the behaviors in a tree, once the behaviors are loaded by an asset system and given a unique id, the `BehaviorTree` class can store an array of pointers to the behaviors, and the tree can store indices into that array, which simplifies the bit field approach.

7.7.5 on_enter/on_exit Behavior

Once a list of previously running behaviors is established, a behavior can define a function for the first-time setup or a cleanup function for when it ceases running. As a part of *Reckoning*, we defined `on_enter` and `on_exit` functions for each behavior. To implement these, the behavior tree class needs to track over subsequent `process()` calls which behaviors were running the previous time, as above. If a list of behaviors run the previous tick is kept, then any behavior in the previous list but not in the current one can call its `on_exit` function before new behaviors are started. `On_enter` and `behavior` functions are then called in order.

7.7.6 Additional Selectors

The algorithm can also be extended by changing the way behaviors are selected. Some different selectors used on *Reckoning* included *nonexclusive, sequential,* and *stimulus* behaviors. Each of these slightly changed how behaviors could be selected to run or altered the logic of how the tree progressed after running a behavior.

Nonexclusive behaviors run as normal behaviors do, but the tree continues checking siblings at that tree level after doing so. For example, a nonexclusive behavior might play a sound or set up some knowledge tracking while leaving it to other sibling behaviors to determine an actual action.

Sequential behaviors run each of their children in order so long as their precondition returned true. An example might be a behavior to perform a melee attack, with children to approach the target, launch the attack, and then back away. So long as the parent melee behavior returns true, the tree will execute the child behaviors in order.

Stimulus behaviors are a way of hooking the behavior tree up to an in-game event system so that agents can define reaction behaviors to events happening around them. Each stimulus behavior defines a particular stimulus, such as spotting the player or hearing a sound, which it can react to. Stimulus behaviors are a way of specializing a commonly used precondition. In *Reckoning*'s implementation, stimulus behaviors were treated exactly as normal behaviors with a separate precondition function that would check for a defined stimulus on the character running the tree. This specialized precondition also handled cleanup of the stimulus when finished.

Any kind of selection algorithm can work with a behavior tree, which is one of the major strengths of the system. For example, a utility-based selector could pick among its children based on their utility scores, or a goal system could be implemented that picks children based on their postconditions. While any selection algorithm can be made to work, often they will change how the behaviors must be defined, either through additional functions or data needed by the selector. The flexibility of using any kind of selector must be weighed carefully against the time and cost of implementing each different algorithm.

7.8 Conclusion

Behavior trees are a flexible, powerful structure to base an agent's decision-making process around, and utilizing script is one method to drive faster iteration and greater ease of behavior authoring. Being able to edit and reload behaviors at runtime is a huge advantage when refining and debugging behaviors, and having a data-driven approach to behavior creation opens up the process to a much wider group of people on the team, helping production speeds. Additionally, with the behavior tree algorithm being as flexible as it is, improvements and game-specific features can be implemented quickly, and with behaviors implemented in script, each can be updated to take advantage of the new features quickly. Changing their parameters can be done without recompiling or restarting the game, so rapid testing of these features can be accomplished.

If a behavior tree is a fit for a game, having script support for implementing the behaviors provides tremendous flexibility. Though careful analysis of the performance costs is necessary any time a scripting language is used, strategies can be employed to minimize the impact while maintaining the advantages of having a rapid iteration environment for behavior development.

Simulating Behavior Trees
A Behavior Tree/Planner Hybrid Approach

Daniel Hilburn

8.1 Introduction

Game AI must handle a high degree of complexity. Designers often represent AI with complex state diagrams that must be implemented and thoroughly tested. AI agents exist in a complex game world and must efficiently query this world and construct models of what is known about it. Animation states must be managed correctly for the AI to interact with the world properly. AI must simultaneously provide a range of control from fully autonomous to fully designer-driven.

At the same time, game AI must be flexible. Designers change AI structure quickly and often. AI implementations depend heavily on other AI and game system implementations, which change often as well. Any assumptions made about these external systems can easily become invalid—often with little warning. Game AI must also interact appropriately with a range of player styles, allowing many players to have fun playing your game.

There are many techniques available to the AI programmer to help solve these issues. As with any technique, all have their strengths and weaknesses. In the next couple of sections, we'll give a brief overview of two of these techniques: behavior trees and planners. We'll briefly outline which problems they attempt to solve and the ones with which they struggle. Then, we'll discuss a hybrid implementation which draws on the strengths of both approaches.

8.1.1 Behavior Trees

A behavior tree in game AI is used to model the behaviors that an agent can perform. The tree structure allows elemental actions (e.g., jump, kick) to be combined to create

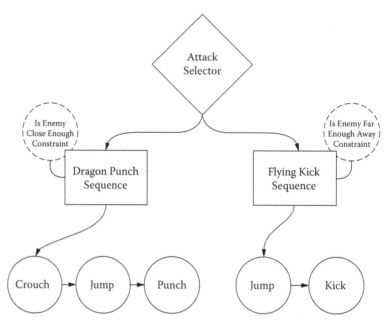

Figure 8.1

Example of a behavior tree.

a higher level behavior (e.g., flying kick). This higher level behavior can then be treated as an elemental behavior and used to compose even higher level behaviors (e.g., attack). Behavior trees also include the concept of *constraints*, which can be attached to behaviors at any level in the tree to keep that behavior from being selected when the state of the world does not match the state required by the constraint (Figure 8.1).

Behavior trees are great at modeling what an AI *can* do. They allow designers to take very low-level actions and combine them to create exactly the set of high-level actions that the designer wants available to the AI. The tree structure easily models any complex design that is thrown at it. Conveniently, this structure also closely resembles the diagrams that designers often use to describe the AI, which allows designers and programmers to speak the same language when discussing AI implementation. The tree structure is also easily configurable, especially if a graphical design tool is available. This allows the designer to rapidly iterate and refine the AI design.

Unfortunately, behavior trees are not so great at specifying what an AI *should* do. In order for the tree to know which action it should perform, it must have intimate knowledge about the world state, including how other AI or game systems are implemented. It must also know how each of its behaviors affects—and is affected by—changes in the world state. This results in a web of dependencies on other systems which are likely to change. If any of these systems change, you'll have to update your behavior tree accordingly. This sort of design is far more brittle than we would like. It is much more preferable that the behavior tree works properly with no modifications even when other systems or its own internal structure changes. Later, we'll discuss ways to solve these issues by taking some cues from AI planners.

8.1.2 Planners

A planner in game AI is used to create a sequence of elemental actions to achieve some goal, given the current world state. This sequence of actions is called a *plan*. The planner maintains a model of the world state, a collection of all elemental actions available to an AI, and a goal heuristic. The world state model contains any information about the world that the heuristic needs. For example, a world state might include a list of available enemies and their health values. The planner understands how each action affects the world state, and since a plan is simply a sequence of these actions, the planner also understands how any plan affects the world state. For example, a kick action deals some damage to an enemy if it is close by, while a jump action moves the AI closer to an enemy.

The goal heuristic scores a given plan by how much it achieves the heuristic's goal. In our example, a combat heuristic would give a high score to a plan that results in enemies being damaged. So, if the AI is close to an enemy, a high scoring plan might consist of just a kick action. However, if the AI is too far from an enemy for the kick to deal damage, the plan will receive a low score. But if we insert a jump action before the kick, now the AI can move in and attack an enemy, a plan which would receive a high score. With all of these pieces available, the planner can create plans that achieve high-level goals dynamically, regardless of the current world state (Figure 8.2).

As you can see, planners are great at managing what an AI *should* do. They allow designers to specify high-level goals for the AI by evaluating world states in the planner's heuristic, rather than trying design specific behaviors for specific situations. Planners are able to do this by keeping a very strict separation between what an AI *does* (actions) and what the AI *should do* (heuristics). This also makes the AI more flexible and durable in the face of design changes. If the jump action gets cut because the team didn't have time to

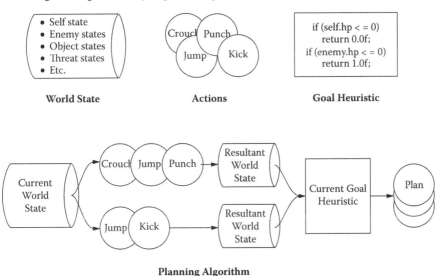

Figure 8.2

Example of a planner.

---

polish the animations, just remove it. The AI will still create the best possible plan for its current world state. If the kick action suddenly also sends out a shockwave, you only need to add that to the kick action's result description. You don't need to change what the AI *should do* just because you changed what it *does*.

While the flexibility of planners is a great strength, it can also be a great weakness. Often, designers will want to have more control over the sequences of actions that an AI can perform. While it is cool that your AI can create a jump kick plan on its own, it could also create a sequence of 27 consecutive jumps. This breaks the illusion of intelligence our AI should produce, which is obviously not what we want to happen. There are techniques to prevent such undesirable plans, but it is difficult to predict all of the situations where a planner can break down. This, understandably, causes distaste for planners among many designers, as they often prefer more control over how their characters behave.

This is the classic tradeoff that AI designers and programmers have to deal with constantly: the choice between the fully designed (brittle) AI that behavior trees provide and the fully autonomous (unpredictable) AI that planners provide. While this battle has been raging for a while now, it is happily not a binary choice. The space between these two approaches is where the best solutions lie. There are numerous implementations of behavior trees and planners and many other techniques that attempt to solve this problem, one of which is our next topic. I'll quickly describe how this approach works, and then we'll dive into how I implemented it on a recent project.

8.1.3 A Behavior Tree/Planner Hybrid

The basic premise of the hybrid approach is simple: combine the strengths of behavior trees and planners to produce an AI system that is flexible and durable in the face of design changes while allowing the designers full control over the structure of the actions available to the AI. It uses a world state model and heuristic, just like the planner. However, where a planner builds sequences of elemental actions dynamically and uses its heuristic to choose the best one, the hybrid approach uses its heuristic to choose between branches of a premade behavior tree.

Using the behavior tree allows the designers to have full control over what actions are available and to easily redesign the structure of these actions while iterating. However, as we mentioned previously, the behavior tree is usually pretty resistant to design changes, as changing the internal structure of an action must be reflected in parent selector nodes back up the tree. This is where our planner half swoops in to save the day.

Remember that our approach also includes a planner's world state model and a heuristic. We incorporate these into the behavior tree by implementing a simulation step for each node type. For *leaf* nodes, this simulation step simply returns a resultant world state just like elemental actions in the planner system. However, the recursive structure of the behavior tree allows us to recursively simulate composite behaviors as well. *Sequence* nodes simulate each of their child behaviors in sequence and then return the accumulated result. *Selector* nodes simulate each of their child behaviors to determine what the resultant world state would be if that node was selected. These results are then fed through the heuristic function to generate a score for each child behavior. The *selector* node then uses these scores to determine which node to select and returns that node's result as its own.

This design allows us to construct behavior trees that know nothing of their internal structure. We can make an *Attack Selector* node that is composed of any number of attack behaviors, and it will choose the one most appropriate to the current world state without knowing about *Dragon Punch* or *Flying Kick* or when they are most appropriate. Any selector node just needs to simulate each of its children and select the one with the highest heuristic score. This allows us to change the internal structure of the tree without changing any code further up the hierarchy. It also allows us to change how a leaf action affects the world without worrying about updating the entire tree to compensate for the changed design. This is what we are looking for. The behavior tree structure allows designers to have full control over what the AI *can* do, while the planner mechanism handles determining what the AI *should* do.

8.2 The Jedi AI in *Kinect Star Wars*™

We developed this behavior tree/planner hybrid approach while working on the Jedi AI for *Kinect Star Wars*™ at Terminal Reality Inc.™, which has been gracious enough to provide the source code for this article as example material. We only have space to go over a subset of the system in this article, but the entire system with sample code is provided on the book's website (http://www.gameaipro.com). The proprietary engine stuff is stubbed out, but all of the Jedi AI bits are there if you are interested in looking them over. Without further ado, let's make a Jedi!

8.2.1 Jedi Memory

The first thing our Jedi needs is an internal knowledge of the world. This is the world state model from our previous discussion, which we called the Jedi AI Memory (see Listing 8.1). It encapsulates everything that our actions can manipulate in the world, including the Jedi, the Jedi's current victim, any nearby enemies, and any incoming threats. It also provides a `simulate()` method, which allows any action to update the parts of memory that change over time (e.g., position), and a `simulateDamage()` method, which allows any behavior to easily simulate damage dealt to a given enemy.

8.2.2 Jedi Behavior Tree

Now that we have our world state representation, let's look at the Jedi's behavior tree implementation. All of our behavior tree nodes, which we called *Actions*, provide the standard begin/update/end behavior tree node interfaces. These nodes return an `EJediAiActionResult` value to their parent from their begin and update operations to let the parent know the Action's current status (see Listing 8.2).

The *Actions* also provide a `checkConstraints()` method, which iterates over a list of attached *Constraint* objects (see Listing 8.3). This method may also be overridden to allow *Action* subclasses to check *Constraints* which are specific to those subclasses. The *Constraint* objects provide options to skip the constraint while the action is in progress or while the action is being simulated, which allow the constraint subclasses a bit of stability. For example, let's consider the *Distance Constraint* attached to the *Dragon Punch* sequence to prevent our AI from executing it when the enemy is too far away. If we start the sequence and the enemy moves far enough away to cause the constraint to fail, the AI will immediately bail out of the sequence, which may not be desirable. It may be more desirable for the AI to continue executing the sequence and simply miss the enemy. If we set up the constraint to be skipped while the action is in progress, this is exactly what will happen.

```
class CJediAiMemory {
public:
    //simulate this AI memory over a given timestep
    void simulate(float dt);
    //simulate damage to an actor
    void simulateDamage(float dmg, SJediAiActorState &actor);
    //data about my self's current state
    struct SSelfState {
        float skillLevel, hitPoints;
        CVector pos, frontDir, rightDir;
    } selfState;
    //knowledge container for world entities
    struct SJediAiEntityState {
        CVector pos, velocity;
        CVector frontDir, rightDir, toSelfDir;
        float distanceToSelf, selfFacePct, faceSelfPct;
    };
    //knowledge container for other actors
    struct SJediAiActorState : SJediAiEntityState {
        EJediEnemyType type;
        float hitpoints;
    };
    //victim state
    SJediAiEntityState *victimState;
    //enemy state list
    enum {kEnemyStateListSize = 8};
    int enemyStateCount;
    SJediAiActorState enemyStates[kEnemyStateListSize];
    //knowledge container for threats
    struct SJediAiThreatState : SJediAiEntityState {
        EJediThreatType type;
        float damage;
    };
    //threat state list
    enum {kThreatStateListSize = 8};
    int threatStateCount;
    SJediAiThreatState threatStates[kThreatStateListSize];
};
```

Finally, the *Actions* provide our simulation interface. Each *Action* contains a simulation summary object which encapsulates everything that our heuristic function cares about. This summary also contains an `EJediAiActionSimResult` value, which is computed by the heuristic and specifies the desirability of the action. Originally, we used a floating-point number between 0 and 1 to specify this value, but it was very difficult to get stable, predictable results from the heuristic that way. We simplified the result to the values in Listing 8.4.

Now that we have specified all of the pieces of an *Action*, we can bring them all together in the `CJediAiAction` class in Listing 8.5. It provides the standard begin/update/end interface, the simulation interface, and the Constraint interface.

Listing 8.2. The returned results of an Action's begin and update operations:

```
//jedi ai action results
enum EJediAiActionResult {
    eJediAiActionResult_Success = 0,
    eJediAiActionResult_InProgress,
    eJediAiActionResult_Failure,
    eJediAiActionResult_Count
};
```

Listing 8.3. The behavior tree's Constraint implementation.

```
//base class for all jedi ai constraints
class CJediAiActionConstraint {
public:
    //next constraint in the list
    CJediAiActionConstraint *nextConstraint;
    //don't check this constraint while in progress
    bool skipWhileInProgress;
    //don't check this constraint while simulating
    bool skipWhileSimulating;
    //check our constraint
    virtual EJediAiActionResult checkConstraint(
        const CJediAiMemory &memory,
        const CJediAiAction &action,
        bool simulating) const = 0;
};
```

Listing 8.4. The behavior tree's simulation summary, which the heuristic uses to score an Action's desirability.

```
//jedi ai action simulation result
enum EJediAiActionSimResult {
    eJediAiActionSimResult_Impossible,
    eJediAiActionSimResult_Hurtful,
    eJediAiActionSimResult_Irrelevant,
    eJediAiActionSimResult_Cosmetic,
    eJediAiActionSimResult_Beneficial,
    eJediAiActionSimResult_Urgent,
    eJediAiActionSimResult_Count
};
//jedi ai action simulation summary data
struct SJediAiActionSimSummary {
    EJediAiActionSimResult result;
    float selfHitPoints, victimHitPoints, threatLevel;
};
```

Listing 8.5. The behavior tree's abstract base Action class.

```
class CJediAiAction {
public:
    //standard begin/update/end interface
    virtual EJediAiActionResult onBegin();
    virtual EJediAiActionResult update(float dt) = 0;
    virtual void onEnd();
    //simulate this action on the specified memory object
    virtual void simulate(
        CJediAiMemory &simMemory,
        SJediAiActionSimSummary &simSummary) = 0;
    //check my constraints
    virtual EJediAiActionResult checkConstraints(
        const CJediAiMemory &memory, bool simulating) const;
};
```

Listing 8.6. The behavior tree's abstract base Composite Action class.

```
class CJediAiActionComposite : public CJediAiAction {
public:
    //child actions accessors
    CJediAiAction *getAction(int index);
    virtual CJediAiAction **getActionTable(int *count) = 0;
};
```

Next, we define a *Composite Action*, the base class of all nodes which are composed of subnodes (e.g., *Sequence* or *Selector*). It is pretty simple, providing a common interface for accessing the list of child nodes (see Listing 8.6).

Next, let's look at the *Sequence Action* (see Listing 8.7). It simply runs all of its child *Actions* in sequence, using the method beginNextAction(). If any of the actions fail, the *Sequence Action* fails as well. Also, simulating a sequence simulates each of its children, starting with the currently running child if the *Sequence* is currently executing. Each child is simulated using the resultant world state of the previous child's simulation. After all children have been simulated, the *Sequence* computes its own simulation result from the resultant world state.

The *Sequence* class provides a few parameters to let you customize how it operates. One thing that you'll notice is that we encapsulate the parameters into their own object. Encapsulating the parameters this way allows a simple memset() to initialize all of the parameter variables, preventing you from forgetting to initialize a new parameter.

Next up is the most important part of the behavior tree: the *Selector* (see Listing 8.8). This class is what decides what the AI will or won't do. The *Selector* does this by calling selectAction(CJediAiMemory *memory), which simulates each of its child behaviors using the provided memory to generate simulation summaries for each. It then calls compareAndSelectAction(), which compares these *Action* summaries and selects the *Action* whose summary has the highest result.

Listing 8.7. The behavior tree Sequence class.

```
class CJediAiActionSequence : public CJediAiActionComposite {
public:
    //parameters
    struct {
        //specify a delay between each action in the Sequence
        float timeBetweenActions;
        //allows the Sequence to loop on completion
        bool loop;
        //allows the Sequence to skip over failed actions
        bool allowActionFailure;
        //specify what action result is considered a failure
        EJediAiActionSimResult minFailureResult;
    } sequenceParams;
    //get the next available action in the sequence,
    //starting with the specified index
    virtual CJediAiAction *getNextAction(int &nextActionIndex);
    //begin the next available action in the sequence
    virtual EJediAiActionResult beginNextAction();
};
```

Listing 8.8. The behavior tree Selector class.

```
class CJediAiActionSelector : public CJediAiActionComposite {
public:
    //parameters
    struct SSelectorParams {
        //specify how often we reselect an action
        float selectFrequency;
        //prevents the selected action from being reselected
        bool debounceActions;
        //allow hurtful actions to be selected
        bool allowNegativeActions;
        //if results are equal, reselect the selected action
        bool ifEqualUseCurrentAction;//default is true
    } selectorParams;
    //simulate each action and select which one is best
    virtual CJediAiAction *selectAction(CJediAiMemory *memory);
    //compare action simulation summaries and select one
    virtual int compareAndSelectAction(
        int actionCount, CJediAiAction *const actionTable[]);
};
```

8.2.3 Jedi Simulation

Now that we've defined our behavior tree components, let's have a look at the planner side of things: the simulation. When we begin simulating an *Action*, we create a summary of the current world state. Then, we modify the world state in the same way that the simulating *Action* actually would if it were executed. For example, when simulating the

Listing 8.9. This shows how we condense a Jedi Memory object into a Simulation Summary.

```
//condense the specified memory into a summary
void setSimSummaryMemoryData(
    SJediAiActionSimSummary &summary,
    const CJediAiMemory &memory);
//initialize a summary from the specified memory
void initSimSummary(
    SJediAiActionSimSummary &summary,
    const CJediAiMemory &memory)
{
    summary.result = eJediAiActionSimResult_Impossible;
    setSimSummaryMemoryData(summary, memory);
}
//compute the resultant world state summary
void setSimSummary(
    SJediAiActionSimSummary &summary,
    const CJediAiMemory &memory)
{
    summary.result = computeSimResult(summary, memory);
    setSimSummaryMemoryData(summary, memory);
}
```

SwingSaber Action, we apply damage to the victim and run the world state simulation forward by the same amount of time that it takes to swing our lightsaber. After the simulation is complete, we create a summary of the resultant world state and compute the desirability of this new state compared to the summary of the initial state (see Listing 8.9). This final summary is passed back to the parent *Action* and will be used by the behavior tree when selecting this *Action* from a set of other *Actions*.

The real meat of this system is the planner heuristic, where we compute the simulation result (see Listing 8.10). This function represents our AI's current goal. In this case, the Jedi's only goal was to avoid damage and threats while causing damage to his victim. The heuristic does this by classifying an *Action*'s post-simulation world state as one of the EJediAiActionSimResult values (impossible, hurtful, irrelevant, beneficial, etc.).

Now that we've defined how our AI's simulation result is computed, let's have a look at how it fits into an actual simulation step: the *SwingSaber Action* (see Listing 8.11).

8.3 Now Let's Throw in a Few Monkey Wrenches …

Game development is an iterative process, and your system will change many times between conception and final product. Even when your system isn't being redesigned, design changes in other systems can change how your implementation behaves. So, it is imperative that our system handles these changes well. As we discussed earlier, the whole point of our hybrid system is to provide flexibility to handle these changes with as few changes as possible. So let's see how well it does by looking at some design changes from *Kinect Star Wars*™.

Listing 8.10. The planner heuristic, which computes the simulation result.

```
//determine the result of a simulation by comparing a summary
//of the initial state to the post-simulation state
EJediAiActionSimResult computeSimResult(
    SJediAiActionSimSummary &summary,
    const CJediAiMemory &memory)
{
    //if we are more hurt than before, the action is hurtful
    //if we are dead, the action is deadly
    if (memory.selfState.hitPoints < summary.selfHitPoints) {
        if (memory.selfState.hitPoints <= 0.0f) {
            return eJediAiActionSimResult_Deadly;
        } else {
            return eJediAiActionSimResult_Hurtful;
        }
    //if our threat level increased, the action is hurtful
    } else if (memory.threatLevel > summary.threatLevel) {
        return eJediAiActionSimResult_Hurtful;
    //if our threat level decreased, the action is helpful
    //if it decreased by a lot, the action is urgent
    } else if (memory.threatLevel < summary.threatLevel) {
        float d = (summary.threatLevel - memory.threatLevel);
        if (d < 0.05f) {
            return eJediAiActionSimResult_Safe;
        } else {
            return eJediAiActionSimResult_Urgent;
        }
    //if victim was hurt, the action is helpful
    } else if (memory.victimState->hitPoints < summary.victimHitPoints) {
        return eJediAiActionSimResult_Beneficial;
    }
    //otherwise, the sim was irrelevant
    return eJediAiActionSimResult_Irrelevant;
}
```

8.3.1 Jedi Skill Level

Kinect Star Wars™ featured three different types of Jedi: Master Jedi, low-level Padawan Jedi, and the second player Jedi. Originally, these were all implemented using the same design. Later, the design team added the caveat that each Jedi should have a skill level to specify how competent he was at combat. This would allow us to make a Master Jedi, like Mavra Zane, more capable in a fight than your Jedi buddy or the other Padawan Jedi in the game.

We implemented this by having the skill level specify how quickly the Jedi could defeat each enemy type. This allowed Mavra to dispatch enemies quickly, while the Padawan Jedi took much longer. To make this work, we added a victimTimer member to our world state to track how much time had elapsed since we acquired our current victim. Then, we added a statement to the heuristic to discourage killing the victim before timer specified by the current skill level had expired (see Listing 8.10).

That was it. We didn't have to change any behavior tree *Actions* or simulation code. The heuristic was already aware if a given action would kill the victim, because we were

The SwingSaber Action's simulation method.

```
void CJediAiActionSwingSaber::simulate(
    CJediAiMemory &simMemory,
    SJediAiActionSimSummary &simSummary)
{
    initSimSummary(simSummary, simMemory);
    EJediAiActionResult result;
    for (int i = data.swingCount; i < params.numSwings; ++i)
    {
        //simulate a single swing's duration
        CJediAiMemory::SSimulateParams simParams;
        simMemory.simulate(
            kJediSwingSaberDuration, simParams);
        //apply damage to my target
        simMemory.simulateDamage(
            simMemory.selfState.saberDamage,
            *simMemory.victimState);
        //if my target is dead, I'm done
        if (simMemory.victimState->hitPoints <= 0.0f)
            break;
    }
    setSimSummary(simSummary, simMemory);
}
```

simulating each action instead of hard-coding the selection logic into the selectors. So the planner held up its end of the bargain, allowing us to change goals without modifying any *Actions*.

8.3.2 Jedi Mistakes

Another wrinkle that arose was the idea of mistakes. It isn't realistic for the Jedi to always defeat their enemies; they should sometimes fail. Also, the designers wanted the Jedi AI to demonstrate what not to do against various enemy types. However, our entire system is built on the idea that the Jedi will choose the **best** option. We could make a custom selector that chooses the worst option instead of the best option, but it would still return a negative simulation result to its parent, which would then not select it to run.

At first this seemed like a flaw in the system, until we thought about what defines a "mistake." Obviously, the Jedi will always *try* to choose the best Action available. But what if they made a miscalculation and chose an Action which actually was hurtful? This would pass correctly back up the behavior tree and the hurtful Action would then be chosen. In order to create this miscalculation, we needed to insert incorrect information into the simulation step for any *Action*. Rather than add these special cases to each *Action*, we added a special *Action* called a *FakeSim*. The *FakeSim Action* is a special type of *Composite Action* called a *decorator*, which wraps another *Action* to add extra functionality to it. The *FakeSim* was responsible for adding incorrect information to the wrapped *Action*'s simulation step by modifying the world state directly. For example, there are some enemies that have a shield which makes them invulnerable to lightsaber attacks. If we want a Jedi to attack the enemy to demonstrate that the enemy is invulnerable while the shield is up, we can wrap the *SwingSaber Action* with a *FakeSim Decorator* which lowers the victim's shield during the simulation step. Then, the *SwingSaber* simulation will think that the Jedi can damage the enemy and give it a good simulation result. This would allow *SwingSaber* to be chosen, even though it won't actually be beneficial.

This ended up being a great way to handle this design requirement. It allows us to insert specific mistakes anywhere in the system without modifying any of the *Action* classes. And it allows us to avoid writing special case code to handle inserting these mistakes. We simply insert a bit of incorrect domain knowledge into the system, which reflects how people make mistakes in real life. So the behavior tree held up its end of the bargain, allowing us to easily design very specific *Action* sequences that the planner couldn't handle on its own.

8.4 Conclusion

We've discussed some of the strengths and weakness with both behavior trees and planners. Behavior trees are great at allowing designers to define exactly what an AI *can* do, and planners are great at allowing designers to easily specify what an AI *should* do. And we've discussed how we can utilize a hybrid approach to realize the strengths of both approaches. Finally, we looked at how this system was used in *Kinect Star Wars*™ to create the Jedi AI. This approach provides designers with all of the control of a behavior tree and all of the durability and flexibility of a planner, allowing it to handle design changes smoothly and with few changes to the code. And that is really the whole point.

9

An Introduction to Utility Theory

David "Rez" Graham

9.1 Introduction

Decision making forms the core of any AI system. There are many different approaches to decision making, several of which are discussed in other chapters in this book. One of the most robust and powerful systems we've encountered is a utility-based system. The general concept of a utility-based system is that every possible action is scored at once and one of the top scoring actions is chosen. By itself, this is a very simple and straightforward approach. In this article, we'll talk about common techniques, best practices, pitfalls to avoid, and how you can best apply utility theory to your AI.

9.2 Utility

Utility theory is a concept that's been around long before games or even computers. It has been used in game theory, economics, and numerous other fields. The core idea behind utility theory is that every possible action or state within a given model can be described with a single, uniform value. This value, usually referred to as *utility*, describes the usefulness of that action within the given context. For example, let's say you need a new toy for your cat; so you go online and find the perfect one. One website has it for $4.99 while another website sells the exact same toy for $2.99. Assuming delivery times are the same, you will likely choose the toy for $2.99. That option typically has a higher utility than the toy for $4.99 because, in the end, you are left with more money.

This process gets more difficult when you need to compare the value of two things that aren't directly comparable. For instance, in the previous example let's assume that the two websites have different delivery times. The toy for $4.99 will arrive at your house in two days while the toy for $2.99 will arrive in five days. In this case, the choice is no longer a simple matter of comparing the two price values. Some conversion between time and money has to be made in order to measure the overall worth of an action. We could say that each day is worth $1, which means that the total cost of the $4.99 toy is $6.99 while the total cost of the $2.99 toy is $7.99. The $4.99 toy is the winner in this case (because it costs you less in combined money + time). You can also weigh things such as website loyalty, recommendations from friends, history, customer reviews, and anything else that you might consider a relevant factor. All of these factors have utility scores of their own, which you can then combine to create the total *expected utility* of for the decision.

It's important to note that *utility* is not the same as *value*. Value is a measurable quantity (such as the prices above). Utility measures how much we desire something. This can change based on personality or the context of the situation. If you were a billionaire, you would likely choose the cat toy for $4.99 because you might value time more than money. The $2.00 you save is a negligible amount. On the other hand, if you were very poor, you would likely choose the cheaper toy and wait the extra time because that extra $2 is really important to you. That money has the exactly same *value*, but the *utility* of the money is variable, based on the context in which it is being considered. This can change from moment to moment. Right now, the utility of having a bandage with you might be pretty small. If you were to accidentally cut yourself, the utility of having a bandage would climb.

9.2.1 Consistent Utility Scores

When calculating utility scores, it's important to be consistent. Because utility scores are compared to each other to come up with a final decision, they must all be on the same scale across the entire system. As you'll see later in this article, scores are often combined in meaningful ways to produce other scores. Therefore, using *normalized scores* (values that go from 0–1) provide a reasonable starting point. Normalized scores combine very easily through averaging, can be easily calculated given any value within a set range of numbers, and are easily comparable since they are on the same scale. It's important to note that any value range will work, as long as there is consistency across the different variables. If an AI agent scores an action with a value of 15, you should know immediately what that means in the context of the whole system. For instance, does that 15 mean 15 out of 25 or 15%?

9.3 Principle of Maximum Expected Utility

The key to decision making using utility-based AI is to calculate a utility score (sometimes called a weight) for every action the AI agent can take and then choose the action with the highest score. Of course, most game worlds are nondeterministic so calculating the exact utility is not usually possible. It's hard to know if an action will be preferable if you can't determine the results of performing that action. This is the heart of utility theory and where it is most useful. For example, if we had the processing power to compute the entire game tree for a chess game, scoring of moves wouldn't be necessary—we would simply determine if sequences of moves resulted in a win, loss, or tie. We currently don't have that ability, so we score each move based on how strong we think the move is. Provided a reasonable scoring system, utility-based AI is very good at making a "best guess" based on incomplete information.

The most common technique is to multiply the utility score by the probability of each possible outcome and sum up these weighted scores. This will give you the *expected utility* of the action. This can be expressed mathematically with Equation 9.1.

$$EU = \sum_{i=1}^{n} D_i P_i \qquad (9.1)$$

In this case, D is the desire for that outcome (i.e., the utility), and P is the probability that the outcome will occur. This probability is normalized so that the sum of all the probabilities is 1. This is applied to every possible action that can be chosen, and the action with the highest expected utility is chosen. This is called the principle of *maximum expected utility* [Russell et al. 09].

For example, an enemy AI in an RPG attacking the player has two possible outcomes—either the AI hits the player or it misses. If the AI has an 85% chance to hit the player, and successfully hitting the player has a calculated utility score of 0.6, the adjusted utility would be $0.85 \times 0.6 = 0.51$. (Note that, in this case, missing the player has a utility of zero, so there's no need to factor it in.) Taking this further, if this attack were to be compared to attacking with a different weapon, for example, with a 60% chance of hitting but a utility score of 0.9 if successful, the adjusted utility would be $0.60 \times 0.9 = 0.54$. Despite having a lesser chance of hitting, the second option provides a greater overall *expected utility*.

9.4 Decision Factors

It is rare that any given decision will only rely on a single piece of data. A decision factor can be thought of as a single point of consideration for a decision. For example, when deciding which website to purchase the cat toy from, we don't usually just consider price, but also consider brand loyalty, shipping times, customer reviews, etc. Each of these data points are factors that we weigh into the calculation of the final utility score for whether or not to buy from that website. Factors can also be further modified by weights that determine how much the AI cares about that particular factor, which emulates personality.

One way to achieve this result is to apply the expected utility calculation in Equation 9.1 to each decision factor to come up with the utility of that factor. Assuming those scores are all normalized, you can average them together to come up with a final utility score for that decision. This lets us define a decision as nothing more than some combination of decision factors.

This principle is best illustrated with an example. Let's say we have an ant simulation game where the AI must determine whether to expand the colony or whether to breed. There are three different factors we want to consider for these decisions. The first is the overall crowdedness of the colony. If there are too many ants, we need to expand to make room for more. The second is the health of the colony, which we'll say is based on how full the food stores are. Ant eggs need to be kept at a specific temperature; so there are specially built nurseries that house the eggs where they are taken care of. The amount of room in these nurseries is the third decision factor. These decision factors are based on game statistics that determine the score for each factor. The population and max population determine how many ants are in the colony and how many can exist based on the current

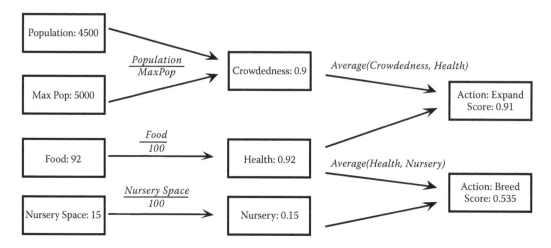

Figure 9.1

An example of combining utility scores from different decision factors to arrive at a final score.

colony size. The food stat represents how full the food stores are and is measured as a number from 0 to 100. The nursery space stat is also measured from 0 to 100 and represents how much space there is in the nursery. You can think of the last stats as percentages.

The scores for the decision factors are then combined to form the final score for the two actions. In this case, crowdedness and health are averaged together to form the score for the expand action while nursery space and health are averaged together to get the score for the breed action. Figure 9.1 shows this combination.

By averaging the normalized scores together, we can build an endless chain of combinations. This is a really powerful concept. Each decision factor is effectively isolated from every other decision factor. The only thing we know or care about is that the output will be a normalized score. We can easily add more game stat inputs, like the distance to an enemy ant colony. This could feed into a decision factor for deciding what kind of ants to breed. You can easily move decision factors around as well, combining them in different ways. If you wanted crowdedness to factor negatively into the decision for breeding, you could subtract crowdedness from 1.0 and average that into the score for breeding.

One of the most powerful uses of this technique is to build a tool that allows you to manipulate decision factors and game state data directly. This tool would allow designers to drag and drop boxes around and connect them with arrows, much like the layout of Figure 9.1. Each arrow would combine the decision factors in different ways. For example, you might average some decision factors together, multiply others, choose the *max* or *min* of another set, etc. Certain decision factors can also be given a weight, making those factors more or less important. There are almost endless possibilities.

9.5 Calculating Utility

So far, we've seen how to calculate the utility given a set of outcomes, and how to combine the utility of multiple decision factors to arrive at the final utility for a decision. The next step is taking an arbitrary game value and converting it to a utility score. Calculating the initial utility for a decision factor is highly subjective; two different programmers will write two different utility functions that produce different outputs, even given the same inputs. In the ant example above, we chose to represent health as a linear ratio by dividing the current amount of food with the maximum amount of food. This probably isn't a very realistic calculation since the colony shouldn't care about food when the stores are mostly full. Some kind of quadratic curve is more of what we want.

The key to utility theory is to understand the relationship between the input and the output, and being able to describe that resulting curve [Mark 09]. This can be thought of as a conversion process, where you are converting one or more values from the game to utility. Coming up with the proper function is really more art than science and is usually where you'll spend most of your time. There are a huge number of different formulas you could use to generate reasonable utility curves, but a few of them crop up often enough that they warrant some discussion.

9.5.1 Linear

A linear curve forms a straight line with a constant slope. The utility value is simply a multiplier of the input. Equation 9.2 shows the formula for calculating a normalized utility score for a given value and Figure 9.2 shows the resulting curve.

$$U = \frac{x}{m} \tag{9.2}$$

In Equation 9.2, x is the input value and m is the maximum value for that input. This is really just a normalization function, which is all we need for a linear output.

9.5.2 Quadratic

A quadratic function is one that forms a parabolic curve, causing it to start slow and then curve upwards very quickly. The simplest way to achieve this is to add an exponent to Equation 9.2. Equation 9.3 shows an example of this.

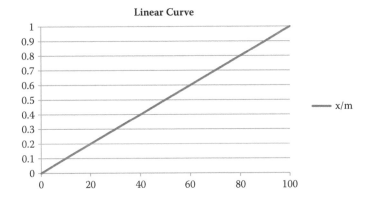

Figure 9.2

A linear curve.

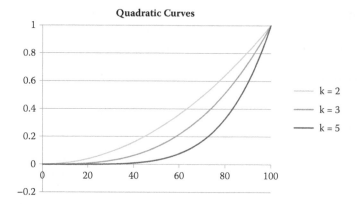

Figure 9.3

Several quadratic curves for various values of k.

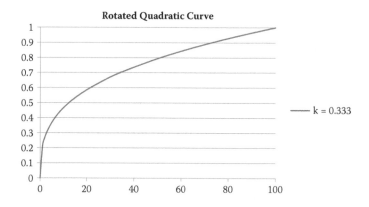

Figure 9.4

A rotated quadratic curve.

$$U = \left(\frac{x}{m}\right)^{k} \tag{9.3}$$

As the value of k rises, the steepness of the curve will also rise. Since the equation normalizes the output, it will always converge on 0 and 1, so a large value of k will have very little impact for low values of x. Figure 9.3 shows curves for three different values of k.

It's also possible to rotate the curve so that the effect is more urgent for low values of x rather than high values. If you use an exponent between 0 and 1, the curve is effectively rotated, as shown in Figure 9.4.

9.5.3 The Logistic Function

The logistic function is another common formula for creating utility curves. It's one of several sigmoid functions that place the largest rate of change in the center of the input

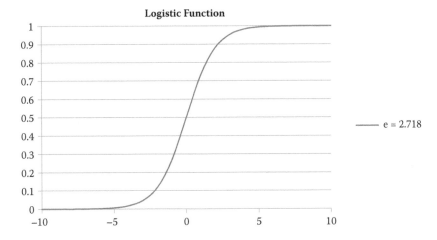

Logistic Function

Figure 9.5

The output of a logistic function.

range, trailing off at both ends as they approach 0 and 1. The input range for the logistic function can be just about anything, but it is effectively limited to [−10 ... 10]. There really isn't much point generating a curve larger than that and the range is often clamped down even further. For example, when x is 6, *EU* will be 0.9975.

Equation 9.4 shows the formula for the logistic function and Figure 9.5 shows the resulting curve. Note the use of the constant e. This is Euler's number—the base of the natural logarithm—which is approximately 2.718281828. This value can be adjusted to affect the shape of the curve. As the number goes up, the curve will sharpen and begin to resemble a square wave. As the number goes down, it will soften.

$$U = \frac{1}{1 + e^{-x}}$$ (9.4)

9.5.4 Piecewise Linear Curves

The curves we've listed so far are by no means a complete list. There are many, many different ways you can transform the input into something else. Sometimes, having a mathematical formula isn't good enough. Designers often need to fine-tune the specific outputs for various given inputs.

For example, consider a problem faced by all Sims games, which is making a Sim eat when they are hungry. All Sims have a *Hunger* stat which measures how full they are. The lower this *Hunger* stat, the more hungry a Sim is. A naïve scoring implementation might be to model hunger with a rotated quadratic curve like the one in Figure 9.4, or perhaps one with a smaller value for k. That would make Sims get really hungry when their *Hunger* stat got low. The problem is that there would still be a chance they would choose to eat, even when their hunger stat was mostly filled up. The chance would be small, but it would eventually get chosen. Designers want a finer degree of control. They want the ability to have a Sim completely ignore hunger until it reaches a threshold, then get a little hungry, then

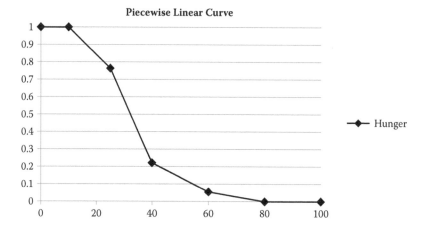

Figure 9.6

A reasonable piecewise linear curve for Hunger.

suddenly get *very* hungry. There's no way to build and tune that specific curve with a simple mathematical formula, so the solution is to create a custom curve. One example of a custom curve is a piecewise linear curve.

A piecewise linear curve is just a custom-built curve. The idea is that you hand-tune a bunch of 2D points that represent the thresholds you want. When the curve is asked for the *y* value given an *x* value, it finds the two closest points to that *x* value and linearly interpolates between them to arrive at the answer. This allows you to create any shaped curve you want and is exactly what *The Sims* uses. Figure 9.6 shows a simple response curve that might be used for hunger.

There are many other types of custom curves. For example, the curve in Figure 9.6 could be changed so that the values from 15 to 60 are calculated with a quadratic curve, while the rest are linear. There's no limit to the number of combinations you can have.

9.6 Picking an Action

Once the utility has been calculated for each action, the next step is to choose one of those actions. There are a number of ways you can do this. The simplest is to just choose the highest scoring option. For some games, this may be exactly what you want. A chess AI should definitely choose the highest scoring move. A strategy game might do the same.

For some games (like *The Sims*), choosing the absolute best action can feel very robotic due to the likelihood that the action will *always* be selected in that situation. Another solution is to use the utility scores as weight, and randomly choose one of the actions based on the weights. This can be accomplished by dividing each score with the sum of all scores to get the percentage chance that the action will be chosen. Then you generate a random number and select the action that number corresponds to. This tends to have the opposite problem, however. Your AI agents will behave reasonably well most of the time, but every now and then, they'll choose something utterly stupid.

You can get the best of both worlds by taking a subset of the highest scoring actions and choosing one of those with a weighted random. This can either be a tuned value, such as choosing from among the top five scoring actions, or it can be percentile based where you take the highest score and also consider things that scored within, say, 10% of it.

This will generally solve the problem at hand, but there could also be times when some set of actions are just completely inappropriate. You may not even want to score them. For example, say you're making an FPS and have a guard AI. You might have some set of actions for him to consider, like getting some coffee, chatting with his fellow guard, checking for lint, etc. If the player shoots at him, he shouldn't even consider any of those actions and only try to score actions that involve combat. In a similar example from *The Sims*, if a Sim is starving to death, she shouldn't bother scoring actions that result in her satisfying her *Fun* motive.

The most straightforward way to solve this is with *bucketing*, also known as *dual utility AI* [Dill 11]. All actions are categorized into buckets and each bucket is given a weight. The higher priority buckets are always processed first. If there are any valid actions in those higher priority buckets, they are always selected before actions in lower priority buckets. In the FPS example above, all combat actions would be in a higher priority bucket than the idle actions. If there are any valid combat actions to take (i.e., they score higher than 0), the guard will always choose one of them and won't consider any of the idle actions. Only when none of the combat actions are valid will the guard choose an idle action.

Buckets can also change priority based on the situation. On *The Sims*, motives are bucketed based on their utility value. The highest scoring motives are grouped into a bucket, and none of the motives below are considered. Once the bucketing is complete, the Sim will score the individual actions on each object, but only the ones that solve for those bucketed motives. Thus, a starving Sim will never even consider watching TV unless they fail to find anything that can solve their hunger. This concept is illustrated in Figure 9.7.

In Figure 9.7, you can see that there are two buckets, one for *Hunger* and one for *Fun*. *Hunger* has scored 0.8 while *Fun* has scored 0.4. The Sim will walk through all possible actions in the *Hunger* bucket and, assuming any of those actions are valid, will choose one. The Sim will not consider anything in the *Fun* bucket, even though some of those actions

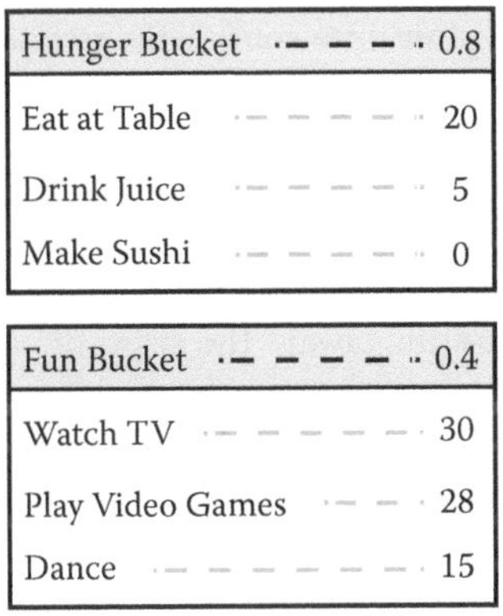

Hunger Bucket	0.8
Eat at Table	20
Drink Juice	5
Make Sushi	0

Fun Bucket	0.4
Watch TV	30
Play Video Games	28
Dance	15

Figure 9.7

The Hunger and Fun buckets, each with three actions.

are scoring higher. This is because hunger is more urgent than fun. Of course, if none of the actions in the *Hunger* bucket were valid, the Sim would move on to the next highest scoring bucket. The buckets themselves are scored based on a response curve created by designers. This causes Sims to always attempt to solve the most urgent desire and to choose one of the best actions to solve for that desire.

9.7 Inertia

One issue that's worth bringing up in any AI system is the concept of inertia. If your AI agent is attempting to decide something every frame, it's possible to run into oscillation issues, especially if you have two things that are scored similarly. For example, say you have FPS where the AI realizes it's in a bad spot. The enemy soldier starts scoring both "attack the player" and "run away" at 0.5. If the AI was making a new decision every frame, it is possible that they would start appearing very frantic. The AI might shoot the player a couple times, start to run away, then shoot again, then repeat. Oscillations in behavior such as this look very bad.

One solution is to add a weight to any action that you are already currently engaged in. This will cause the AI to tend to remain committed until something truly better comes along. Another solution is to use *cooldowns*. Once an AI agent makes a decision, they enter a cooldown stage where the weighting for remaining in that action is extremely high. This weight can revert at the end of the cooldown period, or it can gradually drop as well.

Another solution is to stall making another decision—either for a period of time or until such time as the current action is finished. This really depends on the type of game you're making and how your decision/action process works, however. On *The Sims Medieval*, a Sim would only attempt to make a decision when their interaction queue was empty. Once they chose an action, they would commit to performing that action. Once the Sim completed (or failed to complete) their action, they would choose a new action.

9.8 Demo

The demo on the book website (gameaipro.com) demonstrates many of the concepts from this article. It's a simple text-based combat program similar to the menu-based combat RPG's from the '80s, like *Dragon Warrior* (aka *Dragon Quest*) and *Final Fantasy*. You fight a single monster and each of you has the ability to attack the other, heal with a healing potion, or run away. Attacking will do a random amount of damage, healing will use up one of three healing potions to heal a random amount of hit points, and running away has a 50% chance of successfully running away. The relevant code is in AiActor.cpp, which has all of the scoring functions and is responsible for choosing the action when it's the AI actor's turn. The key function is ChooseNextAction(), which takes in the opponent actor and returns an action to perform. This function calls each of the scoring functions to calculate their scores and chooses one using a weighted random.

9.8.1 Decision Factors

When making decisions, the AI considers four basic factors. The first is a desire to attack, which is based on a tuned value that scales linearly as it becomes possible to kill the player

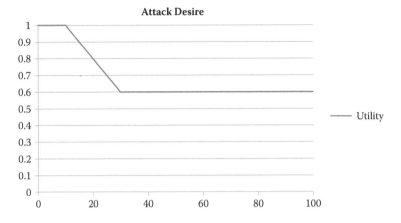

Attack Desire

—— Utility

Figure 9.8

The Attack Desire curve.

in a single hit. This causes the actor to get more aggressive during the end-game and take more risks, as shown in Equation 9.5. This is a good example of a range-bound linear curve. The value of a in the equation is the tuned aggression of the actor, which is the default score.

$$U = \max\left(\min\left(\left(1 - \frac{hp - minDmg}{maxDmg - minDmg}\right) \times (1-a) + a, 1\right), 0\right) \tag{9.5}$$

Figure 9.8 shows the resulting curve from Equation 9.5 where a is set to 0.6.

The second decision factor is the threat. This is a curve that measures what percentage of the actor's current hit points will be taken away if the player hits for maximum damage. It has a shape similar to a quadratic curve and is generated with Equation 9.6.

$$U = min\left(\frac{maxDmg}{hp}, 1\right) \tag{9.6}$$

Figure 9.9 shows the resulting curve for Threat.

The third decision factor is the actor's desire for health. This uses a variation of the logistics function in Equation 9.4. As the actor's hit points are reduced, its desire to heal will rise. Equation 9.7 shows the formula for this decision factor.

$$U = 1 - \frac{1}{1 + (e \times 0.68)^{-\left(\frac{hp}{maxHp} \times 12\right) + 6}} \tag{9.7}$$

The resulting curve is a nice, smooth, sigmoid curve, which is shown in Figure 9.10. Note the addition of +6 to the exponent. This is what pushes the curve over to the positive x-axis rather than centering around 0.

9. An Introduction to Utility Theory

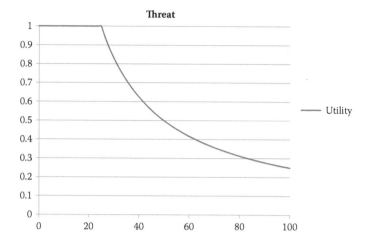

Figure 9.9

The Threat curve.

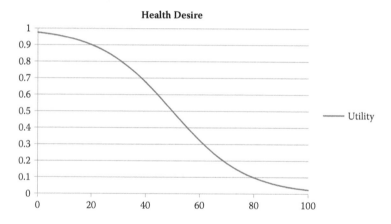

Figure 9.10

The Health Desire curve.

The final decision factor is the desire to run away. This is a quadratic curve with a steepness based on the number of potions the agent has. If the agent has several potions, the likelihood of running away is extremely small. If the agent has none, this desire grows much faster. Equation 9.8 shows the formula for the run desire.

$$U = 1 - \left(\frac{hp}{maxHp} \right)^{\frac{1}{(p+1)^4} \times 0.25} \tag{9.8}$$

The curve itself is dependent on the value of p, which is the number of potions the actor has left. Figure 9.11 shows various curves for various values of p.

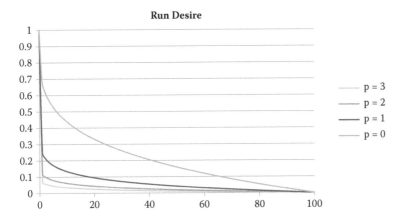

Run Desire

p = 3
p = 2
p = 1
p = 0

Figure 9.11

The Run Desire curve for several values of *p*.

These curves all represent the various decision factors the AI will use to choose one of the three options. The decision to attack is based entirely on the Attack Desire curve. The decision to heal is based on the Health Desire curve multiplied with the Threat curve. This mitigates the case where the actor may want to heal prematurely and changes behavior based on the maximum damage of the player. It's worth noting that we originally had this set to the average damage the player can do since that's more in the spirit of *expected* utility, but this didn't yield strict enough results. This is a good example of how tuning utility curves and formulas is more art than science. The decision to run away works the same way as the decision to heal; it multiplies in the desire to run with the threat.

9.8.2 Decision Making and Gameplay

The demo is a turn-based duel between you and a ferocious utility curve. You start first by choosing one of the available actions, and then your opponent decides how to respond. This continues until one of you is dead or has run away. The AI opponent starts by calculating the score for each decision factor by running through the utility formulas above. The score for each action is calculated by combining the decision factors. The Attack action is just the outcome of the Attack Desire decision factor. The Run action is scored by multiplying the Run Desire decision factor with the Threat. The Heal action is scored by multiplying the Heal Desire decision factor with the Threat. The final decision is chosen with a weighted random.

9.9 Conclusion

Utility theory is a very powerful way to get rich, life-like behavior out of your AI and has been used in countless games of nearly every genre. It can be extremely fast, especially if you choose simple utility functions, and it scales very well. One of the great appeals of this system is the amount of emergent behavior you can get with just a few simple values and a handful of weights to add some personality. By combining decision factors in meaningful ways, you can build up decisions from these atomic components to provide very deep AI.

In this article, we had a whirlwind tour of utility theory and how it can be applied to games. We showed you some basic principles of decision making and dug into the math behind it. With the tools in this article and a bit of work, you can build a powerful, emergent AI system.

References

[Dill 11] K. Dill. "A game AI approach to autonomous control of virtual characters." *Interservice/Industry Training, Simulation, and Education Conference, 2011*, pp. 4–5. Available online (http://www.iitsec.org/about/PublicationsProceedings/Documents/11136_Paper.pdf).

[Mark 09] D. Mark. *Behavioral Mathematics for Game AI*. Reading, MA: Charles River Media, 2009, pp 229–240.

[Russell et al. 09] S. Russell and P. Norvig. *Artificial Intelligence: A Modern Approach*. Reading, MA: Prentice Hall, 2009, pp. 480–509.

10

Building Utility Decisions into Your Existing Behavior Tree

Bill Merrill

10.1 Introduction

While there is no "silver bullet" approach to authoring AI behavior, behavior trees tend to strike a strong overall balance across ease of implementation, ease of visualization, and adoptability for new team members. Building supporting tools is straightforward, and a rapid workflow can be established in relatively short order. On the other hand, behavior trees have a fundamental limitation. They are poor at modeling analog concepts such as uncertainty over multiple valid options. Game characters are simply fun and engaging machines for players to interact with and even exploit, but requirements still often demand more than strictly Boolean selection logic. Because hand-coding analog selection logic everywhere that it is required gets messy quickly, a better solution is needed.

Utility-based decision-making addresses this problem head-on. Rather than creating variation through randomness or forcing agents to arbitrarily take one valid option over another, we can apply existing, well-documented techniques to deal with "gray area" decisions in an elegant manner. Most satisfyingly, we can do all of this without uprooting an existing implementation by imposing structural changes and we don't have to give up any of the most desirable traits of behavior trees.

This article proposes a few simple components that enable the integration of utility considerations into a behavior tree's normal selection process. The express goal of this integration is to overcome much of the behavior tree architecture's biggest weaknesses without sacrificing its strengths.

10.2 Why Behavior Trees?

Behavior trees have been growing steadily in popularity, and for good reason. Put simply, they offer a very pragmatic approach to making decisions. It is their simplicity I find most valuable, and in a world of increasingly complex software, simplicity should not go undervalued. The aggregation of systems comprising AI in modern games is becoming vast, and isn't shrinking anytime soon. It's important to find what works for the team and try not to force new learning curves unnecessarily.

Behavior trees have become somewhat of a standard in the industry. Many AAA studios make use of behavior tree technology, including Bungie with the Halo series [Bungie 07], and Crytek with Crysis 2 [Crytek 11]. A wealth of information on behavior trees is available online and existing toolkits are available for developers looking to get started quickly [Champandard 08, Brainiac 09]. This implementation included with this chapter is basic, but also relatively complete and free for any use. To see more on how developers are constantly improving on the traditional behavior tree, Alex Champandard's behavior tree toolkit provides tips on how to implement your behavior tree to optimize performance and memory access patterns on systems such as consoles that demand the extra attention [Champandard 12].

For my team in particular, the accessibility and scalability of behavior trees has us using them as our primary mechanism for decision making. Productivity depends largely on designers, scripters, and animators gaining a clear understanding of how a given character intends to behave and react to change. We never fully attained this when using a STRIPS-based planner or our finite state machine (FSM) prior to that. In both cases, so much of what was occurring "under the hood" was largely opaque to anyone other than the AI programmer(s). In the case of the planner, it was too organic and mysterious for the designers' comfort. Additionally, emergent behavior is still not a desirable feature most of the time. Planners also make it difficult to string together specific sequences of actions in a defined order when needed. As for FSMs, the lack of true modularity, complex state logic, and a tendency to get messy negatively affected both the designers and programmers alike. This was especially true as NPC characters developed over time, requiring more complex transition logic. Special cases seemed to become the norm, generating many uninvited surprises along the way as we attempted to share functionality with past projects and other game teams.

With behavior trees, our designers can effectively visualize what's happening, in real-time, and can intuitively apply changes or additions with a clear picture of what to expect. Programmers can also easily oversee the changes. Tree structures are a familiar and relatively easy concept to digest, with many designers industry-wide already using them in some form for major aspects of their workflow. This enables us to provide the designers with easily-adoptable debugging and authoring tools. This is invaluable during development when creating complex tools and chasing bugs can steal precious resources from iteration and content creation.

10.3 It's Not All Candy Canes and Gum Drops

The features required by a game change constantly, putting strain on nearly every system in your codebase. AI is particularly susceptible to this problem because it's driven directly by design, and changes more rapidly over the course of a project than other systems of similar breadth and complexity. It's our responsibility as programmers to question the fitness of our solutions in addressing the problems at hand. In terms of decision making, I found myself regularly questioning the fitness of behavior trees while implementing behaviors that didn't have easily quantifiable static priority, or didn't intuitively distill down to simple yes/no criteria.

In a standard behavior tree, priority is static. It is baked right into the tree. The simplicity is welcome, but in practice it can be frustratingly limiting. The same behavior may require different relative priorities, depending on the context. Ensuring our Monster Hunter's primary weapon has a full clip should always be a consideration, even if we're casually patrolling the jungle. But if we're engaged with a savage monster, it's absolutely necessary that we continue to deal damage. Behavior tree authors often deal with this conundrum by duplicating sections of the tree at different branches, with different conditions and/or priorities. Even with slick sub-tree instancing or referencing, this still becomes inefficient, verbose, and potentially fragile.

Even more troublesome cases surface when a simple yes versus no determination isn't easily established. If our *Combat* selector is evaluating its options, should it choose to have us seek a rendezvous with our medic and his space-age healing tech, or should we put everything we have into quickly dropping the giant alien beast threatening to eat us all? This sort of decision is best made only after considering a potentially broad combination of inputs.

Decisions are rarely binary, and many behaviors simply do not have priorities we can comfortably establish offline. Let's start with a simple example behavior tree (Figure 10.1). Having no ability to shoot is a precondition for the *Seek Medic* behavior, forcing us to duplicate the behavior, as seen in Figure 10.2. We could start by giving *Seek Medic* stricter conditions and prioritizing it over *Shoot*, but this will likely create the opposite problem where the Monster Hunter immediately takes the *Seek Medic* action the instant conditions pass. This is the sort of fundamental problem we want to address with the integration of utility.

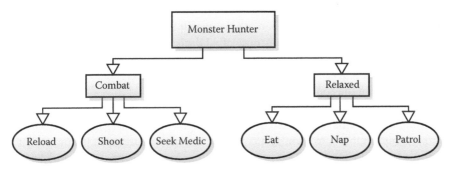

Figure 10.1

Here is a simple, minimal behavior tree for the Monster Hunter.

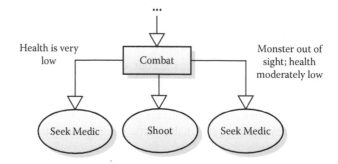

Figure 10.2

In order to implement *Seek Medic* with two different priorities depending on runtime conditions, we're limited to duplication within the tree.

10.4 What Is Utility Theory?

As it applies to game AI behavior, utility theory is simply the process of measuring the relative suitability of a particular action [Mark 09]. To make good decisions, we need to quantify how *worthwhile* an option is, given all the relevant facts, rather than make a determination on validity alone. Industry veterans who advocate the use of utility theory like to remind us that there is rarely just one correct decision to make. So the question is: why do we still favor decision-making architectures that fail to address this problem elegantly?

In reality, an agent of moderate complexity may have dozens of potential options on the table at once. There may even be several perfectly sensible options. Utility theory recognizes that decisions are seldom black and white, and attempts to formally address the complexities of combining various pieces of analog information together to make a final determination. Figuring out how to identify and compare the information in a logical manner is much of the challenge. The most important goal is to ensure that the overall computation is reliable given any combination of inputs, and always results in a reasonable choice.

10.5 Applying Utility in Decision Making

Game agents are *approximations* of autonomous entities within the limited scope of a game's specific design. For this reason, it's not worth the effort in most games to deeply analyze mountains of data for the purpose of AI decision making. Going too broad with the inputs effectively dilutes their meaning, resulting in muddy, or even illogical, formulas. All that should concern us is building an experience that feels believable and engaging to the player within the context of the game.

It's worth first making an effort to represent the input values in a manner that enables direct comparison. This helps avoid a confusing apples-to-oranges quagmire. One easy way to accomplish this is to identify a common unit of measurement. It can be a lot like solving a system of equations. We can substitute one variable with some combination of other, better understood variables. If we're combining two inputs, it makes sense to represent them both in terms of time, health, ammo, a rate of growth/consumption, or something even more abstract. For example, if our Monster Hunter is low on health and wishes to consider rendezvousing with the squad's medic for a health boost, we can measure the benefits of receiving treatment in health points gained. However, running frantically to a safe position is likely to gain the attention of the alien beast, putting us at a risk. If we can measure the risk by predicting the health we're likely to lose in transit, both inputs are now in terms of health points and can be combined and/or compared directly, as in Equation (10.1). We could simply take their sum, and if the net value is positive, taking this action has some benefit we can weigh against other actions.

$$RawUtility = HealthGained - HealthLost \qquad (10.1)$$

More desirably, by attaching more weight to the amount of health we'll lose in transit, we can ensure that we only take this action if we expect to net a significant amount of health, as seen in Equation (10.2). After all, breaking even would be a waste of the time we could've otherwise spent slaying the creature. We also want a high degree of confidence that, even if our predictions were overly optimistic, we're unlikely to end up with a net loss in health and looking rather boneheaded as a result. Naturally there's more we could do, such as apply an exponential scale to *HealthLost*, which causes the utility to fall off more rapidly as the risk grows, as in Equation (10.3).

$$Value = HealthGained - (HealthLost \times 2.0) \qquad (10.2)$$

$$Value = HealthGained - (pow(HealthLost, 1.2)) \qquad (10.3)$$

What happens if we're unable to represent our input values in such easily relatable units, and we wish to consider much more than just a net change in health? One way to combat this scenario is to combine the various influences into higher-level, more abstract values such as "Morale," "Threat," etc. The utility of running to visit our medic could also take into consideration the lost time we could've otherwise spent damaging the monster. Specifically, we could take our formula above, normalize the result, and classify it as a "Heal" factor. Next, we could generate a second formula representing this time lost, normalize it, and classify it as "Delay." We now have two normalized quantities representing higher-level valuations, which we can combine into a final utility value.

$$Utility = \frac{\left(Heal * HealPower - Delay * DelayPower \right)}{HealPower + DelayPower} \qquad (10.4)$$

I have glossed over the concept of normalization in our example above. However, in order to logically compare apples to oranges, the normalization process is fundamentally important, as it essentially "bakes" more complex underlying computations into a single usable value. Typically this involves running a raw value (health, time, ammunition, damage, etc.) through a normalization function to generate a real number from 0 and 1. Normalization functions are most commonly linear, exponential, or sigmoidal, but can be of any form. Response curves are an elegant solution in cases where a single formula is not sufficient for representing the desired normalization, allowing the curve to be broken up into segments that can be further fine-tuned [Mark 10]. The curve you choose can dramatically impact the result, and thus are often the target of on-the-fly tuning. For this reason, I'd recommend building these formulas into components you can represent as reloadable data that you and your designers can tweak. Normalization is a deep subject, and much wisdom can be discovered in available material. Papers available on GameAI.com, the GDC Vault, and the reading material referenced herein all provide excellent background on utility-based AI and behavioral modeling.

10.6 The Utility Selector

The behavior tree structure lends itself well to extensibility. After all, it's nothing more than a tree traversal where the nodes themselves are responsible for and are able to customize the expansion of the tree. The tree already features a component for selecting which branches are taken during execution, namely the *selector*. To introduce utility-based selection, we'll simply create a new specialized type of selector that considers not just the binary validity of its children, but their relative utility as well. We'll cleverly dub the new node type the *utility selector*.

For simplicity's sake, let's consider a vanilla behavior tree implementation. Each execution pass will traverse the tree until a busy node is encountered, at which point execution will yield until the next update. When a utility selector executes, it first queries each child sub-tree for a utility value. If we gather these results first, we can apply any one of several selection methods. For one, we could simply take the child with the highest utility. Alternatively, we could sort the children into buckets and conduct a weighted random selection. Depending on the scenario, we could even apply an unweighted random selection among the children with utility values over some threshold beyond which options are considered desirable. All we're essentially doing is adding utility-gathering to a standard selector, and using the data to determine priority dynamically. With minimal effort, we've busted wide open what is arguably the biggest drawback of behavior tree-based architectures—static priorities. In fact, we can address our problem with *Seek Medic* by switching *Combat* to a utility selector, as we've done in Figure 10.3.

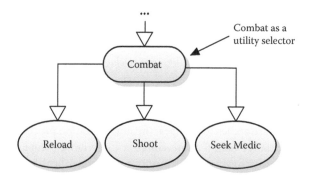

Figure 10.3

The *Shoot* vs. *Seek Medic* conundrum has been solved by converting *Combat* to a utility selector in the original tree.

Listing 10.1. Pseudocode for a basic selector.

```
Status Execute()
{
    if(CurrChild == null) then CurrChild = FirstChild;
    //Execute all children until we encounter a valid one.
    while(CurrChild != null)
    {
        Status s = CurrChild.Execute();
        if(s == Busy || s == Done) return s;
        CurrChild = CurrChild.Next;
    }
    return Failed;
}
```

Listing 10.2. Pseudocode for a basic utility selector.

```
Status Execute()
{
    if(Utility.Size() == 0) then
    {
        //Query for child utility values.
        for(CurrChild = FirstChild; CurrChild != NULL; CurrChild =
CurrChild.Next)
        {
            Utility[CurrChild] = CurrChild.CalculateUtility();
        }
        //Sort from highest utility to lowest.
        SortChildrenByUtility();
        CurrChild = FirstChild;
    }
    //Evaluate in utility order and select the first valid child.
    while(CurrChild != null)
    {
        Status s = CurrChild.Execute();
        if(s == Busy) then return Busy;
        else if(s == Done) then
        {
            Utility.Clear();
            return Done;
        }
        CurrChild = CurrChild.Next;
    }
    Utility.Clear();
    return Failed;
}
```

10.7 Propagating Utility

The utility selector simply queries its children for their utility values. Typically only leaf behaviors will conduct utility calculations, but the utility selector's children may be of any node type, including composite nodes or even another utility selector. For utility information to intuitively propagate up the tree, we need to override `CalculateUtility()` for all composite node types.

For both selectors and sequencers, the simplest method is to return the highest utility value gathered from its own children. Consequently, in order to gather necessary utility data, a utility selector must expand all nodes in its child sub-trees, potentially conducting large quantities of utility calculations in a single pass. This may or may not be a problem depending on the scale you're working with, but with complex utility calculations in large behavior trees on platforms sensitive to random memory access patterns, it's certainly not ideal.

Thankfully, there are ways to mitigate this problem. For one, we could limit utility calculations to some interval within our leaf behaviors' implementations, and return cached values. Alternatively, we could compute utility values for all of our tree's leaf nodes within a completely separate pass, with its own load balancing, leaving only cached values to be used during calls to `CalculateUtility()`.

10.7.1. Transforming Utility During Propagation

For additional flexibility, nodes can choose to modify utility as it works its way up the tree. *Decorators* are a fundamental concept in behavior trees, referring to single-child nodes that can be used to introduce various useful behavior features. Some common examples include repeating the child node *n* times, monitoring a runtime condition, or limiting the child's execution time, but they're a general-purpose tool with infinite potential uses. In fact, there's nothing stopping us from creating a utility decorator that applies some transformation to the utility value of its child. Perhaps it could multiply its child's utility by some factor for weighting purposes, or it could run the value through a custom function.

To provide a simple example, let's say our *Reload* behavior is a black box that internally computes a normalized utility value. Under most circumstances, we may choose to compare *Reload*'s utility directly to that of its siblings. However, we may encounter a case in our game where we wish to limit *Reload*'s utility until we're desperate for ammunition. We can accomplish this goal by adding a utility decorator above *Reload* that runs the utility value through a simple `square()` or `cube()` function, as illustrated in Figures 10.4 and 10.5.

10.8 A Twist on Behavior Trees: Evaluation versus Execution

The behavior tree coupled with this chapter differs from some traditional implementations in that it separates the idea of tree evaluation from actual execution, which I've also done in the version I use for professional work. Doing so provides opportunity for a few improvements over a typical behavior tree implementation. One of those opportunities is to more optimally integrate utility-based decisions. Most notably, the utility selector is able to evaluate its children prior to calculating utility, meaning it must update utility only for valid children. This can be seen in the accompanying source code's `UtilitySelector` implementation. Furthermore, leaf nodes with costly utility calculations can do the work while verifying its conditions in `Evaluate()`, and return a cached value in `CalculateUtility()`.

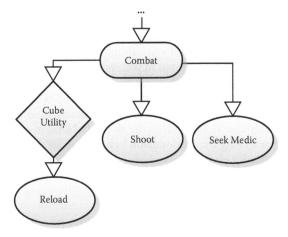

Figure 10.4

We've added a decorator to modify *Reload*'s standard utility value at execution time.

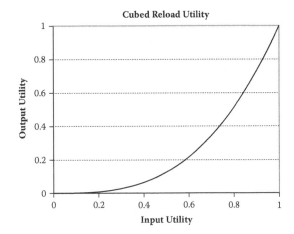

Figure 10.5

Reload's utility is now being cubed as it propagates up the tree, delaying the urgency to reload.

Another useful benefit is the ability to evaluate the tree independently of an agent's behavior execution. While an agent is actively executing behaviors, we can freely evaluate the tree in parallel without interfering with the executing nodes, and only interject if the results vary from the presently executing plan.

Evaluating the tree in its entirety also means we can optionally perform a limited version of look-ahead planning, since we can ensure that an entire plan is valid to the end, at least at the time of evaluation, before committing any of it to the agent. In cases where this is not desirable, nodes can still defer validation until they are executed, enabling them to behave as they would in a typical behavior tree flow.

10.9 Conclusion

Behavior trees and utility are both powerful concepts, made practical by their ease of implementation and experimentation. If you haven't done so already, I highly recommend tinkering with them as a potential solution in your professional endeavors. When combining utility behavior trees, these two otherwise disjointed techniques can help tackle the wide variety of behavioral problems found across genres and scopes.

We started with a straightforward behavior tree implementation, and without making any fundamental changes, we've introduced the ability to blend in utility-based decisions *only where desired*, preserving the tree's default behavior elsewhere. While the examples here are limited in scope for clarity, you've hopefully identified cases where this will help you solve real-world problems you've already encountered while applying behavior trees in practice. Beyond that, hopefully you can make use of utility-based decisions to improve your characters' behaviors further.

I am continuing to develop the coexistence of behavior trees and utility for my own needs in a very demanding commercial project, featuring dozens of unique NPC characters spanning a wide range of classifications. I wanted to share my discoveries thus far, as the results have been pleasantly surprising in practice. We've been able to represent characters ranging from simple wildlife to autonomous beasts with a vast repertoire of special abilities to soldiers with unique and obscure capabilities that must effectively emulate human players, all with the same behavioral foundation and toolset. For example, giant beasts can weigh different types of attacks against multiple targets dynamically, and human soldiers can evaluate and use their deep inventories to cooperatively take down targets, heal and revive teammates, and combine strategies. The integration of utility helped tremendously in mitigating complexity since characters can weigh multiple factors during decision making in a manner that's intuitive and "just makes sense." Rather than fight against the limitations of a single textbook architecture, a simple-to-implement hybrid has provided a great deal of power without sacrificing usability.

If you have questions, suggestions, or simply want to discuss something nerdy, don't hesitate to email bill.merrill at outlook.com.

References

[Brainiac 09] "Brainiac Designer." http://brainiac.codeplex.com/, 2009.

[Bungie 07] M. Dyckhoff. "Evolving Halo's Behavior Tree AI." http://www.bungie.net/images/Inside/publications/presentations/publicationsdes/engineering/gdc07.pdf, 2007.

[Champandard 08] A. Champandard. "Behavior Trees for Next-Gen Game AI." http://aigamedev.com/insider/article/behavior-trees/, 2008.

[Champandard 12] A. Champandard. "Behavior Tree Starter Kit." http://aigamedev.com/ultimate/release/behavior-tree-starter-kit-source-release/, 2012.

[Crytek 11] R. Pillosu. "Coordinating Agents with Behavior Trees." http://staff.science.uva.nl/~aldersho/GameProgramming/Papers/Coordinating_Agents_with_Behaviour_Trees.pdf, 2011.

[Mark 09] D. Mark. *Behavioral Mathematics for Game AI*. Boston, MA: Charles River Media, 2009.

[Mark 10] D. Mark and K. Dill. "Improving AI Decision Modeling Through Utility Theory." http://www.intrinsicalgorithm.com/media/2010GDC-DaveMark-KevinDill-Utility-Theory.pdf, 2010.

11
Reactivity and Deliberation in Decision-Making Systems

Carle Côté

11.1 Introduction

Designing decision-making systems for video games can be quite complex and is typically based on experience, intuition, and continuous refactoring. Over the years, successful games shipped using two main types of decision models: *graphical modeling language-based* decision models such as finite-state machines (FSMs), hierarchical finite-state machines (HFSMs), and behavior trees (BTs), and *symbolic planning language-based* decision models such as goal-oriented action planners (GOAP) and hierarchical task networks (HTNs). Unfortunately, little literature exists that explains how and when each approach should be used and for which family of architectural problems they are best suited.

This chapter will present a collection of considerations and thoughts about **Reactivity** and **Deliberation**, two key decision-making system mechanisms. *Reactivity* is about the ability of an agent to be responsive when stimuli are perceived in its environment, while *deliberation* is about the ability of an agent to make decisions and engage consequent actions. Typically, both are required to some extent in the design of every video game agent. By showing how to integrate these key concepts as core design principles, we'll explain how to avoid common pitfalls and create more scalable and flexible decision-making systems.

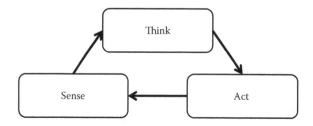

Figure 11.1

Sense-Think-Act paradigm.

11.2 Let's Begin at the Beginning

At its simplest expression, a typical decision-making system revolves around the Sense–Think–Act model, as shown in Figure 11.1. It describes that an agent needs to gather information from its environment (Sense), use the collected information in some decision process to decide what to do next (Think), engage new actions accordingly (Act), and repeat these steps over and over to create autonomy.

While this model shows a very intuitive relationship between an agent's "inner self" and its environment, it doesn't describe anything about the nature of the decision-making mechanisms involved in creating adapted behaviors. In fact, most games require at least two main decision-making mechanisms: reactivity and deliberation. The next sections describe in more detail what they are and their specific roles in a decision-making system.

11.2.1 What Is Reactivity?

Reactivity is the ability of an agent to be responsive to stimuli perceived in its environment. Most of the fun in video games comes from the fact that agents will react to the player's presence—either from direct perceptions (e.g., seeing the player) or indirect perceptions (e.g., hearing broken objects crashing on the ground). In order to be responsive, an agent must engage certain actions in a very short time, otherwise it would create behavioral artifacts that could be perceived by the player as either not believable or not challenging enough compared to their own abilities. These specific actions are called "reactions" and are, as we will see later, crucial when designing decision-making systems. Figure 11.2 illustrates a behavioral timeline with typical examples of reactions.

Reactions can be classified in two categories: *involuntary reactions* and *cognitive reactions*. Involuntary reactions refer to a body's uncontrolled reactions to some events

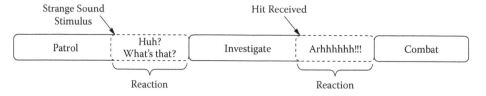

Figure 11.2

Behavioral timeline with reactions.

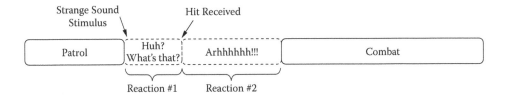

Figure 11.3

Behavioral timeline showing a reaction within a reaction pattern.

like pain, suffocation, or sneezing. Cognitive reactions are reactions that require a minimum of contextual interpretations to be triggered. For example, a loud sound will probably attract attention in a library but would probably be expected on a construction field.

According to our definition, a reaction can have a very short duration (e.g., split second necessary to reorient an agent toward the player) or it can last for a while (e.g., an agent in pain for 10 seconds). This means that during a reaction, other stimuli can be perceived which can potentially create other reactions as illustrated in the timeline in Figure 11.3.

11.2.2 What Is Deliberation?

Deliberation is the ability of an agent to take into consideration many elements of knowledge to decide what to do next. In video games, it's mostly what defines agent behavior in every situation, from high-paced action situations (e.g., combat) to more strategic situations (e.g., investigating an area). In fact, deliberation includes all the rational and irrational introspection mechanisms necessary to execute any tasks. For example, it includes information analysis process, intuition, past experiences, emotions, thinking process, random evaluation, logic, etc. In this article, we'll use the term "decision model" to refer to all these types of introspection mechanisms.

A decision model can take split second, seconds, minutes, days, or even years. For video games, most of the decisions are generally done in seconds or less.

11.3 Common Pitfall #1 : One Decision Model to Rule Them All!

A typical approach to support reactivity in decision-making systems is to use a decision model that can fulfill both reactivity and deliberation requirements. Although this approach seems tempting, it has many drawbacks that are discussed in the following sections.

11.3.1 Different by Nature

Based on reactivity and deliberation definitions, it is effectively possible to conclude that reactivity and deliberation can be merged together as long as the deliberation implementation allows for taking decisions and engaging actions in a very short time. However, this conclusion only considers the responsiveness aspect of the decision model itself; it doesn't consider what triggered the need for a decision and the dynamics of the engaged actions itself. So, let's analyze this a bit.

The first distinction about deliberation and reactivity is the difference between what triggers the need for new actions in both mechanisms. For reactivity, triggering reactions is caused by interruptions that have a higher priority than what is currently ongoing.

For deliberation, the need for a decision comes from two different sources: (1) the current deliberate action (or reaction) is completed and a new action must be engaged, and (2) the current context is changed in a way that it is invalidating or canceling the current action or plan of actions. While some deliberation decisions must be taken rapidly, others can take awhile without causing any problems. This means that deliberation isn't *only* about responsiveness. On the other hand, it is the *main* aspect of reactivity. In video games in general, deliberation tends to be fast because it isn't fun to see inactive agents in a thinking position for a long period of time before taking any action. It is mainly accepted that agents know instantly what to do and how to do it, without hesitation. Still, the very nature of what triggered the need for a decision in both cases is fundamentally different.

The second observation about reactivity and deliberation's nature is related to the nature of their respective undertaken actions. While it is accepted that an agent knows instantly what to do and how to do it, it is also expected that agents will engage in deliberate actions without changing their minds every second for unapparent reasons. Based on this, we can see a second important distinction between reactivity and deliberation: the goal of reactivity mechanisms is to create instantaneous changes in action to reflect body/environmental awareness, while the goal of deliberation mechanisms is to engage the best action possible that can be sustained for the longest time possible according to the context. While this difference seems pretty subtle, it has a big impact on the reactivity and deliberation decision models.

The example illustrated in Figure 11.4 represents a very simple FSM describing the deliberation decision models of an agent in a typical action game.

This FSM can evaluate and execute transitions instantly, that is, it can be used to support reactivity decision models. The states are describing very high-level behaviors like chasing a threat, patrolling the environment, engaging combat, and fleeing a threat. These behaviors can be decomposed in many sub-actions, but they aren't part of the deliberation

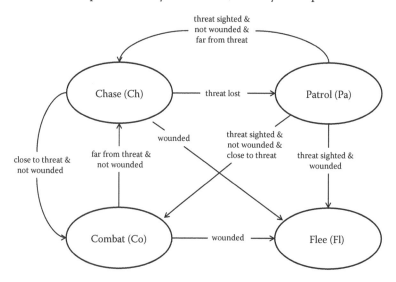

Figure 11.4

Example of a simple FSM describing the deliberation decision model of an agent.

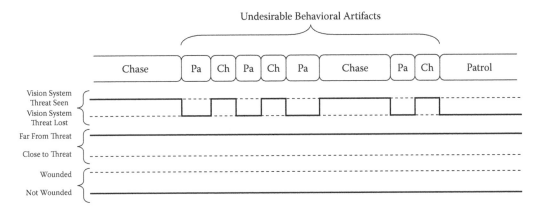

Figure 11.5

Behavioral timeline showing undesirable behavioral artifacts.

decision model expressed into that FSM. The transitions are described using symbols that are also representing high-level concepts such as seeing a threat, being wounded, or being close or far from a threat. It's important to note that no reactivity decision model is shown in this example.

To understand the proper dynamic of this FSM, we need to understand how the agent perceives and analyzes information from its sensors and what it means for this agent to be wounded. For this example, we'll focus on the perception system and presume that the transitions' *threat sight* symbol is directly hooked to the vision system. Figure 11.5 shows a timeline of a situation where the agent can momentarily lose sight of the threat during a chase because of objects preventing the agent to see the threat at all time.

By looking at the timeline, we can observe a lot of transitions in the behavior track. They represent the agent changing its stance from running at the threat to a slow-paced patrol stance multiple times within a couple of seconds because of the vision system losing direct line of sight with the threat. From the player's perspective, the behavior transitions would seem off, and they would most likely be judged as undesirable behavioral artifacts caused for no apparent reason. This is without mentioning that the animation system might not even be responsive enough to execute these fast stance transitions without creating animation popping artifacts. This is a good example to show where responsiveness isn't the only criterion that needs to be considered by deliberation decision models; sustaining actions for the proper amount of time is also crucial to delivering believable behaviors.

In this case, we can solve this issue by hooking the transition's *threat-sighted* symbol to a logical representation of seeing/losing a threat in a chase that would include some form of filtering (using hysteresis algorithms or other similar methods) to avoid creating undesirable oscillations. Figure 11.6 shows an ideal version of the timeline resulting from that logical representation.

11.3.2 Hard to Unify

Considering the different natures of the reactivity and deliberation mechanisms, trying to unify them is very challenging: reactivity is mostly about interruptions while deliberation

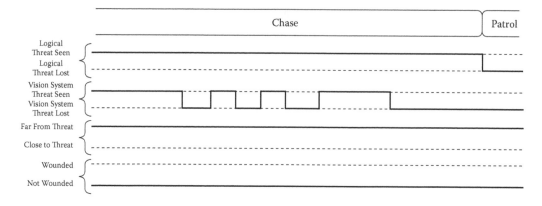

Figure 11.6

Behavior timeline showing the usage of a logical data representation to avoid behavioral artifacts.

is mostly about sustaining states. Any attempt to conciliate them using a unique model is trying to represent conceptual antipodes.

Figure 11.7 represents the same FSM example presented in Section 11.3.1 but including two reaction states: *Hurt* and *Suffocate*.

Because *Chase*, *Patrol*, *Combat*, and *Flee* are deliberation states that are designed to be active as long as possible, they are susceptible to be interrupted at any time. This explains why, in Figure 11.7, we can see that every deliberation state has transitions to every reaction state. Consequently, adding new reaction states to the model would require new transitions from all of the existing deliberation states. The same applies when adding new deliberation states to the model. With increased complexity, it's easy to see that the model will be hard to understand and maintain mostly because it tries to mix two very different kinds of transition dynamics within the same model. To solve this issue, it would be interesting to consider using multiple decision models that can interact together.

11.3.3 Using Multiple Decision Models

It is possible to avoid the limitation of using only one decision model. Figure 11.8 shows an architectural solution allowing multiple decision models. The design principle is pretty simple: create a module (Action Selector) responsible to act as a selector switch between Deliberation and Reactivity modules.

With this architectural solution, Deliberation and Reactivity modules can use their own decision models as long as they can both receive the same stimuli and output their respective set of actions. For example, the Deliberation module could use the FSM presented in Figure 11.4, while the Reactivity module could use a very simple set of rules or a decision tree to evaluate which reaction should be requested according to perceived stimuli. As for the implementation of the Action Selector itself, it can also be done with its own decision model as long as it's able to signal the Deliberation module when a new decision must be taken or to cancel the current deliberate action in order to execute a reaction. Figure 11.9 shows the resulting timeline.

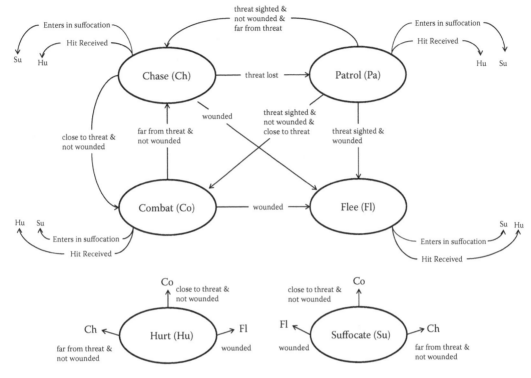

Figure 11.7

Example of an FSM including reaction states.

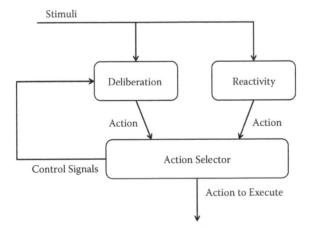

Figure 11.8

Using a selector switch between Deliberation and Reactivity modules.

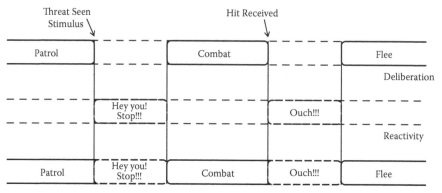

Figure 11.9

Behavioral timeline showing the results of the Action Selector.

11.4 Common Pitfall #2 : One Conceptual Model to Rule Them All!

Another common pitfall is that reactivity and deliberation mechanisms are implemented using the same conceptual model to describe how an agent must behave in every situation. A conceptual model comprises all of the required concepts' definitions and their static/dynamic relationships to create a decision-making system. In fact, when looking closely at each mechanism, we can see many important distinctions that are discussed in the following sections.

11.4.1 Awareness versus Procedural Knowledge

Reactivity is concerned with "danger awareness," whereas deliberation deals with procedural knowledge. Reactions play an important role in a decision-making system that is trying to mimic the physiology associated with the body's inner mechanisms towards self-protection. Two main categories of reaction are presented in Section 11.2.1: involuntary reactions and cognitive reactions. Involuntary reactions are typically created by the body to motivate the individual to withdraw from a dangerous situation. Cognitive reaction is the proactive counterpart where an individual will react preemptively before something can threaten its physical integrity.

By looking closely at these physiological phenomena, we can extract interesting design requirements:

- *Involuntary reactions have a higher priority level than cognitive reactions.* Reactions due to taking physical damages like pain, suffocation, or burning have precedence over any preemptive reactions.
- *Simultaneous involuntary reactions can be combined.* Different physical damages can be received at the same time resulting in simultaneous involuntary reactions. For example, an individual suffocating can simultaneously be hurt by a ranged weapon.
- *Some involuntary reactions have higher priority than others.* Some critical physical damages like being blown away by an explosion or being in heavy pain have precedence over less critical ones.

- *Cognitive reactions depend on the level of danger awareness.* Depending on whether an individual expects danger or not, it might or might not be reacting to some stimuli. For example, hearing a loud broken object sound in the middle of a brawl won't surprise anyone, while it might create a huge surprise reaction in a quiet classroom.

Deliberation isn't tied the same way to the notion of danger awareness. In fact, deliberation is taking this danger awareness notion into account along with many other notions to execute tasks that are important but not necessarily endangering an agent. This means that deliberation's main focus is knowledge and, more precisely, procedural knowledge. Procedural knowledge is the knowledge required to perform any task. When programming an agent to do tasks in its environment, a programmer is actually encoding all of its required procedural knowledge using various decision mechanisms. Depending on what the agent is trying to achieve, different conceptual models can be used. For example, an agent will not use the same decision rules when he's involved in a close-combat situation as when he's involved in a ranged-combat situation. Typically, both situations use different concepts to represent what's important in the environment and the best strategies to use.

11.4.2 Using Multiple Conceptual Models

Using different conceptual models generally allows breaking the complexity in simpler models. This means that, by using the right level of abstraction, it should be easier to write simpler rules and less complex code to maintain. The Action Selector presented in Section 11.3.3 is a good example of this approach. In addition to allowing Reactivity and Deliberation modules to use their own decision models, it also allows them to use their own conceptual models independently. Using the Action Selector as a sequencer between Reactivity and Deliberation modules also simplified the Reactivity module implementation by removing most of the dependencies on Deliberation's conceptual model to select which deliberate action should follow every reaction (as illustrated in Figure 11.7).

The same reasoning applies to the implementation of the Action Selector. It can be implemented with a few simple rules because it uses the right level of abstraction. In this case, the Action Selector only needs to share a minimum set of concepts with the Reactivity and Deliberation modules, that is, knowing if a specific action is a reaction or deliberate action. Figure 11.10 shows the expected timeline from the Action Selector according to its conceptual model.

11.4.3 Separating Decision from Execution

As described in Section 11.4.2, procedural knowledge is a key concept when programming an agent to perform some tasks (or actions). In fact, procedural knowledge generally describes two aspects of what is required to perform a task: the decision model to execute the task (e.g., sequence of actions, various options, how to manage events, etc.) and the decision model to manage the task (e.g., starting conditions, canceling conditions,

| Deliberate Action | Reaction | Deliberate Action | Reaction | Deliberate Action |

Figure 11.10

Action Selector's timeline.

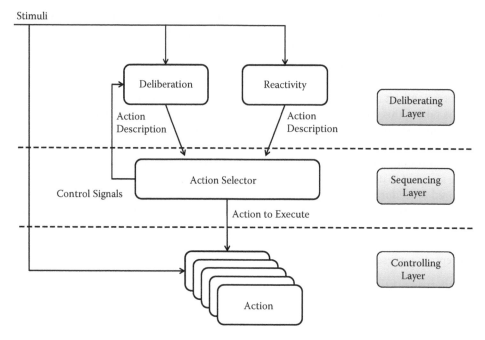

Stimuli

Deliberation

Reactivity

Action
Description

Action
Description

Deliberating
Layer

Action Selector

Control Signals

Sequencing
Layer

Action to Execute

Action

Controlling
Layer

Figure 11.11

An example of a three-layer architecture.

completing conditions, etc). Splitting these decision models can be very useful to reduce the complexity.

In the FSM in Figure 11.4, each state describes a task that an agent should perform if the conditions are met. In fact, it doesn't describe what the agent will do precisely during the execution of this task; it only describes the decision model to manage the task. This means that details of the execution model can somehow be abstracted from the decision model itself without impacting the deliberation mechanisms. This idea has been used many times to create what is called "hybrid architecture" [Murphy 01]. Figure 11.11 illustrates an example of hybrid architecture based on the example presented in Section 11.3.3.

There are only three differences with the example presented in Section 11.3.3. The first one is that the Deliberating Layer explicitly uses decision models to manage actions, instead of the action itself. The second difference is that the role of the Action Selector must not only sequence actions but must also select which actions to execute from the Controlling Layer's action pool. The last difference is the addition of the Controlling Layer, which contains a pool of actions containing the necessary implementations to be executed. Each of these actions can use different decision models and/or conceptual models. They must also be designed to be reactive if required by their respective execution model.

This kind of architecture can be very powerful to use as it offers many ways to break the complexity of a big decision-making system into simpler modules. For example, it can be really easy to change a specific algorithm used to implement an action without impacting other actions or any component from the other layers. Adding a new concept into the conceptual model of an existing action to enhance its implementation could also represent a very isolated modification to the system.

11.5 Conclusion

This article presented deliberation and reactivity mechanisms as two primary elements to consider when designing decision-making systems. And by understanding their fundamental distinctions, it was discussed that it can be possible to reduce inherent complexity of decision-making systems. Consequently, choosing when to use an FSM, a BT, a Planner, or any other decision models can be a lot easier and based on more solid grounds than pure empirical methods.

References

[Murphy 01] R. R. Murphy, *Introduction to AI Robotics*. MIT Press, Cambridge, MA, 2001, pp. 257–274.

12

Exploring HTN Planners through Example

Troy Humphreys

12.1 Introduction

As programmers we may find ourselves perpetually looking for that "better solution" to whatever problems we've encountered—better performance, maintainability, or usability. It's only after we implement those solutions that we understand some of the nuances that come with them. Often, these nuances might be the deciding factor in what solution we go with.

In AI development, a common problem to solve is behavior selection. There are many solutions to this problem, such as finite-state machines, behavior trees, utility-based selection, neural networks, and planners. This article aims to explore the nuances of a type of planner called *hierarchical task networks* (HTN) by using real world examples that one can run into during development.

Planning architectures such as HTN take a problem as input and supply a series of steps that solves it. In HTN terms, the series of steps is called a *plan*. What makes hierarchical task networks unique to other planners is that it allows us to represent the problem as a very high level task, and through its planning process, recursively breaks this task into smaller tasks. When this process is completed, we are left with a series of atomic tasks that represent a plan. Breaking up high level tasks into smaller ones is a very natural way of solving many sorts of problems. In our case, the problem is simply "figuring out what to do." With a high degree of modularity and fast run time execution, HTNs make an attractive choice as a solution. For those of you that are familiar with behavior trees, these benefits might also seem familiar. Unlike behavior trees, however, HTN planners can reason about the *effects* of possible actions. This ability to reason about the future allows HTN planners to be incredibly expressive in how they describe behavior.

There have been many different systems used for HTN planning [Erol 95]. The system we will be exploring is the system that we used on *Transformers: Fall of Cybertron* [HighMoon 12], which is based on a *total-order forward decomposition* planner. The following example will walk through some of the challenges we faced and the benefits we received during development by using a simplified, fictional example.

For our example, we will use a troll NPC called a "Trunk Thumper." The designer's initial description is that he's a big, nasty, lumbering troll that patrols its numerous bridges and attacks passing enemies with a large tree trunk. And just like development in the real world, this design is bound to change.

12.2 Building Blocks of HTN

Before building the behavior for our Trunk Thumper, it's important to go over the basic building blocks of hierarchical task networks so you can get an idea of how it all works. An NPC, in our case the Trunk Thumper, has a *planner* that uses a *domain* and *world state* to build a sequence of tasks called a *plan*. This plan will be run by the Trunk Thumper's *plan runner*. The world state is updated by the NPC's sensors and by the successfully completed tasks executed by the plan runner. A diagram of the system is Figure 12.1.

12.2.1 The World State

Like any type of behavior algorithm, hierarchical task networks need some type of knowledge representation that describes the current problem space. In the case of our Trunk Thumper, this would be a representation that describes what our troll knows about the world and himself in it. Other types of behavior algorithms might query the actual state of different objects in the world. For example, query an object's location or their health. But with HTN, this information needs to be encoded into something it can understand, called the *world state*. The world state is essentially a vector of properties that describe what our HTN is going to reason about. Here is some simple pseudocode.

```
enum EHtnWorldStateProperties
{
    WsEnemyRange,
    WsHealth,
    WsIsTired,
    …
}
```

```
enum EEnemyRange
{
    MeleeRange,
    ViewRange,
    OutOfRange,
    ...
}
vector<byte> CurrentWorldState;
EEnemyRange currentRange = CurrentWorldState[WsEnemyRange];
CurrentWorldState[WsEnemyRange] = MeleeRange;
```

As you can see from the pseudocode, world state can simply be an array or vector indexed by an enum such as `EhtnWorldStateProperties`. Each entry in the world state can have its own set of values. In the case of `WsIsTired`, the byte can represent the Boolean values zero and one. With `WsEnemyRange`, the values in the enum `EEnemyRange` are used. It's important to note that the world state only needs to represent what is needed for the HTN to make decisions. That's why `WsEnemyRange` is represented by abstract values, instead of the actual range. The goal of the world state isn't to represent every possible state of every possible object in the game. It only needs to represent the problem space that our planner needs to make decisions. What this means for our example, of course, is that it only needs to represent what the Trunk Thumper needs to make decisions.

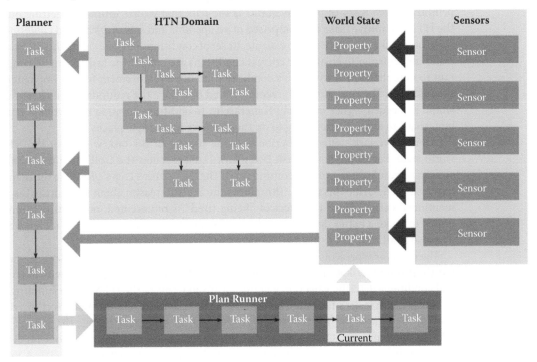

Figure 12.1

Overview of the HTN system.

12.2.2 Sensors

If you recall, an HTN outputs a plan or sequence of tasks. These tasks will have an effect on the world state as it is executed. There are outside influences such as the player or other NPCs, however, that will affect the world state as well. For example, both the enemy and the troll can affect the world state property, `WsEnemyRange`. The tasks executed by the troll could update this property if they were to move the troll. There is nothing in the HTN planner to handle changes produced by the enemy moving, however.

There are many different ways these changes can be translated into the world state. One preferable way is a simple sensor system that manages a set of time-sliced sensors. Each sensor can manage different world state properties. Examples of some different sensors include vision, hearing, range, and health sensors. These sensors would work the same as in any other AI system, with an added step of encoding their information into the world state that our HTN can understand.

12.2.3 Primitive Tasks

As we mentioned already, a hierarchical task network is made up of tasks. There are two types of tasks that are used to build a HTN, called *compound tasks* and *primitive tasks*. Primitive tasks represent a single step that can be performed by our NPC. In our Trunk Thumper example, uprooting a tree or attacking with a trunk slam would be examples of primitive tasks. A set of primitive tasks is the *plan* that we are ultimately getting out of the HTN. Primitive tasks are comprised of an *operator* and sets of *effects* and *conditions*.

In order for a primitive task to execute, its set of conditions must be valid. This allows the task's implementer to ensure the correct conditions are met for the task to run. It's important to note that a primitive task's conditions are not a requirement for the implementation of HTN. They are, however, recommended to reduce the redundancy of checks that would be needed higher in the HTN hierarchy. In addition, doing so will avoid potential bugs that can arrive from having to do these checks in multiple places.

A primitive task's effects describe how the success of the task will affect the NPC's world state. For example, the task `DoTrunkSlam` executes the troll's tree trunk melee attack and results in the troll becoming tired. The `DoTrunkSlam`'s *effects* are the manner in which we describe this result. This allows the HTN to reason about the "future" as was mentioned earlier. Since the effect of "being tired" is represented, our Trunk Thumper is able to make a better decision of what to do after `DoTrunkSlam` or if it's even worth doing so at all.

The *operator* represents an atomic action that a NPC can do. This might sound exactly like the primitive task itself. The difference being that the primitive task along with its effects and conditions describe what the operator means in terms of the HTN we are building.

As an example, let's take the two tasks `SprintToEnemy` and `WalkToNextBridge`. Both of these tasks use the `MoveTo` operator, but the two tasks change the state of our NPC in different ways. On the successful completion of `SprintToEnemy`, our NPC will be at the enemy and tired, specified by the task's effects. `WalkToNextBridge` task's effects would set the NPC's location to the bridge and he'd be a little more bored. As you can see, we are able to use the same *operator* but describe two different uses for it in terms of our network. Here is the notation we will use to describe a primitive task going forward along with the `SprintToEnemy` and `WalkToNextBridge` tasks as an example.

Primitive Task [*TaskName(term1, term2,...)*]
   Preconditions [*Condition1, Condition2, …*]//optional
   Operator [*OperatorName(term1, term2,...)*]
      Effects [*WorldState op value, WorldState = value, WorldState += value*]//optional
Primitive Task [SprintToEnemy]
   Preconditions [WsHasEnemy == true]
   Operator [NavigateTo(EnemyLoc, Speed_Fast)]
      Effects [WsLocation = EnemyLoc, WsIsTired = true]
Primitive Task [WalkToNextBridge]
   Operator [NavigateTo(BridgeLoc, Speed_Slow)]
      Effects [WsLocation = BridgeLoc, WsBored += 1]

12.2.4 Compound Tasks

Compound tasks are where HTN get their "hierarchical" nature. You can think of compound task as a high level task that has multiple ways of being accomplished. Using the Trunk Thumper as an example, he may have the task AttackEnemy. Our Thumper may have different ways of accomplishing this task. If he has access to a tree trunk, he may run to his target and use it as a melee weapon to "thump" his enemy. If no tree trunks are available, he can pull large boulders from the ground and toss them at our enemy. He may have a multitude of other approaches if the conditions are right.

In order to determine which approach we take to accomplish a compound task, we need to select the right *method*. Methods are comprised of a set of conditions and tasks. In order for the method to be the selected approach, the conditions are validated against the world state. The set of tasks, or *subtasks*, represent the method's approach. This subtask set can be comprised of primitive tasks as well as compound. The ability to put compound tasks into the methods of other compound tasks is where hierarchical task networks get their hierarchical nature. Here is an example of the notation we will use to describe a compound task going forward.

Compound Task [*TaskName(term1, term2,...)*]
   Method 0 [*Condition1, Condition2,...*]
      Subtasks [*task1(term1, term2,...). task2(term1, term2,...),...*]
   Method 1 [*Condition1, Condition2,...*]
      Subtasks [*task1(term1, term2,...). task2(term1, term2,...),...*]

In our previous example, using the tree trunk as a melee weapon and throwing boulders are both methods to the AttackEnemy compound task. The conditions in which we decide which method to use depend on whether the troll has a tree trunk or not. Here is an example of the AttackEnemy task using the notation above.

Compound Task [AttackEnemy]
   Method 0 [WsHasTreeTrunk == true]
      Subtasks [NavigateTo(EnemyLoc). DoTrunkSlam()]
   Method 1 [WsHasTreeTrunk == false]
      Subtasks [LiftBoulderFromGround(). ThrowBoulderAt(EnemyLoc)]

By understanding how compound tasks work, it's easy to imagine how we could have a large hierarchy that may start with a `BeTrunkThumper` compound task that is broken down into sets of smaller tasks—each of which are then broken into smaller tasks, and so on. This is how HTN forms a hierarchy that describes how our troll NPC is going to behave.

It's important to understand that compound tasks are really just containers for a set of methods that represent different ways to accomplish some high level task. There is no compound task code running during plan execution.

12.3 Putting Together an HTN Domain

Now that we have an overview of the main building blocks of HTN, we can build a simple *domain* for our Trunk Thumper to illustrate how it works. A *domain* is the term used to describe the entire task hierarchy. As we mentioned before, our troll has numerous bridges that he actively patrols and attacks enemies with a large tree trunk. We start with a compound task called `BeTrunkThumper`. This root task encapsulates the "main idea" of what it means to be a Trunk Thumper.

```
Compound Task [BeTrunkThumper]
    Method [WsCanSeeEnemy == true]
        Subtasks [NavigateToEnemy(), DoTrunkSlam()]
    Method [true]
        Subtasks [ChooseBridgeToCheck(), NavigateToBridge(), CheckBridge()]
```

As you can see with this root compound task, the first method defines the troll's highest priority. If he can see the enemy, he will navigate using `NavigateToEnemy` task and attack his enemy with the `DoTrunkSlam` task. If not, he will fall to the next method. This next method will run three tasks; choose the next bridge to check, navigate to that bridge, and check the bridge for enemies. Let's take a look at the primitive tasks that make up these methods and the rest of the domain.

```
Primitive Task [DoTrunkSlam]
    Operator [AnimatedAttackOperator(TrunkSlamAnimName)]
Primitive Task [NavigateToEnemy]
    Operator [NavigateToOperator(EnemyLocRef)]
        Effects [WsLocation = EnemyLocRef]
Primitive Task [ChooseBridgeToCheck]
    Operator [ChooseBridgeToCheckOperator]
Primitive Task [NavigateToBridge]
    Operator [NavigateToOperator(NextBridgeLocRef)]
        Effects [WsLocation = NextBridgeLocRef]
Primitive Task [CheckBridge]
    Operator [CheckBridgeOperator(SearchAnimName)]
```

The first task `DoTrunkSlam` is an example of how a primitive task can describe an operator in terms of the HTN domain. Here, the task is really executing an animated attack operator and the animation name is being passed in as a term. The next task

NavigateToEnemy is also an example of this, but on the successful completion of this task, the world state WsLocation is set to EnemyLocRef via the primitive task's effect.

12.4 Finding a Plan

With a domain made up of compound and primitive tasks, we are starting to form an image of how these are put together to represent an NPC. Combine that with the world state and we can talk about the work horse of our HTN, the *planner*. There are three conditions that will force the planner to find a new plan: the NPC finishes or fails the current plan, the NPC does not have a plan, or the NPC's world state changes via a sensor. If any of these cases occur, the planner will attempt to generate a plan. To do this, the planner starts with a root compound task that represents the problem domain in which we are trying to plan for. Using our earlier example, this root task would be the BeTrunkThumper task. This root task is pushed onto the TasksToProcess stack. Next, the planner creates a copy of the world state. The planner will be modifying this *working world state* to "simulate" what will happen as tasks are executed.

After these initialization steps are taken, the planner begins to iterate on the tasks to process. On each iteration, the planner pops the next task off the TasksToProcess stack. If it is a compound task, the planner tries to decompose it—first, by searching through its methods looking for the first set of conditions that are valid. If a method is found, that method's subtasks are added on to the TaskToProcess stack. If a valid method is not found, the planner's state is rolled back to the last compound task that was decomposed. We will go into more detail about restoring the planner's state later.

If the next task is primitive, we need to check its preconditions against the working world state. If the conditions are met, the task is added to the final plan and its effects are applied to the working world state. The effects are applied because the planner assumes that task is going to succeed. This allows future methods to consider that new state. If the primitive task's conditions are not met, the planner's state is rolled back such as was done for the compound task. This iteration process is continued until the TasksToProcess stack is empty. Upon completion, the planner will either end up with a list of primitive tasks or the planner will have rolled back far enough that the result was no plan. Below is the example pseudocode that shows this process.

```
WorkingWS = CurrentWorldState
TasksToProcess.Push(RootTask)
while TasksToProcess.NotEmpty
{
    CurrentTask = TasksToProcess.Pop()
    if CurrentTask.Type == CompoundTask
    {
        SatisfiedMethod = CurrentTask.FindSatisfiedMethod(WorkingWS)
        if SatisfiedMethod != null
        {
            RecordDecompositionOfTask(CurrentTask, FinalPlan, DecompHistory)
            TasksToProcess.InsertTop(SatisfiedMethod.SubTasks)
        }
        else
        {
            RestoreToLastDecomposedTask()
        }
    }
```

```
        else//Primitive Task
    {
        if PrimitiveConditionMet(CurrentTask)
        {
            WorkingWS.ApplyEffects(CurrentTask.Effects)
            FinalPlan.PushBack(CurrentTask)
        }
        else
        {
            RestoreToLastDecomposedTask()
        }
    }
}
```

There is a bit of magic going on in the `RecordDepositionOfTask` and `RestoreTo-LastDecomposedTask` functions that should be explained in more detail. The record function records the planner's state onto the `DecompHistory` stack. This includes the `TasksToProcess` and `FinalPlan` containers as well as the method chosen for the decomposition and its owning compound task. By popping off this recorded state to the planner via the restore function, the planner can backtrack either when a compound task cannot be decomposed or when a primitive's conditions aren't satisfied.

As you might have realized, the planner uses a depth-first search to find a valid plan. This does mean that you may have to explore the whole domain to find a valid plan. However, it's important to remember that you are traversing a *hierarchy* of tasks. This hierarchy allows the planner to cull large sections of the network via the compound task's methods. Because we aren't using a heuristic or cost—such as with A* and Dijkstra searches—we can skip any kind of sorting. These features allowed the HTN planner in *Transformers: Fall of Cybertron* to be considerably faster than our GOAP system used in *Transformers: War for Cybertron* [HighMoon 10].

Now that the planner has been explained, we can expand our example and see how a modified version of the Trunk Thumper domain might decompose (Figure 12.2). This domain's root task is still `BeTrunkThumper`, but the `DoTrunkSlam` is now a compound task. `DoTrunkSlam` has two methods—each doing a different version of the trunk slam. The method's conditions for both compound tasks have been omitted for simplicity. Underneath the domain you can see the planner's iterations going from top to the bottom. For each iteration, you can see the left-most task in the `TasksToProcess` stack being processed.

12.5 Running the Plan

Running an HTN plan is pretty straightforward. The NPC's *plan runner* will attempt to execute each primitive task's operator in sequence. As it successfully completes each task, the planner applies the task's effects to the world state. If the task fails for some reason that is specific to the operator it's running, the plan also fails and forces a re-plan.

The plan can also fail if the current or any of the remaining task's conditions become invalid. The plan runner monitors these tasks' preconditions against a "working world state" much like the planner. As it confirms each task's preconditions, its effects are applied

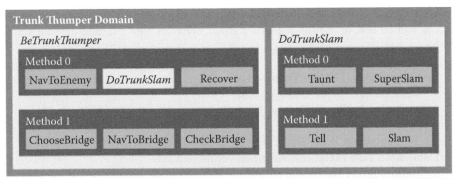

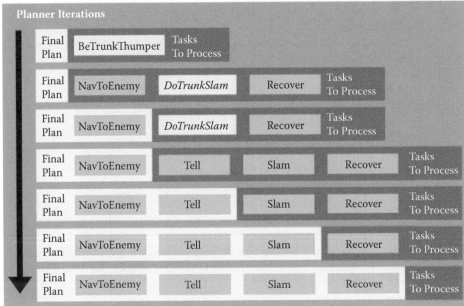

Figure 12.2

Decomposition of the Trunk Thumper domain, showing the resulting plan if BeTrunkThumper. Method0 and DoTrunkSlam.Method.1 were chosen.

to the working world state. It's important that it applies the effects because following task's preconditions might rely on these effects being applied in order to be valid. This plan validation allows the HTN domain to be a bit more expressive and reactive to the changes of the world state.

12.6 Using Recursion for Greater Expressiveness

After seeing our troll in game, the designers think that the tree trunk attack is a little overpowered. They suggest that the trunk breaks after three attacks, forcing the troll to search for another one. First we can add the property WsTrunkHealth to the world state.

By wrapping up the attack method into its own compound task and adding a little recursion, we will be able to modify the troll's attack behavior. The changed domain would now be:

Compound Task [BeTrunkThumper]
    Method [WsCanSeeEnemy == true]
        Subtasks [AttackEnemy()]*// using the new compound task*
    Method [true]
        Subtasks [ChooseBridgeToCheck(), NavigateToBridge(), CheckBridge()]
    Compound Task [AttackEnemy]//new compound task
    Method [WsTrunkHealth > 0]
        Subtasks [NavigateToEnemy(), DoTrunkSlam()]
    Method [true]
        Subtasks [FindTrunk(), NavigateToTrunk(), UprootTrunk(), AttackEnemy()]
    Primitive Task [DoTrunkSlam]
        Operator [DoTrunkSlamOperator]
        Effects [WsTrunkHealth += -1]
    Primitive Task [UprootTrunk]
        Operator [UprootTrunkOperator]
        Effects [WsTrunkHealth = 3]
    Primitive Task [NavigateToTrunk]
        Operator [NavigateToOperator(FoundTrunk)]
        Effects [WsLocation = FoundTrunk]

When our troll can see the enemy, he will attack just as before—only now, the behavior is wrapped up in a new compound task called AttackEnemy. This task's high priority method performs the navigate and slam like the original domain, but now has the condition that the trunk has some health. The change to the DoTrunkSlam task will decrement the trunk's health every successful attack. This allows the planner to drop to the lower priority method if it has to accommodate a broken tree trunk.

The second method of AttackEnemy handles getting a new tree trunk. It first chooses a new tree to use, navigates to that tree, and uproots it, after which it is able to AttackEnemy. Here is where the recursion comes in. When the planner goes to decompose the AttackEnemy task again it can now consider the methods again. If the tree trunk's health was still zero, this would cause the planner to infinite loop. But the new task UprootTrunk's effect sets WsTrunkHealth back to three, allowing us to have the plan FindTrunk → NavigateToTrunk → UprootTrunk → NavigateToEnemy → DoTrunkSlam. This new domain allows us to reuse methods already in the domain to get the troll back to thumping.

12.7 Planning for World State Changes not Controlled by Tasks

So far all of the plans we have been building depend on the primitive task's effects changing the world state. What happens when the world state is changed *outside* the control of primitive tasks, however? To explore this, let's modify our example once again. Let us assume that a designer notices that when the troll can't see the enemy, he simply goes back to patrolling the bridges. The designer asks you to implement a behavior that will chase after the enemy and react once he sees the enemy again. Let's look at the changes we could make to the domain to handle this issue.

Compound Task [BeTrunkThumper]
    Method [WsCanSeeEnemy == true]
        Subtasks [AttackEnemy()]
    Method [WsHasSeenEnemyRecently == true]//New method
        Subtasks [NavToLastEnemyLoc(), RegainLOSRoar()]
    Method [true]
        Subtasks [ChooseBridgeToCheck(), NavigateToBridge(), CheckBridge()]
Primitive Task [NavToLastEnemyLoc]
    Operator [NavigateToOperator(LastEnemyLocation)]
        Effects [WsLocation = LastEnemyLocation]
Primitive Task [RegainLOSRoar]
    Preconditions[WsCanSeeEnemy == true]
    Operator [RegainLOSRoar()]

With this rework, if the Trunk Thumper can't see the enemy, the planner will drop down to the new method that relies on `WsHasSeenEnemyRecently` world state property. This method's tasks will navigate to the last place the enemy was seen and do a big animated "roar" if he once again sees the enemy. The problem here is that the `RegainLOSRoar` task has a precondition of `WsCanSeeEnemy` being true. That world state is handled by the troll's vision sensor. When the planner goes to put the `RegainLOSRoar` task on the final task list it will fail its precondition check, because there is nothing in the domain that represents what the expected world state will be when the navigation completes.

To solve this, we are going to introduce the concept of *expected effects*. Expected effects are effects that get applied to the world state only during planning and plan validation. The idea here is that you can express changes in the world state that *should* happen based on tasks being executed. This allows the planner to keep planning farther into the future based on what it believes will be accomplished along the way. Remember that a key advantage planners have at decision making is that they can reason about the future, helping them make better decisions on what to do next. To accommodate this, we can change `NavToLastEnemyLoc` in the domain to:

Primitive Task [NavToLastEnemyLoc]
    Operator [NavigateToOperator(LastEnemyLocation)]
        Effects [WsLocation = LastEnemyLocation]
        ExpectedEffects [WsCanSeeEnemy = true]

Now when this task gets popped off the decomposition list, the working world state will get updated with the expected effect and the `RegainLOSRoar` task will be allowed to proceed with adding tasks to the chain. This simple behavior could have been implemented a couple of different ways, but expected effects came in handy more than a few times during the development of *Transformers: Fall of Cybertron*. They are a simple way to be just a little more expressive in a HTN domain.

12.8 How to Handle Higher Priority Plans

To this point, we have been decomposing compound tasks based on the order of the task's methods. This tends to be a natural way of going about our search, but consider these attack changes to our Trunk Thumper domain.

```
Compound Task [AttackEnemy]
    Method [WsTrunkHealth > 0, AttackedRecently == false,
CanNavigateToEnemy == true]
        Subtasks [NavigateToEnemy(), DoTrunkSlam(), RecoveryRoar()]
    Method [WsTrunkHealth == 0]
        Subtasks [FindTrunk(), NavigateToTrunk(), UprootTrunk(), AttackEnemy()]
    Method [true]
        Subtasks [PickupBoulder(), ThrowBoulder()]
Primitive Task [DoTrunkSlam]
    Operator [DoTrunkSlamOperator]
        Effects [WsTrunkHealth += -1, AttackedRecently = true]
Primitive Task [RecoveryRoar]
    Operator [PlayAnimation(TrunkSlamRecoverAnim)]
Primitive Task [PickupBoulder]
    Operator [PickupBoulder()]
Primitive Task [ThrowBoulder]
    Operator [ThrowBoulder()]
```

After some play testing, our designer commented that our troll is pretty punishing. It only lets up on its attack against the player when it goes to grab another tree trunk. The designer suggests putting in a recovery animation after the trunk slam and a new condition not allowing the slam attack if the troll has attacked recently. Our designer has also noticed that our troll behaves strangely if he could not navigate to his enemy (due to an obstacle, for example). He decided to put in a low priority attack to throw a boulder if this happened.

Everything about these behavior changes seems fairly straightforward, but we need to take a closer look at what could happen while running the trunk slam plan. After the actual slam action, we start running the RecoveryRoar task. If, while executing this roar, the world state were to change and cause a re-plan, the RecoveryRoar task will be aborted. The reason for this is that, when the planner gets to the method that handles the slam, the AttackRecently world state will be set to true because the DoTrunkSlam completed successfully. This will cause the planner to skip the "slam" method tasks and fall through to the new "throw boulder" method, resulting in a new plan. This will cause the RecoveryRoar task to be aborted mid-execution, even though the currently running plan is still valid.

In this case, we need a way to identify the "priority" of a running plan. There are a couple ways of solving this. Since HTN is a graph, we can use some form of a cost-based search such as A* or Dijkstra, for example. This would involve binding some sort of cost to our tasks or even methods. Unfortunately, tuning these costs can be pretty tricky in practice. Not only that, we would now have to add sorting to our planner, which will slow its execution.

Instead we would like to keep the simplicity and readability of "in-order priority" for our methods. The problem is a plan does not know the decomposition order of compound tasks that the planner took to arrive at the plan—it just executes primitive tasks' operators.

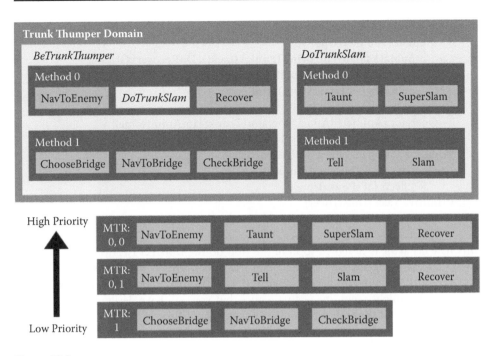

Figure 12.3

All possible plans with the Trunk Thumper domain and the Method Traversal Record for each plan, sorted by priority.

The order of a compound task's methods are what we want to use to define priority—yet the plan isn't aware of what a compound task is. To get around this, we can encode our traversal through the HTN domain as we search for a plan. This *method traversal record* (MTR) simply stores the method index chosen for each compound task that was decomposed to create the plan. Now that we have the MTR we can use it in two different ways to help us find the better plan. The simplest method would be to plan normally and compare the newly found plan's MTR with the currently running plan's MTR. If all of the method indexes chosen in the new plan are equal or higher priority, we found our new plan. An example is shown in Figure 12.3.

We can also choose to use the current plan's MTR during the planning process, as we decompose compound tasks in the new search. We can use the MTR as we search for a valid method only allowing methods that are equal to or higher priority. This allows us to cull whole branches of our HTN based on the current plan's MTR. Our first method is the easier of the two, but if you find you're spending a lot of your processing time in your planner, the second method could help speed that up.

Now that we have the ability to abort currently running plans for higher priority plans, there is a subtle implementation detail that can cause unexpected behaviors in your NPCs. If you set up your planner to re-plan on world state changes, the planner will try to re-plan when tasks apply their effects on successful execution. Consider this altered subsection of the Trunk Thumper's domain below.

```
Compound Task [AttackEnemy]
    Method [WsPowerUp = 3]
        Subtasks [DoWhirlwindTrunkAttack(), DoRecovery()]
    Method [WsEnemyRange > MeleeRange,]
        Subtasks [DoTrunkSlam(), DoRecovery()]
Primitive Task [DoTrunkSlam]
    Operator [AnimatedAttackOperator(TrunkSlamAnimName)]
        Effects [WsPowerUp += 1]
Primitive Task [DoWhirlwindTrunkAttack]
    Operator [DoWhirlwindTrunkAttack()]
        Effects [WsPowerUp = 0]
Primitive Task [DoRecover]
    Operator [PlayAnimation(TrunkSlamRecoveryAnim)]
```

This new behavior is designed to have the troll do the `DoWhirlwindTrunkAttack` task, after executing the `DoTrunkSlam` three times. This is accomplished by having the `DoTrunkSlam` task's effect increase the `WsPowerUp` property by one each time it executes. This might seem fine at first glance, but you will have designers at your desk informing you that the troll now combos a trunk slam directly into a whirlwind attack every time. The problem arises on the third execution of `DoTrunkSlam`. The task's effects are applied and the planner forces a re-plan. With `WsPowerUp` equal to three, the planner will pick the higher priority Whirlwind attack method. This cancels the `DoRecovery` task that is designed to break the attacks up, allowing the player some time to react.

Normally, the whirlwind method should be able to cancel plans of lower priority. But the currently running plan is still valid, and the only reason this bug is occurring is that the planner is replanning on all world state changes, including changes by successfully completed primitive task's effects. Simply not replanning when the world state changes via effects being applied from a primitive tasks will solve this problem—which is fine, because the plan was found with those world state changes in mind anyway. While this is a good change to make, it won't be the full solution. Any world state changes *outside* of the tasks the plan runner is executing will force a replan and cause the bug to resurface.

The real problem here is the domain and how it's currently setup. There are a couple of different ways we can solve this, and it really matters how you view it. One could say that the recovery animation is part of the attack, so it might be worth incorporating that animation into the attack animation. That way the recovery *always* plays after the slam attack. This hurts the modularity of the domain. What if the designers want to chain three slams then do a recovery?

A better way would be to use world state to describe the reason that `DoRecovery` is needed. Consider the change below:

```
Compound Task [AttackEnemy]
    Method [WsPowerUp = 3]
        Subtasks [DoWhirlwindTrunkAttack(), DoRecovery()]
    Method [WsEnemyRange > MeleeRange,]
        Subtasks [DoTrunkSlam(), DoRecovery()]
```

Primitive Task [DoTrunkSlam]
    Operator [AnimatedAttackOperator(TrunkSlamAnimName)]
        Effects [WsPowerUp += 1, **WsIsTired = true**]
Primitive Task [DoWhirlwindTrunkAttack]
    Preconditions [WsIsTired == false]
    Operator [DoWhirlwindTrunkAttack()]
        Effects [WsPowerUp = 0]
Primitive Task [DoRecover]
    Operator [PlayAnimation(TrunkSlamRecoveryAnim)]
        Effects [WsIsTired = false]

Using the `WsIsTired` world state, we can properly describe the reason we need the `DoRecovery` task. The `DoTrunkSlam` task now makes the Trunk Thumper tired, and he can't execute `DoWhirlwindTrunkAttack` until he gets a chance to recover. Now, when the world state changes, the `DoRecovery` task won't be interrupted and yet we save the modularity of `DoTrunkSlam` and `DoRecovery`. When implementing priority plan picking, these subtle details can really throw a wrench in your HTN behaviors. It's important to ask yourself if you are properly representing the world when you run into these types of behavior issues. As we saw in this case, a simple world state is all that was needed.

12.9 Managing Simultaneous Behaviors

A lot of different behavior selection algorithms are very good at doing one thing at a time, but complications arise when it comes time to do two things at once. Luckily, there are a couple ways you can handle this problem with HTN.

One's first reaction might be to roll multiple operators into one. This will work, but this has a couple pitfalls: it removes the ability to reuse operators we have already developed, the combining of multiple operators brings an added complexity that hurts maintainability, and any variation to this combined operator can force us to duplicate code if not handled correctly. Chances are you are going to run into behavior that will need to do multiple things at once, often enough that you are going to want to avoid this method.

A more intuitive way to handle this is to build a separate HTN domain to handle different components of your NPC. Using our troll example, we might have a behavior where we need him to navigate towards his enemy but guard himself from incoming range attacks. We can break this up into multiple operators that control different parts of the body—a navigation operator that would handle the lower body and a guard operator to handle the upper body. Knowing that, we can build two domains and use two planners to deal with the upper and lower bodies.

You may find early on that this can be tricky to implement. The issue that arises is that you need to sync up the tasks in each planner. You can accomplish this by making sure you have world state that describes what's going on in each planner. In our troll example, we can have a world state called *Navigating* that will be set to true when any lower body navigation task is running. This will allow the upper body planner to make decisions based on this information. Below is an example of how these two domains might be set up.

```
Compound Task [BeTrunkThumperUpper]//Upper domain
    Method [WsHasEnemy == true, WsEnemyRange <= MeleeRange]
        Subtasks [DoTrunkSlam()]
    Method [Navigating == true, HitByRangedAttack == true]
        Subtasks [GuardFaceWithArm()]
    Method [true]
        Subtasks [Idle()]
Compound Task [BeTrunkThumperLower]//Lower domain
    Method [WsHasEnemy == true, WsEnemyRange > MeleeRange]
        Subtasks [NavigateToEnemy(), BeTrunkThumperLower()]
    Method [true]
        Subtasks [Idle()]
Primitive Task [DoTrunkSlam]
    Operator [DoTrunkSlamOperator]
Primitive Task [GuardFaceWithArm]
    Operator [GuardFaceWithArmOperator]
Primitive Task [NavigateToEnemy]
    Operator [NavigateToOperator(Enemy)]
        Effects [WsLocation = Enemy]
Primitive Task [Idle]
    Operator [IdleOperator]
```

Now this works great, but there are a couple minor problems with it. A second planner will add a bit of performance hit. Keeping these domains synchronized will hurt their maintainability. Lastly, you will not gain any friends when other programmers run into the debugging headache you just created with your multiple planners—trust me.

There is another alternative for our troll shielding example that does not involve two planners. Currently, navigation tasks complete after successfully *arriving* at the destination. Instead, we can have the navigation task start the path following and complete *immediately*, since the path following is happening in the background and not as a task in the plan runner. This frees us to plan during navigation, which allows us to put an arm up to shield the troll from incoming fire. This works as long as we have a world state that describes that we are navigating and the current distance to the destination. With this we can detect when we arrive and plan accordingly. Below is an example of how the domain would look.

```
Compound Task [BeTrunkThumper]
    Method [WsHasEnemy == true, WsEnemyRange <= MeleeRange]
        Subtasks [DoTrunkSlam()]
    Method [WsHasEnemy == true, WsEnemyRange > MeleeRange]
        Subtasks [NavigateToEnemy()]
    Method [Navigating == true, HitByRangedAttack == true]
        Subtasks [GuardFaceWithArm()]
    Method [true]
        Subtasks [Idle()]
Primitive Task [DoTrunkSlam]
    Operator [DoTrunkSlamOperator]
```

Primitive Task [GuardFaceWithArm]
    Operator [GuardFaceWithArmOperator]
Primitive Task [NavigateToEnemy]
    Operator [NavigateToOperator(Enemy)]
        Effects [Navigating = true]
Primitive Task [Idle]
    Operator [IdleOperator]

As you can see, this domain is similar to our dual domain approach. Both approaches rely on world state to work correctly. With the dual domain, the *Navigating* world state was used to keep the planners in sync. In the later approach, world state was used to represent the path following happening in the background, but without the need of two domains and two planners running.

12.10 Speeding up Planning with Partial Plans

Let us assume that we have built the Trunk Thumper's domain into a pretty large network. After optimizing the planner itself, you have found the need to knock a couple milliseconds off your planning time. There are a couple of ways we can still eek more performance out of it. As we explained, HTN naturally culls out large portions of the search space via the methods in compound tasks. There may be instances, however, where we can add a few more methods to cull more search space. In order to do this, we need to have the right world state representation.

If those techniques don't get you the speed you need, *partial planning* should. Partial planning is one of the most powerful features of HTN. In simplest terms, it allows the planner the ability to not fully decompose a complete plan. HTN is able to do this because it uses forward decomposition or forward search to find plans. That is, the planner starts with the *current* world state and plans *forward* in time from that. This allows the planner to only plan ahead a few steps.

GOAP and STRIPS planner variants, on the other hand, use a *backward* search [Jorkin 04]. This means the search makes its way from a desired goal state toward the current world state. Searching this way means the planner has to complete the entire search in order to know what *first* step to take. We will go back to a simple version of our Trunk Thumper domain to demonstrate how to break it up into a partial plan domain.

Compound Task [BeTrunkThumper]
    Method [WsCanSeeEnemy == true]
        Subtasks [NavigateToEnemy(), DoTrunkSlam()]
Primitive Task [DoTrunkSlam]
    Operator [DoTrunkSlamOperator]
Compound Task [NavigateToEnemy]
    Method [...]
        Subtasks [...]

Here, we have a method that will expand both the NavigateToEnemy and DoTrunkSlam tasks if WsCanSeeEnemy is true. Since whatever tasks that make up

NavigateToEnemy might take a long time, it would make this a good option to split into a partial plan. There isn't much point to planning too far into the future since there is a good chance the world state could change, forcing our troll to make a different decision. We can convert this particular plan into a partial plan:

Compound Task [BeTrunkThumper]
    Method [WsCanSeeEnemy == true, WsEnemyRange > MeleeRange]
        Subtasks [NavigateToEnemy()]
    Method [WsCanSeeEnemy == true]
        Subtasks [DoTrunkSlam()]
Primitive Task [DoTrunkSlam]
    Operator [DoTrunkSlamOperator]
Compound Task [NavigateToEnemy]
    Method […]
        Subtasks […]

Here, we have broken the previous method into two methods. The new high priority method will navigate to the enemy only if the troll is currently out of range. If the troll is not outside of melee range, he will perform the trunk slam attack. Navigation tasks are also prime targets for partial plans, since they often take a long time to complete. It's important to point out that splitting this plan is only doable if there is a world state available to differentiate the split.

    This method of partial planning requires the author of the domain to create the split themselves. But there is a way to automate this process. By assigning the concept of "time" to primitive tasks, the planner can keep track of how far into the future it has already planned. There are a couple issues with this approach, however. Consider the domain.

Compound Task [BeTrunkThumper]
    Method [WsCanSeeEnemy == true]
        Subtasks [NavigateToEnemy(), DoTrunkSlam()]
Primitive Task [DoTrunkSlam]
    Preconditions[WsStamina > 0]
    Operator [DoTrunkSlamOperator]
Compound Task [NavigateToEnemy]
    Method […]
        Subtasks […]

With this domain, assume the primitive tasks that make up the navigation cross the time threshold that is set in the planner. This would cause the troll to start navigating to the enemy. But if the world state property WsStamina is zero, the troll can't execute the DoTrunkSlam anyway because of its precondition. The automated partial plan split removed the ability to validate the plan properly. Of course the method can be written to include the stamina check to avoid this problem. But since both ways are valid, it is better to insure both will produce the same results. Not doing so will cause subtle bugs in your game.

    Even if you feel that this isn't a real concern, there is also the question of how to continue where the partial plan left off. We could just replan from the root, but that would require us to change the domain in some way to understand that it's completed the first part of the full plan. In the case of our example, we would have to add a higher priority method that checks to see if we are in range to do the melee attack. But if we have to do this, what's the point of the automated partial planning?

A better solution would be to record the state of the unprocessed list. With that we can modify the planner to start with a list of tasks, instead of the one root task. This would allow us to continue the search where we left off. Of course, we would not be able to roll back to *before* the start of the second part of the plan. Running into this case would mean that you've already run tasks that you should not have. So if the user runs into this case, they can't use partial planning because there are tasks later in the plan that need to be validated in order to get the correct behavior.

With *Transformers: Fall of Cybertron*, we simply built the partial plans into the domains. For us, the chance of putting subtle bugs into the game was high and we found that we were naturally putting partial plans in our NPC domains anyway when full plan validation wasn't necessary. A lot of our NPCs were using the last example from Section 12.9 for navigation, which is also an example of partial planning.

12.11 Conclusion

Going through the process of creating a simple NPC can be a real eye-opener to the details involved with implementation of any behavior selection system. Hopefully we have explored enough of hierarchical task networks to show its natural approach to describing behaviors, the re-usability and modularity of its primitive tasks. HTN's ability to reason about the future allows an expressiveness only found with planners. We have also attempted to point out potential problems a developer may come across when implementing it. Hierarchical task networks were a real benefit to the AI programmers on *Transformers: Fall of Cybertron* and we're sure it will be the same for you.

References

[Erol et al. 94] K. Erol, D. Nau, and J. Henler, "HTN planning: Complexity and expressivity." *AAAI-94 Proceedings*, 1994.

[Erol et al. 95] K. Erol, J. Henler, and D. Nau. "Semantics for Hierarchical Task-Network Planning." Technical report TR 95-9. The Institute for Systems Research, 1995.

[Ghallab et al. 04] M. Ghallab, D. Nau, and P. Traverso, *Automated Planning*. San Francisco, CA: Elsevier, 2004, pp. 229–259.

[HighMoon 10] *Transformers: War for Cybertron*, High Moon Studios/Activision Publishing, 2010.

[HighMoon 12] *Transformers: Fall of Cybertron*, High Moon Studios/Activision Publishing, 2012.

[Jorkin 04] Jeff Orkin. "Applying goal-oriented action planning to games." In *AI Game Programming Wisdom 2*, edited by Steve Rabin. Hingham, MA: Charles River Media, 2004, pp. 217–227.

13

Hierarchical Plan-Space Planning for Multi-unit Combat Maneuvers

William van der Sterren

13.1 Introduction

In combat simulators and war games, coming up with a good plan is half the battle. Good plans make the AI a more convincing opponent and a more reliable assistant commander. Good plans are essential for clear and effective coordination between combat units toward a joint objective.

This chapter describes the design of an AI planner capable of producing plans that coordinate multiple units into a joint maneuver on the battlefield. First, it looks at how planning for multiple units is different from planning for a single unit. Then it introduces the basic ideas of hierarchical plan-space planning. These ideas are made more concrete for the case of combat maneuvers. The article wraps up with an evaluation of the design and ideas for further application of hierarchical plan-space planning.

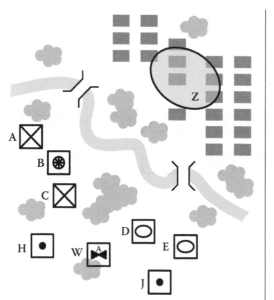

"Our plan:
We'll clear objective Z, with A, B, C, D and E platoons forming up and launching a two pronged simultaneous attack. Afterwards, we'll regroup at objective Z.
B platoon will transport A and C to their form up areas. A and C platoons will attack across the northern bridge, D and E platoons will attack across the southern bridge.
Fire support is provided by batteries H and J and gunships W. Batteries H and J will fire smoke screens to cover the bridge crossings. W flight will be on call."

Figure 13.1

A multi-unit planning problem (left) and the result (right) as briefed to the player.

13.2 Planning for Multiple Units

Creating a plan for multiple units is different from planning for a single unit. Obviously, the plan needs to cater to all the units instead of a single unit, and will involve more actions. In many cases, these units will perform their actions concurrently.

But there is more to it: in most cases, these units will have to interact with each other to accomplish the goal. To coordinate this interaction, the plan needs to tell who needs to interact with whom, where, and at what time.

Another difference is in communication of the plan: the actions making up a single unit's plan typically require no additional explanation. However, when multiple units work together towards an objective, additional explanation is often expected (for example, as part of the briefing in Figure 13.1). How is the work split across subgroups? Who is assisting whom? What is each group's role? And for combat plans, what is the overall concept?

Given these differences, can we take a single-unit planner such as GOAP [Orkin 06] or an HTN planner [Ghallab et al. 04, Humphreys 13] and create plans for multiple units? For all practical purposes, we cannot. Both these kinds of planners construct their plan action for action, and traverse a search space consisting of world states (the state-space [StateSpaceSearch]). Our problem is the enormous state-space resulting from multiple units acting concurrently. For example, assume a single unit has four alternative actions to move about or manipulate its environment, and we are in need of a five-step plan. For this "single unit" case, the total state-space consists of $4^5 = 1024$ states, and can easily be searched. If we attempt to tackle a similar problem involving six units acting concurrently, the state-space size explodes to $(4^6)^5 \sim 1.15 \ 10^{18}$ combinations. GOAP and, to a lesser extent, standard HTN planners struggle to search efficiently in such a large state-space.

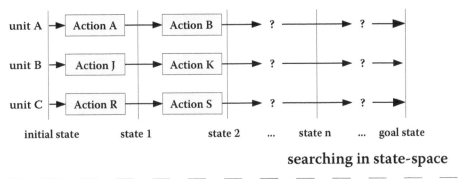

initial state   state 1   state 2   ...   state n   ...   goal state

searching in state-space

searching in plan-space

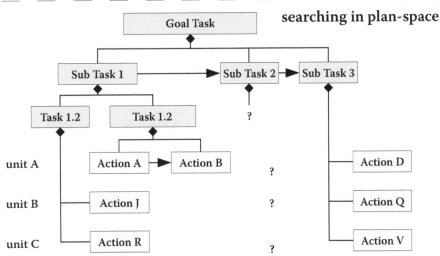

Figure 13.2

State-space search (top) compared with plan-space search (bottom).

Instead of searching in state-space, we can attempt to search in plan-space (see Figure 13.2). Plan-space represents all incomplete and complete plans. This may sound vague, but it actually is quite similar to how human project planners tackle planning problems. Project planners break down the overall problem into smaller tasks that together accomplish the goal. They then repeatedly break down these smaller tasks until the resulting activities are small enough to be accomplished by a single unit's action. See Figure 13.3 for an example of a fully detailed plan.

Working in plan-space offers three key advantages when tackling multiunit planning problems. First, we can make planning decisions at a higher level than individual actions by reasoning about tasks and subtasks. Second, we have the freedom to detail the plan in any order we like, which allows us to start focusing on the most critical tasks first. And, third, we can explicitly represent coordination (as tasks involving multiple units), and synchronization (as tasks not able to start before all actions of a preceding subtask have completed) in our plan. With these advantages, we are able to generate plans describing coordinated actions for multiple units even for a large search space.

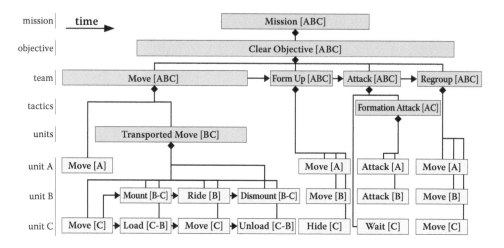

Figure 13.3

A complete plan with higher level tasks (top) and resulting unit actions (bottom).

This article continues by detailing this approach of hierarchical plan-space planning for a combat maneuver problem as illustrated in Figure 13.1.

13.3 Hierarchical Planning in Plan-Space: The Ingredients

We need four ingredients to implement hierarchical planning in plan-space: a planner main loop, the tasks and actions to represent the plan, a set of planner methods which can refine a partial plan by detailing one task in that plan, and finally the plan-space that holds and ranks all partial plans. We will look into these ingredients in this order.

13.4 Planner Main Loop: An A* Search through Plan-Space

The planner main loop executes the search through plan-space. The search starts with a single plan consisting of a single top-level task (the "mission"). Next, the main loop repeatedly picks the most promising plan from the open plans in plan-space and attempts to expand that plan by refining the plan's tasks. The main loop exits successfully when a plan is found that is complete. The main loop exits with a failure when there is no open plan left to be expanded. Figure 13.4 shows the pseudocode for the planner main loop.

The main loop expands a selected plan as follows. It first picks a single task requiring refinement from the plan. It then selects from the catalog of planner methods the methods that can refine this selected task. Each of these methods is applied separately, resulting in zero or more alternative expanded plans (we will discuss this in more detail later). Every expanded alternative plan is assigned a cost and added to the open list.

The main loop is quite generic and similar to an A* path search. Here, we are expanding plans into one or more neighboring plans which are closer to a fully detailed plan, instead of expanding paths into one or more neighboring locations which are closer to the destination. We are expanding plans in a best-first approach, something that is explained in more detail when looking into the plan-space.

```
loop
    current = get most promising plan from open list
    break if current.complete? or current.null?
    add current to closed list
    pick t = current.task_to_detail
    for every method m that applies to task t
        alternatives = m.generate(current, t)
        for every a in alternatives
                plan = clone current
                // refine using method m and alternative a
                m.plan(plan, t, a)
                compute plan's cost
                add plan to open list
```

Figure 13.4

Pseudocode for the planner main loop.

13.5 A Plan of Tasks

A plan consists of interdependent tasks. A task represents an activity for one or more units and consumes time. For our combat maneuver domain, we need tasks to represent basic unit actions, and we need tasks to represent higher level activity. Table 13.1 lists examples of both types of tasks, with unit level tasks in the bottom row. The scope reflects the various levels at which decisions are made and problems are broken down in the military: mission, objective, team, tactics, units, unit.

The basic unit tasks simply follow from the activity that a unit—such as an infantry squad, a tank platoon, or a gunship section—is capable of. We call these tasks "primitive" since we cannot decompose them. The higher level tasks are intended to help us make higher level planning decisions and break down the plan (as shown in Figure 13.3). In general, these tasks are about assigning resources to subgoals and coordinating subtasks. Concrete examples for our combat maneuver domain include a complete team moving to a form-up position, preparatory strikes by artillery and aircraft, or a para drop. These tasks are called "compound" since we can break them down into smaller tasks.

Tasks have a start time and duration. A task's duration is computed as the activity duration for primitive tasks, as the latest subtask's end-time minus earliest subtask's start-time for tasks already refined into subtasks, and as an estimated duration for a compound tasks not yet refined. We'll look into these estimates later.

In the plan, the tasks are organized as a graph. Every task has a parent except for the root task. Compound tasks have children (subtasks implementing their parent). Tasks

Table 13.1 Examples of tasks for combat maneuver domain, arranged by scope

Scope	Task examples
Mission	Mission
Objective	Clear, occupy, defend
Team	Move, form up, attack, air land, defend, counter-attack, para drop
Tactic	Formation ground attack, planned fire support, smoke screen
Units	Transported move, defend sector
Unit	Defend, guard, attack, hide, move, wait, air ingress, air egress, mount, dismount, load, unload, ride, para jump, fire artillery mission, close air support

```
# A LoadTask expects:                                      # An AttackAfterFormUpTeamTask expects:
# - a start_state, indicating the unit's initial state     # - an objective
# - a target state, indicating the unit's loaded state     # - a start state (as unit states preceding the form-up & attack)
# - the passenger                                           # - an avenue of approach to use for this attack
class LoadTask < Task                                       # It outputs:
  is_primitive                                              # - the objective area indicating what terrain to attack & from where
  has_scope :unit                                           # - the assembly area for pre-attack form-up
  has_input :start_state,    :type => :unit                 # - per unit assembly positions in the form-up area
  has_input :target_state,   :type => :unit                 # - an end-state, as unit states after the attack in the objective area
  has_input :passenger,      :type => :unit                 class AttackAfterFormUpTeamTask < Task
                                                              has_scope   :team
  def compute_expected_costs(context)                         has_input   :start_state,    :type => :units
    15.0                                                      has_input   :objective,      :type => :objective
  end                                                         has_input   :avenue_of_approach, :type => :avenue_of_approach
end                                                           has_output  :objective_area, :type => :area
                                                              has_output  :assembly_area,  :type => :area
                                                              has_output  :assembled_state, :type => :units
                                                              has_output  :end_state,      :type => :units

                                                              def compute_expected_costs(context)
                                                                ...
                                                              end
                                                            end
```

Figure 13.5

Two examples of tasks, with inputs and outputs.

may have preceding tasks which require completion before the task can start. For example, a team formation attack won't be able to start until all the form-up tasks of all involved units have been completed. These precedence relations between two tasks also imply all of the first task's subtasks precede the second task. Tasks may have successor tasks in the same way.

Tasks are parameterized with inputs and may provide outputs. In our combat maneuver domain all tasks take the units involved as input, typically with the units in the planned state (position, ammo level) at the start of the task. Primitive tasks deal with one single unit; compound tasks typically take an array of units. Many tasks take additional inputs—for example, to denote cooperating units, assigned targets or zones, or target states (in unit positions at the end of the task).

Figure 13.5 shows an example of two kinds of tasks, each taking inputs. The *LoadTask* represents the loading activity by a transporter unit such as an APC platoon. The *LoadTask* takes three inputs. The start-state input identifies the transporter unit and its initial state consisting of its position, and identifiers for any passenger units already being mounted. The target-state input is similar to the start-state but with the indicated passenger unit mounted. The passenger input identifies the passenger unit.

The *AttackAfterFormUpTeamTask* represents a multi-unit ground attack from a form-up position. It takes three inputs. The start-state input takes an array of units that will execute the attack. The objective input and avenue-of-approach inputs provide additional guidance from "higher up" on how to refine this team level task.

The *AttackAfterFormUpTeamTask* also provides outputs, as do many other tasks. The purpose of an output is to provide values to other tasks' inputs, enabling them to work from a resulting unit state, or from a tactical decision such as an avenue of approach.

A task input need not be set on task creation. It may be left open until the task is being refined. Or it can be connected to the input or output of another task and receive a value when the other side of the connection is set. Figure 13.6 illustrates this.

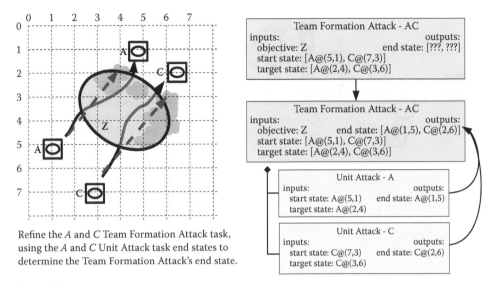

Refine the *A* and *C* Team Formation Attack task, using the *A* and *C* Unit Attack task end states to determine the Team Formation Attack's end state.

Figure 13.6

A parent's task output being determined by child tasks.

In Figure 13.6, a *TeamFormationAttack* task has been created involving tank platoons A and C. The task is given a start-state consisting of the A and C units with their start positions. The task's target-state indicates the tank platoons should move into positions at the far end of objective Z. The *TeamFormationAttack's* end-state output is left open intentionally, leaving detailed positioning of the tank platoons to more specialized subtasks. When the planner refines the *TeamFormationAttack*—for example, by adding two *UnitAttack* tasks, it connects the *UnitAttack's* end-state outputs to the *TeamFormationAttack* end-state output. When the planner refines the *UnitAttacks*, it will set the end-states with values representing positions close to the desired target-state but outside the woods. As soon as these *UnitAttack's* end-states are set, they will propagate to the *TeamFormationAttack's* end-state (and propagate further, if other inputs have been connected to that end-state).

Task outputs thus serve to pass on planning decisions and states along and up the chain of tasks. Connections between outputs and inputs determine how tasks share values. Connections can link inputs and outputs as a whole, but also (for arrays) on a per-element basis. In Figure 13.6, each of the *UnitAttack* tasks sets an element in the *TeamFormationAttack's* end-state.

We call *task* inputs that have all their values set "grounded" tasks. "Ungrounded" tasks lack one or more values in their inputs. We will revisit this distinction when discussing the order in which tasks are being refined.

13.6 Planner Methods

When the planner wants to refine a task in a partial plan, it selects the planner methods that apply to this task. It then applies each of these planner methods separately on a clone of the partial plan, and has the planner method generating alternative and more refined versions of the partial plan.

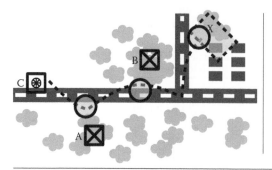

The task is for truck platoon C to pick up infantry squads A and B, and transport them to form-up area X. There A and B are to dismount, and all are to move to their target positions.

This requires decisions on:
- where to pick up A, and where B
- whether to pick up A before B
- where to drop off A and B
- exact final positions for A, B and C

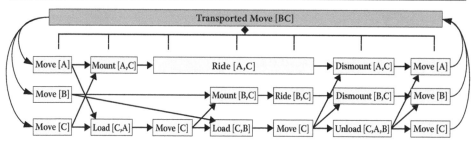

Figure 13.7

Decisions and subtasks when refining a TransportedMove task.

The role of the planner methods (we'll refer to them simply as "methods" from now on) is to refine a specific task in the plan. Methods themselves indicate which task or tasks they are able to refine. If the task to be refined is a primitive task, the method should compute and set this task's outputs. Figure 13.6 shows how the tank platoon's *UnitAttack* is given an output (a destination position outside the woods at the far end of the objective) that matches the tank unit's movement capabilities.

If the task to be refined is a compound task, then the method's responsibility is to decide how to implement that task, create the necessary subtasks, and connect the inputs and outputs of the task and subtasks. The method should ensure the outputs of the task being refined are set or have connections into them. Figure 13.7 illustrates an example of the decisions to be made, and the tasks, relations, and input/output connections to be created by a *TransportedMove* method in order to refine a nontrivial *TransportedMove* task.

To break down a *TransportedMove* task for a truck platoon C and two infantry squads A and B (in Figure 13.7), the *TransportedMove* method first makes a number of decisions. The method selects positions for the truck platoon to pick up squads A and B. Such a pick-up position needs to be accessible for the truck platoon and preferably close to the infantry squad. If the infantry squad had been in the open, the truck platoon might have picked it up at the squads' initial position. In this example, however, the infantry is positioned in the woods and needs to move into the open in order to be picked up. The drop-off point near form-up area X is picked in a similar way. The third decision is about picking up A before B or the other way around. Based on a few path-finding queries, picking up A before B is chosen. The final decision involves picking final positions for A, B, and C if not already given.

Table 13.2 Examples of planner methods and their responsibilities, arranged by scope

Scope	Planner method responsibility
Mission	Arrange objectives, allocate units to objectives
Objective	Define team activities, assign combat units and support units to teams
Team	Execute tasks as a team, distributing the work according to roles
Tactic	Synchronize tactical activity between multiple units
Units	Arrange cooperation between complementary units
Unit	Define end-state

Based on these decisions, the *TransportedMove* method can create the tasks for the two infantry squads and truck platoon. By making one task a predecessor of the other task, the method creates a sequence of tasks for each of the units. In addition, it synchronizes the load/mount actions and the unload/dismount actions by also making specific actions from other units a predecessor of these tasks. For example, the action for C to load A cannot start before both C and A have completed their moves to the pick-up position. Similarly, the infantry squads cannot disembark before the truck platoon has arrived at the drop-off position.

Since the *TransportedMove* method in this example already makes most of the decisions for all units and tasks involved, it can simply set output values and input values for most of the tasks.

To fully cover our combat maneuver domain, we need methods to set end-states for each of the primitive unit tasks, and we need methods to break down each of the compound tasks. For breaking down compound tasks into smaller tasks, we mirror the hierarchy chosen for tasks, from mission level methods down to unit level methods. As a rule of thumb, methods break down tasks into tasks of the next level, sometimes one level more. At each level, the methods have slightly different responsibility, as is illustrated in Table 13.2.

For most tasks, there will be a single corresponding method that is able to break the task down. For a few tasks it makes sense to have multiple methods for refining the task, each specialized in one type of tactical approach. To defend an objective, one method would create subtasks that make the available platoons each occupy a static position around the objective. Another method could create subtasks that have infantry platoons defending from static positions and keeping armor platoons in the rear for a counter-attack.

One benefit of using separate methods implementing different tactics is the ability to configure the planner's tactical approach (doctrine) by enabling or disabling certain methods for planning.

In the example of Figure 13.7, the *TransportedMove* method was able to consider two combinations (picking up A before B, and B before A) and pick the optimal one, because it understood how the task would be implemented in terms of primitive tasks. Methods working with higher level tasks often lack the understanding of how the plan will work out in detail, and have troubles make an optimal (or even "good enough") choice by themselves when facing multiple combinations. In these cases, the method will indicate to the planner main loop that it sees more than one alternative to refine the plan. The planner main loop then will iterate over these alternatives and create new plans by cloning the parent plan and asking the method to refine the plan for the given alternative (see Figure 13.4). Although this adds a little complexity to the planner main loop, the benefit is for us developers having to write and maintain just a single method to break down a specific compound task.

A method may fail to set a task output or break down a compound task and not generate a more refined plan. For example, if an artillery unit has already spent all its rounds in two artillery missions early in the plan, it should not be planned to perform a third artillery mission. If a team of three mechanized platoons is tasked to attack in formation but has to cross a narrow bridge doing so, it won't be an attack in formation and the method should not refine the task.

When one method fails to refine a task, this is only a local dead end in planning if no other method is capable of refining the same task in the same plan. Remember that we're searching through alternative plans with A*: a dead end here doesn't mean there isn't another, perhaps very different, variant of a plan that is feasible.

13.7 Plan-Space

The plan-space is the collection of all generated (partial) plans. We keep track of all plans that can be further refined in an open list. The open list is sorted for the lowest cost (Figure 13.8).

We can choose what to use for costs: plan duration works in most cases and is particularly suited for combat maneuvers, where time plays a considerable role in the plan's quality. The quicker we launch an attack, or the quicker our defending units occupy their positions, the better.

We compute a plan's duration the way project planners do, using accurate data from primitive tasks when available and using estimates for compound tasks that have not been detailed yet. Starting at the root task, we repeatedly pick a child task that has no preceding tasks without a start-time and end-time. For this child task we set as the start-time the maximum end-time of its predecessors, and recursively compute its duration and end-time (start-time plus duration). After doing so for all children, we can set the task's end-time. The root task's end-time minus start-time gives us the plan's duration.

We need to recompute a plan's duration every time we update the plan. Newly added primitive tasks may have a duration different from what their compound parent task estimated. We can, however, cache a compound task's estimate once computed for its specific inputs.

We leave the estimation of a compound task's duration to the task itself. Each compound task should implement an "estimate duration" function. These functions use heuristics to come up with a decent estimate. Since we are using A* to search through plan-space, the estimate should be a close estimate without overestimating the duration. Figure 13.9 illustrates how to come up with a good estimate.

Figure 13.9 shows the same situation and *TransportedMove* task as Figure 13.7. Now we are interested in estimating the duration without going into all the decisions and details that we considered when refining the task. A good estimate would be for C to move to A, then to B and finally to X at its top speed, with time for loading and unloading A and B added. In the estimate, we can decide to move to A before B based on a simple geometric comparison: A is closer to C than is B. Alternatively, we can evaluate path durations for both cases, and pick the lowest estimate. We are underestimating the real costs in most situations, since actual movement will be slower than C due to the terrain.

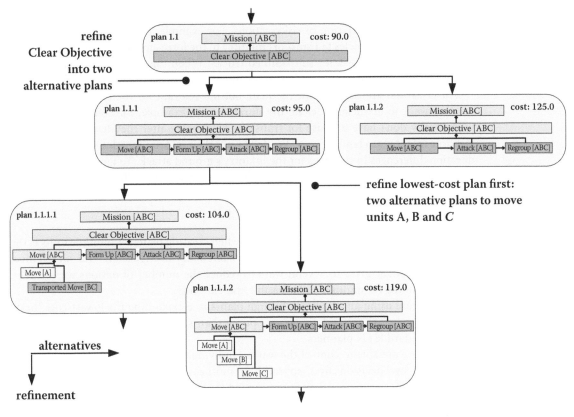

Figure 13.8

Plan-space, with incomplete plans as nodes and links representing refinement.

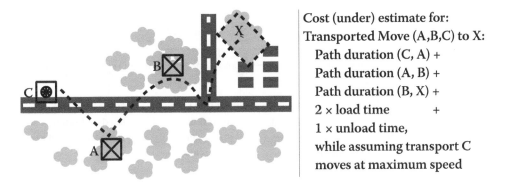

Cost (under) estimate for:
Transported Move (A,B,C) to X:
    Path duration (C, A) +
    Path duration (A, B) +
    Path duration (B, X) +
    2 × load time   +
    1 × unload time,
while assuming transport C
moves at maximum speed

Figure 13.9

Estimating the duration of a compound TransportedMove task.

As with A* pathfinding, we make the planner avoid certain tasks and plans by artificially inflating the duration of risky actions. For example, to make the attacker avoid using soft-skinned vehicles to transport infantry to the form-up location, we can raise the duration of the move task for soft-skinned trucks. When the planner also has available armored personnel carriers, he will be more likely to use these to transport infantry.

For tasks that are required for the plan, but not relevant for the quality of the plan, we may want to artificially deflate the duration. For example, for combat maneuvers, we typically don't have any use for transport helicopters after they have inserted their airborne infantry at a landing zone. We don't want their return flight duration to mask any duration differences in the tasks for the infantry's ground attack. To ignore the irrelevant return flight, we can use a small and fixed duration for the return flight tasks.

13.8 Making Planning More Efficient

As mentioned earlier, the biggest risk we run when creating plans for multiple units is the combinatorics problem (better known as the *combinatorial explosion*). Our hierarchical plan-space planner gives us several ways to reduce the number of options we consider, making planning for multiple units feasible and efficient.

First, we are using an A* search through plan-space expanding the lowest-cost "best" plan first. This helps us considering fewer options than a depth-first backtracking approach used by standard HTN planners.

Second, we are able to control the way an individual plan is expanded, and turn this into a "high-level decisions first" approach. In most cases, a plan will have more than one task that requires refinements and is grounded (has all its inputs set). The planner main loop in Figure 13.3 needs to pick a single task to refine. For the combat maneuver domain, where each task is associated with a command scope, we can have the planner main loop always pick the task with the highest scope as the task to refine first.

In Figure 13.10, this highest scope first task selection is illustrated. The partial plan consists of many compound tasks requiring refinement. Some of these, such as the *Attack* and *Regroup* tasks, cannot be refined yet, since they need inputs from preceding tasks.

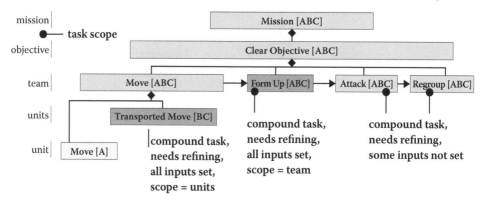

Figure 13.10

Selecting the highest scope task with all inputs set: FormUp.

Two tasks are grounded and ready to be refined: the *TransportedMove*, with "units" scope, and the *FormUp*, with "team" scope. Since "team" scope is higher, the planner will pick the *FormUp* task as the task to be refined first. Refining the *FormUp* task will set the inputs for the *Regroup* task, allowing that task to be refined next.

The benefit of refining higher level tasks first is that these tasks have larger impact on plan feasibility (do we have the maneuvering space for a combined attack by all our mechanized platoons?) and the cost of the plan. The planner should not busy himself detailing seating arrangements for the move to the form-up position before the attack is fleshed out. By making high-level decisions first, the planner needs far fewer steps to find a good plan.

A third way to consider fewer plans is the hierarchical plan-space planner's ability to plan from the "middle-out." In the military, planning specialists mix forward planning and reverse planning, sometimes starting with the critical step in the middle. When starting in the middle (for example, with the air landing or a complex attack), they subsequently plan forward to mission completion and backward to mission start. The military do so because starting with the critical step drastically reduces the number of planning options to consider.

We can mimic this by changing the input/output relations between tasks, and shifting some decisions from one method to another. Keep in mind that the only tasks that can be refined are the grounded tasks. Figure 13.11 shows an example of tasks connected to enable middle-out planning.

In Figure 13.11, a *ClearObjective* task is shown that has been broken down into a *Move*, a *FormUp*, an *AttackAfterFormUp*, and a *Regroup*. These tasks are to be executed in that order. However, refinement of these tasks should start with the *AttackAfterFormUp*. The input/output connections between the tasks are made in such a way that the *AttackAfterFormUp* is the first task having all its inputs set. The *FormUp* and *Regroup* task inputs depend on outputs from the *AttackAfterFormUp* task. The *Move* task depends on outputs from the *FormUp* task. The method refining the *AttackAfterFormUp* task has been

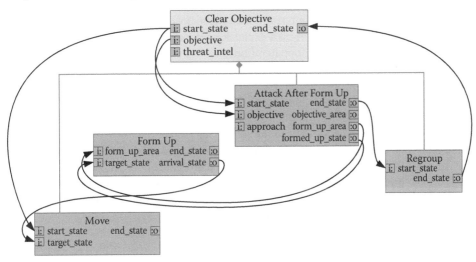

Figure 13.11

Middle-out planning from the AttackAfterFormUp by linking inputs.

modified to work with initial unit positions and the objective, and defines the attack move from the form-up locations through the objective. The *AttackAfterFormUp* task outputs the chosen form-up location and the positions of the involved units after form-up. It also outputs the positions of the units after attacking through the objective. These outputs enable the *FormUp* and *Regroup* tasks to be refined. The method refining the *FormUp* task defines where the units should enter the form-up area and with that output enables the *Move* task to be refined.

Middle-out planning requires changes to tasks and methods but it can greatly reduce the number of plans to consider by making critical decisions first. For combat maneuvers, middle-out planning also resembles a military practice, which makes it easier to translate military doctrine into tasks and planner methods.

13.9 Conclusion

We are able to successfully plan combat maneuvers involving over a dozen mechanized platoons, armor troops, gunship sections, and artillery batteries, taking into account tactical preferences and time. By working in plan-space instead of state-space, by breaking down the problem into high-level and low-level tasks and decisions, and by using a cost-based best-first search that expands high-level tasks first, we can avoid combinatorial explosion and deliver a good plan on short notice. The resulting plan includes not only the actions for each individual unit, but also the relations between these actions for coordination, and all higher level decisions. Turning such a plan into human understandable explanation or briefing is trivial.

The planner's design described here has been in action since mid-2009, generating tens of thousands of combat maneuvers from user input as downloadable missions [PlannedAssault 09]. The current implementation is in Ruby, running single-threaded on a Java VM (through JRuby) on an Intel Core2Quad Q8400, taking some 10s to 30s to generate a maneuver for 4×3 km terrain, with the majority of CPU time spent on terrain analysis and path-finding, not on plan expansion. The majority of plans are constructed in fewer than 200 planner main loop iterations.

13.10 Future Work

One nice side effect of planning in plan-space is the availability of all higher level tasks and decisions in the resulting plan, next to the actions for each of the units. Not only does this availability make it easier to turn the plan into a human readable briefing, it also makes the resulting plan great for use in monitoring the plan's execution. The original plan contains all the information to decide who is impacted by a task running late, which part of the plan needs repairs, and what the maximum allowed duration is for an alternative implementation of a plan part.

References

[Ghallab et al. 04] M. Ghallab, D. Nau, and P. Traverso. *Automated Planning, Theory and Practice*, pp. 229–259. San Francisco, CA: Morgan Kaufmann, 2004.

[Humphreys 13] T. Humphreys. "Exploring HTN planners through example." In *Game AI Pro*, edited by Steve Rabin. Boca Raton, FL: CRC Press, 2013.

[Orkin 06] J. Orkin. "Three states and a plan: The A.I. of F.E.A.R." *Game Developers Conference, 2006*. Available online (http://web.media.mit.edu/~jorkin/goap.html).

[PlannedAssault 09] PlannedAssault on-line mission generator for ARMA/ARMA2 games, http://www.plannedassault.com, 2009.

[StateSpaceSearch] Wikipedia. http://en.wikipedia.org/wiki/State_space_search.

14

Phenomenal AI Level-of-Detail Control with the LOD Trader

Ben Sunshine-Hill

14.1 Introduction

Of all the techniques which make modern video game graphics possible, level-of-detail (LOD) management may very well be the most important, the most groundbreaking, and the most game-changing. While LOD seems like a rather boring thing to think of as "groundbreaking," in order to get the graphical quality we want in the world sizes we want, it's crucial to *not* render everything as though the player was two centimeters away from it. With conservatively chosen LOD transition distances, immense speedups are possible without compromising the realism of the scene in any way. Viewed broadly, even things like visibility culling can be considered part of LOD—after all, the lowest detail possible for an object is to not render it at all. Graphics programmers rely on LOD. It is, in a sense, "how graphics works."

AI programmers use some form of LOD, too, of course, but we don't really *rely* on it. We'll use lower quality locomotion and collision avoidance systems for characters more than ten meters away, or simulate out-of-view characters at a lower update rate, or (similar to visibility culling above) delete characters entirely when they're too far away. But while graphics programmers can use LOD without compromising realism, whenever *we* employ LOD, in the back of our mind, our conscience whispers, "That's just a hack ... someone's going to *notice*." We use LOD only when we absolutely must, because we know that it's bringing down the quality of our AI.

There's another sense in which we don't rely on AI LOD. In graphics, LOD acts as a natural limit on scene complexity. The player can only be next to so many objects at once, and everything that's not near the player is cheaper to render, so framerate tends to even out. It's far from a guarantee, of course, but LOD is the first line of defense for maintaining the framerate. For AI, however, the techniques we'd really like to use often aren't feasible to run on more than a small handful of NPCs at once, and a cluster of them can easily blow our CPU time budget. There's no "LOD threshold distance" we could pick which would respect our budget *and* give most visible characters the detail we want.

So we use LOD. But it's not "how AI works."

What if LOD was smarter? What if it didn't even use distances, but instead could determine, with uncanny precision, how "important" each character was? What if it could read the player's mind, and tell the game exactly when to start using high-quality collision avoidance for a character, and when to stop? What if it knew which characters the players remembered, and which characters they had forgotten? And what if its LOD selections *always* respected the CPU time budget when NPCs decided to cluster around the player, but always made good use of the time available when they didn't?

Well, then, we could *trust* LOD. We could use techniques as expensive as we wanted, because we could rely on LOD to keep them from blowing our budget. We could move away from the endless task of tuning LOD thresholds, and hardcoding hack after hack to compensate for the endless special cases where our LOD thresholds weren't enough. LOD could become "how AI works."

That, in a nutshell, is the LOD Trader. It can't read the player's mind, but its simple heuristics are light-years beyond distance thresholds in determining how important a character is to the player. Rather than relying on fixed transition rules, it treats the entire space of detail levels—for all the AI features we'd like to control—as a puzzle to be solved each frame. It attempts to maximize the realism of the game simulation without going over the computation budget, and does it in a remarkably short period of time (tens of microseconds).

It's not magical. Its heuristics are far from infallible, and the optimality of its LOD solutions is approximate. But it is worlds beyond distance-based LOD, and the first time it outsmarts you—its LOD reductions becoming subtle and then invisible—you'll wonder a bit.

14.2 Defining the Problem

The first thing to do when attacking a problem like "optimal LOD selection" is to figure out what we mean by *optimal*. The graphics guys don't need to do this, because their LOD selections can be made *perfectly*—they can transition far enough away that they're not giving up any realism. But every detail reduction we make is going to potentially reduce realism, so we need to define, in a numeric sense, what we're trying to maximize, and what our constraints are. We need to come up with a metric, a system of units for measurement of realism. Yikes.

Well, let's grab the bull by the horns. I claim that what we're trying to do is pick a detail level for each AI feature, for each character, to minimize the *probability* that the player will notice an issue, an unrealistic reduction in detail. This helps nail things down, because we all know all about probabilities and how to compare and do arithmetic with them. In this model, Choice A won't be "a little less realistic" than Choice B, but will rather be "a little less likely to be noticed." We'll refer to the event of the player actually noticing an issue as a

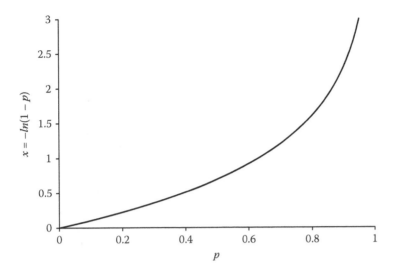

Figure 14.1

Logarithmic probability compared to linear probability.

Break in Realism (BIR). A BIR only occurs when the player notices the issue; just reducing the detail of an entity isn't a BIR if she doesn't notice it as unrealistic.

14.2.1 Diving Into X-Space

Let's make things a little cleverer, though. Suppose that the probability of the user noticing that some entity is unrealistic is p. Rather than work with that number directly, we'll work with the number $x = -\log(1-p)$. That's the negative logarithm (base whatever, let's use the traditional e) of the *complement* of the probability—the probability of getting away with it, of the user *not* noticing. A plot of p versus x is shown in Figure 14.1. As p goes up, x goes up. If p is zero, x is zero; as p approaches 1, x approaches infinity. (The inverse equation is $p = 1 - e^{-x}$.)

Why this complication? Well, actually, it's a simplification; x turns out to be much better-behaved than p. First, if we have two potential sources of unrealistic events, with (independent) probabilities of being noticed p_1 and p_2, and we want to know the total probability p_{tot} of the user noticing either one, that's $p_{tot} = p_1 + p_2 - p_1 p_2$, not especially nice. For three sources it gets even uglier: $p_{tot} = p_1 + p_2 + p_3 - p_1 p_2 - p_1 p_3 - p_2 p_3 + p_1 p_2 p_3$. In contrast, $x_{tot} = x_1 + x_2 + x_3$. Second, this transformation gives us a better interpretation of phrases like "twice as unrealistic." If some event has probability $p_1 = 0.6$ of being noticed, and some other event is "twice as unrealistic" as p_1, what is its probability? Clearly it can't be 1.2—that's not a valid probability. But in x-space things work out fine: $x_2 = 2x_1$, which leads to $x_1 = 0.91$, $x_2 = 1.82$, $p_2 = 0.84$. What is 0.84? It's the probability of noticing it either time, if the first event happened twice. It's extremely useful to be able to describe probabilities relative to each other in that sort of an intuitive way, because it's a lot easier to do that than to determine absolute probabilities. x-space gives us well-behaved addition and multiplication, which (as we'll see later) are crucial to the LOD Trader. In practice, there's actually very little reason to work with p at all.

14.3 Criticality and Probability

The next thing we have to look at is what we'll call the *criticality* of a character. That represents how "critical" the character's realism is to the realism of the scene as a whole—or, if you like, how critical the player is likely to be about the character's detail level. In a sense, that's what distance stood for when we were using distance-based LOD: All else being equal, a closer character is more critical to the scene than a farther character.

But all else is *not* equal. There are other things to use in sussing out criticality. It would be great if we could hook up eye trackers and EEGs and Ouija boards to the player, but even without that, there's plenty of metrics we can pull from the game to help estimate the criticality of a given entity to the player at a given time.

Before we go further, though, there's a really key thing about BIRs, and about criticality, to realize: not all unrealism is alike. Consider two characters. One is a suspected assassin who the player has been following at a distance for some time. The other is a random villager crossing the road a few feet ahead of the player. Both characters are *important*, in a sense. The first character is clearly the object of the player's conscious attention; if we can only afford high-quality path planning for one character, it had better be that one, because the player is more likely to notice if he's wandering randomly. But the second one occupies more screen space, and possibly more of the player's visual attention—if we can only afford high-quality locomotion IK for one, it should probably be that one.

14.3.1 A Field Guide to BIR's

It's tempting to throw in the towel at this point, concluding that there are as many kinds of unrealism as there are AI features whose detail level we'd like to move up and down. But I think there's a small set of categories that nearly all BIR's fall into. Any given reduced detail level will create the potential for a BIR in at least one of these categories, and sometimes more. The reason to categorize things like this is because each category of BIR can have its own criticality model.

14.3.1.1 Unrealistic State

An *unrealistic state (US)* BIR is the most immediate and obvious type of BIR, where a character's immediately observable simulation is wrong. A character eating from an empty plate, or running in place against a wall, or wearing a bucket on his head creates the potential for an unrealistic state BIR. (Not a *certainty*, mind you—the player might not be looking.) US's don't require any long period of observation, only momentary attention, and the attention need not be voluntary—the eye tends to be drawn to such things.

14.3.1.2 Fundamental Discontinuity

A *fundamental discontinuity (FD)* BIR is a little more subtle, but not by much: it occurs when a character's current state is incompatible with the player's memory of his past state. A character disappearing while momentarily around a corner, or having been frozen in place for hours while the player was away, or regaining the use of a limb that had been broken creates the potential for a fundamental discontinuity BIR. These situations can cause US BIR's too, of course. But even if the character is not observed while they happen, as long as the player remembers the old state and later returns, the potential for an FD BIR remains.

14.3.1.3 Unrealistic Long-Term Behavior

An *unrealistic long-term behavior (ULTB)* BIR is the subtlest: It occurs only when an extended period of observation reveals problems with a character's behavior. A character wandering randomly instead of having goal-driven behaviors is the most common example of an unrealistic long-term behavior BIR, but so is a car that never runs out of gas. At any given time, only a small handful of characters are likely to be prone to ULTB BIR's.

14.4 Modeling Criticality

Let's see about coming up with criticality models for these different categories. Each model calculates a *criticality score* as the product of several factors, some of which are shared between multiple models.

For unrealistic state, the factors are observability and attention. *Observability* comes closest to graphical LOD: it measures how feasible it is for the player to see the character in question. *Attention* is self-evident: it estimates how much attention the player is paying to a particular character. As you might guess, it's the most difficult factor to estimate.

For fundamental discontinuity, the two related factors are memory and return time. *Memory* estimates how effectively the player has memorized facts about a character, and how likely they are to notice changes to the character. *Return time* acts as a modifier to the memory factor: It estimates how attenuated the player's memory for the character will be when she returns to the character, or even if she will ever return at all.

For unrealistic long-term behavior, the three factors are attention, memory, and duration. Attention and memory have already been introduced (note that the return time factor is not acting on memory here); the last one, *duration*, simply refers to how much time and attention the player has devoted to that character.

There's the cast of characters. Now let's come up with actual equations for each one. Note that later factors will often use earlier factors in their input; the order we've listed them in is a good order to calculate them in.

Before we go into these, though, we need to introduce a tool which will be used in a lot of them: the *exponential moving average (EMA)*. The EMA is a method for smoothing and averaging an ongoing sequence of measurements. Given an input function $F(t)$ we produce the output function $G(t)$. We initialize $(0) = F(0)$, and then at each time t we update $G(t)$ as $G(t) = (1-\alpha)F(t) + \alpha G(t - \Delta t)$, where Δt is the timestep since the last measurement. The α in that equation is calculated as $\alpha = e^{-k \cdot \Delta t}$, where k is the *convergence rate* (higher values lead to faster changes in the average). You can tune k to change the smoothness of the EMA, and how closely it tracks the input function. We're going to use the EMA a *lot* in these models, so it's a good idea to familiarize yourself with it (Figure 14.2).

14.4.1 Observability

This is a straightforward one—an out-of-view character will have an observability of 0, a nearby and fully visible character will have an observability of 1, and visible but faraway characters will have an observability somewhere in the middle. For character i, you can calculate this factor as proportional to the amount of screen space (or number of pixels) p_i taken up by the character, divided by some "saturation size" p_{sat} referring to how big a character needs to get before there's no difficulty observing them, and limited to 1: $O_i = min(p_i / p_{sat}, 1)$.

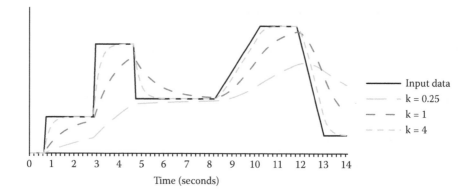

Figure 14.2

The exponential moving average of a data set, with various convergence rates.

We used the amount of screen space taken up by a fully visible character 4 meters away from the camera as p_{sat}. A smaller saturation value may be more appropriate for games intended for high-definition displays.

14.4.2 Attention

As mentioned earlier, attention is the most difficult factor to estimate. There are two steps in determining attention: estimating attempted attention, and applying the effect of interference.

As a first pass, attempted attention $\hat{A}_i$ can be calculated as the EMA of observability: $\hat{A}_i(t) = \alpha \hat{A}_i(t - \Delta t) + (1 - \alpha) O_i(t)$. For observability, you should tune k to have a rapid falloff; we used $k = 2$, which provides a 95% falloff in 1.5 seconds.

You can mix other things into the attempted attention model to improve its accuracy, though. One player behavior strongly associated with attention is *focusing*, where the player attempts to keep the character centered in the camera view. This can be calculated as the EMA of the dot product between the camera's forward vector and the vector to the character, then multiplied by observability. The convergence rate k should be much lower for this term. Other, more game-specific sources can be drawn on for attempted attention as well, such as how much of a threat the character is, or how rapid his motions are. The weighted sum is then used as the attempted attention estimate. For the simple observability-and-focusing model, we found weights of 0.7 and 0.3, respectively, predicted attention well.

The player's attention is not an unlimited resource; the more things they need to concentrate on, the less well they concentrate on each one. Once attempted attention has been calculated for all characters, you should sum the factors up, producing the *total attentional load* L. To compensate for the nonlinearity of this interference effect (as well as interference from sources outside the game), you should also add a constant *ambient attentional load* to L. The actual attention estimate for each character is then the ratio of their attempted attention to the total attentional load: $A_i = \dfrac{\hat{A}_i}{L}$, where $L = \hat{A}_{amb} + \sum_{j=1}^{n} A_j$.
The value $\hat{A}_{amb}$ is a difficult factor to tune; I would suggest setting it such that it represents about 1/3 of L during the most attention-intensive situations in your game. Increasing it

will tend to bias resources towards background characters; decreasing it will bias resources towards foreground characters.

14.4.3 Memory

Our model of memory is a simple one based on cognitive models for an experimental memory task known as *associative recognition*, and on a phenomenon known as *retroactive interference*. In general, a player's memory M_i of a character will tend toward their current attention A_i for that character over time. While memorizing (that is, while memory is increasing), the convergence rate will be a fixed $k = k_m$. While forgetting (that is, while memory is decreasing), we'll use a different convergence rate $k = k_f L$, where L is the total attentional load. So it's an EMA again, but with $k = k_m$ if $M_i < A_i$, and $k = k_f L$ if $M_i > A_i$. We used $k_m = 0.6$ and $k_f = 0.001$, which (for our highest observed attentional load) resulted in a 95% memorization rate in about 5 seconds, and a 50% forgetting rate in 10 seconds under a high attentional load. The latter tended to overestimate long-term retention of memory for characters; this wasn't a problem for us, but you may need to tune that factor upward.

14.4.4 Return Time

Return time is much more objective, because it estimates a player's actions rather than her thoughts. It's somewhat misnamed: the output is not an expected number of seconds until the player's return, but rather an expected attenuation factor to current memory at the moment the player does return, as well as to the probability of the player ever returning at all. It's based on something known as the *Weibull hazard function*. The derivation is rather involved, but the resultant equation is $R_i = k(L)^{-k} e^{Lt_0} \Gamma(k, Lt_0)$. L is the expected future attentional load (you can either use the current attentional load, or smooth it with an EMA), and t_0 is the time since the character was last visible (that is, had an observability greater than 0). k is a tweakable parameter which you can experimentally determine by fitting observed return times to a Weibull distribution; the value we determined was approximately 0.8, and we think that's unlikely to differ much in other games. $\Gamma(s, x)$ is the *upper incomplete gamma function*. Implementations of this function are included in many popular math libraries, including Boost.Math.

14.4.5 Duration

To finish the criticality model factors on a nice, easy note, duration is the total amount of attentive observation: the integral of $O_i A_i$ over time. That is, $D_i(t) = D_i(t - \Delta t) + O_i A_i \Delta t$.

14.4.6 Modeling Costs

Compared to criticality scores, costs are much more straightforward and objective to model. Simply set up your game so that a hundred or so characters are simulating using a particular detail level, then compare the profiler output with a run using a different detail level.

14.5 LOD's and BIR's

Again, the reason to categorize BIR's at all is because each category can have its own criticality score. Having a bit of foot skate is probably less noticeable than running in place against a wall: The latter behavior is more obvious. We will refer to it as having higher *audacity*—that is, a lower LOD will be more *audaciously* unrealistic. But given two characters, if one is twice as likely to be noticed foot skating as the other, it is also twice as likely to be noticed running in place as the other. We don't need to have separate criticality models for the two behaviors, because the same factors affect both. So for a particular category of BIR (in this case, unrealistic state) each character has a criticality score, and each detail level (in this case, a type of local steering which can lead to running into walls) will have an audacity score. To sum up, we have three categories of BIRs, three criticality scores per character, and three audacity scores per detail level. (Note that we're only looking at one AI feature for now—in this example, local steering. We'll move to multiple features later.)

By the way, that "twice as likely" mentioned above should remind you of Section 14.2.1, and not by accident. For a single BIR category, we can think of a detail level's audacity score in that category as a base probability in x-space (for some "standard-ly critical character"), and a character's criticality score in that category as a multiplier to it, the product being the probability of *that* character using *that* detail level causing a BIR in *that* category.

But it gets better! Or, at least, more elegantly mathy! Since we're assuming independence, the probability of that character/detail level combination causing a BIR in *any* category is the sum of the products over all three categories. If we stick the detail level's audacity scores for all categories into a vector, call it the *audacity vector A*, and the character's criticality scores for all categories into another vector, call it the *criticality vector C*, the total BIR probability for the combination is given by the dot product $A \cdot C$. Linear algebra—it's not just for geometry anymore!

14.6 The LOD Trader

Now that we have our model, it's time to introduce the LOD Trader algorithm itself. We'll be adding more capabilities to it through the rest of the article; this initial version controls a single LOD feature (say, how pathfinding is performed) with multiple available detail levels, and limits a single resource (say, CPU time).

As you might guess from the name, the LOD Trader is based on a stock trader metaphor. Its "portfolio" consists of all the *current* detail levels for all characters. The LOD Trader's goal is to pick a portfolio that minimizes the total probability of a BIR. Of course, the best possible portfolio would be one where all characters had the highest detail level; but it must additionally limit the total cost of the portfolio to its available resources, so that's (usually) not an option.

Each time the LOD Trader runs, it evaluates its current portfolio and decides on a set of trades, switching some characters to a higher detail level and other characters to a lower detail level, as their relative criticalities and the available resources change. Remember, the total BIR probability for a character being simulated at a particular detail level is the dot product of the character's criticality vector and the detail level's audacity vector. So the LOD Trader will try to pick detail levels that have low audacity scores corresponding to a character's high criticality scores.

Note that for a given trade, we can find a *relative* cost, but also a *relative audacity* which is the difference in the two detail levels' audacity vectors. Just as the absolute BIR probability for a particular detail level is the dot product of the character's criticality vector and the detail level's audacity vector, the relative BIR probability for a particular trade is the dot product of the criticality vector with the change in audacity. We'll refer to increases in BIR probabilities as *upgrades*, and to decreases in BIR probabilities as *downgrades*.

The heuristic the LOD Trader uses to guide its decisions is a simple *value*-based one: units of realism improvement divided by units of resource cost. If a character is simulated at a low detail level, the value of upgrading it to a high detail level is the relative reduction in the total probability of a BIR divided by the relative increase in resource cost. Valuable upgrades will have a large reduction in BIR probability and a low increase in cost. Likewise, if a character is at a high detail level, the value of downgrading it to a lower detail level is the relative increase in the total probability of a BIR divided by the relative reduction in cost; valuable downgrades will increase BIR probability only slightly and decrease the cost by a lot. To keep the math simple, we'll toss in a negative sign, so that upgrade values are positive, and more valuable upgrades have larger magnitude values. For downgrades, values are positive as well, but the most valuable downgrades will have *smaller* magnitudes. (The exception, which should be handled specially. Under some circumstances, a detail upgrade will result in a reduction in cost, or a detail downgrade may result in an increase in cost. The former should always be chosen; the latter never should.)

During a single run, the LOD Trader runs one or more iterations. In each iteration, it hypothesizes making a set of trades (both upgrades and downgrades) that would respect the resource limits and that might result in an overall reduction in BIR probability. If the hypothetical set of trades does, in fact, reduce BIR probability, the trades are actually performed, and the trader continues to iterate, to try to find additional trades to make. Once it finds a hypothetical set of trades which does *not* reduce BIR probability, it stops (and does not make those trades).

The algorithm for choosing the hypothetical set of trades is simple. First it considers upgrades. It repeatedly picks the most valuable available upgrade to add to its set of trades until it has *over*spent its resource budget. Then, it repeatedly picks the most valuable available downgrade to add to its set of trades until it has not overspent its resource budget. Upgrades and downgrades are stored in priority queues to reduce the search cost. Pseudocode for the LOD Trader is in Listing 14.1; remember that this is the initial version, and we'll add more features and improve performance later.

14.6.1 Multiple Features

One of the most useful effects of the multicategory criticality modeling is the ability to control different *kinds* of LOD at the same time. For instance, we can control pathfinding quality (the quality of which primarily affects the probability of a ULTB BIR) and hand IK (which affects the probability of a US BIR). Put differently, we'd like to control multiple *features* (AI systems whose detail is set on a per-character basis). Of course, we could do that by running multiple LOD Traders, one for each feature. But then we'd have to give each one a separate budget; there'd be no way to automatically shift resources between pathfinding and IK as one or the other became important, or to trade a downgrade in the pathfinding quality of one character for an upgrade in the IK quality of another.

Another problem with the multi-Trader approach is that certain features might depend on each other. For instance, we might control both a character's basic behavior (goal-driven or just standing around) and his pathfinding (high quality, low quality, or disabled). Goal-driven behavior and disabled pathfinding, of course, aren't compatible

Listing 14.1. Initial code for the LOD Trader, supporting only one LOD feature and one resource type.

```
def runLODTrader(characters, lodLevels, availableResource):
    acceptedTrades = []
    while True:
        upgrades, downgrades = calcAvailableTrades(characters,
lodLevels) # returns p-queues, sorted by value
        hypTrades = []
        charactersWithTrades = []
        hypBenefit = 0
        hypAvailableResource = availableResource
        while not upgrades.empty() and availableResource > 0:
            upgrade = upgrades.pop()
            hypTrades.append(upgrade)
            charactersWithTrades.append(upgrade.character)
            hypAvailableResource -= upgrade.costIncrease
            hypBenefit += upgrade.probDecrease
        while not downgrades.empty() and availableResource < 0:
            downgrade = downgrades.pop()
            if downgrade.character in charactersWithTrades: continue
            hypTrades.append(downgrade)
            charactersWithTrades.append(downgrade.character)
            hypAvailableResource += downgrade.costDecrease
            hypBenefit -= downgrade.probIncrease
        if hypAvailableResource >= 0 and hypBenefit > 0:
            acceptedTrades += hypothesizedTrades
            availableResource = hypAvailableResource
        else
            return acceptedTrades
```

as detail levels, but there would be no effective way to coordinate the two traders to avoid that result.

Instead, we let a single LOD Trader balance detail levels of all the features at the same time. A character's current "state" as seen by the LOD Trader will not be a single detail level, but will be the combination of their current detail levels for *all* the features. We refer to a set of levels for all features, which respects all the inter-feature constraints, as a *feature solution*. Rather than picking individual feature transitions, we will pick *feature solution transitions* from one feature solution to another, each of which may result in several feature transitions. For each feature solution, we'll precompute and store a list of possible upgrade transitions and possible downgrade transitions, so that we know which ones to look at for a character currently at any particular feature solution.

If the set of features is small, this has little impact on the algorithm; the only major change is the need to check that we don't pick multiple upgrade or downgrade transitions for a single character. However, the number of feature solutions increases exponentially with the number of features. Since we would have to evaluate every character/feature solution combination and insert it into our priority queues, this could result in a lot of computation, and a *lot* of memory usage. Most of this work would be wasted, because it would be spent on evaluating lots of expensive upgrades for lots of faraway, unimportant characters—ones we should know we won't upgrade in *any* way, given their teeny criticality vectors.

Listing 14.2. Expanding a character.

```
def expandCharacter(char, transType):
    bestRatio = None; bestTrans = None
    for trans in char.featureSolution.availableTransitions[transType]:
        ratio = dotProduct(char.C, trans.A)/trans.cost
        if isBetterRatio(ratio, bestRatio):
            bestRatio = ratio; bestTrans = trans
    return bestRatio, bestTrans
```

14.6.2 The Expansion Queue

Instead, we'll use a new, lazier strategy. Instead of a priority queue of upgrade transitions, we'll start with a priority queue of *characters*; we'll refer to this as the *expansion queue*. The sort key we'll use for the expansion queue will be the *expansion heuristic*, which estimates the *best possible* value that could *possibly* be attainable by *any* transition for that character. This value represents an upper limit on transition value for each character, and may be over-optimistic, but it will never be pessimistic; in this sense it is similar to an admissible heuristic for A* search. We'll select upgrade transitions by "expanding" the character at the front of the queue (the one with the highest expansion heuristic) into all of its possible upgrade transitions, and selecting the most valuable one. The pseudocode for expanding a character is shown in Listing 14.2.

Because the heuristic may be over-optimistic, we can't guarantee that the character at the front of the expansion queue actually has the most valuable upgrade transition among all characters. To compensate for this, we will continue expanding characters from the expansion queue, even after we've overspent our resource budget. Once we're overspent, each time we expand a character and choose a new upgrade for our set of hypothetical trades, we'll then repeatedly remove and discard the lowest-valued trade from the upgrades, until we're only overspending by one trade (that is, removing another lowest-valued trade would make us underspend). To make this efficient, we'll store the set of chosen hypothesized upgrades itself as a priority queue, ordered so that the front element has the *lowest* value. Often, the just-expanded, just-inserted upgrade will itself be the lowest-value trade, and will be removed immediately after being added.

When can we stop doing this? When the worst-value transition already picked—the one at the front of the hypothesized upgrades queue—has a higher value than the heuristically predicted value at the front of the expansion queue. Because of the admissibility of the heuristic, we know at this point that we'll never find a better upgrade than we've already picked, so we can stop without expanding any more characters, and the chosen set of upgrades is the ones remaining in the hypothesized upgrades queue. In practice, this happens quite quickly.

The downgrade phase works analogously: we keep an expansion queue sorted by smallest possible value, and pick the lowest value downgrade for each expanded character, inserting it into our hypothesized downgrade queue. Once our resource constraint is no longer violated, after each pick, we continue to pop largest-value downgrades off the hypothesized downgrades queue until popping the next one would violate the resource constraint. Once the character at the front of the expansion queue has a larger heuristic value than the downgrade at the front of the hypothesized downgrades queue, we stop expanding characters.

14.6.3 Pruning Transitions

Before we get to the best-possible-value heuristic, let's look at a certain class of feature solution transitions. These transitions are what one might call "penny-wise and pound-careless." Or perhaps one might technically refer to them as *stupid*. For instance, a feature transition that upgraded animation IK to the highest possible quality, but kept collision avoidance turned off, would be stupid. It's *allowed*, yes, but it should never be chosen; well before you decide to spend CPU time on high-quality IK, you should first decide to keep the character from walking through walls. The possibility of stupid transitions isn't a problem for the LOD Trader, because it won't ever choose them, but it does spend time evaluating them. As it turns out, a lot of solution transitions—well over half of them, in our experience—are stupid.

What typifies a stupid transition? In a mathematical sense, it's being "strictly dominated" by other transitions; that is, regardless of circumstances, there's always a more valuable transition. Let's examine how we go about identifying those, so we can ignore them.

Remember, the value (for upgrades) is probability benefit—the dot product of criticality and audacity—divided by relative cost increase. To put this in equation form, for switching character i from feature solution α to feature solution β, we'll refer to the change in resource cost as $r_{\alpha,\beta} = r_\beta - r_\alpha$, the change in audacity as $A_{\alpha,\beta} = A_\beta - A_\alpha$, and the resultant value as $V_{i,\alpha,\beta} = -\left(A_{\alpha,\beta} \cdot C_i\right) / r_{\alpha,\beta}$. (Remember the negative sign—we want positive values for upgrades, even though higher quality is lower audacity.) That depends on the criticality vector C_i. The transition from α to β is "stupid" if, for *any possible* criticality vector, there's some *other*, better feature solution χ such that $V_{i,\alpha,\beta} < V_{i,\alpha,\chi}$.

For a given feature transition, figuring out whether it is strictly dominated can be formulated as a linear programming problem. Alternatively, you can just generate a large number of random criticality vectors, and find the best transition for each. Any transition which isn't chosen at least once is assumed to be strictly dominated, and removed from the list of upgrades to evaluate at that starting feature solution. For stupid downgrades the same thing is done but the "best" transitions are the ones with the smallest-magnitude value.

14.6.4 The Expansion Heuristic

Returning to the heuristic, we'll use it for the expansion queue—that is, estimating the best possible value for any transition for each character. Let's look at that value formula again: $V_{i,\alpha,\beta} = \left(A_{\alpha,\beta} \cdot C_i\right) / r_{\alpha,\beta}$. Rearranged, it's $V_{i,\alpha,\beta} = C_i \cdot W_{\alpha,\beta}$, where $W_{\alpha,\beta} = A_{\alpha,\beta} / r_{\alpha,\beta}$. For a particular starting feature solution α, we can gather the W-vectors for all upgrade transitions into a matrix $\mathbf{W}_\alpha = \left[W_{\alpha,\beta}, W_{\alpha,\gamma}, \cdots\right]$. Then we can prune it, removing any column that does not have at least one entry greater than the corresponding entry in a different column. Once we have the W-matrix stored for each starting feature solution, we can calculate the heuristic value quite quickly, as the maximum entry in the vector $C_i \mathbf{W}_\alpha$. We do the same thing for downgrade transitions, using a separate matrix for those. (Remember, for downgrades we want smaller values, so we prune columns that do not have at least one *lower* entry.) This value heuristic calculation is shown in the pseudocode of Listing 14.3.

Listing 14.3. Calculating the value heuristic for a character.

```
def calcValueHeuristic(char, transType):
    elems = matrixMul(char.C, char.featureSolution.W)
    if transType == 'upgrade': return max(elems)
    else: return min(elems)
```

14.6.5 Multiple Resources

CPU time may not be our only resource constraint. For instance, suppose one of the features we'd like to control is whether a character remembers other characters who have been friendly or hostile towards him. That could easily become a large RAM sink, so we'd like to keep our memory usage under a particular budget as well. This is a situation where we might be able to use multiple LOD Traders, one for each resource type, but it's possible that a single feature might have ramifications for more than one resource. As before, we'd like a single trader to do all the work of balancing things. The cost of a detail level will now be vector-valued, as will the total cost of a feature solution and the relative cost of a feature solution transition.

The first thing we have to do is adapt our value heuristic. "Dividing by cost" doesn't work anymore because cost is a vector. We'll use a *resource multiplier vector M* to generate a scalar metric for cost. During the upgrade phase, the resource multiplier for each resource type is the reciprocal of the amount of that resource, which is currently unused. If CPU time is at a premium but there's plenty of free memory, the resource multiplier vector will have a larger entry for CPU than RAM. In case a resource is neither over- nor underspent, it should have a large but not infinite resource multiplier. During the downgrade phase, the resource multiplier is directly proportional to the amount of overspending; resources that are not overspent have a resource multiplier of 0. The resource multiplier vector is recalculated before each upgrade and each downgrade phase, but not during an upgrade or downgrade phase.

Next, we need to adapt our stopping criteria. Rather than picking upgrades such that the only resource is overspent by a single upgrade, we will pick upgrades until *any* resource is overspent. We will then pick downgrades until *no* resources are overspent.

We also need to adapt our definition of stupid feature solutions, and our expansion heuristic. When determining whether a feature solution will ever be chosen, we need to check it against not only a large number of random criticality vectors, but also resource multiplier vectors. And when generating $W_{\alpha,\beta}$, we need to maximize it over all possible resource multiplier vectors: $W_{\alpha,\beta} = A_{\alpha,\beta} / \left(\min_M M \cdot r_{\alpha,\beta} \right)$. (For both of these, you should consider only *normalized* resource multipliers.) In order to get the best performance results out of both feature solution pruning and the expansion heuristic, you should come up with expected limits on the ratios between resource multipliers, and clip actual resource multipliers to these limits.

Finally, note that some feature solution transitions will have both positive and negative resource costs: these should be allowed as upgrades, but not allowed as downgrades.

Listing 14.4. Making the expansion queue over all characters.

```
def makeExpansionQueue(characters, M, transType):
    if transType == 'upgrade': expansionQueue = maxQueue()
    else: expansionQueue = minQueue()
    for char in characters:
        valueHeuristic = calcValueHeuristic(char, M, transType)
        expansionQueue.insert(char, valueHeuristic)
```

Listing 14.5. Final pseudocode for the LOD trader, supporting multiple features and resource types.

```
def runLODTrader(characters, availableResources):
    acceptedTrades = []
    while True:
        M = calcResourceMultiplier(availableResources)
        hypUpgrades, hypAvailableResources =
selectTransitions(characters, M, 'upgrade', availableResources)
        M = calcResourceMultiplier(availableResources)
        hypDowngrades, hypAvailableResources =
selectTransitions(characters, M, 'downgrade', hypAvailableResources)
        hypTrades = hypUpgrades + hypDowngrades
        if calcTotalBenefit(hypTrades) > 0:
            acceptedTrades += hypTrades
            availableResources = hypAvailableResources
        else:
            return acceptedTrades
def selectTransitions(characters, M, transType, availableResources):
    expansionQueue = makeExpansionQueue(characters, M, transType)
    if transType == 'upgrade': transitionHeap = minQueue()
    else: transitionHeap = maxQueue()
    while availableResources.allGreaterEqual(0) or
isBetterRatio(expansionQueue.peekKey(), transitionHeap.peekKey()):
        char = expansionQueue.popValue()
        bestRatio, bestTrans = expandCharacter(char, M, transType)
        transitionHeap.insert(bestTrans, bestRatio)
        availableResources -= bestTrans.costs
        while (availableResources + transitionHeap.peekValue().costs).
anyLess(0):
            discardedTrans = transitionHeap.popValue()
            availableResources += discardedTrans.costs
    return transitionHeap.values(), availableResources
```

14.6.6 Putting it All Together

Listing 14.5. shows the updated pseudocode for multiple features and resources.

14.6.7 Other Extensions to the LOD Trader

In addition to constraining which levels for different features can be used together, it's possible to constrain which levels of a single feature can transition to which other features. For instance, you might transition a character from prerecorded animation to fully dynamic motion, but not be able to transition back from dynamic motion to prerecorded animation. This can be done simply by discarding feature solution transitions that include such a transition.

It's also possible to attach costs and audacities to a feature transition itself, instead of just to feature levels. Attaching costs to transitions can be useful if the transitioning process itself requires nontrivial computation; attaching audacity can be useful if the transition is liable to produce a visible "pop" or if it involves a loss of character information which could later lead to a FD or ULTB BIR.

In some situations it's useful to introduce the concept of a "null" detail level for a particular LOD feature. For instance, the "standing around" behavior detail level would only be compatible with the "null" locomotion detail level, and the "doing stuff" behavior detail level would be compatible with all locomotion detail levels *except* the null level.

An unusual but useful application of the LOD Trader is as an alternative to the "simulation bubble" often used to delete faraway characters. This is done by means of an "existence" LOD feature, with "yes" and "no" levels, where the "no" level is compatible with all other LOD features being "null" and has zero audacity and zero cost, but where the transition from "yes" to "no" itself has US and FD audacity. When a character transitions to the "no" existence level, it is removed.

Another unusual but useful application is to consider "save space" as an additional resource. This can be constrained only when the game is about to be saved, and ensures that the most useful and memorable bits of game state are kept around when saving to a device with limited space.

The LOD Trader can also be leveraged in multiplayer games, simply by adding up the criticality for a given character based on all players currently observing that character. Because of the additive nature of the x-space probabilities, this will result in correct estimation and minimization of BIR probability. Additionally, the LOD Trader can be used to ration network bandwidth by controlling update rates and update detail for different characters; in this situation, a separate LOD Trader instance is run for each player.

Finally, not all characters controlled by the LOD Trader need to have the same LOD features; you need only maintain different transition sets for each "kind" of character, and then have the LOD Trader control, say, both pedestrians and stationary shopkeepers. In fact, not all "characters" controlled by the LOD Trader need be characters at all: it can heterogeneously manage humans, vehicles, destructible objects, and anything and everything which can benefit from criticality-driven LOD control.

14.7 The LOD Trader in Practice

We've had great results with the LOD Trader. We implemented it in a free-roaming game involving hundreds of characters, having it control eight separate features with hundreds of potential feature solutions. We also implemented conventional distance-based LOD picking, so that we could compare the two. The trickiest part of the LOD Trader implementation process was tuning the criticality metrics and audacity vectors, due to their subjectivity. This is an area where playtester feedback could be extremely helpful.

As expected, distance-based LOD picking was only marginally acceptable. In order to guarantee a reasonable framerate, it was necessary to set the threshold distances so close that things like low-quality locomotion could be clearly seen, particularly in sparsely populated areas of the game world and where there were long, unobstructed lines of sight. The LOD Trader, in contrast, was very effective at maintaining framerate in the most crowded situations, and in sparse areas it simulated most characters at the highest LOD.

A controlled, blinded experimental study verified out this impression: Viewers shown videos of the game running with distance-based LOD picking were consistently more likely to experience BIRs, and to experience them more often, than viewers shown videos of the game running with the LOD Trader [Sunshine-Hill 11].

The LOD Trader itself had very good performance: its average execution time was 57 microseconds per frame, or 0.17% of the target frame time. Its memory usage was 500 kB for the transition data and 48 bytes per entity, both of which could easily be halved by picking narrower datatypes, with no reduction in functionality.

14.8 Conclusions

As mentioned in the introduction, the LOD Trader isn't magical. It can't read the player's mind. Its criticality models are approximate, and often very inaccurate.

But that's okay. The goal of the LOD Trader is not to make wildly audacious detail reductions and get away with them. Rather, the goal is to be clever enough to do detail reduction in the *right places* in those moments when detail reduction has to happen *somewhere*. In those moments, the question is not *whether* to reduce LOD but *how* to reduce LOD without causing glaring problems, and we just can't depend on distance-based LOD picking to do that.

And we *need* to be able to depend on our LOD picker. Because detail reduction is always, *always* going to be needed. We'll never have enough computational resources to do all the things we want to do. And when we're not doing detail reduction at runtime, that just means we're doing it at development time, throwing away good techniques because we don't know if we'll always be able to afford them. That's the real benefit of the LOD Trader: the power to implement AI techniques as lavishly detailed as we can imagine, and others as massively scalable as we can devise, with the confidence that our game will be able to leverage each one when it counts the most.

References

[Sunshine-Hill 11] B. Sunshine-Hill. *Perceptually Driven Simulation* (Doctoral dissertation). Available online (http://repository.upenn.edu/edissertations/435), 2011.

15

Runtime Compiled C++ for Rapid AI Development

Doug Binks, Matthew Jack, and Will Wilson

15.1 Introduction

Scripting languages have always been a foundation of rapid AI development but with the increasing demands of AI, their performance drawbacks are becoming ever more problematic. On the other hand, traditional C++ development approaches generally lead to lengthy compile and link times, which limit the amount of iteration and testing that programmers can undertake. Though development tools are progressing in this area, developers still need to run the build and load content to see the end result, and edit-and-continue style approaches do not work for all codebases or changes.

In this article we demonstrate how the same fast iteration times and error-handling can be achieved using pure C++ through a novel approach, which we call Runtime

Compiled C++ (RCC++). RCC++ allows developers to change code while the game is running, and have the code compiled and linked into the game rapidly with state preserved. Programmers can thus get feedback on their changes in seconds rather than minutes or more. The technique has been used in the development of AAA games at Crytek, and gives similar results to Hot Reload as seen in *Epic's Unreal Engine 4*. The RCC++ code is available as a permissively licensed open source project on GitHub and the accompanying disk [Jack, Binks, Rutkowski 11].

15.2 Alternative Approaches

A variety of alternative approaches can be used to achieve fast iteration times in games, each with their own pros and cons. Overall we believe that none offer the main benefits of Runtime Compiled C++, and many techniques can be enhanced by using RCC++ alongside them.

15.2.1 Scripting Languages

Scripting languages provide perhaps the most common solution to achieving fast iteration. A recent games engine survey showed Lua to be the foremost scripting language in game development [DeLoura 09], though UnrealScript [Epic 12a] likely represents a substantial proportion of the market, given the size of the Unreal Engine community. Despite the popularity of scripting languages, we feel that they have a number of issues when used for core features, namely integration overheads, performance, tools and debugging, and low level support such as vector operations and multithreading. In fact, many of the game engine implementations we have encountered do not permit runtime editing of game scripts, which reduces the benefit of using them considerably.

Games written in C++ need an interface to the scripting language in order to allow features to be implemented. A variety of techniques and methods are available to make this relatively simple, but a recompile and game reload will be forced when an interface change is required.

While script performance is improving, it is still well below that of compiled code such as C++ [Fulgham 12]. Indeed, Facebook moved their PHP script code to pre-compiled C++ using the open source cross compiler HipHop, which they developed to address performance issues. They found significant benefits in terms of reduced CPU overhead and thus expenditure and maintenance of systems [Zao 10]. Garbage collection can also be an issue, with optimized systems even spending several milliseconds per frame [Shaw 10]. On consoles, Data Execution Protection (DEP) prevents VMs from Just-In-Time (JIT) compiling, limiting an opportunity for performance optimizations offered by cutting-edge VMs running on PC.

Debugging a C++ application that enters a script VM can prove difficult to impossible, and many of the tools developers use on a day-to-day basis, such as performance and memory profilers, also may not have visibility of the internals of a VM in a way that can be traced back to the original source code.

C++ provides easy integration with native instruction sets via assembly language, as well as direct access to memory. This low level support permits developers to target enhanced, yet common, feature sets such as SIMD vector units, multithreading, and coprocessor units such as the Sony PS3's SPUs.

Havok Script (originally Kore Script) was developed out of the motivation of solving some of these issues [Havok 12], providing an optimized VM along with performance improvements, debugger support, and profiling tools.

15.2.2 Visual Studio Edit and Continue

Edit and Continue is a standard feature of Visual Studio for C++ introduced in Visual C++ 6.0, allowing small changes to code to be made while debugging through a technique known as "code patching" [Staheli 98]. However, there are some major limitations, the most critical of which are that you can't make changes to a data type that affect the layout of an object (such as data members of a class), and you can't make changes to optimized code [Microsoft 10].

15.2.3 Multiple Processes

Multiple processes can be used to separate code and state so as to speed compile and load times, with either shared memory, pipes, or more commonly TCP/IP used to communicate between them. This is the fundamental approach used by many console developers with the game running on a console and the editor on a PC, and as used by client/server style multiplayer games. Support for recompiling and reloading of one of the processes can be implemented reasonably simply if the majority of the state lies in the other process, and since there is a clean separation between processes, this can be a convenient approach to take. However, the communication overhead usually limits this to certain applications such as being able to modify the editor, while having the game and its game state still running while the editor process is recompiled and reloaded. Turnaround times can still be relatively long since the executable needs to be compiled, linked, and run.

15.2.4 Data-Driven Approaches

Many game engines provide data-driven systems to enhance the flexibility of their engine, for example the *CryENGINE 3* uses XML files to specify AI behavior selection trees [Crytek 2012]. Since the underlying functionality can be written in C++, this methodology can overcome many of the issues with scripting languages, while providing designers not fluent in programming languages a safe and relatively easy to use environment for developing gameplay. While frameworks such as data-driven behavior trees can allow a good balance to be struck, this approach can descend into implementing a scripting language in XML, with all the associated problems.

15.2.5 Visual Scripting

Visual Scripting systems such as Epic Games' *Unreal Kismet* and Crytek's *CryENGINE* Flow-Graph provide a graphical user interface to game logic [Epic 12b, Crytek 12]. Functionality blocks are typically written in C++ with inputs, outputs, and data members that can be graphically edited and linked to other functional blocks, thus providing the potential for complex systems to be created. This is fundamentally a data-driven system with an enhanced user interface.

15.2.6 Library Reloading

Dynamic link libraries (DLLs, called "shared objects" on Unix variants) can be loaded during runtime, providing an obvious means to allow fast iteration by recompiling and reloading the DLL. A key feature for game developers is that both the Xbox 360 and PS3 consoles support dynamically loaded libraries, as do iOS (for development purposes only—not in released code) and Android. Function and object pointers need to be patched up, and the interfaces to the DLL can't be changed. If the code for the DLL project is large, compile times can be significant limiting the iteration turnaround. Despite the attraction of this approach, in practice the difficulty of splitting up and maintaining a game with many small-sized DLLs, along with the infrastructure required for delay load linking and state preservation, means this approach is rarely used.

15.3 Runtime Compiled C++

Runtime Compiled C++ permits the alteration of compiled C++ code while your game is running. RCC++ uses DLLs, but rather than building an entire project, the runtime compiler only rebuilds and links the minimal source files required. By using loose coupling techniques, dependencies are kept to a minimum. The resulting dynamic library is loaded, and game state is saved and then restored with the new code now being used. Changes to C++ code are thus possible during a gameplay or editor session with a turnaround time of several seconds. Developers do not need to manage multiple project configurations, as the DLLs are constructed automatically on the fly as required. Indeed, the codebase can be built as a single executable. RCC++ can be seen in action in Figure 15.1.

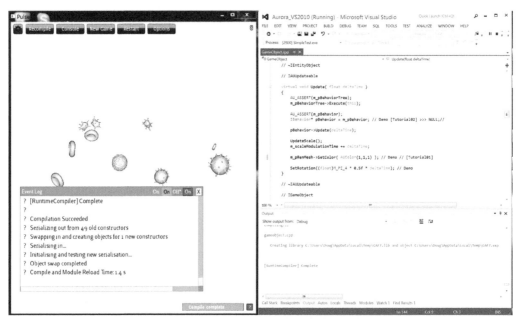

Figure 15.1

The demo game *Pulse* compiling files at runtime after a change, with Visual Studio on the right being used to make the changes. Compiler output goes to both demo event log and Visual Studio Output window to enable navigation to errors with double clicking. Time taken to compile and load changed code is 1.4s as shown by event log in this instance.

Unlike Edit and Continue, RCC++ permits changes to object layout including the addition of entirely new classes, and it works with optimized code as well as debug. Since we're dealing with compiled C++, we enjoy the full feature set this gives along with the ability to use intrinsic functions which access instruction set features like SIMD and atomics, along with OS level functionality such as multithreading. By using one language for development we can use all the tools we have at our disposal, from seamless debugging to performance profilers. Intriguingly, both fixing bugs and optimizing code can now be done on the fly.

We believe that this approach is well suited to replacing scripting as used by programmers for fast iteration, and that designer tools such as data-driven systems and visual scripting languages can be easily enhanced through the use of RCC++. Other developers appear to agree; for example, Epic has dropped UnrealScript entirely in *Unreal Engine 4* by switching to an approach similar in results to RCC++ called Hot Reload. Flexibility for designers is preserved through improvements to the Kismet Visual Scripting system [EPIC 12c].

15.4 Runtime Compiled C++ Implementation

The Runtime Compiled C++ implementation consists of two main components: the Runtime Compiler and the Runtime Object System. The Runtime Compiler handles file change notification and compilation. The Runtime Object System handles tracking of source files and their dependencies. It also provides the `IObject` base class interface and `IObjectFactorySystem` for creating objects and swapping them when new code is loaded. This separation is intended to allow developers to create their own dynamic reloading code while keeping the compiler functionality. Additionally, for console and mobile games, the Runtime Compiler can more easily be moved to a separate process running on the host system.

15.4.1 The Runtime Compiler

The Runtime Compiler provides a simple C++ interface to a compiler. Currently Visual Studio 8.0, 9.0, and 10.0 compilers are supported (Visual Studio 2005, 2008, and 2010) in both the free Express and full versions, and both x86 and x64 targets can be built.

A primary goal of the compiler is to provide rapid turnaround. Compiles are run from a command line process which is instantiated on initialization of the compiler and preserved between compiles. We found that setting up the environment variables for compiles took a substantial amount of time, so by setting these only once and keeping the process active we cut down the time of small compiles significantly. A simple compiler logging interface is provided that can be implemented and passed to the compiler to get compilation output. A handy trick on Windows is to output this using the `OutputDebugString()` function in addition to any other logging; with Visual Studio any errors or warnings can then be doubled clicked to navigate to the offending source.

The Runtime Compiler monitors files that have been registered with the system by the Runtime Object System, and when changes are detected it compiles these files and any dependencies into a DLL module, which is then loaded by the Runtime Object System.

15.4.2 The Runtime Object System

The Runtime Object System provides the functionality needed to have code changes detected, compiled with the correct dependencies, and for the resulting module to be loaded and objects switched over to using the new code. To make compilation as fast as possible, the minimal number of dependencies is compiled.

The runtime object system relies on the C++ virtual function feature to be able to swap objects by simply swapping pointers from the old object to the new object. If the functions were non-virtual, the function pointer would be embedded in any code that calls the function, so the old code would always be run. A simple runtime-modifiable class could be comprised of a header declaring the class as follows:

Listing 15.1. An example runtime object, deriving from IObject.

```
class MyRuntimeModifiableObject : public IObject
{
public:
    virtual void DoSomething();
};
```

In order to be able to make changes at runtime we need to expose this class via a factory style constructor. This is done by applying the macro REGISTERCLASS(MyRuntime ModifiableObject) in the.cpp file, which adds the path of the source file to a list that the Runtime Compiler monitors. When this source file is changed, we compile the source file along with the common Runtime Object System interface code into a DLL and then load the resulting module. Even if the project contains many source files only two need to be compiled and linked into the module in the minimum case. After module load we now have two or more classes called MyRuntimeModifiableObject along with their respective constructors, which is possible as each is in a different module (for example, one is in the executable and another in a DLL). The Runtime Object System can be used to create a new set of objects to replace old ones using the new constructor, and their pointers swapped so that code now references the new class.

We considered several techniques for achieving the runtime swapping of pointers. The two main candidates were a smart pointer, which added one further level of indirection through a pointer table, allowing object pointer swapping to occur at extremely low cost, and serialization of all objects with pointer replacement occurring using an object ID that offered low runtime overhead but a higher cost to swap pointers. In order to preserve object state when changing code we need to have serialization in place anyway, and the reduced runtime overhead seemed a win for serialization. Since the state only needs to be written and read from memory, this serialization can be extremely fast. For non runtime modifiable code, an event system permits developers to use the Object ID to swap object pointers when new code is loaded.

Using virtual functions introduces one level of indirection, so developers of performance-critical areas of code should look at the Section 15.8 on Code Optimizations for

Listing 15.2. Accessing functionality via a system table.

```
//Interface to Runtime Object System
struct IRuntimeObjectSystem
{
public:
    ...
    virtual void CompileAll(bool bForceRecompile) = 0;
    ...
}
//System table to access engine functionality
struct SystemTable
{
    IRuntimeObjectSystem * pRuntimeObjectSystem;
    //other interface pointers can be added here
};
//Example usuage in a GUI button event:
class OnClickCompile : public IGUIEventListener
{
public:
    virtual void OnEvent(int event_id, const IGUIEvent& event_info)
    {
        SystemTable* pSystemTable = PerModuleInterface::GetInstance()->
GetSystemTable();
        pSystemTable->pRuntimeObjectSystem->CompileAll(true);
    }
};
```

suggestions. Note that the use of virtual functions does not imply that the developer needs to implement a complex polymorphic class system with deep inheritance trees.

In order for runtime code to access features of nonruntime modifiable code, we provide a mechanism for passing a System Table object pointer to runtime modifiable code. This System Table can then be used to store pointers to interfaces of the game engine's subsystems, such as rendering, audio, physics, etc. In Listing 15.2, we make accessible the Runtime Object System subsystem itself to allow the user to force a full recompile. This example is taken from the Pulse demo in the code sample included with this book (called SimpleTest in the code base).

The overall architecture of the Runtime Object System is best illustrated by looking at a full example of its application, which we'll do in the next section.

15.5 Runtime Compilation in Practice—a Step-by-Step Example

In this example we'll look at implementing a simple Win32 console application which runs a main loop every second, calling an update function on a runtime object. In the following listings we've removed some of the implementation so as to focus on the main elements. Once again see the included source code for full details, in the ConsoleExample project.

The main entry point of the project simply constructs a `ConsoleGame` object, calls its `Init()` function, and then calls the `MainLoop()` function in a loop until this returns

Listing 15.3. The ConsoleGame class declaration in ConsoleGame.h.

```cpp
class ConsoleGame : public IObjectFactoryListener
{
public:
    ConsoleGame();
    virtual ~ConsoleGame();
    bool Init();
    bool MainLoop();
    virtual void OnConstructorsAdded();
private:
    //Runtime Systems
    ICompilerLogger*        m_pCompilerLogger;
    IRuntimeObjectSystem*   m_pRuntimeObjectSystem;
    //Runtime object
    IUpdateable*    m_pUpdateable;
    ObjectId        m_ObjectId;
};
```

Listing 15.4. ConsoleGame initialization. The string "RuntimeObject01" refers to the class name of the object we wish to construct.

```cpp
bool ConsoleGame::Init()
{
    //Initialize the RuntimeObjectSystem
    m_pRuntimeObjectSystem = new RuntimeObjectSystem;
    m_pCompilerLogger = new StudioLogSystem();
    m_pRuntimeObjectSystem->Initialize(m_pCompilerLogger, 0);
m_pRuntimeObjectSystem->GetObjectFactorySystem()->AddListener(this);
    //construct first object
    IObjectConstructor* pCtor =
m_pRuntimeObjectSystem->GetObjectFactorySystem()->
GetConstructor("RuntimeObject01");
    if(pCtor)
    {
        IObject* pObj = pCtor->Construct();
        pObj->GetInterface(&m_pUpdateable);
        if(0 == m_pUpdateable)
        {
            delete pObj;
            return false;
        }
        m_ObjectId = pObj->GetObjectId();
    }
    return true;
}
```

false. The `ConsoleGame` class, which derives from `IObjectFactoryListener`, receives an event call when a new constructor has been added after a code change, allowing us to swap the runtime object pointers using an ID lookup. The data member `m_pUpdateable` is where we store the native pointer, while `m_ObjectId` stores the id of the runtime object.

ConsoleGame.cpp contains the fundamental aspects required for a RCC++ implementation. The initialization requires creating a logging system (which simply writes the log output to `stdout`), and the Runtime Object System, followed by adding the `ConsoleGame` as a listener for events and then creating our runtime object—in this case, a class called simply `RuntimeObject01`.

When new code is loaded, the `IObjectFactoryListener::OnConstructors Added()` method is called, and we use this to swap our object pointer to the new code as in the listing below.

Listing 15.5. Swapping runtime object pointers after new code is loaded.

```
void ConsoleGame::OnConstructorsAdded()
{
    if(m_pUpdateable)
    {
        IObject* pObj =
m_pRuntimeObjectSystem->GetObjectFactorySystem()->GetObject(m_ObjectId);
        pObj->GetInterface(&m_pUpdateable);
    }
}
```

The main loop first checks for compilation completion, and loads a new module if a compile has just completed. We then update the file change notification system and our runtime object through the `IUpdateable` interface.

If we want to change the class declaration at runtime, a separate virtual interface is needed for nonruntime modifiable code. This interface shouldn't be modified at runtime, though header tracking allows the interfaces between different runtime source files to be changed. In practice, the more code that is moved to being runtime compiled, the less restrictive this becomes. Our console example has a simple interface as in Listing 15.6; this defines the `Update()` function and also derives from `IObject`.

Listing 15.6. The update function is declared as an abstract interface.

```
struct IUpdateable : public IObject
{
    virtual void Update(float deltaTime) = 0;
};
```

Listing 15.7. The runtime object. This code can be modified while the console example is running, with saving the file out causing compilation and reloading of the code.

```
class RuntimeObject01 : public TInterface<IID_IUPDATEABLE,IUpdateable>
{
public:
    virtual void Update(float deltaTime)
    {
        std::cout << "Runtime Object 01 update called!\n";
    }
};
REGISTERCLASS(RuntimeObject01);
```

The runtime object code is correspondingly simple. The class, defined in Listing 15.7, derives from a template which implements the `GetInterface()` member function, which in this case allows us to get hold of a pointer to an `IUpdateable*` using the interface ID, `IID_IUPDATEABLE`.

Putting this together, and running the sample, we're able to change the `Update()` function and save out, seeing our changes in action in the console. Listing 15.8 shows example output from a session where we've added "NEW!" to the output.

15.6 Runtime Error Recovery

We felt that for RCC++ to be really practical, it had to have a form of crash protection. After all, it would be a frustrating experience if you could avoid quitting, recompiling, reloading only until your first simple mistake, when a null pointer forces you to close it all down and start over. We looked at two main approaches to achieving this: using a separate process, and structured exception handling.

Google Chrome uses the process approach for each of its tabs, allowing one to crash without affecting any of the others. This is a very robust approach, but unless your engine's architecture has this in mind, it may result in a very large number of interprocess function calls, which would have severe performance impact. We wanted an approach that would be easy to drop into existing projects.

Structured exception handling (SEH) is a Win32 API feature that allows handling of runtime errors such as access violations. It behaves much like standard exceptions but is in fact quite separate; there are various reasons why standard exceptions are not used on games consoles, but these don't affect SEH. When a runtime error such as a null pointer dereference occurs, the OS checks a stack of possible handlers registered by the application to see how to proceed. The crash dialogs you see in Windows are, in fact, the default handler; when Visual Studio's debugger is attached, that adds another.

Using SEH it is quite easy to catch an error and carry straight on. In our case, the key place for this is around the update calls on our game objects. When an update fails, we disable it until the code has been runtime-recompiled, then we try again. During this process the rest of the application—rendering, GUI, logging—all keep running.

But actually, you don't want to handle a crash silently—you'd really like to find out what caused it first! You could add code to produce a stack trace. However, debuggers like

Listing 15.8. The console example compiling files at runtime after a change. Note the added 'NEW!' to the output of the update function.

```
Main Loop - press q to quit. Updates every second.
Runtime Object 01 update called!

Main Loop - press q to quit. Updates every second.
Runtime Object 01 update called!

Main Loop - press q to quit. Updates every second.
FileChangeNotifier triggered recompile of files:
Compiling...
Created intermediate folder "Runtime"
cl /nologo /O2 /LD /Zi /MP /Fo"Runtime\\" /D WIN32 /EHa /FeC:\Temp\
BFCB.tmp "e:\aurora\examples\consoleexample\runtimeobject01.cpp"
"e:\aurora\runtimeobjectsystem\objectinterfacepermodulesource.cpp"
echo _COMPLETION_TOKEN_
Runtime Object 01 update called!
Microsoft Windows [Version 6.1.7601]
Copyright (c) 2009 Microsoft Corporation.  All rights reserved.

E:\Aurora\Examples\ConsoleExample>
Setting environment for using Microsoft Visual Studio 2010 x64 tools.

runtimeobject01.cpp
objectinterfacepermodulesource.cpp
    Creating library C:\Temp\BFCB.lib and object C:\Temp\BFCB.exp

[RuntimeCompiler] Complete
'ConsoleExample.exe' (Win32): Loaded 'C:\Temp\BFCB.tmp'. Symbols loaded.
Compilation Succeeded
Serializing out from 1 old constructors
Swapping in and creating objects for 1 new constructors
Serialising in...
Initialising and testing new serialisation...
Object swap completed

Main Loop - press q to quit. Updates every second.
NEW! Runtime Object 01 update called!

Main Loop - press q to quit. Updates every second.
NEW! Runtime Object 01 update called!
```

that in Visual Studio already provide a really ideal interface when crashes occur, allowing you to inspect state easily. So really, we would like to crash, but then continue.

In fact, this is exactly what we do; we first allow the crash to proceed as normal so we can use Visual Studio to debug it, after which the user can hit the "continue" button in the IDE. Usually the "continue" option is quite useless but in our case we catch the crash on the second attempt—and proceed with execution. We get the best of both.

As an aid to productivity, we include a runtime assert macro that is compatible with the runtime exception handling process.

15.6.1 Handling Errors on Loading New Code

When new code is loaded (see the `ObjectFactorySystem::AddConstructors` function in the prototype), we need to construct the new objects, serialize state into them, and initialize them (if required). Since the process is reliant on working serialization, we also test serializing out from the newly constructed objects. Structured exceptions (crashes) could occur during this process, so we use the runtime exception filter to handle them, and revert to running the old code and state. This gives the developer an opportunity to fix the problem and reload the new code without restarting the application.

Should an error be caught, the new objects that were constructed are deleted. This introduces a new failure path in the destructor, so this also uses runtime exception handling and simply leaks the objects when an error occurs.

Another issue which can commonly occur is that the new code pollutes the data during this process in such a way as to not crash, but to render the application instance unusable. A trivial solution, which has not yet been implemented in our codebase, would be to maintain an undo list of code and data to allow developers to revert back to a previously working state and make further changes from there.

Further stability could be added by unit testing new code prior to loading, and/or creating a save point on disk. If developers intend to use the Runtime Compiled C++ approach in an editing tool we would recommend adding these features, but for a programming productivity tool we believe these steps would be counterproductive due to the extra delay in turnaround.

15.7 More Complex Code-State Preservation and Header File Handling

When swapping new code for old, it is desirable to ensure that the state of the old object is propagated to the new one. The Runtime Object System includes a simple serialization system designed for the needs of runtime modification of code.

The SERIALIZE macro can be used for any type that implements the operator = method, which also permits types to be changed to compatible types, such as float to double or int etc. Non runtime pointers can be serialized by their value since the address doesn't change, but runtime pointers are serialized through their ObjectId.

Listing 15.9. An example serialization function.

```
virtual void Serialize(ISimpleSerializer *pSerializer)
{
    IBaseClass::Serialize(pSerializer);
    //any type which implements operator = including pointers
    SERIALIZE(m_SomeType);
    //serialize a runtime object pointer
    SERIALIZEIOBJPTR(m_pIObjectPointer);
    if (pSerializer->IsLoading()) {
        //do something only when loading values
    }
    //serialize something whose name has changed
    pSerializer->Serialize("m_Color", m_Colour);
}
```

To save developer time, the same serialization function is called on both load and save of state. For situations where different behavior is needed, the `IsLoading()` function can be used.

Values are serialized by name, so if the name of the object changes the developer should use the `Serialize` function directly rather than the macro, and replace with the macro once it's been loaded.

A simple header file dependency tracking method has been implemented. To use this, add the `RUNTIME_MODIFIABLE_INCLUDE` to the header file (defined in `RuntimeInclude.h`), and when this file changes any code which includes it and has a runtime modifiable class will be recompiled. This macro expands to a recursive template specialization that, when such headers are included from a.cpp file, uses the _COUNTER_ macro to assign successive numbers to the filenames of each. This enables the system to iterate through all of the include files for a given class.

15.8 Code Optimizations for Performance-Critical Code

We use virtual functions to give runtime redirection of function calls when new code is loaded. This adds a small performance penalty to the function call. For many AI and scripting style use cases, this is still equal or better performance than alternatives such as running a script VM or using a data-driven approach. However, some simple approaches can reduce or eliminate this penalty.

For developers who only use the virtual functions for runtime compiling of code, it is possible to write a macro for final release builds which declares the appropriate functions to be nonvirtual, so long as polymorphic behavior is not required. This introduces a potentially substantial difference between builds, so a strong test regime is required.

Listing 15.10. Optimization for final release builds by removing virtual from performance-critical functions. Note that we don't declare an abstract interface, so the developer must take care to ensure they only use virtual or RUNTIME_VIRTUAL functions in nonruntime code.

```
#ifdef RUNTIME_COMPILED
#define RUNTIME_VIRTUAL virtual
#else
#define RUNTIME_VIRTUAL
#endif
class SomeClass : public Tinterface<IID_ISOMECLASS,IObject>
{
public:
    virtual void SomeVirtualFunction();
    RUNTIME_VIRTUAL void OnlyVirtualForRuntimeCompile();
private:
    //members which are not virtual or RUNTIME_VIRTUAL
};
```

A simpler alternative is to base the high performance areas of the code around aggregated calls, similar to the approaches taken in data oriented programming. For example, if we consider the following function performing operations on a game object:

Listing 15.11. Simple virtual function example declaration and definition.

```
virtual void Execute(IGameObject* pObject)
{
    //perform actions on one game object
}
```

If we have many calls to execute in our game the virtual call overhead may become significant. So we could replace this by aggregating all calls as follows:

Listing 15.12. Redesigned function to reduce virtual function call overhead and improve cache coherency by processing multiple objects per call.

```
virtual void Execute(IGameObject* pObjects, size_t numObjects)
{
    //perform actions on many game objects
}
```

Here, we've defined this based on a new interface that requires the developer to pass in an array of game objects to process, and so have reduced the cost of the virtual function call to $1/numObjects$ times the original cost. Additionally there are potential benefits from cache coherency, which could give even further performance benefits.

15.9 Use Case: A Behavior Tree and Blackboard Architecture

The ability to change code freely at runtime doesn't just speed up iteration on existing workflow. It can also allow us to approach problems in an entirely different manner. Some of the first techniques we reevaluated this way were behavior trees and blackboards.

Bastions of modern game AI, behavior trees provide a framework for breaking down complex AI into modular pieces with structured reactive decision making, and have been described widely, including in this very book. Blackboards are a simple approach to sharing data between aspects of an AI while remaining loosely coupled. Often the two are used together, with conditionals within the behavior tree reading primarily from the blackboard, while that data is updated regularly from sensory systems and written to by the operations of the behaviors themselves.

15.9.1 A "Soft-Coded" Behavior Tree

Here, we take as an example a "first-generation" behavior tree—essentially a decision tree with behavior states as its leaves, a very common design in modern games including *Crysis 2*.

Implementations have included the use of snippets of Lua to form flexible conditions at each node, or in *Crysis 2* a simple virtual machine executing a tree specified by XML [Martins 11]. However, in essence, the structure is a simple tree of if-else statements—the rest of the behavior tree architecture deriving from the requirement for rapid iteration, as a set of hardcoded C++ if-else clauses would bring AI development to a near halt.

We can now reevaluate that assumption. Under RCC++ such decision code can be thought of as "soft"-coded—we can change it at will while the game is running. So, assuming some nicely formatted code, let's consider its properties: being raw C++, it is obviously extremely fast, it will handle errors without crashing, it has easy access to all the state in our AI system, it can share sub-trees as function calls, it can use all our C++ math and utility routines, we can make use of our existing debugger, we can apply our existing profiler if we need to, you can see useful diffs from source control … the list goes on. In a few lines of code you've implemented a behavior tree—in fact, an unusually fast and powerful behavior tree.

The main aspect for improvement is that of the interface for designers. Simple parameters may, of course, be exposed through XML or a GUI. In this author's experience more structural changes are best kept the responsibility of AI programmers, who often find a simple text specification better to work with than a graphical one. However, such if-else code may be very easily generated from a graphical representation should one be required, with the simple act of replacing the source file triggering runtime-compilation.

15.9.2 A Blackboard

Blackboards may be naturally represented in languages such as Lua or Python as a table of key-value pairs, comprising strings and dynamically typed values. While similar constructions are possible in C++, they represent a possible performance bottleneck. In an analogous approach to our behavior tree, we can represent our blackboards under RCC++ as simple structs—each key-value pair becoming a named member variable of appropriate type.

Reading and writing from the blackboard becomes as simple as passing its pointer to our sensory systems and to our RCC++ behavior tree. The main difficulty we must resolve is that of dependencies, as all the code that uses it must include the struct definition as a header, and must be recompiled should it change.

The header-tracking feature of RCC++ makes this simple, with a change to the include file triggering recompilation of all the dependent code. We advise using a hierarchical form of blackboards with, for example, a particular agent's full blackboard inheriting from one shared blackboard across all agents, and one shared by its species, and with separate access to any blackboard used solely by the current behavior. This approach helps ensure that only relevant AI code needs to be recompiled when the blackboard definition is changed, keeping recompiling as efficient as possible.

15.10 Crytek Case Study

Following a presentation at the Paris Game/AI conference in 2011, Crytek implemented a similar system internally which they call SoftCode. The system has been used on several game projects currently active in Crytek and has been used for systems as diverse as render effects, UI, and animation. It is most heavily employed currently on the AI system in use for *Ryse* for authoring behaviors and managing behavior selection.

SoftCode builds upon the approach of RCC++ in several interesting directions. The first is that it provides the compilation and change tracking functionality of the runtime compiler as a Visual Studio 2010 add-in, which works for 32-bit and 64-bit Windows builds as well as Xbox 360. Additionally, it generalizes the concept of the runtime object system, allowing developers to expose their own system through a type library. Thus, rather than having to derive from a single `IObject` base class, each SoftCoded type can derive from their own base interface. Like RCC++, SoftCoding has an error-handling mechanism using structured exceptions, but its lambda functions allow call state capture so that individual methods can be retried after failure. To simplify development, SoftCode types use a `SOFT()` macro to expose class member variables rather than through an explicit Serialize function, and globals can be exposed through an `SC_API` macro.

15.11 Future Work

With Mac and even Linux becoming more popular targets for games, we feel support for these platforms is a natural next step for the project. Beyond this, moving to a client/server model for the Runtime Object System and Runtime Compiler would permit further targets such as Consoles and mobile devices to be targeted.

An interesting further step would be to support a simpler interface to programming than C++ with an intermediate compiler that generates C++ code, using RCC++ to permit runtime usage. A basic graphical interface to construct object data members and function declarations with function bodies editable in a variant of C++, which limits operator arithmetic and what functions can be called, may be sufficient for many technically oriented designers. Alternatively, full blown graphical scripting methods like Unreal's Kismet or Crytek's Flow-Graph could output C++ rather than data, allowing the compiler to make optimizations where possible. A hybrid approach permitting existing building blocks to be connected together, and new ones constructed in code on the fly, seems a good solution for allowing designers freedom of expression in a safe and highly productive environment.

Meanwhile, we will continue to evolve the current codebase in our search for faster iteration times, easier development, and the potential for maximum performance. Check the author's blog at RuntimeCompiledCPlusPlus.blogspot.com for updates.

15.12 Conclusion

Our initial goals with Runtime Compiled C++ were to demonstrate that compiled code could replace scripting for iterative and interactive development of game logic and behavior, particularly in performance-critical areas of code such as AI. We believe we have not only succeeded in this goal, but have also developed a technique (and permissively licensed open source code base), which permits developers to go further and develop substantial proportions of their game code this way.

Changing behavior, fixing bugs, adding new functionality, and even optimizing are now all possible without needing to restart the process, with turnaround times on the order of a few seconds.

With special thanks to Adam Rutkowski

References

[Crytek 12] Crytek. "CryENGINE 3 AI System." http://mycryengine.com/index.php?conid = 48, 2012.

[DeLoura 09] M. DeLoura. "The Engine Survey: General Results." http://www.satori.org/2009/03/the-engine-survey-general-results/, 2009.

[Epic 12a] Epic Games. "UnrealScript." http://www.unrealengine.com/features/unrealscript/, 2012.

[Epic 12b] Epic Games. "Unreal Kismet." http://www.unrealengine.com/features/kismet/, 2012.

[Epic 12c] Epic Games. "Unreal Engine 4." http://www.unrealengine.com/unreal_engine_4, 2012.

[Fulgham 12] B. Fulgham. "The Computer Language Benchmark Game" http://shootout.alioth.debian.org/, 2012.

[Havok 12] Havok. "Havok Script." http://www.havok.com/products/script, 2012.

[Jack, Binks, Rutkowski 11] M. Jack, D. Binks, and A. Rutkowski. "Runtime Compiled C++" https://github.com/RuntimeCompiledCPlusPlus/RuntimeCompiledCPlusPlus.

[Martins 11] M. Martins. Paris Shooter Symposium 2011. Available online (https://aigamedev.com/store/recordings/paris-shooter-symposium-2011-content-access.html).

[Microsoft 10] Microsoft. "Supported Code Changes." http://msdn.microsoft.com/en-us/library/0dbey757%28v = VS.100%29.aspx, 2010.

[Shaw 10] J. Shaw. "Lua and Fable." Presentation, Games Developer Conference (GDC), 2010. Available online (http://www.gdcvault.com/play/1012427/Lua-Scripting-in-Game).

[Staheli 98] D. G. Staheli. "Enhanced Debugging with Edit and Continue in Microsoft Visual C++ 6.0." http://msdn.microsoft.com/en-us/library/aa260823%28v = vs.60%29.aspx, 1998.

[Zao 10] H. Zao. "HipHop for PHP: Move Fast." https://developers.facebook.com/blog/post/2010/02/02/hiphop-for-php—move-fast/, 2010.

16

Plumbing the Forbidden Depths
Scripting and AI

Mike Lewis

16.1 Introduction

Lurking deep in the mists of contemporary artificial intelligence work is a controversial and hotly debated technique—a "black magic" that has been rumored to accomplish fantastical things, but at perilous cost. This forbidden ability has been responsible for some of the most cherished game AI in the industry's history … and also for some of its worst embarrassments. I speak of scripted AI.

Scripting, however, need not be feared. Like any good black art, it must be understood and mastered to be wielded safely [Tozour 02]. Here, we will explore the good, bad, and dangerous aspects of scripting as it pertains to developing game AI—all with an eye towards delivering the kind of dynamic, adaptive, challenging-but-entertaining experiences that modern gamers demand.

There are, of course, a multitude of ways to integrate scripting techniques into a game's architecture, but for the most part they comprise two basic philosophies. These rival points of view can be thought of as the "master" and "servant" ideologies. While both have their proper place, it can be tremendously useful to consider which role scripts will play in a given game's implementation. It is also of paramount importance to maintain as much adherence to that role as possible, for reasons which will be considered later.

By the same token, there is a vast spectrum of complexity in scripting systems, ranging from simple tripwire/response mechanisms to full-blown programming languages. Once again, each possible approach has its merits and drawbacks. As with any technology or tool, the situation at hand must be carefully examined and considered in order to decide how best to deploy scripting systems and what their implementations should look like.

16.2 The Master and the Servant

From the very beginning of working with an AI scripting mechanism, it is important to understand the system's place in the overall architecture of the game—not just how it interacts with other AI features, but how it will function in terms of the totality of the game's systems. Moreover, it is deeply beneficial to remain true to that decision for the duration of development. Without this discipline, scripts can quickly become unruly monsters that suck up huge amounts of debugging time, deliver subpar gameplay experiences, or even drag down development as a whole.

The most successful approaches to scripting will generally fall into one of two camps. First is the "scripts as master" perspective, wherein scripts control the high-level aspects of agent decision making and planning. The other method sees "scripts as servant," where some other architecture controls the overall activity of agents, but selectively deploys scripts to attain specific design goals or create certain dramatic effects.

In general, master-style systems work best in one of two scenarios. In the optimal case, a library of ready-to-use tools already exists, and scripting can become the "glue" that combines these techniques into a coherent and powerful overarching model for agent behavior. Even in cases where such a library is not immediately available, master scripts are often the superior approach when it is known in advance that agents must be able to fluidly transition between a number of different decision-making or planning techniques.

By contrast, servant scripts are most effective when design requires a high degree of specificity in agent behavior. This is the typical sense in which interactions are thought of as "scripted"; a set of possible scenarios is envisioned by the designers, and special-case logic for reacting to each scenario is put in place by the AI implementation team. Servant scripts need not be entirely reactive, however; simple scripted loops and behavioral patterns can make for excellent ambient or "background" AI.

Most game designs will naturally lend themselves to one side or the other of the master/servant divide. Even when the game itself does not clearly lean towards a preferred approach, the human factor almost always will. Different teams will work more effectively in one style or another, depending on any number of circumstances: the ratio of programmers to designers, relative experience of the engineers working on the AI, time and budget constraints, and so on.

One such factor worth considering is the investment required to implement either approach. A master system will tend to work best with developers who can draw upon a diverse bag of tricks to help flesh out the overall implementation of the AI. Servant systems are much easier to design and implement in terms of code, but require extra care from gameplay design to avoid falling into the classic trap of producing agents that feel like cardboard cutouts.

Alternative philosophies surely exist, but they can be difficult to tame. Interspersing "scripted" logic with other architectural approaches is often a recipe for creating exactly the kind of rigid, inflexible agents that have (rightfully) earned scripting a bad reputation. Without clear boundaries and responsibilities, different systems will begin competing for dominance—either at an abstract level in the code's design and details, or in the worst case, while the game is being played.

16.2.1 Scripts as Benevolent Overlords

The master-script philosophy derives its power from one fundamental principle: delegation. It is not the responsibility of the script to dictate every detail of how an agent behaves, or even to anticipate every possible scenario that might occur during the game experience. Instead, a good master script seeks to categorize and prioritize, and hand off responsibility for the mundane details to other systems.

Categorization is all about recognizing the nature of what is going on in the simulation at a given moment. Knowledge representation is often the key to doing this effectively; it is mandatory that agents have coherent and believable ideas about the world they inhabit so they can interpret events in a manner that is consistent with their worldview, and thereby take appropriate action. Note that it is not necessary for agents to have *accurate* or *precise* beliefs, so long as they do things which seem *sensible* from the perspective of the player. It can be tempting to build highly complex knowledge systems, but this often leads to inscrutable decision-making processes that wind up feeling arbitrary or mysterious to an outside observer.

Prioritization, on the other hand, boils down to choosing what to do with the gathered knowledge of an agent's surroundings and situation. For the master script, this is not a matter of selecting behaviors or states per se. Rather, during prioritization, the master script examines a set of lower-level control mechanisms, decides which are most appropriate for the moment, and selects one or more of those mechanisms to contribute towards the final decision-making process.

For example, consider a typical open-world role-playing game in which a large number of agents populate a town. The master script shouldn't concern itself too much with the minutiae of what an agent happens to be doing at any given moment. Instead, it acts like a sort of abstract state machine, governing which systems might control an individual agent at any point in time.

During peaceful spells, the master may choose between simple idle animation loops for a stationary blacksmith agent or perhaps it might assign a utility-based system to monitor the desires and needs of that agent and select activities based on those demands. The script might gather a group of agents to take on the role of the town militia, patrolling for nearby threats and policing the streets; these agents might be controlled using group tactical reasoning and movement systems, whereas a stray dog might simply wander around randomly and attempt to eat various things it encounters in the world.

All of this is simply prioritization. The master oversees the "peaceful" environment and delegates responsibility for agents to specific subsystems. This works elegantly alongside traditional subsumption architectures, where the details of an agent's activities are divided into increasingly abstract layers. At the highest layer, the master script plays the role of benevolent overlord, coordinating the activities of the lower-level agents and systems, and if necessary, dealing with situations that are otherwise problematic or insurmountable for the more specific layers.

Categorization enters the picture when the peaceful little hamlet becomes embroiled in a vicious battle with the local band of roving goblins. Suddenly, the master script must detect that the once-sensible actions it has been assigning to its minions are no longer appropriate. It is here that the abstract state machine makes a transition, and begins issuing a different set of prioritizations and orders.

The blacksmith, once happily pounding away on his anvil, might suddenly shift from making horseshoes to making swords. This might be accomplished by changing his idle animation, or simply adjusting the relative merits of sword-making in his utility inputs. The militia must cease worrying about pickpockets in the local market and begin establishing a line of defense against the marauding goblins; they still act as a tactical unit, but now with a very different set of priorities and behaviors that may not fit well with their peacekeeping patterns. Even the poor, mangy, stray dog must not be forgotten: instead of rooting around in the trash for scraps, he might be found behind the barred gates of the town, bristling and growling at the shadowy enemy that lurks outside.

Note that the master script need not transition to the wartime state in any particular fashion; in fact, it is precisely the freedom to choose how this transition occurs that makes scripting a powerful tool for this type of scenario. If the game leans towards the sandbox style, the master might simply examine how many goblins are near the town and trip the transition when their "threat level" exceeds some threshold. In a more narrative-driven title, the master script might simply wait for twenty minutes after the player enters the area and then initiate the invasion.

In any case, the important flexibility of master-scripting lies in the general abstractness of the script's activities. Throughout this example, the master script is rarely, if *ever*, in the position of actually controlling the blow-by-blow activities of any given agent. This is, of course, always an option, but should be used sparingly. The whole purpose of a master architecture is to enable more appropriate control schemes to come into play as necessary. It is through this philosophy that the master script evades the trap of brittle, predictable, boring behavior. Since the script is only guiding the broad strokes of the simulation, other systems retain the freedom to act in interesting and meaningful ways based on the details of that simulation.

16.2.2 Scripts as Humble Indentured Labor

It is, of course, hardly necessary for a scripting system to maintain the high-level "master" overview of how agents behave in a simulation. A perfectly viable alternative is to invert the priority hierarchy and place a traditional behavior control system in charge of the overarching flow of the simulation, while relegating scripts to handling certain particular details. This is the "servant" approach to scripting.

In this view, scripted logic is deployed only when other techniques cannot deliver the precise behavior desired in an easily configurable manner. Most commonly, servant scripts are used to plug the gaps where design requirements have asked for a very specific outcome. For instance, a standard behavior tree could be used to dictate an agent's actions for the majority of a simulation, while a script is activated at a particular node (typically a leaf node) of the tree in order to realize a step in a story progression, or a highly crafted response to a particular stimulus, and so on.

Servant scripts derive the bulk of their power from their specificity. Unlike master scripts, which aim for the exact opposite, servant scripts are generally designed to handle a narrow range of scenarios in a simulation. The "triggers" for these scripts are, for the most part, looking for very precise combinations of events or inputs, and the scripts themselves create agent reactions (or even proactive behaviors) that make sense only in that exact context.

As a tool for rounding out the suite of techniques used to create robust AI, servant scripts certainly have their place. The principal danger in using scripts in this manner lies in the fact that servant scripts are, by far, most effective when used sparingly as supplements to other behavior control systems.

From the perspective of a player, overuse of servant scripts produces brittle, predictable, and—after the first few encounters with the script—stale interactions. One commonly (and fairly) criticized use of scripting is the "tripwire" technique, where agents mindlessly repeat some particular pattern of action until the player crosses an invisible line in the sand, which switches the script to the next set of behavior.

Tripwires are of course not inherently bad; the issue is in using servant scripts in a vacuum. When there is no high-level system producing interesting behavior, scripted actions are no longer exceptional. Once scripted behavior becomes the norm in a simulation, players are likely to become frustrated or bored very quickly with the repetitive and overly patterned interactions they can have with the AI.

Heavy reliance on servant scripts requires an exacting attention to detail and an exhaustive capacity for predicting the sorts of situations players are likely to create. This is certainly possible, and a few noteworthy titles have created exceedingly memorable and believable experiences using extensive scripting. A serious risk, though, is the creation of an "uncanny valley" effect. Good scripting can produce very immersive results up until the point where a player does something the scripts could not have anticipated. At that point, the realism is shattered and the player often comes away feeling disappointed at the discontinuity of the illusion.

Much like in master scripting, it is imperative to maintain a selection of alternative techniques for producing interesting and compelling AI behaviors. The key difference between the two approaches is simply a matter of which extreme the scripts control—generalized, or specialized scenarios.

16.2.3 The Evils of Cross-Pollination

As mentioned earlier, wrangling a herd of AI scripts successfully requires consistent adherence to either of the servant or master models. Straying from these recipes can have disastrous consequences.

The reasons for this are primarily organizational. Without a clear set of guidelines about how scripts are to be deployed, it is virtually inevitable that a project will become inconsistent and variegated in its views on what exactly scripts are meant to do. As a result, different interactions with AI agents within the simulation will feel very different. Some might be highly scripted and controlled to exacting detail, while others are loose and rely on other AI techniques to be interesting.

In the best case, this haphazard use of scripts will produce a disjointed and inconsistent experience for the player. In the worst case, the confusion and wildly varying level of "quality" of interactions will render the experience painful and unpleasant.

The aforementioned uncanny valley effect is nearly certain to appear if agents have highly variable degrees of believability. Certainly, for practical reasons, we may not be able to craft every single agent's entire life in crystal-clear detail for the duration of the player's experience. Indeed, most large-scale simulations are forced to embrace the idea of "ambient" or "throw-away" agents who exist solely as background or filler and generally are low level-of-detail creatures.

However, there is a fine line between level of detail and level of fidelity. Players are, for the most part, willing to accept agents who forego excruciatingly detailed existences within the simulation. What causes problems, however, is lack of fidelity in the behaviors of those agents. A particularly egregious flaw is to intersperse carefully scripted behavior of a particular agent with other control techniques acting on the same agent, without regard to the player's perception of the changes. This is a classic recipe for ruined immersion. Agents will feel inconsistent, arbitrary, or even random in their responses to simulation stimuli, and the net effect is almost universally negative.

This is not to say that all scripting must remain at one polar extreme or the other; to be sure, it is possible to inject scripted logic at various degrees of generalized or specialized control over a simulation, which can even be done to great effect if planned carefully. The key is to remain mindful of the effect that this can have on the end-user experience. To that end, heavy design, oversight, and constant testing and iteration are essential.

16.2.4 Contrasting Case Studies: The X Series

In the "X Series" of space-simulation games by Egosoft, we used a range of scripting technologies to implement the agent AI. Across the span of three titles, the overall philosophy of scripting shifted dramatically, although it never really landed on a clear footing with regards to the master/servant paradigm.

For *X²: The Threat* agents were controlled via a haphazard blend of servant scripts. Each individual "quest" or mini-story in the game was a separate scripted encounter. Moreover, content could be implemented in any of three layers: the C++ core engine, a bytecode-based language called KC, or a third layer known only as "the script engine" which was in turn implemented on top of KC.

This rapidly created the sort of uncanny valley experience described earlier; with no consistent quality or degree of fidelity to the agents and their behavior, the game offered a typically less-than-compelling patchwork of content. As a result, players tended to gravitate towards a tiny fraction of the in-game world that had been implemented with the most attention to detail.

The game's sequel, *X3: Reunion*, saw the introduction of the so-called "God Module" which represented a shift towards master-style scripting, at least in part. The purpose of this module was to observe the state of the simulated game universe and arbitrarily introduce events which would change the world to some degree. At the most extreme, entire swaths of space stations could be built or destroyed by this master script throughout the course of gameplay.

Unfortunately, due to limitations on time, the master philosophy was not consistently applied to all AI development. Much of the old servant style remained, and a large part of the game's content again suffered from a consistent lack of quality and detail. This was addressed post-ship via a number of downloadable patches. Even after extensive updates, however, the disjointed fidelity of agent behavior remained a common complaint among players.

Finally, in *X3: Terran Conflict*, we introduced a system known as the "Mission Director." Interestingly, this represented far more of a shift back towards servant-style scripting than the name might suggest. Instead of attempting to control the experience from a high level, the Mission Director allowed developers—and, eventually, enterprising players—to write highly concise and expressive scripts using a common framework and tool set.

The net result of the Mission Director was to allow the servant philosophy to flourish. With access to rapid development tools and a unified policy for how to create new game content, *Terran Conflict* shipped with substantially more hand-crafted AI behavior and quests than any of the game's predecessors.

Ultimately, the most compelling conclusion to be drawn from this experience is that the actual selection of a design philosophy is not as important as consistent application of that decision. Once again, it is also extremely beneficial to select a design approach that fits nicely with the development resources available for a given project.

16.3 Implementation Techniques

Once a guiding philosophy for scripting's role has been chosen for a given project, it's time to begin considering implementation details. There are numerous mechanisms that could be considered degrees of "scripting" to some extent. These range from simple observation and reaction systems all the way to full-fledged programming languages embedded within the larger simulation itself.

For the most part, implementation choices are orthogonal to the philosophical choices outlined previously. Generally speaking, any of the techniques detailed in the following sections can be applied equally well to master or servant script models. There are a few exceptions to this, which will be specifically called out, but the predominant factors involved in choosing a script implementation approach pertain to the team involved more than the master/servant distinction itself.

Before embarking on the journey of building a scripting system, it is worth taking some time to evaluate the situation's particulars in order to ensure that the most appropriate techniques are selected. For example, observation/reaction systems have a distinct advantage when the majority of the simulation "script" logic needs to be emplaced by designers or nonprogrammer staff. At the other extreme, rolling a custom language is best reserved for engineers with prior language creation experience—although depending on the nature of the custom language, the audience may not necessarily need much technical programming experience, as we shall see later.

In the realm of implementation decisions, there are far more potentially profitable approaches than can be exhaustively enumerated here. Instead, we'll look at both extremes of the implementation spectrum, and then examine a happy medium that can be deployed to balance out the strengths and weaknesses of other approaches.

16.3.1 Observation and Reaction Systems

The canonical observation/reaction system is the "tripwire." This is a simple mechanism which observes the location of an agent within the simulation's world space, and when the agent enters (or exits) a particular locale, a reaction is triggered [Orkin 02].

Tripwires are trivial to implement in the context of most engines, because they rely only on testing intersection of an agent's bounding volume with some other (typically invisible) bounding volume within the simulation space. Such functionality is almost always necessary for other aspects of the simulation, such as generalized physics or collision detection and response, so very little new code needs to be written to accomplish a simple tripwire.

The simplest case of a tripwire resembles the ubiquitous automatic sliding doors found at the entrances to supermarkets; when something moves into the sensor volume, the door opens, and when nothing has moved there for a time, the door shuts again. This is fine for trivial interactions—where things get interesting with tripwires is in selective reaction.

Suppose we want to have a security system on the door, so that it only opens if someone carrying the appropriate keycard walks into the sensor volume. This can become an arbitrarily complex task depending on the nature of the rest of the simulation. Is a "keycard" just a Boolean flag on an agent, or might agents have inventories which need to be enumerated in order to find a key? To selectively activate the tripwire, it is suddenly necessary to interface with a large part of the rest of the simulation logic.

The challenge here is in providing appropriately rich tools. Those responsible for creating the AI technology must ensure that those actually using the technology have all the hooks, knobs, levers, and paraphernalia necessary for accomplishing the design goals of the project. While it can be tempting to throw in the kitchen sink, there is tremendous benefit in careful up-front design of both the game systems themselves and their interactions with the tripwire AI systems. Otherwise, the tools can become overwhelmingly complex and detailed, even to the point of obscuring the most commonly needed functionality.

Context is supremely important when making these decisions. What is appropriate for a team creating a general-purpose engine for licensing purposes will be dramatically different from what makes the most sense for a small, nimble team producing mobile titles at the rate of several per year. While the two systems may bear a striking resemblance to one another in the broad strokes, it is generally straightforward to keep the feature set of a tripwire system minimalistic if the scope of the simulation is well defined up front.

Any number of considerations may be useful for an observation/reaction system. Again, context is extremely important in selecting them. However, there are a few patterns that are so broadly applicable that they are worth considering—even if only to mutate them into something more specifically useful for the project at hand.

The first and most common consideration is **classification**. Put simply, this consideration examines the "kind" of thing that has just tripped the sensor: perhaps it only examines player agents, or only AI agents, or only agents on the Blue Team, and so forth. An even more powerful option is to allow things besides agents to trip the sensors. If a sensor volume moves along with an agent, and the volume is "tuned" to trip a response when a grenade enters it, it becomes trivial to build grenade evasion logic into an agent using nothing but observation/reaction architecture.

A sister technique to classification is **attribute checking**. An attribute check might look for the presence (or absence) of a particular inventory item, or compare values based on some threshold, and so on. Attribute checking is also convenient when needing to make decisions that are not strictly binary. For example, an attribute check might look at a player's health and ammunition levels before triggering a reaction that sends out squads of enemies in response to the perceived threat.

Another useful consideration is **sequencing**. A sequence requires that one tripwire be activated before another can become active. Sequencing allows designers to create linear flows of connected events. Combined with configurable timings, sequencing can be used to unfold entire story arcs based simply on having one event follow logically after another.

Deduplication is yet another handy technique. This is a trivial state flag which simply ensures that a particular tripwire cannot be triggered more than once, or more often than at some prescribed rate. This avoids the classic blunder of AI systems that repeatedly greet the hero as he steps back and forth across the threshold of the city gates.

It is worth noting that observation/reaction does not necessarily lead to strictly linear behavior, in contrast to the images that the term "scripted AI" typically conjures up. Branching logic can be accomplished easily with the use of attribute checks and sequences. Deduplication can be applied to ensure that logic does not become repetitively applied to the simulation. Last but not least, there is the potential for movable trigger zones to be employed, as suggested in the grenade evasion example from earlier.

If a single agent has a set of tripwires applied to itself, it can quickly become prepared to handle all kinds of contingencies in the simulation world. Indeed, the limitations are predominantly found in the foresight and creativity of the designers rather than technical details.

Obviously, however, if everything in a complex simulation is handled by tripwires of various kinds—and especially if intricate, nonlinear storytelling becomes involved—the number of tripwires required can explode exponentially very easily. This is the primary weakness of simple observation/reaction systems; since they are essentially data driven mechanisms, they scale proportionally with the number of situations that the simulation must present and/or respond to. Even if the feature set of the tripwire technology is minimalistic and elegant, the number of actual triggers needed to realize a sophisticated project might be prohibitive.

16.3.2 Domain-Specific Languages

At the opposite extreme of implementation technique lies the **domain-specific language**, or DSL. A DSL is simply some kind of tool for expressing specialized types of logic. Strictly speaking, DSLs can run the gamut from little more than textually defined observation/response systems, to intricate monstrosities that rival the complication of full-blown traditional programming languages.

As the name hopefully suggests, however, domain-specific languages should be precisely that: constrained heavily to accomplish one particular task—or *domain*. The further a language strays from this self-imposed limitation, the more likely it is to become a liability rather than an asset [Brockington et al. 02]. General-purpose languages require extraordinary amounts of effort to develop to the point where they are suitable for general-purpose tasks; rolling a custom general-purpose language almost automatically entails giving up on existing tools, programmer knowledge, and battle-tested code. As such, it pays to keep the "domain-specific" part in mind at all times.

In a nutshell, the goal of a good DSL is to allow implementers to talk (in code) about what they want to happen using the same vocabulary and mental patterns that they use to think about it. DSLs are by nature very heavily tied to their intended audience; a language for helping helicopter pilots navigate automatically is going to look very different from a language used to help physicists calibrate particle accelerator experiments.

A key realization in the creation of DSL-based AI is that it is not necessary to lump *all* functionality of the AI into a single language. In fact, it is almost universally detrimental to do so, given that such accumulation of features will by necessity cause the language to stop being specific and start being more general.

Another important thing to keep in mind is that DSLs are often most useful for people who are not primarily programmers [Poiker 02]. There is no need for a DSL to be littered with squiggly symbols and magical words; on the contrary, a good DSL will tend to resemble both the terminology and the overall structure of a design diagram of the intended logic. If the intended audience tends to use certain symbols or incantations to describe their goals, then those things should be considered perfectly at home in a DSL. However, a good language design will avoid bending over backwards to "look" or "feel" like a general-purpose programming language.

Put simply: a good DSL should not look like C++ code, nor should it require a complex parser, compiler, interpreter, virtual machine, or any other trappings of a typical general-purpose language. In fact, a simple whitespace-based tokenizer should be amply sufficient to power most DSLs. Another common option entails using existing file formats such as XML or JSON to encode the logic, and providing thin user interfaces on top of these formats for creating the actual programs in the language. End users need not write XML by hand; they can use comfortable, visually intuitive tools to craft their logic [McNaughton et al. 06]. Meanwhile, there is no need to roll yet another parsing system just to load the generated scripts. Good DSLs are about leveraging existing technologies in new ways, not reinventing wheels.

For most DSL implementations, the real work is in specifying a compact yet usable language; actually parsing and executing the code is relatively straightforward. Simple techniques include large `switch` statements, or groups of "executable" classes derived from a simple abstract base class or interface, where virtual dispatch is used to trigger the corresponding code for each language "keyword" or operation.

Of course, from a theoretical standpoint, there exists the possibility of writing an entire virtual machine architecture just for executing game logic; this has in fact been explored in numerous successful titles, including the *X Series* described earlier. However, rolling a true, custom VM is almost always a serious crime of excess when a DSL is concerned.

An effective guideline for designing DSLs is to create a language that expresses the sort of things that might be useful in a more simplistic observation/reaction architecture. All the standard considerations apply: classification, attribute checking, sequencing, and so on are all fundamental control flow techniques for the language.

In sharp contrast to a general-purpose language, DSLs need not worry about handling every contingency under the sun in terms of writing agent behavior logic. Rather, the language designers craft the vocabulary and syntax with which the AI implementers assemble the final resulting scripts—the language is the bricks and mortar, and the actual building is up to the AI programmer or designer to accomplish.

The nature of those bricks can have profound consequences for the final constructed building. As such, just as with a tripwire architecture, DSLs require a large degree of context-specific decision making to be effective. It is exceedingly unlikely that a DSL from one genre of game could be readily reused in a totally different kind of simulation experience, for example.

It is worth mentioning again that confining a game to a single DSL is usually a mistake. Even within the AI system, it can be highly effective to deploy multiple DSLs in concert. Subsumption architectures are a perfect match for this approach, and master-script systems may see tremendous benefit from deploying DSLs for various subsets of the fine-detail control mechanisms.

The basic idea is to divide up agent behavior into discrete, well-defined, compact groupings, and write a language for each grouping. Describing the behavior of an agent wandering freely about the world might require a very different linguistic framework than

```
; Robot.dsl
set energy = get energy of robot
set mypos = get position of robot
set chargepos = get position of charger
compute homedist = distance mypos to chargepos
trigger if energy <= homedist
    path robot to chargepos
    wait until energy equals 100
trigger if energy > homedist
    set mywidget = get closest widget to robot
    set targetpos = get position of mywidget
    path robot to targetpos
    wait until mypos equals targetpos
    pickup mywidget
repeat
```

describing the exact same agent's split-second reactions during intense combat. Moreover, DSLs can even be nested—a high-level enter combat command in one DSL might invoke a far more detailed script implemented in a different, lower-level language.

Listing 16.1 illustrates a simple DSL fragment used to control a widget-gathering robot. For sake of brevity, the robot isn't terribly intelligent, but it should have enough basic logic to accomplish its mission and get lots of widgets. Unfortunately, it might eventually try for a widget that is too far from home, and run out of power before it can return to recharge; but extending the logic to safely avoid such widgets should be straightforward.

The key advantage of using a DSL for this logic is that any number of robot behaviors can be crafted without having to write any general-purpose control code in a more traditional programming language. As alluded to earlier, this enables a far wider audience to create AI scripts for the simulation project—a very effective force multiplier.

Note that the DSL snippet can be parsed using a trivial tokenizer; it looks readable enough, but the vocabulary is carefully chosen so that the code can be parsed and broken down into a sequence of simple command objects in program memory at runtime. For example, consider the line, set mywidget = get closest widget to robot. We can split this into a series of whitespace-delimited tokens using the string parsing facilities of our implementation language of choice. In most modern languages, this is no more than a line of code or a single library function call.

Next, we traverse the list from left to right. The intention is always clear without having to peek ahead to additional tokens in the stream—we want to set a variable called widget. The equals sign can be thought of as decoration to help make the program more readable. It can simply be discarded by the parser.

Once we have ascertained that the statement is a variable assignment, we proceed—again, from left to right. We determine that we will perform a lookup of some kind (get). This lookup should specifically find the closest of two entities in the simulation. Lastly, we realize that the two entities we want to look for are of type widget and robot. Each section of the phrase can be converted directly into some kind of in-memory representation for later execution without complicated parsing algorithms or nightmarish flashbacks to compiler architecture courses.

A typical approach to executing DSL code is to process the scripts once during load time and then store them in an in-memory format that is easy to handle for fast execution. If load time performance is an issue, most DSLs can be trivially preprocessed into binary formats that are faster to convert into the in-memory format.

There are many subtly different approaches to execution models, but for the most part, they boil down to a simple decision: should execution of a single instruction in the DSL code be accomplished by virtual function dispatch or by a switch statement? The particulars of making this decision will of course tend to vary widely between teams, levels of experience, architectural preferences and policies, and platform performance considerations.

In the virtual dispatch model, individual instructions are implemented as classes which derive from a common interface or abstract base class. During loading, instructions from the raw source are converted into instances of these classes as appropriate. During execution, the scripting engine simply stores a container of these objects and sequentially invokes a virtual function such as Execute on each one.

Parameters to each instruction can be stored in a variety of formats, but typically a simple typeless DSL will only need to store strings (or enumeration "tokens" for built-in strings) that represent each parameter's value. This allows each instruction to have a simple interface that accepts a generic, untyped container of parameters which it interprets according to the semantics of the instruction itself. Implementation of a full type system is certainly possible, but it is important to weigh the work of building a type system against the (typically marginal) gains that this offers for the sort of code likely to be written in the DSL.

The switch-based model is slightly more involved. Instructions are simple constant numerical values, typically stored in the host language's notion of an enumeration. Executing a stream of DSL code consists of reading an instruction value, performing the switch to invoke the correct functionality, and then parsing off parameters for the instruction.

This approach generally requires the notion of an explicit execution stack as well as other forms of storage. One powerful model is to have parameters to each DSL instruction passed via a stack, and other state accessible via a blackboard mechanism. The blackboard can be shared between different DSLs and even the core language of the engine, allowing seamless passing of knowledge between various AI layers. This can be especially useful if certain routines need to be implemented directly in low-level code for performance or storage reasons.

Flow control (conditions, loops, and so on) can also be more difficult in a switch-based implementation. It is generally advantageous to have assembly language experience when working with this model, as many of the same concepts are in play—explicit jumps to certain addresses for flow control, typeless storage, an execution stack, and so on.

By contrast, flow control in a virtual dispatch model is trivial: simply create an instruction class such as loop (for example) that stores its own container of attached instruction objects, and executes them repeatedly based on the loop conditions.

In general, virtual dispatch-based execution models are simpler to implement and maintain—particularly to extend—but come at the obvious cost of requiring virtual functions to operate. If the DSL is focused on high-level behavior rather than per-frame behavior, however, this may not be a significant loss; if an agent only needs to complete a "thought tick" every 3 seconds on average, the cost of virtual dispatch and storing the code as objects in memory is well worth it for the advantages in ease of use.

16.3.3 Integrated Architectures

Either way, though, rolling a DSL execution engine is a considerable undertaking, and should be carefully considered against other options. One particularly effective alternative is to use existing scripting engines—or even the low-level implementation language itself—in concert with specially crafted code structures that look and feel like a DSL but require none of the implementation investment.

These "integrated architectures" are built by constructing a library of classes or functions (or both) which represent the sum total of functionality that should be available to the scripted system. The "scripts" are then simply modules in the program that access only that limited subset of functionality, and nothing else.

Listing 16.2 illustrates the same robot and widget logic, implemented entirely in C++. This is the high-level "script" only—the implementation of each of the invoked functions is left up to the imagination. Obviously, some elements such as the Wait(); function would require some thought to implement successfully, but for the most part, this is simply good code architecture put into practice. There is no reaching out to the renderer, or the physics model, or even much of the world state itself. Everything is implemented in terms of simple routines that have been deemed appropriate for use by the AI.

Listing 16.2. This is the robot from Listing 16.1, reimplemented in C++ as part of an integrated architecture. Note that the logic looks very similar aside from superficial syntax differences; the idea is that the script logic is implemented in terms of lower-level functionality provided by a library.

```
//Robot.cpp
while (robot.IsActive()) {
    FloatValue energy = robot.GetEnergy();
    Position mypos = robot.GetPosition();
    Position chargepos = charger.GetPosition();
    FloatValue homedist = mypos.DistanceTo(chargepos);
    if(energy <= homedist) {
        robot.PathTo(chargepos);
        while(energy < 100.0f)
            Wait();
    }
    else {
        Widget mywidget = AllWidgets.GetClosest(mypos);
        Position targetpos = mywidget.GetPosition();
        robot.PathTo(targetpos);
        while(robot.GetPosition() != targetpos)
            Wait();
        robot.PickUp(mywidget);
    }
}
```

Clearly, this is predicated heavily on programmer discipline. There is little stopping a programmer from accessing functionality directly in the rendering system, or even the operating system itself, for example. Certain measures can be taken (limiting the use of `#include` in C and C++, or `using` in C# and `import` in Java, and so on) but ultimately it is up to the leadership of the team to ensure that all code complies with the restrictions on what functionality should be used from the "script" modules.

At first blush, integrated architecture may not sound like a scripting solution at all—there is no special language in use, no external tools, and only a minimum of specially crafted logic to support the system. However, upon closer examination, integrated architectures still fit into the paradigms of master and servant architectures described earlier and can accomplish precisely the same things as a separate scripting language.

There are several major advantages to using an integrated architecture over a separate language implementation. First, it allows programmers to use their existing language knowledge and skills without much modification. Second, using an existing language opens up access to all of the existing tools for working in that language—IDEs, debuggers, compilers, profilers, and so on. Third, it removes a layer of execution abstraction between the logic and the underlying platform, which can be a substantial performance win on lower-end hardware or when the team lacks an experienced optimizations engineer to work on the scripting language implementation.

Last, but certainly not least, integrated architectures provide an illustrative method for writing almost any large-scale code. The layered approach has been heavily encouraged for decades, with notable proponents including Fred Brooks and the SICP course from MIT. Learning to structure code in this way can be a powerful force multiplier for creating clean, well separated modules for the rest of the project, even well outside the scope of AI systems.

Although the example in Listing 16.2 uses C++, it is not necessarily the most effective language for building an integrated architecture. Lua is an immensely popular option, and provides a powerful and high-performance framework on which to build scripted systems. An embedded Python implementation can use `yield` statements instead of the `Wait()` function to accomplish cooperative multitasking between agents with very little work. For programmers who happen to be familiar with JavaScript, an embedded implementation of that language can easily use a callback-oriented event model for interleaving agent processing, as used in notable stacks such as `Node.js`.

The critical tradeoff here is giving up access to existing debugging and instrumentation tool support, in exchange for a bit of extra safety (the high-level scripting language can be trivially prevented from accessing unrelated functionality such as the renderer) and a potentially large productivity boost. This is yet another judgment call that must be made on a per-team and even per-project basis, taking into account the team's skill levels, experience levels, development preferences, and so on as well as the requirements of the target platform and the scope of the project itself.

16.4 Writing the Actual Scripts

With the dominating technical issues considered, it is time to move on to actually building a complete and functional AI using the scripting technologies of choice. Although the selection of a master or servant architecture and the details of the scripting system's implementation can play a significant role in the outcome of a scripted AI, the real artistry—and the real black magic—lies in building effective scripts on top of the technical foundation.

There are a number of challenges to creating a compelling gameplay experience via scripting. First and foremost, it is important to realize that scripting cannot and should not be used for everything. Whether in a master or servant role, scripting is most effective when used in concert with other techniques, as the project in question requires.

The chief problem with overusing scripting is combinatorial explosion. Trying to anticipate every possible circumstance that needs to be scripted for is a losing proposition. Inevitably, players will encounter some situation that the AI was not preprogrammed to handle, and the immersion will be lost entirely as the AI does something incredibly stupid. Worse, the more robust the AI seems to be, the harder these failures hit when they do occur; perfection cannot be achieved, and for the most part, the closer a scripted system comes to appearing perfect, the more disappointing its shortcomings will seem.

This can be mitigated by relying on other technologies where scripting is liable to become too hard to manage manually. The selection of these supplemental techniques is highly sensitive to the demands of each individual and unique project, but the primary guideline to keep in mind is that general situations call for general solutions. Scripting is, for the most part, a highly specific and focused approach to creating agent behavior, particularly in the servant role. It is not generally all that effective at responding to an unpredictable diversity of situations. Even in the master configuration, scripting must be carefully planned to anticipate the categories of behavior to be selected, and deferring to alternative systems is advisable when the lines get fuzzy.

16.4.1 Iteration

When implementing an AI that involves heavy use of scripting, rapid iteration is vital. As the scripts take shape, there will inevitably be gaps in the range of scenarios that the scripts are prepared to handle. Moreover, there will also be discrepancies between what the player expects an agent to rationally or believably do, and what actually occurs.

Because of this, it is crucial to test and refine scripted logic as often and thoroughly as possible. Teams with work environments set up for rapid iteration will benefit greatly, as the tiny problems can be ironed out and turned into a cohesive result. Slow or nonexistent iteration is a recipe for disaster. Because of scripting's inherent tendency to slide towards hard-coded and fixed solutions, neglecting iteration will almost inevitably result in brittle and boring behavior.

The flip side of this, of course, is that once a system passes a certain degree of flexibility and adaptability, it becomes increasingly difficult to test exhaustively. Substantial changes at this point run the serious risk of introducing more potential side effects than can be reliably checked and validated. So while iteration remains important, it is also key to limit the scope of changes made in each pass, so as to avoid constantly creating wildly different experiences that are virtually impossible to test to a satisfactory degree.

16.4.2 Transitions

There are any number of transitions that may occur during the course of a simulation unfolding: transitions between behavior control systems when scripting is used in the master role, transitions between scripts in the servant approach, transitions between levels of detail when using a subsumption architecture, and so on.

All of these transitions represent a significant challenge to creating seamless and believable scripted experiences. Any time the control of an agent undergoes such a change, it opens the possibility of a discontinuity in the perception of that agent on the part of the player.

To help alleviate this, it is important to know what transitions will occur up front during the design of the AI itself. Each transition must be carefully considered to ensure that the handoff is smooth and convincing. There are a few tricks for assisting with this, such as shared knowledge systems. If both the outgoing and incoming scripts have access to the exact same set of information, it becomes simpler to ensure that they behave consistently. Another useful variant on this technique is to explicitly communicate between the two scripts, such as handing off internal state data from one to the other.

Going a step further, it can be useful to inject special-case logic for certain transitions. For example, when moving between levels of detail, there can be great gains in believability to be had by adding extra transitory levels. These exist specifically to smooth out the jump from one degree of fidelity to another; they should be designed to come and go quickly, and give way to more long-lasting levels. In general, the larger the potential discrepancy between the behavior generated by two systems, the more appropriate it can be to use interstitial logic.

16.4.3 Variety

One of the harshest but most applicable criticisms leveled against a typical scripted AI system concerns lack of variety. Overly simplistic use of tripwire systems, for example, can easily lead to this undesirable result: if the hero is hailed by another character—using the exact same dialogue—every time he walks back and forth over some invisible line, players will inevitably lose their immersion into the simulation and come away with a less than optimal impression of the AI. Larger scale examples tend to be even more disruptive to the experience.

For this reason, it is well worth spending some time up front in design to make sure that the scripted behavior can avoid feeling canned or stale. Deduplication of tripwire activations, as discussed previously, is one simple but effective technique for doing this. In general, making sure that events do not repeat (or do not repeat too often) is a good policy for improving the feel of a scripted AI system.

Of course, past a point, adding more variety to a game's content becomes a practical problem. Content is not free to produce, and the increase in required assets may be prohibitive. In this case, simple limitations on the frequency of scripted events repeating themselves can go a long way.

Another useful trick, especially with master-style control systems, is to stagger the scripts and their execution across time. In other words, rather than having all agents begin their scripts at the exact same moment, they are dropped into the action at various points midway through the script. This avoids the eerily robotic look of dozens of ambient AI agents performing the exact same routine in a sort of zombie lockstep. A great advantage of this approach is that it requires no additional content assets; just trigger behaviors on different timetables for each agent, and over time their routines will tend to spread out and form interesting emergent interactions.

Master systems tend to be a little easier to use when it comes to creating variety. Because the master script is delegating to one or more of a handful of actual control systems for agents, a natural variegation will emerge from the fact that not every agent is executing in the same control scheme at a given time. Servant style scripting can be just as diverse and interesting, but at the expense of requiring much more special-case logic and design work up front.

Either way, scripts should generally be seen as a sort of "glue" that interconnects other techniques for creating convincing agent behavior. Some game implementations may be largely constructed out of scripts, but in the end, reliance on other mechanisms becomes paramount. Even if it is as simple as delegating to steering and navigation systems, handing off control from a purely hard-wired script to another system goes a long way toward creating good variety and ensuring that different situations can be handled by the AI agents effectively.

16.4.4 Surprise

Next to variety, surprise is one of the most commonly lacking elements in a script-heavy AI. Unfortunately, it is also one of the most ethereal and subjective qualities to pursue in game creation. Creating experiences that can surprise and entertain players is a difficult design challenge, regardless of scripting's role in the project itself.

Working closely with designers and testers (for iterative feedback) is, of course, central to accomplishing this goal. However, there are a few technical decisions that can heavily affect how practical it is to create surprising and engaging encounters with a game's AI agents. For example, excessively complex scripting systems (such as entire full-blown programming languages) can cost far more in terms of implementation effort than they deliver in terms of final game quality. This is true not only of the core technology's implementation itself, but also of the scripts built using that technology.

Because of this, it is advisable to favor simple solutions that require a little bit of creativity over excessively complex and deceptively "powerful" systems. Carefully designed tripwire systems, minimalistic DSLs, and well-crafted integrated architectures can all be set up in such a way as to provide tremendous amounts of flexibility for design purposes without becoming overly complicated.

The important factor here is giving designers and script implementers the ability to efficiently handle a diverse range of possible scenarios in which the player may find herself. However, it is just as important to resist the urge to anticipate every possible situation in advance. The specifics of this depend on whether a master or servant approach is taken.

For the master ideology, it is sufficient to categorize a broad range of situations and react to them appropriately via delegation. The servant perspective requires a little more care. Generally, the goal is to avoid creating scripts for all possible scenarios, and allowing generalized behavior control schemes to dominate as much of the time as possible. This enables the AI to provide a varied and interesting experience while retaining the potential for carefully crafted encounters created via scripts.

16.4.5 Narrative

Perhaps the most effective home for scripting is in the creation of rich narrative experiences. When specific sequences of events are meant to unfold in a particular way during gameplay, scripting is the logical choice for implementing such a design. As has hopefully become clear, this is not the only venue in which scripting can be an effective tool, but it is certainly one of the most natural.

Creating a compelling interactive narrative experience is no small task. For its part, AI must be designed to help further the experience, and not fight against it [Barnes et al. 02]. Everyone has stories of watching a hapless character stoically continue their idle animations while chaos and battle rage all around them. Slightly less common but just as egregious are situations where the AI actively seems to refuse to do what it is meant to do.

A major component of creating good narrative AI is visibility. The developer must always be able to understand why the AI has done something particular. When using scripting, this often simply boils down to keeping a trace log of the steps that have been performed by the agent, and, where applicable, what branches have been selected and how often loops have been repeated. Being able to select an agent and view a debug listing of its complete script state is also an invaluable tool.

In the end, interactive narratives are most compelling when everything works together to create a harmonious gameplay experience. Careful iteration, attention to transitions, provision of variety, and the occasional surprise all play key roles in fulfilling this objective.

16.5 Conclusion

Scripting is all too often treated as a brittle, boring, and undesirable approach to creating game AI systems. Unfortunately, this stigma is largely justified by the negative experiences of players struggling to enjoy games with little depth or variety to their AI interactions. The good news is that this is not an inevitable outcome; with proper care and investment, scripting can be a very powerful tool.

To wield this tool effectively requires intimate coordination between the design and technical concerns of the project. Knowing the design plans and requirements is critical to success, as is forethought on how to accomplish those plans.

Moreover, scripting must be viewed as simply one tool in a diverse toolbox. Over-reliance on scripts is bound to wind up producing the exact brittle, boring results that we are trying to avoid. Scripts should be seen as a sort of glue that attaches various decision-making, planning, and knowledge representation systems into a cohesive and powerful whole.

By the same token, it is important to resist the urge to try to anticipate everything that a script might need to handle. Delegation to other technologies and techniques is crucial to upholding the quality of the final game experience. Whether this is done via a "master" or "servant" approach, consistency of application is also vital. Staying true to a design philosophy, chosen early on, will help guide the creation of all of the scripted logic and underlying technologies.

As is often the case in software engineering, simpler is better when it comes to script systems. Designers have a persistent knack for creatively using (some might say abusing) any tool set before them; this can be leveraged for great effect. Instead of creating overly complicated and intricate systems, focus on creating simple ones that are flexible and can be used in creative and interesting ways.

Last but not least, never ship blind. Play testing and iteration are critical to refining and drawing out the fun in a game, and this applies just as strongly to scripted AI as anything else. Always be prepared to rapidly tweak an interaction based on player feedback or design decisions, and stay nimble.

Scripts are a sharp blade. They can accomplish amazing feats, but one false move can be hazardous. There is no need to fear, however; with proper care and control, scripting remains one of the most powerful techniques available to the AI creator. Whether it is a simple looping behavior or a complex, blossoming tree of intricate narrative possibilities, scripting is everywhere.

It takes only some imagination and some discipline to unleash.

References

[Barnes et al. 02] J. Barnes and J. Hutchens. "Scripting for undefined circumstances." In *AI Game Programming Wisdom*, edited by Steve Rabin. Hingham, MA: Charles River Media, 2002.

[Brockington et al. 02] M. Brockington and M. Darrah. "How not to implement a basic scripting language." In *AI Game Programming Wisdom,* edited by Steve Rabin. Hingham, MA: Charles River Media, 2002.

[McNaughton et al. 06] M. McNaughton and T. Roy. "Creating a visual scripting system." In *AI Game Programming Wisdom 3*, edited by Steve Rabin. Charles River Media, 2006.

[Orkin 02] J. Orkin. "A general purpose trigger system." In *AI Game Programming Wisdom*, edited by Steve Rabin. Hingham, MA: Charles River Media, 2002.

[Poiker 02] F. Poiker. "Creating scripting languages for non-programmers." In *AI Game Programming Wisdom*, edited by Steve Rabin. Hingham, MA: Charles River Media, 2002.

[Tozour 02] P. Tozour. "The perils of AI scripting." In *AI Game Programming Wisdom*, edited by Steve Rabin. Hingham, MA: Charles River Media, 2002.

PART III
Movement and Pathfinding

17

Pathfinding Architecture Optimizations

Steve Rabin and Nathan R. Sturtevant

17.1 Introduction

Agent path requests are notorious for devouring huge proportions of the AI's CPU cycles in many genres of games, such as real-time strategy games and first-person shooters. Therefore, there is a large need for AI programmers to all be on the same page when it comes to optimizing pathfinding architectures. This chapter will cover in a priority order the most significant steps you can take to get the fastest pathfinding engine possible.

All game developers understand that A* is the pathfinding search algorithm of choice, but surprisingly, or not so surprisingly, it is not a panacea. There is a huge realm of knowledge that is crucial to crafting the fastest engine. In fact, even if a large number of pathfinding design choices have already been made, there is still much you can do.

17.2 Orders of Magnitude Difference in Performance

What is the difference between the fastest and slowest A* implementations?

At the DigiPen Institute of Technology video game university, the introductory AI course has students program a simple A* implementation on fixed regular grid as one of the first assignments. As extra credit for the assignment, there is a contest held to see who can write the fastest A* implementation. So if you were to guess the difference between the fastest and slowest solutions, what would you guess? Would you guess that the best solution is several times faster than the slowest?

The true answer is quite surprising. Given hundreds of students who have taken the course over the years, the fastest implementations are 2 orders of magnitude faster than the slowest implementations (a 100× difference). The fastest implementations are also 1 order of magnitude faster than the average implementation (a 10× difference). To put concrete numbers behind this example, on a given map, the fastest implementation finds a path in ~200 us, the average takes ~2500 us, and the slowest implementations take upwards of 20,000 us. Given that these are junior, senior, and master's students, how do you think you would rank if given the same task? It's a strange question, since as a professional game programmer you would never be put in such a position. Wherever you might rank, it is a scary thought that you might be 1 to 2 orders of magnitude slower than the best solution.

Although with fewer students, the second author has had similar experiences with his students in both regular assignments and competitions. The insights of both authors have been distilled here. Thus, you might want to scour this chapter for the nuggets of wisdom that will keep you within spitting distance of the best implementations.

17.3 Optimization #1: Build High-Quality Heuristics

This first optimization is the epitome of the classic programming trade-off between memory and speed. There are many ways that heuristics can be built; we will go through several useful approaches here.

17.3.1 Precompute Every Single Path (Roy–Floyd–Warshall)

While at first glance it seems ridiculous, it is possible to precompute every single path in a search space and store it in a look-up table. The memory implications are severe, but there are ways to temper the memory requirements and make it work for games.

The algorithm is known in English-speaking circles as the Floyd–Warshall algorithm, while in Europe it is better known as Roy–Floyd. Since the algorithm was independently discovered by three different mathematicians, we'll give credit to each and refer to it as the Roy–Floyd–Warshall algorithm [Millington 09].

While we won't explain the algorithm in enough detail to implement it, you should be aware of its basic advantages and properties so that you can make an informed choice whether to pursue implementing it for your game. Here are the facts:

- Roy–Floyd–Warshall is the absolute fastest way to generate a path at runtime. It should routinely be an order of magnitude faster than the best A* implementation.
- The look-up table is calculated offline before the game ships.
- The look-up table requires $O(n^2)$ entries, where n is the number of nodes. For example, for a 100 by 100 grid search space, there are 10,000 nodes. Therefore, the memory required for the look-up table would be 100,000,000 entries (with 2 bytes per entry, this would be ~200 MB).
- Path generation is as simple as looking up the answer. The time complexity is $O(p)$, where p is the number of nodes in the final path.

Figure 17.1 shows a search space graph and the resulting tables generated by the Roy–Floyd–Warshall algorithm. A full path is found by consecutively looking up the next step in the path (left table in Figure 17.1). For example, if you want to find a final path from B to A, you would first look up the entry for (B, A), which is node D. You would travel to node D, then look up the next step of the path (D, A), which would be node E. By repeating this all the way to node A, you will travel the optimal path with an absolute minimum amount of CPU work. If there are dynamic obstacles in the map which must be avoided, this approach can be used as a very accurate heuristic estimate, provided that distances are stored in the look-up table instead of the next node to travel to (right table in Figure 17.1).

As we mentioned earlier, in games you can make the memory requirement more reasonable by creating minimum node networks that are connected to each other [Waveren 01, van der Sterren 04]. For example if you have 1000 total nodes in your level, this would normally require $1000^2 = 1,000,000$ entries in a table. But if you can create 50 node zones of 20 nodes each, then the total number of entries required is $50 \times 20^2 = 20,000$ (which is 50 times fewer entries).

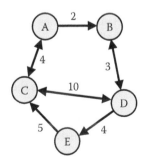

Next Node Look-Up Table

	A	B	C	D	E
A	A	B	C	B	B
B	D	B	D	D	D
C	A	A	C	A	A
D	E	B	E	D	E
E	C	C	C	C	E

Cost to Goal Look-Up Table

	A	B	C	D	E
A	0	2	4	5	9
B	16	0	12	3	7
C	4	6	0	9	13
D	13	3	9	0	4
E	9	11	5	14	0

Figure 17.1

A search space with its corresponding Roy–Floyd–Warshall path look-up table on the left and a very accurate heuristic cost look-up table on the right.

17.3.2 Lossless Compression of Roy–Floyd–Warshall

Another approach to reducing the memory requirement is to compress the Roy–Floyd–Warshall data. Published work [Botea 11] has shown the effectiveness of compressing the data, and this approach fared very well in the 2012 Grid-Based Path Planning competition (http://www.movingai.com/GPPC/), when sufficient memory was available.

An alternate way to compress the Roy–Floyd–Warshall data is to take advantage of the structure of the environment. In many maps, but not all maps, there are relatively few optimal paths of significant length through the state space, and most of these paths overlap. Thus, it is possible to find a sparse number of "transit nodes" through which optimal paths cross [Bast et al. 07]. If, for every state in the state space, we store the path to all transit nodes for that state, as well as the optimal paths between all transit nodes, we can easily reconstruct the shortest path information between any two states, using much less space than when storing the shortest path between all pairs of states. This is one of several methods which have been shown to be highly effective on highway road maps [Abraham et al. 10].

17.3.3 Lossy Compression of Roy–Floyd–Warshall

The full Roy–Floyd–Warshall data results in very fast pathfinding queries, at the cost of memory overhead. In many cases you might want to use less memory and more CPU, which suggests building strong, but not perfect heuristics.

Imagine if we store just a few rows/columns of the Roy–Floyd–Warshall data. This corresponds to keeping the shortest paths from a few select nodes. Fortunately, improved distance estimates between all nodes can be inferred from this data. If $d(x, y)$ is the distance between node x and y, and we know $d(p, z)$ for all z, then the estimated distance between x and y is $h(x, y) = | d(p, x) - d(p, y) |$, where p is a pivot node that corresponds to a single row/column in the Roy–Floyd–Warshall data. With multiple pivot nodes, we can perform multiple heuristic lookups and take the maximum. The improved estimates will reduce the cost of A* search.

This approach has been developed in many contexts and been given many different names [Ng and Zhang 01, Goldberg and Harrelson 05, Goldenberg et al. 11, Rayner et al. 11]. We prefer the name *Euclidean embedding*, which we will justify shortly. First, we summarize the facts about this approach:

- Euclidean embeddings can be far more accurate than the default heuristics for a map, and in some maps are nearly as fast as Roy-Floyd-Warshall.
- The look-up table can be calculated before the game ships or at runtime, depending on the size and dynamic nature of the maps.
- The heuristic requires $O(kn)$ entries, where n is the number of nodes and k is the number of pivots.
- Euclidean embeddings provide a heuristic for guiding A* search. Given multiple heuristics, A* should usually take the maximum of all available heuristics.

Why do we call this a Euclidean embedding? Consider a map that is wrapped into a spiral, such as in Figure 17.2. Points A and B are quite close in the coordinates of the map, but quite far when considering the minimal travel distance between A and B. If we could just unroll the map into a straight line, the distance estimates would be more accurate. Thus, the central problem is that the coordinates used for aesthetic and gameplay

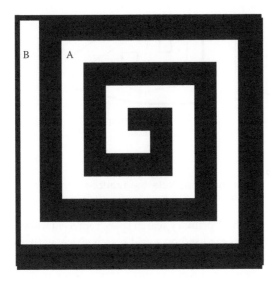

Figure 17.2

A map where straight-line distances are inaccurate.

purposes are not the best for A* search purposes. That is, they do not provide accurate heuristic estimates. If we could provide a different set of coordinates optimized for A* search, we could use these coordinates to estimate distances between nodes and have a higher quality heuristic. This process of transforming a map into a new state space where distance estimates are (hopefully) more accurate is called an *embedding*. A single-source shortest-path search from a pivot node is equivalent to performing a one-dimensional embedding, as each node gets a single coordinate, and the heuristic in this embedding is the distance between the embedded points. Other types of embeddings are possible, just not yet well understood.

The key question of this approach is how the pivots should be selected. In general, a pivot should not be at the center of the map, but near the edges. The heuristic from pivot p between nodes x and y will be most accurate when the optimal path from p to x goes through y. In many games, there are locations where characters will commonly travel, which suggests good locations for pivots. In a RPG, for instance, entrance and exit points to an area are good locations. In a RTS, player bases would be most useful. In a capture-the-flag FPS, the location of the flag would probably work well.

17.4 Optimization #2: Using an Optimal Search Space Representation

If you have to search for a path at runtime, then the number one optimization you can make is to use an efficient search space representation. The reason is that the time spent looking for a path is directly proportional to the number of nodes that must be considered. Fewer nodes equates to less time searching. A more in-depth discussion on choosing a search space representation can be found within this book [Sturtevant 13].

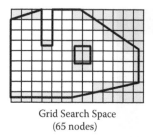 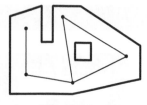 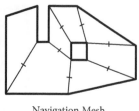

Grid Search Space
(65 nodes)

Waypoint Graph
(5 nodes)

Navigation Mesh
(7 nodes)

Figure 17.3

Three search space representations. Note the number of nodes in each representation, which affects search speed.

Figure 17.3 shows the three primary search space representations available. As you can plainly see, the most nodes are used by a grid search space, with an order of magnitude fewer nodes in the waypoint graph and the navigation mesh (navmesh).

If you have a large world, none of the three search space representations will be sufficient to keep CPU load to a minimum. Instead, you need to resort to subdividing the search space with a hierarchical representation. *Hierarchical pathfinding* is the concept that the search space can be subdivided into at least two levels: a high-level zone-to-zone representation and a low-level step-by-step representation [Rabin 00]. In this scheme, a path is first found in the high-level representation from the starting zone to the goal zone (think of rooms in a castle, starting in the foyer and finding a room-to-room path to the balcony). Then, to begin moving, the low-level path is found from within the starting zone to the next zone on the path (for example, from the standing place in the foyer to the next room on the path). Once the second zone is entered, a step-by-step path is then found from the second zone to the third zone, and so on.

Two concrete examples of hierarchical pathfinding in shipped games include *Dragon Age: Origins* [Sturtevant 08] and *Company of Heroes* [Jurney et al. 07]. The final architecture in *Dragon Age: Origins* used two levels of grid-based abstraction above the low-level grid. In *Company of Heroes*, the high-level search space representation was a hex-grid and the low-level representation was a regular square grid. If there isn't enough memory to store the Roy–Floyd–Warshall solution in memory for the low-level state space, there is usually enough memory to store this information in an abstract state space.

17.5 Optimization #3: Preallocate All Necessary Memory

Once you have optimized the search space, the next step is to ensure that absolutely no memory is allocated during the search. Although this knowledge should be ingrained among all game programmers, it can't be stressed enough. Memory allocation during a search can increase search times by at least an order of magnitude.

How do you avoid memory allocations? Simply preallocate a pool of memory at start time and reuse it. Since nodes are all the same memory size, they can easily be pulled out of a pre-allocated buffer without any fragmentation issues.

The memory needed for A* can also be part of the map representation. This avoids the need to explicitly store a separate closed list, as each node in the map can have a flag indicating whether it is on closed or not. If an id is used instead of a Boolean flag, the search can avoid having to reset the nodes in the closed list between most searches.

17.6 Optimization #4: Overestimating the Heuristic

In order for A* to guarantee an optimal path, the heuristic must be admissible, meaning that the heuristic guess of the cost from the current node to the goal node must never overestimate the true cost. However, by using an overestimating heuristic, you can get a tremendous speed-up at the possible expense of a slightly nonoptimal path. While this sounds like a terrible trade-off initially, it turns out that a small amount of overestimating has large benefits with very little noticeable nonoptimality. In the world of search algorithms this once might have been seen as heresy, but in the video game industry it's a shrewd and worthwhile optimization.

In order to understand how to overestimate the heuristic, let's first look at Equation 17.1, which is the classic A* cost formula. As you can see, the final cost, $f(x)$, is the sum of the given cost, $g(x)$, and the heuristic cost, $h(x)$. Each node added to the Open List gets this final cost assigned to it and this is how the Open List is sorted.

$$f(x) = g(x) + h(x) \tag{17.1}$$

Equation 17.2 shows the addition of a weight on the heuristic portion of the formula.

$$f(x) = g(x) + \left(h(x) \times weight\right) \tag{17.2}$$

By altering the weight, we can tune how A* behaves. If the weight is zero, then the formula reduces down to just $g(x)$, which is identical to the Dijkstra search algorithm. This approach is guaranteed to find an optimal path, but is not a "smart" search because it explores uniformly outward in all directions. If the weight is 1.0, then the equation is the classic A* formula, guaranteed to expand the minimal number of nodes needed to find an optimal path given the current heuristic estimate, modulo tie-breaking. If the weight is larger than 1.0, then we are tilting the algorithm toward the behavior of Greedy Best-First search, which is not optimal but focuses the search on finding the goal as quickly as possible.

Thus, we can tune A* with the weight to lean it toward Dijkstra or Greedy Best-First. By using weights in the neighborhood of 1.1 to 1.5 or higher, we can progressively force the search to more aggressively push toward the goal node, at the increasing expense of a possible sub-optimal path. When the terrain is filled with random obstacles that resemble columns or trees, then a larger weight makes a lot of sense and the path is not noticeably suboptimal. However, if significant backtracking away from the goal is required for the final path, then a lower weight is advisable.

The correct weight for your game or parts of your game must be discovered experimentally. There is also the possibility of adaptively discovering the ideal weight for an area given a particular error tolerance on how suboptimal the path is allowed to be. See [Thayer and Ruml 08] for one such algorithm. At any rate, overestimating the heuristic is a tried and true optimization for games that you will want to explore.

17.7 Optimization #5: Better Heuristics

There are two ways to use better heuristics. First, some heuristics are more suited to solve certain problems, and so selecting the correct heuristic can significantly reduce the work required to solve a problem. The second approach is to build and store improved heuristics, of which the Roy–Floyd–Warshall algorithm is just one example. Building a new heuristic is most useful when the map topology is relatively static, as changing the world can invalidate a heuristic.

As for heuristic selection, consider pathfinding on a grid, with 8-directional movement. Three possible heuristics are straight-line (Euclidean) distance, octile distance, which assumes that only 45° and 90° angles are allowed, and Manhattan (city-block) distance. Manhattan distance is a poor heuristic, because it will overestimate distances, not taking diagonal movement into account. A straight-line heuristic is also poor, because it will underestimate distances, assuming that paths can take any angle. The octile heuristic, which corresponds exactly to movement in the world, is the most accurate and best heuristic to use on a grid. The octile heuristic between two points can be computed as $max(\Delta x, \Delta y) + 0.41 \cdot min(\Delta x, \Delta y)$, assuming that diagonal movement has cost 1.41.

17.8 Optimization #6: Open List Sorting

A textbook description of A* states that the node with the lowest f-cost should be expanded at each step. A more efficient implementation will break ties between nodes with equal f-costs towards those with largest g-cost, as these nodes are expected to be closer to the goal. This results in better tie-breaking, which can be quite significant in some maps. The sorting for the Open list can be done in a priority queue structure such as a heap, although researchers have spent significant effort improving these data structures, so if full sorting is required, a weak-heap [Edelkamp et al., 12] is just one option for speeding up A*. It is very often the case that the last node inserted into priority queue is immediately removed again for the next expansion. Caching an inserted node before inserting it into the Open List can reduce this overhead.

An even more efficient approach is to avoid explicitly sorting states. In state spaces where the number of unique f-costs will be small, a list can be maintained for each unique f-cost; finding the best node on the Open List is as simple as taking the first node off the list with the smallest f-cost. It would seem that this would preclude tie-breaking by higher g-costs, but treating each f-cost list as a LIFO stack will produce similar tie-breaking.

In some searches, the number of nodes considered is limited, such that the Open List typically has under 10 or so nodes with a max of 20 or 30. In such a case, an unordered Open List represented as an array might actually be the best choice, although this should always be verified experimentally. Inserting new nodes is essentially free, O(1), and finding the cheapest node is a matter of simply walking the short list. Without the overhead of even a trivial scheme, an unordered Open List can be extremely fast since it simply doesn't execute that many instructions. To offer a little more detail, the unordered Open List is held as an array, with inserted nodes placed at the end of the array. When a node must be removed, it is replaced with the node at the end, in order to stay packed. With this data structure, the overhead in maintaining the data structure is almost nonexistent and its minimalist size (one pointer per node) means that it is very cache-friendly, thus resulting in even more speed.

17.9 Optimization #7: Don't Backtrack during the Search

It might seem obvious, but no path ever backtracks along the same nodes it's already visited, so similarly an A* search should also not consider nodes that backtrack. In practice, this is as simple as not considering a neighboring node if it is the same as the parent node. This simple optimization will speed up a search by roughly one over the branching factor. For a grid search space this is 1/8, but for a navmesh search space it's about 1/3.

In grids there are many short cycles, meaning that there is overhead from redundantly looking up a given state from many different neighbors. An inexpensive scan through the state space can allow the search to skip many intermediate nodes to avoid these redundant lookups. The full details of this approach are part of the Jump-Point Search algorithm [Harabor and Grastien 11].

17.10 Optimization #8: Caching Successors

One of the most common operations in an A* search is to look up the neighbors of a node. Thus, it follows that this operation should be as cheap as possible. Storing the neighbors of each node explicitly, rather than traversing more expensive data structures, can result in significant improvements in speed, at the cost of additional memory.

17.11 Bad Ideas for Pathfinding

The following are a list of bad ideas that usually result in slower pathfinding searches.

17.11.1 Bad Idea #1: Simultaneous Searches

When many pathfinding search requests are required all at once, an architectural decision must be made as to how many simultaneous search requests should be processed at the same time. For example, if 10 requests are all needed, it's a tempting thought to time-slice between all of the requests so that one very slow search doesn't hold the others up.

Unfortunately, supporting many simultaneous searches at the same time is fraught with disaster. The primary problem is that you'll need to support separate Open Lists for each request. The implications are severe as to the amount of memory required, and the subsequent thrashing in the cache can be devastating.

But what is to be done about a single search that holds up all other searches? On one hand, this might be a false concern because your pathfinding engine should be blindingly fast for all searches. If it isn't, then that's an indication that you chose the wrong search space representation or should be using hierarchical pathfinding.

However, if we concede that a single search might take a very long time to calculate, then one solution is to learn from supermarkets. The way supermarkets deal with this problem is to create two types of check-out lanes. One is for customers with very few items (10 items or less) and one for the customers with their cart overflowing with groceries. We can do a similar thing with pathfinding by allowing up to two searches at a time.

One queue is for requests deemed to be relatively fast (based on distance between the start and goal) and one queue for requests deemed to take a long time (again based on distance between the start and goal).

17.11.2 Bad Idea #2: Bidirectional Pathfinding

One innovative approach for a search algorithm is to search the path from both directions and complete the path when the searches meet each other. This bidirectional pathfinding reduces the amount of nodes visited with breadth-first and depth-first searches [Pohl 71], but what about A*?

One brilliant reason to consider this approach is the continent and island problem. Consider a search that begins on the continent and the goal is on an island, but we are unable to cross water. With a traditional A* search starting on the continent, the entire continent must be explored before the search concludes that no path exists, which is very, very time consuming. With bidirectional pathfinding, the search starts at both ends, the island side quickly runs out of nodes, and the search concludes that there is no path (with a minimal amount of work).

The continent-island argument however is better solved using a hierarchical approach. At a minimum, the continent would be considered one zone and the island another zone. For a hierarchical architecture, the top-level search would almost instantly discover that no path connects the two zones and the search would fail quickly.

But even without considering the continent-island argument, the truth is that bidirectional pathfinding for A* often requires twice the amount of work. This can be seen when the two searches are separated by a barrier and both searches back up behind the barrier until one spills over and connects. Since we care more about the worst case than best case, this is an important case to avoid. For these reasons, bidirectional pathfinding for A* is usually a poor choice.

17.11.2 Bad Idea #3: Cache Successful or Failed Paths

While caching results for expensive operations is generally good optimization advice, it is not a good idea for paths. The reason is that there are simply too many unique paths. The memory requirements would be very large (similar to Roy–Floyd–Warshall), and the chance that you'll request exactly the same path again is very small.

17.12 Conclusion

This article has covered the techniques for improving the speed of your A* implementation. Using these ideas can ensure that your code is on par with the best possible implementations, and several orders of magnitude faster than more naïve implementations.

References

[Abraham et al. 10] I. Abraham, A. Fiat, A. V. Goldberg, and R. F. F. Werneck. "Highway Dimension, Shortest Paths, and Provably Efficient Algorithms." *ACM-SIAM Symposium on Discrete Algorithms*, pp. 782–793, 2010. Available online (http://research.microsoft.com/pubs/115272/soda10.pdf).

[Bast et al. 07] H. Bast, S. Funke, P. Sanders, and D. Schultes. "In Transit to Constant Time Shortest-Path Queries in Road Networks." Workshop on Algorithm Engineering and Experiments, 2007. Available online (http://www.siam.org/proceedings/alenex/2007/alx07_transit.pdf).

[Botea 11] A. Botea. "Ultra-fast optimal pathfinding without runtime search." *AAAI Conference on Artificial Intelligence and Interactive Digital Entertainment*, pp. 122–127, 2011. Available online (http://www.aaai.org/ocs/index.php/AIIDE/AIIDE11/paper/view/4050).

[Edelkamp et al., 12] S. Edelkamp, A. Elmasry, and J. Katajainen. "The weak-heap family of priority queues in theory and praxis." *Proceedings of the 18th Computing: The Australasian Theory Symposium, Conferences in Research and Practice in Information Technology*, pp. 103–112, 2012. Available online (http://www.cphstl.dk/Paper/CATS12/cats12.pdf).

[Goldberg and Harrelson 05] A. V. Goldberg and C. Harrelson. "Computing the shortest path: A search meets graph theory." *ACM-SIAM Symposium on Discrete Algorithms*, pp. 156–165, 2005.

[Goldenberg et al. 11] M. Goldenberg, N. R. Sturtevant, A. Felner, and J. Schaeffer. "The compressed differential heuristic." *AAAI Conference on Artificial Intelligence*, pp. 24-29, 2011. Available online (http://www.aaai.org/ocs/index.php/AAAI/AAAI11/paper/view/3723).

[Harabor and Grastien 11] D. Harabor and A. Grastein. Online Graph Pruning for Pathfinding On Grid Maps, *Proceedings of the AAAI Conference on Artificial Intelligence (2011)*, pp. 1114–1119. Available online (http://www.aaai.org/ocs/index.php/AAAI/AAAI11/paper/view/3761).

[Jurney et al. 07] C. Jurney and S. Hubick. "Dealing with destruction: AI from the trenches of company of heroes." *Game Developers Conference*, 2007. Available online (https://store.cmpgame.com/product.php?cat=24&id=2089).

[Millington 09] I. Millington. "Constant Time Game Pathfinding with the Roy–Floyd–Warshall Algorithm." http://idm.me.uk/ai/wfi.pdf, 2009.

[Ng and Zhang 01] T. S. Eugene Ng and H. Zhang. "Predicting Internet network distance with coordinates-based approaches." *IEEE International Conference on Computer Communications (INFOCOM)*, pp. 170–179, 2001.

[Pohl 71] I. Pohl. "Bi-directional search." In *Machine Intelligence 6*, edited by Meltzer and D. Michie. American Elsevier, 1971, pp. 127–140.

[Rabin 00] S. Rabin. "A* Speed optimizations." In *Game Programming Gems*, edited by Mark DeLoura. Hingham, MA: Charles River Media, 2000, pp. 272–287.

[Rayner et al. 11] C. Rayner, M. Bowling, and N. Sturtevant. "Euclidean Heuristic Optimization." *AAAI Conference on Artificial Intelligence*, pp. 81–86, 2011. Available online (http://www.aaai.org/ocs/index.php/AAAI/AAAI11/paper/view/3594).

[Sturtevant 08] N. Sturtevant. "Memory-efficient pathfinding abstractions." In *AI Game Programming Wisdom 4*, edited by Steve Rabin. Hingham, MA: Charles River Media, 2008, pp. 203–217.

[Sturtevant 13] N. Sturtevant. "Choosing a search space representation." In *Game AI Pro*, edited by Steve Rabin. Boca Raton, FL: CRC Press, 2013.

[Thayer and Ruml 08] J. T. Thayer and W. Ruml. "Faster Than Weighted A*: An Optimistic Approach to Bounded Suboptimal Search," *Proceedings of the Eighteenth International Conference on Automated Planning and Scheduling (ICAPS-08)*, pp. 355–362, 2008. Available online (http://www.cs.unh.edu/~ruml/papers/optimistic-icaps-08.pdf).

[van der Sterren 04] W. van der Sterren. "Path look-up tables—small is beautiful." In *AI Game Programming Wisdom 2*, edited by Steve Rabin. Hingham, MA: Charles River Media, 2004, pp. 115–129.

[Waveren 01] J. P. van Waveren. "The Quake III Arena Bot," pp. 40–45, 2001. Available online (http://www.kbs.twi.tudelft.nl/docs/MSc/2001/Waveren_Jean-Paul_van/thesis.pdf).

18

Choosing a Search Space Representation

Nathan R. Sturtevant

18.1 Introduction

The choice of a path planning architecture for a game will help determine what features the game can support easily, and what features will require significant effort to implement. There are good articles describing different types of path planning architectures [Tozour 04], and there have been debates in different forums [Tozour 08, Champandard 10] about the correct choice for a path planning architecture. Each choice comes with its own set of benefits and drawbacks, the strength of which will depend on the type of game being developed and the time allotted to developing the architecture. The goal of this article is to summarize and extend some of the arguments made for different architectures.

It is important to know that, for most games, all feasible path planning architectures are abstractions of the space through which characters can walk in the game. This is because the physics that are used to simulate the world are not directly used as the path planning representation. So, in some sense, much of the debate here is related to what representation most closely matches the underlying physics of the game world.

This article focuses on the primary representations: grids, waypoint graphs, and navigation meshes. We assume that most readers are familiar with these representations, as they are probably the most common architectures used today. Furthermore, examples of several of these architectures can be found in this book. But, for reference, an example map is shown in Figure 18.1(a). Figure 18.1(b) shows the grid decomposition of the map, Figure 18.1(c) shows a waypoint graph on the map, and Figure 18.1(d) shows a triangle decomposition, which is a type of navigation mesh. This article is primarily directed

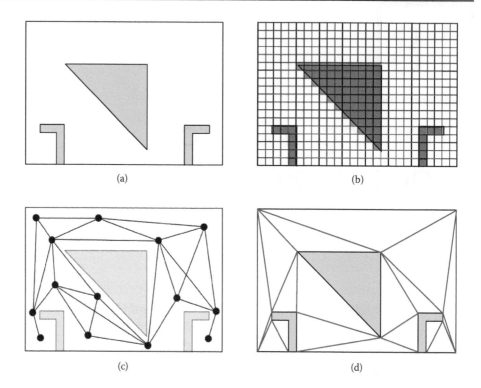

(a)

(b)

(c)

(d)

Figure 18.1

Three common world representations. (a) Original map, (b) grid decomposition, (c) waypoint graph, (d) nav mesh.

towards independent or small developers, as they are more likely to have a choice in the architecture they use.

18.2 Tasks

To begin, we briefly highlight the characteristics that we will consider when comparing path planning representations. These include memory usage, the ease of localization, planning, smoothing, path following, and dynamic modification of the representation. We also discuss the time required for implementation.

Memory usage is measured simply by the overhead of building and storing the representation of the map in memory. *Localization* is the process of moving from a spatial coordinate to a representation that is native to the path planning representation. When a user clicks the mouse, for instance, the coordinates of the click are recorded. This must then be converted into a grid cell or polygon in a navigation mesh. *Planning* is the cost of finding a valid path between two locations. *Smoothing* and *path following* is the process of taking a planned path and removing sharp turns or discontinuities to improve the overall quality. This can be done as part of planning, postplanning, or while the path is being followed by a character. *Dynamic modification* is the cost of performing changes to the representation on the fly, while the game is being played.

Note that the exact combination of each of these tasks depends on the game being created, and so the weight of each argument below depends on the importance of each task in your game. Grids, for instance, are a suitable representation for tower-defense games, but large open worlds in a MMORPG are usually too large for grids.

In addition to representing space for path planning, the representation can often be used for more generic queries to facilitate AI behavior. These may include positioning in battle, the best location for new buildings to be constructed, or the most protected location during battle. These queries are game-dependent, and so we will not directly consider them here.

18.3 Grids

The simplest implementation of a grid represents the world via an array of blocked and unblocked cells. More sophisticated implementations can include information on slope, terrain type, or other meta-information which is useful for planning. Grids traditionally represent only two-dimensional worlds, but can be used to represent three-dimensional worlds as well [Sturtevant 11].

The pros are:

- Grids are one of the simplest possible representations and are easy to implement. A working implementation can be completed in a few hours.
- A grid representation can be easily edited externally with a text editor. This can save significant tool-building efforts [Van Dongen 10].
- Terrain costs in grids are easy to dynamically update. For example, player-detected traps in Dragon Age: Origins are easily marked with a few bits in the relevant grid cells. It is easy for A* to account for these costs when planning, although the cost of planning will be increased if too many cells are re-weighted.
- Passable cells can be quickly modified in a grid in a similar way to terrain costs being updated.
- Localization in a grid is easy, simply requiring the coordinates to be divided by the grid resolution to return the localized grid cell.

The cons are:

- Grids are memory-intensive in large worlds. Note that a sparse representation can be used when the world is large, but the walkable space is relatively small [Sturtevant 11].
- Path smoothing usually must be performed to remove the characteristic 45° and 90° angles that are found in grid-based movement, although any-angle planning approaches can also be used [Nash et al. 07].
- Path planning in grids can be expensive due to the fine-grain representation of the world. This can be addressed using some form of abstraction [Rabin 00, Sturtevant 07].
- Grid worlds often contain many symmetric paths, which can increase the cost of path planning. Some techniques can be used to avoid this (e.g., [Harabor and Grastien 11]), but this can also be avoided with different state representations.

18.4 Waypoint Graphs

Waypoint graphs represent the world as an abstract graph. Importantly, waypoint graphs do not have an explicit mapping between nodes in the graph and walkable space. Waypoint graphs were widely used before the popularity of navigation meshes grew. While they have been criticized for their shortcomings [Tozour 08], they have also been praised for their strengths [Champandard 10].

The pros are:

- Waypoint graphs are relatively easy to implement.
- Waypoint graphs are easy to modify if the changes are known ahead of time. For instance, if a door in the world closes and is locked, it is easy for the developer to mark the edges in the graph that cross the opening of the door and block them when the door is shut.
- Waypoint graphs represent only a small fraction of the points found in a grid. This sparse representation of walkable space is both cheap to store and leads to inexpensive path planning requests.

The cons are:

- Path quality can suffer if there are not enough walkable edges in the graph, but too many walkable edges will impact storage and planning complexity.
- Waypoint graphs may require manual placement of nodes to get good path quality.
- Localization on waypoint graphs requires mapping between game space and the graph. If a character is knocked off of the graph, it may be unclear where the character should actually be within the waypoint graph.
- Because there is no explicit representation of the underlying state space, smoothing off the waypoint graph can result in characters getting stuck on physics or other objects.
- Dynamic changes are difficult when they aren't known ahead of time. If a character can create an unexpected hole in a wall, new connections on the waypoint graph are needed. However, it can be expensive to check all nearby connections to verify if they have become passable due to the changes in the map.

18.5 Navigation Meshes

Navigation meshes represent the world using convex polygons [Tozour 04]. A special case of navigation meshes are constrained Delaunay triangulations [Chen 09], for which the world is only represented by triangles. Note that grids can also be seen as a special case of navigation meshes, as both representations use convex polygons, but their usage is significantly different in practice.

The pros are:

- Polygons can represent worlds more accurately than grids, as they can represent non-grid-aligned worlds.

- With the accurate representation of a polygon it is easier to correctly perform smoothing both before and during movement. This accuracy can also be used for tighter animation constraints.
- Path planning on navigation meshes is usually fast, as the representation of the world is fairly coarse. But, this does not impact path quality, as characters are free to walk at any angle.
- Navigation meshes are not as memory-intensive as grids as they can represent large spaces with just a few polygons.

The cons are:

- The time required to implement a navigation mesh is significant, although good open-source implementations are available [Mononen 11].
- Navigation meshes often require geometric algorithms, which may fail in special cases such as parallel lines, meaning that implementation is much more difficult [Chen 09].
- Changes to navigation meshes can be difficult or expensive to implement, especially when contrasted with changes to grid worlds.
- Localization on navigation meshes can be expensive if poorly implemented. Good implementations will use additional data structures like grids to speed up the process [Demyen 06].

18.6 Conclusion

To conclude, each path planning architecture has its own strengths and weaknesses. The choice of an architecture should depend on the type of game being developed, the tools already available, and the time available for implementation and debugging. Many game engines ship with their own path planning representation, but for the cases where a new implementation must be performed, we summarize the pros and cons as follows:

Grids are most useful when the terrain is fundamentally 2D, when implementation time is limited, when the world is dynamic, and when sufficient memory is available. They are not well suited for very large open-world games, or for games where the exact bounds of walkable spaces are required for high-quality animation.

Waypoint graphs are most useful when implementation time is limited, when fast path planning is needed, and when an accurate representation of the world is not necessary.

Navigation meshes are best when there is adequate time for testing and implementation. They are the most flexible of the possible implementations when implemented well, but can be overkill for smaller projects.

Ultimately, the best representation is the one that minimizes developer effort and helps make the game-playing experience as compelling as possible. This may be different in any game, but being aware of the trade-offs between each architecture will help you make the best decisions on any new project.

References

[Champandard 10] A. Champandard. "Are Waypoint Graphs Outnumbered? Not in AlienSwarm." http://aigamedev.com/open/review/alienswarm-node-graph/, 2010.

[Chen 09] K. Chen. "Robust Dynamic Constrained Delaunay Triangulation for Pathfinding." Master Thesis, 2009.

[Demyen 06] D. Demyen. "Efficient Triangulation-Based Pathfinding." Master Thesis, 2006. Available online (https://skatgame.net/mburo/ps/tra.pdf).

[Harabor and Grastien 11] D. Harabor and A. Grastein. Online graph pruning for pathfinding on grid maps, *Proceedings of the AAAI Conference on Artificial Intelligence (2011)*, pp. 1114–1119. Available online (http://www.aaai.org/ocs/index.php/AAAI/AAAI11/paper/view/3761).

[Mononen 11] Mikko Mononen. "Recast." http://code.google.com/p/recastnavigation/, 2011.

[Nash et al. 07] A. Nash, K. Daniel, S. Koenig, and A. Felner "Theta*: Any-angle path planning on grids." *Proceedings of the AAAI Conference on Artificial Intelligence (2007)*, pp. 1177–1183. Available online (http://idm-lab.org/bib/abstracts/papers/aaai07a.pdf).

[Rabin 00] S. Rabin. "A* Speed Optimizations." In *Game Programming Gems*, edited by Mark DeLoura, Hingham, MA: Charles River Media, 2000, pp. 272–287.

[Sturtevant 07] N. R. Sturtevant, "Memory-efficient abstractions for pathfinding." *Artificial Intelligence and Interactive Digital Entertainment*, pp. 31–36, 2007. Available online (http://web.cs.du.edu/~sturtevant/papers/mmabstraction.pdf).

[Sturtevant 11] N. R. Sturtevant. "A sparse grid representation for dynamic three-dimensional worlds." *Artificial Intelligence and Interactive Digital Entertainment, 2011.* Available online (http://web.cs.du.edu/~sturtevant/papers/3dgrids.pdf).

[Tozour 04] P. Tozour. "Search space representations." In *AI Game Programming Wisdom 2*, edited by Steve Rabin. Hingham, MA: Charles River Media, 2004, pp. 85–102.

[Tozour 08] P. Tozour. "Fixing Pathfinding Once and For All." http://www.ai-blog.net/archives/000152.html, 2008.

[Van Dongen 10] J. Van Dongen. "Designing Levels without Tools." http://joostdevblog.blogspot.com/2010/12/designing-levels-without-tools.html, 2010.

Creating High-Order Navigation Meshes through Iterative Wavefront Edge Expansions

D. Hunter Hale and G. Michael Youngblood

19.1 Introduction

When placing AI-driven characters into your immersive game world, one large problem needs to be addressed, and that is the issue of a meaningful representation of the environment. The only source for information about the layout of the environment available to these characters is that which is provided to them by the game designers usually in the form of the geometric models that are assembled spatially to create the world. In all but the simplest of games, the level of detail in those model files is often too complex, too detailed, and organized more for display than spatial reasoning. Instead, some form of spatial abstraction is needed to group similar areas in single regions of space for the character to consider.

Historically, this representation was generally presented in the form of a waypoint map (i.e., valid points of known open points in a space with a collection of known good routes between them). Searching such a structure allowed AI characters to make paths through traversable space that appeared reasonable [Tozour 04]. The usage of waypoint graphs has been in decline as the navigation mesh spatial representation has risen in usage [McAnils 08]. A navigation mesh (often referred to as a *navmesh*) is composed of a listing of regions, which are well-defined convex groupings of traversable space (usually defined by polygons or poly-hedrons) and an additional listing describing connectivity (as a topological graph). This collection of regions organized as a graph can be rapidly searched to generate a path and characters can walk from region to region knowing they will remain in traversable areas.

Traditionally, navigation meshes have been created either by hand or using some form of automated spatial decomposition algorithm that examines the obstructions present in the environment and then breaks down the area between them into as few regions as pos-sible. Reducing the number of regions present in a world yields a smaller search space and is generally considered to be highly important to a spatial decomposition. Unfortunately, creating a decomposition for a game environment with an optimal (absolute minimum) number of regions is NP-Hard [Lingas 82]. This means that there is no *best* technique. Instead there are many techniques that attempt to approach the optimal one. These approaches generally start with some form of triangulation of the environment [Delaunay 34] and then attempt to minimize the number of regions present in the environment through combining these triangles [Hertel 83].

The problem with this approach is that the triangles that remain in the navigation mesh cause problems for character navigation in areas where many triangles come together at a single point. It is all but impossible for a character to say which region they are standing in at the confluence points. These confluence points unfortunately show up all too often in complex environments. This leads to localization and pathfinding issues (i.e., if the char-acter does not know where it is, then how can it find a path to its destination) [Hale 11].

The alternative to the triangular decomposition approaches, and one that will help minimize the character localization problem, is a growth-based approach. In our previ-ous work we have presented 2D (PASFV) and 3D (VASFV) growth-based spatial decom-position algorithms [Hale 08, Hale 09], which were inspired by the Space-Filling Volumes algorithm [Tozour 04]. While these approaches do generate quality navigation meshes they can be slow when executed on large environments (the runtime of the algorithm increases based on the area to be decomposed). This is due to the fact these algorithms perform many unnecessary collision tests since they have to verify that every growing region has not intruded into another region or obstruction on every growth step. The vast majority of the time this is not the case, and this test will return a negative result. This unnecessary testing is a consequence of the sequential iterative expansion in traditional growth-based algorithms.

We have developed the Iterative Wavefront Edge Expansion Cell Decomposition (referred to as *Wavefront* for brevity) algorithm to address the problems of previous tech-niques by reducing collision tests and iterative growth. This algorithm works by scanning the world geometry visible from each region we place in the world and determines where possible collisions might occur (i.e., interesting places to expand toward). By forcing our regions to expand directly to these locations, we eliminate all but a handful of collision tests. This alters the runtime of the growth-based algorithm such that it increases with the complexity of the world (number of obstructions) instead of the area of the world. Not only is this technique faster than existing growth-based techniques, but the resulting navigation meshes produced using the Wavefront algorithm retain the high mesh quality exhibited by the PASFV and VASFV algorithms by providing regions of higher-order polygonal/polyhedron geometry [Hale 11].

19.2 Wavefront Spatial Decomposition

The Wavefront Edge Expansion Cell Decomposition (Wavefront) algorithm is derived from the PASFV and VASFV algorithms [Hale 08, Hale 09] and shares several implementation steps with them. The algorithm generates decompositions via a four-step process. First, unit-sized potential regions (seeds) are placed into the world. Next, one of these regions is selected at random and obstructions present in the world are analyzed from this region's perspective. In the third step of the algorithm the selected region enters a phase of accelerated expansion. This expansion is towards the obstructions found by the analysis in the second step of the algorithm. Steps two and three of the algorithm repeat for each region; this expands each region to their maximum possible size. Finally, in the fourth step of the algorithm new seeds are placed into any traversable space (a.k.a., empty space, unconfigured space, negative space) adjacent to the regions just created and the algorithm returns to step two, allowing these new regions to expand. If no new seeds are placed the algorithm terminates.

19.2.1 Initial Seeding

Traditionally, growth-based algorithms start using a grid-based pattern to place the initial unit-sized regions into the world. These approaches then iteratively give every region the chance to grow and expand outward in the direction of the normal of each edge (or face in 3D—we will use edge for simplicity here since they are both effectively boundaries for occupied space) of that region.

When using the Wavefront algorithm on our initial entry into the seeding phase we generate a list of *potential* seed points using a seeding algorithm that places a potential seed next to every exposed obstruction edge. This results in better overall coverage of the environment with fewer unit-sized quad (or cube in 3D) regions placed into the world over simple grid seeding [Hale 11]. Then one of these seed points is randomly selected to use as our initial region. The other potential seed points will be retained for later seeding passes, but will only be used if they are still in areas of traversable space that are as yet unclaimed by any regions. If on later passes through the seeding phase this list is empty, we will attempt to refill it by looking for areas of unclaimed traversable space adjacent to the regions we have placed. If this list remains empty after that point then the Wavefront algorithm will terminate.

19.2.2 Edge Classification

After a seed region has been generated, we proceed to the edge classification step of the Wavefront algorithm. These next two steps are the most computationally intensive steps of this algorithm, and we only wish to perform them on valid regions that we know are going to expand. Therefore, we only expand one region at a time and discard region seeds that are covered by earlier expansion. During this step, we iterate through each of the edges of obstructions present in the world as well as any edges present in regions that we have already placed into the environment. We then discard any edges whose normal faces away from the target seed point of the region as these edges are back facing and they cannot interact with the region. We then sort these edges into categories based on their relative spatial position when compared to the target seed location ($+x$, $-x$, $+y$, $-y$, $+z$, $-z$). Note that this technique creates axis-aligned edges between decomposed regions (obviously not guaranteed between regions to obstructions), which makes it easier for AI characters to reason and traverse regions. Edges that span multiple categories are placed in the first applicable one, depending on the evaluation order used in the implementation of the algorithm. Our reference implementation uses the following ordering +*y*, -*y*, +*x*,-*x*, +*z*, and -*z*. Any ordering will work as long as it is consistently followed.

Once the edges have been sorted, we locate all potential event points. Our region will have an edge that is perpendicular to each of the sorting classifications and whose normal matches the sorting classification (we will refer to this as the classification edge). By comparing the slope of each of our sorted obstruction edges to the appropriate classification edge, we can determine in advance how the expanding region would interact with the obstruction. This can be visualized by thinking of a radial half-plane sweep drawn from the initial seed point and then rotated in 90 degree arcs along each edge as shown in Figures 19.1 and 19.2. This sweep line will report the orientation of the edges it finds as well as the closest point on the edge to the initial seed point. The interactions between these edges of occupied space and the edge of the region we just placed can be reduced down to a series of cases.

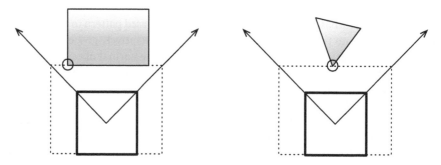

Figure 19.1

Two simple cases for event-based spatial decompositions: the case on the left shows expansion towards a parallel element and the case on the right shows the discovery of an intruding vertex.

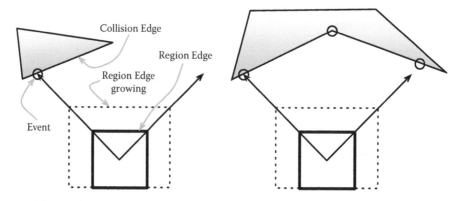

Figure 19.2

Two complex cases for the Wavefront decomposition involving splitting events.

Part III. Movement and Pathfinding

The first of these cases occurs if the tested edge is found to be parallel to the classification edge as shown on the left side of Figure 19.1. In this case, we will wish to move the classification edge such that it is adjacent and co-planar to the target edge. We accomplish this by calculating the closest point on the edge to the initial seed point of the region we are evaluating. We then log this point and the distance from it to the region's initial seed point as an event. Incidentally, since all of our placed regions only expose axis-aligned edges and our expanding regions also only expose axis-aligned edges, any events involving other regions of traversable space will fall into this category.

A slightly more complicated case occurs when the edge is examined and found to be sloping inward towards the classification edge (i.e., region edge under evaluation) as shown in the right side of Figure 19.1. In this case, we will only be able to expand such that the closest vertex of that edge lies on the classification edge without changing the slope of the classification edge. We cannot change this slope as this would result in previously claimed areas of traversable space being relinquished, which would violate one of our invariants (claimed region space must always remain claimed by that region). This case is also resolved by storing the location of the closest vertex on the edge under evaluation along with the distance to that vertex from the initial seed point of the region.

Finally, we come to the most complicated case, which might result in the potential addition of new edges to the expanding region. In this case, as shown on the left side of Figure 19.2, the closest obstruction edge is sloping away from the midpoint of the classification edge, and it would be possible to move the classification edge such that one of its vertices could intersect the edge under consideration. This is an edge splitting case, and in order to calculate where this split should occur, the closest point on the edge under evaluation to the initial seed point of the region is found. This point is then stored as an event point along with the distance between this point and initial seed point of the region. Additionally, we wish to store the two end points of the edge under consideration (assuming the closest point was not an end point) so that we will be able to increase the order (order indicates the relative number of sides of a polygon/polyhedron, so a triangle has order three, an octagon order eight, and so forth) of this region such that it adds a new edge that is adjacent to the entire length of the edge under consideration. However, instead of calculating the distance between each of these end points and the initial seed point, we will treat them as a special case that looks at them as if they are only slightly further away from the initial point than the point we are using to split. This will prevent those points from interfering with other calculations in the process.

A more complex case with multiple splitting events can be seen on the right side of Figure 19.2. The events should be processed in order based on the distance from the initial seed point of the expanding region, and by altering the distance of these two end points we will ensure that the region tries to fully encompass all of the space that is adjacent to the edge it splits on as that point is processed.

At this point we have a collection of potential events for our new region to expand towards; however, we need to do two things before we can begin the expansion. First, if the edges of the world are defined as some boundary conditions rather than nontraversable space, events will need to be inserted to allow each region to expand outward to the edges of the world. Then this list will need to be sorted based on the distance between each event and the initial seed point of the region. This results in the processing of closer events first as we are more likely to reach them as further events are oftentimes unreachable due to the presence of more immediate obstructions.

19.2.3 Edge Expansion

With the completed event list for this region we are able to proceed to the expansion phase of the Wavefront algorithm. First, the expansion rates of all of the edges of the region are reset to zero. Then, the first (closest) unprocessed expansion event is selected and removed from the list of potential events. The distances that the edges of the region would have to move such that they reach this expansion event are then calculated. This is done by calculating the distance between the current location of the two (three in 3D) closest edges and the target expansion location. This result is then broken down into its principal components (x, y, z) and if these values are positive they are set as expansion rates for the edge or edges that have a normal that points toward the target event. The use of rates is a legacy from stepwise growth, but here the rates indicate jumps directly to event points. Expansion should then occur with each edge iteratively moving outward. Once all the edges have moved, then the check for any collisions or invalid expansion conditions can be executed. This happens because there are splitting events that may result in invalid configurations if only half of the event (i.e., one rather than two edges are allowed to expand) is executed.

Once the region has finished expanding, any collisions with other regions or obstructions must be resolved. Any vertices of the expanded region that collided with an obstruction must be split, and the region must be converted to a higher-order polygon/polyhedron by inserting a new edge. To construct this new edge take the opposite normal of the obstruction edge and constrain this new edge to the extents of the obstruction edge. Since expansion events are calculated in isolation with no consideration for other regions or potential obstructions, it is possible that a collision will occur and that the region will have to contract from a potential expansion event. If this happens, then the edge involved in the collision should cease further attempts to expand. The algorithm will then select another expansion event, repeating this process until there are no more events or all of its edges have ceased attempting to expand due to collisions.

19.2.4 Reseeding

After all regions have finished expanding, additional regions will be placed as per the seeding process discussion earlier. If the algorithm enters the seeding phase, and is unable to place any new regions, it terminates. This results in a collection of regions that is ready to serve as a navigation mesh. Additionally, if desired, this collection of regions can be cleaned up by combining adjacent regions such that the result would still be convex.

19.3 Postdecomposition

Existing growth-based spatial decomposition algorithms (e.g., PASFV, VASFV, and SFV) took advantage of a postprocessing step to improve the quality of the resulting navigation mesh. Occasionally, two or more region seeds will grow into an area of the environment that could be filled by a single convex region. This is a natural consequence of placing and growing multiple seeds at the same time, and is generally corrected by combining the regions. However, this combining takes time and effort, and it would be nice if it was not required. A strength of the Wavefront algorithm is that it avoids most of this form of cleanup due to the fact it only grows one region at a time. Since two regions are never growing at the same time, they cannot both attempt to subdivide the same convex area of traversable space, thus yielding a cleaner decomposition.

19.4 Wavefront Runtime

The Wavefront algorithm enjoys a worst case runtime, bounded by the complexity of the environment it is executed on of $O(n*m)$. In this case n is the number of obstructions present in the world, each of which will have to be evaluated by m regions that will be seeded by the algorithm. This runtime might seem to be worse than existing growth-based spatial decomposition algorithms (they generally increase fractionally, $O(n^{1/x})$ where n is the number of square units in the world, and x is the number of regions), but remember that the runtimes of these increase based on the size of the world (due to the additional growth steps that have to be performed to fill the world).

The runtime of the Wavefront algorithm only increases with the actual complexity of the environment and not due to the introduction of additional unoccupied space. In general, across a variety of game environments of different sizes and complexities, our reference implementations of these two algorithms average runtimes in the milliseconds to seconds range for Wavefront in comparison to a range of seconds to minutes for our growth-based implementations. The memory footprint of the Wavefront algorithm grows linearly as each newly generated region only needs to interact and know about existing regions and obstructions at any given point in time.

19.5 Comparisons to Existing Techniques

The Wavefront algorithm has been compared to existing methods of generating spatial decompositions with particular focus on those currently in use in industry, namely Delaunay Triangulation, Hertel–Melhlorn Decompositions, and Trapezoidal Cellular Decompositions. We only targeted algorithms for comparison that also generate full coverage decompositions in order to ensure the comparisons were valid. Evaluations were conducted on 25 procedurally generated worlds composed of randomly generated and placed obstructions with no axis-aligned restrictions and a basic set of rules that generated test worlds similar in geometry to those found in many games (the generation rules were influenced from public *Quake 3* levels, which were used in initial testing).

We generated decompositions for the worlds using each algorithm under consideration (one of these levels and the Wavefront Decomposition for it is shown in Figure 19.3). We then evaluated the decompositions based on the number of regions present, and the quality of the decomposition (using navigation mesh evaluation metrics [Hale 11] to determine the number and shape of any degenerate or low quality regions). We found that the decompositions generated with the Wavefront algorithm contained both fewer total regions and fewer near-degenerate regions than the Trapezoidal Decompositions or Delaunay Triangulation Decompositions. We define a near-degenerate region to be one that an AI character would have difficulty moving into or out of. Such regions are characterized as oddly or bizarrely shaped areas (e.g., fans of triangles all coming together at a single point, long thin slivers of quad-based regions spanning an environment, regions

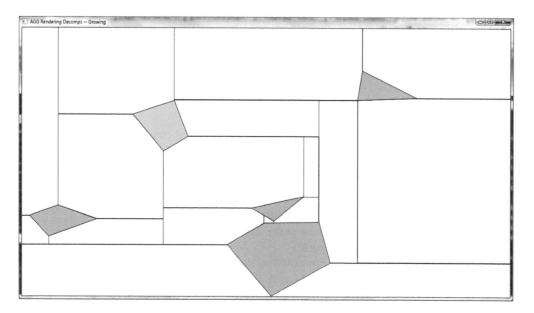

Figure 19.3

A decomposition produced by the Wavefront algorithm. Obstructions are shown in gray, while the decomposition regions are shown with black outlines.

with very narrow adjacencies to other regions, or disjoint/poorly connected regions), which we are able to test for and detect.

The number of regions was consistent between the Wavefront algorithm and the Hertel–Melhlorn decomposition; however, the Wavefront decompositions had fewer near-degenerate regions than the Hertel–Melhlorn decompositions [Hale 11]. It is not surprising that the Wavefront algorithm has fewer of these near-degenerate regions as it possesses a unique property not shared by the other decomposition techniques we tested against. Namely, there is an upper limit on the number of regions that come together at a single point of traversable space of five (10 in 3D); mathematical proof in [Hale 11]. The other commonly used techniques have no upper bound on how many regions can converge at a single point of traversable space. This convergence of many regions onto a single point is what often leads to the creation of near-degenerate regions and should be avoided if possible.

It is worth noting that the Wavefront algorithm generates decompositions that appear to be similar to those generated by the Trapezoidal cell decomposition algorithm. However, they are distinct decompositions, due to the fact the Wavefront algorithm will consistently produce decompositions with fewer regions. This is due to Trapezoidal Decomposition being restricted in only decomposing the world in a single direction (vertical or horizontal) while the Wavefront algorithm is in effect a multidirectional decomposition (both vertical and horizontal wavefronts originate from the initial region seeds).

For detailed information on the evaluation of the Wavefront technique, quantitative numbers, and navmesh quality metrics, please refer to Hale's *A Growth-Based Approach to the Automatic Generation of Navigation Meshes* [Hale 11].

19.6 Conclusion

Overall, the Wavefront algorithm generates fast, high-quality decompositions for use as navigation meshes via a quad-based expansion algorithm. Such decompositions have fewer small and degenerate regions (generally triangles) that can interfere with character navigation. This algorithm improves on previous growth-based approaches by performing fewer expansion steps, which reduces the number of collision tests that must be performed. This yields an algorithm whose runtime scales with the complexity of the world rather than the size of the world as existing growth-based approaches do. Additionally, since this algorithm only grows one region at a time, there is less post processing that would normally be caused by multiple regions competing to fill the same convex area. The decompositions generated by this algorithm compare favorably with those produced by existing popular algorithms (e.g., Hertel–Melhlorn or Trapezoidal Cell Decomposition).

References

[Delaunay 34] B. Delaunay. "Sur la sphere vide" *Classe des Sciences Mathematiques et Naturelle* 7. 1934.

[Hale 08] D. Hunter Hale, G. Michael Youngblood, and P. Dixit. "Automatically-generated convex region decomposition for real-time spatial agent navigation in virtual worlds." *Artificial Intelligence and Interactive Digital Entertainment (AIIDE)*. 2008.

[Hale 09] D. Hunter Hale and G. Michael Youngblood. "Full 3D spatial decomposition for the generation of navigation meshes." *Artificial Intelligence and Interactive Digital Entertainment (AIIDE)*. 2009.

[Hale 11] D. Hunter Hale. A Growth-Based Approach to the Automatic Generation of Navigation Meshes. Doctoral Dissertation. University of North Carolina at Charlotte, December 2011.

[Hertel 83] S. Hertel and K. Mehlhorn. " Fast triangulation of the plane with respect to simple polygons." *International Conference on Foundations of Computation Theory*. 1983.

[Lingas 82] A. Lingas. "The power of non-rectilinear holes." *Proceedings 9th International Colloquium on Automata, Language, and Programming*. 1982.

[McAnils 08] C. McAnils and J. Stewart. "Intrinsic detail in navigation mesh generation." In *AI Game Programming Wisdom 4*. Hingham, MA: Charles River Media, 2008, pp. 95–112.

[Tozour 04] P. Tozour. "Search space representations." In *AI Game Programming Wisdom 2*. Hingham, MA: Charles River Media, 2004, pp. 85–102.

Precomputed Pathfinding for Large and Detailed Worlds on MMO Servers

Fabien Gravot, Takanori Yokoyama, and Youichiro Miyake

20.1 Introduction

Precomputed solutions for pathfinding were common on old generation consoles, but have rarely been used on current hardware. These solutions give the best results in terms of computation cost, as all path request results are precomputed in a lookup table. However, they have two drawbacks: memory cost and loss of flexibility. Currently most games use dynamic algorithms like A* for navigation.

In the context of MMO games, however, precomputed solutions are still used. While the corresponding servers are typically equipped with ample memory, they have very few CPU cycles available for each request. This article will show how precomputed pathfinding has been implemented for *FINAL FANTASY XIV: A Realm Reborn.*

This game has very large and detailed maps (about 4 km² each), with cliffs from which the agent can fall (unidirectional path). We will present an accurate navigation system with navigation mesh autogeneration and a component based hierarchical lookup table. We define a component to be a group of connected polygons (at the lowest layer) or connected sublayer components (at other layers). We will first give an overview of the whole navigation system, followed by a brief explanation of the navigation mesh autogeneration, finally focusing on the precomputed data generation.

20.2 System Overview

The navigation system presented in this article has been developed for *FINAL FANTASY XIV: A Realm Reborn*, "a Massively Multiplayer Online Game," developed by SQUARE ENIX. The choices made for this system are mostly driven by this game's needs; however, the techniques presented here can also be used in other environments.

The game performs all the navigation path computations on the servers. One server can simulate several maps. One map can be as large as 4 square kilometers with several thousand NPCs and players. Figure 20.1 shows an in-game screenshot of part of the world to explore. Because the pathfinding system must be very fast, meaning A* was not an option, a precomputed path lookup table was chosen.

Another important requirement was to have the pathfinding system be mostly automatic. It has to be able to generate accurate navigation for hundreds of maps without expert or manual input, but if necessary, it must be possible to edit the data directly. As a game rule, any NPC can go where the player can go (except when specified by the level designer). The navigation system must be as close as possible to the collision system used by the player. Since players can jump or fall off (from almost anywhere) the navigation system must support those features. It also means that large NPCs can go through narrow passages if the player can use them. The NPC size is not used to find a path, but it is still used to smooth it at run-time. To fill the role of world navigation representation, a navigation mesh was chosen.

The precomputed navigation data is generated from the navigation mesh, and this generation is the core concept of this article. The precomputed data is stored in a hierarchical lookup table. This approach was chosen to reduce the memory footprint while maintaining very fast computation time. These tables are used on the server to perform all the navigation system tasks.

Figure 20.1

FINAL FANTASY XIV: A Realm Reborn screenshot.

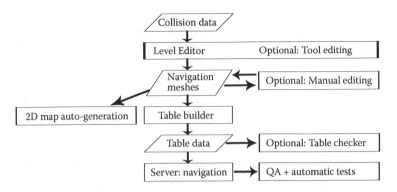

Figure 20.2

Tools flow chart from the collision data to the table data used by the server navigation system.

20.3 Tool Chain

The main tools used to generate the navigation table data are the Level Editor and the Table Builder (Figure 20.2). The Level Editor gathers all the collision data to generate the navigation mesh. The navigation mesh auto generation is done by Recast, an open source software library developed by Mikko Mononen [Mononen 12], released under the MIT license. The mesh is generated after a voxelization phase to identify the walkable areas [Miles 06, Axelrod 08]. The main modification made to Recast was the addition of the game-specific "falling mesh" into the generation process.

The level editor also allows editing the navigation mesh through various tools. For example, it is possible to remove the mesh generation inside a box or mark an area as only accessible by the player. Doors can also split and tag the mesh underneath, thus forbidding motion when closed. The most important feature is the navigation mesh seed point. It allows designers to remove all the polygons that are not connected to this point. Falling polygons are kept only if they allow the connection between two valid walkable polygons.

The navigation mesh by itself is simply a 3D polygon mesh model that can be edited or manipulated by other appropriate tools. For instance, it can be used by the 2D map auto-generation tool (Section 20.9.4).

Figure 20.3 shows a screenshot of a navigation mesh generated by this system, viewed in Maya. It is possible to edit it manually, but doing so invalidates further autogeneration. This option, if used, must be done in the final stages of the project.

The main purpose of the navigation mesh is to be used to compute table data through the Table Builder. This data is used in the server navigation system, which is checked by QA and other automatic tests (Figure 20.2). It is also possible to analyze the table data directly with the Table Checker tool. All of these quality checks expose problems in either the input data (collision data) or the algorithm. Quality checking is one of our main concerns in creating a system as robust as possible for autogeneration of navigation data.

20.4 Mesh Generation

Early in the project, navigation meshes were chosen for the navigation system. They describe a free moving space usable for steering.

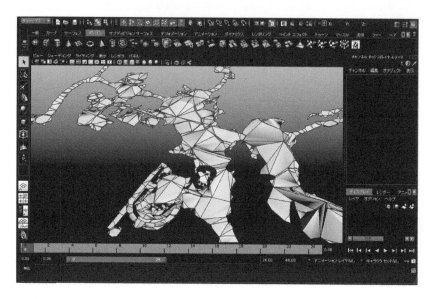

Figure 20.3

Navigation mesh of walkable areas generated for a town-like environment, viewed inside Autodesk® Maya®.

Since the world is very large, the navigation mesh generation splits it into a regular grid. Each tile generates a navigation mesh independently. We have chosen to keep this grid information in the precomputed data using small tiles of 32x32 meters.

Figure 20.4 shows a more detailed view of the navigation mesh. At its borders, the mesh is shrunk by the player radius, so that NPCs, or more precisely their centers, can move freely on the entire mesh surface. The generation process must try to minimize the number of polygons and match the collision data as much as possible.

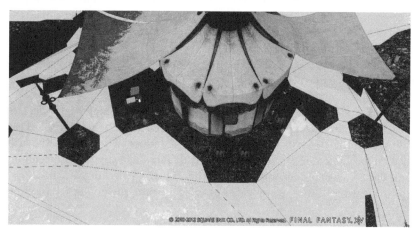

Figure 20.4

Navigation mesh autogenerated around a tent.

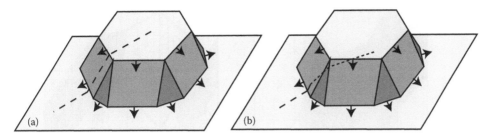

Figure 20.5

The falling mesh, in dark gray, and the desired output direction; (a) shows the unidirectional edges and how pathfinding is done; (b) shows how knock-back motion can cross falling polygon boundaries (dotted line).

As mentioned, we added falling meshes to the mesh generation algorithm. The generation of these is outside the scope of this article but some details are useful as it strongly influenced the Table Builder algorithm. The player can fall from anywhere from any height without taking damage. NPCs must be able to follow the player and avoid long detours. Designers can add an invisible wall to prevent the player from falling.

Moreover we added support for NPC knock-back, giving the player the ability to knock an NPC off a cliff. Figures 20.5a,b show how the falling mesh is used to support knock-back functionality, covering all possible falling directions. Figure 20.6 shows a falling mesh generated from a game map.

It is possible to use the mesh connectivity for the knock-back length (dotted line in Figure 20.5b). If the knock-back path stops in the middle of a falling mesh, a falling motion is appended to it.

The advantages of using falling meshes for knock-back in place of collision checks are computation speed and the guarantee that the NPC will always end up in a valid pathfinding position on the navigation mesh. The main drawback is the complexity of the autogeneration process.

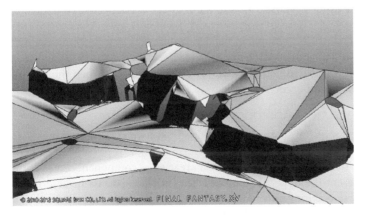

Figure 20.6

Falling mesh generated for a game world. The falling polygons are darker. In those areas the slope of the collision data is too steep to allow walking.

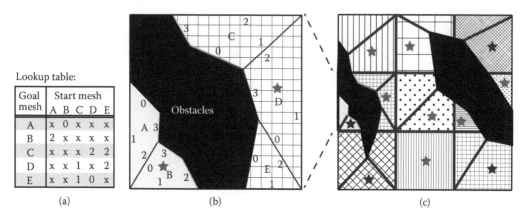

Lookup table:

Goal mesh	Start mesh A	B	C	D	E
A	x	0	x	x	x
B	2	x	x	x	x
C	x	x	x	2	2
D	x	x	1	x	2
E	x	x	1	0	x

(a)

(b)

(c)

Figure 20.7

Black shapes represent obstacles, while polygons within the same component have the same pattern. The gray stars show the polygons that are used as component centers. Figure (b) shows the detail of one tile of the whole navigation mesh (c). Figure (a) shows the lookup table of (b) with the polygon letter and the output edge number, or 'x' when there is no path.

20.5 Table Generation Overview

The precomputed navigation data is generated from the navigation mesh. For this purpose, lookup tables are built. Figure 20.7a shows such a lookup table. For instance, it indicates that traversing from C to E implies using Edge 1 of Polygon C. The lookup tables give the correct output edge to use when moving from one polygon to another. However, with the number of polygons generated (N) the table size will quickly become prohibitive ($N \times N$). A hierarchical approach is used to avoid the memory explosion [Dickheiser 03, Sterren 03]. With a hierarchical approach, we can split the N polygons into K groups and have K tables of size $(N/K) \times (N/K)$ and one portal table of size $P \times P$ where P is the number of portals connecting the polygon groups.

Instead of using portals to divide the regions, a connected component approach is used. This method is derived from the work done on *Dragon Age: Origins* (Bioware, 2009) [Sturtevant et al. 10]. A component is defined as a set of fully connected polygons. This component will be a node for the upper hierarchical level table. Since we use a hierarchical approach, we will use the term "node" in place of polygon when the description can be generalized to an upper hierarchical layer.

20.5.1 Component Approach

Figure 20.7b shows how 5 nodes are gathered into two components inside one tile. Since there is connectivity between the nodes C, D, and E, it is possible to gather them as one component. The stars show the nodes that are used as component centers. The component centers represent the upper layer nodes. They replace portals in describing component connectivity in our implementation. In general, the component center is the node which minimizes the distance to the other nodes inside this component.

Due to the size of the world, the navigation mesh autogeneration splits it into a regular grid and generates the mesh for each tile. The lowest level of the lookup tables is based on these tiles (Figure 20.7c). We define the following elements:

- *Node*: a polygon or a sublayer component.
- *Component*: a group of connected nodes. There is always a path between any two nodes in a component.
- *Tile*: a cell in the grid partitioned layer. It can have any number of components or nodes.

20.5.2 Table Connectivity

Each tile has a lookup table describing connectivity between all of its nodes. To avoid discontinuities at its borders, each tile also has a lookup table describing connectivity between its nodes to all its neighbor tiles' nodes (Figure 20.8b, left table). This ensures that when moving from tile to tile, there is always a detailed table showing which edge to choose.

Each tile also has a lookup table that describes connectivity between each of its nodes and the component centers two tiles away (Figure 20.8b, right table). As we will see in the next subsection, having this last table increases the quality of the pathfinding heuristic given by the upper layer. Figure 20.8a shows 25 tiles with the navigation mesh. The central tile (vertical line pattern) has a lookup table describing connectivity between its two nodes with each other, with all the 15 nodes of its eight neighbor tiles (horizontal line pattern) and with the component centers (14 nodes with gray star) of its 12 next neighbor tiles (grid pattern). In summation, the central tile has a lookup table from its two nodes to 31 (2 + 15 + 14) nodes.

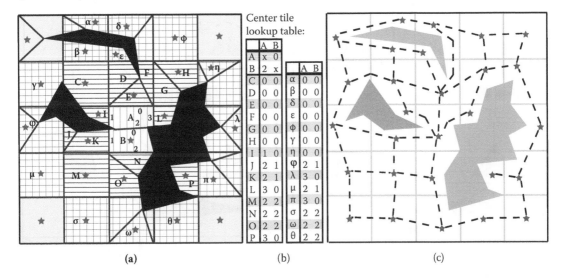

(a) **(b)** **(c)**

Figure 20.8

Figure (a) shows the local table connection levels. Latin letters represent polygons. Stars or Greek letters represent component center. The edge index of the polygons A and B is also shown. Figure (b) shows the center tile lookup table. It has a node-to-node table (left side) for the nine center tiles (line pattern) and node-to-component center table (right side) for the 12 border tiles (grid pattern). Figure (c) shows the top level node graph corresponding to Figure (a). Component centers of the lower layer, shown as gray stars, are the nodes of the top layer. The connections are shown with dashed lines.

20.5.3 Falling Meshes Outside the Table

When falling, the player loses control. In the same way, moving through a falling mesh changes the NPC's motion. We decided that for the purpose of simulating an agent falling, the falling mesh's polygons would each have only one output edge. The Table Builder uses this property to optimize the lookup table size. It first reorders the falling polygon edges so that the output edge is the first one. Thus, the output edge of any falling polygon will be Edge 0 for any goal in the lookup table (i.e., the lookup table column of a falling polygon is a null column). Moreover, we decided that any goal on the falling mesh will be changed to its ending fall point. This allows predictive motion and removes the need to have the falling polygon as a goal in the lookup table (i.e., the lookup table rows). This means that the falling mesh doesn't need to be stored in the lookup table. This method reduces the size of the lookup table by up to 20%.

20.5.4 Pathfinding Requests

Figure 20.9 shows an example of the pathfinding process. The path subgoals are in fact the component centers. The choice of which component center to use is made by the upper layer. In this simple example, there is only one upper layer with one lookup table in which to find the next node link to use. If a solution cannot be found at the lowest level,

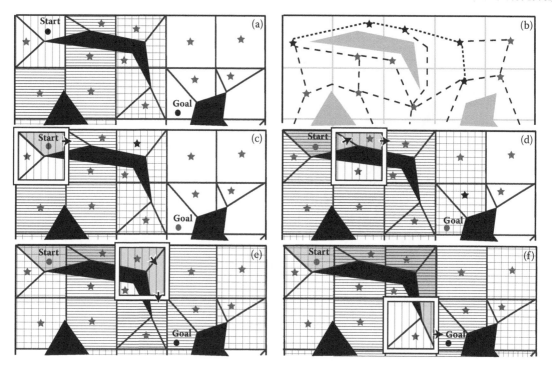

Figure 20.9

Example of pathfinding using precomputed data. Figure (a) shows the query start and goal point. Figure (b) shows the top level with the top level path. Figures (c,d,e,f) show the path planning process for the current tile (vertical line pattern) in each pathfinding iteration, as well as the edges chosen (black arrow). The resulting mesh path is shown in gray.

it is searched for in the upper level (b). Figures 20.9c,d show how the subgoal is chosen. It is the furthest component center on the upper layer path that is still inside the local lookup table (patterned tiles). The current tile's lookup table contains the next edge to use. The Figures 20.9e,f show that once the goal is inside the neighbor tiles, the direct node–node table is used. This example shows the complete pathfinding process, but if the goal is sufficiently far, it is not necessary to compute the complete path for every hierarchical layer. This allows for very fast path computation.

20.5.5 Hierarchy

In order to further reduce memory usage, we use not just two, but three hierarchical levels on the largest maps. For instance, with one of our tested maps, the table size is 16.5 mega octets with 2 levels, 8.8 with 3 levels, 8.7 with 4 levels, and more than 400 without any hierarchy.

We use the same process as previously described to create the upper level. Figure 20.10 shows the second level added to the example of Figure 20.8. In Figure 20.10, the second level has a tile size of 2 by 2 sublevel tiles. For the upper level tiles, the nodes (dots or stars in Figure 20.10a) are the component centers of the lower layer (stars in Figure 20.8a). For each tile it is possible to compute its component centers (stars in Figure 20.10a), which become the nodes of the highest layer graph (Figure 20.10c).

In our test, the mean and maximum number of components for the lowest layer (mesh) are 1.5 and 15, respectively, and for the middle layer, 3.2 and 19, respectively. This approach gives a good compression, minimizing the table size.

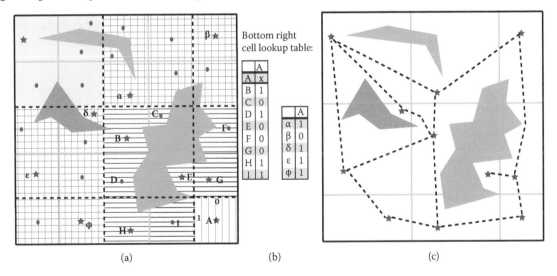

(a) (b) (c)

Figure 20.10

Figure (a) shows the second layer tile (dashed line) with dots for nodes and stars for component centers. The edge index of Node A is also shown. Figure (b) shows the bottom right tile lookup table. It has a node-to-node table (left side) for the center tiles (line pattern) and node-to-component center table (right side) for the border tiles (grid pattern). Figure (c) shows the top level node graph corresponding to Figure (a). Component centers of the lower layer, shown as gray stars, are the nodes of the top layer. The connections are shown with dashed lines.

Listing 20.1. Pseudocode of the table building process, showing the main steps of the algorithm.

```
ComputeConnectivity();
FallingMeshSetup();
BuildMeshTable();
for(int i = 0; i<max_level; ++i) {
    ComponentComputation(i);
    SplitProblematicComponents(i);
    ComputeComponentCenter(i);
    if (i+1 != max_level) {
        AddHierarchy(i);
        BuildHierarchicalTable(i);
    }
}
for(int i = max_level-1; i>0; --i) {
    RemoveInvalidSubLink(i);
}
```

20.6 Table Generation Algorithm

The previous section explained the main ideas behind the hierarchical table data used for navigation. In this section we will explain the algorithm computing this data in more detail and discuss some pitfalls that need to be avoided in order to obtain reliable data.

Listing 20.1 shows the table builder algorithm pseudocode. It iterates over the hierarchy of levels and applies specific functions to the lowest level (mesh data). In order to avoid several inconsistencies in the generated tables, some additional measures are taken. We will detail all those steps in this and the following sections.

20.6.1 Compute Connectivity

The ComputeConnectivity() function is probably the simplest one. Since the navigation mesh generation algorithm produces a 3D mesh file, it is necessary to compute the connectivity between its polygons. Our code is based on the "building an edge list for an arbitrary mesh" algorithm [Lengyel 05]. The only modifications made were to add support for falling polygons. Since these can overlap, additional rules were added based on the falling polygon's material (i.e., falling output, falling portal between tiles, falling path from edge, etc.).

20.6.2 Falling Mesh Setup

To simplify manual editing of falling meshes, the only requirement imposed on them is that a special output marker is placed at the end of a fall (a special triangle denoting the output edge). Because it is possible to have an output edge connected to several walkable polygons, the table must split falling edges to match the underlying polygon boundaries. FallingMeshSetup() is also in charge of computing the falling path and setting up the falling output edge.

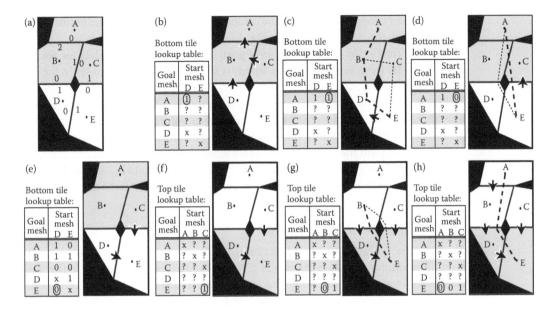

Figure 20.11

Figure (a) shows the two tiles used with the dots at the polygon center and the edge number. Figures (b), (c), and (d) show the table building process for the goal A and the bottom tile. Figure (b) shows the edge selection of D. Figure (c) and (d) show the edge selection of E, respectively, for the additional and smoothed distances. Figure (e) shows the table update for the last goal: E. Figures (f), (g), and (h) show the table building process for the top tile with the goal E for the starting polygons C, B, and A, respectively.

20.6.3 Distances Between Polygons

To build the lookup table, we tried to minimize the distance between the polygons' centers. We experimented with two ways of computing this distance: additional and smoothed.

The additional distance is the sum of the intermediate distances. Going from Polygon A to Polygon E through Polygon D, we have the distance AE equal to the sum of the distances AD and DE (Figure 20.11c).

The smoothed distance uses the smoothed path between centers as distance. In that case the distance from Polygon A to Polygon E through Polygon C is smaller or equal to the sum of the distances AC and CE (Figure 20.11d). Note that we will discuss the pros and cons of both distances in Section 20.9.

20.6.4 Table Builder

To decrease the computation time and memory usage, we decided to build the complete map lookup table data only for the highest layer (which has only one tile). For lower layers, the lookup tables take only the 21 neighboring tiles into account. In Figure 20.8a, these neighbor tiles are shown with line or grid patterns. Because we have not yet determined the component centers, a node–node table is computed instead of the node–component table.

The algorithm builds a lookup table for each tile independently (in fact, this process is multithreaded). Note that the shortest path result may change with the neighborhood; it is not possible to reuse it from tile to tile. For instance, in Figure 20.8a the path between π and θ makes a long detour inside the center cell neighborhood. In the bottom right tile neighborhood, the path from π to θ is the shortest one.

To avoid conflicting paths to one fixed goal, we compute the table data for one goal to all other nodes (reversed search). The search is stopped when all the nodes in the current tile are updated (Figure 20.11e).

Figure 20.11 shows the table building process for the Dijkstra algorithm at the mesh level (function `BuildMeshTable()`). As shown in Figure 20.11c,d, the smoothed-path distance can give a better result than the additional distance. However, this approach does not necessarily yield the shortest path (as for example in Figure 20.11h). Since it has been decided that going from B to E is done through D (Figure 20.11g), the path from A to E must go through D. Note also that with smoothed distance, paths are not symmetric (Figure 20.11d,h).

20.6.5 Hierarchical Table Builder

The function `BuildHierarchicalTable()` is in charge of the upper hierarchical levels. It is similar to the function `BuildMeshTable()`, explained previously. For this algorithm we also tried the smoothed and additional distances. The smoothed distance uses the distance computed in the lower layer between nonadjacent nodes (Figure 20.12a). This is valid only if the lower layer is not using additional distance. The smoothed distance significantly increased the quality of long paths.

Note that with smoothed distance, paths are not required to go through the component center as shown in Figure 20.12a. The shortest path from B to J is B, A, F, G, I, J. The shortest upper layer path, α, γ, δ, traverses through Component γ: {F, G, H, I}, but not through its center, Node H.

The function `BuildHierarchicalTable()` includes an additional constraint we refer to as the "subnode path" constraint. Its purpose is to ensure the validity of the algorithm responsible for solving the table inconsistencies presented in Section 20.7.2.

This constraint applies when the subnode center and one other subnode have different next components for the same goal. The Figure 20.12b shows such a situation. Imagine that the start point is B and the next subgoal is H. For the upper layer node there is a direct

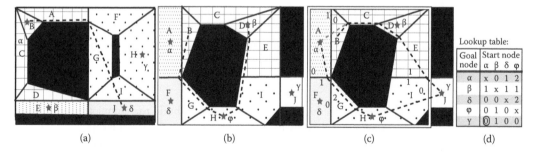

(a)   (b)   (c)   (d)

Figure 20.12

Problematic cases to take into account during the hierarchical table building process. The Greek letters represent the upper layer nodes (i.e., the polygon components). Mesh layer tiles have different patterns. Figure (d) shows the lookup table generated for the upper layer tile, which is a group of 2-by-2 mesh layer tiles shown inside the white border rectangle of Figure (c).

link β-φ, that is, the subnode path goes from D to H with only one change of component. However, for B, the shortest subnode path to H is B, A, F, G, H, which goes through α (A). Since the path β, φ can imply going through α, the upper layer path α, β, φ can yield a table inconsistency α, β, α (i.e., the subnode path A, B, A).

The algorithm detects all the cases where the component subnodes have a path not going directly to the adjacent components. These result in forbidden 3-node paths (e.g., α, β, φ) that are added as rule-based constraints. For instance, β cannot have α as previous node if its next node is φ. During the Dijkstra search process from goal to start, if one of these rules applies, the previous possible node is rejected. Figure 20.12c shows the table building process from the goal γ. The paths from β (β, φ, γ), δ (δ, φ, γ), and φ (φ, γ) have already been decided; α cannot be chosen as the previous node of β even if it is the shortest distance. Instead, the output of α must be δ (Figure 20.12d). Note, however, that in this example, the mesh tables have no inconsistencies between each other. The path from A to J will use the mesh table resulting in the shortest path A, B, C, D, E, I, J.

20.6.6 Add Hierarchy

The `AddHierarchy()` function is responsible for building a higher hierarchical level from the lower level component centers. The links between the upper layer nodes are defined as the paths between their subnode centers, as explained in Section 20.5.5.

20.6.7 Component Computation

Component computation is done in two phases. The first phase, performed by the function `ComputeComponent()`, calculates components using the node connectivity information see (Section 20.5.1). The only thing to keep in mind for the first phase is the use of unidirectional connections. For instance, with 3 nodes N_1, N_2, N_3, with the unidirectional connections N_1 to N_2, N_2 to N_3, and N_3 to N_1, we have N_1, N_2, N_3 in the same component.

The second phase splits those components, and will be explained in the following section.

20.7 Table Inconsistencies

If used as described previously, the table generation will produce inconsistencies. These are defined as infinite loops within the node path that ultimately prevents reaching the goal. Without unidirectional links, inconsistencies always occur between two bordering nodes (i.e., linked nodes in different tiles). With unidirectional links, the loop can include an indefinite number of nodes but at least two border nodes. These inconsistencies are due to both the local nature of the lookup table generation and the hierarchical approach, and are solved during the table building process.

20.7.1 Split Problematic Components and Compute Component Center

`SplitProblematicComponents()` is responsible for solving two possible inconsistency scenarios within the tables: the opposite path inconsistency and another one we refer to as the convexity problem. The methods of solving each of these are similar. For each node in a component, determine whether it is compatible with the other component node(s). This implies computing paths within the tile neighborhood. These paths are based on the 21 neighbor tiles in the lookup table computed in Section 20.6.

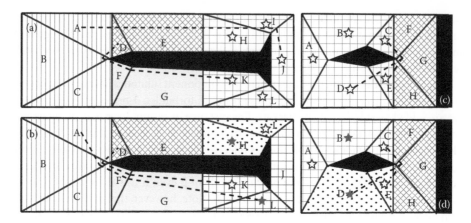

Figure 20.13

This figure shows how grid tile components are split. Areas with the same pattern correspond to the same component, while empty stars indicate potential component centers. Figures (a) and (b) show the opposite path inconsistency, while figures (c) and (d) show the convexity problem. Figures (a) and (c) show the components before and figures (b) and (d) show them after the split.

20.7.1.1 Opposite Path Inconsistency

The opposite path inconsistency is shown in Figures 20.13a,b. Going from D to K using the node–node table yields a shortest path of D, A, B, C, F, G, K. However, going from A to K is done through the node–component center table. If the center of the component including K is H, I, or J, the shortest path is A, D, E, H, I, J. This creates an inconsistency. In the same way K, L, J cannot be the center of the component including H or I. This shows that the pairs H, I, and K, L cannot be in the same component, and therefore we must split them.

This problem occurs only on the edge border of neighbor tiles (nodes D and F).

20.7.1.2 Convexity Problem

All paths inside a component are supposed to stay inside the component. An upper level node should not have a link to itself through another node. Figures 20.13c,d show such a case where the shortest path from C to D is C, F, G, H, E, D, and goes outside the component. This implies that C and D cannot be in the same component and should be split.

20.7.1.3 Component Center

Once the splitting constraints have been found the component is computed again. This time there are several possible choices of components. For instance, in Figure 20.13b we can have the components {H, I, J} and {K, L} or the components {H, I} and {J, K, L}. The algorithm selects the components with the smallest surface area first.

Afterwards, the component centers can be calculated. However, due to problems such as the opposite path inconsistency, some component centers may be illegal. For instance "J" cannot be a component center in Figure 20.13b.

Currently, the component center is chosen from within the set of allowed centers to be the barycenter of the component. It is possible to optimize center selection by, for instance, decreasing the distances between linked centers.

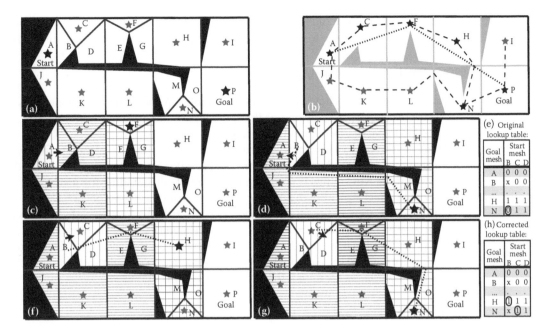

Figure 20.14

Invalid sublink. The pattern shows the table access method (line for node–node, grid for node–component). Dotted lines represent the shortest distances. Figure (a) shows the problem arising when the start point is within A, and the goal within P. Figure (b) shows the top layer nodes with links shown as a dashed line, the shortest path with black stars, and the smoothed distance is shown as a dotted line. Figure (c) shows how the subgoal F is used to go from A to B. Figure (d) shows that if the subgoal N is used from B, there is an inconsistency. Figure (f) shows that the inconsistency is solved if the subgoal H is used instead. Figure (g) shows that the path from C to N is valid. Figures (e) and (h) show the lookup table used in figures (d) and (e), respectively, before and after the sublink removal.

20.7.2 Remove Invalid Sublink

The function `RemoveInvalidSubLink()` is responsible for removing table inconsistencies due to both the local nature of the table building process and the path heuristic, which chooses the farthest component center as a subgoal. Depending on the tile neighborhood, the subgoal selection may produce a path that doubles back on itself. This is solved by disallowing the selection of the farthest subgoal by removing its link in the lookup table. Figures 20.14e,h show how the subgoal is changed by removing the output edge in the lookup table for the path B to N.

Since the hierarchical building process ensures that the upper layer tables are consistent for adjacent nodes (constraints in Section 20.6.5), removing the farthest subgoals will still result in a valid path.

This type of inconsistency can only occur on tile borders when the subgoal is changing, and is mainly a problem with long paths. In these cases, the upper layer data is more accurate than the lower layer and for this reason, the algorithm validates the layers from top to bottom.

Figure 20.14 shows a problem arising from the dynamic nature of the subgoal selection. In some cases, selecting the farthest possible subgoal can lead to doubling back. In the example shown in Figure 20.14d, the node-component table access from B to N is removed. The last valid subgoal to go to P will be H, removing the inconsistency in Figure 20.14f.

20.8 Table Use on Server

In Section 20.5.4, we saw how a path request is handled. As previously mentioned, it is not necessary to compute the polygons or the upper layer nodes path until the goal. Since no searching is required, the request is very fast.

However, this only yields a polygon sequence rather than the actual path to follow. An optimized version of the Funnel algorithm [Douglas 06] is used to calculate a smoothed path. Even if the NPC radius is not taken into account when finding the mesh path, it is used by the Funnel algorithm to push the path away from the border polygons.

The use of the agent radius for path smoothing leads to better looking paths but does not prevent large NPCs from intersecting with a collision boundary. It is possible to create a new table (not necessarily a new mesh) to avoid narrow passages, but this can result in long detours.

To further improve the path quality for small distances, a straight path search is done to the goal. If obstacles are found, the pathfinding algorithm is used.

20.9 Results

The presented navigation system provides very fast query speed at the cost of a loss of flexibility. One query takes about 4 micro seconds. The main problem with precomputed data is that any dynamic change requires a new table; therefore, this approach is best suited to static worlds. However, some dynamic changes such as opening/closing doors are supported by allowing/forbidding to cross the door polygons. This check is done at runtime.

This disadvantage is outweighed by the dramatic reduction in processing power needed at run-time by the navigation system. The most costly task is the relatively simple query for the nearest polygon, which is also facilitated by the regular grid partitioning. Even the smoothed path computation is less expensive.

20.9.1 Smoothed Distances

Using smoothed rather than additive distances for computing the lookup table (Section 20.6.3) improved the path quality.

Benchmarking with random trajectories showed that the length of more than 70% of the paths was unchanged. Of the remaining paths there were both increases and decreases in length. However, the number of trajectories reduced by more than 5% was 10 times greater than those that had increased by the same proportion.

The smoothed distance technique came at a cost: asymmetric paths, increased complexity of the algorithm, and twice the table computation time. However, the computational time is still within an acceptable range with less than 80 seconds for the largest maps tested.

20.9.2 Table Builder Algorithm

We experimented with three algorithms to compute the lookup table: Floyd–Warshall, Dijkstra, and A*. The best result in terms of path quality was given by Dijkstra using the smoothed distance. The fastest algorithm was given by the combination of A* using the additional distance. The heuristic used by A* was the distance to the tile being processed.

The Floyd–Warshall algorithm was slower, and it was difficult to add new constraints or to use the smoothed distance. It calculates all the shortest paths between all the nodes of all the 21 neighbor tiles. In the example in Figure 20.8a, this means that 42×42 paths were needed instead of 2×42 (Figure 20.8b).

The heuristic for A* with smoothed distance is the Euclidean distance to the nearest border of the currently processed tile. Even if this algorithm returned the shortest possible path for all the polygons in the processed tile, its global result would be worse than the Dijkstra version. The tiles tables' inconsistencies increased and, to resolve them, longer paths were used.

It is worth noting that all three algorithms yielded similar results when used in conjunction with the additional distance metric.

20.9.3 Table Size

The biggest table size is about 4 mega octets (Mo) for a 1.5 km² forest. Dungeon and town sizes are under 500 kilo octets. Note that this data is not based on the final maps, and that during the map design process, table sizes sometimes reached up to 10 Mo.

20.9.4 Alternative Uses

Other than navigation, the mesh was also used for checking the collision data, but its most interesting secondary application is the in-game 2D map autogeneration. The player has access to a 2D map of the world that must represent the areas accessible by the player. This map is basically a projection of the navigation mesh. Unfortunately, the details of its generation process are out of the scope of this article. However, it is worth showing in Figure 20.15 one of the maps that this cool feature enabled us to generate.

20.10 Conclusion

This article has described the steps taken for automatic generation of a precomputed navigation system. We have underlined ways to handle unidirectional paths and evaluated different methods of performing distance measurements. The resulting system allows very fast navigation requests for large and detailed worlds. It is a good solution for all server-based applications where there are strong constraints on security or client hardware limitations.

The whole generation system is completely automatic, freeing up the rest of the team to concentrate on more creative work. We hope that this article will be useful to others creating a precomputed navigation system and help them avoid potential pitfalls.

Acknowledgments

We would like to thank all the FFXIV team, and especially Shinpei Sakata who worked on the 2D map autogeneration, allowing us to share this unexpected use of the navigation mesh.

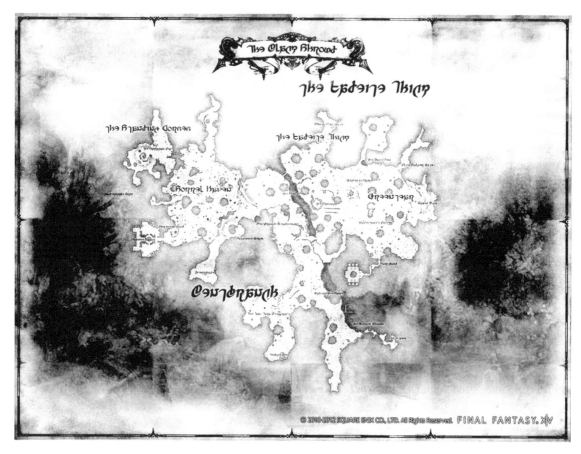

Figure 20.15

2D Game world map autogenerated from the navigation mesh.

References

[Axelrod 08] R. Axelrod. "Navigation graph generation in highly dynamic worlds." In *AI Game Programming Wisdom 4*, edited by Steve Rabin. Reading, MA: Charles River Media, 2008, pp. 124–141.

[Dickheiser 03] M. Dickheiser. "Inexpensive precomputed pathfinding using a navigation set hierarchy." In *AI Game Programming Wisdom 2*, edited by Steve Rabin, Reading, MA: Charles River Media, 2003, pp. 103–113.

[Douglas 06] D. Jon Demyen. "Efficient Triangulation-Based Pathfinding." Master Thesis, 2006. Available online (https://skatgame.net/mburo/ps/tra.pdf).

[Lengyel 05] Eric Lengyel, "Building an Edge List for an Arbitrary Mesh." Terathon Software 3D Graphics Library, 2005. http://www.terathon.com/code/edges.html.

[Miles 06] D. Miles. "Crowds in a polygon soup: Next-Gen path planning." Presentation on *Game Developers Conference (GDC)*, 2006.

[Mononen 12] M. Mononen, "Recast." http://code.google.com/p/recastnavigation/

[Sterren 03] W. van der Sterren. "Path look-up tables—small is beautiful." In *AI Game Programming Wisdom 2*, edited by Steve Rabin. Reading, MA: Charles River Media, 2003, pp. 115–129.

[Sturtevant et al. 10] N. Sturtevant and R. Geisberger. "A comparison of high-level approaches for speeding up pathfinding." *In Artificial Intelligence and Interactive Digital Entertainment (AIIDE), 2010.* Available online (http://web.cs.du.edu/~sturtevant/papers.html).

21

Techniques for Formation Movement Using Steering Circles

Stephen Bjore

21.1 Introduction

Moving formations around open terrain is fairly easy. However, it becomes more difficult to generate a path such that the formation ends at a specific point in a specified orientation, given the limitation that formations can only turn so quickly. A solution to this problem is presented in this chapter, and is an extension of the idea of using steering circles from Chris Jurney's GDC presentation [Jurney et al. 07]. The solution can be broken into two parts:

1. Generate the path to follow.
2. Navigate the formation along the path.

It's worth noting here that the first part of generating the path isn't limited to formations. It can be used for individual characters, vehicles, or any other moving object for which a steering circle can be defined. The second part is specific to formations and describes two different techniques for moving the formation along the path.

21.2 Generate the Path

Using two steering circles, one based on the current position of the formation and one based on the target position, we can calculate the path the formation needs to take.

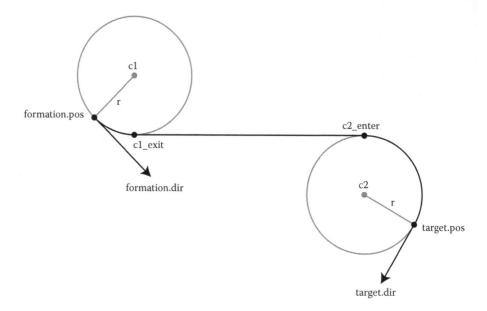

Figure 21.1

The final path starts at *formation.pos*, facing *formation.dir*, and ends at *target.pos*, facing *target.dir*. *c1* and *c2* show the centers of the steering circles. *c1_exit* is where the path breaks away from the starting circle and *c2_enter* is where the path joins the ending steering circle.

Figure 21.1 shows the most important information, as well as an example of what our final path could look like.

When we first begin generating the path, we start with five pieces of information: the current position of the formation (*formation.pos*), the current orientation (*formation.dir*), the target position (*target.pos*), the target orientation (*target.dir*), and the radius of the steering circles (or the turn radius of the formation, r). Based on this data, we need to calculate four additional values:

- $c1$, the center point of the starting steering circle.
- $c1\_exit$, the point where the formation will break away from the starting circle.
- $c2$, the center point of the ending steering circle.
- $c2\_enter$, the point where the formation will join the ending circle.

21.2.1 Calculating c1 and c2

The first step towards calculating the path is to generate the steering circles that will be used at the start and end points. To do this, we need to calculate the vector *target.pos–formation.pos*, which we will refer to as *dirVec*.

Next, we will calculate the center point of starting circle, $c1$. For this, we need the perpendicular vector of *formation.dir* in the same direction as *dirVec*. We can calculate this by taking the dot product of both perpendiculars of *formation.dir* with *dirVec*. We will use the perpendicular with the positive result, labeling it *formation.perp*. Scale *formation.perp* to have length equal to r, and then add it to *formation.pos* to get $c1$. The center point for the ending circle, *c2*, is calculated in the same way, using *–dirVec* (instead of *dirVec*) and the perpendicular vectors of *target.dir*. The vector with the positive dot product will be referred to as *target.perp*.

The only exception is when the distance between *c1* and *c2* is less than *2r* (i.e., the steering circles are overlapping). The solution in this case is to invert both *formation.perp* and *target.perp*. This will cause the formation to steer in the opposite direction, thereby giving it enough space to turn. For example, if we originally used the right-hand perpendicular of *formation.dir*, we will use the left-hand perpendicular instead, essentially flipping the steering circle to the other side of *formation.dir*.

21.2.2 Calculating c1_exit and c2_enter

The goal of this section, finding *c1_exit* and *c2_enter*, has two different cases that we need to consider. In order to determine which case we have, we first need to look at whether *position.perp* and *target.perp* are the left or right perpendiculars of *position.dir* and *target.dir*. For brevity, we will say *formation.perp* is equal to "Left" if it is the left-hand perpendicular of *formation.dir*; otherwise it is "Right." Likewise, *target.perp* is equal to "Left" if it is the left-hand perpendicular of *target.dir*; otherwise it is "Right."

The first case is for when *formation.perp* and *target.perp* fall on opposite sides (e.g., *formation.perp* equals *Right* and *target.perp* equals *Left*). In this instance, our goal is to calculate the angles where the points *c1_exit* and *c2_enter* are on the circumference of the two circles, relative to the x-axis (these angles are *a3* and *b3* in Figure 21.2). Once we have those angles, we can then calculate the two points.

The second case is when *formation.perp* and *target.perp* are on the same side. This case doesn't require us to calculate any angles, but instead relies on the observation that the important angles involved are all 90 degrees.

21.2.2.1 Calculation if Formation.Perp and Target.Perp Are on Opposite Sides

In the case where *formation.perp* is not on the same side as *target.perp*, our goal is to calculate the angles *a3* and *b3*. We will get into the details momentarily, but it should be noted that the calculation for *a3* and *b3* will change slightly, depending on which sides *formation.perp* and *target.perp* are on, which is why there are two diagrams in Figure 21.2.

Before we start the calculations, we will make several observations. First, the line from *c1* to *c1_exit* and the line from *c2* to *c2_enter* are both perpendicular to the line between *c1_exit* and *c2_enter*. Second, the lines *c1* to *c2* and *c1_exit* to *c2_enter* intersect each other at the midpoint of both lines. Third, we know the radius of the steering circles, *r*. And fourth, we are able to calculate the distance between *c1* and *c2*, which is labeled *d*. Looking at Figure 21.2, we can see that we now have two right-hand triangles, and that we know two sides of the triangles (one side is *r*, the other is ½*d). This means that we can calculate the angle *a1*: `a1 = acos(r/(1/2 * d))`. We can also calculate *a2* by finding the angle of the vector *c2-c1* relative to the x-axis.

For *a3*, the calculation we need to use will depend on the values of *formation.perp* and *target.perp*. If *formation.perp* is Right, then we can refer to Diagram A, and *a3* is calculated by adding *a1* to *a2*. Else, if *formation.perp* is Left, we refer to Diagram B, and *a3* can be calculated by subtracting *a1* from *a2*.

The calculation for *c2_enter* is very similar to the calculation for *c1_exit*. The angle *b1* is calculated using the exact same equation and values that we used to find *a1*. The angle *b2*

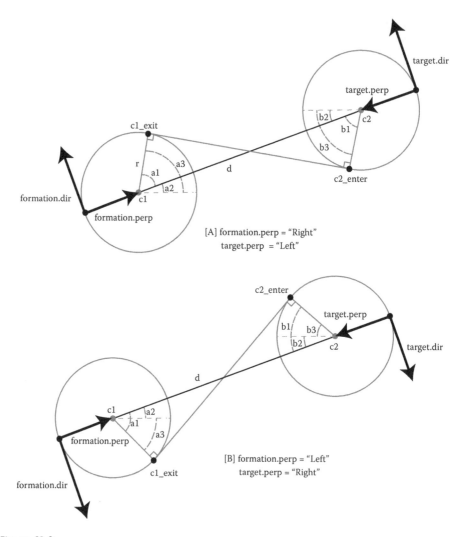

Figure 21.2

This diagram shows everything necessary to calculate the angles *a3* and *b3* when *formation.perp* and *target.perp* are on opposite sides. [A] shows the angles to be calculated when *formation.perp* is Right and *target.perp* is Left. [B] shows the angles for when *formation.perp* is Left and *target.perp* is Right.

is the angle of the vector *c1-c2* relative to the x-axis (unlike *a2*, which is the angle of *c2-c1* relative to the x-axis). The calculation for *b3* is also the same as the one we used for *a3*, and is simply *b2-b1* or *b2+b1*, depending on the values of *formation.perp* and *target.perp*.

Finally, now that we've calculated *a3* and *b3*, we can generate the points on the circles, *c1_exit* and *c2_enter*:

- $c1\_exit(x,y) = (c1.x + r * \cos(a3), c1.y + r * \sin(a3))$
- $c2\_enter(x,y) = (c2.x + r * \sin(b3), c2.y + r * \sin(b3))$

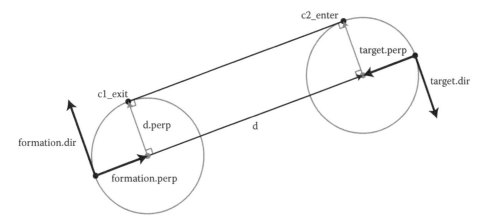

Figure 21.3

This shows what needs to be calculated when *formation.perp* and *target.perp* fall on the same side; in this case, they are both "Right."

21.2.2.2 Calculation if Formation.Perp and Target.Perp Are on the Same Side

In the case where *formation.perp* and *target.perp* both fall on the same side (meaning that they are both Right or Left), the calculation is a bit simpler. Here, we start by calculating the vector *c2-c1*, which we called *d*. As seen in Figure 21.3, if *formation.perp* is equal to Right, then we will use the left-hand perpendicular of *d*, labeled *d.perp*. Similarly, if *formation.perp* is equal to Left, then *d.perp* will be the right-hand perpendicular of *d*. In either case, once we have *d.perp*, add it to *c1* and *c2* to get *c1_exit* and *c2_enter*.

21.2.3 Generate the Points Along the Path

Finally, we can generate the points along the path for the formation to navigate by. The points will start at *formation.pos*, and move around the circle *c1* to *c1_exit*, move on to *c2_enter*, and finally around the circle *c2* until we arrive at *target.pos*.

The direction of travel around the circles is determined by *formation.perp* and *target.perp*. When they are equal to "Right," then we will generate points on the corresponding circle going around in the clockwise direction, and when they are "Left," we will generate points going around in the counter-clockwise direction.

21.3 Navigate the Formation

Moving a formation around in a way that looks reasonable requires the positions within the formation to be fluid. The following examples will keep the first row of the formation static, and the rows behind will follow in a couple of different ways. Here, we will look at two styles: the first style involves moving each unit within the formation towards the unit ahead of it, and the second style requires each unit to preserve its row by staying next to the units to its left and right.

Note that the points within the formation described here are intended to be pathfinding targets, not necessarily the actual locations of the units within the formation. This flexibility could allow units to go off and do other things, such as dealing with attacking enemies, gathering nearby resources, or navigate around smaller obstacles. Once the unit has completed whatever subtask it had, it can then resume pathfinding to its target position within the formation.

21.3.1 "Column" Formation

This technique involves moving each unit within the formation towards the unit in front of it, while maintaining a set distance. While this will result in a fairly fluid look, and maintain a connection between each unit in a column, it does not preserve the rows.

The first step is to update the position and direction of the formation, based on the velocity of the formation and the next point in the path. To keep the units of the first row in a straight line, their positions are calculated such that the line they form is perpendicular to the formation's updated direction, and is centered at the formation's position. Starting on the second row, calculate the direction between each target, and the target ahead of it in the same column. We then move the target in that direction until it's touching the unit ahead of it, repeating this process for the units in all of remaining rows in the formation.

21.3.2 "Band" Formation

For this movement style, the formation preserves the rows as it steers around corners. The first row is calculated in the same manner that was used for the *Column Formation* style.

Next, we need to determine whether the second row is turning left or right, based on the direction that the first row moved in. To do this, first calculate the direction from any unit in the second row to the unit in the same column of the first row, and then take the right-hand perpendicular, which we will call *rPerpendicular*. Next, take the dot product of the direction that the first row moved in with *rPerpendicular*. If that result is positive, the second row will be turning right, or else it will be turning left.

For the moment, let's assume that the second row is turning left. The next step will be to move the leftmost unit in the second row towards the unit ahead of it in the same column until they are touching. Next, starting with the second unit in the row, set each unit's position to be touching the unit to its left, moving in the direction of *rPerpendicular*.

If the row is turning right, there are only two minor differences. The main one is that we will want to calculate the position of the rightmost unit first, moving it towards the unit in front of it until they are touching. The other difference is that you will start with the second unit from the right, and will set each unit's position to be touching the unit to its right, moving in the direction of *-1*rPerpendicular*.

In either case, once we have the positions for all of the units in the second row, we can repeat this process for the remaining rows in the formation.

21.4 The Demo

A demo provided on the book's website (http://www.gameaipro.com) was created to be used as a proof-of-concept for the ideas presented in this paper. It was written in HTML5 and Javascript, with the intention of being as portable as possible. Nearly all of the logic for generating the path can be found within "main.js," while the logic for drawing, updating, and moving the formation and the units within the formation can be found in "formation.js."

21.5 Conclusion

This article has shown that steering a formation to end in a specific place and direction, with the use of some simple linear algebra, is not difficult. By calculating two steering circles based on the formation's current position and the destination position, it's possible to generate a path for the formation to follow that will ensure that the formation will never need to make turns sharper than it is capable of.

Further development of this concept could include the ability for the formation to take obstacles into account, on both a large and small scale. For smaller obstacles, the intention is that the formation can largely ignore them. This is because it is intended that the pathfinding targets within the formation will deal with finding a way around anything small. Large-scale obstacles would need to be dealt with separately, but could potentially be handled by taking into account the size of the entire formation, and then perform pathfinding for the formation as a whole.

References

[Jurney et al. 07] C. Jurney and S. Hubick. "Dealing with destruction: AI from the trenches of company of heroes." *Game Developers Conference, 2007*. Available online (https://store.cmpgame.com/product.php?cat=24&id=2089).

22

Collision Avoidance for Preplanned Locomotion

Bobby Anguelov

22.1 Introduction

Collision avoidance for NPCs is a critical component of any character locomotion system. To date, the majority of collision avoidance approaches are based either on Reynold's seminal steering articles [Reynolds 99] or one of the many reciprocal velocity obstacle techniques (RVO) [Guy et al. 10, v.d. Berg et al. 08]. In trying to increase the visual fidelity of our character locomotion by reducing artifacts such as foot sliding, some developers are moving away from traditional steering-based locomotion in favor of *animation-driven locomotion* (ADL) systems in combination with preplanned motion. This article discusses the implications of moving your locomotion system to a preplanned ADL system with regards to avoidance and why traditional collision avoidance systems may be overkill for preplanned motion. We present the collision avoidance approach used in *Hitman: Absolution* (HMA) and discuss how this system can be adapted for use with any preplanned locomotion system.

In traditional steering systems, characters are usually simulated as moving spheres and character trajectories are calculated based on the current velocities of these spheres. Appropriate character animations are then layered on top of this simulation to give the illusion that the character is actually moving. Since there exists a disconnect between the animation and the simulation, the animation is not guaranteed to exactly match the simulation and results in noticeable artifacts like foot sliding. ADL takes the opposite approach wherein a character's trajectory updates are read directly from the animation, meaning that the character's position updates and animations are in-sync, completely eliminating foot sliding. Unfortunately, in using ADL, we constrain character motion to the set of animations available, thereby potentially sacrificing the wide range of motion offered by steering systems. Furthermore, ADL systems have an inherent latency associated with them resulting from the fact that we can only change our motion whenever a foot is planted on the ground, meaning that we often have to wait for a footstep to complete before we can adjust our movement. A detailed discussion of these systems is beyond the scope of this article and interested readers are referred to [Anguelov et al. 12] for more information.

Once we have our characters moving around, we would ideally like to have them navigate from one location to another in our game world. The key difference, at least with regards to collision avoidance, is due to the path-following behavior in the locomotion system. In most cases, path points are simply treated as rough goals, and the steering system is tasked with navigating between them. In steering-based systems, the path resulting from the steering actions can deviate significantly from the original path found. Unfortunately, depending on the ADL motion constraints as well as the ADL latency, we could end up in problematic situations where characters clip corners or potentially leave the navigation mesh (navmesh).

This can occur when the steering desires are too fine grained for the locomotion system to satisfy or the locomotion system doesn't take the ADL latency into account, which is extremely problematic at high movement speeds. These problems can be ameliorated through complex adjustments to the steering system taking the ADL constraints into account as well as other measures such as constraining characters to the navmesh. Unfortunately, the complexity of such adjustments rapidly increases to the point where our locomotion system is significantly complex, without even taking collision avoidance into account. Now this is not to say such an approach will not work, since many developers use exactly this approach with great success, but we feel there is a simpler solution.

We think the important thing is to not look at the ADL reduced motion set as a disadvantage, but rather as a benefit, since the reduction in options makes it feasible for us to preplan our motion for the entire path. What we mean by preplanning is to plan the exact path, and potentially the set of animations needed, to reach our end goal prior to starting locomotion. This means that we can, for any given point in time, predict both the exact position and velocity of an agent. There are various ways to achieve this preplanning, and readers are referred to [Champandard 09] and [Anguelov 12] for more information.

It is with these preplanned systems that traditional avoidance techniques start to lose their applicability due to the exact precomputation of our locomotion. Standard RVO systems resolve collision by trying to find a local, collision-free velocity for a character, relative to other characters in the scene. The character's velocity is then adjusted to match the collision-free velocity. This is all done within a local neighborhood and only returns the immediate collision-free velocity, not taking anything else into account; this can potentially result in anomalous behavior such as agent oscillation. Discussing the potential problems with RVO is beyond the scope of this article and we simply wish to point out that RVO is a local avoidance system, which, given our global knowledge of our agents' locomotion, may not be the best approach to solving the avoidance problem.

22.2 Collision Avoidance for Preplanned Locomotion

We built a very simple yet robust avoidance system that allows us to detect collision on a more global scale than what RVO would have allowed. Our solution also allows us to resolve collision in a high fidelity manner entirely within the constraints of our ADL system. *Hitman: Absolution's* locomotion is a preplanned ADL-based system, with each character following a smoothed path precisely. These smoothed paths are created by postprocessing an existing navmesh path, and then converting this path into a set of continuous quadratic Bézier curves. Interested readers are referred to Anguelov [12] for information on the path postprocessing used in HMA.

Our characters will then follow these smoothed paths precisely, with the distance traveled per frame being read from the currently selected animation. Simply put, you could think of our characters as being on rails. These paths serve as the primary input to our avoidance system with the secondary input being the characters' current state and motion data, which is populated by the locomotion system.

Our avoidance system consists of three distinct stages: collision detection, trivial collision resolution, and nontrivial collision resolution. Our avoidance system is run once per agent per frame, and each agent is checked for a collision with every other agent (now termed *colliders*) in the scene sequentially. The result of this collision check is either a speed modification/stop order or a request for path replanning.

The first stage and the core of our avoidance approach is the collision detection mechanism. Our characters (now termed *agents*) are modeled as collision spheres with a fixed collision radius, and the premise behind the collision detection system is to simply slide our spheres along our paths and check whether they make it to the end of their paths without colliding with any other spheres.

During the frame update of each agent's animation/locomotion programs, the agent will query the avoidance system to see whether its current path is collision-free. The avoidance system will perform a collision detection pass as well as attempt to trivially resolve a detected collision. The details of this system are too complex to discuss here, since it is built around our locomotion system, so we will not attempt to do so but rather we will try to describe the higher level concepts the best we can to try to inspire you to build similar systems.

22.3 Collision Detection and Trivial Collision Resolution

Our collision detection works as follows: We first calculate a collision detection range for our agent. In our case, we know exactly how much time and distance is necessary for our agent to stop if we had to immediately issue a stop command. This stopping distance is then added to a specified time horizon length (in seconds) multiplied by our current velocity, the result being the collision detection range for our agent (refer to Figure 22.1a).

Stopping distance is important as we don't want to trigger a "stop" command which will result in our agent stopping in the path of another agent or, even worse, end up stopping inside another agent. The time horizon window allows us to detect collisions much further in advance than an RVO system could. In our testing, we've found it sufficient to only check two seconds ahead for a good balance of performance and fidelity.

Before we actually check the agent's path, we perform two exclusion checks on the collider. We first run a simple dot product check to determine whether the collider is in

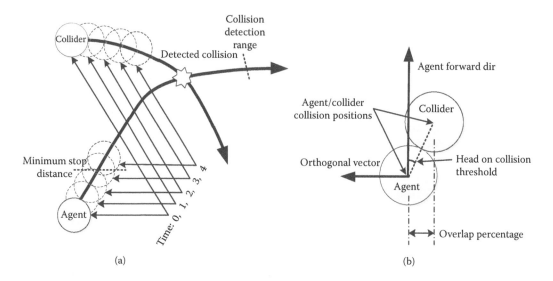

Figure 22.1

(a) Collision detection along an agent's path. (b) The stored collision data for a given collision.

front of the agent relative to the movement direction. In ignoring any colliders behind the agent, we implicitly delegate the responsibility for any potential collisions that may occur to those colliders. If the collider is determined to be in the direction of our movement, we perform a simple sphere–sphere intersection test [Ericson 05a] using the agent and collider positions for the sphere origins and the agent and collider's calculated collision detection ranges as the sphere radii. If both tests succeed, we then proceed to check the agent's path for a collision with the collider.

The path checking is performed by moving the agent along its path by the *agent's collision radius* (ACR). By moving the agent along its path in discrete intervals, we are discretizing our continuous path into ACR length pieces. The time needed for the agent to complete one ACR length movement (i.e., the *time per movement* or TPM) is determined by the agent's current velocity and is used to calculate the average velocity vector for the move. We then proceed to move the collider along its path by calculating the collider's position at the end of the TPM interval to ensure temporal consistency; this position and time is used to calculate a collider velocity vector.

In our case, our agents always move with a fixed velocity so this calculation is trivial, but it will be more complex if you have varying velocities per animation clip. This process of moving an agent's collision sphere along the path is visualized for 4 TPM intervals in Figure 22.1a. Once we have the agent and collider final positions and the average velocity vectors, we perform a moving-sphere–moving-sphere check [Ericson 05b].

If we detected an intersection between the spheres, we need to record some data regarding the collision for later use. This data initially contains the positions of the agent and collider at the point of collision. We also store whether the collision was head-on by checking whether the angle between the agent's forward direction and the vector to the center of the collider is within some threshold (in our case ~10 degrees). A rough estimate of the potential overlap percentage between the two collision spheres for that collision is then calculated and stored. The overlap percentage is calculated as the actor collision sphere diameter minus the min distance between the two spheres (along their respective paths) divided by the actor collision diameter. The final bit of data we store is the orthogonal vector to the agent's forward direction, away from the collider's direction of movement. This orthogonal vector is used for the path modification later on. All the necessary data we store for a detected collision is visualized in Figure 22.1b.

If no collision is detected, we calculate the collision sphere motion for the next TPM interval and repeat the check until we reach the end of the agent's collision detection range. If we have detected a collision then we immediately terminate the detection stage and move onto the trivial resolution stage. It is important to note that our system is only concerned with the first detected collision and so only tries to resolve that collision. The assumption is made that any further collisions along the agent's path will be detected and resolved on subsequent frames.

The trivial resolution stage attempts to resolve the detected collision through simple speed modification. We attempt to do this by performing the path checking algorithm at a different agent speed. If this new agent speed results in a collision-free path, then we simply instruct the agent to change speed. This adjustment is immediate, and any subsequent calls into the avoidance system will make use of the updated agent speed. This means that any other agents running an avoidance check will make use of the updated agent speed.

The speed modification check is run for all available speeds, and if all the speeds still result in a collision, then we check whether our stopping distance is collision-free; if it is then we instruct the agent to stop and wait until he can continue on a collision-free path.

This simple system resolved the bulk of our existing in-game collisions, but we needed an additional system to handle collisions that couldn't be avoided through simple speed modification (e.g., stationary agents or head-on collisions). This secondary system is used for what we termed nontrivial collision resolution, but before we carry on we need to discuss some details regarding the collision detection stage.

First, we've made an assumption that all of our characters are moving but that is not always the case. In many situations characters are stationary, either performing some level-specific or idle act (e.g., using an ATM or leaning against a wall). These stationary characters have to be handled differently since they have no paths allocated. The collision checks are performed in the same way, except now the agent is stationary so we simply don't need to calculate an update position for the collider.

Second, even though agents are moving, they might be in a transition animation for starting or stopping. In our case, our agents travel with a linear velocity, which greatly simplifies the math in the path collision check. When starting or stopping, we had a nonlinear velocity during the transition, so our prediction of agent velocity and position during those transitions was rather complex. We didn't want to unnecessarily increase complexity by modeling the nonlinear transition velocity in our avoidance code, so we simply resorted to estimating the velocity within those transitions.

Agent velocities during transitions were estimated by dividing the remaining distance of the transition by the time of the transition. We also tried to ensure that our start-and-stop animations were as short as possible, further reducing the error of this estimation. Something to keep in mind is that your transitions may have long periods wherein the agent is not actually moving. For example, we had a *turn-on-spot* starting transition where the agent would be turning for more than half of the transition, but didn't actually change position; this broke our estimation code and required us to have to pre-process all animations to determine the portion within the animations that actually move the character. Luckily, these nonmoving intervals are usually only at the start or end of an animation, which makes it easy to deal with by simply decreasing the transition time and treating the collider as stationary for that time.

Since our default avoidance query is for already moving agents, we also need to take into consideration agents that are stationary and wish to begin moving. We created a custom *'CheckForCollisionFreeStart'* avoidance query that takes into account our nonlinear start transition and determines when it is safe to start moving. This additional check allows us to wait for other agents to get out of the way before we start moving. We added two additional game-specific queries to the avoidance system dealing with combat sidesteps and *shoot-from-cover* acts. Since we don't want an agent to step out into another agent's path, we provided an interface for the combat programs to query whether a proposed new position was collision-free before issuing any move/act orders.

22.4 Nontrivial Collision Resolution through Path Modification

Our nontrivial collision resolution is a path modification system: we modify an agent's path around an obstacle without any need for replanning on a pathfinder level. Making use of the collision data stored during the detection stage, we calculate an *avoidance point* (AP) that will resolve the collision and a *reconnection point* (RP) on the original path.

The entire path starting from the agent's current position to the RP is replaced with a new path that is made up of two cubic Bézier curves and which goes through the AP. The AP is calculated as a point that lies at some distance along the orthogonal vector to the agent's forward vector at the point of collision. We apply a relatively large distance of around 5× the agent collision radius along the orthogonal vector to calculate the avoidance point. It is important to note that the actual position of the avoidance point is not all that important; in simply altering the length of the path, we also affect the time at which we would reach the previous collision point, which in itself is often enough to resolve the collision.

After calculating the avoidance point, we perform a navmesh query to ensure that the avoidance point is both on the navmesh and straight-line-reachable from the agent's collision position. If the point is off the navmesh, we simply truncate the point to the furthest on-navmesh point along the orthogonal vector that is further than some minimum avoidance threshold. We then set the tangent of the AP to be the same as the tangent on the original path at the point of collision. This means that the avoidance point simply acts as an offset to the path. If we have truncated the AP onto an exterior edge of the navmesh, we have to modify the tangent at the AP to be the same as the tangent to the exterior edge of the navmesh; doing this will help ensure that the cubic Bézier curves stay within the navmesh at the AP (refer to Figure 22.2b).

The next step is to find the furthest straight-line-reachable navmesh point along the path from the point of collision; this is the RP. It is important to ensure that the tangent at the AP and the vector to the reconnection point are dissimilar by some threshold (in our case 8 degrees) to ensure that reconnection curve doesn't cross over the original path. Finally, we then cut the path segment from the agent's current position to the RP

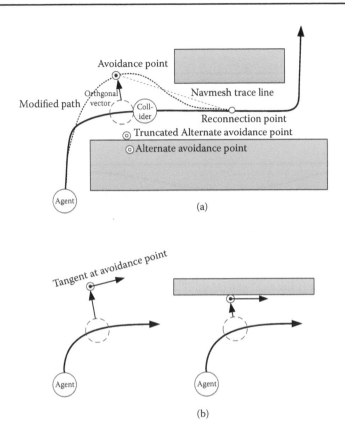

Figure 22.2

(a) Path modification. (b) Avoidance point tangents.

and replace it with the two cubic Bézier curves which pass through the avoidance point respecting the set avoidance point tangent.

Before we can accept this modified path, it is necessary to run some validation checks on it. The first check discretizes the path into short straight line segments, and we run navmesh straight-line-reachable queries for each segment to ensure that the path does not leave the navmesh. If the path leaves the navmesh, it is immediately discarded. The second check performed is a path collision detection check, exactly the same as in the detection stage, at the current agent speed on the newly modified path though. Unlike the detection stage, this check is considered successful if the result is either collision-free or is a speed modification instruction. If we receive a speed modification instruction, then we can safely accept the path, knowing that on the next frame the speed modification instruction will be received and executed.

Sometimes the modified path will result in an unavoidable collision; so what do we do in that case? We decided to try to find an alternate modified path by calculating a new AP using the negated orthogonal collision vector. We validate this alternate path and if it once again results in an unavoidable collision, then we simply pick between the two modified paths by selecting the path which results in the lowest collision overlap percentage.

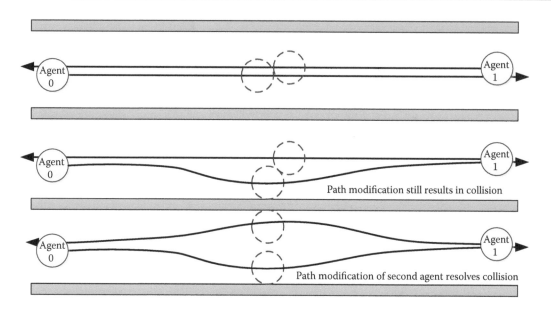

Figure 22.3

Collision resolution through multiple agent path modification.

In many cases, neither of the paths will resolve the collision, so we try to minimize the collision as much as possible. In many cases, upon running the avoidance query upon the collider and again trying to minimize the collision, you will potentially resolve it. This is exactly what we see happening when several agents try to navigate through a narrow corridor. The added benefit is that it results in flow channels forming. An example of collision resolution through collision minimization is illustrated in Figure 22.3.

22.5 Performance and Visual Quality

Visual quality was extremely important to us, so we added a few things to the avoidance system to help with the overall visual fidelity of our locomotion. We noticed that when sending groups of agents to investigate events, the agents would tend to bunch up and move together. Even though the agents were collision-free, the result looked poor. We decided to add a further check at the end of our collision detection stage (if we don't detect any collisions) to ensure that we maintain a minimum distance from any agents walking in the same direction as ourselves. We simply checked that if an agent was walking in the same direction as a collider and the agent was less than the minimum distance from the collider, we simply slowed down until we satisfied the minimum distance requirement. This simple check had a huge impact on the visual quality of our agents. We also had a problem where bugs in our AI would sometimes send more than one agent to the same position, so we leveraged the path modification to allow us to modify the end point of our path, ensuring that agents did not end up right on top of one another.

In general, the visual fidelity of our avoidance system is extremely high, having agents modify their speeds or simply stop and wait looks quite good (and in our opinion quite natural) especially within confined spaces. Furthermore, our system doesn't exhibit any of the oscillation side effects that are quite prevalent in the RVO family. Since our collision detection is performed along the agent's path, we have the added benefit over RVO that our detection works around corners allowing us to resolve collision well in advance of the agent reaching the corner.

It has been suggested that most of the problems with RVO can be ameliorated through tweaking of the parameters or the algorithm, but this only further increases the cost and complexity of such an approach, which is in stark contrast to the simplicity of our approach. Performance-wise, we found our system to be extremely cheap in that we are able to perform avoidance queries, in our production levels, for around 30 agents at a max total cost of around 1~1.5% (0.3~0.5 ms) of the frame time on Playstation 3.

22.6 Conclusion

We have presented a very simple alternative to RVO-based avoidance for use with preplanned locomotion. The system makes use of simple geometric intersection tests to perform collision detection and had two stages of collision resolution. The trivial stage made use of speed modification and stopping to resolve collisions, while the nontrivial stage calculated a new path in an attempt to avoid the detected collision. We discussed the high level concepts of such a system in *Hitman: Absolution* and the results thereof. This system is able to handle multiple agents in a complex environment and results in emergent flow fields developing in confined spaces. Furthermore, the premise behind the system is extremely simple and easy to extend, allowing developers a large degree of freedom in applying these concepts to their future games.

References

[Anguelov et al. 12] B. Anguelov, S. Harris, and G. Le Blanc. "Animation driven locomotion for smoother navigation." *Game Developers Conference (GDC)*, 2012.

[Champandard 09] A. J. Champandard. "Dynamic Locomotion by Example with Alex Champandard." http://aigamedev.com/premium/tutorial/dynamic-locomotion/, 2009.

[Ericson 05a] C. Ericson. *Real Time Collision Detection*. San Francisco, CA: Elsevier, 2005, pp. 88–89.

[Ericson 05b] C. Ericson. *Real Time Collision Detection*. San Francisco, CA: Elsevier, 2005, pp. 223–226.

[Guy et al. 10] S. J. Guy, M. C. Lin, and D. Manocha. "Modeling collision avoidance behavior for virtual humans." *Proc. of the 9th Int. Conf. on Autonomous Agents and Multi-agent Systems (AAMAS)*. 2010.

[Reynolds 99] C. W. Reynolds. "Steering behaviors for autonomous characters." *Game Developers Conference, 1999*. Available Online (http://www.red3d.com/cwr/steer/gdc99/).

[v.d. Berg et al. 08] J. v.d. Berg, M. Lin, and D. Manocha. "Reciprocal velocity obstacles for real-time multi-agent navigation." *IEEE International Conference on Robotics and Automation (ICRA 08)*. 2008.

23

Crowd Pathfinding and Steering Using Flow Field Tiles

Elijah Emerson

23.1 Introduction

Crowd pathfinding and steering using flow field tiles is a technique that solves the computational problem of moving hundreds to thousands of individual agents across massive maps. Through the use of *dynamic flow field tiles*, a more modern steering pipeline can be achieved with features such as obstacle avoidance, flocking, dynamic formations, crowd behavior, and support for arbitrary physics forces, all without the heavy CPU burden of repeatedly rebuilding individual paths for each agent. Furthermore, agents move instantly despite path complexity, giving AI and players immediate feedback.

23.2 Motivation

While working on *Supreme Commander 2*, we were given the task of improving movement and pathfinding behavior. As in many games with pathfinding, each unit in *Supreme*

Commander would move along a fixed, one-way A* path. Eventually, units would collide with other units, especially when they were moving in formation or moving into battle. When paths cross and units collide, the existing code would stop the units and wait for the conflict to resolve, rather than rebuilding a new path around the obstacle. This is because rebuilding a path every time there is a collision turns into a compounding problem, especially in large battles, where the new path will likely lead to a second and third collision, causing the game to grind to a halt. This behavior repeats across a thousand units, whose controlling players are all frantically clicking at each other's units, essentially begging for them to clash and collide with each other.

To overcome this path rebuilding problem, all movement was engineered to prefer to stay on the same path, resulting in limited physics, formations, AI, hit reaction, and so on. In this way, the pathfinding was limiting the entire user experience.

Because of *Supreme Commander's* one-track pathfinding solution, players would baby-sit their units as they moved across the map. They would spend their time watching and clicking, watching and clicking, all to help their units cope with the game's ever changing obstacles and environment.

23.3 World Layout

In the *Supreme Commander 2* engine, the world is broken up into individual sectors containing grid squares, where each grid square is 1×1 meter and each sector holds 10×10 grid squares. There are also portal windows, where each portal window crosses a sector boundary. Figure 23.1 shows an example.

In Figure 23.1, sectors are connected through pathable portal windows. Portal windows begin and end at walls on either side of sector boundaries. There is one portal for each window side, and each portal center is a node in an N-way graph with edges that connect to pathable, same sector portals.

23.4 The Three Field Types

For each 10×10 m grid sector there are three different 10×10 m 2D arrays, or fields of data, used by this algorithm. These three field types are *cost fields*, *integration fields*, and *flow fields*. Cost fields store predetermined "path cost" values for each grid square and are used as input when building an integration field. Integration fields store integrated "cost to goal" values per grid location and are used as input when building a flow field. Finally, flow fields contain path goal directions. The following sections go over each field in more detail.

23.4.1 Cost Field

A cost field is an 8-bit field containing cost values in the range 0–255, where 255 is a special case that is used to represent walls, and 1-254 represent the path cost of traversing that grid location. Varying costs can be used to represent slopes or difficult to move through areas, such as swamps. Cost fields have at least a cost of one for each grid location; if there is extra cost associated with that location, then it's added to one.

If a 10×10 m sector is clear of all cost, then a global static "clear" cost field filled with ones is referenced instead. In this way, you only spend memory on cost fields that contain

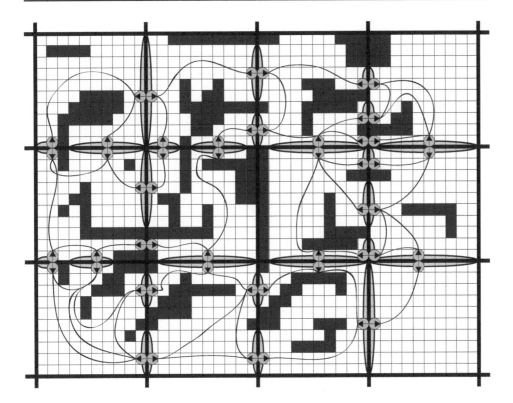

Figure 23.1

An example of the terrain representation used in *Supreme Commander 2*. Each sector is 10 x 10 grid squares with portals connecting sectors.

unique data. In an RTS game, there are a surprising number of clear sectors. In *Supreme Commander 2*, we had roughly 50–70% of the pathable space marked as clear due to widespread areas of open and flat land, lakes, and oceans.

Cost field data was prebuilt by our editor, which converted walls and geometry slope into cost values. Our design team could also visualize this path cost information, as well as make changes to it.

23.4.2 Integration Field

The integration field is a 24-bit field where the first 16 bits is the total integrated cost amount and the second 8 bits are used for integration flags such as "active wave front" and "line of sight." You can optionally spend more memory for better flow results by using a 32-bit float for your integrated cost making it a 40-bit field.

23.4.3 Flow Field

Flow fields are 8-bit fields with the first four bits used as an index into a direction lookup table and the second four bits as flags, such as "pathable" and "has line of sight." The flow field holds all the primary directions and flags used by the agent's steering pipeline for steering around hills and walls to flow toward the path goal.

23.5 Path Requests

Once you have a valid goal position and one or more source positions, you can create a *path request*. The path request will first run A* through the portal node graph. The A* walker starts at the source position, travels through portal nodes, and ends at the goal, thus producing a linked list of "next" portal nodes. This process continues with the next path request source, but this time the portal walker runs "merging" A*, in which the walker prefers to stop and point to a previously traveled portal node to "merge" with previous A* results. With "merging" A* you are more likely to share flow field results and sources are more likely to path closer together, which is the desired behavior when selecting multiple sources to move toward a single goal.

If your A* path to goal is successful, the next step is to walk through your list of next portal nodes and submit a flow field request for each one. At this point you're done with the path request and, because you've only traversed the portal node graph using merging A*, you've used very little CPU.

23.6 The Integrator

We define the *integrator* as the class responsible for taking a single flow field request and, over one or more ticks, building out a single flow field tile. This is achieved by taking the request's cost field data as well as the request's "initial wave front" as input. The initial wave front is a list of goal locations, each having a predetermined integrated cost value.

The integrator takes the initial wave front and integrates it outward using an Eikonal equation [Ki Jeong 08]. Visualize the effect of touching still water, creating a rippling wave moving across the water surface. The Integrator's active wave front behaves similarly in how it moves across the pathable surface while setting larger and larger integrated cost values into the integration field. It repeats this process until the active wave front stops moving by hitting a wall or the sector's boarders. To better understand the integration process, let's go over the Integrator's integration steps.

23.6.1 Integration Step 1: Reset the Integration Field

The integrator's first step is to reset its integration field values and apply the initial goal wave front. If the requested flow field has the final 1×1 goal, then its initial goal wave front is a single 1×1 location with a zero integrated cost value. However, if the flow field request is from a 10×1 or 1×10 portal, then there will be ten goal locations with ten different integrated cost goals.

For higher quality flow results you can integrate at least one flow field ahead in the portal path. Then you can carry over the previously integrated costs as your initial portal window costs instead of using zeros, effectively making the flow across borders seamless. This quality improvement comes at a cost of making flow tiles order dependent, and thus harder to reuse by other path requests.

23.6.2 Integration Step 2: Line Of Sight Pass

If we are integrating from the actual path goal, then we first run a line of sight (LOS) pass. We do this to have the highest quality flow directions near the path goal. When an agent is within the LOS it can ignore the Flow field results altogether and just steer toward the exact goal position. Without the LOS pass, you can have diamond-shaped flow directions around your goal due to the integrator only looking at the four up, down, left, and right neighbors.

It's possible to improve flows around your goal by looking at all eight neighbors during the cost integration pass, but we wouldn't recommend it; marking LOS is cheap and when within the LOS, you get the highest quality path direction possible by ignoring the flow field altogether.

To integrate LOS you have the initial goal wave front integrate out as you normally would, but, instead of comparing the cost field neighbor costs to determine the integrated cost, just increment the wave front cost by one as you move the wave front while flagging the location as "Has Line of Sight." Do this until the wave front hits something with any cost greater than one.

Once we hit something with a cost greater than one, we need to determine if the location is an LOS corner. We do this by looking at the location's neighbors. If one side has a cost greater than one while the other side does not, we have an LOS corner.

For all LOS corners we build out a 2D line starting at the grid square's outer edge position, in a direction away from the goal. Follow this line across the grid using Bresenham's line algorithm, flagging each grid location as "Wave Front Blocked" and putting the location in a second active wave front list to be used later, by the cost integration pass. By marking each location as "Wave Front Blocked" the LOS integration wave front will stop along the line that marks the edge of what is visible by the goal.

You can bring LOS corner lines across sector borders by carrying over the "Has Line of Sight" and "Wave Front Blocked" flags at portal window locations. Then, when you build out the neighbor's integration field, for each portal window location that has the "Wave Front Blocked" flag, consider it an LOS corner to the goal and build out the rest of the line accordingly. This will make the LOS seamless across sector borders.

Continue moving the LOS pass wave front outward until it stops moving by hitting a wall or a location that has the "Wave Front Blocked" flag. Other than the time spent using Bresenham's line algorithm, the LOS first pass is very cheap because it does not look at neighboring cost values. The wave front just sets flags and occasionally detects corners and iterates over a line.

Figure 23.2 shows the results of a LOS pass. Each clear white grid square has been flagged as "Has Line Of Sight." Each LOS corner has a line where each grid square that overlaps that line is flagged as "Wave Front Blocked."

23.6.3 Integration Step 3: Cost Integration Pass

We are now ready for cost field integration. As with the LOS pass, we start with the active wave front list. This active wave front comes from the list of "Wave Front Blocked" locations from the previous LOS pass. In this way we only integrate locations that are not visible from the goal.

We integrate this wave front out until it stops moving by hitting a wall or a sector border. At each grid location we compute the integrated cost by adding the cheapest cost field and integrated cost field's up, down, left, or right neighbors together. Then repeat this Eikonal equation process again and again, moving the wave front outward toward each location's un-integrated, non-walled neighbors.

During integration, look out for overlapping previously integrated results because of small cost differences. To fix this costly behavior, make sure your wave front stops when it hits

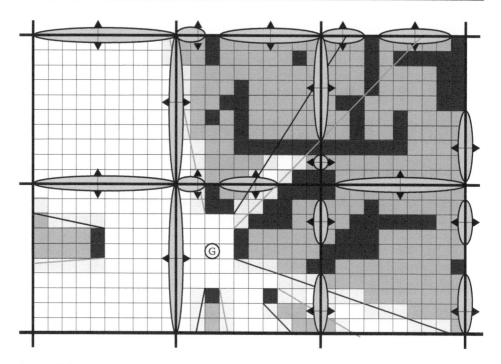

Figure 23.2

The results of an LOS pass.

previously integrated results, unless you really have a significant difference in integrated costs. If you don't do this, you risk having wave fronts bounce back and forth, eating up results when it's not necessary. In other words, if a different path is slightly cheaper to take, then don't bother backtracking across the field just to save that small pathfinding cost difference.

The following is an example of when it's appropriate to overlap previously integrated cost results. Imagine a single path that splits into two paths, where each split path leads to the same goal location. However, one split has a long and costly sand trap, while the other does not. The integration wave front will move away from the goal, split into two, and converge on each other at the beginning of the path. When they meet, the cheaper wave front will overlap the more expensive wave front's results and continue to integrate, backtracking down the expensive path until the cheaper integrated costs do not have a significant difference with the previously integrated costs. This backtracking behavior will have the effect of redirecting the flow field directions away from the sand trap and back toward the cheaper path. This is no different than backtracking in A*; it's just good to point this behavior out as it's more costly when integrating fields.

23.6.4 Integration Step 4: Flow Field Pass

We are now ready to build a flow field from our newly created integration field. This is done by iterating over each integrated cost location and either writing out the LOS flag or comparing all eight NW, N, NE, E, SE, S, SW, W neighbors to determine the "cheapest" direction we should take for that location.

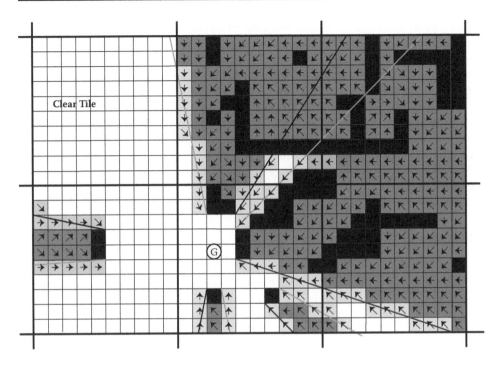

Figure 23.3

The final flow field directions.

Figure 23.3 shows what the final flow field directions look like. Notice that no work was done for locations that have goal LOS or locations within the clear tile. Once the flow field is built out we submit it to the *flow field cache*.

23.7 The Flow Field Cache

The flow field cache contains all of our built flow fields, each with their own unique ID based on the portal window they take you through. In this way, work can be shared across path requests despite having different goals.

If there is a two-way hallway in your map, the odds are pretty good that multiple paths will want the same hallway flow field results. A flow field can also be reference tracked so when there are no more references to it, it can be discarded or put on a timer to be discarded later. You can also prebuild all flow field permutations and store them on disk so that you only need to build the flow fields that have custom LOS goal information.

23.8 Supporting Dynamic Environments and Queries

The whole point of inventing this technique was to better handle the dynamic nature of our game environments in real-time. To that end, we built everything with dynamic change in mind.

We can easily support moving sources by running another "merging" A* across portal nodes if the agent's position moves outside the sectors in the planned path.

We support moving goals by rebuilding the goal's flow field. If the goal crossed a sector boundary, the path's portal nodes are rebuilt behind the scenes. Most of the flow fields requested by the new path will already have been built and will be in the cache, so very few flow fields need to be rebuilt. Once the new path is ready, the agent will seamlessly switch over to it from the old path.

We support changing walls and hills by marking the cost field of the sector that contains them and their associated portals as dirty. Then the portal graph is rebuilt for nodes that are on the borders of the dirty sectors as well as their neighbors. Finally, the paths that were affected by those changes are rebuilt.

All of this is done by marking things dirty and rebuilding them based on a priority queue, where each item in the queue is given a time slice of a fixed number of milliseconds. This allows us to control what, when, and how rebuilding happens over time.

23.9 Cost Stamp Support

Cost stamps represent a custom set of costs values you can "stamp" into the world. In *Supreme Commander 2*, we needed to place buildings down that had custom walls as well as custom pathable areas. The player can essentially paint whole new pathable landscapes by using varying sized structures, including 1×1 grid walls.

Cost stamps record the original cost field values before replacing them with a new set of costs. After placing a cost stamp down, the overlapping sectors would be flagged as dirty and the dynamic graph and path rebuilding process would take care of everything else.

23.10 Source Cost Data

The map editor would build the cost field data from looking at geometry, placing down walls and hills where appropriate. We would run a blur pass to add a cost gradient near walls to improve flow results when going down hallways and around jagged edges.

All cost data was also shown in the editor so that designers could manually add and remove path cost as they saw fit. This was a huge benefit to the design team as they could finally control where and how units moved in their maps.

23.11 Different Movement Types

Each agent in the *Supreme Commander 2* engine has its own movement type. Each movement type has its own cost field data and hence produces its own portal graph. In this way, a land-only tank would have a different path than a hovercraft that can travel over lakes and swamps.

The editor would build out the different cost data for each movement type. To support large units, a special wall cushioning process was run over the map that moved the walls outward. This had the effect of closing off skinny gaps that are too small for large units as well as pushing out wall and mountain sides so large units can't visually overlap them when near.

If the user selected units with different movement types, such as a squadron of jets, a few land-only tanks, some hovercraft, and a super large experimental robot, the game would use the "most restrictive movement type" path for all compatible units before building more paths for the incompatible units.

23.12 Steering with Flow Fields

When agents steer with flow fields, there are some if-else conditions to look out for. For starters, if the agent doesn't have a valid flow field, it should steer to the next portal position. Once the agent has a flow field, it should look for an LOS flag to steer to its goal; otherwise, it should use the specified flow field direction.

When an agent is receiving new flow field directions, we recommend storing off a path direction vector and blending in new flow directions as you cross grid squares. This has the effect of smoothing out the flow field directions as the agent traverses the field.

23.13 Walls and Physics

With flow fields, your pathfinding agents can move in any direction without the high expense of rebuilding their path. Once your agents move in any direction, they are bound to hit a wall or another agent. In the *Supreme Commander 2* engine, agents could push each other around as well as slide along walls using physics.

Having physics in our game allowed for new game play scenarios such as explosions that push back units or super large robots that could push back a hundred tanks. We had a structure that could arbitrarily push or pull units across the map, as well as a large unit that could suck units into a whirlwind, spinning them around and around until they smashed together. These new game play scenarios would not have been possible without the cheaper movement cost associated with using flow field tiles.

23.14 Island Fields

An optional *island field* type can be implemented containing island IDs, where each island ID represents a single pathable island. Imagine the different islands of Hawaii: if you are on one island, you can only drive to locations within the same island.

For each sector you store its island ID. If there is more than one island ID in the sector, then the sector has an island field breaking the IDs down to individual grid locations. With this information you can quickly determine if a path request is valid.

In the *Supreme Commander 2* engine, you can move your mouse over any location on the map and see the mouse icon change from an arrow to a stop sign, indicating that you cannot reach that location. This feature was implemented by retrieving Island IDs at the source and destination locations to see if they match.

23.15 Minimizing CPU Footprint

You can enforce low CPU usage by capping the number of tiles or grid squares you commit to per tick. You can also easily spread out integration work across threads because the Integration Field memory is separate from everything else.

23.16 Future Work

The following is a list of ideas to further improve this technique.

- Support 3D spaces by connecting portal graph nodes across overlapping sectors.
- Pre-process and compress *all* flow field permutations and stream them from disk.
- Add support for arbitrarily sized maps by using a hierarchy of sectors and N-way graphs.
- Build out the flow field using the GPU instead of the CPU [Ki Jeong 07].
- Support multiple goals. Multiple goal flow fields are perfect for zombies chasing heroes.

23.17 Conclusion

Our work on *Supreme Commander 2* shows that it's advantageous to move beyond single path-based solutions and start looking at field-based solutions to support dynamic crowd pathing and steering in RTS games with hundreds to thousands of agents. In this article, we demonstrated how to represent and analyze the pathable terrain to generate flow fields that can drive hundreds of units to a goal. Additionally, we showed that this method is computationally cheap, compared with individual unit pathfinding requests, even in the face of dynamic terrain and queries. Hopefully you can benefit from our experience with the *Supreme Commander 2* engine and continue to expand and refine field-based pathfinding in your next game.

References

[Ki Jeong 07] W. Ki Jeong and R. Whitaker. "A fast Eikonal equation solver for parallel systems." *SIAM Conference on Computational Science and Engineering*, 2007.

[Ki Jeong 08] W. Ki Jeong and R. Whitaker. "A fast iterative method for Eikonal equations." *SIAM Journal on Scientific Computing* 30(5), 2008.

24

Efficient Crowd Simulation for Mobile Games

Graham Pentheny

24.1 Introduction

Crowd simulation is a topic of ongoing exploration and experimentation in the game AI industry [Pelechano et al. 07, Sung et al. 04]. Modern games are filled with more and more AI-controlled agents. It is therefore imperative to create a movement system that is realistic, robust, and designer-friendly.

Traditional pathfinding approaches compute separate paths for individual agents, even though many paths may have similar sections. These redundant path calculations inhibit simulations of large numbers of units on mobile hardware.

The mobile tower defense game *Fieldrunners 2* used a combination of vector flow fields and steering behaviors to efficiently simulate thousands of agents, referred to as units. This article will describe the systems of flow-field generation, flow sampling, and unit movement employed by *Fieldrunners 2*. The process of constructing and balancing a dynamic crowd simulation system will be described in detail from the ground up.

24.2 Grid

The grid provides a discretization of the game world and defines the areas within which units may travel. For *Fieldrunners 2,* a grid cell was sized slightly wider than the widest unit, so that every computed path was traversable by every unit. Each grid cell can either be *open,* indicating that a unit may pass through it, or *blocked* indicating that the cell is impassible.

24.3 Flow Field

Units move through the grid following a static vector *flow field.* The flow field represents the optimal path direction at every cell in the grid, and is an approximation of a continuous *flow function.* Given a set of destination points, the flow function defines a vector field of normalized vectors, indicating the direction of the optimal path to the nearest destination. The flow function is similar to common methods for describing flows in fluid dynamics [Cabral and Leedom 93], with the difference that all flow vectors are normalized. Given this definition, we can define a flow field to be a discretization of a *flow function.*

Flow fields guide units to the nearest destination in the same manner as a standard pathfinding system; however, the units' pathing information is encoded in a flow field, removing the need for units to compute paths individually.

The vector flow field is specific to each set of potential destinations and thus can be used by all units sharing a set of destination points. Because the flow field expresses pathing information for the entire game world, it does not need to be updated unless the pathable areas of the grid or the set of destination points changes.

For example, if a bridge across a river is destroyed, the flow field only needs to be recomputed once to account for the change to pathable areas. Units following that flow field will implicitly change their respective paths in response to the change in the game world.

The flow field is comprised of a single normalized vector for each grid cell, as shown in Figure 24.1. A flow field and a unique set of destination points together are called a *path.* For example, a path corresponding to an m by n grid is a set of $m*n$ normalized vectors and a set of one or more destination points. Due to the number of vectors required to represent the flow function, this approach can potentially yield prohibitively high memory usage. Memory consumption is linearly dependent on the product of the number of grid cells and the number of independent paths. Maps in *Fieldrunners 2* were restricted to three unique paths at most, and map grid sizes were small enough that flow-field memory usage did not prove to be a significant issue.

The grid size, and thus the resolution of the flow field, does not need to be high to yield believable movement characteristics. Using bilinear interpolation, a continuous flow function can be approximated from the four closest vectors in the low-resolution flow field [Alexander 06]. As the grid resolution increases, the flow field computes a higher and higher sampling of the same flow function. Bilinear interpolation of vectors in a flow field improves the continuity and organicity of unit paths.

24.4 Generating the Flow Field

The flow field is generated via a modified traditional point-to-point pathfinding function. The algorithm used in *Fieldrunners 2* was based on Dijkstra's algorithm

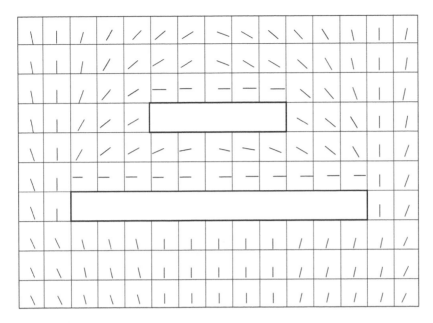

Figure 24.1

A flow field for a sample environment. The flow for a given cell is shown as a line starting at the center of the cell and pointing in the flow direction. Blocked cells are outlined with a thick black line. This particular flow field moves characters around the two rectangle obstacles and towards a destination along the bottom edge of the environment.

Dijkstra [59]; however, alternate pathfinding algorithms are aptly capable of generating a flow field.

The algorithm used in *Fieldrunners 2* begins by adding the grid cells for each of the paths' destinations to the open list. As the normal iterations of Dijkstra's algorithm progress, nodes are removed from the open list and linked to a nearby cell with the lowest computed path cost. As cells from the open list are expanded, the flow vector for the newly expanded cell is set to point in the direction of the cell it was linked to. Instead of terminating when a path is found, the algorithm expands all traversable cells added to the open list, assigning a flow vector to each, and terminating when the open list is empty. The demo code included with this article on the book's website (http://www.gameaipro.com) contains a full implementation of flow-field generation within the `GenerateFlowField()` function.

This preceding algorithm is used to generate a flow field for each path every time a change is made to either the path's destination set or the traversable area of the grid.

24.5 Units

Fieldrunners 2 required a crowd dynamics system capable of supporting dozens of different units, each with unique movement characteristics. Units in *Fieldrunners 2* are simple autonomous agents based on Craig Reynolds' *Boid* model [Reynolds 99]. Each unit has a set of both physical attributes and steering behaviors that together control its movement.

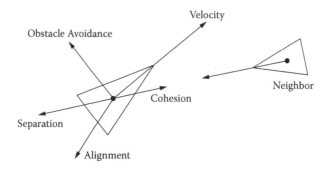

Figure 24.2

This figure shows all the steering forces acting on the left unit, with the exception of flow-field following.

The set of steering behaviors and their implementations are consistent across all unit types. A unit's physical attributes (e.g., total mass, size, agility) define its unique movement characteristics.

Units in *Fieldrunners 2* are represented as point-masses with respective velocities. A unit's steering behaviors control its point-mass by applying a set of forces to it. The prioritized combination of these steering forces imparts an acceleration on the unit, resulting in realistic, perceptively intelligent movement. Steering behaviors are widely used in games to control unit movement, and are described in numerous publications [Reynolds 99, Millington and Funge 09]. In *Fieldrunners 2*, specific modifications were made to the standard implementations of some steering behaviors to support more dynamic unit interactions.

Units in *Fieldrunners 2* use a limited, greedy, prioritized summation of five steering behaviors (four of which are shown in Figure 24.2). The five behaviors listed in descending order of priority include flow-field following, obstacle avoidance, separation, alignment, and cohesion. In each simulation step, a unit is only influenced by a specified total magnitude of steering forces. The forces resulting from steering behaviors are added to the running total in priority order until the maximum magnitude has been reached. Any steering forces that have not been added to the total are ignored.

The separation, alignment, and cohesion steering forces together describe flocking behavior [Reynolds 99]. In *Fieldrunners 2*, flocking is used to encourage units to move cohesively as a group when near other units.

Obstacle avoidance helps faster units maneuver intelligently around slower units. The implementations of the obstacle avoidance and separation behaviors differ slightly from Reynolds' original implementation [Reynolds 99]. The obstacle avoidance steering behavior generates a "side stepping" force perpendicular to the unit's velocity, and proportional to the position and relative velocity of the neighbor. The force generated by the separation steering behavior is scaled by the ratio of the kinetic energy of the neighbor to the kinetic energy of the unit the force is applied to. Units with smaller masses and velocities (presumably being more nimble) will more readily yield to larger, less maneuverable units.

Finally, flow-field following moves the unit in the direction specified by the flow field. The flow-field direction at the position of the unit is computed by linearly interpolating the four closest flow vectors.

The mass, maximum force, maximum velocity, and neighbor radius attributes describe a unit's unique behavior. The mass is used to calculate the unit's kinetic energy in addition to the accelerations resulting from steering behaviors. The maximum force value dictates the maximum combined magnitude of steering forces that can influence the unit in a single simulation step. A unit's agility value is defined as the ratio of a unit's maximum force to its mass—the unit's maximum acceleration. Finally, the maximum velocity attribute limits the magnitude of the unit's velocity, and the neighbor radius attribute restricts the set of neighbors used in calculating flocking forces to those within a certain radius.

24.6 Adjusting Unit Movement Values

It is necessary to find the correct set of attribute values for a unit to yield a desired behavior. In simulations based on steering behaviors, this is notoriously difficult and arduous. A systematic approach was developed and used by designers to balance unit attributes in *Fieldrunners 2*. For reasons of simplicity, all units used an identical set of weighted, prioritized steering behaviors, relying on their physical attributes for unique behavior.

First, the maximum velocity attribute is set to a reasonable value, and the remaining attributes are given an arbitrary base value. Because the maximum velocity of a unit is most easily visualized, it provides a good starting point. The remaining values will each be adjusted individually.

Next, the maximum force value is adjusted to yield believable movement characteristics for a single unit of that type. Because the maximum force affects the agility of the unit, it will alter visual aspects such as turning speed and braking.

Given a group of homogeneous units, the result of changes to the unit's neighbor radius attribute can easily be observed in isolation. Smaller neighbor radiuses will allow units to cluster more closely, while increasing the neighbor radius will spread units out.

Finally, all units' masses are adjusted relative to each other. When adjusting the mass of a unit, its agility must remain constant, or the previously adjusted movement characteristics of the unit will change.

24.7 Mobile Limitations and Performance Considerations

The largest runtime performance issue in this approach is the generation and processing of neighboring unit lists used in computing the flocking steering forces. In *Fieldrunners 2*, performance issues were mitigated through use of a *loose quad tree* [Ulrich 00] to reduce the neighboring unit search space. Units with large neighbor radiuses will yield a large set of neighbors to consider, decreasing performance. Combining the calculations of flocking forces can provide measurable performance improvements, as intermediary values can be reused in subsequent computations.

Floating-point operations on mobile processors can be slow, and minimizing the number of operations required in pathing and movement calculations can also yield improvements. Storing scalars that represent vector magnitudes as their respective squared values was a common optimization in *Fieldrunners 2*. This allowed vector length comparisons to use the squared vector magnitude, removing the need to compute many floating-point square root values.

Flow-field-based systems provide the greatest benefits when large numbers of units need to navigate to a set of common goals. A separate flow field is required for each unique set of goal positions among units. As the number of unique sets of goals increases, the calculations and memory required to maintain the necessary flow fields can become prohibitively complex and large. The memory required to represent a flow field grows linearly with the number of grid cells, while the pathfinding computational complexity is equivalent to the worst-case complexity of the pathfinding algorithm used. In the case of *Fieldrunners 2*, Dijkstra's algorithm was used, which yielded quasi-linear time complexity dependent on the number of grid cells. One approach to minimizing flow-field memory consumption is to save flow vectors as a specific rotation of the "north" vector (usually <0,1>). When accessing the flow direction for a given cell, the known basis vector is recreated and rotated the amount specific to that cell. Alternatively, if flow vectors are restricted to specific directions (e.g., cardinal directions), they can be stored as a one byte integer where its value corresponds to the specific potential direction.

As mobile hardware moves towards multicore processors, correct utilization of multithreaded algorithms becomes important. The problem of generating multiple flow fields can easily be modeled as a parallel process. The mutual independence of flow fields allows each to be computed in parallel with the rest, potentially in different threads or processes. The composition and independence of steering behaviors allows them to be computed in parallel as well, so long as they're accumulated and applied to the unit collectively. Together, the intrinsic parallelizability of flow-field generation and steering behavior computation make multithreading optimizations trivial.

24.8 Benefits

This approach to unit movement was chosen for *Fieldrunners 2* due to a specific set of unique benefits that it provided. Pathing information is precomputed and stored in the flow field; thus it is only ever calculated once for a given world configuration. This property of flow fields offered notable performance benefits in *Fieldrunners 2*, as the pathability of the world is modified infrequently.

Pathing information for all locations in the world is computed in a single pass, yielding a grid size-based complexity comparable to Dijkstra's algorithm. Compared to traditional pathfinding methods where the time complexity is linear with respect to the number of units, this approach is constant with respect to the number of units simulated. For *Fieldrunners 2*, this enabled complex scenarios with thousands of independent and diverse units to run on mobile devices at interactive frame rates.

Steering behavior-based approaches like this one provide great flexibility in defining unique unit behavior. Steering behaviors rely on composition to define complex behavior, making specializations and additions modular and encapsulated. The composition of a new steering behavior or the modification of an existing steering behavior can both easily be applied to a unit to define a unique movement style.

24.9 Conclusion and Future Work

The system used in *Fieldrunners 2* used static vector flow fields and steering behaviors to simulate thousands of units on mobile devices. Unlike traditional pathfinding techniques, the proposed navigation system minimizes redundant path calculations by encoding pathing information from all areas in a vector flow field.

Flow-field-based pathfinding techniques provide a unique way to reduce redundant pathfinding computations by computing the optimal path from every point. The flow-field generation technique used in *Fieldrunners 2* was based on Dijkstra's algorithm for simplicity and design reasons. More advanced pathfinding algorithms, such as Theta* [Nash et al. 07], can generate smoother, more organic flow fields. Flow fields can be extended to incorporate alternate motivations and concerns for units by blending static and dynamic flow fields [Alexander 06]. Despite this potential improvement, static flow fields and steering behaviors provided a robust, realistic crowd simulation for *Fieldrunners 2*.

References

[Alexander 06] B. Alexander. "Flow fields for movement and obstacle avoidance." In *AI Game Programming Wisdom 3*, edited by Steve Rabin, pp. 159–172. Boston, MA: Charles River Media, 2006.

[Cabral and Leedom 93] B. Cabral and L. Leedom. "Imaging vector fields using line integral convolution." *SIGGRAPH '93 Proceedings of the 20th Annual Conference on Computer Graphics and Interactive Techniques*, pp. 263–270, 1993. Available online (http://www.cg.inf.ethz.ch/teaching/scivis_common/Literature/CabralLeedom93.pdf).

[Dijkstra 59] E. Dijkstra. "A note on two problems in connexion with graphs." *Numerische Mathematik* 1, pp. 261–271, 1959. Available online (http://www-m3.ma.tum.de/foswiki/pub/MN0506/WebHome/dijkstra.pdf).

[Millington and Funge 09] I. Millington and J. Funge. *Artificial Intelligence for Games*, pp. 55–95. Burlington, MA: Morgan Kaufmann, 2009.

[Nash et al. 07] A. Nash, K. Daniel, S. Koenig, and A. Felner. "Theta*: Any-angle path planning on grids." *Proceedings of the AAAI Conference on Artificial Intelligence (2007)*, pp. 1177–1183, 2007. Available online (http://idm-lab.org/bib/abstracts/papers/aaai07a.pdf).

[Pelechano et al. 07] N. Pelechano, J. M. Allbeck, and N. I. Badler. "Controlling individual agents in high-density crowd simulation." *SCA '07 Proceedings of the 2007 ACM SIGGRAPH/Eurographics Symposium on Computer Animation*, pp. 99–108, 2007. Available online (http://www.computingscience.nl/docs/vakken/mpp/papers/12.pdf).

[Reynolds 99] C. W. Reynolds. "Steering behaviors for autonomous characters." *Proceedings of the Game Developers Conference (1999)*, pp. 763–782, 1999. Available online (http://www.red3d.com/cwr/papers/1999/gdc99steer.pdf).

[Sung et al. 04] M. Sung, M. Gleichar, and S. Chenney. "Scalable behaviors for crowd simulation." *Computer Graphics Forum*, Volume 23, Issue 3, pp. 519–528. September 2004. Available online (http://www.computingscience.nl/docs/vakken/mpp/papers/21.pdf).

[Ulrich 00] T. Ulrich. "Loose octrees." In *Game Programming Gems*, edited by Mark DeLoura, pp. 444–453. Hingham, MA: Charles River Media, 2000.

25

Animation-Driven Locomotion with Locomotion Planning

Jarosław Ciupiński

25.1 Introduction

In the race to increase immersion in video games, every aspect of a game has to be improved. Animation-driven locomotion is one way to increase the realism of character movement. This doesn't just mean having lots of animations, as playing them in a random order will look unrealistic. The solution to this problem is to plan actions so that every animation is perfectly coordinated with *future* movement. To sum it up in few words: in animation-driven locomotion, a character's movement comes directly from the animations.

However, due to the dynamic nature of games, just playing the animations is not enough. Some adjustments are required to move a character in the desired direction and to the desired spot. For that reason, the execution of a plan is important for making animation-driven locomotion work and using it to fulfill its aesthetic requirements.

This article approaches the task as follows: A high-level path is used to guide the incremental generation of an animation-driven path. An animation-driven path is comprised of *actions*, which are broken into three categories. *Transfer actions* are used to cover longer distances in roughly a straight line. *Pretransfer* and *posttransfer* actions are optionally used to move into and out of transfer actions. The entire system described here is a revised version of what shipped in the game *Bulletstorm*.

25.2 Animation and Movement Architectures

In many cases, locomotion does not exist as a separate subsystem. Responsibility for a character's movement is often divided between the AI, gameplay, physics, and animation systems. To have more control over "what is happening and why" in locomotion, it is better to move as many responsibilities related to movement (creation of the navigation path, taking care of actual movement, queuing, checking if the target is reached, etc.) together, providing a clean and easy-to-use interface. The best place to put locomotion code, if not in a separate layer between AI/gameplay/scripting and animation, is in an animation subsystem itself.

Animation-driven locomotion uses data from animation to move a character. What this means is that movement conforms to animation data and velocity data contained in the animations. Locomotion subsystems may make further changes to adjust velocities to fulfill movement requests. To make animations easier to work with, they should follow some basic rules. For example, the root bone (if root motion in your animation code translates directly to the character's velocity) should move as closely as possible to a straight line or curve.

While this is not a hard requirement and in some cases may not even be desired (e.g., for drunk characters), it will make locomotion planning more predictable (characters will be less likely to leave the planned path), and move execution will be easier.

If only simple looped animations are used, then there is no need for any planning and the locomotion can be fully reactive. This means that played animations are chosen to match movement which is already planned. The character's AI then selects its own velocity and animations to try and make everything look appropriate. Such approaches are simple to implement, but in many cases do not look natural, especially when movement is starting or stopping.

To make movement look more natural, transition animations are used. These are animations for starting, stopping, changing directions, and other nonlooped actions. Note that these animations take time and require space to be played properly. Therefore, a system that just responds to current requests will work, but only in some simple and straightforward situations. For example, such a system will have no problem with a character running forward 10 meters and starting to stop 2 meters before the destination point. But, if the path is more complicated, a character may easily miss the point where it was requested to stop. There are often several variants for stopping animations, but checking against all possibilities for every frame is too expensive. As the AI knows what path to take to get to its final destination, preplanning animations is the natural solution.

25.3 Preparation

When starting work on animation-driven locomotion, it is strongly advised that you talk to animators and AI programmers as much as possible to decide what you want to achieve. For example, animators may desire really long, nice-looking animations to cover various situations in order to achieve nice aesthetics. However, these may be problematic to handle, as long animations will result in a less responsive system and will require more physical space to perform. This may mean that the system will need to plan ahead more than just a few steps.

You should also decide the kinds of movement that you want to have. Running and walking, for example, might only be done in the forward direction, while other directions will be covered with short steps or in sequence (making turns and moving forward). Also, it is important to decide whether obstacles can be traversed before starting work on animations and the planning system. If so, consider what kind of obstacles there will be, how they should be approached by the character, how they should be stored in the navmesh, and how they are processed. Animators, AI programmers, and/or designers may want to have other features and rules present. An example might be a rule to have specific animations for shooting when taking steps in any direction, instead of allowing shooting to be overlaid onto walking or running animations.

25.4 Locomotion Planning

It is best to divide planning for locomotion into separate modules, each having a distinct and clearly defined purpose:

1. A navigation path-processor
2. A planner that creates an action-stack
3. An animation system that executes the action-stack

It is strongly advised to add an additional module that works as an interface to other game subsystems. This module would accept new requests, prepare orders for animation modules (what they should do now), and work as a central hub for exchanging data. Such a module really helps with finding problems with locomotion; it makes it easier to find invalid requests and decide whether it was the animation/locomotion subsystem problem or another module that failed.

25.4.1 Navigation Path-Processor

The handling of movement requests starts with the creation of a navigation path. It is worthwhile to store the navigation path as both polygons and points. Due to unexpected events that may take place during movement (e.g., other objects moving in the way), the navigation path might require adjustment or complete recreation of the whole path. Storing polygon data will reduce the need to access the navmesh. It also gives more freedom when adjusting point-based paths, which are the base representation of the planner (Figure 25.1).

The creation of point-based paths should start with a simple approach such as string-pulling or the funnel algorithm that will give the shortest path connecting the start and end points. Please refer to the following resources for more information on pathfinding, string-pulling, and the funnel algorithm [Demyen et al. 06, Cui et al. 11].

The first job for the path processor is to take care of points that are close to each other, as they don't provide any extra information and may just complicate the subsequent steps in locomotion planning. It is easier to assume that every segment of the path is of minimum length, chosen arbitrarily, or based on the shortest stopping animation. This means that the three subsequent segments (starting at the current location of the character) will cover, for example, at least 2 or 3 meters.

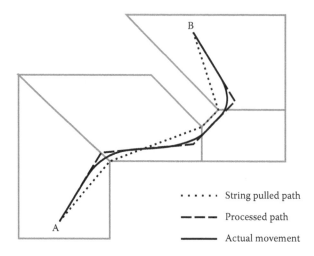

······ String pulled path

— — — Processed path

———— Actual movement

Figure 25.1

A path from point A to point B is provided to the locomotion system as polygons and is further processed. Actual movement doesn't exactly correlate to the processed path, as for locomotion planning it is more important where the animation should start and where it will end.

In some cases, when dealing with longer movement animations (that require more space), it is better to do further adjustments to the location of points. For example, after string-pulling a path, there might be two subsequent points that change the direction of movement by 90° in opposite directions and are very close to each other. If they are too close, it will be impossible to play two "sharp-turn-while-running animations" one after another and to (roughly) stay on path. If there is enough space around these points, they might be moved further away from each other to give enough space to play both animations. If it isn't possible to move the points further away, there should still be a fail-safe solution provided: stopping at the first turn point, taking a step towards the next point, and starting to run from there. In order to avoid affecting the fluidity of movement, such fail-safe solutions should be used rarely.

In some cases it might be useful to add extra points along the path that would make approaching some locations easier. For example, instead of running to an obstacle that should be jumped over, stopping next to it, and then jumping, an extra point could be used to run at the obstacle from a better angle. Due to memory limitations, there might be just two animations for "jumping from standing" and for "jumping while running straightforward" and both might look terrible when running toward an obstacle from a wide angle; therefore, approaching from a better angle is critical to making it look good.

25.4.2 Action-Stack

The *action-stack* is a list of actions required to follow the current segment of the path. It is more feasible to choose actions starting from the end (from the desired goal state). This means that the first actions to be chosen are last to be executed (Figure 25.2).

When the path has been processed, it should be in the form of points with some extra data describing how to behave at each given time (crouch, do not run, jump over). Only

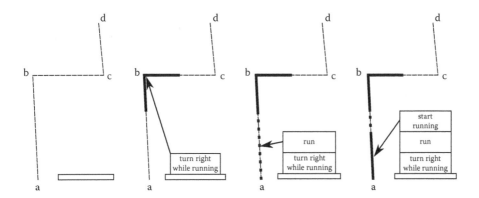

Figure 25.2

In this example we are creating an action-stack for segment "ab" of the path, starting at point "a". It is essential to know how much space animations need (for animation-based actions this is marked as a thick line) so only animations that can fit in given segment are chosen. The space required to execute an animation-based action is also used to determine when to first trigger the action (a dotted line represents a "run" action that at some point should be interrupted with the "turn right while running" action).

two or three segments of the path should be considered when creating an action-stack for the following reasons:

1. The creation of the action-stack is computationally intensive, and if done for whole path, would result in significant performance spikes.
2. We have no idea what will happen in the future, so there really is no need to plan everything ahead. A character may run into another character or may be ordered to do something else.

Ideally, just one segment of the path needs to be covered by the action-stack. When all actions from the stack are performed, the character should be at the best point to go on to the next segment, and a new action-stack can be created at that time. However, the two or three subsequent segments should still be considered when creating the first action-stack, in order to best enter subsequent segments. There is also another reason for considering subsequent segments: In some of the cases it might be possible to use one animation to cover several segments. One example might be entering cover behind a corner.

Even if planning actions are only performed for one segment, knowledge of what the character will be doing afterwards is valuable. Will the character run or slide? Does it need to stop there or should it proceed at full speed? This tells it what state (location, direction, gait, or pose) the character should be in at the end of the current segment. There is also, of course, the current state of the character. Other information might describe the current segment, such as distance, and what animations are allowed or disallowed (e.g., character can't run here). Given this data we have two options to cover the segment:

1. Do one action that will directly transition the character from current state straight to the desired state.

2. Do several actions:

A pretransfer action that will ready the character for a transfer action (e.g., start running in specific direction).

A transfer action that will move the character over longer distances (e.g., walk, run).

A posttransfer action that will bring the character into the desired state (e.g., stop at a point, perform sharp-turn while running).

25.4.2.1 Direct Transition

A direct transition gives the best-looking results but requires lots of animations that cover many possibilities. In an actual game these should only be used to cover special cases. For example, walking extremely short distances can be accomplished by an animation taking a single step or two steps. For such short distances there is no need, and it might look strange to start running and then immediately stop.

25.4.2.2 Transfer Action

Using a transfer action is more feasible for longer distances. It requires animations to be divided into three basic groups (as described previously: pretransfer, transfer, and posttransfer), which can be heavily reused in different combinations resulting in smooth character animation.

Each action (pretransfer, transfer, and posttransfer) is optional. Since a character may already be in a "transfer" state, there may be no need to do anything at the end of the segment. Additionally, the transfer itself may be omitted as in some cases it might be practical to just play pretransfer and posttransfer animations back-to-back.

In games, it is not possible to have pretransfer or posttransfer animations for all possible situations. This may happen because of memory limitations, budget limitations, or development time limitations. Therefore, we might remove or not create animations for rare situations. When dealing with cases for which there is no appropriate animation, the planner will have to solve the problem in a different way.

An example of such a case is starting to run when the character is crouching. Let's assume that there is no animation for this case and follow what the planner does. The planner first tries to find one animation that will take the character from a crouched stance (current state) to running 20 meters away (desired state). There, of course, is no such animation. The planner then tries to find posttransfer, transfer, and pretransfer actions, but it can't find an action to take the character from crouching to running. Suppose there are just animations for "character starting to run from standing" in eight directions, and there are animations that bring a character from a crouch to a standing stance. The planner should then try to use the crouch to standing animation, execute one action-stack, and try to approach the problem again. After playing the animation of the character crouching to standing, it is possible to use one of eight "stand to run" animations.

In some cases it might be possible to use actions or animations that take a character from the current state to the desired state, but only with an extra action. For example, there could be an animation that is walking to the right while shooting, but in the beginning the character faces away from the target, so before the walking-shooting animation plays, the character should turn toward the enemy.

Similar extra actions may be required when a transfer action brings a character to a desired location, but it is not yet in the desired state (e.g., the character isn't turned in the right direction or is not in the desired stance).

Part III. Movement and Pathfinding

25.4.2.3 *Implementation Suggestions*

For implementation, we strongly suggest dividing data into three groups:

1. Transfer information (walk, run, walk crouched, jump over, slide under) that has:

A list of transfer animations.

A list of posttransfer animations with info about the final character state (e.g., rotation, stance, how much space does it take, or any other information needed). Note that some of the posttransfer animation entries may store that this is not the final animation to reach a desired state and the planner needs to do something more.

2. Stance information (standing, crouching, stealthy) that has

A list of stance idle animations.

A list of pretransfer animations with information about the state they take a character into (transfer state, in which direction the character will move, how much space is required, etc.).

A list of animations that change directly from one stance to another.

3. Direct transitions:

A list of animations that take a character from any state to any other state, although in most of the cases it might be enough to have such a list just for stances.

Pretransfer, posttransfer, and direct transition animations may also be described in a separate place with details irrelevant to the decision taken by the planner, but having general information about the transfer which is useful during execution.

Some of this information can be collected algorithmically. For example, how does every animation connect to the transfer animation (to start a transfer animation, to match a pose, or to adjust movement in such a manner that the posttransfer animation will be triggered at the right moment).

Other information (mostly those required by the planner) may be collected automatically, although it is often useful to enter the data or at least tweak it by hand. An example is the space required for an animation. Some "starting to run" animations may need 2 meters of space. Some animations that are taking characters from one spot to another may only cover from 1 to 3 meters. While this can be computed automatically, entering data by hand gives much more cohesion and control over what each system will do in a given situation.

Note that it is important to have fail-safe solutions that would prevent the character from being stuck in one pose, even if it means turning towards the final destination and walking there step-by-step.

25.4.3 Executing Actions

During planning, actions are divided into a few different types, including pretransfer, transfer, posttransfer, whole segment animations, and extra actions. Conversely, *execution* of actions can be divided into only two groups: transfer and nontransfer actions. The following sections describe the execution of each group.

25.4.3.1 *Nontransfer Actions*

Nontransfer actions just play an assigned animation with small adjustments to velocity and rotation, if required.

When changing stance (standing up or crouching), it is enough to play an animation without any adjustments. For pretransfer actions, a directional adjustment is required in order to get the character moving in the correct direction when the pretransfer animation reaches its end. Most of the posttransfer actions require characters to be at a precise spot facing the right direction, so there is a requirement to adjust these as well. Adjustments to both location and direction are needed for actions that take a character from one place to another.

Parameter adjustments should be determined by the planner, meaning that the execution of all such actions does not differ.

25.4.3.2 Transfer Actions

Transfer actions are looped animations (although there can be random or in-order animations following one another) that take a character from one point in space to another. Besides matching the correct direction and ending at the required location, a character might be required to end in a specific pose in order to make a seamless blend to a posttransfer action. For example, a stopping animation that starts with a character on the right foot requires a character to be on that same foot when the stopping animation begins.

This may require altering character velocity, such as slightly speeding up or slowing down movement. This works nicely for longer distances, but adjusting a pose over short distances can result in a velocity adjustment that is too big or results in the character switching to a posttransfer animation too far away from the target location. In such cases the pose either has to be ignored, or there should be posttransfer animations that differ in the starting pose (on the left foot or right foot). Although variants can be decided during planning, they can also be picked up during execution. This may come in handy if a character had to adjust its path slightly for other reasons.

An alternative to speeding up or slowing down the character's velocity is modifying the playback rate of the animation. It is important to remember to maintain the playback rate when switching animations and to adjust the playback rate gradually. If the playback rate is not kept, animations may seem to speed up and slow down immediately, resulting in strange-looking character behavior.

Code for handling transfer actions should try to deal with any obstacles, keep characters in formation, or perform any required path adjustments. With navigation corridors and information about the end-point of transfer actions, it is possible to do some adjustments to the movement of a character and still end at the point requested by subsequent actions. For example, if a character runs and notices a new obstacle in front of it, it may alter the direction of movement early enough to avoid hitting the obstacle, without risking that the character won't be able to end at a point where the next action should start.

There are also situations in which a character will end up outside of a known navigation corridor or at some point of execution it might become obvious that it will miss the next action's starting point or won't get there at all. In such cases, either the action-stack should be rebuilt or the whole navigation path should be reconsidered.

Hitting an obstacle should be handled in a similar way. It may be impossible to avoid hitting an obstacle or it may be decided that a character may not even try to avoid running into one. The latter solution works well enough in practice. When a character hits an obstacle, it can play an evasive animation and, after it is finished, request a new navigation path (although in some cases rebuilding of action-stack may be enough).

25.4.4 Inverse Kinematic (IK) Controllers

As the system makes lots of adjustments to movement, IK controllers for feet should be used to cover corrections by removing, hiding, or at least reducing the foot-sliding effect. A simple two-bone IK solver is enough for human limbs [Juckett 08]. A proper animation will have no foot-slide, which means that when a foot is put down on the ground, it doesn't move until it is picked up.

During execution of the action-stack, the velocity of a movement animation is increased or decreased without speeding up or slowing down the animation playback rate (as the reason to speed up or slow down is to match a pose at a given point), which unfortunately results in foot sliding. For example, if the velocity is increased, the foot will slide forward; if there are additional rotations or other adjustments, the foot may also slide sideways. In these cases, an IK controller tries to keep the foot where it was originally placed.

Other IK controllers may be used to adjust the torso location in reference to the feet to help with situations in which the feet are kept behind or in front of the character. This may happen if the character stopped and antisliding controllers kept the feet in places other than originally expected.

25.5 Other Information about Locomotion Planning

The following is additional information about locomotion planning.

25.5.1 Performance

Locomotion does not require significant CPU resources during the execution stage. Everything is already planned, and it is just about keeping the character's movement faithful to the plan. In contrast, reactive locomotion requires checking and possibly updating all possible actions during every frame.

However, while the execution stage causes no problems with performance, it is important to note that locomotion planning may cause significant CPU spikes. If there is a need, most of the spikes can be neutralized by delaying any of the following processes, trying to delay actions with lowest priority first:

1. Lowest priority: handling a new navigation path
2. Middle priority: action-stack creation for standing characters
3. Highest priority: action-stack creation for moving characters

In the worst-case scenario, some characters might get stopped. Please keep in mind that when a character is stopped (playing a stopping animation), the CPU situation may get much better. In-game, the resulting behavior may look like a bug, as the character has stopped and started running again, but remember that there is always the potential to play a new animation. In particular, an animation for looking around, scratching your head, or stumbling will all offset the user perception of poor AI behavior.

25.5.2 AI Requests for Movement

An AI that relies on animation-driven locomotion should be patient; that is, it should not send too many requests in too short of a time period. If the AI changes its mind too often, a character may get stuck in repeating "start" and "stop" animations over and over. This can be partially prevented through locomotion systems that provide extensive feedback, so the AI does not have to "worry" that a character is not moving yet or is doing something else. Not every AI request can be handled immediately, as pre- and posttransfer actions are usually not interruptible and should be left until they're finished.

The locomotion system should be careful not to treat every AI request as something completely new and unconnected, as this results in creating completely new paths. New paths often mean that the character will stop and start to move again in the same direction. In many situations, the AI just needs to change the very end of a requested path, so the currently executed action-stack (with part of the navigation path already processed) is still sufficient for local movement.

25.6 Commercial Implementation

Planning, as described in this article, is a revised version of the planning implemented for *Bulletstorm* (developed by People Can Fly, part of Epic, published by Electronic Arts in 2011). The actual implementation relied on finite-state machines—generalized versions of transfer and stance descriptions mentioned in previous sections. This means that the whole system was data driven, although some cases required a separate approach, which was handled by special code. Mantling over and sliding under objects, for example, were added late in production.

The code for this implementation was part of the animation tree (distributed over a few animation nodes) with a separate structure (called AnimationProxy) used for communication with other game systems. Source code is available for UE3 licensees.

25.7 Conclusion

Animation-driven locomotion with planning brings a believable look and feel to a game. Characters move in a more natural and fluid manner. The basic implementation of planning is quite easy and, as it is data driven, adding more animations is simple. The same code can be used for characters that have different behaviors, although the fine-tuning of the system may require experience and time.

References

[Cui et al. 11] X. Cui and H. Shi. "Direction oriented pathfinding in video games." *International Journal of Artificial Intelligence & Applications (IJAIA)*, Vol. 2, No. 4, October 2011. Available online (http://airccse.org/journal/ijaia/papers/1011ijaia01.pdf).

[Demyen et al. 06] D. Demyen and M. Buro. "Efficient Triangulation-Based Pathfinding." Department of Computing Science, University of Alberta Edmonton, 2006. Available online (http://www.aaai.org/Papers/AAAI/2006/AAAI06-148.pdf).

[Juckett 08] R. Juckett. "Analytic Two-Bone IK in 2D." http://www.ryanjuckett.com/programming/animation/16-analytic-two-bone-ik-in-2d, 2008.

PART IV
Strategy and Tactics

26

Tactical Position Selection
An Architecture and Query Language

Matthew Jack

26.1 Introduction

Agent movement is arguably the most visible aspect of AI in any game, and this is particularly true of shooters. Choosing between positions—and generating those positions to consider in the first place—is critical to the success of these games. Not only is it key to an agent's effectiveness in combat, but it also visibly communicates his role and status in that combat. More generally in games, an agent's movement helps define his personality and often much of the core gameplay.

In this article, we describe a complete architecture for choosing movement positions as part of sophisticated AI behavior. We outline a query language for specifying those positions, consider how position selection integrates with our behaviors, and give some specific building blocks and best practices that will allow us to develop queries quickly and to the best effect. Performance is given special attention, both to ensure our results reach the final game and to allow us to employ more powerful query criteria. We also discuss techniques for handling group movement behavior and the tools required for effective development.

Techniques developed for the Tactical Position Selection (TPS) system, a CryEngine component used in *Crysis 2* and other upcoming titles, provide the core of this chapter [Crytek 11]. We supplement this with a number of approaches seen in other games, as well as promising directions for future work.

26.2 Motivation

Any system used for choosing movement locations faces design pressures from many directions. It must be flexible and expressive, as it will define the movement possible for our agents. It must be capable of rapid, iterative development, and it must include powerful tools, as these will limit the quality of our final behaviors. Finally, since it is used frequently and in reaction to the player, it must be a fast and efficient workhorse, delivering results within a few frames while always remaining within CPU budgets.

The core problem of tactical position selection comes down to the question that designers will ask you when they are working with your behaviors: "Why did he move here, when it's just common sense that he should move there instead?" It's a question you should be asking yourself as you test your AI, because it's the question that players will ask themselves too.

Modeling that "common sense" is what makes this such a tough problem. Indeed, many shooters decide to use triggers and scripting to orchestrate the movements of their AI, leaving it to designers to provide that human judgment in each and every case—and this can be highly effective. However, this is a time-consuming process not suited to all development cycles, inherently limited to linear gameplay, and unsuitable for open sandbox games.

With the right abstractions and efficient processing, we can describe that human intuition for the range of contexts that our agent will encounter, and strike a powerful balance between specification and improvisation. In the process, we greatly speed up our behavior prototyping and development and gain a versatile tool for a wide range of gameplay applications.

26.3 Fundamentals

At their core, systems of this kind typically take a utility-based approach [Mark 09, Graham 13], evaluating the fitness of a set of points with respect to the requirements of a particular agent in order to identify the best candidate. Sources for these points are discussed in the Generation section, but they may be placed by designers, generated automatically, or some combination of the two. Usually we will collect or generate points within a specified radius of our agent's current position before beginning evaluation.

Evaluation will first filter out unsuitable points based on criteria such as the minimum distance from a threat and the direction(s) from which they provide cover. It will then score the remaining points based on desirability criteria such as how close they are to a goal point or how exposed they are to a number of threats.

We then choose the highest-scoring valid point as the result and use this as a movement target for our agent. By combining various criteria in different ways and weighting their effect on the score, we can produce effective queries for different agent types, environments, and behaviors. We can also use the same system for other applications, such as targets to shoot at or spawn locations. Good examples of tactical position selection have been given in previous work [Sterren 01, Straatman et al. 06] and in this book [Zielinski 13].

26.4 Architecture

Our tactical position selection system comprises a number of subsystems, and it must also integrate with the rest of the AI framework. Figure 26.1 shows the overall structure of the architecture.

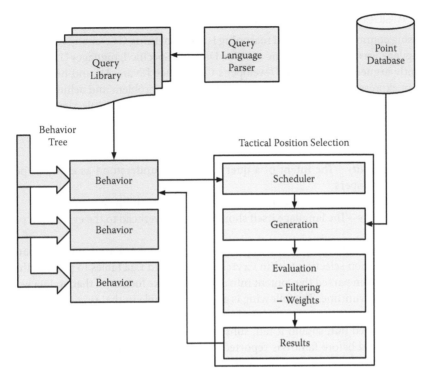

Figure 26.1

An architecture for tactical position selection.

The specification of individual queries can be thought of as the first step in the process of position selection, and a powerful *specification language* forms the first component in our architecture. We use this to build a *library* of context-specific queries to express each of our agent's behaviors in each of the environments it will encounter.

We employ a high-level AI framework, such as a behavior tree or finite-state machine, to provide the current *context*, which is the combination of the agent's current behavior and its current environment. We then use the context to select the appropriate query from the library. Should a query fail to find a valid location, this can serve as an input to the high-level framework, allowing it to respond should circumstances change.

We use a *database* of points, which may be manually placed or procedurally generated, to form the main input data for the evaluation process. A *scheduler* will often be required to help manage asynchronous queries and to amortize their cost.

Evaluation itself begins with *generation*, where points are collected from the database or generated on the fly, as required by the query specification, to form the set of candidate points for each query. We then *filter* those candidates with conditions, and apply *weights* to those that remain, as described above. In practice these two tasks may be interleaved for more efficient evaluation and spread over multiple frames by the scheduler. Finally, the full *results* of that evaluation may be displayed in the world graphically and summarized in the log for debugging before being reduced to the one or more points required by the query. In addition, each of these stages may be monitored by profiling systems.

26.4.1 A Query Specification Language

Expressing common-sense spatial reasoning is not something C++ or any common scripting language was designed for. The case for Domain-Specific Languages (DSLs) has been eloquently argued at the Game Developer's Conference [Evans 11] and here a powerful means of expression allows us to focus on the intrinsic problem and achieve rapid iteration. The key attributes of a successful query language for position selection are:

- *Abstraction*—We gain a lot of power if we can reapply existing criteria (keywords) in new ways.
- *Readability*—The intent of a query should be understood as easily as possible by developers.
- *Extensibility*—It should be easy to add new criteria to the language.
- *Efficiency*—The language itself should not add overhead to the evaluation process.

Many DSLs are built on top of existing languages. When developing the query language for tactical position selection within Crytek, we exploited Lua tables to provide the basic structure, but then parsed the content into a bytecode-like format so that no Lua was used by the system at runtime. The following is a simple example in that syntax.

Listing 26.1 shows a query that is made up of two subqueries, called "options." The first option is preferred but, should it fail, subsequent options will be tried in the order that they are specified before failure is reported. In this example, the first option will collect hidespots effective against the current attack target within a radius of 15 m around the agent, discarding any that are less than 5 m from the agent and discard any point closer to the attack target than the agent himself. Of the points that remain, it will prefer any hard cover that is available to any soft cover and prefer the closest point. The second option

Listing 26.1. A simple example in the Crytek query language syntax.

```
Query_CoverCompromised_FindNearby =
{-- Chiefly for use when our current spot has been compromised
    {    -- Option 1
         -- Find hidespot from our target a short distance from us
         Generation = {hidespots_from_target_around_puppet = 15},
         Conditions = {min_distance_from_puppet = 5,
                         canReachBefore_the_target = true},
         Weights = {softCover = -10, distance_from_puppet = -1.0},
    },
    {    -- Option 2 (fallback)
         -- Move away from target, taking a position in the open
         -- but preferring any that blocks line-of-sight
         Generation = {grid_around_puppet = 10},
         Conditions = {min_distance_from_puppet = 5,
                         max_directness_from_target = 0.1},
         Weights =   {visible_from_target = -10,
                     distance_from_puppet = -1.0}
    }
}
```

(the fallback) generates a grid of points to move sideways or away from the target and prefers to block Line-of-Sight (LOS). Both options share the goal of moving to a new, safe location at least 5 m away. Thus, this query might be used in reaction to a grenade landing at the agent's feet.

The Generation section of each option specifies the source of our candidate points. The Conditions section contains the filters that should be applied during evaluation, which must all pass if a point is to be valid. The Weights section tells the AI how to score the fitness of those valid points.

Each line in those sections is a Lua table entry comprising a string and a value. The string, in the syntax of our DSL, is formed from a sequence of keywords joined by underscores, which is trivially parsed back into the keywords themselves. Usually the most important keyword comes first—for example, `hidespots` or `distance`—and specifies the evaluation or generation method that we are going to apply. This can be referred to as the *criterion*.

Criteria often take an object, which allows the same method to be applied in different ways. For example, rather than having a `distanceFromTarget` keyword, we allow the same keyword to be used with many different objects, such as `puppet` (the requesting agent), `referencePoint` (general-purpose position), `player` (in single-player contexts), `leader` etc., and in particular `target` (the agent we are attacking if any). Objects are key to turning a set of parameters into a versatile query language. Some criteria do not take any objects—e.g., `softCover`, which is simply a property of the point.

The `min` and `max` keywords may prefix a criterion string, such as `distance`, that represents a float value. This changes the way the criterion is applied and also where it is used. Without the `min` or `max` keyword, it would simply be applied as a weight, but with these keywords we instead produce a Boolean result, depending on whether the actual value is above or below the specified limit. This allows us to use the same criteria in either the Weights or the Conditions section, as needed. In the example above, for instance, `min_distance_from_puppet = 5` is used to specify that points must be at least 5 m from the requesting agent.

There is also a set of "glue" keywords such as `from`, `to`, `at`, and `the`, which must be put between the criterion and its object, serving only to produce a more human-readable sentence—such as `distance_from_puppet`. The user is free to pick the word that forms the most natural expression in each case; the glue word is simply discarded during parsing.

Each keyword is registered with type markers as to where it can be employed. This allows us to detect and reject invalid queries during the parsing process, and to provide useful debug output.

While Lua was the most natural choice in the Crytek codebase, JSON, XML, or a simple custom format would also be reasonable vehicles for this kind of language. Queries can, of course, be changed while the game is running, in this case by editing and reloading the appropriate script files. A similar language has been implemented with a Kismet-style graphical interface under *Unreal 3* [Zielinski 13].

Documentation of the Crytek TPS system can be found online [Crytek 11] and it is available for use in the *CryEngine Free SDK* [Crytek 12]. Should you try any queries from the article, note that the common keyword `target` is shortened here; the correct keyword is `attentionTarget`.

26.4.2 Contexts and Query Library

As we discussed in the Motivation section, our agents face a complex and dynamic world, and players expect the agents to consistently make judgments similar to the ones that they themselves would make. One approach to achieving believable, reactive movement behavior across the range of environments in our game is to build a very complex "über-query." However, the problem becomes much more tractable if we break it down into bite-size chunks, each consisting of a specific behavior (such as flanking, retreating, or providing covering fire) that we wish to perform in a specific environment (such as a dense forest or a postapocalyptic New York street). We refer to each combination of behavior and environment as a context, and we can form a library of such queries.

It is much easier to describe exactly where to move if we make assumptions about our environment. For example, while we might be able to tweak a query until it allows us to advance effectively both between trees in a dense forest and from car to car in a city street, if we consider them separately, then our separate queries become much simpler. In fact, with the right criteria available, query construction becomes very predictable to the developer, and with some thought good results can be achieved without spending a lot of time tuning the queries. We discuss this further in the Best Practices and Specific Criteria section.

26.4.3 Integrating with Behavior Selection

To make use of a library of queries specific to context—the combination of behavior and environment—we must be able to choose the appropriate context at any given time. This can be achieved by viewing each behavior as having a core movement query and incorporating the current environment type as part of our behavior selection framework. This maps well onto a "first-generation" behavior tree, such as that used at Crytek [Martins 11], consisting essentially of a decision tree with behaviors as the leaves; different environments can form branches of the tree. Alternatively, the same behavior might use different queries in different environments; which is best will depend how much behavior is shared between environments. In *Bulletstorm*, a FPS game from People Can Fly, a similar system was used with a more sophisticated behavior tree [Zielinksi 13], and it could also be done with other architectures.

Basic knowledge of our current environment can be based on simple high-level cues, such as a per-level setting, or designer volumes or triggers. However, the behavior selection framework can also receive feedback from the queries we run and use this both to guide the selection of behavior and to inform us reactively about our environment. This feedback takes the form of failed queries—queries that return no valid results—which can occur for a couple of different reasons.

One way failure could occur is that we have designed our query for a common case, and this is an unusual example. For instance, our behavior and thus our queries might be designed for a dense forest, but obstacles or a path could mean there are very few trees in the local area. This might be a level design problem, but we may choose to provide a fallback for such cases—a second "option" in the query.

The fallback might often relax the filters and/or extend the query radius, especially if we used that smaller radius simply for performance reasons. It might also use different generation criteria: perhaps generating some points without cover around us and looking for one that at least has blocked line-of-sight to our target. The fallback essentially hides the failure from behavior selection and lowers our quality bar on this occasion, to get us smoothly past this tricky spot.

However, there is a more informative case: our context isn't as we thought, and what we are trying to do is wrong for this situation. If we have designed our query correctly, it has not simply ranked all the points in order of preference, but also eliminated all the points that were not appropriate. If, for example, we are flanking left around a target in a forest, failure indicates that there is no suitable location to our left—we have run out of cover or our way is blocked. We can acknowledge this—for instance, by flagging this state in our blackboard—in order to choose a different behavior or indeed, in a squad context, to inform allies that a group action may have to be aborted. In the Crytek system, a query specification can include a specific signal to send or blackboard state to set in the event of failure.

26.4.4 Forming a Database of Input Points

Most games will form a static database of hidespots for consideration, and these form a mainstay of the candidate points for evaluation. These may have been placed by designers—for instance, the oriented "hide anchors" of *Far Cry* and *Crysis*, which indicated a position for the point as well as having a directional cone from which cover was provided. They may be automatically embedded in certain objects, such as trees; manually embedded in static or dynamic objects, such as vehicles; or generated automatically around complex objects. All of these have been combined in Crytek titles—with *Crysis 2* introducing automatic generation based on designer hints [Martins 11]. Notably, *Killzone 3* pregenerated its hidespots with an automatic process [Mononen 11], while *Brink* had no such static database and relied entirely on dynamically generated points [Nelson 11].

In general, such a database allows more time to be put into offline processing or designer work and provides a cheap resource of reliable points as input to a TPS system. Of course, the database can contain other types of positions in addition to (or instead of) hiding locations. Locations representing choke points, doorways, sniper spots, vantage points, respawn points, etc. may also be used as candidates, using specific criteria to generate a particular type or to distinguish between them. This represents a rich source of designer hints about the environment.

26.4.5 Collection and Generation

The first part of evaluating any query is to form a set of candidate points, whether by collecting them from a database or generating them at runtime. Typically, our primary source is to collect them from the static database described above, using a criterion such as that in our example:

```
Generation = {hidespots_from_target_around_puppet = 15}
```

This finds hidespots from a target and illustrates three parameters that are key to this phase: the center of the query—here, the `puppet` object, the agent itself; a radius for collection/generation—15 m; and an object, which for this criterion represents the primary target from which we wish to hide—in this case, the `target` object.

The best basis for an efficient query is to generate points in the specific location or locations we're actually interested in and within as small a distance as possible; the choice of center and radius should be made with this in mind. Centering on the requesting agent is not always the best choice: for instance, when entering close combat we might center it on our target or the center of our squad (as we will discuss in the Group Techniques section). A common technique for designer control is to restrict agent movement to an area—for example, to defend, patrol, or advance upon. We can provide generation criteria for this based on an associated point or polygon, rather than relying upon conditions.

If we provide a primary hide-target (in this case `target`, the current attack target), this enables a range of powerful and efficient generation criteria. In *Far Cry* and *Crysis*, hide-spots around trees were neatly handled by generating a hidespot on the opposite side from the hide-target. These omnidirectional hidespots are also useful in that they were refreshed on each hide request, moving an agent around the obstacles as its hide-target moved. The hide-target also allows us to use directional hidespots effectively—immediately rejecting cover points that are not correctly oriented for this hide-target using a dot-product test.

As well as collecting from our database, we may generate points on demand—for example, as we do in our fallback option in the query above:

```
Generation = {grid_around_puppet = 10}
```

In this case, we generate the candidate positions in a 10 m square grid around the agent. These arbitrary points can then be analyzed for their potential as cover or other properties. For example, if there is no explicit cover nearby, we may still try to block line-of-sight to our target; we may simply want to escape an overriding threat, such as a grenade, or specifically to move out into the open.

Brink generated points in concentric rings to find all of its cover dynamically [Nelson 11]. We could simulate something similar with a query such as the following (which would find the nearest point to the agent which blocks LOS to the target):

```
Generation = {circles_around_puppet = 10},
Conditions = {visible_from_target = false},
Weights =   {distance_from_puppet = -1.0},
```

Cover rails, as used in *Crysis 2*, are a relatively recent development that avoids representing cover as discrete points and instead stores a path, anywhere along which an agent may take cover or move in cover. On demand, we generate locations on the rail for tactical position selection. This allows us to, for instance, generate at least one location at the closest point on the rail to the agent or to generate locations at an optimal spacing from other agents using the rail.

Given the benefits of these different kinds of points, the role of this phase is to collect or generate relevant candidates from all these possible sources and to present them in a uniform manner to the rest of the process. While explicit hidespots may come with properties such as flags for high or low cover, cover quality or direction, grid points will have none of these, but ideally we will otherwise be able to treat them just the same in our conditions and weights.

26.4.6 Filters

Filters (or conditions) are criteria that will check the validity of a point and may then reject it. We can think of them as logically forming a second phase of the process, but in practice it can make sense to interleave them with weights for performance reasons (as we will discuss in the Performance section).

Filters may simply be a property of a point, such as whether it provides high or low cover, soft cover, or hard. They may also involve some kind of evaluation against an object or position, such as raycasts to check whether, from relevant firing stances, we would be able to shoot our target. We can require these criteria to be either true or false—it can be useful, for instance, to find points that are visible from a target or to find those that are not.

When points have been generated from multiple sources, some filters may not make sense on some points. For instance, the condition `providesHighCover` simply looks up a Boolean flag in a collected hidespot, while a point generated in the open has no concept of direct cover at all. The Crytek system handles this by criteria returning the value that makes the most intuitive sense—for instance, a non-cover point returning false for `providesHighCover`—but a system might also be structured to skip over criteria that are irrelevant to a given point.

26.4.7 Weights

Weights are criteria that make a contribution to the score of a point. In most such systems the value returned by the evaluation itself is multiplied by a user-defined weight, allowing the contribution to be balanced against other weights. In the Crytek system, the values returned by all such criteria are first normalized to the 0–1 range, which makes balancing more intuitive. The user-specified weights we multiply those values by are over any range and can be either positive or negative. The results are summed and the best point is that with the highest, or least negative, score.

Most commonly, criteria that return a continuous value, for instance representing distance, will be used as weights but Boolean criteria may also be employed, returning simply 0 or 1. This allows us to give a fixed advantage or disadvantage to points in an easily balanced manner, for instance based on high or low cover.

Many weights are based on distances, and here clamping to known limits makes an enormous difference to the ease of specifying a query. If we simply return the raw distance, say, from a goal point or the closest enemy, then the maximum value is simply unknown, and while we may tweak for a common case of, say, 0–20 meters, when less common cases occur, our scores may be quite unbalanced. We can avoid this problem by choosing an appropriate maximum useful range for our game—say, 30 meters—and clamping to this, normalizing all distance criteria within that range. This means that we can then confidently predict the range of values when choosing our multiplier and comparing those to the expected effect of other weights in the query.

To achieve this, each criterion that returns a continuous value has declared limits for its output, so that when used as weights all such criteria are normalized in output to the [0–1] range. This also facilitates some of the optimizations we will discuss in the Performance section. When `min` or `max` are applied to make it a condition, we do not apply these limits; instead, we use the original, unnormalized value.

26.4.8 Returning Results

We have considered our context and chosen the relevant query, generated the appropriate candidate points for that query, applied conditions to filter them down to those that are acceptable, and evaluated their weights to score their fitness. We can now take the top points and return them as the result of the query.

In the ideal case, we are only interested in one point: the point that our agent will now move to. However, there can be good reasons to return multiple results, such as to help with hidespot contention, as we will discuss later. In general we should not need to return a set of points for a subsequent system to choose between; if our API or query language is flexible enough, we should be able to do this within our system. Further, each point returned forces us to fully evaluate its criteria and lose the potential optimizations that we will discuss in the Performance section.

We can widen the applicability of the system by returning more than just a position vector. For example, we might return the type of point (i.e., cover point, point generated in the open, etc.), and any type-specific metadata. If the point is a hidespot from a database, we can specify this and give its unique ID, useful when marking the hidespot as occupied. In the Crytek system, points can be generated at the position of all entities of a specific type, and with these we return the original entity ID. Regarding results as objects in the world, rather than just points, allows us to consider reusing the architecture for a host of other AI and gameplay applications: from choosing which of our squad mates to signal for assistance, to prioritizing between opponents in target selection, to finding nearby objects to interact with.

26.5 Best Practices and Specific Criteria

For great results from your tactical positioning system, you don't just need a good architecture, you also need powerful criteria that fit the task at hand, and you need to use those criteria effectively. Here, we discuss some criteria and approaches that have proven effective in the development of games at Crytek or elsewhere.

26.5.1 Weights and Balancing

Queries can be built by using a large number of weights and tweaking and tuning them until your desired results are seen. However, more rapid and robust development can be achieved by preferring to use criteria as conditions rather than weights, by making use of fallbacks, and by further breaking down our queries to be more context-specific.

For example: when we want to flank left, rather than weighting all points according to "leftness," just invalidate any point that is not left of your current position; rather than tweaking a tradeoff between hard/soft cover and distance, write an option that only considers hard cover, then a fallback that only considers soft.

Keeping the number of weights down—ideally to one or two—results in queries with predictable results for given contexts and saves a lot of tuning time.

Effective criteria will also help you keep your queries simple—we examine some examples now.

26.5.2 Directness

When approaching a goal, an obvious basis for our query would be a weight based on inverse distance to the goal:

```
Weights = {distance_from_referencePoint = -1.0}
```

However, in many cases we do not wish to reach the goal directly, but to approach it in a series of hops—for example, ducking from cover to cover along the way. When this is the case, pure distance to the goal quickly becomes hard to work with and to balance other weights against. It is encouraging us to get as close to the goal as possible, when what we're really looking for is a succession of carefully selected waypoints. In other words, what we really need is a measure of progress towards the goal, with distances to be specified separately.

Directness is a measure of how much closer a point will get us to a goal for the distance traveled.

$$\text{directness} = \frac{\text{distance from agent to goal} - \text{distance from point to goal}}{\text{distance from agent to point}} \quad (26.1)$$

Using Equation 26.1, if we are 50 m from our goal, a point that is 10 m away from us and 45 m from the goal will score 0.5 on directness. This measure is very predictable: the closer to a straight line to our goal, the higher the score, regardless of distance. We can ignore distance and simply request the point closest to a straight line to the goal:

```
Weights = {directness_to_referencePoint = 1.0}
```

Even simpler, rather than using it as a weight, we can make it a condition by specifying that it should just be positive, so we will always make progress towards our goal, however small, or that it should be at least 0.5, so that for every 10 m we move, we will get at least 5 m closer to our target. These are easy to reason about and orthogonal to other criteria we might introduce, so we can apply it to existing queries without long sessions of retweaking.

```
Conditions = {min_directness_to_referencePoint = 0.5}
```

Further, this simple measure of `directness` actually offers a lot of power beyond goal-seeking. We can, of course, retreat from a goal in the same way by using a negative weight or requiring a negative directness:

```
Conditions = {max_directness_to_referencePoint = -0.5}
```

However, we can also get quite different behavior from the same criterion. By making a condition that the weight must fall in a set range around zero—for instance [−0.1, 0.1]—we specify locations where, by moving to them, we will have made no real progress towards or away from the target. This is a great basis for flanking, which we might specify as the following (note that this query does not imply any particular direction—which we can easily add):

```
Generation = {hidespots_from_target_around_puppet = 15},
Conditions = {min_directness_to_target = -0.1,
              max_directness_to_target = 0.1},
Weights =    {distance_from_puppet = -1.0}
```

Directness can also bring out zigzagging. In one case, core to gameplay on a Crytek project, designers desired agents to approach the player rapidly through forests, dashing from cover to cover, often without stopping. If they approached directly, their movements would be very predictable and offer too easy a target. Here, we can specify directness both as conditions with a maximum value and as a negative weight:

```
Generation = {hidespots_from_target_around_puppet = 15},
Conditions = {min_directness_to_target = 0.5},
Weights =    {directness_to_target = -1.0}
```

Thus we take a route that is as indirect as it can be, while always making minimum progress of 1 m towards the player for every 2 m traveled, with irregularly placed trees and player movement providing a "random" factor. The result is zigzagging movement converging rapidly on the player.

26.5.3 CanReachBefore

If an agent runs towards a hidespot only to have an opponent occupy it before him, it can hurt us twice: first by the agent appearing to lack any anticipation of his opponent, and second by leaving him stranded in the open and abruptly changing direction towards other cover.

This is easy to prevent with a couple of provisions. The simplest is to focus on our current primary opponent and discard any point closer to our enemy than to us, effectively assuming that both agents will move with the same speed. We can implement this as a simple condition, such as:

```
Conditions = {canReachBefore_the_target = true}
```

This rule of thumb is so pervasive to good behavior that in the *Crysis 1* hiding system it was not optional; you might make it a default in all queries.

This focuses on just one opponent. *Far Cry* and *Crysis* also exploited perfect knowledge of which hidespots all agents are moving towards, never picking a hidespot that another agent had already claimed. Here prominent visual debugging is advised, since queries from one behavior or agent will have non-obvious interactions with others.

26.5.4 CurrentHidepoint

Often, it can be useful to generate just the point that we have already chosen, either to adjust it or to verify that it is still good enough.

Sometimes the exact position of a point will be determined on demand—for instance, the hidespots for trees in *Crysis*, mentioned earlier, that would always be generated on the opposite side from the hide-target. If we are using cover rails, we might just want to adjust our position on the rail, to reflect the movement of our target or to maintain separation from a nearby squadmate who is sharing the rail.

Once we have started to move towards a point, we usually want to show a certain amount of inertia behind that decision: changing direction if it becomes slightly less desirable, or, as a slightly better spot becomes available, will often look artificial to players. However, if circumstances change considerably—perhaps as a grenade lands or an enemy movement leaves a position clearly exposed—we do need to react.

Hence, once we have chosen a point, we can periodically check it with a simplified query that generates just that single point, where weights are irrelevant and just the critical conditions are employed—making it cheaper, simpler, and more tolerant than the original query. This query is verifying that the point is still "good enough." When this does fail, we may fall back to the full version of the query to pick a new point with the same criteria, or go back to our behavior tree to reevaluate our context. Should the situation change dramatically—for instance, due to the presence of a grenade—we rely upon the behavior tree to switch us to a different behavior and thus a different query.

Bulletstorm used a similar validation of chosen hidespots, but implemented it as a specific type of criteria within a single query, rather than separate versions [Zielinksi 13].

26.6 Group Techniques

So far we have discussed individual agents making the best decisions about their own movement. When we start to consider agents as members of groups or squads, or indeed companions, then new criteria can help us build their behaviors while coping with this added complexity.

26.6.1 Spatial Coherency—A Squad Center

In considering a squad, our most fundamental property is spatial coherency—that is, keeping the squad together. We can do this by defining a center for the squad—for instance, its current average position—so that each member's queries can specify they should stay close to that point. We can implement this by reapplying our existing criteria with a new object, squadCenter.

Perhaps the most obvious approach is to weight our queries to prefer points inversely proportional to their distance from the center.

```
Weights = {distance_to_squadCenter = -1.0}
```

This is very useful when our squad needs to converge (perhaps reacting to being surrounded) or, conversely, to spread out (perhaps under threat of mortars). However, as a building block, it has the problem of being a weight that must be balanced against any others in our query. Coherency is not a behavior in itself, but a property of all the other behaviors we would like to show—hence, ideally we would specify this in a manner orthogonal to other criteria.

A simple way to achieve that is to simply limit the maximum distance. Our members are then entirely free to move within that radius of the squad center, which will travel with the squad as its members progress [Champandard et al. 11]. Note that we can achieve this very efficiently by centering our collection/generation on the squad center and setting the radius appropriately.

```
Generation = {hidespots_from_target_around_squadCenter = 10}
```

The results have some very nice properties. If some of our squad is trailing behind while moving towards a goal—for instance due to a scattered starting configuration or some members taking long paths around obstacles—then those at the front will find their queries return no new valid points, as the only ones that progress towards the goal are outside of range of the squad center. In this case they should handle this "failure" by waiting, until those at the rear catch up and the squad center moves forward. This gives rise to a loose leapfrogging behavior without any explicit consideration of the relative position of squad members.

Here, we generally assume that the goal we are progressing towards is a common one across the squad—and by choosing that goal's location appropriately we can present that as the squad advancing or retreating, or even give designers direct control of the goal, allowing them to direct the squad according to scripted events.

However, individuals can also choose a completely different behavior and move independently for a time without disrupting the group. If, for example, an individual is avoiding a grenade, or collecting nearby ammo, he may well ignore the group coherency criteria in that query. While he may appear to leave the group, he still contributes to the squad center and so they will not proceed too far without him, allowing him to catch back up.

26.6.2 Hidespot Contention

Whenever we operate within a group while maintaining spatial cohesion, there will be more contention for available hidespots. This can present both behavioral and architectural problems.

Whenever individuals are responsible for the choice of location, they can only optimize choices, given their own preference and the points currently available. Hence, the rifleman who occupies the ideal location for a grenadier, or the agent who takes the nearest available cover for himself, leaving his squadmate to run awkwardly around him to reach any at all.

This can be resolved by performing queries at the squad level rather than the individual level, maintaining a central set of points that are assigned to squad members with the whole squad in mind. This approach was used effectively for the group behaviors in *Crysis*. However, this can lead to tightly coupled behaviors that are hard to extend.

There is also the problem that if we have queries in progress on multiple agents at the same time—for instance, running in parallel on multiple threads—they may both try to take the same point, which we must somehow resolve. One way to do this is to return multiple results for each query, so there are other points to fall back to. As we will note in the Performance section, returning the full list of results would mean we cannot take advantage of some important optimizations—but one or two extra results will usually be sufficient and can be generated with only an incremental increase to the cost of the query.

26.6.3 Companions and Squadmates

An NPC designed to interact closely with the player is one of the biggest challenges in game AI. When the NPC shares movement locations such as hidespots with the player, their movement choices must become like cogs in a machine, meshing closely with the unpredictable movements of the player if we are to avoid a painful clash of gears.

In first-person and third-person games, the problem is especially acute as we face the conflicting demands of remaining in the player's field of view to keep her aware of our movements and activity, while trying to avoid getting in the way or stealing a location from the player; in shooters, we also have to keep out of the player's Line-of-Fire (LOF) … the list goes on. There are some specific criteria that can help us in finding solutions:

`cameraCenter` returns a value indicating where this point is in the players' view frustum. It interpolates from 1 for the dead center to 0 at the edges and negative values off-screen, allowing us the control to specify positions towards the edge of our view or just off-screen. Variations on this can specifically prefer positions to the left or right.

`crossesLineOfFire` takes an object to specify whose LOF to consider, usually the local player. Our implementation uses a simple 2D line intersection test, comparing the line from the specified object to the candidate position against the forward vector of the player, although more complex implementations are certainly possible.

Using these two criteria we can form a simple squadmate query:

```
Generation = {hidespots_from_target_around_player = 15},
Conditions = {crossesLineOfFire_from_player = false
              min_cameraCenter = 0},
Weights =    {distance_from_player = -1.0,
              cameraCenter = -1.0}
```

This query is for a context where we already have a target we are attacking and try to find a cover point from that target, insisting that it must not cross the player's LOF to get there and that it must be on-screen, but as close to the edge of the player's view as possible and balancing that against staying as close to the player as possible.

Of course, this is just a starting point in a long process of design and development. For instance, the player's view changes constantly as he looks around and our companions should not run back and forth to remain in view; nor does the player's forward vector at any given moment always represent his likely line-of-fire. We can begin to address these by averaging these vectors over time, by considering a "golden path" representing likely movement flow through the level and by considering the targets the player is likely to fire at.

As we try these new ideas, we can add them as new criteria, exploiting the rapid proto-typing capabilities of our query system to help us try out all their permutations quickly and effectively.

26.7 Performance

In developing a system of this kind, work on its performance must go hand-in-hand with the expansion of its capabilities and its use. The more efficient the system and the more sophisticated its handling of expensive criteria, the more freely we will be able to use the system and the more powerful criteria we will be able to add to our toolset. Tactical position selection is one of the most productive uses to which we may put our AI cycles, but unless we have performance under control, our ideas will not make it into a shipped product. Here, we discuss ways to reduce and manage the cost of our queries.

26.7.1 Collection and Generation Costs

When collecting points from your database, an efficient lookup structure designed for cache coherency is essential on consoles. Without this, it is quite possible for the cost of collecting the points to exceed the cost of their evaluation. Crytek games have used various schemes for storing points and hidespots, including storing them in the navigation graph, using spatial hashes, and separating them by type. We could also maintain only the set of points relevant to this section of the game, swapping them out as we might an unused part of the navigation graph.

In generating points dynamically or verifying the cover of collected points, prefer to generate the candidates as cheaply as possible and defer any expensive tests—for instance, for occlusion from a target, for later in the evaluation process where we may be able to avoid their cost altogether.

26.7.2 Minimizing Raycasts

Raycasts are commonly used for a host of purposes, including establishing that you are hidden from a particular target, or establishing whether you could shoot at a particular target using a particular stance. In many games, they are the dominant cost of position selection or of the whole AI system, and as such deserve special consideration.

A physics raycast operation is always expensive and will generally traverse a large number of memory locations. Should it be performed synchronously, this will be painful in terms of cache misses, cache trashing, and possibly synchronization costs with any physics thread; on consoles this is quite prohibitive. Asynchronous operations allow batching and smooth offloading of the work to other cores such as PS3's SPUs. TPS systems thus should prefer an asynchronous API, even if only for the efficient handling of raycast-based criteria.

We may be able to form points in our database such that we can assume occlusion from some directions and avoid raycasts completely. In a static environment we can use a very simple approach of implied direction for every hidespot, such as the "hide anchors" in *Crysis*. We can then simply test if a target falls within a cone from the hidespot's direction. In a dynamic environment we may also need to periodically check that the cover object is still valid. Taking this a step further, *Crysis 2*'s cover generation system actually maps the silhouette of associated cover objects and is able to remap them upon destruction [Martins 11]. This allows us to test occlusion from a point against this nearby geometry without raycasts.

When minimizing an agent's exposure from multiple targets we will need to be able to consider cover from a number of angles and also consider what other geometry might be blocking line-of-sight, which means that we are likely to require raycasts. However, in many games such attention to exposure is not required, and in many contexts, in terms of believability, digital acting, and gameplay, it can be more effective to focus on hiding well from the single opponent we are actively engaged with, rather than attempting to hide from several.

One source of raycasts that is very hard to avoid is those which verify we can shoot at the target effectively from a location, usually by aiming over or around our cover geometry. After all, when we request a place to hide, what we usually really mean is a firing position with cover; we must verify that we can shoot at, or near, our target if gameplay is going to be interesting.

We need our system to handle the raycasts that we must perform as efficiently as possible. This means that we should leave raycast-based conditions until late in the position selection process, so that other conditions will screen out as many candidates as possible. We should also limit the number of raycasts that we initiate per frame, so as to avoid spikes, and allow the raycasts to run asynchronously. In many systems, raycast tests are treated specially for this reason—and this may be sufficient for your needs. In the Crytek system and in this discussion, we treat them as one example of a range of expensive and/or asynchronous operations we would like to support in our criteria.

26.7.3 Evaluation Order

The simplest thing we can do that will make a big difference to performance in general is to pay attention to the order we evaluate our criteria. The rule of thumb for evaluation order is:

- *Cheap filters first,* to discard points early
- *Weights,* to allow us to sort into order
- *Expensive filters,* evaluating from highest scoring down, until a point passes

It is reasonable to class many criteria as simply "cheap," because a great many criteria consist of simple Boolean or floating-point operations, with cache misses on data likely the dominant cost. These filters should be run first, as they can be used to quickly eliminate candidates, thus avoiding more expensive criteria. A few criteria, on the other hand, may be many orders of magnitude more costly (such as raycasts). We should defer these tests as long as possible, so as to minimize the number of candidates we have to run them for. By discarding points quickly with cheap filters, then evaluating weights, then performing expensive filters on the remainder in order from the highest-scoring to the lowest, as soon as a point passes we can stop evaluation, returning the correct result but often at much reduced cost.

We note that there is little we can do about expensive weights in this approach (such as a relative exposure calculation or an accurate pathfinding distance); also, that in the worst case we will fully evaluate all of our points before a valid one, or none, is found.

26.7.4 A Dynamic Evaluation Strategy

If we had the ability to skip expensive weights, as well as conditions, this would allow us a greater freedom in the development and use of such criteria. We might measure relative exposure to multiple targets, for example, or make use of accurate path lengths rather than straight-line distance. Of course, we would want to ensure that we return the same results as if full evaluation had been employed. Here, we present an approach that allows this.

We first note that in general we do not need to have the final score of a point to establish that it is better than any other may be. To illustrate this, consider two criteria that return floating-point values, normalized to the 0–1 range: A, assigned a weight of 2/3 in this query and B, assigned a weight of 1/3. If one point gains the full score on weight A, while the second scores less than half of that, then there is no reason to evaluate weight B on these two points; the highest score that B could provide would still not cause the second point to score more highly than the first.

Based on this observation, we should focus our evaluations on the point which currently has the potential to score highest out of all those considered. In order to do this, we need to know how many criteria have been evaluated so far on each point, and the maximum score that each point might achieve. We can use a struct to hold this metadata and the point itself:

```
struct PointMetadata
{
    TPSPoint point;
    int evalStep;
    float minScore, maxScore;
}
```

We employ a binary heap [Cormen et al. 01] to maintain a partial sort of these structures as we proceed, based on the maxScore value. Often used for priority queues, heaps ensure that the maximal element is kept at the top of the heap with a minimum of overhead. In a binary heap, removing the top element (pop_heap) is an O(log *n*) operation and, usually implemented in a single block of memory such as an STL vector, they are also relatively cache friendly.

Nonetheless, we noted earlier that many criteria are inexpensive to evaluate, and in these cases the overhead of heap maintenance would be comparable to the evaluations themselves. Hence, we deal with these "cheap" criteria before forming the heap in a straightforward manner similar to that discussed in the previous section: we evaluate all of the cheap conditions and discard any points that fail, then we score the remaining points based on the cheap weights—that is, summing the products of their normalized return values and the multipliers (weights) specified by the user.

This leaves us with a reduced set of points upon which to evaluate the more expensive conditions and weights. The next step is to establish the minimum and maximum possible score that each remaining point might achieve when all of the weights have been evaluated. Since all weights will be normalized to return values in the [0–1] range, we can do this just by reference to the user-defined multipliers. We sum the values of the negative user-defined multipliers (weights) in the query to find the greatest amount they could subtract from the overall score. We do the same for the positive user-defined multipliers to find the greatest amount they could add to the overall score. We then go through each point and add these amounts to the actual score that was computed when we evaluated the cheap weights, finding the lowest and highest potential scores for that point—the minScore and maxScore metadata described above.

Having dealt efficiently with the cheap criteria and established potential scores, we create the heap from these structs, populated as described above, and all further evaluation is based on that data structure. We now look at the core evaluation loop in detail. The blocks of code in this section can be combined to describe the whole loop, but we have split it into parts so that we can explain each step in the process.

Each iteration begins by checking if we have exhausted all candidates, in which case this query option has failed. Otherwise, we take the top point from the heap and check to see if it has been completely evaluated. If it has, we have a final result and either return immediately (as below) or remove that point from the heap and continue evaluation to find multiple results.

```
while (!empty_heap(pointHeap))
{
    PointMetadata& best = pointHeap[0];
    if (best.evalStep > finalEvaluationStep)
        break;
```

We then check what the next evaluation step is for this point. There is a single defined evaluation order, further discussed in the coming text, which may alternate between conditions and weights. If the next criterion is a condition, we perform that evaluation and then either remove the point from the heap (should the condition fail) or advance to the next evaluation step (should it pass).

```
    if (isCondition(best.evalStep))
    {
        bool result = evaluateCondition(best);
        if (!result)
            pop_heap(pointHeap);
        else
            best.evalStep++;
        continue;
    }
```

When the criterion is instead a weight, we make use of the "heap property." In a binary heap this dictates that the second and third elements, which are the two child nodes of the first element, will each be maximal elements of their subtrees within the heap. Hence, by comparing with these two elements, we can check if the *minimum* potential score of the top element, best, is greater than the *maximum* potential score of any other point. If this is the case, we can skip this and any other weight evaluations on this point—based on our observation at the start of this section—but we must still check any remaining conditions.

```
    if (isWeight(best.evalStep))
    {
        if (best.minScore > pointHeap[1].maxScore
            && best.minScore > pointHeap[2].maxScore)
        {
            best.evalStep++;
            continue;
        }
    }
```

If that is not yet the case, we must evaluate the weight criterion for the point, lookup and apply the defined range to normalize it to the [0, 1] range, and then fetch the user multiplier that will determine its final contribution to the score.

```
        float value = evaluateWeight(best.point);
        float normalized = normalizeToRange(value, best.evalStep);
        float multiplier = getUserMultiplier(best.evalStep);
```

We then need to adjust the minimum and maximum scores for this point. Performing a weight evaluation has narrowed the range of potential scores, in effect resolving some of the uncertainty about the score of this point. Where the user-defined multiplier for this criterion is positive, a weight that returns a high normalized value will raise the minimum score by a lot and lower the maximum score just a little; conversely, a weight returning a low normalized value will raise the minimum score by a little and lower the maximum score by a lot. Note that in both cases, minScore goes up and maxScore goes down.

```
        if (multiplier > 0)
        {
            //A positive contribution to final score
            best.minScore += normalized * multiplier;
            best.maxScore -= (1 - normalized) * multiplier;
        }
```

```
        else
        {
            //A negative contribution to final score
            best.minScore -= (1 - normalized) * multiplier;
            best.maxScore += normalized * multiplier;
        }
```

With the effect of that weight evaluation applied, we now reposition this point in the heap since it may no longer have the maximum potential score. This operation is equivalent to a pop_heap operation immediately followed by a push_heap operation, removing and then replacing the top element. We advance to the next evaluation step and begin the next iteration:

```
        best.evalStep++;
        update_heap(pointVector);
    }//Matches if (isWeight(best.evalStep))
}//Matches while (!empty_heap(pointHeap))
```

In deciding the evaluation order of criteria we are free to interleave weights and conditions. Ordering them by increasing expense is a reasonable strategy, but we might instead evaluate the largest weights earlier and likewise conditions that in practice usually fail. There is scope for considerable gains in performance based on profiling and feedback.

This approach improves over the simpler approach in cases where we have expensive weights that we hope to avoid evaluating. Where we have no such weights, the evaluations it performs will be the same as the approach described in the previous section. In the worst case, when none of the points are valid, it may be able to perform better since the evaluation order can be more freely adjusted, as above. However, if we are to be sure of returning any valid point that exists, this worst case will of course require us to check at least enough conditions to discard every point regardless of the approach we take to do so.

When a query takes significant time to evaluate, due to expensive criteria or a worst-case evaluation on a large number of points, we must be able to spread evaluation over a number of frames. It may also be useful to share evaluation time between multiple agents, to avoid all active agents waiting upon a single slow query. The heap structure described is suitable to pause evaluation at any stage to continue later—as we will exploit in the next section.

26.7.5 Asynchronous Evaluation and Timeslicing

A synchronous approach, returning results in a single function call, is the simplest execution model and the most convenient for the developer, but as we place greater load on our system and provide more powerful criteria, synchronous queries can easily lead to unacceptable spikes in processing time. Further, certain criteria may depend on asynchronous operations—for instance, efficient raycasts, as discussed. As a result, we will almost certainly need to support the ability for queries to be handled asynchronously.

In order to better handle asynchronous queries, we employ a scheduler, which will keep track of which requests are pending and which are currently being processed. *Crysis 2* employed a simple first-come-first-served scheduler working on a single query at any time—however, a scheduler that shared time between agents would be a useful improvement. With a scheduler in place, we can timeslice our evaluation, checking evaluation time periodically during execution and relinquishing control when our allocated budget for the frame has expired.

The Crytek system performs the entire generation phase and evaluates all of the cheap weights and conditions in one pass, before checking evaluation time. Since, by design, these stages are low cost, we do not expect to greatly overrun the budget by this point, and only synchronous operations are supported so we will not need to wait for any operations to complete. Once this is complete, the system forms the heap, which is compatible with timeslicing.

When we continue evaluation of the heap, we evaluate a single criterion—either a weight or a condition—on the point with the highest potential score, and then check the elapsed time before continuing with the next or putting aside the heap until next frame. Since by definition all of the criteria evaluated in this heap stage are of significant expense, the overheads of checking the CPU clock and heap manipulation are acceptable.

The same infrastructure provides the basis to handle criteria that use asynchronous operations such as raycasts. Whenever we reach one of these we start that deferred operation in motion before putting the heap aside much as if we had used up our timeslice. On the next frame we reevaluate the heap in much the same state as before—except this time we find our deferred operation is waiting for a result, which should now be available. We can then complete the results of that criterion on that point just the same as if it has been synchronous—and proceed to the next.

The latencies resulting from criteria that employ asynchronous operations are significant and could limit their use in our queries. There are a number of ways we can address this. First, we should evaluate asynchronous criteria last for each candidate point, so that we will avoid them if we can. Second, if we have remaining time available we could continue evaluation on another query, increasing our throughput. Finally, we could speculatively start deferred criteria on a number of other points near the top of the heap at the same time as the first.

26.8 Tools

As with all such systems, our TPS system is only as effective as the tools we build for it and the workflow we develop around it. The query language is one such tool, but we also need to be able to visualize the query results if we are to effectively develop and tune queries and track down problems.

The Crytek system allows us to render query results for a specific agent in the world in real time. A sphere is drawn for every candidate point, with color indicating their status: white for the highest-scoring point, green for a point that passed all conditions, red for a point that failed a condition, and blue for a point that would have been only partially evaluated. The final score is displayed above each sphere. At the same time, a representation of the parsed query is output to the log, to confirm which query was used and also to allow us to double-check what criteria were used in the evaluation.

While we did experiment with grading the colors by their relative score, we found that the differences in score were often small—though significant—and so very hard to judge visually.

Some criteria have custom debug rendering. For instance, criteria that include raycasts draw the corresponding line in the game world, and more complex dynamic generation criteria could draw indications of where and how they considered generating points.

BulletStorm used a similar visual debugging approach, but also annotated every invalid point with a short text string indicating the specific condition that failed [Zielinksi 13].

26.9 Future Work

There are some avenues for future work that are particularly promising.

As the industry standardizes on efficient navmesh solutions, a family of powerful new criteria become affordable in a TPS system. *Accurate path distances* for individual agents between locations would provide subtly improved movement choices across the board and a greater robustness to dividing obstacles such as walls and fences, compared to the Euclidean distances we take for granted. *Generation of points* could be done only in nav polys connected to our agent, ensuring that points generated in the open, such as the grid method described, are always reachable. *Navigational raycasts* could be very useful for maintaining line-of-sight within a group and might in some cases make a cheap approximation for full physics raycasts.

Game environments continue to become richer, more dynamic, and increasingly they make use of procedural content generation. All these trends represent a scalability challenge to conventional search methods. There is increasing interest in the use of *stochastic sampling*, seen in games such as *Love* [Steenberg 11], which could scale better. This comes at a risk of missing obvious locations, with a cost in believability and immersion that is often unacceptable in current AAA titles, but such games might be tuned to make this very rare, or such points might be used to supplement a conventional database of points.

Finally, when working on a squad-based game, there is currently a stark choice between individual position selection, offering decoupled interaction between members of a group in different roles; and centralized position selection that can coordinate the allocation of points to the advantage of the whole group, but at the cost of tightly coupled behavior code. Work towards *coordination between decentralized queries* would be an area of special interest to the author.

26.10 Conclusion

Tactical Position Selection is a keystone of shooter AI and a potential Swiss army knife of AI and gameplay programming. When we break out of rigid evaluation methods and provide an expressive query language, we can drive a wide variety of behavior with only small data changes. By creating a library of queries specific to the environment and desired behavior, and by considering best practices and making use of specific building blocks, we can keep queries simple and create them quickly. Feedback from our query results to our behavior and query selection allows our AI to adapt when circumstances change.

We have discussed how we can architect such a system, from query specification to final result and how we can integrate it with our behaviors. We have considered performance and tools for debugging that help ensure we make the best use of the system in the final shipped product. In particular, we have referred to details of the system used in *Crysis 2*.

Acknowledgments

The author would like to thank Crytek for their assistance with this article and AiGameDev.com for the valuable resources that they provide. Thanks also to the other developers involved, in particular, Kevin Kirst, Márcio Martins, Mario Silva, Jonas Johansson, Benito Rodriguez, and Francesco Roccucci.

References

[Champandard et al. 11] A. Champandard, M. Jack, and P. Dunstan. "Believable Tactics for Squad AI." GDC, 2011. Available online (http://www.gdconf.com/).

[Cormen et al. 01] T. H. Cormen, C. E. Leiserson, R. L. Rivest, and C. Stein. *Introduction to Algorithms*. MIT Press, 2001, pp. 127–144.

[Crytek 11] Crytek. "The Tactical Point System." http://freesdk.crydev.net/display/SDKDOC4/Tactical+Point+System, Crytek, 2011.

[Crytek 12] Crytek. "Crydev.net." http://www.crydev.net. 2012.

[Evans 11] R. Evans et al. "Turing Tantrums: AI Developers Rant." GDC 2011. Available online (http://www.gdcvault.com/play/1014586/Turing-Tantrums-AI-Developers-Rant).

[Graham 13] David "Rez" Graham. "An introduction to utility theory." In *Game AI Pro*, edited by Steve Rabin. Boca Raton, FL: CRC Press, 2013.

[Mark 09] D. Mark. *Behavioral Mathematics for Game AI*. Boston, MA: Course Technology PTR, 2009.

[Martins 11] M. Martins. Paris Shooter Symposium 2011. Available online (https://aigamedev.com/store/recordings/paris-shooter-symposium-2011-content-access.html).

[Mononen 11] M. Mononen. "Automatic Annotations in Killzone 3 and Beyond." Paris Game/AI Conference. 2011. Available online (http://aigamedev.com). Slides available online (http://www.guerrilla-games.com/publications).

[Nelson 11] J. Nelson. Paris Shooter Symposium 2011. Available online (https://aigamedev.com/store/recordings/paris-shooter-symposium-2011-content-access.html).

[Steenberg 11] E. Steenberg. "Stochastic Sampling and the AI in LOVE." Paris Game/AI Conference. 2011. Available online (http://aigamedev.com).

[Sterren 01] W. van der Sterren. "Terrain reasoning for 3D action games." In *Game Programming Gems 2*, edited by Steven Rabin. Boston, MA: Charles River Media, 2002.

[Straatman et al. 06] R. Straatman, A. Beij, and William van der Sterren. "Dynamic tactical position evaluation." In *AI Game Programming Wisdom 3*, edited by Steve Rabin. Boston, MA: Charles River Media, 2006.

[Zielinski 13] M. Zielinski. "Asking the environment smart questions." In *Game AI Pro*, edited by Steve Rabin. Boca Raton, FL: CRC Press, 2013.

27

Tactical Pathfinding on a NavMesh

Daniel Brewer

27.1 Introduction

Traditional pathfinding has been focused on finding the *shortest* route from A to B. However, as gamers demand more realism, this is no longer sufficient. Agents should instead find the most *appropriate* route from A to B. In action-shooter or strategy games, this usually means the most tactically sound route—the route that provides the most concealment from the enemy and avoids friendly lines of fire, rather than the shortest, most direct path.

Many tactical pathfinding solutions require a regular waypoint grid and numerous line-of-sight raycast checks to determine the safer, more concealed route between two points. However, regular waypoint grids are known for poor memory efficiency and the large number of waypoints to check increases the run-time pathfinding load, especially with the numerous visibility checks required for tactical pathfinding.

Navigation meshes (NavMeshes) are an alternative approach to grids and have become a widely used, efficient representation of navigable space. This article will present a method of cover representation and modification to the A* algorithm to perform tactical pathfinding directly on a NavMesh.

27.2 Other Methods

At its core, tactical A* pathfinding can be achieved by modifying the cost of nodes in your navigation graph [van der Sterren 02]. A node that is visible or exposed to the enemy should have a higher cost, while a node that is concealed from the enemy should have a lower cost. This way, the A* algorithm will favor the lower cost, more concealed nodes over the high cost, exposed nodes. An agent following such a path will seem more cautious, preferring to keep out of line-of-sight of his enemy as much as possible.

The common practice in tactical pathfinding is to use a grid or a regular waypoint graph. The high resolution and regular spacing of nodes allows the A* algorithm to better take into account the differing costs for exposed versus concealed nodes over the distance traveled. The accuracy of these techniques depends on the density of the grid; the tighter the grid spacing, the greater the number of nodes and the better the accuracy of the paths generated. A high grid density has significant costs, not only in memory for storing all the nodes, but also in processing at run-time when the A* algorithm has many more nodes to compute.

There are a number of possible methods to determine how exposed a particular node is to an enemy threat. The crucial question is "Can an enemy standing at position A see me at position B?" Performing visibility raycast checks at run-time during pathfinding can drastically hamper performance. Exhaustive visibility calculations can be performed offline and stored for use in game via look-up tables [Lidén 02]. As the environment increases in size and the number of nodes grows, this $O(n^2)$ approach requires exponentially larger amounts of memory.

An alternative to relying on exact line-of-sight raycast checks is to use approximations. A possible approximation is to store a radial distance field for each node [Straatman 05]. This approach can be extended to 3D with depth-buffer cube-maps [van der Leeuw 09]. This allows a quick look-up to approximate how far an agent can see in a particular direction from a specified point in the world. By comparing the distances in each direction between two points, it is possible to determine if these points are visible to each other. Another form of approximation is to rasterize cover objects into a grid [Jurney 07]. The enemy's view cone can then be rasterized into the grid to add a weighting factor against waypoints that are exposed to his line-of-sight. This rasterizing approach can be used to deal with dynamic, destructible cover, too. After an object is destroyed, simply perform the rasterization again with the remaining objects, and the navigation grid will reflect the current run-time changes.

These approximations actually enhance the robustness of the solution against small movements of the enemy threat. In an environment filled with complex geometry it is possible for a raycast to pass through a tiny gap in an object and so report a clear line-of-sight, when in fact the location would be concealed. The opposite can also occur, reporting an obscured line-of-sight when the location would in fact be visible. Even with simple geometry, a small adjustment of the raycast origin could return different results. The low resolution of the distance fields, or rasterized cover grids, makes these approximations much less susceptible to these slight variations in position.

Navigation meshes are a popular, efficient method of representing navigable regions of a virtual environment [Tozour 04]; however, it is not as straightforward to perform tactical pathfinding on these navigation representations. The irregular spacing and large area covered by the navigation polygons results in poor overall visibility accuracy from raycast tests. To overcome this drawback, it is possible to dynamically calculate a regular waypoint graph at run-time by sampling positions from a static NavMesh [Bamford 12]. This tactical graph need only be generated locally for the areas of the world where combat encounters take place. However, this does lead to a duplication of navigation information and at worst case may even require a separate, independent pathfinding code for the two different representations.

The following section presents an approach to tactical pathfinding that can work directly on a NavMesh without requiring the duplication of navigation information.

27.3 Tactical Pathfinding Method

The technique is split up into three parts. The first part will deal with ways to partition and annotate the NavMesh. The second part will deal with cover representation, and the final part will deal with calculating the cost of navigation polygon traversal in A* in order to calculate a more appropriate route.

27.3.1 Tessellating and Annotating the NavMesh

There has been a lot of work on creating an optimal NavMesh representation of a virtual environment [Tozour 02, Farnstrom 06], though this is not necessarily required for the purposes of tactical pathfinding. The NavMesh can be more finely tessellated to provide increased detail in areas of different movement properties or tactical significance.

Polygons in which it is more difficult, or more tactically unsafe, to move can be flagged with additional costs, just as in a regular grid representation. Areas of water could be flagged as "slow movement" or "only passable by amphibious units." Regions of high grass could be flagged with "provides concealment." Dense undergrowth could be flagged as "slow movement" and "provides concealment." The center of a courtyard with overlooking balconies can be flagged as "vulnerable" or "unsafe" so that agents will move through the area while staying near the edges. These flags and costs modify the traversal costs for the pathfinding algorithm to get agents to follow more appropriate paths rather than simply the shortest route.

An optimal NavMesh will be made up of large, convex polygons in order to provide the most coverage of the navigable space with the least number of polygons. The aforementioned courtyard could be represented by a single polygon as shown in Figure 27.1. This would prevent the differentiation between the exposed center and the covered edges under the balconies. Additional polygons are required in order to represent the tactical difference between these areas.

A quick and easy way to achieve these benefits is to provide tools allowing level designers to mark-up areas of the NavMesh with this extra detail. The designers need to be able to specify the contour boundaries of the marked up areas, and then these boundaries need to be kept fixed in the polygonal tessellation of the map. It is possible to use terrain analysis algorithms during NavMesh generation to automate some of the tedium of manual mark-ups, but this is beyond the scope of this article. In most cases, this manual mark-up may only be necessary in very specific game-play instances and the general cover approach below will suffice for most tactical pathing needs during combat.

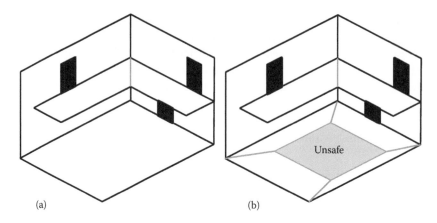

Figure 27.1

Optimal NavMesh for a courtyard with an overhanging balcony (a). The same courtyard is shown with an exposed designer region flagged as "unsafe" (b).

27.3.2 Cover Representation

Cover spots in game levels can be represented as discrete points. This is often the case with waypoint graph navigation representations. Connected areas of cover are represented by links between these cover waypoints. It can be beneficial to instead consider cover as connected, linear segments rather than discrete points. These line segments follow the contour of the cover-providing obstacle and a height property can differentiate between tall, standing cover and waist-high, crouching cover. This annotated line segment is called a "cover segment" and provides a simple polygon approximation of the line-of-sight blocking obstacle.

It is important to quickly be able to look up which pieces of cover can provide concealment to an avatar at a given location in the world. Each polygon in the NavMesh can store a small table with the indices to the most significant cover segments affecting that polygon. This table of cover segments per polygon is called the Cover Map (CoverMap). This allows a quick look-up of the objects that could provide cover or block line-of-sight to a character on a particular polygon in the NavMesh (Figure 27.2).

This data is only an approximation of the line-of-sight blockers, since only the most relevant cover for each NavMesh polygon is stored. A heuristic for selecting cover segments for a navigation polygon should take into account the direction of cover provided, the distance of the cover segment from the polygon, and whether that cover is already occluded by other cover segments. For the purposes of allowing agents to make better tactical choices during combat, this approximation is sufficient. It is possible to improve the accuracy by increasing the number of cover segments stored per polygon and by tweaking the selection criteria.

27.3.3 Pathfinding

When searching for the shortest path, the primary concern is distance or movement time. Tactical pathfinding, on the other hand, is concerned more with finding a safe path. This can be accomplished by taking a standard pathfinding algorithm and biasing the node

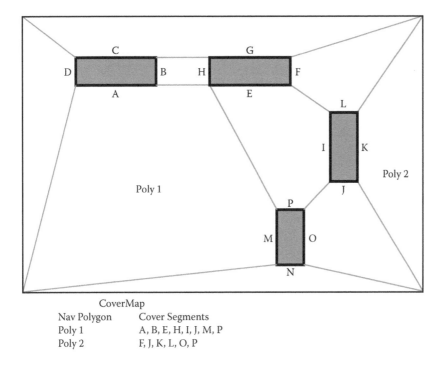

CoverMap

Nav Polygon	Cover Segments
Poly 1	A, B, E, H, I, J, M, P
Poly 2	F, J, K, L, O, P

Figure 27.2

Example NavMesh showing some cover segments and how they are stored in the CoverMap.

traversal cost by how exposed or concealed that node is to the enemy. By increasing the cost of exposed nodes, the pathfinding algorithm will return a route that avoids more of these exposed nodes and thus one that is more concealed. The method below will not cover how to perform A* on a NavMesh, which can be found elsewhere [Snook 00], but will focus on how to modify the A* costs to take cover into account in order to find a safer path. The core of the algorithm is first presented in a simpler, 2D form in order to clearly illustrate the concept. The next section will explain some extensions to the algorithm to operate in more complex environments.

To start finding a safe path from an enemy, the algorithm requires a list of cover segments that can potentially shield the agent from his enemy. The navigation polygon containing the enemy's position can be used to index into the CoverMap and obtain the list of cover segments. When considering a potential path segment, it is now possible to calculate how much of that path segment is concealed from the enemy.

The next step is to construct a 2D frustum from the cover segment (A–B in Figure 27.3) and the lines joining the enemy's position to each end of the cover segment (C–A and C–B). The normals of all these planes should point inwards to the leeward area behind the cover. The path segment is then clipped by this frustum. The portion of the segment left in front of all three planes is the concealed portion of the path segment.

These steps are repeated for each cover segment in the enemy's CoverMap. By comparing the total clipped length to the original segment length, the proportion of exposed to

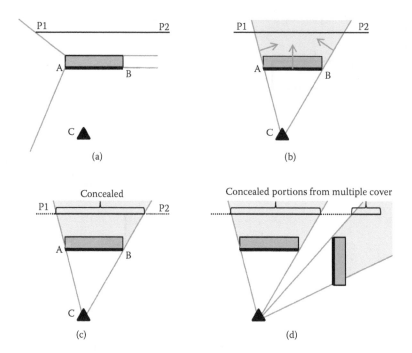

Figure 27.3

Calculating the proportion of the path segment that is concealed from an enemy (a) by first constructing a frustum from the cover segment (b) and then clipping the path segment by this frustum (c) and repeating for each cover segment in the CoverMap (d).

concealed is calculated. This is then multiplied by the cover-bias factor and added to the base cost of the segment, as shown in Listing 27.1. The A* search will thus be biased away from exposed segments. The greater the cover-bias factor, the more it will cost the agent to move along exposed segments and this will result in him going further out of his way to find a safer, more obscured path.

Listing 27.1 also shows how designer mark-ups and agent biases can affect the pathing costs. When dealing with these, it is important to remember that biases above 1.0 will increase the cost of traversing the polygon, while biases below 1.0 decrease it and may cause the cost of traversing the node to drop below the actual straight-line distance. In general, this should be avoided as it is preferable to keep the heuristic admissible and always modify the costs to make nodes more expensive. Care should also be taken not to increase the costs too much, as if the heuristic is drastically different to the cost, the A* algorithm will explore many more nodes than necessary.

27.4 Extending the Technique to 3D

The previously presented algorithm is good for 2D or slightly undulating terrain. This is to present the core algorithm in a simple, digestible manner. However, not all environments are this simple. A character on a tall hill will be able to draw a line-of-sight over some intervening cover. Vertical structures can prove problematic as a character may not be able

Listing 27.1. Pseudocode functions to calculate the exposed portion of a path segment and the cost of traversing that segment for A* pathfinding.

```
Line ClipLineByPlane(Line, Plane)
    returns the segment of the input Line in front of the Plane

float GetSegmentExposedLength(Line pathSegmentP1P2, Point C)
    float ConcealedLength = 0
    For each Line coverSegmentAB do
        Plane planeAB = CalcPlaneFrom3Points(A, B, A + up_axis)
        Plane planeAC = CalcPlaneFrom3Points(A, C, A + up_axis)
        Plane planeCB = CalcPlaneFrom3Points(C, B, C + up_axis)
        Line clippedLine = ClipLineByPlane(pathSegmentP1P2, planeAB)
        clippedLine = ClipLineByPlane(clippedLine, planeAC)
        clippedLine = ClipLineByPlane(clippedLine, planeCB)
        ConcealedLength += Length(clippedLine)
        ExposedLength = Length(pathSegmentP1P2) - ConcealedLength
        return ExposedLength

float CostForSegment(Line pathSegmentP1P2, polyFlags)
    float segmentLength = Length(pathSegmentP1P2)
    float exposedLength =
        GetSegmentExposedLength(pathSegmentP1P2, enemyPosition)
    float cost = exposedLength * agentCoverBias +
        (segmentLength - exposedLength)
    cost += segmentLength * polyFlags.isUnsafe * agentSafetyBias
    return cost
```

to draw a clear line-of-sight through the floor or ceiling, but if the visibility approximation only considers cover segments, it will not take the floor or ceiling into account. Fortunately, the technique can be extended to work with these more complex environments.

If the terrain has large height variance, a more accurate result can be obtained by treating the cover segment as a rectangular polygon representing the length and height of the cover. A frustum can be constructed from the enemy's position and the edges of the cover polygon, as shown in Figure 27.4. This frustum can be used to clip the path segments to determine how much of the segment is obscured, just as in the planar example presented above. If the environment includes more vertical structures, it may be necessary to add extra cover planes for floors and ceilings into the CoverMap.

27.5 Conclusion

Agents that can navigate an environment in a tactically sound manner can greatly enhance a video game experience. A good approximation of cover is crucial for run-time tactical pathfinding. Using linear cover segments is an effective way of reasoning about cover and line-of-sight blocking obstacles. This representation makes it simple to calculate how much of a path segment is obscured by each cover segment. By combining this cover representation with a NavMesh, it is possible to perform fast tactical pathfinding without having to resort to high memory usage grids, regular waypoint graphs, or comprehensive visibility look-up tables.

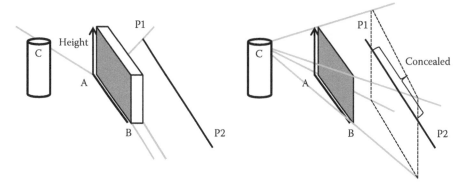

Figure 27.4

To extend the algorithm into 3D, a full frustum needs to be created from the edges of the cover segment polygon to clip the path segment.

References

[Bamford 12] N. Bamford. "Situational Awareness: Terrain Reasoning for Tactical Shooter A.I." AI Summit, GDC 2012. Available online (http://www.gdcvault.com/play/1015443/Situational-Awareness-Terrain-Reasoning-for).

[Farnstrom 06] F. Farnstrom, "Improving on near-optimality: More techniques for building navigation meshes." In *AI Game Programming Wisdom 3*, edited by Steve Rabin. Charles River Media, 2006, pp. 113–128.

[Jurney 07] C. Jurney and S. Hubrick. "Dealing with Destruction: AI From the Trenches of Company of Heroes." GDC 2007. Available online (http://www.chrisjurney.com/).

[Lidén 02] L. Lidén. "Strategic and tactical reasoning with waypoints." In *AI Game Programming Wisdom*, edited by Steve Rabin. Hingham, MA: Charles River Media, 2002, pp. 211–220.

[Snook 00] G. Snook. "Simplified 3D movement and pathfinding using navigation meshes." In *Game Programming Gems*, edited by Mark DeLoura. Charles River Media, 2000, pp. 288–304.

[Straatman 05] R. Straatman, W. van der Sterren, and A. Beij. "Killzone's AI: Dynamic Procedural Combat Tactics." GDC 2005. Available online (http://www.cgf-ai.com/docs/straatman_remco_killzone_ai.pdf).

[Tozour 02] P. Tozour, "Building a near-optimal navigation mesh." In *AI Game Programming Wisdom*, edited by Steve Rabin. Hingham, MA: Charles River Media, 2002, pp 171–185.

[Tozour 04] P. Tozour, "Search space representations." In *AI Game Programming Wisdom 2*, edited by Steve Rabin. Charles River Media, 2004, pp. 85–102.

[van der Leeuw 09] M. van der Leeuw. "The PlayStation 3's SPU's in the Real World—A KILLZONE 2 Case Study." GDC 2009. Available online (http://www.gdcvault.com/play/963/The-PlayStation-3-s-SPU).

[van der Sterren 02] W. van der Sterren. "Tactical path-finding with A*." In *Game Programming Gems 3*, edited by Dante Treglia. Hingham, MA: Charles River Media, 2002, pp. 294–306.

Beyond the Kung-Fu Circle

A Flexible System for Managing NPC Attacks

Michael Dawe

28.1 Introduction

Action games featuring real-time combat have an interesting balance to strike when approaching difficulty and player challenge. Frequently, such games may have encounters featuring several adversaries in a group attacking the player, often with differing types of attacks. This can be desirable from a game design standpoint, for reasons ranging from total combat duration to narrative requests. However, inexperienced players may become overwhelmed by the sheer number of enemies attacking simultaneously, and so these games typically restrict opponents to attacking one at a time.

For *Kingdoms of Amalur: Reckoning*, the game design called for an authentic action game inside a traditional RPG setting, complete with a large number of enemies taking on the player at once. After evaluating several approaches of restricting attackers within a combat encounter, we used a technique capable of changing the number of attackers and even the types of attacks allowed against the player dynamically based on the attackers themselves and the player's chosen difficulty level.

28.2 The Kung-Fu Circle

Requiring that opponents attack the player one at a time is a technique known as the Kung-Fu Circle, named after classic scenes from martial arts movies in which the protagonist faces off against dozens of foes who launch their attacks one at a time. This is a simple algorithm to write and employ, and can make sense in games where focusing on a single opponent is desirable. However, this restriction may be too strict for a game with quick-flowing combat. To allow for a faster pace of combat and to give the player opportunities to use wider-affecting area attacks, it is advantageous to ease these restrictions and allow more than one enemy to attack at a time. A naïve approach might be to simply allow two or three enemies to attack simultaneously, but this will not account for different enemy types or the relative strength of their attacks. For *Reckoning*, we employed an approach known internally as the "Belgian AI" system (so-called for the iconic sketches of waffles used to describe the algorithm) to allow the combat team to design encounters utilizing a variety of creatures while always employing the same underlying rules to determine the number and types of creatures allowed to attack at the same time.

28.3 Belgian AI

At a high level, the Belgian AI algorithm is built around the idea of a grid carried around with every creature in the game. While every NPC had a grid for itself, in practice the player is the game entity we are most concerned about, so we will use the player as our example throughout this article. The grid is world-space aligned and centered on the player with eight empty slots for attacking creatures, much like a tic-tac-toe board with the player at the center. In addition to the physical location of those slots, the grid stores two variables: *grid capacity* and *attack capacity*. Grid capacity will work to place a limit on the number of creatures that can attack the player at once, while attack capacity will limit the number and types of attacks that they can use.

Every creature in the game is assigned a *grid weight*, which is the cost for that creature to be assigned a spot on someone's grid. The total grid weight of the creatures attacking a character must be less than that character's grid capacity. Similarly, every attack has an *attack weight*, and the total weight of all attacks being used against a character at any point in time must be less than that character's attack capacity.

The easiest way to show the impact of these variables is to describe an example of them in action. Let's look at a situation where an enemy soldier has become aware of the player and decides to launch an attack. Before doing so, the soldier needs to request a spot from which he can attack the player. For *Reckoning*, we kept all spatial reasoning out of the individual creatures and had a centralized AI responsible for handling the positioning of creatures in battle called the *stage manager*. Our soldier will therefore register a request to attack the player with the stage manager and wait to be assigned a spot. On its next update, the stage manager will process the request and compare the soldier's grid weight against the player's current grid capacity. For our example, we'll say that the soldier's grid weight is 4 and the player's grid capacity is 12. Since the grid weight of the soldier is less than the available grid capacity, the stage manager will assign the soldier the closest available grid position and reduce the player's available grid capacity to 8. The soldier now has

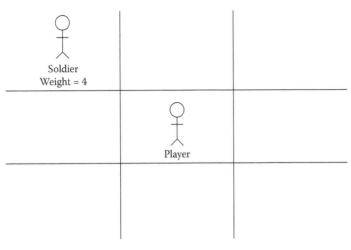

Available Grid Capacity = 12 − 4 = 8

Figure 28.1

A soldier is granted permission to attack the player and takes up position on the grid, reducing the player's available grid capacity.

permission to approach the player and launch an attack. Figure 28.1 shows an example of what the grid might look like at this point.

Next, suppose a troll notices the player. Similarly to the soldier, the troll must request of the stage manager a position on the grid, but since trolls are larger and more powerful than mere humans a troll's grid weight is 8, double that of our ordinary soldier. Since that's still within the player's available grid capacity, the stage manager can assign a slot to the troll and reduce the player's available grid capacity to 0. Now when another soldier comes along (Figure 28.2), he can request a spot to attack the player, but the stage manager will not assign him a slot, since his grid weight is larger than the player's available grid capacity. This second soldier cannot approach the player and must wait outside the grid area.

Attack capacity and weight work similarly, but for individual attacks. So far in our example, both a troll and a soldier have been granted permission to attack the player, but they haven't picked out an attack to use yet. Suppose the player's attack capacity is 10. The troll may have two attacks to pick from: a strong charge attack with an attack weight of 6, and a weaker club attack with a weight of 4. Since the player's attack capacity is 10, the troll can pick the charge attack and inform the stage manager, which reduces the player's attack capacity to 4. Now the soldier picks from his attacks: a lunge with cost 5 or a sword swing with cost 3. Since the player's current attack capacity is 4, he's unable to use the lunge attack, so he'll have to settle for the sword swing this time.

28.3.1 Grid Sectors, Inner Circles, and Outer Circles

Though the algorithm often refers to grid positions, it is more natural to think of the grid slots as defining positions equidistant from the player, forming a circle some arbitrary distance away. For Reckoning, we further subdivided the grid into inner and outer circles, which we called the "attack" and "approach" circles. The radius of the attack circle

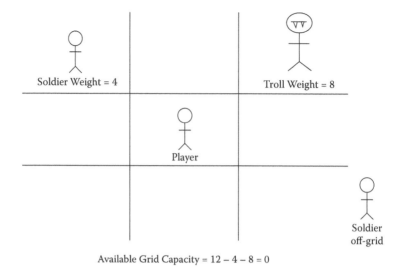

Available Grid Capacity = 12 − 4 − 8 = 0

Figure 28.2

A troll is also granted permission to attack, bringing the grid capacity down to 0. The second soldier is not allowed to approach the player to attack.

is defined by the minimum and maximum distances for melee attacks. When a creature first passes the grid capacity check and is granted permission to approach the player, it will move to stand inside the approach circle. When it is granted permission to perform a particular attack (such as the troll's charge or the soldier's sword swing), it will move into the attack circle to do so. Meanwhile, characters that have not yet passed the grid capacity check (such as the second soldier in our previous example) will stand outside the approach circle, awaiting their chance to step in. This helps the player to determine which creatures are immediate melee threats. Figure 28.3 shows what it might look like.

28.4 Behavior Integration

To fully take advantage of the grid system, creatures in *Reckoning* had a series of specific common behaviors to enforce positioning and attack rules. This also increased behavior reuse, as any creature that could use melee attacks would share these common behavior sets.

First, any creature that was within the distance defined by the outer circle but without permission to attack had to leave the circle as quickly as possible. This helped make it clear to the player which creatures were attacking. Additionally, it prevented monsters from getting in the way of each other when making their actual attacks.

Creatures waiting on the outside of the grid but not assigned grid slots were not given permission to approach, but would instead be given the location of a slot on the grid that was not currently occupied. The creatures would attempt to stand in front of their given slots, even if they did not have permission to attack, which made for natural flanking behavior without any creature explicitly needing to know about any other creature in combat.

Finally, creatures would relinquish control of their grid slot back to the stage manager immediately after launching an attack. Thus, the stage manager could queue requests for

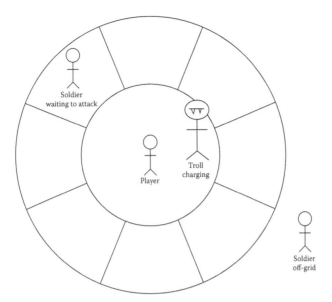

Figure 28.3

The inner- and outer-circle approach. Creatures assigned a grid slot move to their assigned section on the outer circle, but only creatures launching attacks are allowed inside the innermost circle. Any creature not assigned a slot must wait outside the outer circle.

attack slots and rotate the creatures allowed to attack throughout a combat encounter. This kept creatures moving into and out of immediate melee range of the player and ensured no single creature could monopolize attack opportunities. In the case of encounters with a small number of creatures, any creature that gave up its position after making an attack could immediately be assigned a slot again.

28.5 Scaling Difficulty

Grid capacity and attack capacity work together to limit both the number and types of creatures and attacks that can be thrown at the player at any given time. One advantage of this system is the immediate difficulty scaling that can come out of changing the player's grid capacity and attack capacity, all without changing the carefully balanced individual grid and attack weight set for each creature. As the player increased the difficulty in *Reckoning*, we scaled up the grid and attack capacities accordingly. The change to grid capacity allowed more creatures to surround the player during combat, while the change to attack capacity allowed more of those creatures to attack simultaneously and to use more powerful attacks as well.

28.6 Additional Concerns

While the Belgian AI is straightforward enough, care needs to be taken to ensure that it works well with a fast-paced action combat game. Additionally, there may be other design goals concerning creatures and their attacks that the system can be adapted to.

28.6.1 Maintaining Grid Assignments in the World

As mentioned previously the grid is world-oriented, so slots on the grid move around with the player. Sometimes, this would lend itself to situations where the slot that creatures had been assigned would no longer be the closest slot to them. This would frequently occur when the player rolled out of the way of an attack towards other creatures.

To solve this, we gave the stage manager full control over the assignment of the slots on the grid. On any given frame, it could decide which creatures to assign to slots in order to make the best use of the player's grid capacity. In the case of an empty grid, creatures could be assigned the slot closest to their current position. If creatures were already on the grid, the stage manager could assign a slot that was not the closest, or perhaps shift assignments of creatures already granted slots to make room for the newcomers. Creatures would never remember their grid slot assignments and were responsible for checking with the stage manager to get their current slot assignments every frame.

Creatures that had previously been determined to be in the best position to attack could also suddenly not be the best choice to attack the player. For a concrete example, suppose the player had encountered the troll and soldier as before, with a second soldier waiting to attack on the outside of the grid. If the player suddenly moves towards the second soldier who is currently without permission to attack, it would be best if the stage manager could move permission from the first soldier to the second to take advantage of the second soldier's new position.

To solve this, the stage manager could "steal" slot assignments from one creature to give to another or otherwise reassign creatures as it saw fit. In practice, this was tweaked such that it tended to leave creatures with permission to attack alone, unless the assigned creature was outside of the attack grid while some other creature was within the space of the grid, in which case the creature assignment would shift. Shifting could also occur in order to move attacking creatures to different positions on the grid. This shifting would attempt to reduce the total travel time for all creatures to their assigned places in combat. Further, creatures that were actively launching an attack would "lock" their assignment with the stage manager, so they wouldn't lose their slot during an attack and accidentally overload the player's attack capacity. Such an algorithm might look like the following:

```
Attacking list = all attacking creatures
For each creature in Attacking list
    Find closest slot for creature
    If closest slot is locked, continue
    Assign closest slot to creature
    Remove creature from Attacking list
    If closest slot was already assigned,
    Remove assignment from that creature
```

28.6.2 Further Restrictions on Enemy Attacks

While the attack capacity restricts the total number of attacks that can be launched at the same time, it doesn't prevent many creatures from launching the same type of attack simultaneously, especially at higher difficulty levels where the attack capacity is increased, and especially in encounters with many of the same type of creature. In order to help ensure that a variety of attacks occur in a given combat encounter, *Reckoning* also imposed cooldowns on individual, creature-wide, and global bases to prevent creatures from launching too many of the same attacks within a certain window of each other. This helped tremendously in preserving game balance at the most difficult setting, as even with an increased attack capacity, particular enemies could be prevented from using too many area-of-effect type attacks at once.

28.7 Conclusion

Managing game difficulty is an area worthy of serious consideration and research. While it's important to not overwhelm a player learning the game, flexible systems are imperative in order to provide challenging gameplay for more experienced players. Simple approaches, like the grid-based one presented here, can help empower game designers to create different and interesting encounters that can scale for a multitude of difficulty levels simply by adjusting a small set of initial values.

While the implementation of this algorithm is simple enough, its real strength lies in how the positioning logic is centralized to the stage manager. Simply having behaviors to move characters out from slots they aren't assigned to can work to get characters to flank and avoid each other, but it's easy to see how this algorithm could easily be paired with an influence map technique to help characters avoid each other and move around the battlefield more naturally. Other techniques could similarly be combined with the idea of a battle grid to tailor the technique to the needs of an individual game while maintaining the flexibility of adaptive difficulty levels.

29

Hierarchical AI for Multiplayer Bots in Killzone 3

Remco Straatman, Tim Verweij, Alex Champandard, Robert Morcus, and Hylke Kleve

29.1 Introduction

First-person shooter (FPS) games often consist of a single-player campaign and a large competitive multiplayer component. In multiplayer games, some players' slots can be taken by *bots*, AI controlled players that mimic human players for training purposes. This section describes the AI techniques used to create the bots for Killzone®3, a tactical FPS released on the Playstation®3.

Killzone bots have been used both in an offline training mode with only one or two human players in the game and in multiplayer games with any number of human and bot players. Killzone's main multiplayer mode, *Warzone*, has a number of features, such as multiple team-based game modes being played on the same map in succession and class-based player abilities, which lead to specific requirements for the AI. The chosen approach is inspired by AI techniques from strategy games (hierarchical chain-of-command AI, use of influence maps) and leans heavily on planning and position picking techniques developed for our single-player campaigns.

In this article we describe the scope of the system, the chosen architecture, and the three layers of the architecture. We provide details on the techniques that make up the various layers and describe how we model behaviors. We conclude by describing our experiences, experiments, and future directions.

29.2 Scope

Warzone pits two teams (called *ISA* and *Helghast*) of up to 12 players against each other. During one round on a single map, seven different game modes play out in random order and the team that wins the most game modes wins the round. The game modes are:

- *Capture and hold* (teams gain points by controlling objects on the map)
- *Body count* (teams compete for the most kills)
- *Search and retrieve* (both teams try to return an object to their respective return point)
- *Assassination* (attacking team tries to eliminate one specific player on the other team)
- *Search and destroy* (attacking team tries to destroy an object of the defending team)

The last two game modes are played twice, with each team playing the defending role once.

Players and bots can pick one of five classes which give them access to specific weapons and abilities. For example, the engineer class can place automated turrets, while the medic class can heal teammates. Other abilities include calling in flying drones, disguising as an enemy, cloaking, placing mines, etc.

Each map contains a number of tactical spawn points (TSPs) that can be captured by the tactician class. Team members can spawn at captured TSPs. Mounted guns, ammo boxes, and vehicles (exoskeletons called Exos) are placed at fixed spots on the maps; these can be destroyed or repaired by engineers so that they are usable by the team. For a new player joining *Warzone*, there are many things to learn. To assist in the players' learning process, the bots should mimic experienced human players, master the maps, use the abilities, and work together to win each specific game mode. They should show high level strategies, tactics, and appropriate use of abilities.

29.3 Architecture

The multiplayer AI system is set up as a three-layered hierarchy, where each layer controls the layer below it and information flows back from the lower layers to the higher one. Figure 29.1 illustrates the architecture. Each team has a hierarchy responsible for its bot players. The *strategy layer* is responsible for playing the current game mode, and contains the *commander* AI. The commander monitors the state of the game mode, assigns bots to squads, and issues objectives. The *squad layer* contains the AI for each of the squads. The *Squad AI* is responsible for translating objectives into orders for its members, group movement, and monitoring objective progress. At the lowest level, the *individual layer* consists of the individual AI of the bots. The *bot AI* follows squad orders, but has freedom in how to execute those orders. Bot AI mainly deals with combat and using its class abilities.

The communication between the layers consists of orders moving downward and information moving up. The commander can order squads to *Attack area*, *Defend area*, *Escort player*, or *Advance to regroup point*. Squads will report to the commander on successful completion of orders or imminent failure—for instance, when the squad has been decimated during an attack. Squads will order their members to move to an area, attack a target, use a specific object, or restrict bots to specific areas. Bots will report back completion of orders and send information on observed threats.

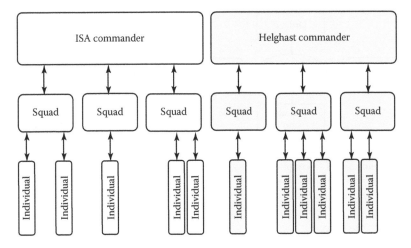

Figure 29.1

Hierarchical layered AI for both teams.

The previous sections have shown the scope and overall architecture. The following sections describe the individual, squad, and commander AI layers in more detail.

29.4 Individual Bot AI

At the lowest level in the hierarchy we find the individual AI for each bot. Even though the bots get orders from their squad, they are still highly autonomous agents. The squad does not micromanage each bot; bots gather information and decide how to fulfill their role. For example, bots can select their own attack target, the position to attack from, the weapon to use, and so forth. They can also decide to temporarily ignore orders in order to survive. Bots have the same weapons and abilities as human players.

29.4.1 Individual Update Loop

The bot AI takes a typical agent-based approach, as shown in Figure 29.2. First, the NPC gathers information about the current world state, either through *perception* or by messages from other team members. Agents perceive *stimuli* in the game world through various *sensors*. There are different sensors for seeing, hearing, and feeling, and different types of stimuli (visual, sounds, and contact). The sensors have limitations such as view cones and maximum distance. See [Puig08] for general information on perception systems. Abilities such as cloaking and disguise further influence perception and make the AI react believably. The information on threats derived from perception is placed in each individual's *world database*. Because of the limitations in perception, the bot's idea of the world may be believably wrong. Besides perception and messages from other agents, a number of *daemons* fill the agent's database with other data. A daemon is a component that adds facts about a specific type of information such as the state of the bot's weapons and health.

In the next step, the *planner* either generates a *plan* or continues execution of the current plan. A plan consists of a sequence of *tasks*. The set of tasks available to the bots is typical for a shooter (such as move to destination, select weapon, reload weapon, etc.).

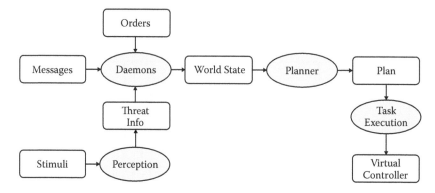

Figure 29.2

Individual update loop.

Each update, the current task of the plan gets executed. Completion of the task advances the plan to the next task, while failure will invalidate the whole plan. Executing a task updates the lower level *skill planner* that takes care of coordinating lower granularity actions such as looking, aiming, walking, crouching, etc. The skills finally update the bots' *virtual controller*, the interface both bots and players share to control their humanoid game avatar. The virtual controller enforces a strict separation between AI and the game engine, so that AI code does not directly control animations or guns, and thus ensures that the bots' capabilities are identical to those of the player.

29.4.2 Individual Planner

We use a custom planner that is based on the Hierarchical Task Network (HTN) planner architecture [Nau 00]. This planner was chosen because it provides good control over what plans can be generated and a clear definition of priorities between plans.

The individuals' behavior is defined in HTN by a *domain*, which consists of *constants* and *methods*. A method defines one or more ways to achieve a *task* by defining a list of *branches*. Each branch has a *precondition* and a *decomposition* consisting of a list of tasks. A task can be *primitive*, meaning it can be executed by the agent, or *compound*, meaning it needs to be further decomposed using a method.

Planning begins by instantiating a plan for a top-level task. The branches of the method for this task are attempted in listed order. When a branch's precondition matches, the planner recursively tries to create plans for all compound tasks in the branch's plan. The planner will backtrack over branches, variable bindings of preconditions, and plan instantiations for compound tasks. The resulting plan is the first one fully consisting of primitive tasks.

The primitive tasks modify their agent's memory, make the bot do things in the world, and add information for debugging. Table 29.1 shows some of the primitive tasks.

Listing 29.1 shows the method that turrets (which use the same planner as the bots) use for selecting a weapon to fire at some threat (represented by the variable ?threat). Variables are prefixed by a question mark, constants by an @ sign, and the keyword call precedes C++ function calls. Each of the weapons of the turret has its own branch, with preconditions matching against facts in the agent's world database (e.g., distance_to_threat), resulting in the instantiation of local variables (e.g., ?dist). The plan of both branches

Table 29.1 Example of primitive tasks (prefixed with !) for individual bots

Primitive task	Description
`!remember`	Add a (temporary) fact to agent database.
`!forget`	Remove fact(s) from agent database.
`!fire_weapon_at_entity`	Fire current weapon at specified entity.
`!reload_weapon`	Reload current weapon.
`!use_item_on_entity`	Use current inventory item on other entity.
`!broadcast`	Send a message to nearby bots.
`!log_color`	Add text to the debug log of an agent.

Listing 29.1. Example methods for selecting a weapon to fire. The syntax is based on the SHOP HTN planner, which was written in Lisp. Our HTN compiler converts this domain description into C++ code.

```
(:method (attack ?threat)
    (:branch "use bullets"
        (and (distance_to_threat ?threat ?dist)
            (call le ?dist @bullet_rng)
            (call request_line_of_attack ?threat bullets)
            (line_of_attack ?threat bullets) )
        (    (!begin_plan attack_using_bullets)
            (select_weapon bullets)
            (!fire_weapon ?threat)
            (!end_plan) )
    )
    (:branch "use missiles"
        (and (distance_to_threat ?threat ?dist)
            (call ge ?dist @bullet_rng)
            (call le ?dist @missile_rng)
            (call request_line_of_attack ?threat missiles)
            (line_of_attack ?threat missiles) )
        (    (!begin_plan attack_using_missiles)
            (select_weapon missiles)
            (!fire_weapon ?threat)
            (!end_plan) )
    )
)
```

contains a number of primitive tasks and one compound task (`select_weapon`). To form an instantiated plan that compound method needs to be decomposed further by another method.

The example in Listing 29.1 also shows how a request for information (`request_line_of_attack`) can be part of the precondition; the result will be placed in the database and is tested in the next condition (`line_of_attack`).

For bots, plan generation always starts with a root task (called `behave`). The methods in the domain determine the plans that can be generated and in which order they are tried. Listing 29.2 shows the final decomposition that led to a medic bot's plan to use the revive

Listing 29.2. An example decomposition tree for the HTN domain. "+" denotes a successful branch choice, "-" a branch that was considered but failed. Variable bindings are in italics. Not all successful decompositions are shown expanded.

```
behave
+ branch_mp_behave
   - (do_behave_in_vehicle_mp)
   + (do_behave_on_foot_mp)
      - branch_self_preservation
      + branch_medic_revive
         + (do_medic_revive)
            - branch_medic_revive_abort
            - branch_medic_revive_continue
            + branch_medic_revive
               (!begin_plan medic_revive [Soldier:TimV])
               (!log_color magenta "Medic reviving nearby entity.")
               (!broadcast 30 10 medic_revives [Soldier:TimV])
               (!select_target [Soldier:TimV])
               + (walk_to_attack 5416 crouching auto)
               + (wield_weapon wp_online_mp_bot_revive_gun)
                  - branch_dont_switch_weapon
                  + branch_switch_weapon
                     (?wp = wp_online_mp_bot_revive_gun)
                     + (wield_weapon_internal wp_mp_bot_revive_gun)
               (!use_item_on_entity [Soldier:TimV] crouching)
               (!end_plan)
```

tool on a teammate. The decomposition illustrates the way the HTN planner solves a plan, but also illustrates the way the domain is structured.

The final plan consists of all the primitive tasks in the decomposition. Starting at behave, the first branches decide between behavior in a vehicle or on foot, followed by a choice between self-preservation behavior (such as fleeing a grenade) and doing one of its class abilities, revive.

As described above, planning starts at the root node, generating a plan for behave. It does this by going through behave's branches in the order specified, so that branches pertaining to self-preservation are considered before those for healing friendlies for instance. If it selects a branch that contains composite tasks, the planner recursively generates a plan for that branch.

Once the planner has finished, the agent can execute the plan. Each update the current task in the plan is executed. The current task can continue running for multiple updates before succeeding and moving to the next task in the plan, or fail. If the plan has reached the end or a task has failed the agent needs to generate a new plan.

In practice, making sure the agents' plan is still the best one given the ever-changing situation is more complicated. Because of this, the agent reruns the planner at a fixed rate and replaces the current plan if it finds one which is better (that is, one that traverses branches that are farther up the list than those in the current plan). For example, if the AI is in the process of healing a buddy when it replans, and it discovers that there is a grenade nearby, it will abort the heal in favor of a self-preservation branch (such as fleeing from the grenade).

Plans will also be interrupted if they are no longer relevant. For example, if the AI is running toward a buddy that it wants to heal, but that buddy has since died, then it is time to select a different plan. This is implemented by adding extra branches to the domain that contains the "continuation conditions." These branches are selected when a plan is active and the plan's continuation conditions are met. They contain a single `continue` task, which lets the planner know that further planning is unnecessary, and the current plan is still the best.

Within this general planning and reasoning framework the domains need specific information to make good tactical decisions. The next section briefly describes the types of information that are available, and how they are used.

29.4.2 Individual Tactical Reasoning—Waypoint Graph and Cover Data

The basis for the combat reasoning of our single and multiplayer bots is a combination of *waypoints* and *cover data*. The *waypoint graph* defines waypoints, positions for which tactical data is available, and links between them that allow the AI to plan paths and navigate. This waypoint graph is generated by our automated tools (described in [Mononen 11]). For each waypoint, cover data is stored that describes the cover available in each direction. The cover data is automatically created in an offline process.

This data, in combination with dynamic information on threats, is used for various tactical decisions. For instance, selecting a suitable position to attack a threat is done by *position picking*, where the waypoint graph is used to generate nearby potential waypoints and score these candidates based on a number of properties. Properties can include cover from known threats, distance from threats or friendlies, line of fire to threats, travel distance to reach the position, etc. The properties that are used and how they influence the score can be specified differently for different behaviors. Another use of this data is *threat prediction*, where the most likely hiding waypoints for a hidden threat are calculated. Our agents' tactical reasoning has been discussed in more details in our previous work [Straatman 06, Van der Leeuw 09].

These tactical services are available to the domains in a number of ways. Position picking or path planning queries can be used in preconditions of branches and will instantiate variables with the best position or path (if any). Predicted positions of threats can be queried in preconditions of branches and plans can use the resulting lists of hiding waypoints in a variety of ways—for example, to search or scan for the threat. In this way we combine a more specific, optimized tactical problem solver with the general HTN planner to generate tactical behavior.

29.5 Squad AI

The previous section described how our autonomous bots make decisions on combat and ability use. We now turn to squads, which will make these bots work together as a group to achieve a goal. A *squad* is an agent that controls a collection of bots. The squad AI structure is similar to an individual's: it collects information into a world state, generates and monitors a plan using the HTN planner, and executes the tasks in that plan. The difference lies in the data collected, domains, and primitive actions.

29.5.1 The Squad Update Loop and Planning Domain

During data collection, the squad AI gathers information on the state of its members. Instead of using perception to collect this information, however the squad bases its world

Table 29.2 Primitive tasks (prefixed with !) for squads

Primitive task	Description
!start_command_sequence	Start a sequence of commands to send to an agent
!order	Send command to agent's queue
!end_command_sequence	End a command sequence
!clear_order	Pop current command from own command queue

state on messages received from its members. Based on this state and the orders given to it by the commander AI, the squad planner generates a plan. The squad does not act directly, but through its members. As a result, most of its primitive tasks simply send an order to a member's *command queue*. Table 29.2 shows some of these primitive tasks.

Each squad and individual has a command queue (similar to RTS units). Newly arriving orders overwrite existing orders, unless they are part of a sequence, in which case they are queued. The individual's domain will try to handle the current command and removes it from the queue when the order is completed.

Listing 29.3 shows a part of the squad method for making one member defend an area. The branch advance takes care of the case where the squad needs to move to the area that must be defended. The plan starts by resetting the squad's bookkeeping on what the member is doing, and then commands the member to stay within the areas the squad pathfinder defines (discussed below), orders the member to move to defend, orders the member to send a message to the squad (so the squad knows it arrived), and on arrival orders the member to stay within the defending area.

Listing 29.3. Part of a squad method showing one branch for defending an area.

```
(:method (order_member_defend ?inp_mbr ?inp_id ?inp_level ?inp_marker
?inp_context_hint)
    ...
    (:branch "advance"
        ()//no preconditions
        (   (!forget member_status ?mbr **)
            (!remember - member_status ?inp_mbr go_defend ?inp_id)
            (!start_command_sequence ?inp_mbr ?inp_level 1)
            (do_announce_destination_waypoint_to_member ?inp_mbr)
            (!order ?inp_mbr clear_area_filter)
            (!order ?inp_mbr set_area_restrictions
                (call find_areas_to_wp ?inp_mbr
                (call get_entity_wp ?inp_marker)))
            (!order ?inp_mbr move_to_defend ?inp_marker)
            (!order ?inp_mbr send_message completed_advance ?inp_id)
            (set_defend_area_restriction ?inp_mbr
                (call get_entity_area ?inp_marker))
            (!order ?inp_mbr defend_marker ?inp_marker)
            (!end_command_sequence ?inp_mbr)
        )
    )
)
```

As stated before, when the individual bot AI has `DefendMarker` as its current order its planner can make different plans to achieve this. The branches of the method that deals with this order specify both character class specific plans and generally applicable plans. The engineer specific branch specifies: "move there, place a turret nearby," the tactician specific branch specifies "move there, call in a sentry drone," and the generic branch just specifies "move there, scan around." The generic branch is always available, so after an engineer placed his turret he can generate a plan to scan around.

Similar to the individual bots, the squad planner needs information about static and dynamic aspects of the world to make tactical plans. The next section will describe the tactical reasoning available to squads.

29.5.2 Squad Tactical Reasoning—Strategic Graph and Influence Map

The squad AI reasons about the terrain using the *strategic graph*. This is a hierarchical summary of the waypoint graph and consists of *areas* (groups of waypoints) and connections between areas. A connection between two areas exists when there is a link between the waypoints of the two areas in the waypoint graph. This ensures that when a path exists between areas in the strategic graph, it also exists in the waypoint graph, and vice versa. The abstraction of detail the strategic graph provides makes squad reasoning more efficient. This is necessary because the squad's plans typically cover larger areas, and sometimes even the entire map, which would be prohibitively expensive if done on the waypoint graph. Since we do not want to micromanage the individual bots, reasoning at the area level also leaves choices for individual bots, when doing their tactical reasoning at the waypoint level.

The strategic graph is automatically generated from the waypoint graph at export time. The clustering algorithm incrementally groups areas together, starting at one area per waypoint. Clustering is done based on connection properties, number of waypoints in an area, and area surface. This process leads to logical areas that have good pathfinding properties. Similar clustering algorithms have been described elsewhere [van der Sterren 08].

An *influence map* provides dynamic information to complement the strategic graph. Each of the factions updates its own influence map. The map assigns an influence float value to each area expressing whether the area is under enemy or friendly control. Influence maps are a standard technique in strategy games and have been documented in detail [Tozour 01]. The influence map is calculated by counting the number of friendly and enemy bots and players in an area as well as automated turrets and drones. Recent enemy and friendly deaths also change the influence values. Next the values are smoothed based on distance and combined with the previous values in the influence map for temporal smoothing.

Each squad has a strategic pathfinder. Using the influence values in strategic pathfinding allows the squads to avoid enemy controlled areas. Another use is the selection of *regroup markers*, which are safe locations near the objective where squads will gather an attack. Choosing between regroup markers is done by taking the influence map values of the area containing each marker into account. Additionally a penalty is given to areas chosen by any friendly squad as part of their paths, which provides variation for repeated attacks and spreads out simultaneous attacks.

The pathfinder is implemented as a single source pathfinder which calculates the cost towards all areas in the level using the position of the squad as source. Figure 29.3 illustrates the results of this pathfinder.

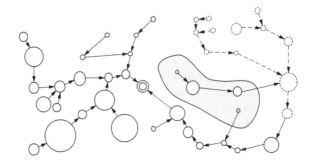

Figure 29.3

The spanning tree of the squad pathfinder in a section of the Salamun Market map. The ultimate destination of the squad is the double circle. The left section of the figure shows a spanning tree that follows the shortest Euclidean path. The shaded dotted zone in the middle right is marked as high cost for the squad, so the dotted nodes on the right avoid that area due to the pathfinder taking into account the costs from the influence map.

The approach allows the squad HTN planner to do many position and path queries as it plans. The squad pathfinder returns a *strategic path* (a sequence of areas) which is then used as a corridor for the squad members by restricting them to these areas. These restrictions constrain the portion of the waypoint graph available for individual path planning and position picking, which allows the individual bots to make their own decisions while still taking the more global tactical decisions of the squad into account. Furthermore the corridor restricts the search space of individual path planning, thus improving performance.

The strategic path planners are updated incrementally using an anytime algorithm to minimize performance impact [Champandard 02]. The incremental nature is less of an issue at the squad level as updates are less frequently needed.

29.6 Commander AI

The highest layer in our AI system is the commander AI for each of the two factions (Helghast and ISA). The commander understands how to play the game modes, and will assign objectives and bots to squads as appropriate for the particular mode being played. Because of the varying number of bots in a faction, the multiple objectives in the game modes, and aspects such as tactical spawn points (TSPs) and vehicles, the commander must be able to create new variants of strategies; a fixed policy for a game mode will not do.

29.6.1 Commander Objectives and Assignment

The commander consists of three parts:

1. A game mode specific part that generates objectives
2. A system for assigning objectives and bots to squads
3. A system for monitoring the objectives assigned to squads

The commander can create squads, delete squads, reuse previous squads, assign a bot to a squad, reassign a bot, and assign objectives to squads and to individual bots. There are four types of objectives: `AdvanceToWaypoint`, `DefendMarker`, `AttackEntity`, and `EscortEntity`. Each objective has a weight, which expresses its importance relative to the other objectives, and an optimal number of bots.

The mission specific AI consists of C++ classes, one for each mission type. These classes use the current information from the game state to add and remove objectives. For example, the class for the Capture and Hold mode needs objectives for attacking or defending the three conquerable areas. Initial objectives will be created to capture all three areas, but if a faction is ahead in score and owns two of the three areas, it can decide to only generate defend objectives for the areas it has already captured.

For Search and Destroy, objectives are added for each of the two destructible targets. The type of objective depends on whether the commander's faction is the defending or attacking side.

In Search and Retrieve there is one object that both factions want to return to their base. When the object has not been claimed, an objective will be generated to advance on the location of the object. If it is claimed, the holding faction will create an escort objective for the carrier, and the other faction will create an objective to attack the carrier to reclaim the object. Both factions may decide to add objectives to defend the enemy's base to prevent returning the object, or to attack their own base to make it easier for the (future) carrier to return.

Some objectives are relevant for all game modes. The tactical spawn points are important because of the shorter travel distances to objectives for re-spawning team members, so capturing or defending them is also a lower priority objective. Furthermore, one level contains vehicles (called Exo's), so there is a *Harass with vehicle* objective that will make a bot in a vehicle attack enemies near the most important objective.

The commanders are custom coded based on input from the multiplayer designers and QA testers. By specifying a list of current objectives, one can make the commanders for a game mode as simple or subtle as needed while the code for the commander stays small.

The algorithm for assigning bots and squads to objectives is as follows:

1. Calculate the ideal distribution of bots, then squads.
2. Create new squads if necessary.
3. If the previous assignments had too many squads assigned to any one objective then remove the excess squads.
4. Assign the best objective to each squad.
5. If too many bots are assigned to a particular squad or objective then unassign them.
6. Assign each free bot to the best squad.

In step 1, all active objectives' weights and desired number of bots are used to calculate the desired number of squads and their sizes. Step 2 and 3 ensure that the actual number of squads matches the desired number as closely as possible. Step 4 prefers to keep squads assigned to previously assigned objectives and otherwise assigns them based on the distance between the squad and the objective. Squads reassigned to new objectives may have too many bots, so step 5 makes these extra bots leave their squad. Step 6 takes care of assigning all bots without a squad to the closest squad in need of more bots. Bots can be assigned to a squad when they are about to re-spawn and then will select the spawn point with the best travel cost (including influence map cost) to their squad. Class selection on spawning by bots is done by a fixed heuristic. This ensures that there are some tacticians and engineers because of their importance for achieving objectives, and randomly assigns a class to the rest of the bots.

29.6.2 Commander Strategic Data

The Commander AI uses a number of *level annotations* to make better map-specific strategic decisions. We chose to manually place these, because they would require complex terrain reasoning to generate automatically but can be identified easily for each map by observing play tests. Some of the annotations are also used by the squad and individual AI at the lower layers when formulating their plans.

Generic level annotations include:

- *Regroup locations*, which are strategic locations that are good to control. Squads are sent here to form up before attacks.
- *Sniping locations*, which specify areas that have good visibility over key locations. Squads are sent here to help defend or attack objectives.

Mission specific annotations include:

- *Assassination hiding locations*. These are markers that specify good locations for the target bot to hide during Assassination missions. Good locations are typically inside defensible buildings. The commander for the defending team initially picks one of these locations, and may decide to move the target to another one based on distance and the influence map later.
- *Defend locations*. Missions with static objectives, such as Capture and Hold, use these locations to define where the defenders should stand or patrol.

Our previous work includes more details on the use of annotations [Straatman 09], as well as on the architecture itself [Verweij 06].

29.7 The AI in Action

As an example, in a Capture and Hold mission the ISA commander might send a squad to defend a capture point, another squad to take the nearby Tactical Spawn point (TSP), and a third squad (which consists of a bot manning an Exo vehicle) to harass any enemies in the areas near the capture point. The squad attacking the TSP plans a path from the base, avoiding another capture point that is owned by the Helghast. Once it has arrived, the tactician captures the TSP and the engineer places a turret on a defend marker near the TSP. After capturing the TSP, the tactician and engineer will patrol and scan the area to defend it. Meanwhile, the squad defending the capture location has come under attack. In response, the tactician calls in drones to help with the defense. Individual bots use the cover data to find cover and attack locations. ISA medics use their revive tool to revive wounded comrades. Engineers repair the supporting Exo when needed. ISA defenders that did not survive will spawn at the nearby TSP to get back to defending the capture point. The overall result is that, by using the architecture described in the sections above, the bots master all gameplay aspects of the *Warzone* mode.

29.8 Future Work

The process of shipping a title always brings new lessons and ideas. Based on what we learned creating *Killzone 3* we are considering the following improvements:

- The squad assignment component of the Commander AI was much harder to get working than it was for *Killzone 2*. This was probably because in *Killzone 3* there are more objectives to consider, but fewer bots to accomplish them with. Therefore we created an agent-based Commander AI that uses the same HTN planner. We expressed our current capture and hold commander and squad assignment in an HTN-based commander and would consider using this approach in future titles.
- It is relatively easy to express different strategies for a game mode using either the objective system or the HTN commander described above. Interviews with our internal testers, game designers, and watching games in public beta will lead to many possible strategies. However, deciding between strategies is harder. We have used reinforcement learning to adapt branch ordering and preconditions in the commanders' HTN domain based on the outcomes of bot versus bot games.

Both these changes are described in more detail in a paper by Folkert Huizinga [Huizinga 11].

29.9 Conclusion

This article described the AI systems we use for our multiplayer bots. We have shown the architecture, algorithms, the way we structure the planning domains, and the extra data (both static and dynamic) involved in making decisions. This approach divides the responsibility for decisions in a hierarchical manner that reduces complexity and maximizes opportunities for adding interesting dynamic behavior.

The use of hierarchical layers is one way we reduce complexity and maximize reuse. Within one agent we often combine static terrain data, a generic problem solver, and dynamic game state data to achieve a nice combination of predictability and reactiveness. Between hierarchical layers the translation from commands to behavior introduces choice and character-specific ways of achieving a goal.

We use various existing techniques in a complementary way. In some places we automatically generate tactical data whereas in others we rely on designer-provided input. We use a generic domain-independent HTN planner to define most of our behavior, but use specific problem solvers for position picking, squad path planning, and lower level humanoid skill planning.

We believe this section shows a way in which various established techniques can be used for combined effect, and that the architecture described here can be applied to many AI engines.

Acknowledgments

The work described here is the result of development over a number of projects and collaboration with numerous other developers. We want to thank the developers at Guerrilla, especially Arjen Beij and the multiplayer design team, for their contributions, feedback, and support. Furthermore, we thank Guerrilla and Sony Computer Entertainment for providing us with the environment that led to the development of the techniques described above.

References

[Champandard 02] A. J. Champandard. "Realistic Autonomous Navigation in Dynamic Environments." Masters Research Thesis, University of Edinburgh, 2002.

[Huizinga 11] F. Huizinga. "Machine Learning Strategic Game Play for a First-Person Shooter Video Game." Masters Research Thesis, Universiteit van Amsterdam, 2011. Available online: (http://www.guerrilla-games.com/publications/index.html#huizinga1106).

[Mononen 11] M. Mononen. "Automatic Annotations in Killzone 3 and Beyond." Paris Game/AI Conference 2011, Paris, June 2011. Available online: (http://www.guerrilla-games.com/publications/index.html#mononen1106).

[Nau 00] D. S. Nau, Y. Cao, A. Lotem, and H. Muñoz-Avila. "SHOP and M-SHOP: Planning with Ordered Task Decomposition." Tech. Report CS TR 4157, University of Maryland, College Park, MD, June, 2000.

[Puig 08] F. Puig Placeres. "Generic perception system." In *AI Game Programming Wisdom 4*, edited by Steve Rabin. Hingham, MA: Charles River Media, 2008, pp. 285–294.

[Straatman 06] R. Straatman, A. Beij, and W. van der Sterren. "Dynamic tactical position evaluation." In *AI Game Programming Wisdom 3*, edited by Steve Rabin. Hingham, MA: Charles River Media, 2006, pp. 389–403.

[Straatman 09] R. Straatman, T. J. Verweij, and A. Champandard. "Killzone 2 multiplayer bots." *Paris Game/AI Conference 2011*, Paris, June 2011. Available online (http://www.guerrilla-games.com/publications/index.html#straatman0906).

[Tozour 01] P. Tozour. "Influence mapping." In *Game Programming Gems 2*, edited by Mark Deloura. Hingham, MA: Charles River Media, 2001, pp. 287–297.

[Van der Leeuw 09] M. van der Leeuw. "The PlayStation®3's SPUs in the Real World: A KILLZONE 2 Case Study" Presentation GDC 2009, San Francisco, March 2009. Available online (http://www.guerrilla-games.com/publications/index.html#vanderleeuw0903).

[van der Sterren 08] W. van der Sterren. "Automated Terrain Analysis and Area Generation Algorithms." http://aigamedev.com/premium/masterclass/automated-terrain-analysis/

[Verweij 06] T. J. Verweij. "A Hierarchically-Layered Multiplayer Bot System for a First-Person Shooter." Masters Research Thesis, Vrije Universiteit Amsterdam, 2006. Available online: (http://www.guerrilla-games.com/publications/index.html#verweij0708).

30

Using Neural Networks to Control Agent Threat Response

Michael Robbins

30.1 Introduction

Neural networks are one of the oldest and most widely used machine learning techniques, with a lineage dating back to at least the 1950s. Although there has been some concern within the game AI community that they might not be the right fit for games, our experience with using them in *Supreme Commander 2* has been tremendously positive. Used properly, they can deliver compelling behaviors with significantly less effort than it would take to hand-code them. In *Supreme Commander 2*, neural networks were used to control the fight or flight response of AI controlled platoons to great effect. Far from being useless, neural networks added a lot of value to the AI without an exorbitant amount of effort.

There are numerous resources both in print and on the web that describe the basics of neural networks, and even provide sample code. The books *Artificial Intelligence for Games* [Millington 09] and *AI Techniques for Game Programing* [Buckland 02] are great resources for getting started, while *Game Programming Gems 2* [Manslow 01] provides sample code and a wide range of practical hints and tips. This article will focus on the specifics of how neural networks were used in *Supreme Commander 2*.

30.2 What Is a Neural Network

There are many different types of neural networks but this article will focus on multilayer perceptrons (MLPs), which were chosen for *Supreme Commander 2* because they're relatively easy to implement and simple to use.

MLPs typically consist of three layers of neurons or "nodes," as they are often called in the neural network literature. These layers are the input layer, the hidden layer, and the output layer. Each node has a value associated with it that lies in the range zero to one and indicates its level of excitation. Nodes are connected to other nodes by unidirectional "weights," which are the analog of biological synapses and allow the level of excitation of one node to affect the excitation of another. In an MLP, each node receives stimulation only from nodes in the preceding layer and provides stimulation only to nodes in the next layer.

Data is fed into an MLP by setting the levels of excitation of the nodes in the input layer. Each node in the hidden layer then receives an amount of stimulation that is equal to an internal bias plus the sum of the products of the levels of excitation of each node in the input layer and the weight by which it is connected to it. The excitation of each node in the hidden layer is then calculated by applying a nonlinear activation function to the value that represents its level of stimulation. The logistic function is the standard choice of activation function for MLPs and produces a level of excitation in the range zero to one.

This process is repeated with each layer in the network receiving stimulation from the preceding layer until the levels of excitation of the network's output nodes have been updated; these levels constitute the network's output and hence its response to the earlier input. The behavior of an MLP is determined entirely by the values of its weights and biases, and the process of training it consists of finding the values of the weights and biases that minimizes some measure of the difference between the network's outputs and some ideal target values.

30.3 Setting Up a Neural Network

For *Supreme Commander 2*, it was decided to use an MLP to control a platoon's reaction to encountering enemy units. We decided to use a total of four MLPs, one for each platoon type: land, naval, bomber, and fighter. We split the MLPs this way so that each platoon type could learn what it needed to without interfering with the other platoon types.

The bulk of the AI's platoon logic would exist inside of a finite-state machine that would use the MLP to decide what to do when the platoon encountered enemy resistance and would continue to use the MLP to reevaluate the constantly changing situation. MLPs provide a great way to accomplish this because they can quickly size up a situation based on their training. In any situation, an MLP can give an AI the ability to determine which enemy targets it should attack first or to retreat if it found itself outmatched. To accomplish this, the first thing that needs to be done is to decide what information the MLP needs to make these decisions and how it should be represented.

30.3.1 Choosing Inputs

Inputs are supplied to an MLP by setting the values that represent the levels of excitation of its input nodes. These values are typically bounded to lie in the range zero to one, though the range minus one to plus one also works well with MLPs. For *Supreme Commander 2*, inputs were created by taking the ratio between the friendly and enemy values of certain statistics which included number of units, unit health, overall damage per second (DPS), movement speed, resource value, shield health, short-range DPS, medium-range DPS, long-range DPS, and repair rate. All input values were clamped to lie in the range zero to one, so the reciprocals of the ratios were also included to provide the network with useful information about the relative sizes of the statistics even when the friendly statistic exceeded the enemy statistic. These statistics were gathered from friendly and enemy units in a radius around the AI's platoon. Altogether, 17 ratios were calculated, and hence the network had 34 inputs.

This relatively large number of inputs worked well in *Supreme Commander 2* but could be problematic in other applications, particularly if there were only a few thousand examples that could be used in training. This can lead to what is called "overfitting," which is where a network effectively learns certain specifics of the training data rather than the general patterns that lie within it. Overfitting is apparent when a network performs significantly better during training than it does when tested. Overfitting is most easily prevented by retraining with a simpler network (or by providing a larger set of training data, of course). Thus, in general, it's a good idea when choosing inputs to find as small a set as possible. At the same time, the MLP will only be able to account for information that you provide to it, so the desire to have a small input set needs to be balanced against a desire to include as much of the relevant information as possible. At the end of the day, you'll need to experiment to find what works for your project.

30.3.2 Choosing Outputs

When inputs are applied to an MLP, it computes outputs in the form of values between zero and one that represent the levels of excitation of its output nodes. For *Supreme Commander 2*, it was decided that each output node would represent the expected utility of one of the actions that the platoon could take. These actions included attack the weakest enemy, attack the closest enemy, attack the highest value enemy, attack a resource generator, attack a shield generator, attack a defensive structure, attack a mobile unit, attack an engineering unit, and attack from range. Although the platoon could run away, the act of running away was not associated with any individual output. Instead, it was decided that the platoon would run away if none of the network's outputs were above 0.5, because that indicated that no individual action was expected to have particularly high utility.

30.3.3 Choosing the Number of Hidden Nodes

It is the hidden nodes in an MLP that are responsible for its ability to learn complex nonlinear relationships, and the more hidden nodes a network has, the more complex are the relationships that it can learn. Unfortunately, increasing the number of hidden nodes also comes at the cost of increased training time and, as with increasing numbers of inputs, an increased risk of overfitting. Unfortunately, the optimum number of hidden nodes is problem dependent and must be determined by trial and error. One approach is to initially test your network with only two or three hidden nodes, and then add more until acceptable performance is achieved. For more complex decisions, it's reasonable to start with a larger network, but you will want to ensure that the trained network is thoroughly tested to make sure that its performance under test is consistent with its performance during training.

For *Supreme Commander 2*, we found that a network with 98 hidden nodes achieved good and consistent performance during both training and testing. Such a network would be too large for many other applications, particularly when the amount of training data is limited, but given our ability to generate arbitrarily large amounts of training data and the complexity of the decision being made, this worked well for us.

30.4 Training a Neural Network

Training an MLP usually involves repeatedly iterating through a set of training examples that each consist of a pairing of inputs and target outputs. For each pair, the input is presented to the network, the network computes its output, and then the network's weights and biases are modified to make its output slightly closer to the target output. This process is repeated for each example in the training set, with each example typically being presented hundreds or thousands of times during the course of training.

In *Supreme Commander 2*, we decided not to create a fixed set of training examples but to generate examples dynamically by making the AI play against itself. This was achieved by putting two AI platoons on a map and having them battle against each other as they would in a regular game, except we would run the game as fast as possible to speed up iteration time. During the battle, the AI's platoons would act the same as they would in a regular game. The AI's neural networks would make a decision as to which action should be performed whenever opposing platoons met on the battlefield by gathering data about the friendly and enemy units in a radius around the platoon and feeding that data into the MLP. Instead of actually taking the action suggested by the network, however, each platoon was made to perform a random action and a measure of how good those actions were—a measure of their utility—was derived using a fitness function. The utility measure then formed the target output for the output node corresponding to the random action, and the target outputs for all other output nodes were set to each node's current level of excitation; in this way, the network updated its weights and biases to improve its estimate of the utility of the random action but didn't attempt to change any other outputs. Random actions were used instead of the actions suggested by the networks to ensure that a good mix of actions were tried in a wide range of circumstances. An untrained network will typically repeatedly perform the same action in a wide range of circumstances and hence will learn extremely slowly—if it learns at all.

This training process produced an MLP that responded to an input by estimating the utility of each of the different actions. Choosing the best action was then a simple matter of choosing the action associated with the output that had the highest level of excitation. The key to ensuring that these actions were appropriate was to make sure that the fitness function—which assessed the utility of actions during training—assigned the highest utility to the action that was most appropriate in each situation.

30.4.1 Creating the Fitness Function

The fitness function's job is to evaluate the results of the selected action to determine how much better or worse the situation became as a result of its execution. For *Supreme Commander 2*, this was achieved by gathering the same set of data (number of units, DPS values, health, etc.) that were used to make the initial decision, and then examining how those data values changed when the action was taken.

Listing 30.1. Fitness function snippet from *Supreme Commander 2*.

```
float friendRatio = 0.0f;
int numData = 0;
for (int i = 0; i < mFriendData.size(); ++i)
{
    if (mFriendData[i] > 0.0f)
    {
        ++numData;
        friendRatio += (newFriendData[i]/mFriendData[i]);
    }
}
if (numData > 0)
    friendRatio /= numData;
float enemyRatio = 0.0f;
numData = 0;
for (int i = 0; i < mEnemyData.size(); ++i)
{
    if (mEnemyData[i] > 0.0f)
    {
        ++numData;
        enemyRatio += (newEnemyData[i]/mEnemyData[i]);
    }
}
if (numData > 0)
    enemyRatio /= numData;
DetermineNewOutputs(friendRatio, enemyRatio, mOutputs, mActionIndex);
network->FeedAndBackPropagate(mInputs, mOutputs);
```

Listing 30.1 gives a snippet of the fitness function we used on *Supreme Commander 2*. It first takes the ratio between the new and old values for each type of data. Note that since all of these values are likely to have stayed the same or gone down, all of these ratios should be between 0 and 1, which constrains the magnitude of the later calculations to something reasonable. Next, we take the average of the ratios for the friendly units and for the enemy units. This gives a sense of how much the overall tactical situation has changed for each side not only in terms of damage taken, but also in terms of every significant capability—shields, damage output, number of units remaining, and so forth. The resulting averages are passed into `DetermineNewOutputs` which determines what the correct output—called the *desired output*—value should have been using Equation 30.1.

$$desiredOutput = output \times \left(1 + \left(friendRatio - enemyRatio\right)\right) \qquad (30.1)$$

This desired output value is then plugged into the corresponding output node of the MLP, and the MLP goes through a process of adjusting weights and biases, starting at the output layer and working its way back to the input layer in a process called *back propagation*. This is how an MLP learns.

30.4.2 Adjusting Learning Parameters

The training of an MLP is typically controlled by a learning rate parameter that controls the sizes of the changes the network makes when adjusting its weights and biases. A higher learning rate allows for larger changes, which can lead to faster learning but increases the risk of numerical instability and oscillations as the network attempts to zero in on optimum values; a lower rate can make training impractically slow. One common trick is therefore to start training with a higher learning rate and decrease it over time—so you initially get fast learning but, as the weights and biases approach their optimum values, the adjustments become more and more conservative. For *Supreme Commander 2*, we initially started with a learning rate of 0.8 and gradually lowered it down to 0.2.

MLP training algorithms usually also have a parameter called *momentum*, which can be used to accelerate the learning process. Momentum does this by reapplying a proportion of the last change in the value of a weight or bias during a subsequent adjustment, thereby accelerating consistent changes and helping to prevent rapid oscillations. As with the learning rate, a higher value for the momentum parameter is good initially because it accelerates the early stages of learning. For *Supreme Commander 2* we started with a momentum value of 0.9 and eventually turned momentum off entirely by setting it to zero.

30.4.3 Debugging Neural Networks

A neural network is essentially a black box, and that makes debugging them difficult. You can't just go in, set a breakpoint, and figure out why it made the decision it did. You also can't just go in and start adjusting weights. This is a large part of the reason why neural networks are not more popular. In general, if an MLP is not performing as desired, then it's usually a problem with the data its receiving as input, the way its outputs are interpreted, the fitness function that was used during training, or the environment it was exposed to during training.

For example, if an MLP performs well during training but performs less well during testing, it could be because the environment the network was exposed to during training wasn't representative of the environment it experienced during testing. Maybe the mix of units was different, or something changed in the design? It could also be due to overfitting, in which case a network with fewer inputs or fewer hidden nodes might perform better. If an MLP performed well during training but its behavior isn't always sensible, then it might be that the fitness function that was used during training was flawed—perhaps it sometimes assigned high utility to actions that were inappropriate or low utility to actions that were appropriate—more on this point later. If an MLP fails to perform well even during training, then it's usually because either its inputs provide too little relevant information or it has too few hidden nodes to learn the desired relationships.

If you are using neural networks in a game, these points need to be stressed. When debugging neural networks, the solution is usually not to find the point of failure by setting a breakpoint. You have to think about the network's inputs, its outputs, and how your fitness function is training your neural network.

30.4.4 Case Study: Repairing a Bug in the Fitness Function

In *Supreme Commander 2*, each player starts with a unit called an ACU and whichever player destroys their opponent's ACU first wins the game. However, when an ACU is destroyed, it blows up in a large nuclear explosion, taking out most of the smaller units and buildings in a wide area. For the neural network this posed a problem: since the network was trained on tactical engagements, it didn't know about winning or losing. All it saw was that when it sent units up against an ACU, most of them were destroyed.

This introduced a bug that made the AI unwilling to commit troops to attack an ACU. It would overwhelm players with massive groups of units but, as soon as it saw an ACU, it would turn tail and run. The problem wasn't in the behavior code, and it wasn't something that could be tracked down by setting a breakpoint; the problem was in the fitness function.

Once we realized what the problem was, the solution was simple: we needed to modify the fitness function to take into account the destruction of an enemy ACU. Basically, we needed to teach the neural network that it was worth taking out an ACU whatever the cost. This was done by modifying the fitness function to provide a very positive measure of utility whenever an enemy ACU was destroyed. Instead of relying on the results of Equation 30.1, the fitness function would return a desired output of double whatever the original MLP output was, clamped to a maximum of 1.0. After retraining the network with the new fitness function, we saw a huge improvement. The AI would run from the ACU if it only had a small number of units but, if it had a large enough group to take it down, it would engage, winning the game as the enemy's ACU blew up in spectacular fashion.

30.5 Adjusting Behavior

Even though the behavior of an MLP is fixed once it's been trained, it's still possible to use it to generate AI that exhibits a variety of different behaviors. In *Supreme Commander 2*, for example, we added an aggression value to the AI personality. This value was used to modify the ratios that were input to the MLP to mimic the effect of the AI's units being stronger than they actually were. This made the MLP overestimate the utility of more aggressive actions, producing an overall more aggressive AI.

Rather than always having the AI perform the action for which the MLP estimated highest utility, different action selection schemes could be considered. For example, the AI could select one of the N highest utility actions at random or select an action with probability proportional to its utility. Both of these schemes would produce behavior with greater variety though they both involve selecting actions that are probably suboptimal and hence would probably produce AI that is easier to beat.

30.6 Neural Network Performance

The run-time performance of an MLP is determined by how many nodes it has. In *Supreme Commander 2*, each MLP has 34 input nodes, 15 output nodes, and 98 hidden nodes and we never saw a network take longer than 0.03 ms to compute its output (during an eight-player AI match). Since feeding a MLP forward is basically just a bunch of floating-point math, this is not surprising. Performance will, of course, vary depending on hardware and the details of your implementation, but it is unlikely that the time taken to query an MLP will be a problem.

30.7 Benefits of Using a Neural Network

Probably the most notable benefit of using a neural network over something like a utility based approach is that you don't have to come up with the weights yourself. You don't have to figure out whether health is more important than shields in any particular decision or how they compare to speed. This is all worked out for you during training. Each of *Supreme Commander 2*'s neural networks took about an hour of training to reach a shippable level of performance. We did, however, have to complete the training process several times before we ended up with a set of neural networks that worked well, mostly due to snags such as the ACU problem that was mentioned earlier.

A major benefit of the input representation that was used in *Supreme Commander 2* was that it provided an abstract representation of the composition of a platoon that remained valid even when the statistics of individual units changed; the neural network is not looking at specific units, only their statistics. As long as there weren't any radical changes in the game's mechanics, the networks were able to continue to make good decisions as the statistics of individual units were modified to produce a well-balanced game.

30.8 Drawbacks of Using Neural Networks

Like most things in life, using a neural network solution doesn't come free. There are certainly some drawbacks to using them over more traditional methods, the foremost of those being their black box nature. With most solutions you can come up with a tool that designers can use to adjust the behavior of the AI; at the very least you can make small adjustments to alter its behavior to suit their needs. With neural networks this is difficult, if not altogether impossible. On *Supreme Commander 2*, we got lucky because we had a separate AI system for the campaign mode than we did for skirmish mode. The designers could make any changes they wanted for the campaign but they did not want to have control over skirmish mode. Unfortunately, most projects are not that lucky.

The other issue is the training time. Unlike with other techniques, where you can easily make small changes, if you change anything to do with a neural network—its inputs, the interpretation of its outputs, the fitness function, and the number of hidden nodes—you have to start training from scratch. Even though training is hands-off, the time it takes makes it difficult to quickly try things out.

30.9 Conclusion

Whenever the subject of neural networks in *Supreme Commander 2* comes up, two questions are frequently asked: Was it worth using them, and would you use them again? The answer to both is yes. We firmly believe that the AI in *Supreme Commander 2* would not have had the same impact without the use of neural networks. Moreover, if someone proposed doing *Supreme Commander 3*, you can bet neural networks would play a part.

That being said, neural networks are not for every project, and they are certainly not the be-all and end-all of AI. Neural networks are a tool like any other in that they have specific strengths and weaknesses. They are very handy if you have a well-defined set of actions or responses and designers don't require a lot of control. If your designers are going to want to fine-tune things or you have to work with multiple sets of responses to accommodate things like different AI personalities, however, you may want to look at other options.

References

[Buckland 02] M. Buckland. *AI Techniques for Game Programming*. Cincinnati, OH: Premier Press, 2002, pp. 233–274.

[Manslow 01] J. Manslow. *Game Programming Gems 2: Using a Neural Network in a Game: A Concrete Example*. Hingham, MA: Charles River Media, 2001, pp. 351–357.

[Millington 09] I. Millington and J. Funge. *Artificial Intelligence for Games*. Burlington, MA: Morgan Kaufmann, 2009, pp. 646–665.

PART V
Agent Awareness and Knowledge Representation

Part V

31

Crytek's Target Tracks Perception System

Rich Welsh

31.1 Introduction

All our knowledge has its origins in our perceptions.

—Leonardo da Vinci

Perception is something that we all take for granted on a day-to-day basis. Without the ability to see, hear, smell, touch, and taste, we would know nothing of the world around us, nor would we have the means to communicate with one another.

One of the greatest challenges in writing good, believable AI is making "artificial intelligence" appear as "natural intelligence." As developers we have omnipotence in the virtual world that we create—passing information to AI agents without the limitations of mimicking human perception is as easy as calling a function.

```
pAIAgent->ThePlayerIsHere(position);
```

A scene in the film *The Matrix* features the protagonist being guided out of an office to avoid capture by a disembodied voice over a phone. With our access to the state of the game world, we could easily pass knowledge about targets and/or threats to AI agents in this way; however, once players realize that the AI are cheating, then they naturally tend to feel cheated. In this sense, "natural intelligence" could also be considered "artificial stupidity." The AI agents have access to any and all information about the state of the

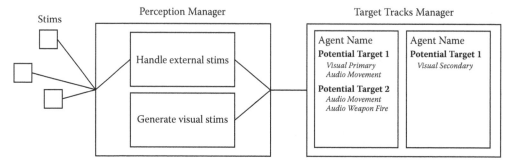

Figure 31.1

System overview. (The term *stim* is an abbreviation for "stimulus.")

game world at any time, but in order to make them act more believably, more human, we intentionally withhold this knowledge from them.

So if allowing the AI agents to directly query information from the game gives them too much knowledge, what other options are available? Quite simply, the best way to keep agents from knowing too much is to give them limitations similar to those of a human player's. Since the player determines the state of the game world through interpreting sights and sounds, the AI should attempt to simulate that as convincingly as possible.

While trying to simulate the perception of stimuli by AI, the primary focus of this system is target selection and prioritization. When faced with several potential targets (e.g., hostile agents, the player, etc.), which should an AI agent select to engage?

The system that Crytek implemented to both simulate limited perception and handle target selection is called the Target Tracks Perception System (TTPS). Originally written for *Crysis 2* by Kevin Kirst, the TTPS has proven robust and adaptable enough to be used again for all of Crytek's current projects, becoming an integral part of the *CryENGINE 3's* AI system.

31.2 System Overview

The TTPS comprises three main sections:

- *Stims*: These are data representations of perceivable events (or stimuli) that occur in the world. (See Figure 31.1.)
- *Perception manager*: This is responsible for handling, processing, and, in some cases, generating stims.
- *Target Track manager*: This manager is responsible for storing and updating every agent's perceptions over time, as well as containing logic for prioritizing targets.

31.3 Stims

Any in-game stimuli originating from a potential target (any current targets included) need to be handled in a consistent manner. By creating a simple structure that contains data about perceivable events and a handler that can interpret them, we're able to create an interface that allows AI agents to start making sense of the world around them. In the TTPS, this structure is referred to as a stim (an abbreviation of the word stimulus).

Stims need to contain the following information in order to describe an event: The type of stimulus being generated (discussed later in this section), the entity ID of the source, the position or direction from which the stimulus originated, and a radius within which that stimulus can be perceived. Additional information such as a second entity ID can be useful as more special case events are added to the game, though the majority of events can be described using the initial set of data outlined above. For example, a stim generated by footsteps would contain the type `AUDIO_MOVEMENT`, the position of the footstep, and the entity ID of the character that generated it. However, a stim generated for a box that was thrown will need the type `AUDIO_COLLISION`, the position in which the box collided with the world, the entity ID of the box, and the entity ID of the character that threw the box (in order to determine whether the action was performed by a friendly character or a hostile one).

Before stims even reach the perception handling logic, there must be a way to filter them to avoid unnecessary processing of unimportant stims. Not every agent is interested in every event, so ignoring those stims from the start is an immediate way of cutting down the amount of stim traffic that needs to be handled. Having agents subscribe to event types that they are interested in and comparing that to the event type of a stim makes this a very cheap test.

The second way that stims can be filtered is by looking at both the perception range of each agent and the perceivable radius that is part of the stim data. If the agent is too far away to perceive this stim, then it can be discarded.

Finally, in each agent's perception configuration, event types can be registered with flags such as "hostile only," allowing events of this type generated by friendly agents to be ignored. This can make quite a big difference in reducing the volume of stims that need handling, as in a lot of FPS games the only hostile target that AI agents will encounter is the player, meaning that any events generated by other AI agents will not be processed.

31.3.1 Types of Stims

With a well-defined stim structure and a simple interface to pass stims through to the perception manager, stims can be created from anywhere in your codebase. While the majority of stims that get generated tend to fall into the categories of sight and sound, there are some that don't fit either category and as such are a more special case. The three types are discussed in the following sections.

31.3.1.1 Sound

While initially it may seem like every sound would generate a perceivable event, generally there are only a few sounds that the AI would be interested in. For example, most environmental sounds are of no interest to AI agents—ambient sounds such as birdsong or mechanical whirrs add ambience to the game for a player, but they don't give the AI any useful information about potential threats and targets. On the other hand, aggressive sounds such as explosions and weapon fire are of high importance to the agents, as identifying the source may keep them from harm or perhaps allow them to come to the aid of a colleague in combat.

In *CryENGINE*, the code that handles weapon firing generates these stims in parallel to firing the weapon. Since the "fire" event is triggered from the animation system, this means that the animation, audio cue, visuals (muzzle flash, tracer, etc.) are synced up with the gunshot audio stim. Although it might be too late for the agent to react and dodge, it lends itself to a more realistic perception model. Explosions are handled similarly, with the code that is responsible for generating the explosion generating the stim as well.

Collision sounds are a more complex type of event. While they are generated in the same way as regular stims, the notion of a collision having hostility is difficult to represent. In these cases, we "cheat" by having both the entity ID from the source of the sound (the item that caused the collision) and an additional entity ID of the character that was responsible for the collision stored in the stim. For example, an AI agent bumping into a barrel would send a stim with the barrel's ID as the source, and the clumsy agent's ID as extra data. By doing this, the perception manager is able to use the secondary ID to determine if a friendly agent caused the collision (and thus potentially ignore the stim). If a player caused the collision noise (by throwing a prop or knocking something over), then the collision would be treated as suspicious by the AI, since the collision was generated by a hostile.

31.3.1.2 Sight

In order to tell whether an AI agent is able to see something, most games tend to use a raycast from the agent to the target. While this does test whether there's a clear line of sight between the two, it can start to get expensive very quickly. For example, in our games we try to limit the number of active AI agents to 16. This means that every agent can potentially see 15 other AI characters. In the worst case scenario, this could mean 120 raycasts being requested to check visibility between all the AI agents, even before the player is considered!

In the AI system used for *Crackdown 2*, each agent could register how hostile a target needed to be before visibility checks should be done. These hostility levels were *hostile*, *neutral*, and *friendly*. By having AI agents register an interest in only hostile targets, this meant that any nonhostile targets became invisible to the agent, dramatically reducing the amount of raycasts required. Should a target change hostility (for example, going from being a neutral to a hostile target), the AI system will start or stop visibility tests as required.

When originally developing the AI for *Crackdown 2*, every agent tested against every other agent and the player. This would mean that in an environment with 16 active agents and the player, 136 raycasts would be required. After the optimization of having agents only register interest in hostile targets, only 16 raycasts would be required (assuming all of the AI agents were regarded as non-hostile to one another).

Further optimizations can be made to the generation of visual stims. In the *CryAISystem*, every agent has a view distance and a field of view. A lot of unnecessary raycasts can be avoided by doing these much cheaper tests to see if potential visual targets are even within an agent's view cone before requesting a raycast.

31.3.1.3 Special Case

The remaining few stims tend to be events that you want to make your AI aware of, but don't fit under the normal categories of sight or sound. For some of these events, you can effectively treat them as a dog whistle—create a sound stim without playing any audio and send that to the perception manager. These stims are then just handled in whatever way you need them to be.

Table 31.1 Examples of events that could generate stims

Stimulus type	Stimulus name	Description
Visual	Primary FOV	An agent is visible within the agent's primary FOV
Visual	Secondary FOV	An agent is visible within the agent's secondary FOV
Visual	Thrown object	An object that was thrown has been seen moving
Visual	Dead body	A body has been seen
Audio	Movement	Target has made sound while moving, e.g., footsteps
Audio	Loud movement	Target has made a loud sound while moving, e.g., landing from a fall, footsteps while sprinting
Audio	Bullet rain	Bullets are passing nearby
Audio	Collision	A physics collision has occurred
Audio	Loud collision	A "loud" physics collision has occurred
Audio	Weapon	A weapon has been fired
Audio	Explosion	An explosion has occurred

For stims that can't be treated as a sound, extra data is usually required. An example from our games is *bullet rain*. When bullet rain is occurring, the AI don't necessarily know the point of origin (or the hostility, though we pass the shooter's ID with the stim so that we can add the bullet rain to the appropriate *target track*—as explained in Section 31.5 Target Tracks); however the direction the bullet rain is coming from is known. As such, this type of stim needs to be handled slightly differently to a sound, having the agent react to being under fire without knowing the shooter's position immediately (Table 31.1).

31.4 Perception Manager

The perception manager is the middle management of the TTPS. It provides a single point of entry for stims into the system while also doing some specific case handling and stim generation of its own. Since stims can come from anywhere in the codebase, having this single entry point means that only one interface needs to be opened up to the rest of the game. Stims all share the same basic structure, which means that further encapsulation is possible by having only a single function exposed within that interface. After this point, the TTPS can become a black box to the rest of the code base, with a minimal interface consisting of functions for registering stims and querying the best current target for a given agent.

As mentioned earlier in the article, the perception manager is responsible for not only receiving external stims, but also generating some internally. As it's a centralized place to forward valid stims to the target tracks manager, it makes sense to put this logic here.

The stims that are generated from within the perception manager are all visual. Having a list of all active AI agents, the perception manager can iterate through each in turn, testing to see whether that particular agent can see any of the known observables (in the case of the *CryAISystem*, the list of known observables is a list containing all active characters, including players). If an observable is within the view distance and FOV for the active AI, an asynchronous raycast is performed. (As raycasts are expensive to perform and the visibility tests aren't urgent enough to require the results within the same frame, requesting deferred raycasts is perfectly acceptable.) On receiving the result of the raycast, a clear line of sight means generating a visual stim and passing that to the target tracks manager.

Having sight stims generated in such a way works fine for the majority of cases, but doesn't allow agents to have a peripheral vision. In order to accomplish that, we use another set of values for a secondary view distance and FOV. If an observable is within this secondary range of vision but not the primary (and still receives a clear raycast), then a secondary visual stim is sent to the target tracks manager. This stim has both a lower peak perception value (this value is used for stim prioritization when selecting a target, and is explained further in Section 31.6 ADSR Envelopes) than the primary stim and a longer attack time. By having a longer attack time, a target that is in the peripheral will take longer to identify than one that is in the primary FOV. Should the target move from the peripheral FOV into the agent's primary FOV, the primary visual stim will take priority over the secondary. These values are explained in more detail in a later section.

31.5 Target Tracks

Each agent in the game world needs to keep track of any targets that they identify. This is important when developing the behavior of the agents, as it can be used to identify which target to prioritize in a situation where several are present.

Once a stim has been sent from an event and passed through to the target track manager, that target has been perceived by the agent and becomes tracked. When keeping track of a target, any and all stims received (and converted into envelopes, as explained in Section 31.6 ADSR Envelopes) from that target are then stored together in a single *Target Track*. This container of envelopes represents all the perception that a particular agent has of a single target. By storing the envelopes in this way, we can make *Target Tracks* responsible for the envelopes that they contain—updating the perception values over time and eventually removing them once they have expired.

Each *Target Track* will only remember a maximum of one envelope per event type. As each *Track* is associated with a specific target, new envelopes received with an event type equal to that of an existing envelope in that *Track* will simply update the outdated one.

By using the highest envelope value within a *Track* as the overall value of that *Track* (and therefore the value for that *Track*'s target), finding the best target for an agent is as simple as choosing the *Track* with the highest value.

31.6 ADSR Envelopes

Once the stims have been filtered by the perception manager, the data used to test their validity isn't required by the target tracks manager. The only information that is needed at this point is the source of the stim. Rather than store stims directly, the target track manager creates ADSR envelopes (the terminology is based on the system used in music synthesizers; see Figure 31.2).

When a stim is initially received, an envelope is created and given a *perception value*, which will be used to compare the importance of this stim against others. This value is ticked over time, remaining constant as stims of the same event type from the same source continue to be received. Once stims stop being received, the event is no longer perceivable and as such the value starts to decrease.

Each event type can have a different peak value. This means that if a single target (e.g., the same agent or player) is the source of multiple different stimuli, some will have a

Part V. Agent Awareness and Knowledge Representation

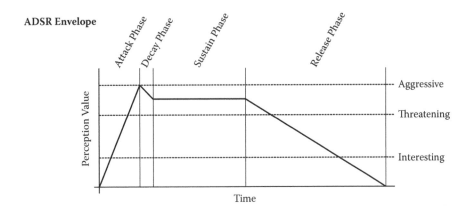

ADSR Envelope

Attack Phase · Decay Phase · Sustain Phase · Release Phase

Perception Value

Aggressive

Threatening

Interesting

Time

Figure 31.2

Graph demonstrating how the perception value for an ADSR envelope changes over time.

heavier weighting towards target selection. This peak value is an arbitrary number defined in a configuration file, but should be balanced across all event types. For example, in our current stim configuration, footsteps peak at a perception value of 25, weapon sounds peak at 50, and primary FOV visual stimuli peak at 100. This means that if one target can be heard firing a weapon and also seen, then the visual stim would be considered the most important event that's currently being perceived.

31.6.1 Envelope phases

ADSR envelopes are broken down into the following four phases.

31.6.1.1 Attack

The attack phase has three parameters, ignore time, peak value, and time. When a new stim is received, an envelope is created and started in the attack phase. During this phase the value of the envelope will rise from 0 to that peak value over the specified amount of time. The ignore time is the delay from after a stim is generated to when the AI will perceive it. This is usually set to 0 as most stims want to be registered immediately; however, in some special cases (such as faking speed of sound delays) it can be useful.

31.6.1.2 Decay

The decay phase only takes time as a parameter. After the peak of the attack phase has been reached, the envelope value can drop slightly over the time specified in the decay phase. The value that the envelope decays to is specified in the sustain parameters. This decay is so that new stims have a chance of being recognized as a higher priority over stims that have been sustained for a while.

31.6.1.3 Sustain

The sustain phase takes a fraction of the peak value. Once the decay phase has finished, the envelope will be sustained at the perception value equal to the fraction specified of the peak. This phase remains active for as long as the stim is still valid, and as such the envelope value will remain constant throughout. By having a sustain fraction of 1, the envelope will remain at peak value until it enters the release phase.

31.6.1.4 Release

The release phase takes a time as a parameter. Once the stim is no longer valid, the envelope enters the release phase. For a sound this is immediately after the sound stops and for a visual it is when stims for that visual are no longer being received (usually because line of sight with the source has been lost). During the release phase, the envelope value slowly decreases until it either reaches 0 or the stim becomes valid once more.

31.6.2 Modifiers

While the base value of the envelope can be used to determine target prioritization, all stims of the same type (for different targets) that are in the sustain phase will have equal weighting. With this in mind, modification multipliers are applied to the base envelope values in order to help further weight them based on user specified criterion.

The TTPS supports a whole range of multipliers for different stims. The most beneficial of the multipliers that we use is one based on distance; targets that are close to the AI get a multiplier of 1, whereas targets 50 m or further away receive a multiplier of 0. This multiplier scales linearly based on distance, that is, a target 25 m from the AI would have its envelope value multiplied by 0.5.

31.6.3 Pulses

Pulses are artificial boosts to an envelope's value that are triggered through code. In the example configuration below (see Listing 31.1), there is a pulse set up to add an extra 12.5 to the primary visual envelope's threat value, that will decay down to 0 over 7.5 seconds. To trigger a pulse, a signal is sent to the perception manager with the name of the pulse and the agent to whom it's being applied. The one in the example is used if the agent is chasing ("sticking to") a target. By sending a pulse, it helps keep the target currently being chased the best target, even if a second target is spotted in the primary FOV.

31.6.4 Threat Levels

Threat levels are used more for the agent's behavior than in choosing a target. Once a target has been designated as the best available option for an agent, the threat level of that "best target" can be obtained and the behavior responds accordingly. Threat levels are stored as a percentage of the peak envelope value, as seen in the example perception configuration file in Listing 31.1.

31.7 Data Driving Perception

Stims need to be converted to ADSR Envelopes for the perception manager, though different agents may want to weight stims differently when it comes to target prioritization. For example, should you have an agent that is blind, then visual stims wouldn't register at all, but audio stims would have much higher weightings. The way that we've chosen to do this is by having a set of configuration files for stim/envelope setup written in XML. (In the case where all AI agents want to have the same perception, only a single configuration file would be needed.) Listing 31.1 is an example of how a stim is configured in the TTPS.

Listing 31.1. A perception configuration file.

```
<Stimulus name = "VisualPrimary" attack = "2" hostileOnly = "1"
peak = "100.0" sustain = "1.0" release = "40.0">
    <Modifiers>
        <Distance value = "1"/>
    </Modifiers>
    <Pulses>
        <Pulse name = "Stick" value = "12.5" duration = "7.5"/>
    </Pulses>
    <ThreatLevels>
        <Aggressive fraction = "1"/>
        <Threatening fraction = "0.625"/>
        <Interesting fraction = "0.25"/>
    </ThreatLevels>
</Stimulus>
```

Having such a flexible perception system has been very useful during development; it has allowed us to more easily tune the AI for various stealth and combat sections of the game by changing parameters in the perception configuration file. For example, increasing the time of attack on a visual stim gives the player more time to lean out of cover and look around, or dash to the next cover location without the AI spotting him immediately.

Exposing these values to the designers in data is incredibly important as well. It allows them to experiment and rapidly iterate on the AI's perception model without needing a new build of the game every time or requiring a programmer to assist them.

31.8 Conclusion

While there are plenty of different ways to model perceptions and prioritize targets, the Target Tracks perception system has proven itself to be both robust and flexible over the course of several different AAA titles. Since it was originally written, there have been very few modifications to the system, the most notable being the recent addition of the Threat Levels in the configuration file. This addition was made almost exclusively to extract more information from the TTPS, rather than to change the underlying logic or flow of the system.

Having a perception management system that is well encapsulated with a clean, minimal interface helps you keep the generation of stimuli simple. When working in large teams, the single-function interface to the perception manager makes it very easy for the rest of your team to start adding stims as and when they need to.

A free copy of the CryENGINE 3 SDK for noncommercial use is available online [CryENGINE 12], which uses the TTPS for perception handling.

References

[CryENGINE 12] CryENGINE 3 Free SDK, 2012. Available at http://mycryengine.com.

How to Catch a Ninja

NPC Awareness in a 2D Stealth Platformer

Brook Miles

32.1 Introduction

Mark of the Ninja is a 2D stealth platformer game by Klei Entertainment. The player, as the Ninja, sneaks through levels keeping to the shadows, crawling through vents, and ambushing unsuspecting guards. The engine we used, however, was based on Klei's previous game *Shank 2*, and if Shank knows one thing … it sure isn't how to be sneaky.

The AI enemies in *Shank* and *Shank 2* only cared about attackable targets (the player, or multiple players in a coop game). They would spawn, choose an appropriate player to attack when one came within range, and do so until they killed, or were killed by, that player.

This worked well for the *Shank* games, which focus on constant, head-on combat. But for *Mark of the Ninja* we needed more subtle behavior. Guards needed to have multiple levels of alertness; the player needed to be able to distract them with sounds or movement, or break line of sight to escape detection before circling back to strike from behind. Guards needed to display some awareness of their surroundings, notice when something is amiss, investigate whatever catches their attention, and respond to fallen comrades.

To address the need for AI characters to be aware of events and objects in the world around them, one of the changes we implemented was a data-driven interest system that allows designers or scripters to define **interest sources** in the world, and have agents detect and respond to them appropriately.

In *Mark of the Ninja*, targets and interests are similar concepts; they each represent an object with a position in the game world that an agent is aware of and should react to. However, there are a significant number of differences, both in the data used to represent each concept and in the associated behavior of the agents, which resulted in the decision to implement them as separate entities within the game.

Perhaps most importantly, all targets are basically created equal: if it's an enemy, shoot it! Most of the processing going on while an agent has a target is dedicated to tracking its position and attacking it. An agent that has a target will always be on high alert, and will disregard most other stimuli until either it or its target is dead. Interests, on the other hand, represent things that are not targets; they are assumed to be stationary but are much more numerous and varied, as we will see later. When an agent has an interest, it will usually attempt to investigate the interest and search the surrounding area, all the while keeping an eye out for targets, or other potential interests of greater importance.

32.2 From Shank to Ninja—Noticing Things Other Than Your Target

As part of the *Ninja* branch from the *Shank 2* source tree, agents initially gained the ability to notice **points of interest**. A point of interest consisted simply of a 2D point in the level, something to approach but not necessarily shoot at.

These points of interest were created in the update loops of each agent's brain from sources such as sounds, dead bodies, and broken lights. The update loop would collect and iterate over each type of game object or, in the case of sounds, a simple list of 2D points. After the list of potential interests was collected, one would be chosen based on proximity, or other hard-coded criteria, to be the current interest which the agent would then respond to. This setup worked in some cases, but there were significant problems that we wanted to overcome.

First, if the designer wanted an agent to take interest in any new and previously undefined object or event, they would need to request a programmer to add a new set of checks into the brain, and possibly new data structures to track whatever was being sensed. It was already apparent at the time that this process could be tedious and time consuming, but it ultimately would have proven to be a serious limitation. We ended up with around 60 different types of interest sources in the game and development may have been seriously hampered by this programmer-dependent process.

Second, there was no accounting for multiple agents reacting to the same point of interest. If you made a loud noise, everyone nearby would come running, which makes some sense, but what if you just broke a light? Does it make sense for a group of four guards all to walk over and stare dumbly up at the light, each remarking separately to themselves that somebody really ought to do something about that broken light?

If a group of agents standing together detects an interest source, ideally one or two of that "group" (see Section 2.5 for more on how *Ninja* deals with groups) would be dispatched to check it out, while the rest are simply put on alert and hang back waiting for the result of the search. Not only does this feel more natural, it provides more interesting gameplay opportunities to the player, allowing them to separate closely clustered guards and deal with them individually off in a dark corner, instead of running into a brightly lit room and getting shot by five guys with automatic weapons.

32.3 Senses

We determined that fundamentally there were two broad categories of interest sources our agents needed to detect in the world, things they could see, and things they could hear, which gave us our two senses: **sight** and **sound**.

Detection by the sight test involves a series of checks including these questions: Is the interest source within one of the agent's **vision cones**? Is the game object associated with the interest source currently lit by a light source, or does the agent have the night vision flag, which removes this requirement? Is there any collision blocking line of sight between the agent's eye position and that of the interest source?

A vision cone, as shown in Figure 32.1, is typically defined by an offset and direction from the agent's eye position, an angle defining how wide it is, and a maximum distance. Other vision geometry is possible as well; we have some which are simply a single ray, an entire circle, or a square or trapezoid for specific purposes.

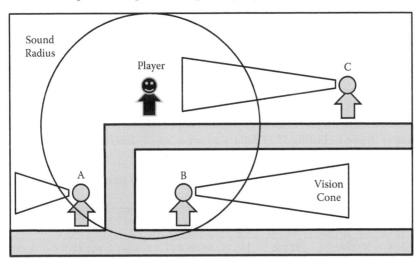

Figure 32.1

The player has made a noise by running, represented by the Sound Radius circle. Guard A will hear the sound and turn around to investigate. Guard B is within the Sound Radius but can't hear the sound because there is no path from the guard to the sound source. Guard C is outside the Sound Radius and can't hear the sound; however, if the player enters Guard C's vision cone, the player will be spotted.

Detection by sound is determined by pathfinding from the interest source's position to the position of the agent's head. When a designer exports a level from our level editor, one of the steps is to generate a triangle mesh from all of the empty space within the level (we also generate the inverse mesh, of all of the solid collision in the level, for the purposes of rendering the map). We use this "sound mesh" at runtime to perform A* pathfinding [Millington 06] from the "sound" interest source to any agent who might potentially hear it.

This same pathfinding operation is performed by the audio system between the player character and the source of sound events within the world to determine the amount of filtering to apply. Both the sound and map meshes were generated using the program **Triangle** by Jonathan Shewchuck [Shewchuk 05], which generates very clean meshes and has a variety of useful options to control mesh quality, density, and other interesting properties for those more mathematically inclined.

For both performance and gameplay reasons, sight and sound interest sources define a maximum radius, and only agents within that radius are tested to determine whether they can detect the interest source.

32.4 Definition of Interest Sources

From our two core senses, we can now allow the designers to create an **interest source** representing whatever object or event they want, so long as it can be detected via the sight or sound tests. Designers can specify a "gunshot" sound, or a "footstep" sound, a "corpse" sight, or a "suspect" sight. The agent's behavioral scripts can use the specified interest source type to determine any special behavior, but the backend only needs to know how to determine whether the agent can see or hear the interest source.

You can also bend the definition of "sight" and "sound" somewhat. One special case of agent in *Mark of the Ninja* is guard dogs, who we want to be able to "smell" the player in the dark but, for gameplay reasons, only over a very short distance. In this case, instead of needing to create an entirely new smell test, we can simply define a sight interest source which is attached to the player game object, and require that any agent noticing it have the "dog" tag as shown in Listing 32.1. Voila, we have a "smell" interest.

Listing 32.1. Just a couple of the 60 or so different interest source declarations used in the final game.

```
CreateInterestSource {sense = "sound", priority =
    INTEREST_PRIORITY_NOISE_LOUD, radius = RUN_ON_LOUD_RADIUS,
    ttl = 4*FRAMES, offset = {0, 1.5*TILES}, forgetlosttarget = true}

CreateInterestSource{sense = "sight", source = "suspect", priority =
    INTEREST_PRIORITY_SUSPECT, radius = INTEREST_RADIUS_SUSPECT, ttl =
    INTEREST_TTL_FOREVER, canberediscovered = true, noduplicateradius = 0,
    removeduplicates = true, followowner = true, condition =
    HasAttributeTag("dog")}
```

32.4.1 Interest Sources Live in the World, Interests Live in Your Brain

An **interest** is just the record in the agent's brain of what he's interested in right this moment. It may have a reference to the interest source that created it (if there was one), but even if it doesn't, it still has a copy of all of the necessary information, the sense for the interest, the source type, its position, priority, and so on. When an agent is determined to have detected an interest source, an interest record is added to its brain, and this is the information that the agent uses from that point on.

While sight and sound are the only available sense types for interest sources in *Mark of the Ninja*, interests of any arbitrarily defined sense can be added directly to an agent's brain by the designer through a script call, as no additional testing needs to be done against them; the designer or script writer has already determined that this agent should be interested in whatever it is.

For example a "touch" interest may be added to an agent's brain when he is struck with a dart projectile, or a "missing partner" interest can be added if the agent's partner goes off to investigate a sound and fails to return.

32.5 Driving Updates from Interest Sources and Lightweight Group Behavior

A question that arose early on was how groups of agents should respond when they all sense an interest simultaneously. At first it was every man for himself; each agent did its own test and upon sensing an interest would react, most likely by running to investigate it. This typically resulted in entire groups of agents running towards the slightest noise or converging on the player en masse. This wasn't the kind of gameplay we were looking for. We want the player to be able to manipulate the agents, distract them, split them apart, and dispatch them on the player's own terms.

We looked for ways in which we could have some level of apparent cooperation between the agents without going so far as to explicitly manage group behavior or coordinated movement. We really only needed guards reacting to the same thing, at the same time, to have a variety of responses. Some should go and investigate, one might play a line of audio dialog telling another nearby guard to go check it out, and others might just glance over and wait for the previously mentioned guards to deal with the situation. Instead of driving this scenario from the agent side and attempting to coordinate updates, or creating a separate concept of grouping, we chose to rely on the implicit group that already existed: the set of agents who detected an interest.

By driving the detection of interest sources from the interest source itself, instead of from each agent individually, we can easily collect all of the information we need in order to determine who should be reacting, and how they should react.

The sensory manager update loop tests each interest source against all possible "detection candidates." Given this list, it makes some decisions based mainly on group size, but possibly also by location or distance from the interest source. If only a single agent can detect the interest, our work is done, the agent is notified, and he goes to investigate. If more than one agent can detect the interest, we can assign **roles** to each agent, which are stored along with the interest record in the agent's brain. Roles only have meaning within the context of a specific interest, and when that interest is forgotten or replaced, the role associated with it goes away too.

If multiple agents can detect the interest, one is chosen as the "sentry" or "group leader" and he plays audio dialog telling the other agents nearby to go check out the interest and then hangs back waiting. One or more agents are given the "investigate" role and will go and investigate, seemingly at the command of the "group leader." Any remaining agents will get the "bystander" role, and may indicate they've seen or heard the interest but otherwise hold position and decrease the priority of the interest in their mind so they are more likely to notice new interests for which they might be chosen as leader or investigator.

The key is that once the roles are assigned, and the sensory update is complete, there is no "group" to manage. Each agent is acting independently, but due to the roles that were assigned, they behave differently from each other in a way that implies group coordination.

32.6 Prioritizing Interests

If you are investigating a broken light and come across a dead body, should you stop and investigate the body, or continue to look at the light? What if you hear your partner being stabbed by a Ninja, and then discover a broken light on your way to help him? Should you stop to investigate? Clearly, certain types of interest must be prioritized over others.

Interest sources, and by extension interest entries in agents' brains, contain a simple integer value of **priority**, where higher priority interests can replace lower or equal priority interests, and the agent will change his focus accordingly. If the agent currently holds a high priority interest, lower priorities interests are discarded and never enter the agent's awareness.

Balancing the priority of various interests turned out to be a challenging and ongoing task all throughout development. Listing 32.2 shows what the priorities for various types of interest sources were near the end of the project, but they had changed many times during development in response to unanticipated or blatantly unrealistic behavior, resulting from the current set of interest priorities. Making them easy to change and try out new combinations was a big help.

Initially, we assumed that finding corpses would be one of the highest priority interests in the game, superseded only by seeing a target (the player), but it turned out to be not so

Listing 32.2. *Mark of the Ninja's* priority definitions for interests.

```
INTEREST_PRIORITY_LOWEST = 0
INTEREST_PRIORITY_BROKEN = 1
INTEREST_PRIORITY_MISSING = 2
INTEREST_PRIORITY_SUSPECT = 4
INTEREST_PRIORITY_SMOKE = 4
INTEREST_PRIORITY_CORPSE = 4
INTEREST_PRIORITY_NOISE_QUIET = 4
INTEREST_PRIORITY_NOISE_LOUD = 4
INTEREST_PRIORITY_BOX = 5
INTEREST_PRIORITY_SPIKEMINE = 5
INTEREST_PRIORITY_DISTRACTIONFLARE = 10
INTEREST_PRIORITY_TERROR = 20
```

simple. If you hear a sound, and while investigating the sound you discover a body, clearly it makes sense to pay attention to this new discovery. But what if the situation were reversed? If you're investigating a body and you hear a sound, should you ignore it? This is potentially very unwise, especially if the noise is footsteps rapidly approaching you from behind.

It turns out that corpses, noises, and a variety of other specific interest types should all be treated on a newest-first basis. The last thing you notice is probably the most important thing. Our solution here was simply to make this set of interests all the same priority. However, new interests of equal priority (to your current interest) are treated as more important.

Other interests truly are more or less important than others, regardless of the order they are encountered. Seeing a broken pot is always less interesting than a shadowy figure or a gunshot. Seeing your partner impaled on a spike trap is always more important than the sound of glass breaking in the distance.

32.7 Investigation and Rediscoverability

Once an interest source has been noticed by an agent, the agent has an opportunity to "investigate" it, which might simply mean looking at a broken light and commenting that it should be fixed. Or it could involve seeing a fallen comrade, running over to check for a pulse, and then calling the alarm.

Once an agent determines that an interest source has been dealt with, particularly in the case of mundane things like broken lights, we really don't want every guard that walks past to stop and take notice. This would be repetitive and doesn't make for especially compelling gameplay. Even worse would be the same agent noticing the same interest source over and over. When an agent has completed whatever investigation is called for, the interest source associated with the agent's interest record is marked as investigated, which then removes the interest source (but not the game object it was associated with) from the world, never to be seen or heard of again.

This still doesn't completely solve our problem, though; in the case of corpses, for example, what happens if you draw the attention of a guard who is investigating a body before he has a chance to thoroughly investigate and sound the alarm? After losing his target, he may turn around and see the body again. It doesn't make sense for him to be as surprised to see his fallen comrade as he was a moment ago. It would be natural for him to return to complete his initial investigation, but this ultimately felt like going a little bit too far down the rabbit hole. We made the decision that each agent would be aware of only one interest at a time and there would be no stack or queue of interests. Once the highest priority interest was dealt with at any given time, we wanted the situation to naturally reset to a default state and not have the guard continuing on to revisit every past source of interest they may have come across during an encounter.

By default then, we only want each agent to detect or notice each interest source once. When that happens, we record that this discovery took place and that agent will be excluded from noticing the interest source again. Since we drive updates from the direction of interest sources looking for agents to discover them, the interest source keeps a list of discoverers and doesn't cause itself to be noticed by the same agent twice.

In rare cases, we do want an interest source to be noticeable multiple times by the same agent, the primary example being the "suspect" interest source attached to the player. This interest source is detectable from farther away than the agent's ability to see the player as a target, and so draws them in to investigate without immediately seeing and shooting the player. We want this to happen every time the agent detects the player, and so this particular interest source is marked as being rediscoverable, and it doesn't bother keeping a list of who has seen it in the past.

32.8 Using Interests for Lightweight Agent Scripting

In addition to allowing agents to passively notice events or objects in the world, there are various situations in the course of designing the game levels where some level of scripted encounter is desired. In some cases that scripting is quite rigid; you want an agent to play specific animations at certain times and at specific places. For these cases, more specific level scripts are created.

Other times, however, it's acceptable or desired to set up a more natural situation and let it play out, possibly with interference from the player. Instead of scripting an agent to follow a specific path to a specific point, play a specific line of dialog, and so on, an interest can be added directly to the agent's brain. The agent will then pathfind normally to their destination interest point, opening doors and so on as he goes. On reaching his destination, he will perform his normal search pattern. When he gets there, he may notice the object placed there for him to notice, in which case he can comment on it and continue investigating as usual or perform other contextual actions as a result.

The benefit of this simple approach is that no special handling needs to occur if the player alters the parameters of the situation. Perhaps the player distracts the agent before he reaches his goal. Or perhaps the player turns off the lights in the room the agent is headed towards, preventing him from noticing what he would have in the first case, causing him to give up and return to his patrol. No special cases need to be scripted for these situations, as the agent's behavior wasn't a script to begin with.

Other objects that the agent encounters, as this situation plays out, can be handled locally by behavior scripts independently of (or in conjunction with) the agent's current interests. Agents know how to open doors and turn on lights as they encounter them, and it's not necessary for these actions to interfere with interest handling.

Creating an interest for every possible little thing in the world that the agent can interact with is unnecessary and unwieldy, partly because of the rule of having only a single interest at a time. When an agent comes across a door, he doesn't need to be interested in it; his navigation and behavior scripts simply determine he needs to walk through a door and acts accordingly, after which he continues on his way investigating whatever his current interest is.

32.9 Limitations and Improvements

We found it difficult to achieve sensible behavior from agents who are receiving quickly repeating or alternating interests. It's not always immediately obvious what an agent should do when his current interest changes or moves from moment to moment. While this is primarily a problem outside the scope of interest detection, there was some special handling done in order to help address the issue. Specifically, when acquiring a new interest, the agent will compare the incoming interest to the current interest if any. If it's the same sense, source type, priority, and is relatively close to the previous interest, then it's not handled as a new interest, but the timers and position of the current interest are updated to reflect the new information. A primary example of this is the player creating a series of footstep interests while running. It's not desirable to treat each footstep as a new interest.

Similarly, there is no direct support for tracking the movement of a single source of interest, as the vast majority of interest sources in the game have a fixed position. This imposes some limitations on their use; for example, one of the player's inventory items in *Mark of the Ninja* is a box made of cardboard that you can hide in. One implementation involved attaching an interest source to the box when the player (hiding inside) moved, as a way to draw the attention of nearby agents. However, this didn't result in the desired behavior, as most of the interest source handling code and scripts relied on an interest's position not changing after detection.

Section 32.4 touches on the idea of providing a "condition" that is evaluated against agents who may potentially detect an interest source. This functionality was added towards the end of the project and as a result didn't end up being used extensively. When used with caution, it can provide an extra dose of flexibility for all of those special cases that will invariably crop up during a project, but attention must be paid to avoid embedding too much complicated logic in the condition that would be better placed elsewhere.

32.10 Conclusion

What was originally intended to deal with the issue of noticing dead bodies and broken lights soon expanded to an ever increasing variety of other purposes, as described in this chapter. While by no means a silver bullet, this system granted the designers more control over the behavior of game characters, while reducing the need for special case scripting or programmer intervention. Overall, the sense detection architecture which assigns agent rates during the update of an interest source, combined with the designers' ability to data-drive interest source definitions and priorities, resulted in a simple but flexible system that created believable guard awareness and even provided light-weight group behavior with minimal additional complexity.

Acknowledgments

We would like to thank the entire team at Klei for making *Mark of the Ninja* a joy to work on, in particular Kevin Forbes whose work on *Shank 2* provided the foundation for the AI and who provided much helpful direction in expanding on those systems; and fellow AI/gameplay engineer Tatham Johnson who also contributed to the work described in this article.

References

[Millington 06] I. Millington. *Artificial Intelligence for Games.* San Francisco, CA: Morgan Kaufmann, 2006, pp. 233–246.

[Shewchuk 05] J. R. Shewchuk. "Triangle: A Two-Dimensional Quality Mesh Generator and Delaunay Triangulator." http://www.cs.cmu.edu/~quake/triangle.html, 2005.

33

Asking the Environment Smart Questions

Mieszko Zielinski

33.1 Introduction

Finding your way in a complex and dynamic environment such as in a shooter game is a challenge, especially if you're just an AI actor with very few CPU ticks to spare every frame. Life is tough. "How do I know where to go? If there are a number of places, how can I tell which one is better? Oh! There's an enemy! Two! Three of them! Who do I shoot first?"

It's a tricky task to create a service that will supply AI with all the data it needs, at low CPU time cost, while being flexible and easy to use. It needs to be able to look for different things, filter them, and score them. For *Bulletstorm*, we created a system that serves all of the spatial awareness needs of the AI while not taking much CPU time and is also intuitive for designers. We concentrated on creating a system which takes input that is easily understandable by humans, rather than making humans produce counterintuitive data that the system will have an easy time consuming.

33.2 Motivation

Early in the development of *Bulletstorm*, two new systems were designed and implemented: one for AIs' logic (our Behavior Tree implementation) and the other for centralized environment querying. This article will describe the latter system, which we called Environment Tactical Querying (ETQ for short).

Environmental queries in *Bulletstorm* can take two forms: object types and object properties. *Enemies, covers,* and *locations* are examples of object types. *On navmesh, not visible to enemy,* and *some distance away from leader* are examples of object properties. These object properties could also take the form of preference: *prefer ones not visible, prefer ones closer to me,* and so on.

33.3 Goals

The following are goals that we pursued throughout the development of the system.

- *Think of "What to ask" not "How to ask"*: Creating and asking questions was to be made as simple as possible. We wanted nothing to stand in the way of our creativity.
- *Let nonprogrammers do the job*: We aimed from the start to create a dedicated editor for designers, so that whenever they wanted to change or tweak the way an AI picks cover or an enemy, they can do it themselves just by clicking.
- *Code reusability*: That was our main coding commandment, and it resulted in really clean and compact code.
- *Performance*: It was essential to have this system perform its duties without any other system noticing a hit on performance.
- *Asynchronous*: Even though the ETQ system itself was running on the game thread, we made it asynchronous so that questions asked would not block the game. Instead the system was scheduling query processing to be performed during system's regular update. It also allowed us to time slice the main query processing loop.

33.4 Our Philosophy

We wanted our idealized data creator to author queries just by asking him or herself simple questions:

- *What to generate?* Those could be covers, enemy locations, points—anything that has a location in the game world.
- *Who's asking?* What is the context object of the query—which entity is asking the question. Most often that was an AI actor, but questions could also be asked about an enemy being tracked by an AI ("Where could he go?"), a cover or a spawn point for example.
- *Where to look?* What are the spatial restrictions for candidate items? We could generate items in a radius around a context object, for example, or in the object's assigned combat zone, or so on.
- *Which items are good enough?* What are the minimal qualities of an acceptable item? We might require items visible from some reference object or items that are no closer than X to the context object, etc. These formed conditions.
- *Which items are better?* How can we tell one item is better than the other? We could prefer items that are closer or further from something, or prefer items having some property, or have some property's value lower than a set limit, etc.

33.5 Anatomy

The ETQ system is a data-driven solution, and most of its power lies in the design of data representation. Much care went into making it both flexible and efficient. It's time to look a bit more into the details of our design.

33.5.1 Query

A Query has three main components:

- *Context object*: The game entity that is asking the question (or more precisely on behalf of whom the question is being asked). What is the spatial context for this query? This is crucial since this actor's properties will be used to define a subjective world view, like, "Is that spot visible from here?" and, "Is it within my view range?" Note that a context object need not be an AI actor
- *QueryTemplate Id*: Which one of the user-created questions are we asking? All query templates registered with the system have their unique id, and this is the place to indicate which one to use.
- *Items*: All items found are returned as a list. Later, we will remove all items that fail subsequent filtering tests.

To trigger query processing, one calls the ETQ system supplying information on what query template to run and what is the spatial and gameplay context of that query. One might also request a query to be processed instantly rather than in the background.

33.5.2 Query Template

Now that we know how a question is asked at runtime, how do we define one? We need to express what we're looking for and what properties we'd like our "good items" to have. We might want to require some properties while using others just for item scoring.

A question is defined in the editor, with a special tool we created, and saved as a regular asset. This asset is referenced in code as a Query Template. A Query Template consists of one or more *Options* which in turn are made up of several Tests.

First, the Query Template defines an Option, which contains information on how to generate the item population that will be processed in later steps. This creates a collection of items representing entities in the game world. We implemented a number of generators, for example:

- *Context Object's Enemies*: Gathers all enemies that a given AI is aware of.
- *Covers*: Results in a collection of cover points within a parameterized radius of a context object.
- *Points on grid*: Generates points on a configurable grid around a context object.

ETQ makes the authoring of new generators extremely easy, at times requiring only two or three lines of code.

Once the generator for a Query Template's Option is set, the ways of filtering out and scoring those items is specified. Items are conditioned out and scored by *tests*. Take a look at Listing 33.1 for a pseudocode look at a Test structure. A Test structure designates a

Listing 33.1. Pseudocode of a Test structure.

```
struct Test
{
    TestType;           //Distance, Reachability,...
    ConditionModifier;  //None, Min, Max
    Reference;          //Self, Enemy, Leader, Item,...
    TestedValue;        //float, int, bool,...
    SymbolicValue;      //Melee distance, Weapon range,...
    Weight;             //float in [-1,1]
    /** flags */
    bCondition;         //boolean flag indicating this test is
                        //used as a condition
    bValidityTest;      //and/or as a validity test (see 33.5.3)
    bWeight;            //or as a weight
}
```

property to test for (`TestType`), a list of references for the test (`Reference`), a comparison type (`ConditionModifier`), and a value to compare against (`TestedValue`). We can also assign tests a weight if they are to be used for scoring.

The order in which tests are set up is irrelevant. Tests will be reordered by the system according to their computational cost. The cost is estimated by a programmer with a relative list of which tests are more expensive than others (Section 33.7), and whether it's a condition or just a scoring test. Even the most expensive tests are performed first before any scoring takes place. This results in fewer items while scoring, which may or may not save time in the long run. We address this issue in Section 33.10 with *final test*.

In the case where tests are too restrictive and no item gets past the conditions, we might relax the constraints rather than simply fail on the whole query. The system supports this scenario. If a query template has more than one option, then all of them are processed in a sequence until one produces some items which become the result of a query.

33.5.3 Validity Test

A test declared in the query template's option can be a condition, a weight, or both. However, ETQ also allows you to designate certain tests as *validity tests*. These tests will be used not at cover generation time, but later, when an AI is moving to that cover, or sitting in it, to check if the cover is still valid (not exposed to enemy fire for example). Of course, a test can be both a regular test and a validity test at the same time. This way all of the configuration information on how to pick a cover point and, later, how to tell if it is still good (oftentimes not the same thing) are nicely gathered in one place.

We could achieve the same functionality by rerunning a query on that one item in question, but that would result in a number of tests we don't need while performing an ongoing validation. We could also create a separate lightweight query just for validity testing, but that on the other hand would require keeping both queries in sync whenever one of them is changed. Marking some tests as a validity test is the best of both worlds. During the ongoing testing, we only run the tests we need, while at the same time having all of the logic for picking items and for ongoing validation in one query asset.

Table 33.1 Shows how different tests can be used as both conditions and weights

Test	Condition	Weight
Visibility	Is (not) visible	Prefer (not) visible
Distance	More/less/equal to X	Prefer closer/further away
Configurable dot	More/less/equal to X	Prefer more/less
Within action area	Is (not) in action area	Prefer (not) in action area
Reachable	Is (not) reachable with navigation	Prefer (not) reachable
Distance to wall	More/less/equal to X	Prefer more/less
Current item	Is (not) current item	Prefer (not) current item

33.5.4 A Test in Any Role

In order to have a nice unified interface to all tests, we decided we'd have every test make sense in both roles, as a *condition* as well as a *weight*. For example if we use "distance to enemy" as a condition, we can require it to be less or more than 2000 units. But if we use it as a weight, then we interpret it as preferring a smaller or greater distance to the enemy. We express how much we prefer a tested property by setting the test's weight value. The higher the value, the more a given property is desired. Table 33.1 gives some more examples.

33.6 The Heart

The core ETQ algorithm is captured in the pseudocode in Listing 33.2.

Listing 33.2. The core ETQ query algorithm.

```
foreach Option in QueryTemplate.Options:
    Query.Items = (generate items with QueryTemplate.Generator
        using contextual data from Query);
    if Query.Items is empty:
        continue to next option;
    foreach Test in Option.Tests:
        Reference = (find world object Test refers to);
        if Reference not empty or not required by Test:
            //explained in Section 33.7 under "Fail Quickly"
            if Test has a fixed result:
                apply result to all Query.Item elements;
            else:
                perform Test on all Query.Item elements;
            if Test.bCondition is true:
                filter out Query.Item elements that failed Test;
            if Test.bWeight is true:
                foreach Item in Query.Item:
                    calculate weights from every test result
    if Query.Items not empty:
        foreach Item in Query.Items:
            sum up all weights calculated by weighting tests;
        sort Query.Items descending with computed weight;
        return success;
return failure;
```

33.7 Implementation Details

There are always some little tricks you can perform while implementing even the simplest algorithm. The following are some of the optimizations we implemented.

- *Start with cheaper tests:* We manually presorted test-types according to expected performance. For example, a Distance test is more expensive than checking if an actor has a tag, but is less expensive than finding out if a point is on the navmesh.
- *Fail quickly*: For some tests it's possible to fail early, thus saving computation. For example, checking whether a point is on the navmesh will always fail if there's no navmesh. Tests can fail even sooner if they require a reference that doesn't exist in a given context, like the squad leader or an enemy for example.
- *Normalize test results and weights*: We quickly discovered that trying to weight a distance test against a "has a property" kind of test was an impossible undertaking. Even if it could be done with a known maximum distance, it would fall apart as soon as we change the maximum value and would require retweaking. So we decided to normalize all test results. While performing a test we store the maximum result value and once the test is finished, we normalize all the results with the stored maximum. In some cases we would also use the item generation range of a processed option. We also made sure that weights are always within the range [-1, 1] (via the editor), which together with normalizing results gave us some good mathematical properties and allowed reliable query tweaking.
- *Debug-draw whatever you can*: It's impossible to overvalue debug drawing. While developing a system like this it's crucial to be able to trigger any query on any target of your choice, during runtime, and you need to see the results. Countless times we found bugs in a query just by debug-drawing its results, which proved a significant time saver.

33.8 Editor

Taking advantage of the ease of creating tools with *Unreal Engine 3*, we created a tool for ETQ. Using the tool made working with query assets a lot more pleasant. As a direct consequence, we were more willing to work with queries, tweak them, and instantly see if something was set up wrong. Figure 33.1 shows a Query Template in our editor with examples of option and test node properties.

The tool further provided the following features:

- *Weights auto-scaling*: Whenever a weight of a test has been changed to something outside of the range [–1, 1], the editor rescaled all weights in a given query option proportionally, so that they again fit in the range mentioned in the implementation section.
- *Auto-arranging visuals*: A query was represented as a tree-like structure. All elements that were used to visualize tests were put in columns with an option node as a head, to achieve a unified look for every query, regardless of who created it. This made it a lot easier to find your way around in someone else's queries.
- *Descriptive labels*: We made every test node in a query asset produce a non-programmer understandable description string for itself and displayed it on

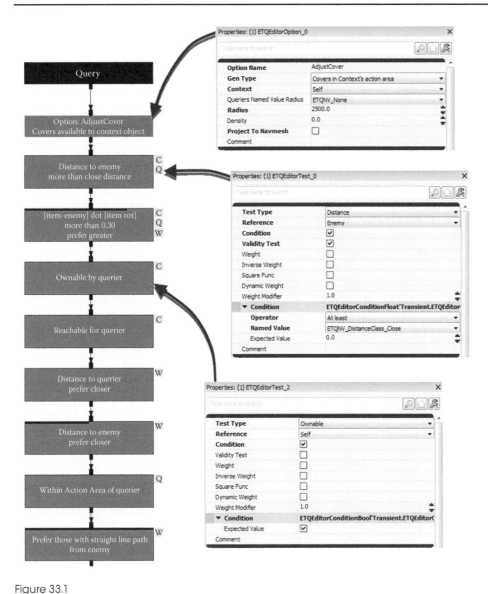

Figure 33.1

A Query Template in our editor with examples of option and test node properties.

its visualization in the editor. For example, we had labels like "Leader has a straight line path to (condition)" or "Distance to context object, prefer less (weight)." The idea was that even an untrained person could more or less tell what a given query will generate just by looking at it.

- *Coloring*: This one's pretty obvious, but we colored with yellow (as opposed to everything else being in dark colors) everything that was incorrectly set up or was missing some values. This way we instantly knew where a given query was broken at the very first glance.

33.9 Pros and Cons

There are a number of good properties ETQ achieved. Some examples include:

- *Intuitive query creation*: With the tool we created, designers were able to construct a query with minimal tutoring. The idea itself was so close to the way people express these kinds of queries that even less technical designers had no trouble understanding it.
- *Data driven*: Having data control the way code behaves is the holy grail of game development. For example, programmers no longer need to be involved in every change to the way AIs pick enemies or cover.
- *Efficient*: By having our system time-sliced and our queries set up to not generate insane numbers of items, we were able to squeeze ETQ to under 0.02 ms per frame on average, while still having it look for game entities of specified properties with very sophisticated queries.
- *Flexible*: Adding new tests or generators was so easy that whenever someone needed to do something that the current tests or generators did not provide, adding a new one was simple—very easy to add and still efficient at runtime (due to time-slicing).

The main issue with ETQ is it can take some time or experience to tweak the queries to get the desired behavior. On the other hand, iterations while working with queries were very fast (we also had some runtime tools for it) and inexperienced users developed the required intuition quickly.

The ETQ system was also used in *Gears of War: Judgment*. On that project, it exhibited a number of issues. One major issue was that in some scenarios it generated huge CPU usage spikes of up to 15 ms. This was due to performing expensive tests on a large collection of items, since we treat each test on a single collection of items atomically and don't time-slice it. These spikes resulted from the query generator reading cover gathering range from level-placed entities (in this case "Goal Actors"), a value that was set up by level designers. This is in fact a problem inherent in data-driven systems and care needs to be taken to make sure data supplied by designers doesn't kill the system's performance. The quick fix was to limit the radius to some experience-based maximum value.

33.10 Things to Fix and Improve

There were a number of improvements that we were unable to get to in the final stages of shipping *Bulletstorm*. These include:

- *Merging tests*: Certain tests tend to show up as a group. For example, while querying for cover points, *dot product to enemy more than X*, *distance to enemy more than Y*, and *not my current cover* would routinely come up as group. Intuitively it would make sense to have one special test that does all three things instead of three individual tests executed one after the other.
- *Final test*: Often, even numerous filters were not able to reduce enough the total number of items to test. When the system reached the expensive tests, there were far too many items to process and performance was poor. The idea of the *final test*

Part V. Agent Awareness and Knowledge Representation

is to pick the required first N items that pass that test and abort testing the rest. The final tests would be the very last ones to process, and this way we'd get good enough results without calculating expensive tests for all items.

- *Reversed processing*: [Robert 11] presented a scheme to quickly pick a cover better than the one our AI is currently using. The same could be added to ETQ. Thus instead of running regular processing of a query, we could take the AI's current cover point, grade it first, and then accept the very first item that passes all of a query's filters and has a higher score.
- *Multigenerators*: Allow a Query Template to use multiple generators to be able to run unified testing on a collection of different items (like regular points and cover points in one pass).
- *Multithreaded implementation*: There was neither a need nor CPU resources to run ETQ in a separate thread, but with the trend toward more CPU cores, this is a promising future direction.

33.11 Conclusion

Even though the described system was very simple in its design, it proved to be very powerful. We gained a lot of environment querying power without eating up a lot of CPU time. Having ETQ driven by data and queries, created with our dedicated authoring tool, allowed very rapid iteration over how AI picks enemies or covers, further enhanced with runtime debugging tools.

There's also a higher level gain. From the very start we were thinking about ETQ in asynchronous service terms and it helped us make the rest of our AI system components asynchronous as well. Designing and implementing asynchronous AI takes a slightly different mindset, but it results in solutions that scale well on multiple cores, which is a requirement in coming years.

Acknowledgments

I'd like to thank my wife, Agata, for talking me into writing this article. I also would like to thank Łukasz Furman for helping me make all my crazy ideas for *Bulletstorm* AI happen.

References

[Robert 11] G. Robert. "Cover Selection Optimizations in GHOST RECON." Paris AI Conference Shooter Symposium, 2011.

34

A Simple and Robust Knowledge Representation System

Phil Carlisle

34.1 Introduction

Knowledge comes in many forms, and how the knowledge is represented can have a significant impact on the efficiency and development time of any game AI. The representation chosen is particularly important for any game that involves complex characters. This chapter describes a system that was created for the game *EverSky*, an indie first-person exploration game for the PC and tablet devices.

The goal of the game was to push the boundaries of companion style AI and allow for a cast of characters that would be constantly alongside the player. This required that each character have deep knowledge of the world and each be capable of portraying complex attitudes to events, other characters, and objects within it. The complexity of the knowledge required led to a number of iterations on the design of how the data was represented, leading to a system that favored flexibility and iteration speed over raw efficiency, both in terms of memory and CPU usage.

34.2 Design Requirements

Before we begin, we note that increasing the longevity of characters also increases the requirements on the knowledge supporting the characters' behaviors. We focus on long-lived companions that require a complex knowledge representation. It is often the case that nonplayer characters in a video game have a relatively short lifespan and thus do not require any form of complex knowledge representation.

That said, the guiding design principles for this system were:

- Minimize iteration time (sometimes at the expense of execution speed, we could always optimize later).
- Trade memory for efficiency (as a PC-based game, memory is not that restrictive).
- Easily integrate with scripts.
- Work flexibly with a component-oriented architecture (more on that later).
- Allow for varying types of knowledge and be flexible in structure.

If we think of logic as simple sets of `if (condition) do action` clauses, then we must consider what the condition part of that clause actually means. In order to obtain any form of complex behavior, the conditional part of any logical clause must contain any number of conditions, the complexity of the conditions being generally proportional to the complexity of the behavior. The key realization for anyone working on game artificial intelligence is that these conditions rely heavily on knowledge and that knowledge representation can form a large part of the requirements for any complex behaviors.

The knowledge representation for *EverSky* went through a number of iterations on the basic structure of knowledge. The first iteration involved a simple blackboard architecture that contained a number of get and set functions to add and retrieve information from the blackboard, which were also available to scripts. It soon became apparent that this was not a very well structured approach to the problem of knowledge representation for a character with complex behavior and high expected longevity. The problem was that having get and set methods for every single type of information was simply not possible. The amount of time required to add a new type of knowledge to the blackboard code was too great and added to the iteration time. It was time to go back and rethink the problem.

What should we consider as the basis for a knowledge representation system?

Knowledge generally consists of elements such as:

- entity attributes (position, velocity)
- existence
- classification or type
- set membership
- relationships/attitudes
- knowledge of others
- semantic knowledge
- knowledge of events

Let's examine these types of knowledge in more detail:

34.2.1 Entity Attributes

Entity attributes are simply data associated with a particular entity. It could be things like position, velocity, name, facing direction, current animation, etc. Each entity that a particular character senses (more on that later) needs to be stored along with useful attributes of that entity. This information goes in an `Entities` array, which is a dynamic array of all entities a given character is aware of.

34.2.2 Existence

The notion of existence is very important as often we can gain efficiency by only considering objects or sets of objects about which the character has knowledge. For instance, conditional logic required to select the appropriate enemy to target during combat requires the knowledge that an enemy exists, before it is useful to consider knowledge for which enemy is the most desirable. In many ways it is useful to use the existence of something as the primary condition and then to drill down into secondary conditions, only if that primary condition is true. So in a typical situation, you may see an `is_enemy_seen()` method that returns true if an enemy is seen by the NPC, which then feeds into other conditions such as selecting from a list of seen enemies. This concept of "existence" can be easily represented by the count of any specific set membership, a nonzero value representing the existence of an enemy in the `enemies` set for instance.

34.2.3 Classification

The notion of "enemy" in this example is an interesting one. What we mean by "enemy" is that the particular entity belongs to a set of entities which elicit a specific reaction from our logic relating to that particular classification. But is it enough to simply classify entities as a single type? Imagine the case of Romeo and Juliet. Both could be classed as Montague or Capulet, but they could also be classed as male and female, they could be classed both as human, or they could both be classified as lovers. The problem is that any given entity may be part of a number of classifications depending on the context. Romeo can be classified as male, human, Montague, and lover all at the same time. If the number of classifications is relatively small, then it is possible to use a simple bit-flag representation and binary logic to represent them, but a more flexible approach is often preferable.

34.2.4 Set Membership

Sets can be represented as a simple dynamic array of member ID's. If we allow for an arbitrary number of sets, each containing an arbitrary number of members, along with a way to name the sets and lookup the members, then we can cope with any number of different classifications.

34.2.5 Relationships

Relationships are a slightly more complex version of set membership. In relationships we have a membership, as well as a positive or negative value on each member in the set or on the set overall. Consider the relationship between Romeo and Juliet again. In this case there is the overall relationship between Montague and Capulet (which implies that Romeo and Juliet are members of those sets), but there is an overall negative relationship value between those two sets.

But in the specific case of Romeo and Juliet themselves, they also have a positive relationship, which implies another set membership, where the members are the two lovers. Ultimately, the representation chosen for relationships is a simple one. Each membership set is represented as a named dynamic array of members, where members are stored using their ID value. Each entity stores the names of each set it is a member of in a dynamic array that basically forms a hierarchy of membership from most to least specific. So the first element might be membership of the "lover" set, the next might be "Montague," and the final set might be "human."

Each membership set also has a `valence` value that can be positive or negative to denote the positive or negative associations with that set. The reason for this flattened hierarchy is that when considering a behavior we will often want to consider more specific behavior first, followed by more generalized behavior. If we store the set membership in this fashion, we simply need to read the array from left to right and consider the behavior for each set membership as appropriate. So for example, if we find we are in the set "lover," we might choose a display of affection. However, if we are not a member of this set, then we may be a member of "Montague" and subsequently select a display of dominance, with the final fallback of "human" allowing a default for when no other membership is available.

34.2.6 Attitudes

Attitudes are dealt with using the exact same structure as relationships (attitudes in this sense are just relationships to simple objects or events rather than characters).

34.2.7 Knowledge of Others

If we are creating behavior for companions, we need them to appear as though they also have a model of what those around them know. In this case, we can simply store a set of "companions" for each entity and then query their knowledge via lookup if required.

34.2.8 Semantic Knowledge

Perhaps the thorniest issue in knowledge representation is the concept of semantic knowledge. Suppose we have a character that likes fruit; as we are exploring, we come across an object we have not encountered before. It looks like a fruit that the character is familiar with, so the character decides to try and eat it. The question is, what made the character decide to try and eat it? It was the semantic knowledge that this new object was "like-a" fruit.

Terms such as "like-a" and "is-a" are interesting concepts. A potato is not a fruit and yet it is edible. It has an "is-a" relationship with the concept "food" in the same way that fruit has an "is-a" relationship with the food concept. In order to allow for inference of this kind, we need to consider representing semantic knowledge. We note that experience shows that the vast majority of game AI behavior does not require semantic knowledge like this; thus we will leave experimenting with this semantic knowledge as an exercise for the reader.

34.2.9 Events

These are records of any events relevant to the character; they might be events such as "just heard a grenade land" to "just seen Romeo kiss Juliet." Event knowledge is useful for rapid reactions to things that require immediate attention, and they are also useful as aggregate statistics that affect things like mood. They can be used for example to change a value that represents battle fatigue or to alter a value that aggregates combat experience over time.

To sum up, what is needed is a system that allows storing of arbitrary information in arbitrary data structures that nonetheless allows efficient retrieval and querying, while also allowing automated access to knowledge representations from within scripts and conditional statements from the decision logic.

34.3 Implementation

Each entity in *EverSky* is represented by a unique per-instance integer value, which allows for fast lookup of entities by using the entity ID as the hash in a hashtable. Entities themselves are represented using the `GameObject` class, which is a simple container for a flat list of `GameComponent` derived classes. For more information on component-based architectures, it might be useful to refer to Jason Gregory's excellent book *Game Engine Architecture* [Gregory 09], but in general you can think of components as classes which deal with specific functionality in a narrow scope.

The advantage of component-based architectures is that you can composite entities by simply adding or removing components and get quite different behavior. All entities in the game are composed at runtime from a named XML template that describes all the components of the entity. Levels are described in another XML file, which contains the entity template name, unique ID, and other relevant attributes for each entity in the game.

It might be useful to refer to the first *AI Game Programming Wisdom's* chapter on blackboards [Isla and Blumberg 02]. In general, a blackboard is a simple repository of data with corresponding access methods. Initially, when designing the knowledge representation for *EverSky*, a simple blackboard with a number of lists of named integers, floats, and ID values with member functions (used to retrieve information from each list) was used. In addition, it had a number of floating-point and integer values used to represent knowledge such as emotional state and counts of items owned, etc. The downside to this approach is that every new piece of information had to have some method of setting and getting that information added to the blackboard class, along with defining the interface for access by scripts, etc. This ended up being overly complicated and not particularly useful for the purpose of prototyping gameplay. Eventually, it was decided to use variant type data, which allowed arbitrary data to be stored, but also simplified the interface for both native code and script code. In reality there is always a trade-off between performance and accessibility and the use of variant data types was deemed to be a reasonable compromise.

In the knowledge representation system described in this chapter and available on the book's website (http://www.gameaipro.com), you will find a system that is based around the blackboard concept. However, it has been modified to appear very similar to a property-based system, in that it stores arbitrary named data in a variant format that allows querying of the data by name, but also retrieval of the data in any suitable format with reasonable conversion. The data itself is stored in variants which have a name string and a notional "type" with methods to convert to other common types. In practice this means that most data is stored as native types with no conversion, but has the advantage that common conversion such as string access for passing to scripts is trivial.

While this system is not as efficient as a simple list of integers or floats, it is efficient in terms of ease of use and automation of access; this trade-off is one that is appropriate for a system which is meant to change as the design of the behaviors adapts to gameplay requirements. The main caveat to this approach is that it is not always possible to convert from one type of data to another. For instance it is not possible to convert from any arbitrary string to a numerical format. The way *EverSky* deals with mismatched data type access is to use the POCO class libraries exception handling routines; however, in a nonprototype game context, or on a shipping title, it would make more sense to simply assert the data access and fix the code that is incorrectly accessing or storing data.

Because this was an indie project and in general we are supporters of open source code, the implementation is built using an open source variant implementation provided by the POCO C++ class libraries [Applied Informatics 12]. In particular the variant type `poco::dynamicany` allows the storage of variant data without type in much the same way dynamically typed languages allow variable storage.

The variant system used in the example code was extended in three ways. First, we added hierarchies of variant types. This means that each variant can store either a single value or a dynamic array of other variants, which enables any single data access to be able to access anything between a single value and a complete hierarchy as part of that access. Second, we added a "name" property to the variant such that variants can be queried by name, which is useful for script access. Finally, we added a method to describe the expiry value for the variant data. This expiry value is either zero to denote a nonexpiring piece of data, or any nonzero value, which is then counted down during the update of the blackboard. The variant system requires that any variant data access specifies the type of data that is returned through the use of a template parameter. The variant data is stored and accessed via the blackboard class.

34.4 Execution

In the case of *EverSky*, an AI component stores a blackboard instance within it, plus it allows for accessing other "named" blackboards. The AI component also stores a behavior tree instance, which has an `Execute` method called during update of the AI component. This execute method is passed a pointer to the AI component along with the elapsed time. As the behavior tree executes, it can access the blackboard via the AI component interface, as well as add actions for the AI component to execute. In this way, the decision logic of the behavior tree class is separated from the action execution logic of the AI component.

During the AI component update, the blackboard itself is updated with the elapsed time, which allows for the blackboard data to be cleaned up as expiring data can be pruned from the dataset. This expiry is simply a loop over the entities list. Values that are nonzero have the elapsed time subtracted from them and any that would lead to either a zero or negative value are considered to have expired and are removed from the list. Note that this expiry system allows for any individual piece of data to expire either at the aggregate level, as in the case of an individual entity and all its attributes, or at the attribute level for specific features of an entity such as position or velocity. During this update, another method allows for new event data to be aggregated using an `appraisal` class. This class is game specific and allows for aggregation of events and other knowledge generally useful for implementing features such as character emotions and moods.

34.5 Sensing

Data can be added to the blackboard during entity construction via an XML file reference or it may also be added in the game update loop via the sensory system. As each entity is sensed, it is added to the blackboard along with a number of common attributes such as position, direction, velocity, etc. If an entity is sensed and is already in the blackboard, the variant for that entity is updated with a new expiry time, if appropriate, along with any new attributes that may have changed.

34.6 Handling Events

Events are added as they are received from the central event handling system called `MessageManager` and are parsed into variant structures for adding to the `Events` variant array in the blackboard class using the `AddEventMemory` member function.

34.7 Accessing the Knowledge

Accessing the various representations of knowledge can either be by named element or by index values if a variant array is stored. Typically, access takes the form:

```
<type> variable = blackboard<type>[elementname];
```

where `<type>` is any supported data type and `elementname` is the string name given to the element.

In place of `elementname`, an integer index can be used for variants which are known to store arrays of other variants. The Boolean member function `IsArray()` can be used to determine whether the variant storage has an array stored within it. The unsigned integer member function `Count()` returns the number of elements in the array.

The reader is advised to consult the various `condition` nodes available in the source code for examples of accessing the various variant data types.

34.8 Debugging, Scripts, and Serialization

One of the primary benefits of the variant approach is that exposing the data to other systems becomes trivial. Each variant knows how to serialize itself to any given data stream, whether this be for debugging, logging, or entity serialization. So the process becomes a recursive one where you simply call a function on the topmost variant and allow it to serialize itself and its child hierarchies automatically. Because each variant has a name, it is relatively easy to understand what each value represents visually within the stream. For example, this feature is used within *EverSky* to serialize the blackboard to a JSON format for display in a web browser, which is accessed via an embedded web server. Script interfacing is similarly simplified, because a simple function can be written which exposes a given named variant to the script engine via a string conversion using the variant name to allow access. Variant types that store arrays are usually exposed as tables in scripting languages that support them such as LUA.

34.9 Conclusion

While developing the behavior for a game, reducing the iteration time required to get any single behavior implemented is of paramount importance. The knowledge representation system described builds on the concept of blackboards and adds a more dynamic form of data representation that more easily deals with changing requirements. While this allows for a flexible data representation, it does have tradeoffs in terms of performance that may not be desirable in a final shipping product. It is useful to point out that this system derives many of the benefits and pitfalls of dynamically typed languages. A good solution to the pitfalls is to optimize the representation once it is known what the final behavior implementation requires and to allow type specific data accesses once this has been finalized.

Although we have not explored the use of semantic knowledge, this is perhaps the last area of development for *EverSky* that is required to build fully adaptive and believable characters. It is left as an exercise for the reader to consider what use of semantic knowledge might add to their own games.

References

[Applied Informatics 12] Applied Informatics. "Poco Project." 2012. Available at (http://pocoproject.org/)

[Gregory 09] J. Gregory. "*Game Engine Architecture.*" Boca Raton, FL: CRC Press, 2009.

[Isla and Blumberg. 02] D. Isla and B. Blumberg. "Blackboard architectures." In *AI Game Programming Wisdom*, edited by Steve Rabin. Hingham, MA: Charles River Media, 2002, pp. 333–345.

35

A Simple and Practical
Social Dynamics System

Phil Carlisle

35.1 Introduction

One of the issues with current games that have large numbers of characters is that they often do not portray many of the coordinated interactions seen in any social group in the real world, for example, when friends cluster together at parties or when long-separated relatives hug each other after finally meeting each other again. Social interactions are an important part of how we understand the structure of social groups, and we would be wise to portray them in order to make the experience of the world more compelling.

This article will describe a social dynamics implementation based on modular components that together form a system that enables characters to take part in and portray social interactions. Building on a foundation of commonly used components such as behavior trees, blackboards, animation, and locomotion controllers, we will discuss aspects of nonverbal behavior commonly seen in social situations and will provide source code examples and practical implementation details (source code available on the book's website: http://www.gameaipro.com).

35.2 The Importance of Observation

When animators work on characters, they do so by implementing motions that they have observed, either through their own experience or from seeing other similar characters.

Similarly, many of the methods implemented here are intended to reproduce aspects of social interactions observed by both academics and animators. At the foundation of all of this work is the notion that observation of interactions is key to our being able to implement them. We must study life if we are to approximate the illusion of life in our characters.

AI programmers who are interested in working towards believable characters are strongly urged to become keen observers of human interaction. It is relatively easy to spot subtle interactions that can help sell any given relationship or social dynamic, especially if we film a number of such interactions and later analyze the footage. Small digital cameras that are suitable for capturing social interactions without being observed are relatively cheap and are a powerful tool to have available when working on any given scene.

35.3 What Is a Social Dynamic?

A social dynamic is any social interaction that has to happen in real-time between two or more characters. Typically, there is an element of spatial position, timing, and orientation involved in the interaction, hence the term "dynamic." There are a number of different elements that could be classified as social dynamics, and each of them can contribute to a more believable set of social interactions for characters, which will ultimately add to the believability of the world.

Typical examples are:

35.3.1 Gaze Control

We learn a lot about characters by looking at their face. One of the key things we understand is that if a character is gazing (looking) at an object, then it is likely aware of that object. The other aspect of gaze is that it focuses our attention on what is important to the character. For example, we can understand if one character is interested in another if their gaze is held for any significant time. This is useful to signal to the player that a character is attracted to another. Similarly, if a character we see suddenly gazes in a given direction, it is likely that we should pay attention in that direction, too, which can be useful for leading the players' view towards a particular visual event.

35.3.2 Proxemic Control

When we interact with other humans, we tend to keep a specific distance from them, depending on how well we know them, whether we like them, etc. This field of study is known in social psychology as *proxemics* and is important because it gives us a model of how humans move around within any social group.

As humans, we have a preferred distance which we maintain during different social interactions. For instance, when chatting socially, we have a relatively relaxed distance, but when trying to be intimate with someone we generally get a lot closer, often within easy touching distance. We should pay attention to proxemics because it gives us a general guide for forming small social groups, especially in spatial terms. Readers are referred to a useful paper on the application of this proxemic distance for use in games by Claudio Pedica [Pedica and Vilhjálmsson 08].

35.3.3 Posture

When interacting with another, we often adopt a given posture, depending on the nature of the interaction and the relationship we have with them. In a context where we are chatting with friends, we might adopt a relaxed posture where our arms are by our sides or gesturing. We might have a wider stance, too, and we will often lean towards people we are attracted to. Conversely, if we encounter someone in a position of authority over us, or in a role that puts social pressure on us to act with restraint, we might show this by having a more closed posture, with feet planted more firmly and closer together, our back straight or even leaning away slightly. These relatively subtle changes in posture can be used to signal differences between characters during social interactions. In addition, our posture can also affect elements of our gait when walking. Animators often exaggerate certain motions to affect changes in posture that imitate good or bad moods, for instance.

35.3.4 Gesture

This is perhaps the most challenging aspect of social dynamics in that it appears simple. It is easy to simply play gesture animations on a character, but the underlying reasons for why we gesture and what gestures we make are quite complex. The biggest area where we have problems in games is in the area of coordinated character gestures. If we observe real world social interactions we see many examples of gestures where one character touches another. A simple greeting might result in a handshake for instance. Yet in games, coordinating animations is actually quite difficult, not least because of the cost of animating a wide enough range of gestures to allow coordination to occur.

Readers are advised to review literature in the area of embodied conversational agents for more information on a number of posture and gesture studies; a good reference is the book *Embodied Conversational Agents* [Cassell 00].

We also note that the stated social dynamic elements are not an absolute requirement for every situation. They should be considered as extra details that provide subtle but useful hints to the player, much in the same way that additional texture data is used to add detail to rendered objects. However, it is likely that future games will feature more depth of social interaction as we develop our understanding of how this affects player perception.

35.4 Implementation

Rather than attempt to create a single system that portrays all social dynamics, instead we construct a number of systems that deal with individual aspects of social behavior and rely on the composition of these systems to implement the whole. In the example code, you will notice that all entities are simply composites. Please refer to the companion chapter number 34 "A Simple and Robust Knowledge Representation System" for more detail on the component-based architecture used.

The component implementations for the social dynamics system fall roughly in line with the aspects of social dynamics discussed previously. Components for gaze, proxemics, posture, and gesture control are simply added to characters at run time during instantiation of the character template. Where possible, a component performs a narrow subset of behaviors without requiring aspects of other components, but in the case of many of these social behaviors, other components are required. Frequently, social components delegate actions to other components. For instance the `ProxemicComponent`, which controls the social distances at which a character interacts, requires that there is a `LocomotionComponent` or other movement oriented component available in order to request the character to change position.

Before we describe the various components involved in the social dynamics system, we should describe how they are coordinated. Some aspects of social interactions are entirely based around the individual involved. For instance, an individual chooses the focus of their gaze and thus their attention. Yet most social interactions involve dynamically reacting to another person. These interactions can often involve groups of characters that may change over time. A chat may start out with two or three characters, expanding to five or six as more join the group, eventually having the original characters leave the chat, leaving none of the original group members involved. The initial group members instigated a social interaction that outlasted the participation of the instigators. This leads to the realization that another entity must be instantiated to monitor and control participation in the group activity.

35.4.1 SocialObjectComponent

This component performs the task of coordinating much of the group formation aspect of the system. At its core, it is a component that handles set membership, allowing characters to request access to the group, removing characters that are no longer participating, and allocating resources and/or positions in the group structure. This system is also responsible for advertising the availability of the social interaction as well as organizing flow control for when resources are limited, which as an example is useful to control how many people are talking at once during a group discussion.

This `SocialObjectComponent` is usually either added to the world during instantiation of an object or it is added dynamically during the update of a character that is receptive to a social encounter. An example of the former is a hot dog stand, where the `SocialObectComponent` is instantiated to control the behavior of the characters as they use the stand to buy hot dogs. An example of the latter would be when a character has true conditions for <idle>, <wants_social>, <sees_friend>, and <friend_also_wants_social>. When the conditions for social activity are met, the character spawns a `GameObject`, which has a `SocialObjectComponent` added. This becomes a proposal for social interaction and the `SocialObjectComponent` begins its role in coordinating the interaction.

35.4.2 SocialComponent

The intracharacter coordination of the various social dynamics components is controlled by the `SocialComponent`. This component is responsible for querying the world as to available potential interactions, forming requests to participate, controlling the focus of attention, etc. Much of the work of this component is involved in handling events propagated through the game and sending events to the different components of the social dynamics system to handle. For instance, the social component sends an event to its parent `GameObject` to indicate that the attention of the character has changed.

35.4.3 GazeComponent

This is perhaps the easiest component to implement in that it functions as a simple modifier to the animation component. Adding a `GazeComponent` to a character's xml template schema will mean that the component first initializes itself by requesting access to the `AnimationComponent` of the character `GameObject`. If this access fails, the `GazeComponent` asserts the failure, alerting the programmer to the dependency. The next step is for the `GazeComponent` to add itself as a listener of the `AnimationComponent`, which allows it to alter the animation prior to the animation being submitted for rendering the final character. During the listener callback method, the `GazeController` simply changes the orientation of the head bone within specific limits, along with the spine bones as in Figure 35.1.

Please refer to the method `UpdateGaze()` for the actual math involved in modifying the animation, but it is perhaps useful to note that for a character with more spine nodes, the rotation of each spine bone should be scaled the further away from the head bone they are in the hierarchy. This allows for some amount of torso twist, which is desirable to mimic the twist available in the human torso. Obviously the number of spine links in a typical game character is less than the number in a human so there will always be some visual discontinuity, but in general some torso twist is enough to sell the motion. It should be noted that the amount of rotation that both torso and head bones are allowed should be carefully selected so that they are in a range of motions that would be generally considered comfortable for any given character type, depending on age, build, etc.

Figure 35.1

The skeleton of a character is manipulated by rotating the bones of the head and spine in order to allow the head to "look at" a given position. Note the restricted range of the vertical and horizontal motion (horizontal restriction not shown) and the reduced proportion of the horizontal motion as we get further away from the head.

The `GazeComponent` reacts to events sent via the `SocialComponent` to "look at" another entity and/or position. The duration of the gaze is modified by the intensity of the interaction as noted in the "look at" event. Eventually the gaze controller resets the gaze direction, or may even modulate the current gaze direction to temporarily look away from the gaze target for a brief period. The character personality data specified in the `AIComponent`'s blackboard allow for the gaze to be modified such that a shy character looks away more often than an assertive one.

35.4.4 The Social Origin

A key aspect of coordinating movement for social interactions is having a shared social origin. It is useful to think of many social interactions as a spatially oriented set of timed actions; in order to have coherent animations, we must assume that the social interaction is performed with respect to a shared origin. This allows for each interaction to function anywhere in world space as coordination acts in a space relative to the social interaction which is propagated to all participants.

This role of coordinating the shared origin is part of the `SocialObjectComponent` class as part of its responsibility as arbiter of the interaction. Individual characters involved in the interaction must respect this shared origin as they calculate their own movements while also respecting the movements of other characters. This approach bears some resemblance to the moving origin techniques used for animating a character during parkour-like behavior. For more information see an interview with Laurent Ancessi of Naughty Dog on AIGameDev.com [Ancessi 10].

35.4.5 ProxemicComponent

Controlling the proximity to other characters during social interaction requires access to the `LocomotionComponent` of the character (or other functionality which serves to move the character and orient them in space). The `ProxemicComponent` request is constrained by the locomotion, navigation, and collision avoidance strategy of the character movement. The `ProxemicComponent` is responsible for calculating the ideal position of the character during any movement of agents in the social group.

This means that, for instance, if a character leaves the group, the other characters may change position in order to stay in reasonable proximity for the social interactions. In practice, this means that each character tries to maintain a comfortable proxemic distance from all other characters in the group, while still maintaining other constraints such as line of sight or being close enough to touch with gestures for characters that have positive affection. Acting in a very similar manner to steering behaviors, the proxemic distance is maintained via a simple vector length calculation which relates character distance away from a group circle. This behavior approximates what has been observed by social scientist Adam Kendon who referred to the phenomenon as an "O frame" [Kendon 90], although it must be noted that it is useful to dampen any movement force such that the character is not continually shifting position (Figure 35.2).

35.4.6 PostureComponent

Posture is one of the easier components to implement as it simply relies on animation selection and/or blending to achieve the desired effect. The implementation provided demonstrates the simplest form of this animation selection to simply affect a bias in the

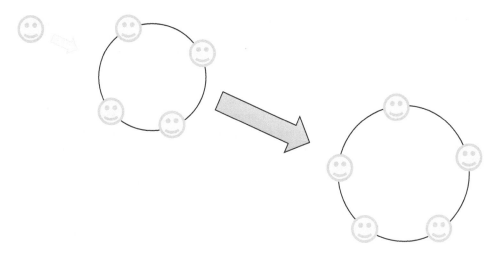

Figure 35.2

Proxemic distance is controlled by the `ProxemicComponent` that calculates a position offset relative to a circle known as an "O frame" and attempts to maintain that position as members of the group change.

choice of available animations. A more complex implementation would be to add blend nodes into an animation blend tree that would blend different postural clips at different weights based on the overall mood of the character. This requires that a number of similar animation clips be prepared that correspond to the changes in mood that would normally affect posture.

Effects such as fatigue, happiness, sadness, and excitement can then be portrayed by simply selecting the appropriate clip from the available animation set. In the case of the Floyd character in the demonstration provided, there are a number of animation clips that are chosen based on a notional "mood" value held in the blackboard of the character. With this we are able to portray a number of moods through postural changes that can be quite subtle; elements such as slumping of the shoulders, making the eyelids droop, or in the case of Floyd, who is intended as a comedic sidekick worker robot, his "eye" glows slightly less to denote a more somber mood.

35.4.7 GestureComponent

Gestures play a large part in the portrayal of a character, in that they allow the player to quickly appraise the feelings of the character by observing the gestures made. Characters that gesture often, with wide arm movements and large shifts of body weight, are generally considered more energetic and positive. Once again, the `GestureComponent` essentially modifies the animation of the character by selecting different animation clips. In this case, the clips are usually additively blended on top of basic motion clips. In the case of a humanoid character we must take care not to attempt a gesture while performing other animations that would look out of place. So, for instance, we only play gestures that require arm movements when no other animation is playing that would affect the arms too strongly. More specifically, it makes no sense to incorporate greeting gestures when the character is doing a forward roll.

One of the more challenging aspects of the `GestureComponent` functionality is in knowing when to initiate a gesture. Typically, we gesture more when we are trying to make a point or guide a conversation. Usually this gestural "language" underlies a discussion by punctuating key words with gestures, known by social scientists as *nonverbal communication*. Fully describing the role of nonverbal communication is beyond the scope of this chapter, but it is very important for believable characters. The reader is recommended to seek out academic work in this area such as *Bodily Communication* by Michael Argyle [Argyle 88].

Given that gestures often accompany speech, it may be useful to allow audio engineers to trigger gestures by allowing them to send events at appropriate points in the audio clip. Another issue is when gestures are required to touch another character. This requires a great deal of precision in order to achieve the touch without problems of penetrating the mesh of the other character. Although it is not implemented in the example code, a simple 2 bone inverse kinematic controller is often used to control the exact position of the hand during gestures involving other characters.

While the class diagram in Figure 35.3 may seem complex, the beauty of this system of components is that each component is relatively simple to implement. Because each component deals with a single aspect of behavior, we can structure the code to be straightforward in dealing with only that single aspect. In practice, this means that we can implement each component optionally; components are tied together via events and generally do not know about one another or rely on each other to function. The exceptions to this case are that

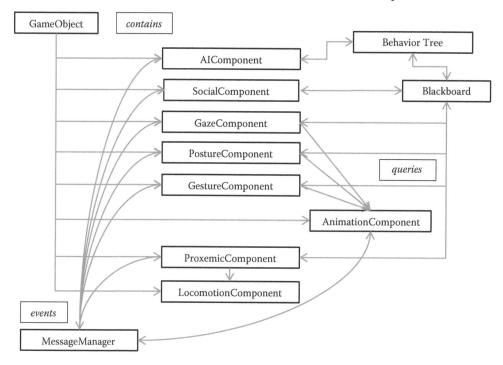

Figure 35.3

Shows how the individual components communicate with one another and with the behavior tree and blackboard implemented within the AIComponent.

Part V. Agent Awareness and Knowledge Representation

most of the components discussed require access to the `AnimationComponent` and that the functioning of many of the components requires that the `SocialComponent` be added to the character in order to coordinate the behavior. Even this is not a strict requirement, as it is possible to debug behavior by simply injecting the relevant events into the event stream to be read by the various components.

35.5 Execution

As is shown in Figure 35.3, the individual components are contained within a `GameObject` parent container. Each component can access data from the `AIComponent` via the blackboard. When a character becomes aware of available social interaction possibilities, either via the sensory system or via the event system, this information is placed into the blackboard. This in turn makes the behavior tree conditions become true, which cause an event to be sent to the `SocialComponent` of the parent `GameObject`. The `SocialComponent` in turn sends an event to the `SocialObjectComponent` of the sensed object to request participation in the interaction.

Once the `SocialObjectComponent` receives enough requests to fulfill its role, it sends an event to all participants notifying them of their role in the interaction. Prior to this notification, all agents are continuing with their previous behavior. It should be noted that the number of potential social interactions in which a given agent can request participation should be determined by the requirements of the game and can have an impact on overall performance. Too few requests mean agents appear to be unsociable, but too many requests create unnecessary processing to occur when agents have to remove their requests upon successfully starting an interaction. Events to set the origin for the interaction, as well as participant information, turn taking, and other coordination information, are sent periodically. Finally when the interaction is deemed completed, the `SocialObjectComponent` sends an event to release all remaining participants, allowing them to continue seeking other interactions or to pursue alternative behavior.

Each update of the `AIComponent` in the main game loop executes the character behavior tree, which in turn updates data in the blackboard. During the same update loop, the `SocialComponent` reads the updated data and sends events to the other components that respond with appropriate changes in position/orientation/posture/gaze/etc. The final effect of these changes is then either assimilated into the current animation or is output as forces which are then incorporated into the next locomotion update.

35.6 Conclusion

The requirement for social dynamic behavior for game characters is compelling. As we strive for ever increasing visual realism, we should also strive for behavioral realism. This is not to say that we need to restrict ourselves to "realistic" behavior so much as to propose that we pay attention to the facets of behavior that increase the believability of our characters. A component-based approach to these facets of behavior allows us to iteratively implement and refine our approaches to these aspects. We can start off with a simple "look at player" component and extend the system over time. The goal is to create characters that enable the player to believe they are alive and ensuring that they play their part in making the game a compelling experience. Incorporating the finer details of character social dynamics helps lead us to worlds in which the player believes in the illusion of life.

References

[Ancessi 10] Laurent Ancessi interview with Alex Champandard (aiGameDev.com). Available online (http://aigamedev.com/premium/masterclass/interactive-parkour-animation/).

[Argyle 88] M. Argyle. *Bodily Communication*. Taylor & Francis, 1988, p. 363.

[Cassell 00] J. Cassell. *Embodied Conversational Agents*. MIT Press, 2000, p. 440.

[Kendon 90] A. Kendon. *Conducting Interaction: Patterns of Behavior in Focused Encounters (Studies in Interactional Sociolinguistics)*. Cambridge University Press, 1990, p. 308.

[Pedica and Vilhjálmsson 08] C. Pedica and H. Vilhjálmsson. "Social perception and steering for online avatars." *Intelligent Virtual Agents*, Springer, 2008, pp. 104–116.

36

Breathing Life into Your Background Characters

David "Rez" Graham

36.1 Introduction

Background AI is an important component of any game that contains nonplayer characters, critters, and other background elements, as it adds to the believability and immersion of your game. For the purposes of this article, NPCs are background characters, as opposed to enemy agents or major, story-driven characters, although there's nothing stopping you from applying these same principles to other characters as well.

It's important to provide the illusion that these background NPCs have their own lives and personalities so that your game world comes to life. If you have static NPCs that don't look like they're busy with their lives, your world will feel stale. The catch is that since these are minor NPCs, they can't cost very much in terms of memory, CPU time, or development time.

The chosen technique must also be able to scale in the number of NPCs processed, the complexity of their AI, and how often they're processed since it's likely that NPC behavior and content will get scaled back as cuts to the development schedule need to be made. There are performance and memory concerns as well. As the game comes to a close, CPU and memory intensive systems will end up getting scaled back, and it's important that the chosen solution can easily be scaled in either direction.

36.2 Common Techniques

There are a number of common techniques that many games use when adding background NPCs to their games. One approach is to use looping idles, where the NPC loops a single animation over and over. You might have a blacksmith who does nothing but hammer away at a sword for the entire duration of the game, or perhaps you have an innkeeper who is constantly wiping down the counter. This is often paired with other NPCs running random walk cycles where they simply choose a random location, walk there, idle for a minute, and then do it all over again. Unfortunately, neither of these techniques looks very good, which is not surprising when you consider that old RPGs from the NES and SNES era did the exact same thing.

Another common pitfall is to swing the pendulum in the other direction and attempt to implement a deep, rich AI system. If you already have a complex AI system you use for major NPCs or enemies, it might make sense to reuse that system for background characters, but this is often a mistake. By their very nature, background characters are not the focus of the player. They are just there for flavor. A much simpler system that is faster and uses less memory is usually the better choice here, because it allows you to have more background NPCs, which is important for creating the illusion of a large city. Only seeing four or five NPCs wandering around is not enough to convince the player that he's in a city, but seeing 20 or 30 might be. The goal here is to get the best of both worlds and be able to scale your solution towards either direction.

36.3 Description of the Schedule System

Three important criteria for determining if a strategy for background AI is feasible are high performance, scalability, and ease of implementation. Performance is important because you will want to run dozens or even hundreds of NPCs at one time. Running complex scoring functions during updates is often too expensive to be a viable solution. Having a modular system that lets you swap out complex components for simple ones lets you throttle the performance of the system without having to rewrite anything. The final solution needs to be very low-risk from an implementation and maintenance point of view as well. It should be as data-driven as possible so that once it's built, the designers and animators should be able to do 90% of the work necessary to create as many background NPCs as they desire.

One way to meet all three criteria and still get reasonable-looking behavior is to use a schedule system. A schedule can be thought of as a black box where the input is the current time and the output is an action. Under the covers, these actions are really nothing more than "go here and run this animation." By itself, a single NPC will still be rather predictable and stale, but if you have a dozen or more NPCs all running different schedules, you suddenly have a living, breathing world. At its heart, a schedule is really just a set of time blocks where each block defines the behavior for an NPC executing that schedule. The system is a lightweight, data-driven, hierarchical state machine, where the top-level state selection is based on time.

We used a system similar to this one on *The Sims Medieval* to give designers the flexibility they were after. It's also been used successfully on a number of RPGs and simulation games, which is where this kind of system works well. It can be used on other types of games, like first-person shooters, adventure games, etc., but you may have to make some modifications. We'll discuss this further later in the chapter.

36.4 Schedule Architecture

There are three key components to this schedule system: *schedules*, *schedule entries*, and *actions*. Together, these concepts form the core of the background AI system.

36.4.1 Schedules

Schedules are linked to NPCs with a pointer, an ID, or anything else that's appropriate to the system. The schedule is the top-level interface for accessing any schedule data on the NPC and manipulating the schedule during runtime. Schedules contain a number of schedule entries, each of which represents a slice of time (see the following). With this system, NPCs may only be in one schedule entry at a time, though it wouldn't be too difficult to allow schedule layering as long as the rules were simple enough. One example would be to allow NPCs to consider all possible actions for all schedules they were in. Another idea is to allow an NPC to have multiple schedules but only one active schedule at a time. On *The Sims Medieval*, we chose the latter method.

Schedules are responsible for moving to the appropriate schedule entry based on the current time. They are also responsible for calling into the currently running entry and returning the appropriate action for the NPC to perform. Any functionality of a running schedule that needs to be accessed by the rest of the game should go here.

In the example code that accompanies this article (available on the book's website, http://www.gameaipro.com), the schedule component is implemented with the `ScheduleInstance` and `ScheduleDefinition` classes. `ScheduleInstance` represents the runtime data for a schedule, such as which entry is currently active, while `ScheduleDefinition` represents the static data that never changes, such as the ID and which schedule entries are tied to that schedule.

36.4.2 Schedule Entries

A *schedule entry* is a single slice of time within the schedule. It manages the lifecycle of the schedule entry and determines when it's time to move to the next entry. Schedule entries also encapsulate the decision-making an NPC performs when it is looking for something to do. For this reason, schedule entries are typically implemented with a strategy pattern, or other design pattern that enables you to easily swap one entry for another [Gamma et al. 01].

Whenever an NPC is idle within a schedule, it calls into the schedule to find a new action. The schedule calls into the currently active schedule entry, which in turn runs the actual decision-making logic to find a new action for the NPC to perform. This is returned up to the NPC, which then performs the appropriate action. The function in the schedule entry for choosing a new action is a pure virtual function whose implementation is dependent on the specific subclass that's instantiated. Schedule entries are all interchangeable and conform to a single interface. The specific schedule entry that is instantiated is determined by the type set in the data, which is passed to a factory.

Defining different schedule entry subclasses and overriding the action chooser function gives you a lot of control over how complex you want your background NPC AI logic to be.

You could return a single action, or a random action from a list, or you could run through a bunch of complex scoring algorithms that weigh NPC desires and goals based on the current world state. This is exactly what *The Sims Medieval* does. Each schedule entry had a set of desires for the Sim to fulfill above and beyond their standard desires. For example, the Blacksmith might attempt to satisfy his "Be a Blacksmith" desire by working at the forge.

Schedule entry types can also be mixed and matched. Some schedule entries could return a single action while others might use a more complex form of scoring. Changing the decision-making strategy is as simple as changing the schedule data. You can then build a library of various decision-making strategies and let your designers choose the one they want for each situation. This is the power of a data-driven scheduling system.

In the example code that accompanies this article, the schedule entry system starts with the `ScheduleEntry` base class, which declares the pure virtual function `ChooseNewAction()` as the action chooser. This class, along with the sample subclasses, is defined in the ScheduleEntry.cpp file.

36.4.3 Actions and Object Ownership

Actions are the output of schedules and represent things that NPCs do. They usually define a target object, the duration of the action, maybe an animation, and any other bits of data necessary to execute the action. Actions are very game-dependent; each game will likely have its own way of making NPCs interact with the world. This part of the system is the interface into your world. The actions returned by the action chooser in the schedule entry should be in whatever format works for your game. On *The Sims Medieval*, we called them *interaction definitions*. They were objects that contained the necessary information to instantiate an interaction on a Sim.

It's usually not enough to have an NPC interact with a targeted object. It's much more common to tell an NPC to sleep in its own bed or to work at its particular forge. We want the best of both worlds, so the action system needs to deal with the concept of object ownership as well.

All game objects that can be interacted with should have a type ID, which defines the type of object it is. The object type is really just metadata for the designer to label groups of similar objects. For example, all beds could be grouped under the "bed" type. This allows NPCs to own an object of a particular type, which greatly simplifies the scheduling data. For example, a schedule could have an action that tells the NPC to go to bed. The NPC will look in its map of owned objects and check to see if it has a "bed" object. If it does, it will use that bed. If not, some default behavior can be defined. Perhaps the NPC will choose a random bed, or perhaps it will fail the action and choose a new one. This same action could be applied to multiple NPCs without modification and it would work just fine. Each NPC would go to its own appropriate bed.

Defining object ownership is also game-specific. One common approach is to set up object ownership in your NPC tool as a set of object type to object ID mappings. This way, it can be specified by designers. Another approach is to support larger, more encompassing tags. For example, on *The Sims Medieval* designers had a spreadsheet that allowed them to map NPCs to their home and work buildings. This gave them permission to use all of the objects in those buildings so when they were told to "go home," they went to the appropriate place.

As an example, consider the sample action XML definition in Listing 36.1.

Listing 36.1. This is an example of an XML definition for an action.

```
<Action name = "bake_in_oven" target = "baker_oven"
        minDuration = "0.1" maxDuration = "0.2"
        animation = "bake_bread.anm"/>
```

The target of the action is an object type ID. This is not a specific object in the world, but rather a type of object. This will cause the NPC to search its mapping of objects it owns and, if it owns the appropriate type of object, perform the action on that object. If it doesn't, it will run some sort of default behavior, such as finding the closest object of that type.

This also allows you to target a group where multiple NPCs may own different objects. In the example above, there may be multiple oven objects with the "baker_oven" type, each owned by a different NPC. This cuts down on data duplication quite a bit.

The system as described only allows NPCs to own a single object of any given type. As long as you have reasonable rules for handling it, there's nothing stopping you from allowing NPCs to own multiple objects of the same type. One example would be to always choose the closest object.

In the example code that accompanies this article, actions are split into instances and definitions, just like schedules. There's the `ActionInstance` class and the `ActionDefinition` class. The `ActionInstance` class handles all the runtime data while the `ActionDefinition` handles the static data.

36.4.4 Putting It All Together

Putting all three of these systems together gives you a great framework for creating a simple scheduling system. To illustrate the point further, take a look at Listing 36.2.

Listing 36.2. An example of an NPC schedule with two entries. The first entry is a simple sleep entry that causes the NPC to sleep in its bed. The second entry has two actions which are chosen from a weighted random distribution. The NPC has a 25% chance to work at the copier and a 75% chance to work at its desk.

```
<Schedule name = "Drone">
        <Entry name = "Sleep" type = "Simple" startTime = "22">
                <Action type = "sleep"/>
        </Entry>
        <Entry name = "work_at_desk" type = "WeightedRandom"
                        startTime = "8">
                <Action type = "work_at_desk" weight = "3"/>
                <Action type = "work_at_copier" weight = "1"/>
        </Entry>
</Schedule>
```

36.5 Schedule Templates

One downside of schedules is that they tend to result in a lot of data duplication. For example, if your game has a day/night cycle, it's likely every NPC will have a schedule entry for sleeping. In fact, many of the entries will be very similar with each other. You can mitigate this by allowing templates and data inheritance.

Let's say that you have a guard schedule entry that determines where a guard should stand. If you build this entry in a template, you can apply that template to every guard's schedule and override just the data that's specific to that particular schedule. Adding this functionality is pretty straightforward. The template itself should have the exact same schema as the schedule entry, so all you need to do is create a schedule entry for each template and store it in a table for easy lookup.

Take a look at Listing 36.3 for an example of what this template might look like in XML.

Listing 36.3. Two schedule entry templates, one for sleeping and one for guarding.

```
<ScheduleEntryTemplates>
        <Entry name = "SleepTemplate" type = "Simple">
            <Action type = "sleep"/>
        </Entry>
        <Entry name = "GuardTemplate" type = "WeightedRandom">
            <!-- prefer to guard the residential area -->
            <Action type = "guard_west" weight = "2"/>
            <Action type = "guard_east" weight = "1"/>
        </Entry>
</ScheduleEntryTemplates>
```

Defining the guard schedules is just a matter of pointing to the templates and overriding the values you care about, as shown in Listing 36.4.

Listing 36.4. Two schedules using the same templates with overrides.

```
<Schedule name = "DayGuard">
        <Entry name = "Sleep" template = "SleepTemplate"
            startTime = "16"/>
        <Entry name = "StandGuard" template = "GuardTemplate"
            startTime = "8"/>
</Schedule>
<Schedule name = "NightGuard">
        <Entry name = "Sleep" template = "SleepTemplate"
            startTime = "8"/>
        <Entry name = "StandGuard" template = "GuardTemplate"
            startTime = "16"/>
</Schedule>
```

36.6 Improvements

There are a number of improvements that can be made to this system. First, only schedule entries use the template system, when in fact all of the schedule components could benefit from it. Every part of a schedule should be inheritable so that designers can build up a toolbox of different schedule parts to compose into final schedules for their NPCs.

Another improvement is in the handling of schedule caching. Currently, every schedule, template, action, and entry is stored in memory. This was done for simplicity and ease of explanation. A more appropriate implementation will depend on the design of your game. If your NPCs rarely switch schedules, you can flush out the schedules that are currently not being used and load them dynamically when necessary. This could potentially even be done on the schedule entry layer, since moving from one entry to another doesn't happen very often.

In the demo, IDs are handled as strings. This is how schedules are linked to actions and NPCs. This is another place where we chose this method due to its simplicity and ease of explanation. Every game uses something different for object IDs and has its own method of linking objects together. However, it's worth noting that doing string compares to match IDs is not a good strategy. At the very least, you'll want to hash those strings into unique IDs.

Another thing to consider is the rigid nature of schedules. If you have a schedule that sends NPCs to an inn for dinner and drinks at 6:00pm every day, you could easily have a pile of NPCs all stopping whatever they're doing and immediately heading to the inn at the exact same time. A better solution is to randomize the schedule update time with a Gaussian distribution function centered on the end time for that schedule entry. This will cause NPCs to move to their next entry at a time reasonably close to the tuned time, as long as you don't mind them being a little early sometimes. You can also rely on the action itself to inject some randomization. This is what we did on *The Sims Medieval*. Sims who changed to a new schedule would finish their current interaction before going to their scheduled location.

Integrating a scheduling system into your existing AI system can be very powerful. The core AI system needs to be able to override the schedule system when necessary. For example, if the player attacks the baker, the baker's schedule should be thrown out the window and he should either fight back or run away. Once the threat is gone, he can resume his schedule. This can work for enemies as well. You could assign a schedule to all enemies that will get overridden as soon as they notice the player.

Right now, schedule entries are defined by time. They represent what an NPC should be doing at a particular time, but not all games have the concept of time. Fortunately, it's easy to change this to anything else. For example, you could have schedules that choose schedule entries based on game events or player movements. You could have NPCs exist in a guarding schedule entry that changes when an alarm is raised.

You could even mix the two and have some schedule entries that are controlled by time and others that are controlled by events. This would allow you to have NPCs that run around on schedules but can also react to the world around them. For example, you could have a shopkeeper with a typical work schedule who can also respond when the town is attacked by orcs. Remember, the underlying structure behind this schedule system is a hierarchical finite-state machine. It's relatively easy to bring it closer to its roots.

Another limitation of the current system is that NPCs can only own a single object of any given type. As long as you have reasonable rules, there's nothing stopping you from allowing NPCs to own multiple objects of the same type.

Finally, all of the schedule data is in XML. Asking a designer to hand-edit this XML is not very realistic, so you will need to build a scheduling tool that can generate the necessary data and link it to game objects. A simple C# application with a grid control should suffice.

Note that this is a place where having a component-based object hierarchy [Rene 05] can really help. You can simply build a component that handles all the schedule data and attach it to any game object that needs to be controlled through a schedule. You could have another component that tracks the object type and allows objects with that component to be targets for schedules. This would allow you to easily slot in the schedule system.

36.7 Conclusion

NPCs can make or break the player's suspension of disbelief in your game. If you have an NPC that spends the entire game nailing in a board on a wall or polishing a sword, the illusion of a living world starts to go out the window. Fortunately, building believable background characters can be achieved quickly and easily using a scheduling system. NPCs are locked into schedules and updated with very simple behavioral AI. With just a handful of schedules, the hustle and bustle of a town will begin to emerge. Players will see NPCs going about their regular day and begin to infer a story from them. With a very small amount of work, your game worlds can come alive.

References

[Gamma et al. 01] E. Gamma, R. Helm, R. Johnson, and J. Vlissides. *Design Patterns: Elements of Reusable Object-Oriented Software*. Reading, MA: Addison-Wesley, 1995, pp. 315–323.

[Rene 05] B. Rene. "Component based object management." In *Game Programming Gems 5*, edited by Kim Pallister. Reading, MA: Charles River Media, 2005, pp. 25–37.

37

Alibi Generation
Fooling All the Players All the Time

Ben Sunshine-Hill

37.1 Introduction

The sandbox just keeps growing. Recent open-world games let players roam freely over tens or hundreds of square miles. And it's not just raw size: the bar for density and variety of content keeps being raised. Of course, the bar keeps being raised! We don't just want to give players a *space*; we want to give them a *world*. A living, reacting, interacting world, where a player's actions can have far-reaching consequences, and where a new plot lies in wait behind every doorway, behind the eyes of every individual character going about his virtual life. Where things are happening, and the player—if she dares—can become a part of them.

That's the ideal, anyway. But while a combination of large content teams, efficient level building techniques, and careful use of procedural content generation have given us larger and more varied worlds, we're still trying to figure out how to populate and simulate them. We tend to spawn randomly generated characters in the area around the player (the "simulation bubble"), giving the impression of a fully populated world. But it's tricky to keep up the illusion. If the player blocks a just-spawned NPC's path, how will he replan? If the player picks his pockets, what will she find? If the player follows him, where will he turn out to be going? With a careless approach to character generation, the answers are likely to be "back the other way," "`rand(0,10)` money," and "endlessly wandering"... and that's just not good enough anymore. The bar's up *here* now.

Alibi generation is a more considered, consistent kind of character generation. NPCs are still generated randomly to fill the simulation bubble, but as necessary, they are given *alibis*: filled-out backstories, goals, and states of being; everything necessary to play the part of a living, breathing character in a living, breathing world. Done properly, it is *impossible* for the player to determine whether an NPC has always been around or whether they were just given an alibi a couple of seconds ago.

37.1.1 Background

The underpinnings of alibi generation rely heavily on probability theory. To get the most out of this article, you should be familiar with terminology such as *joint distribution*, with notation such as $E[PQ] - E[P]E[Q]$ and $P(\neg A | B = 1)$, and with tools such as Bayesian networks. For an introduction to this field, I highly recommend the Khan Academy series of videos on probability.

37.2 Your Ideal World

Suppose your game was meant to execute on the ultimate hardware: An infinitely fast processor with unlimited memory. There would be no reason for the simulation bubble, of course; it is much more straightforward to simulate all the characters in the world, all the time. And no reason to start them *in media res*, either: Just start everyone at home and run them for a few in-game hours as part of the first frame of simulation.

That's not to say that you'd have no need for procedural generation. Since your content team *wouldn't* be infinite, you'd still need to use it to create your world's populace in the first place. But rather than generating them as a current state, you'd have the system generate the information *about* them: Where they live, where they work, how they dress, what sorts of activities they engage in; their AI rules would take care of the rest. As the content creator, you'd create the following items:

1. A list of immutable "fact" features about a character. This list might include "where the character lives" and "how tall the character is." Some of these things might be immediately visible ("what color the character's hair is"), but most will be only indirectly observable ("what food the character prefers").
2. A list of possible values for each fact and how likely each of those values is. (In the case of features like "where the character lives," this will probably be generated from information in the world.)
3. A list of mutable state features about a character. Most of these will be immediately visible things like "what the character is currently doing," but some may be less visible, like "how hungry the character is."
4. Rules for how a character chooses actions, based on their immutable facts and their current state, and for how those actions affect the character's state.

You'd probably spend much of your time on the second item, deciding which facts were correlated with which other facts, and how likely each value was. In contrast, you wouldn't bother coming up with information like "How likely is it that the character is in a Mexican restaurant *right now*," because there'd be no need for it. Each character would go about his life, and the interaction between his immutable facts, his mutable state, and his rules of behavior would lead to a mutable state which either included "in a Mexican restaurant" or didn't. Put differently, a character's immutable facts would be the cause, and the character's mutable state would be the effect. A character whose facts included "prefers Mexican food" would be more likely to be in a Mexican restaurant at any given moment than a character whose facts didn't, without you needing to specifically hard-code that in.

Alibi generation turns this around. It starts by generating only the visible information about a character. Later, if necessary, it treats the visible information as the cause, and generates the invisible information (the alibi) as an effect. For instance, if a character is generated with visible information including "in a Mexican restaurant," and later the player gets into a conversation with the character and an alibi is needed, the alibi generated for the character would be more likely than average to include "prefers Mexican food."

But—and here's where it gets a bit tricky—how often *should* you generate people in Mexican restaurants, and exactly how much more likely *is* it that someone in a Mexican restaurant prefers Mexican food? The key feature that makes alibi generation useful is that you, as the content creator, are still responsible *only for coming up with the four original items*. All of the dependent information used to generate characters *in media res*, and to give them alibis later, is generated in a preprocessing step based on that original information.

Let's go into this a little more. There are three parts to the runtime component of alibi generation: Generating initial, alibi-less characters, identifying when an alibi is necessary, and generating an alibi for a character. We'll explore each of these in turn.

37.2.1 Heisenburgh

It's difficult to go too far into this "ideal world" stuff without an example application, so we'll present ours: Heisenburgh. Heisenburgh is a simple simulation of pedestrians in a city, about the size and population of Manhattan. (Its street layout is adapted from a region of Basra, Iraq.) There are thousands of potential points of interest in the city, such as homes, office buildings, restaurants, banks, and theaters. In the full simulation, a character has a home and a workplace. They pick a next goal (such as "go to work" or "eat at a nice restaurant") based on their current location, walk there via the shortest path, then stay there for a random amount of time dependent on the type of goal. Goals can be round-trip errands or one-way journeys. For some types of goals (e.g., getting a hot dog), characters pick the closest destination of its type; for others (e.g., visiting a friend) they pick a particular one in the world. Afterward, they either return to their previous location, or pick a new goal, depending on the goal type.

Heisenburgh's mechanics are simple, yet simulating millions of its characters in real time is beyond the capabilities of current-generation video game hardware.

We broke the world into sectors of about eight city blocks each and simulated only the sectors visible to the player, using alibi generation to manage characters. Each sector was connected to neighboring sectors by "portals," which tended to be in the middle of blocks. We precomputed the shortest path through a sector from any portal to any other portal, from any building within the sector to any other building within the same sector, and between any portal and any building in the sector. These precomputed paths were known as "path segments," and a character got from place to place by following a sequence of these path segments. A character's initial information consisted of their current path segment

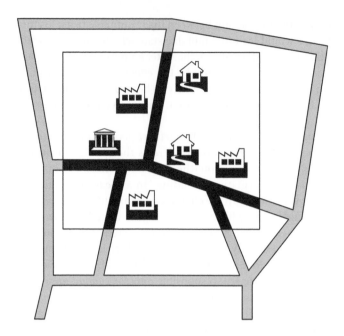

Figure 37.1

A single sector (rectangular outline) in Heisenburgh. This sector contains six buildings and five portals, and results in 110 path segments: 20 from portal to portal, 30 from portal to building, 30 from building to portal, and 30 from building to building.

(including direction); their alibi consisted of the building they had previously left and the building they were heading towards, as well as their reason for the trip (Figure 37.1).

37.3 Initial Generation

Initial generation of characters, of course, is something we already know how to do, because we've been doing it all along. It needs to be really quick to do, because we'll be doing it for every character, including unimportant background characters. From the point of view of alibi generation, the most important aspect of initial generation is that it has to be consistent with the distribution of characters in the full simulation. If you generate a character walking down an alley toward a dead end and there aren't any destinations at the end of the alley (or other AI reasons why a character would go there), it'll be impossible to generate an alibi for that character. More subtly, if there's only one destination in that direction, every character walking down it will get an alibi which includes going to that destination, so the alley had better be exactly as populated as that destination is popular.

37.3.1 Population Size

The first part of initial generation we need to look at is deciding how *many* characters to generate in a particular place (say, in a bookstore when the player first walks in), and how often to generate new ones (new customers walking through the door). The most important aspect of this is that the two processes match up. If the entry rate is too high, the bookstore will start out deserted and quickly fill up; if it's too low, the bookstore will become deserted over time.

For Heisenburgh, after breaking the world into sectors, we identified all possible paths through each sector, each end of a path being either a sector boundary or a building entrance. We calculated and stored the average population of each path. (Note that a "path" may be several blocks long and a single block of sidewalk will have many "paths" which go down it.)

To generate the initial population when a player moves into view of a new sector, we used the *Poisson distribution*. This is a random distribution over populations, which takes the average population as its only parameter and assumes that characters' positions are independent of each other. Sampling from the Poisson distribution can be done using a simple iterative algorithm [Knuth 69].

To generate new characters entering a sector at the beginning of a sector path when the adjacent sector was not visible, we used the *exponential distribution* to generate the "time until next arrival." This distribution takes the average entry rate as its only parameter. If the average population of a path segment is p and the time to travel all the way along this path segment is t, the average entry rate is p/t. After sampling a time until next arrival, a delayed event is set for that future time; when the event fires, a new character enters that path segment, and a new next-arrival-time is generated. A global priority queue manages all arrival times. When two adjacent sectors are both visible, we didn't generate new entries from one into the other, as that would result in characters visibly popping into being. Instead, characters got into the sector the normal way: by previously being in the other sector.

The Poisson and exponential distributions are, mathematically, the "correct" distributions to use for these tasks, assuming simple independence and homogeneity properties. There's little reason to deviate from them. Moreover, since the distributions depend on only two numbers per path, this data can simply be precalculated and stored.

37.3.2 Position and Other Information

For each character starting on a path, it's necessary to define where they are on that path. That's done simply by sampling a random position on the path, then offsetting by a small random amount to bootstrap collision avoidance. A character's appearance—face, clothing, etc.—is also randomly generated as a set of meshes, which are then merged.

37.4 Identifying When an Alibi Is Necessary

When deciding whether to generate an alibi for a given character, you need to strike a balance between realism and performance. Simulating a character may become more expensive once they have an alibi, and the alibi generation process itself may also be expensive. However, waiting too long to generate an alibi may make it impossible to find one which is consistent with everything the player has already observed about the character.

Ideally, you want to generate an alibi at some point before the alibi-less and alibi-ful behavior of the character could diverge. If a character has just started walking down a block with no destinations on it, there's little uncertainty about what their short-term behavior will be. It's only once they get to the end of the block and need to decide which way to turn that they would draw on their hidden, internal state. Interaction with the player can also necessitate an early alibi.

For Heisenburgh, splitting character-traveled regions into paths through sectors worked in our favor here. Since a character's initial state usually included several blocks of walking, it wasn't necessary to generate an alibi for them the first time they turned a corner. It was only once they approached a sector boundary—and the end of their path through the sector—that an alibi was needed. Moreover, if a character came into being almost at the end of their sector path, we did not immediately generate an alibi; instead, we picked a random path through the next sector for them, relying on the player's inability to reason about their path given the tiny portion of it they were able to see.

37.5 Generating the Alibi

Successfully generating an alibi starts with the groundwork laid out by the initial generation. Like initial generation, the goal is to come up with a set of data that is consistent with certain prior conditions. Storing the entire conditional probability table for alibi generation, however, would be utterly infeasible—it's much too large. The real trick, then, is finding a compact representation for the alibi distribution and a way to sample from it. There are a few options for this; we'll present one here, and others in Section 37.6.

Enter the Metropolis–Hastings algorithm. This is a technique for generating random samples from a distribution which is difficult to sample—or even compute—directly. It is a *random walk* technique, which starts from some initial condition and then incrementally modifies that condition over many iterations. Although the initial condition is not random, over time the distribution of the current state converges to the desired probability distribution. In conventional Metropolis–Hastings, the goal is usually to generate a large number of samples from the same distribution; the first few hundred iterations are known as the *burn-in*, and are discarded because they are likely to be correlated with the initial state. For alibi generation, however, we spend all of our iterations on burn-in; after that, we take the last state as the alibi.

The best part of Metropolis–Hastings is that we don't actually need to compute conditional probabilities. Given initial data D, to sample an alibi $A|D$, we need to compare the *relative* probability of two alibis, $P(A_1|D)/P(A_2|D)$. By Bayes' Rule, this is the same as $P(A_1,D)/P(A_2,D)$. So we need to provide a function $f(A,D) \propto P(A_1,D)$. We also need to provide a transition function which randomly chooses a "nearby" candidate alibi A_2 given A_1 as input, and a function $q(A_1 \rightarrow A_2)$ which tells us the probability of that transition – the probability of choosing that candidate alibi A_2 when moving from A_1.

During each iteration, we perturb A_1 into A_2 using our random transition function. Then we compute the acceptance probability, $a = \min\left(\dfrac{f(A_2,D)\, q(A_2 \rightarrow A_1)}{f(A_1,D)\, q(A_1 \rightarrow A_2)}, 1 \right)$. We accept A_2 with probability a; if we do not accept it, our current alibi remains as A_1.

For Heisenburgh, we analytically generated a small set of tables that could be used to generate $f(A,D)$ [Sunshine-Hill 11]; these consisted of conditional probability tables and tables of per-destination probability distributions (like entry rate). Remember that an alibi consisted of source and destination buildings; to perturb an alibi, we perturbed the source building, then the destination building. Each building in the world held a table of nearby buildings (including the building itself), and perturbed source and destination were sampled uniformly from the current source and destination buildings' tables. To avoid a division by zero, we removed unidirectional transitions from the tables, which often made them differently sized. That meant that $q(A_1 \rightarrow A_2)$ was the reciprocal of the product of the source and destination table sizes.

Alibi generation took place in two steps: First, determining *where* a character was going, and second, determining *why*. The "where" consisted of both their source and destination. The "why" consisted of whether their current destination is a one-way trip, going to a round-trip errand, or returning from a round-trip errand, and what their goal was. The second step was important because it helped determine what the character's *next* action would be and because it determined whether the source or destination had any particular significance to them. If the player were to see a character going home to a particular building, that character had better keep going home to that same building in the future.

37.6 Options for Alibi Generation

The most difficult part of alibi generation is designing and building the data which is used for the sampling. I've shown you the gold standard—the Metropolis–Hastings sampling from closed-form probability distributions—but there are a few options.

37.6.1 Exact Calculation

For Heisenburgh, we built a representation of the alibi distribution which was provably identical to the stationary distribution of the "ideal world" (the full simulation). I won't lie to you: Doing this is *very, very difficult*. Even for the simple character AI we used, solving the full set of equations took weeks and invoked deeply obscure areas of stochastic process theory. Doing things this way is great if you can pull it off, since its results are dependably correct; but if your AI rules are significantly complicated, it's just not feasible.

For more information on Metropolis–Hastings, I recommend [Chib and Greenberg 95].

37.6.2 Canned Alibis

A really, really simple approach to alibi generation is to store, for each unique set of initial conditions, a list of prerecorded alibis. For instance, you might have a list of alibis specifically for men who are wearing suits, carrying paper bags, and walking east on a particular block. A randomly (or sequentially) chosen alibi from the list is applied whenever one is needed.

The benefit of this approach, of course, is simplicity. There's no need for elaborate probability calculations, and it's by far the fastest way to "generate" an alibi. It's a one-size-fits-all solution. The drawback is the need to strike a compromise between space requirements and variety: The more alibis per initial condition set, the larger the space requirement; but the fewer alibis, the less variety that alibi generation can create.

The space requirement is dependent on both the world size and the variety of initial conditions. The former affects both disk space and RAM space; the latter affects only RAM space, since alibis will only need to be generated for characters who were created near the player's current position, so the lists can be paged in and out. It's especially important, therefore, to limit the dimensionality of initial conditions, at least those which delineate alibi lists. For instance, in the above example you might choose not to have separate lists for carrying paper bags versus not carrying paper bags.

The recording process is simple: Have an option to simulate the entire world fully populated, run it for a while, and take snapshots of people in different initial conditions. It's useful to disable graphics, sound, and any other subsystems with no bearing on the simulation. If your characters all start at deterministic locations, remember to give them time to wander for a while before you start sampling. Additionally, don't sample too frequently, or alibis for contiguous paths may end up overly correlated. This process can be informally parallelized; run it on several machines overnight and combine their alibi lists.

37.6.3 Hybrid Generation

There's a potential middle path for people who want variety and a large space of initial conditions, but still want to use recording to generate alibi lists. The basic idea is to start with canned alibis, then add variety to some aspects of the alibi—but not others—using random perturbation.

The most likely way to employ this strategy is to perturb the character's current destination, but only among destinations of the same type. As in the Metropolis–Hastings method, each building has a transition table of nearby buildings, but now it is only among buildings of the same type. And as in the canned alibis method, each set of initial data has a table of alibis to choose from. First, a canned alibi is chosen; then, that alibi's destination's transition table is used to move the alibi destination around. Only a few burn-in iterations, or even just one, need to be run, and $f(A_2, D)/f(A_1, D) \sim 1$ (as long as the current path is along the shortest path to A_2; otherwise, it is 0), so the acceptance probability is only the ratio of the table sizes. It's perhaps a stretch to even call this Metropolis–Hastings; it's basically just a random walk over the space of possible destinations.

37.7 Maintaining and Deleting Characters

An important question to ask about alibi generation, particularly if we're looking at it as an improvement to the "simulation bubble" approach, is when to *remove* characters. As a first approach, we can simply delete characters when their current sector becomes invisible. That's akin to the simulation bubble, but it creates obvious potential problems. Even if the player hasn't been watching a character for long, she still might notice if she goes around a corner, comes back, and he's gone. We can make this a little less likely by depopulating invisible sectors only if the player is more than a specified distance away or only once they've been invisible for a certain period of time; this way, the player would not be assured of being able to find the same characters even in the full simulation. In the case of interior locations where characters may remain for some time, a longer invisibility cutoff time should be used.

It's a good idea to extend the lifetimes of characters with alibis. A character with an alibi often has one because they were specifically important to the character in some way, so they may be memorable to the character for longer. This can create a situation where an invisible sector has a couple of characters with alibis in it, but it is otherwise unpopulated. When you initially populate a sector which already has characters in it—alibi-ful or otherwise—you should subtract this population from the "average population" parameter used for the Poisson distribution, but not from the parameter used for the exponential distribution.

As an alternative to these strategies, the LOD Trader (discussed in the chapter "Phenomenal AI Level-of-Detail Control with the LOD Trader") is an ideal tool for managing alibis. Whether a character has an alibi or not can be treated as an LOD feature, with the no-alibi level given a ULTB penalty. Likewise, as discussed in the LOD Trader, rather than deleting characters based on thresholded distance or time, existence can be treated as a feature, with the transition to nonexistence given US and FD penalties. Creating initial characters is still done when a sector becomes visible, and as mentioned before, when generating the initial population, subtract any current population from the average population parameter.

37.8 Conclusion

Alibi generation, in its most fundamental form, is a simple idea: Generate details lazily. That's "lazy" in the computer science sense: When first required, not before, and not after. There's a variety of ways to do this, from the simple and informal (canned alibis) to the complex and theoretically precise (Metropolis–Hastings). The most important objective, regardless of approach, is to keep the concept of the "ideal game world" in mind and design your alibi generation system so as to seamlessly replicate the experience of that ideal game world.

References

[Chib and Greenberg 95] S. Chib and E. Greenberg. "Understanding the Metropolis-Hastings algorithm." *The American Statistician*, vol. 49, no. 4 (Nov. 1995). pp. 327–335, 1995. Available online (http://elsa.berkeley.edu/pub/reprints/misc/understanding.pdf).
[Sunshine-Hill 11] B. Sunshine-Hill. Perceptually Driven Simulation (Doctoral dissertation), 2011. Available online (http://repository.upenn.edu/edissertations/435).

PART VI
Racing

38

An Architecture Overview for AI in Racing Games

Simon Tomlinson and Nic Melder

38.1 Introduction

This article describes the requirements, architecture, and best practices for high-speed vehicle racing AI. We mainly consider high production value simulation games, but arcade style games can also be built using simplified elements of the approach here. Subsequent articles in the Racing section of this book will then expand in greater detail some of the critical aspects of the racing AI system.

Many of these techniques have been known for some time [Biasillo 02a, 02b, 02c] but in racing, the difference between winning and losing can be small fractions of a meter or second. Because of this it is important to push for accuracy and detail with the objective of convincing the user that his AI opponents are as expert on the track as he is.

38.2 Understanding the Physics

Before designing the AI system, it is important that the developer fully understands the type of physics in play and how that will affect the implementation. In very simple games the AI will advance along a predefined spline, and all that is needed is emulation of cornering speed, acceleration, and braking based on parametric formulas and basic collision detection—examining if the spline ahead is blocked within the braking distance.

There is no physics required. But in a full simulation, the AI car will be similar to that experienced by the player, including an engine model, transmission, tire models, braking model, and all the vehicle quirks and characteristics this encompasses.

Vehicle physics is mainly about forces and tires. Any acceleration on the car, either a speed change or a change of direction, results in forces being applied through the tires. The magnitude of the forces is limited by the capability of the tire and, if that limit is exceeded, the tire will no longer grip the road surface and the car will slide. In corners this can result in oversteer (the car digs in towards the apex and the rear slides out) or understeer (the car drifts to the outside of the bend). When accelerating or braking, the tires might spin or lock, reducing the effectiveness of the speed change, so a key action of the AI is to ensure that the available tire grip is not exceeded. This is done by ensuring corners are taken at the correct speed, braking is done in good time, and acceleration is managed with gradual pressure on the throttle. If the AI is too conservative it will be slow, so the best AI, like the best human drivers, will need to work very near "the limit of grip" at all times. This is what the whole AI design is geared towards.

The details of racing physics are beyond the scope of this article, but it is highly recommended that the AI developer gains a solid grounding in this area [Pacejka 06].

38.3 The Architecture

It is best to consider the AI in terms of four layers and one subsystem that extends through these layers. The top layer is the *character layer* or *persona layer*. This layer works on a fairly long timescale and is responsible for the individual driver's skill levels which affect the performance of the AI. The next layer is the *strategic layer,* which works on short timescales between a single frame and a few seconds. The strategic layer houses the behavioral elements of the system and determines broad steering and speed goals based on an examination of the track representation in the near and medium distance. The next layer down is the *tactical layer,* which will normally be processed every frame and is responsible for refining the steering and speed goals into solid values. Typically, there will be a number of competing goals produced at the strategic and tactical level, and these will be analyzed and combined in the final *control layer*. This layer is responsible for calculating the controller inputs (steering, brake, and throttle) in order to achieve the previous layers' strategy.

Alongside these layers is the vitally important *collision avoidance subsystem*. This can usually be split into two sections based on the immediacy of the analysis they perform. At a longer range, the AI will need to look at the track some distance ahead of the car and plan safe routes around any obstacles, such as debris or damaged vehicles. At a shorter range, the AI will need to make small but rapid adjustments due to static or dynamic obstacles. Examples include racing close to a solid wall, alongside another car when overtaking, or driving close behind an opponent to 'slipstream' in preparation for an overtake.

38.4 The AI Driver Persona

In real life no two drivers will be the same, they will have different abilities and approach racing with slightly different strategies. In a fixed formula race, such as Formula 1 or IndyCar, where the performance of the vehicles is quite similar, differences in driving skill will substantially contribute to the race result. At a minimal level, a spread of driver skill will produce a spread of the physical positions of the cars on the track. This is not just more realistic, but also helps to ensure the player experiences a number of micro challenges as they progress through the field. Done well, driver personas can feed into the observed behaviors and add significant color to the game experience. However, such color is only really worthwhile if the actions of the AI driver are distinguishable in the game. It also helps to support these traits with driver profiles viewable pre-game or perhaps in-game signals like audio commentary.

The primary characteristic will be *skill*, a measure of their ability to drive at the limit; secondary characteristics may include *aggression*, *vehicle control*, and *mistakes*. Primarily, the skill characteristic would be applied where any speed related calculations are used, such as multiplying the actual available grip in calculations of cornering speed and braking distances. This will have the net effect of reducing the overall speed. While this characteristic might be exposed to the user and designer in the range [0, 100], the requirement that we always drive close to the limit means that, within the AI strategic layers and below, this should be mapped onto a smaller range of say 98–99%. Although this may appear as a small range, a 1% variation accumulated over several laps can have a surprisingly large effect, especially when applied in several places in the code. It may be found that a much smaller range in the skill factor is necessary to avoid the AI spreading unrealistically. Similarly, by mapping to a lower range (e.g., 80%–82%) the overall race experience should become easier so the skill characteristic can also be used to modify the overall game difficulty.

Using a smaller range makes it more difficult for the user to discern the speed variance between the different drivers. To counter this, a *biorhythm* can be applied to the driver's skill. The skill factor will vary slowly with time, for example using a sine wave with a period of 100 seconds. In this way, the driver's average skill measured over a number of laps might be 99%, but for some short periods of time, the skill factor could be significantly lower. This will make the AI driver temporarily vulnerable to being overtaken without having an overly large long term effect. It is not necessary to use a sine wave as the biorhythm, and it is worth experimenting with different waveforms, for example, a square wave with a low duty cycle that produces a skill factor near the upper limit for 90% of the time but perhaps a skill as low as 90% or 95% for short periods. With a defined set of rules, this idea can be further extended to encompass a full race-pace system [Jimenez 09, Melder 13].

Secondary characteristics can be used to affect behavioral changes such as the probability of entering overtaking mode, the rate that the throttle is applied, or the number of unforced mistakes that they make. A driver with a high *aggression* characteristic will drive closer to the cars in front and will require less space to overtake a vehicle, a driver with a low *control* characteristic may take twice as long to push the throttle in, and a driver with a high *mistake* characteristic might lead to random errors in corner speed calculation.

38.5 Racing Behaviors

The breadth of behaviors in a racing AI system is not large, so generally a finite-state machine (FSM) is sufficient to represent them. At any time most of the behaviors may become valid and so they usually all compete to be the active one, and should be reviewed on every update of the strategic layer. A good way to manage this is for each valid state (as defined by the current state exit transitions) to evaluate a 'utility' score. Provided that this utility score is larger than the current state's, a state transition would result. In order to avoid short-lived states and rapid transitioning, a small additional threshold should be added to the current state utility. This will produce hysteresis which will tend to retain the current behavior state unless a significantly stronger alternative arises. Some of the more common behaviors are described below.

38.5.1 Normal Driving

The objective of this behavior is to simply get around the main track as fast as possible. The AI should stay reasonably close to the optimum racing line, but remain conservative in terms of avoiding other cars: allow a reasonable amount of space between any car in front or that happens to be alongside. The utility for this behavior is a baseline constant for the whole system that other behaviors must beat. If using a utility range of [0, 1000] a value of 500 is appropriate.

38.5.2 Overtake

In *overtake* mode, the AI is actively seeking a line which will allow it to pass one or more cars in front. The AI is still basically driving along the track, but this is modified in order to achieve an overtaking maneuver. Dealing with more than one overtaking target simultaneously can be necessary in situations such as the race start, as otherwise the resultant behavior may look uncompetitive and mechanical. The analysis for the state is to look ahead down the track. If there are one or more opponents in range and the AI has a speed advantage, the analysis will determine a safe (wide enough) window across the track width for overtaking.

The deeper this analysis, the better overtaking events will be and anticipation is key. For example, the car ahead may not be slow enough *now*, but if it is approaching a corner it is likely to slow down and offer an opportunity. Another example is the car in front is under-steering and will shortly open up a viable gap on the inside.

Not every overtaking opportunity should be taken and randomness or a biorhythm trait should contribute to the utility calculation. Generally, overtaking is less likely on a straight where all cars are at full throttle, so the current and future track features should figure in the utility. If there is a significant speed advantage (such as an opponent slowing due to a mechanical failure), then overtaking should always be activated. Note that this behavior should not go into too fine a grain in terms of dimensional precision, since when the AI does overtake, the tactical layer and short range avoidance subsystems will deal with the detail of driving past the opponent(s) safely.

Once overtaking mode is activated, the driver should become a little more aggressive and even closer to the limit. Not withstanding any mechanical boost, such as using nitro, the AI skill levels should be increased close to saturation or indeed beyond. For example a driver might deliberately choose to accept the risk of exceeding their grip limits temporarily and skidding slightly (under-steering) by braking late to get past the opponent as they enter the bend on the inside, in the knowledge that once they have claimed the position and blocked the other car they can then regain composure and complete the turn. Avoidance tolerances should also be reduced; the AI will be prepared to get closer behind or alongside an opponent while overtaking. Indeed in some game types some light, controlled contact might be allowed.

The strategic analysis of the overtaking opportunity should continue so that, for example, if the gap closes, the overtake is aborted and the AI returns to normal driving mode. To avoid erratic AI switching, it is also good to disallow re-activation of the overtaking state for a few seconds after an aborted attempt. A successful overtake is where the AI has passed the opponent and is some distance ahead, in which case it can return to normal driving. The AI should not switch too early, though, as a small reduction in speed due to the state change could mean the positional advantage is quickly lost as the opponent comes back past the AI.

38.5.3 Defend and Block

In some racing styles it is acceptable to try to defend an overtake by moving across into the path of the opponent. This state would be triggered using a utility where an opponent was approaching from behind, not directly on the same line and with some current or future potential speed advantage.

The *defend and block* state operates by making small steering moves to match the AI's line on the track with the opposing vehicle behind. Depending on the racing rules in force, defending may be aborted once the opponent gets alongside or even after a set duration or lateral movement has been exceeded (Formula 1 rules for example allow a single lateral move, i.e. you cannot weave back and forth).

In all but the most aggressive racing genres, defending should be terminated if you are putting the opponent in danger—for example, pushing him off the track. A good way to manage this is to allow the opposing AI or human to post a *complaint message* if they feel they are in danger, so that the defending mode is aborted. Similar to overtaking, while the AI is performing a defend and block, the speed margins should be pushed to the limit.

38.5.4 Branch

Some racing genres use tracks with multiple routes and branches; even in classic simulation games, there may be a pit lane. The utility value to decide to take a branch could be based on all sorts of strategic considerations: tire wear, fuel levels, and position relative to other cars in a simulation genre, or an analysis of the value of a short cut against the risk in a more arcade style game. In either case, the key detail is to make the decision early enough so that the correct line into the branch can be followed. Also, the AI needs to be extra aware of nearby vehicles that might block access to the branch—if necessary, braking to fall behind the other vehicle in plenty of time. For that reason, this behavior should not end until well into the alternative track or, for example, the branch is aborted due to obstructive vehicles.

38.5.5 Recover

In the most realistic games, the AI can make occasional mistakes resulting in going off road or spinning within the track bounds. Thus, the objective of a recovery behavior is to get back racing. In practice, on- and off-track recovery may be separate behaviors triggered using metrics, such as pointing the wrong way along the track or being too far out of the main track bounds. In either case, the first task is to stabilize the car, stop sliding, and slow down or even stop if facing the wrong way or close to a barrier.

In off-track recovery, the goal is to drive towards the nearest edge of the track at a modest speed, giving way to any cars that are approaching from behind. For on-track recovery, the AI can do a slow tight turn or may even try to spin up the back wheels for a *donut*. In either case, good driving manners mean that, until the upstream road is clear, the AI should just stay put to avoid causing a collision.

Because the recovery process is very disadvantageous in terms of competitiveness, the AI should be allowed every chance to carry on racing where possible, so it is best not to trigger recovery based on a single update of the utility value, but rather to integrate up the utility over a few seconds. For example, at a strategic update rate of 10 frames per second and a utility range of [0, 1000], one might add 10 points for every meter off the track and 10 points for every wheel that has lost grip, but also subtract 20 points every frame even if off-track. Once the car is on-track, stable, and facing the correct way, the points are quickly subtracted, leading to the completion of this behavior.

38.6 The Race Choreographer

The race choreographer is essentially a scripting system that can be used by designers to affect storyline aspects within the course of a race. It is a separate AI object, receiving event triggers from the individual AI vehicles, the physics system, or the main game code. It then interacts with the AI at the persona or strategic level (although it could also implement actions on the physics or other systems). Examples of events include changing a specific driver's skill level halfway through the race, causing a tire blowout, or triggering an AI custom behavior (e.g., try to collide with the player).

38.7 Interfaces

The main interface between the AI and the vehicle should be the same as that between the human controller and the car, so that the AI and a human are interchangeable. The AI will also need an interface to extract metrics from the physics, such as available grip and whether each tire is currently sliding. And there is no harm in one AI vehicle asking another for detailed information such as, "Are you about to turn left?" This may seem like cheating, but a real life experienced driver will always be able to read the signs and interpret an opponent's intentions. Of course, a real driver may not get it right all the time, so adding some fuzziness and randomization within the AI request interface might be appropriate.

38.8 Balancing the AI

The AI must always be balanced and tuned to make sure each car can drive as quickly as possible, but also to maintain a good distribution of vehicles through the track so that the player always feels "involved" with the other cars. Balancing the AI can often be the most difficult part of the game development process. It can be very time consuming and stressful, so it is always worth considering how this process will work and what tools can be built to ease the pain.

The objective is to maximize the experience for the player; we want them to have to work hard to compete and overtake, but ultimately we want players of varying abilities to still have a reasonable likelihood of winning the race. In a scenario with tightly restricted car specifications, like Formula 1, the problem is mainly to bring a group of quite similar

AI opponents' performance into proximity with the player. In a game with a wider range of vehicle performance on the same track, the problem is even greater.

It is for this reason that many games employ a system called *rubber-banding* [Melder 13] which attempts to change the AI speed to best match the player's over the course of the race. Normally, the objective is to be beating the player at the start of the race, but to be losing at the finish, ideally such that the player reaches a winning position in the last few hundred meters of the race. Note that the mechanics of balancing may not lie solely within the AI. If the AI is pushed past the 100% grip limit it will make mistakes, slide, and ultimately its performance will suffer, thus hindering the balancing process.

It is usually better to consider the AI balancing as a process of achieving the correct spread of performances over the group, while the overall balance against the player is better achieved using adjustments within the vehicle physics such as tire grip, engine power, and torque. Also bear in mind that in some implementations, the AI uses a "cut-down" version of the physics, which may not produce the same outcomes as the human's vehicle, even where all the parameters are equal. This must also be accounted for with balancing adjustments in the physics.

38.8.1 Offline Automated Learning

Even where a dynamic in-game system is not used, there is substantial opportunity for optimizing the AI performance using offline automated learning. Initially during development, the definition of the racing line is usually specified by the designer placing splines directly on the track, but this can then be improved. One simple improvement is to use bisection to optimize each node on a racing line one by one [Biasillo 02c]. However, those who are familiar with multivariate optimization know that this sort of strategy can be prone to false solutions.

Broadly, the issue is that a racing line is a sum of its parts, or rather each part or node is not independent of those around it. Consider a single node on a curve containing 10 nodes which is smooth but not optimal. If a single node is moved 0.5m laterally, all this will do is produce a kink in the racing line that is likely to have the effect of slowing down the AI. In practice, what needs to happen is that several points should be moved coherently and in proportion. A good technique to achieve this is a modified genetic algorithm. This is based on the random Monte Carlo technique where a number of variables are randomly selected and randomly modified and, if the measured process metric (usually the average lap time) improves, the new solution is kept, otherwise it is discarded, and a new attempt is tried.

In a multivariate problem, Monte Carlo is generally of the order of $\sqrt{N}$ faster than a linear search, where N is the number of variables. Where genetic algorithms improve efficiency is that they deal with groups of variables in the problem together, patching lines of several nodes together from two parents. If this is combined with coherent mutation (modifying a run of adjacent nodes), then this automated technique can be improved greatly. Moreover, it can be very advantageous to use knowledge of the track in the construction of the GA. For example, marking up groups of nodes that are known to form a curve and encouraging mutations that follow a pattern which is likely to be favorable will help the GA find a good solution. Note also that optimization of the racing line is not the only area for automated learning. Parameters used with the strategic layer, such as utility weights and the constants within the control layer or PID controller, are also ripe for this technique.

There are a number of pitfalls and tips when using automated learning. As with any numerical optimization method, the difficulty increases geometrically with the number of parameters being optimized in the problem. Thus, if automated learning is to be used, the AI should be designed from the start in a way which minimizes the amount of data. For example, in defining the racing line, nodes should be placed wider apart to minimize their number around the track.

Another pitfall with automated learning is that it can be difficult to see how the solution has arisen, and any changes to the underlying system that require a re-evaluation of the solution can be time consuming. For this reason, a manual editing method should always be provided as a fallback. However, other optimization methods can also suffer similar issues. For example, in a regime where the racing line is simply recorded using a human player, a substantial change in the track will still require the whole track to be re-learned, recorded, and tested.

Ultimately, though, the final arbiter of whether a balancing process has worked or not must be a human. In such a complex process as a race, even though AI lap times say they are optimized, it may be that the AI is not competitive in real terms. This is perhaps the case because the AI runs slower when other cars are on the track or perhaps because the AI are too easy/hard to overtake. Testing with a range of player abilities over varying scenarios will always remain an essential balancing tool.

38.9 Conclusion

This article has described in detail a broad architecture for the AI in a high-speed racing game. The detail and depth of the implementation will depend on the style of racing game, but most games will require most, if not all, of the elements described. However, in real life, racing can often depend on small fractional details, and the same is true in a high-end racing simulation. In that respect we have only really provided a starting point; there is much more to learn and many areas to experiment with in the quest for realism, performance, and excellence.

A racing AI implementation is full of paradoxes. The principle paradox is that the AI must operate in real-time, making complex decisions in order to not only remain in control of the car, but to drive it at the very edge of its capabilities. However, the success of the AI lies in long hard hours preparing prebaked data, tweaking parameters, and anticipating solutions to potentially difficult scenarios. Thus, the paradox is that a successful racing AI is the careful balance of real-time control and carefully thought-out data. Moreover, you should not skimp on the design phase; in a highly connected AI system the discovery of a weakness in the latter stages of development can be very difficult to remedy.

References

[Biasillo 02a] G. Biasillo. "Representing a race track for AI." In *AI Game Programming Wisdom*, edited by Steve Rabin. Hingham, MA: Charles River Media, 2002, pp. 439–443.

[Biasillo 02b] G. Biasillo. "Racing AI logic." In *AI Game Programming Wisdom*, edited by Steve Rabin. Hingham, MA: Charles River Media, 2002, pp. 444–454.

[Biasillo 02c] G. Biasillo. "Training an AI to race." In *AI Game Programming Wisdom*, edited by Steve Rabin. Hingham, MA: Charles River Media, 2002. pp. 455–459.

[Jimenez 09] E. Jimenez. "The Pure Advantage: Advanced Racing Game AI." http://www.gamasutra.com/view/feature/3920/the_pure_advantage_advanced_.php, 2009.

[Melder 13] N. Melder. "A rubber-banding system for gameplay race management." In *Game AI Pro*, edited by Steve Rabin. Boca Raton, FL: CRC Press, 2013.

[Pacejka 06] H. B. Pacejka. *Tyre and Vehicle Dynamics,* 2nd edition. Oxford: Butterworth-Heinemann, 2006.

39

Representing and Driving a Race Track for AI Controlled Vehicles

Simon Tomlinson and Nic Melder

39.1 Introduction

One of the most important elements in an AI racing system is the representation of the track. The amount and diversity of data contained in this structure will depend on the genre, but there will always be a representation of the physical layout. There will also usually be some sort of racing line—a guide that is used by the AI as a primary (fastest) route along the track. However, the nature of the racing line and other data depend on the details of the genre.

An arcade style game may require detours to retrieve pickups and, in this case, the racing line may be less about the fastest route and more about choosing the best tactical route; that is, the track will be heavily branched with alternative routes. In a very tightly defined game, such as a Formula 1 simulation, there will be a single, highly optimized racing line that contains detailed tactical information all the AI vehicles can reference. Because all the vehicles have similar characteristics, the optimal speed for any corner can be "baked-in" to the track data during development. In a game where a wide range of vehicles can race on the same track, there may be too much data to bake-in and so techniques are required that allow parameters such as the optimal speed to be evaluated in real time. Indeed, real-time evaluation will account for variations in the current situation (such as a non-ideal corner entry) and is therefore preferred if computing resources allow. Ideally, any AI solution should use both approximate baked-in data at the strategic (behavioral) level and detailed real-time evaluation at the tactical (driving) level.

39.2 Physical Track Representation

As a minimum, the objective of the track representation is to define the boundaries of the racing area. A good standard representation is to mark up the track as a series of nodes along the nominal track center, with perpendicular and normal vectors defining the width of the track and its orientation. These nodes are then arranged in an array or bi-directional linked list to form a series of quadrilateral segments, as shown in Figure 39.1. This is quite similar to previously published representations [Biasillo 02a] but is strongly node-centric rather than focusing on the area of the segment. Note that the track is normally projected onto the 2D ground plane; height variations in the track are important, but are dealt with separately. However, this is not possible if the track is truly 3D and has loops or many over-/underpasses.

The track width need not be symmetric and rarely is in practice. It is more important to keep the path defined by the track nodes and links reasonably smooth. The definition of track width is also fluid. A good definition is the main area of tarmac on which the vehicles race. However, in real-world tracks, there are often rumble strips, runoff areas, road junctions in a street track, and so on, all of which might be drivable to some extent. Therefore, the edge of the track is best considered to be *fuzzy* and represented by three values on each side: the main track boundary (w_t), the extended runoff boundary (w_r), and the hard width, which defines solid walls or barriers (w_w) as shown in Figure 39.1. These widths are defined separately for each side of the track and can vary independently. However, on a track with close-in walls, these three widths will be the same. Also, the track width should be smooth, as sudden changes or kinks can prove troublesome in later processing.

Note that the node orientation as defined by the normal vector, **n**, is not the same as the link vector between nodes, **l**. Because the representation is node-centric, this should be

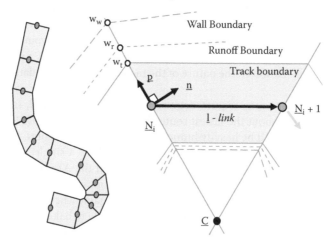

Figure 39.1

Track segments making up the physical track representation.

derived from the track tangent at the node which is the average of the forward and backward links, as shown in Equation 39.1.

$$\underline{t} = \left[\left(\underline{N}_{i+1} - \underline{N}_i \right) + \left(\underline{N}_i - \underline{N}_{i-1} \right) \right] / 2 \tag{39.1}$$

39.2.1 Generating the Track

It is possible to generate the physical track representation of nodes and widths by processing the "polygon soup" that defines the track surface. However, this method is not recommended. It can become confused at street track junctions or tarmac runoff areas, for example, and will often require designer intervention to correct such issues.

It is much better to allow the track designers to mark up the track nodes, links, and different widths, within a track editor tool. Using a tool has large advantages. Such a tool can provide a lot of programmatic assistance in placing the nodes—for example, by suggesting widths for a new node placement or supplying metrics, such as link and edge smoothness. Last minute edits to the track are easier to deal with, and the human eye is a much better arbiter of the fuzzy track edges than a simple algorithm. The designer will also have the option to adjust the track in order to affect the AI behavior—for example, by narrowing the main track and hard track widths as a last resort to reduce AI collision avoidance failures in difficult areas.

39.2.2 Branches and Open-Ended Tracks

Normally, a racing track will be a single list of nodes, where the last node connects back to the first node to form a closed loop. However, other configurations are also possible. A track may have one or more branches that will require multiple link references in the data. If the branches are high speed, it is a good idea to make the branch in the track representation some distance before the actual physical branch on the track, so that the most appropriate racing lines on the approach to the branch can be stored. Bear in mind that the two routes overlap physically, so code that considers the two vehicles to be immune to collision, based on the track frame of reference, should be avoided. Tracks can also be point-to-point rather than looped, in which case there will be null links at the first and last node on the track. This can be problematic for the AI if they drive beyond the first/last track node, but the physical track should always contain a run-out distance beyond the finish line for cars to slow down and stop or drive through. Once off-camera, they can then be removed, so the AI should never actually reach the final AI track node.

39.2.3 Track Node Spacing

There is a trade off with the track node spacing between accuracy and development time. Shorter spacing means that the angle change between any pair of nodes is smaller, that is, the track is more linear, so any calculations are more accurate. It also means variations in curvature or other data, such as track width, are better represented. However, longer segments mean less work for designers in laying out the AI data. Furthermore, any kind of automated learning relating to the track will be more tractable if there are fewer nodes.

A good compromise is variable spacing, concentrated in highly curved regions and more widely separated on long straights. If this method is used, there is some extra overhead in the AI since distances along the track must always be summed segment by segment; they can no longer be derived as a number of nodes multiplied by a constant separation. Also, sudden changes in length between adjacent segments will lead to difficulties with the tangent/normal evaluations, which will become dominated by the longer link. These undesirable effects can be reduced by gradually transitioning the length over several segments (preferably only on straights) and by precalculating and caching the link lengths.

39.3 Calculating Track Data

There are two principle types of track data. First, the AI needs to know where it is on the track; essentially its position in the frame of reference of its nearest track nodes. This can be called the "track registration" and from this, other information such as the vehicle orientation relative to the track can be derived. This data will almost always be baked-in. The other type of information is driving hints, such as the maximum viable speed in an upcoming track section. This can also be baked-in but, since it potentially depends on vehicle specific parameters, it must often be calculated in real time. Instead, we can bake-in solid physical information on which the corner speed depends, such as the radius of curvature of the track, the racing line, or both.

39.3.1 Track Registration

Track registration involves calculating three things: the nearest consecutive pair of track nodes which define the link segment that the vehicle is on, the distance along that segment, and the perpendicular distance from a reference line, such as the link vector between nodes.

Finding the nearest node pair is a simple process of stepping through the nodes and seeking the smallest squared distance to the vehicle position. The second node in the pair depends on whether the vehicle is in front or behind the nearest node, as determined using a dot product with the node normal. Coherence may be used [Biasillo 02b] where the nodes are searched outwards from a previously known nearest node. If no previous node exists, a full search is necessary, but this can be sped up using a preliminary coarse search of every n^{th} node. Once a node pair is identified, it is customary to store the lowest index node as the registered node, with the vehicle being in the segment between that node and the next node in the list.

The distance along the segment is then calculated using the vector between each node and the vehicle position, **R**. Because corner track segments are not simple rectangles, projecting a position vector onto the link vector between the nodes will be inaccurate—indeed, it could show the vehicle as within a segment when in fact it is not. Similarly, projecting onto the $\mathbf{n}_i$ normal alone may be inaccurate if the vehicle is at the far end of a segment. To resolve this issue a combination of projections can be used as a ratio, as shown in Equation 39.2.

$$d = \frac{(\underline{R} - \underline{N}_1) \cdot \underline{n}_1}{(\underline{R} - \underline{N}_1) \cdot \underline{n}_1 - (\underline{R} - \underline{N}_2) \cdot \underline{n}_2} \tag{39.2}$$

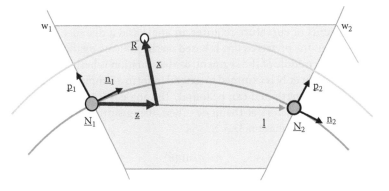

Figure 39.2

Track registration.

This provides the longitudinal registration (d) as a normalized value between 0.0 and 1.0 along **l**. To find the lateral position, simply calculate **z**, and hence the length of **x**, as shown in Figure 39.2.

Note that the registration should be considered undefined if a vehicle is beyond the inner intersection of the two perpendiculars (point **C** in either Figure 39.1 or Figure 39.3) as the logical forward direction of the track is no longer consistent. Furthermore, while the registration to the track center line is useful at a strategic level, the tactical driving calculations need registration to the racing line. This means that a track node will ideally need to store not only a position along the perpendicular where the racing line passes into the segment, but also the racing line normal (tangent) and perpendicular at this point. Using a fixed lateral offset from each node combined with the primary node orientation vectors is an alternative, but this can be inaccurate as the racing line angle will not be the same as the node normal angle around corners.

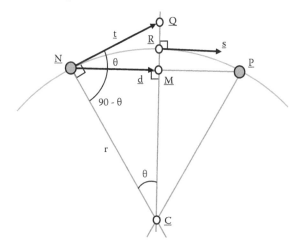

Figure 39.3

Radius of curvature.

39.3.2 Radius of Curvature

Calculating the radius of curvature requires an angle and a distance. Various constructions are possible, but the preferred one is based on the node using the tangent of the track curve rather than the middle of the segment, as the situation is better defined as shown in Figure 39.3. The tangent at **N** is assumed to extend to form a simple arc to **P** (the next track node) from which the length of **d** can be found. The angle is found from the dot product of the tangent and link vectors at the node. Then, using similar triangles, the radius of curvature, *r*, is shown in Equation 39.3.

$$r = d/\sin(\theta) \qquad\qquad (39.3)$$

The radius of curvature of the racing line is generally more useful than that of the center of the track, as this is used to calculate maximum cornering speed. However, where the AI driver is off the racing line, some other radius is apparent and the center track radius is then useful as an upper value in approximating a revised radius.

39.3.3 Curved Nature of the Track

Although the track representation is piecewise linear, being simple straight links between nodes, it should be understood that any segment of track is in fact curved to some degree. What this means is that any reference to position within the track frame of reference is approximate. We can still interpolate information along the linear link, such as the track width, but these calculations are only accurate close to the line across the track at a node formed by its perpendicular. For this reason you should also avoid using the track frame of reference for fine-grain collision avoidance, if possible. For vehicle-to-vehicle avoidance, always use physical world coordinates, but for strategic planning, the approximate track registration is sufficient. Similarly, the radius of curvature, defined in Equation 39.3, is strictly the instantaneous value at **N**. On a real track, the tangent at **P** will differ, so the radius of curvature will vary throughout the segment.

39.4 Driving the Track

In this section we discuss the frame-by-frame driving along the main racing line. However, the AI code should also account for situations where it is not on the ideal line and be prepared to make approximate adjustments to the calculations. Indeed, because the practice of a race will never match the ideal of the racing line, one should be aware that ultimate accuracy within the driving calculations may in fact be superfluous.

39.4.1 Steering the Line Using a Look-Ahead or Runner

Track steering is based on using a *racing line* as a guide. This is defined as a series of positions associated with each track node, but can be interpolated between nodes using a lateral distance within the segment. If the steering is calculated, based on the racing line immediately in front of the car's track registration position, the AI will tend to make a lot of small corrections, which results in weaving left and right across the line. In the worst case, this can build up, become noticeable to the user, and ultimately cause the vehicle to spin out.

Instead, it is better to steer towards an aiming point some distance ahead of the vehicle, with steering based on the angle between the vehicle's current direction and the vector between the car center and the aiming point. This tends to smooth out the steering. However, it can lead to unusual behavior; on a sharp corner, a larger look-ahead will make the AI cut across the inside of the corner. To counter this, the look-ahead distance should be related to the track curvature and/or the current speed; the exact formulation tends to be a matter of trial and error.

This technique can be further improved by making the steering aim at an actual AI object called a *runner* or *rabbit*. On every frame, the runner is updated along the racing line by a distance equal to the current speed of the vehicle, with a correction for any re-evaluation of the look-ahead distance. Using a runner can have other advantages, as it is an object that can be operated upon to affect the steering. It is also possible to drive parallel to the racing line, but at a small offset distance, by using interpolation of the scaled node perpendicular vectors through the segment.

39.4.2 Corner Speed and Braking Distance

The maximum cornering speed at any node is based on a simple function of the local radius of curvature (r), the vehicle mass (m), and its velocity (v) compared to the limit of grip force available from the tires (G_{max}), as shown in Equation 39.4.

$$\frac{mv^2}{r} \leq G_{max} \tag{39.4}$$

However, there are other factors—the vehicle suspension, weight distribution, down force, and even steering lock can play a roll. For that reason a preferred method is to request the maximum speed from the vehicle physics interface, based on a value of radius. This request might use Equation 39.4 with modifications or it might use a lookup table.

In an ideal corner, the radius of curvature would change from infinity to a fixed value for the direction of the bend and all braking would happen in the preceding straight. However, real corners are not like that, and the best drivers can brake into the start of a bend before committing fully to steering.

A good solution is to predict the vehicle's speed under braking and compare this to the maximum viable speed at each future track node on the racing line. If the predicted speed with full braking is greater than the maximum speed at a node, then the driver must brake. If the speed prediction reaches zero or less without exceeding a node speed, the car is safe to continue accelerating. Recalculate this every few frames in the tactical layer and, if possible, factor in the braking rate at each node (which will not be 100% if the vehicle also needs to steer). This can be expensive computationally, so alternative methods include baking in the maximum speeds at each node or having a designer define the speeds in an editing tool. A comparison of "distance to the speed hint" with "braking distance to that speed" can then be used as a braking initiator.

39.4.3 Wall Avoidance

Wall avoidance can be considered as either a medium or short-range problem. The medium range problem is to extrapolate the future vehicle position and take corrective action if that position is outside the track [Biasillo 02b]. However, there are some caveats. First, if a vehicle is successfully steering around a bend, then the extrapolation should account for the turn rate; otherwise, a vehicle on the outside of a bend may conflict with a wall without reason. Also, any turning should be "under control," that is, within grip limits. Furthermore, the corrective action should be based on available spare grip; if extra steering would force the vehicle beyond the grip limit then braking might be preferred (even though this still may not help, it is more realistic as the inevitable wall impact should be at a lower speed). If the extrapolation is in conflict with a non-hard track boundary, the reaction might be less severe, thus allowing the car to run off and recover rather than risk a spin. If a runner object is used, this can also be validated to be within the track, and this can be used alongside extrapolation.

However, it is also a good idea to look directly sideways as well as ahead; that is, make small corrections based on the proximity to any wall alongside the car in order to maintain a safe buffer distance. This can be more effective in tight tracks where the vehicle must travel close to walls, as extrapolation is an approximation and can be overly conservative. This kind of short-range adjustment works particularly well with a PID-based control layer [Melder and Tomlinson 13], when mixed into the main steering target as a correction.

39.5 Racing Lines

What is the optimal racing line? Strictly speaking, it is the resultant path driven by a vehicle that is optimized to complete the track in the minimum amount of time. This is not necessarily the same thing as the fastest line in any local region, as it may be more important to set up the entry for a future corner than pass through the current corner at top speed in complex sections.

Even where this line can be defined, the use of a runner usually means the actual path steered by a vehicle can be different from the racing line guide. This apparent disconnection between the stored racing line and emergent path should be borne in mind when editing the data; the most important thing is the final resultant driving performance, not necessarily what the stored racing line data looks like. In code, the racing line should be stored as a width offset at each track node. This can easily be converted to a real-world position using the reference node position and the normalized perpendicular.

Generation of the racing line can be a complex process and space here is insufficient to explore all of the issues and techniques; however, here are some general points. Asking designers to include an initial estimate of the racing line in the track editing tool, manually moving points and measuring the lap times, is a time consuming and tedious process. Another method is to record a racing line as driven in-game by an experienced user. This does work, but the recorded route can be prone to kinks and weaker areas. A human does not steer absolutely smoothly and almost always tends to include increments or corrections in the steering graph. Any kinks in the recorded line will lead to an overestimate of the radius of curvature in that track section and hence a lower speed than may actually be possible. Furthermore, it is unlikely that any one lap will be "perfect"; even the best player will make one or more small mistakes, which will invalidate some sections. This is not to say the recording method is to be avoided, but it should be backed up with some postprocessing to average or patch over several laps and generally smooth out kinks. No matter which of the above approaches is used, remember that the AI uses the racing line as a guide only and therefore even the most "perfect" stored racing line will not result in the most perfect driven line.

By far the best approach is some form of automated learning [Tomlinson and Melder 13]. Not only does this speed up the optimization process, but it can also nullify artifacts within the tactical driving calculations as the learning is based on the output results and not the input racing line format. However, bear in mind that the nodes in the line are correlated, that is, if one is moved, those around it should move in a coherent fashion. For example, if the learning algorithm moves a node 0.5m laterally (which is the only degree of freedom if the racing line is constrained to be on a track node perpendicular), then forward and backward nodes should be moved a smaller amount based upon a function related to their distance from the primary perturbation node. Also, make sure the metric (lap time) is averaged over several laps; in particular, the AI should have half a lap run-up on a looping track, rather than a standing start that will not be representative. Randomization in the AI should be switched off, or rather set to fixed mid-values. Even where learning is used, the generated racing line only really applies to that particular car's capability, as differences in braking or cornering grip will subtly affect the line. It is impractical to record a line for each and every vehicle, but some averaging with different car types or using two or three lines for different car groups should be considered.

39.6 Alternate Lines and Other Tactical Information

In a competitive race, the actual racing line may also account for strategic considerations, for example, making it more difficult for an opponent to overtake where small losses in time or speed are tolerable. This means there is conceptually a *best defending* line, which might be stored in the same way as the racing line. Similarly, one or more overtaking lines might be stored. Typically, there are multiple possible lines in a corner, including pushing up the inside of a slightly wide opponent or entering a corner wide in order to gain speed earlier on the exit ("the undercut"). Of course, all these lines can be a lot of additional work to optimize and additional data to store, so emergent solutions may be preferred that use lateral offsets from the single racing line. Markers at track nodes can still be useful though, for example, to indicate to the AI what overtaking entries might be available at a future corner.

39.7 Using Splines

In the discussion of track segments, it was noted that the piecewise linear approximation is only accurate near the nodes. This can be improved by using a spline between the nodes, so that the curve of the track center, edge, or racing line is fully defined throughout the segment. Various types of splines are available, such as Catmull–Rom or Bézier. However, splines are a mixed benefit. Registration is not direct and must generally be done using an iterative process such as bisection. Similarly, local tangents must be estimated using a finite difference.

39.8 Conclusion

We have discussed a highly detailed representation of a race track and how to use that track in real time to guide AI vehicles at their limit of speed and performance. The level of detail and complexity here is probably only appropriate for simulation type racing games, but the methods described can be simplified for more arcade style games. It has also been suggested that the piecewise linear representation can be improved upon by using splines. Further areas to explore include learning techniques to improve the racing line and more subtle driving considerations such as the effect of height variations, in particular crests, which can cause a vehicle to temporarily lose downward force and hence grip.

References

[Biasillo 02a] G. Biasillo. "Representing a race track for AI." In *AI Game Programming Wisdom*, edited by Steve Rabin. Hingham, MA: Charles River Media, 2002, pp. 439–443.

[Biasillo 02b] G. Biasillo. "Racing AI logic." In *AI Game Programming Wisdom*, edited by Steve Rabin. Hingham, MA: Charles River Media, 2002, pp. 444–454.

[Melder and Tomlinson 13] N. Melder and S. Tomlinson. "Racing vehicle control systems using PID controllers." In *Game AI Pro*, edited by Steve Rabin. Boca Raton, FL: CRC Press, 2013.

[Tomlinson and Melder 13] S. Tomlinson and N. Melder. "An architecture overview for AI in racing games." In *Game AI Pro*, edited by Steve Rabin. Boca Raton, FL: CRC Press, 2013.

40

Racing Vehicle Control Systems using PID Controllers

Nic Melder and Simon Tomlinson

40.1 Introduction

A *control system* is defined as the entirety of the mechanical, physical, or digital machinery, including the environment in which it operates (the *plant*), and the device used to manage it (the *controller*). In a real-world control system, whenever we are trying to achieve a desired value (such as setting a temperature via a wall thermostat or a speed using a vehicle's cruise control), a controller is used to modify the externally defined target input to achieve the desired output. Characteristics of the plant can be accounted for and designed into the controller, such that the time taken to reach the desired target can also be optimized. The response of the plant at different rates of change of the desired target value can also be analyzed and controlled.

In order to design the controller, the control engineer will typically analyze the plant and represent it as a series of linear differential equations, using complex mathematical techniques to obtain the required responses under all conceivable steady state and transient conditions. Thankfully, in computer simulations or games, the effect of a badly designed controller is never catastrophic as it might be in a chemical plant, for example, and so instead of a fully specified controller, the much simpler and easier to operate Proportional

Integral Derivative (PID) controller can be used. This PID controller is "good enough" that it can be used in most situations where we are trying to control a single input target and output value system and absolute precision is not necessary. For the curious, a more complete introduction to control theory and plant analysis is available [Ogata 09] as is advanced instruction on bespoke controller design [Warwick 96].

40.2 Basic Control Theory

Any system that we are trying to control contains two parts, the plant and the controller. The plant is what is being controlled but is not necessarily a physical machine. In a home heating system the plant is the boiler, radiator, and the room environment; the controller is the thermostat. In racing games, the plant is typically the digitally simulated vehicle and track.

There are two types of control strategies: open-loop and closed-loop control as shown in Figure 40.1. The key difference between these is that closed-loop control feeds a measurement of the output of the plant back into the input to the controller. This type of system is also referred to as a feedback system. An open-loop controller does not measure the actual output as a reference and so cannot adjust for the effects of the environment. For example, consider a car driving along a flat surface with throttle held at 20%. The vehicle will accelerate slowly until it reaches a maximum speed. Now, if the car is driving up a constant incline or decline, the speed will decrease or increase to a new speed. Similarly, if a different car undertakes the same test, it will reach a different maximum speed. That is, an open-loop system is not able to compensate for any external changes or disturbances to the system.

In contrast, the closed-loop circuit takes the output value (Y) and feeds that back to the input where it is subtracted from the required target value (R). This error value (e) is then acted on by the controller. In the constant speed scenario above, a closed-loop controller will allow the vehicle to maintain the constant required speed even if there is a change in environment or plant (an incline or a different car) because the measured speed error will alter and the controller can react by adjusting the throttle. Furthermore, with a closed-loop controller, the car will accelerate more quickly to its desired speed by starting

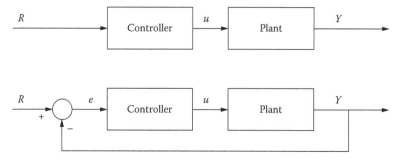

Figure 40.1

An open-loop control system (top) and a closed-loop control system (bottom). Note the output feeding back into the input for the closed-loop system.

with 100% throttle and then reducing the throttle input as it approaches the required speed, that is, the error decreases.

From this example it would seem that open-loop control systems have no practical use. However, if there is a direct relationship between the input and output value, then open-loop control is sufficient. Turning the wheels on a vehicle (for steering) can be done using open-loop control as the mechanics in a vehicle's steering system are well defined so that an applied angle at the steering wheel results in a specific angle on the wheels.

While closed-loop control has many advantages over open-loop control, it can suffer from undesirable effects due to a badly designed controller. These include *overshoot*, where the actual value exceeds the target value, *oscillations* or *ringing* where the actual value oscillates around the target value, and *positive feedback* where an increase in error actually pushes up the plant input resulting in a continual runaway build-up around the feedback loop. Figure 40.2 shows the response of a plant to a step of the input target and the different types of responses that can occur.

There are four major characteristics of the closed-loop controller in response to a step change in the required target value, R:

1. *Rise time:* The time for the plant output to rise to 90% of R.
2. *Overshoot:* The peak value the plant output rises above R, if any.
3. *Settling time:* The time it takes for the system to settle to its steady state.
4. *Steady-state error:* The difference between R and the output Y once the system has settled to a constant state.

Even for the simple PID controller, these effects must be addressed when designing the solution.

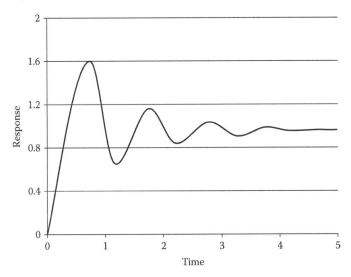

Figure 40.2

A typical response to a step input. This is not the ideal desired response but shows an overshoot, diminishing oscillations, and settling to a constant state.

Table 40.1 A summary of how the three parts of a PID controller affect various aspects of the output

Response	Rise time	Overshoot	Settling time	Steady-state error
K_p	Decrease	Increase	Minor	Decrease
K_i	Decrease	Increase	Increase	Removes
K_d	Minor	Decrease	Decrease	Minor

40.3 Introducing the PID Controller

The closed-loop PID controller is comprised of three parts. The first term (K_p) is proportional to the error (e) between the required target value (R) and the plant output (Y). The second term (K_i) is proportional to the integral of the error, and the last term (K_d) is proportional to the derivative of the error. The output is the sum of these three components:

$$e(t) = Y(t) - R(t) \qquad (40.1)$$

$$u(t) = K_p \cdot e(t) + K_i \cdot \int e(t)\,dt + K_d \cdot \frac{d}{dt} e(t) \qquad (40.2)$$

Calculating the error, integral error, and differential of the error is straightforward; it is the selection of *gain* for K_p, K_i, and K_d that give the controller its characteristics. Note that the error can be either positive or negative, that is the measured speed could be above or below the required speed. Similarly K_p, K_i, and K_d can be negative. The effect of increasing the different parameters on the four main system characteristics is summarized in Table 40.1.

40.3.1 Proportional Control

Proportional control simply multiplies the error by a constant gain (K_p). If K_p is too large, this can cause the system to start to oscillate due to too much input being applied to the plant. This causes the output to overshoot, which could then require a large correction in the opposite direction. Positive feedback can also occur where the average error continuously increases, resulting in an unstable and uncontrollable system.

For a vehicle driving around a circular track (the error is the distance from the center of the vehicle to the center of the road), if K_p is too large, a small error will result in the vehicle turning too much, then overcorrecting and ultimately weaving across the line uncontrollably with larger and larger amplitude. When K_p is small, the vehicle will slowly turn in the correct direction to reduce the error. However, the smaller the error gets, the smaller the processed input to the vehicle will become. In this example, Y will never reach R so the error will never become minimized to 0. It can be seen that our vehicle will never reach the racing line as the steering corrections become minuscule. As the steering corrections are insufficient, the car will settle a fixed distance away from the racing line. This is known as the steady-state error.

40.3.2 Integral Control

In order to counter the steady-state error caused by the proportional term, an integral component can be added to the controller. This integrates the error over time, which is then added back into the input. Therefore, as the steady-state error persists, the integral term builds up, pushing the input further in that direction, thus reducing the steady-state error.

One effect of using an integral component is that oscillations can be introduced into the output. Once the steady-state error has been reduced to zero, the integral error will still be nonzero and contribute to the controller output. It is this residual error (or memory) that causes the overshoot. Furthermore, as the integral and proportional term try to correct for the overshoot, oscillation around the target value can develop. However, unlike positive feedback instability, this oscillation will diminish over time.

40.3.3 Derivative Control

Derivative control generates an input to the plant based upon the rate of change of the error. Because of this, it can be used to either dampen or exaggerate the effects of the proportional term. If the error is changing slowly, the derivative component will have little effect, but if the error suddenly increases, a positive derivative output will also increase giving the system a "kick start." This effect can be used to reduce the rise time of the controller response. Conversely, if K_i is negative, the derivative component can be used to hold back sudden changes in the input, that is, it dampens sudden changes so that the system can focus on long-term changes in R.

40.4 Implementing the PID Controller

When implementing the PID controller, there are a number of additional factors that must be accounted for. This section discusses some of these more fine grain design points.

Limit and reset the integral error. Because the integral error builds over time, if the system has a constant error (such as waiting for the start lights to change) the integral error will be constantly increasing. To counter this, it is desirable to be able to reset the integral error based upon external events (such as the lights changing). Similarly, capping the integral error may also be desirable to limit the effects of the *error memory*.

Maximum history of the error (time constants). In a real-world system, the integral and derivative terms are governed not only by a constant multiplier (gain) but also by what is known as a *time-constant*. For the integral terms, this affects how long in the past the integral is based upon. This effectively limits the amount of "history" stored in the integral, which would otherwise contain information going back as far as the initialization of the controller. This is best implemented by calculating the integral error as a rolling average, that is, on each frame the current integral is reduced by (1–T%) and T% of the current error is added back. This also has the effect of normalizing the integral error.

The choice of the time constant affects the length of the history. A small value will look back in time a significant number of frames while a large value will look only a few frames. Larger histories make the plant output smoother, while shorter histories make the plant output more responsive to changes in R. Using longer time constants does come with a cost, though; it takes longer for the integral error to build up after a step change resulting in a greater lag before the controller responds.

Similarly, the derivative error can be sampled at varying time constants; current and last frame, current and second to last frame, and so on. Using a longer time constant has the effect of making the derivative term less spiky. If you want to use a continuously variable time constant in the derivative, simply estimate interframe error values using interpolation. Optimizing time constants is a useful secondary tool in shaping the controller characteristics.

Filtering input data. If the input data (R) is noisy, the derivative term can fluctuate in an undesirable manner. Smoothing the error data with a low-pass filter (i.e., a rolling average of the last few frames) can help to eliminate this. However, this is effectively adding another integrator. If a low-pass filter is placed either in the input stage or in the feedback loop, this can result in a further time lag in response to changes in R. Alternatively, a separate low pass filter can be added at the input of each individual PID term so that the filtering can be adjusted to suit each component.

Varying the K-coefficients. It may be the case that in different situations, different K values work better. For example, at low speed the vehicle may require much larger K values to get it to start to move, compared to when it is running at high speed. In this case, it would be useful to linearly vary the K values as a function of speed. Be careful with this, though, because if the coupling is too great, a hidden positive feedback loop can be set up, resulting in instability. Similarly, the values used when the vehicle is on tarmac may be unsuitable when driving on dirt. For this case, we would want to use a state-based system where the K values are determined by the surface the vehicle is on.

Record metrics for tuning and debugging. When tuning the K values it is desirable to use a fixed, easily repeatable scenario and record metrics every frame to see the effect that the parameter changes have made. For a steering controller, this would involve recording the vehicle position perpendicular to the racing line. Furthermore, there may be situations where the controller does not behave as expected and being able to record and visualize the controller internals can greatly aid in debugging instabilities.

Determining success. When tuning the controller it is important to be able to define what a good controller is. This "success" value could be time to hit target speed, time taken to do a lap around the track, minimum distance traveled around the track, or smoothness of controls, depending on the game requirements. Properly identifying the correct metric is important and, once such a metric has been found, it can be used as a basis for automated learning.

Using an error offset. Instead of trying to minimize the error, by having a nonzero target error it is possible to give some variety to the systems being controlled. For example, a steering controller would normally try to minimize the distance of the vehicle to the racing line, but by using an error offset, this would cause the vehicle to drive a short distance to the left or right of the racing line. Similarly, if different vehicles use a different error offset when setting a desired speed, there will be some variation in the final speed, which may be appropriate in a traffic simulation. Such effects can also be achieved by offsetting the target value (R) directly, but in some cases, it is easier to work within the controller error domain.

40.5 Designing and Tuning the PID Controller

When designing a PID controller, it is important to properly associate parameters from the tactical AI layers with the input target value R, parameters in the vehicle physics simulation with the output, and also recognizing the significance of the closed-loop error value.

If using a controller designed to manage speed, the input is our desired speed, the output is a value fed into the pedal system, and the error is the speed difference. In this case, the scaled controller output might vary from –1.0 (need to slow down) to +1.0 (need to accelerate). This value will need to be further distributed into actual brake and accelerator pedal inputs.

When used in a steering controller, the input may be the vehicle's required position, the scaled output is fed into the vehicle's steering wheel, and the error is the perpendicular distance of the vehicle to the racing line.

Understanding the input, output, and error allows the specific characteristics of the controller to be defined. For example, steering should be reasonably responsive, but smooth, for normal driving. Additionally, we should certainly avoid over-steering and zigzagging, so we should aim for an overshoot free characteristic. Speed control can also be smooth, but in collision avoidance situations, we might switch in a set of PID values tuned for fast response and accept some oscillations.

Tuning PID controllers is normally done through trial and error, but it is possible to analytically calculate what the gain values should be. However, this requires a good knowledge of the mechanics of the system and is beyond the scope of this article. It is important to only vary one parameter at a time so that the effects on the metric graph in the training scenario are not obscured.

Once the desired characteristics are determined, the following sequence is recommended for tuning the controllers:

1. Set all gains (K) to 0 and increase K_p until the system behaves in a desirable manner with no overshoot or oscillation. Tuning this value first is advisable, as it will generally have the biggest effect on the output.
2. Increase K_i to eliminate the steady-state error.
3. Adjust K_d to reduce any overshoot or reduce the settling time as required.

In practice, it is often found that K_d and K_i are approximately half of K_p. As a general rule, if the system is unable to reach its desired value, increase K_i. If it oscillates, reduce K_p and K_i. If it is too slow to change, then increase K_d. Remember that the properties of the plant also play a part, so if there is a lot of time lag in the plant, the controller may need to work harder to compensate.

40.6 Adaptive Control

In a system that is constantly changing (such as the weight of a vehicle as it burns off fuel or when traveling over different surface types), the initial K values chosen for our PID controller may cease to be appropriate and the controller must adapt. State switching or simple linear variation of the controller parameters has already been outlined, but more intricate methods are also available.

One adaptive control method is to use *gain scheduling*. This is where the controller parameters are directly adjusted by an external factor, such as the vehicle's speed or the surface grip, through a simple linear relationship or a more complex polynomial equation. Gain scheduling can work well when the system is largely dependent upon only one value, but can become particularly difficult to tune when the values are dependent upon multiple factors.

Model reference adaptive control (MRAC) is a form of adaptive control where a model of the system characteristics is predetermined (e.g. given an error of 20, we want to reduce the error at a rate of 5 per second). While the system is running, a comparison between the measured response and the reference model response is made, and the difference is used to adjust the controller parameters. Although MRAC is a more complex form of adaptive control, it is much easier to understand and to tune than other, simpler methods. More information on how the described adaptive control schemes work and can be implemented can be found elsewhere [Forrester 06].

40.7 Predictive Control

Predictive control looks ahead into the future to try to respond to changes in R ahead of time and hence compensate for time lags in the plant. A well known technique used in industrial controllers is *model predictive control* [Alba 02], but this type of system is probably overkill in games.

In practice, we can use a simpler form of predictive control where we generate the input based upon what we are expecting to happen, by using knowledge of the problem. Using a steering system as an example, we can change the input from perpendicular line position to use a *runner* object that leads the vehicle [Tomlinson and Melder 13]. In this case, the input is now the angle between the forward direction of the vehicle and the line between the vehicle and the runner, and the controller error is the difference in angles. This is predictive because the runner will begin a turn before the vehicle needs to. Note that the lead distance of the runner is part of the "plant" and needs to be considered when tuning. Similarly, the speed controller can use a predicted speed by looking down the track.

40.8 Other Controller Applications in Racing

There are many more areas that the PID controller can be applied to beyond the speed and steering management discussed so far. Here are a few further applications.

Types of steering controller. When the driving simulation is high grip, requires smooth driving (e.g., Formula 1 or IndyCar), and the vehicles respond quickly, the controller will be tuned for smoothness (K_p is generally low with a small or even negative K_d). In contrast to this, for off-road racing on low grip surfaces where sliding and drifting is expected, the K values are much larger. This is to compensate for the lag between the input and the effect on the vehicle due to the lower grip of the surfaces.

Speed controller—split channels. There are actually two methods of speed control: throttle only and exact tracking. Using the throttle only technique, if the vehicle is going too fast, then engine braking and tire friction is used to slow the vehicle down. Exact tracking also uses the brake to slow down. A real-world racing driver will use engine braking to deal with small reductions in speed and only use braking for larger reductions. Also, because braking force is usually distributed to all tires and acceleration is only through one axle, the characteristics of the PID for acceleration and braking can be different. So, for more realistic speed control, two subchannels of PID controllers should be implemented: an acceleration channel that responds only to positive errors whose output is the throttle and a braking channel responding only to negative errors. A dead band may also be required so that for small negative errors both the throttle and brake are off and engine braking is used.

Stopping at a point. This can be implemented by using an error equal to the distance to the point minus the vehicle's rolling distance. In order to stop at a point, it is necessary to know the vehicle's braking and rolling distance over a range of speeds. The rolling distance is the stopping distance under engine braking and friction. By comparing the distance to the target and the rolling distance of the vehicle at that speed, the difference can be used to control the brake. When both the braking distance and rolling distance are shorter than the actual distance, it is necessary to apply the throttle. Using this method, the author has been able to make the AI drive a distance of 10 m and stop within an average of 2 mm of its target in less than 5 s. This controller was used for the staggered start mode in Codemasters' *DiRT2* and *DiRT3*.

Drifting. Drifting is where the car is deliberately slid sideways along the track so that the direction of movement is different from the orientation of the vehicle; the difference between the two is the drift angle. The controller is set up where the error is the difference between the desired and measured drift angles.

The usual way to instigate a drift is to sharply turn the vehicle and break the traction on the back wheels (either with the handbrake or by applying a huge burst of throttle power). Once the traction has been broken, the angular momentum of the car will continue to push out the rear against the friction of the tires which are sliding sideways. The drift can be controlled by applying more throttle for more angle and less throttle for less angle, to affect the balance between the friction and angular momentum. Although PID controllers can be used to manage drifting, it is very difficult to achieve, and in practice, it is easier to cheat a little and modify the power and grip on the back wheels directly! In normal circumstances, the drift management should be disabled and only enabled when specific drift situations can occur.

Grip loss prediction, recovery, and channel cross-over. In a race where the driver is at the very limit of grip, circumstances may force them to step over that limit on occasion and slide the car a little. The driver must then take positive action to avoid the slide becoming more significant. It is therefore useful to design a PID controller where the error is a direct measurement of how much the tire is sliding, that is, in normal conditions the error is zero but it becomes nonzero when grip is lost. The response to sliding is to reduce the amount of steer, brake, or acceleration that is causing it, so ideally up to three channels of grip loss monitoring are implemented to feed into the brake, accelerator, and steering inputs of the plant. However, these should work alongside the normal PID driving controllers rather than instead of. This makes it necessary to either mix the different channels before input to the plant, or better still cascade the "slide controllers" into the main driving controllers in a sort of gain scheduling scheme. When active, each of the slide controllers should reduce the K values in each channel. This technique is stepping a bit beyond a simple PID controller, but it does allow the AI to realistically test the limits of the car.

Priority mixing. Although state changes can be used to switch the controller parameters, some situations call for a more analog approach. Consider the situation where two cars are driving around a corner alongside each other. The steering can then have multiple possible required values (R), one for corner turning and one to avoid collision, both acting simultaneously. This can still be dealt with using controllers by mixing the two inputs based on a nominal priority value, P:

$$R = \frac{R_1 P_1 + R_2 P_2}{P_1 + P_2} \qquad (40.3)$$

Mixing can be applied to the required values (R) before the single PID controller, but if the characteristics of the two inputs are different, it can be implemented as two separately tuned PID channels and mixed before input to the plant (u). If this latter arrangement is used, bear in mind that the feedback loop will be sampling the same steering output Y, so the two PID channels are not separate, but are in fact cross coupled. This can be used to advantage by careful tuning to balance the two channels, but it can also lead to instability.

40.9 Conclusion

The PID controller is one of the simplest, yet most versatile, tools that an AI programmer has in order to control specific aspects of a physically based system. It acts as a link between the tactical layer of the racing AI, which defines required steering and speed goals, and the vehicle simulation, which takes action toward the goals. PIDs can be used at a fairly simple level to achieve tailored responses to changes in tactical requirements or can be explored in more depth to deal with driving issues such as grip loss. The closed-loop PID also makes things easier for the programmer, in that it operates by controlling the actual actions of the vehicle on the track, and so the programmer is relieved of the onerous task of having to manually convert abstract tactical requirements into actual driving inputs.

References

[Alba 02] C. B. Alba. *Modern Predictive Control*. London: Springer, 2002.
[Forrester 06] E. Forrester. "Intelligent Steering Using Adaptive PID Controllers." In *AI Game Programming Wisdom 3*, edited by Steve Rabin. Hingham, MA: Charles River Media, 2006, pp. 205–219.
[Ogata 09] K. Ogata. *Modern Control Engineering*. New Jersey: Prentice Hall, 2009.
[Tomlinson and Melder 13] S. Tomlinson and N. Melder. "Representing and driving a race track for AI controlled vehicles." In *Game AI Pro*, edited by Steve Rabin. Boca Raton, FL: CRC Press, 2013.
[Warwick 96] K. Warwick. *An Introduction to Control Systems*. World Scientific, 1996.

The Heat Vision System for Racing AI

A Novel Way to Determine Optimal Track Positioning

Nic Melder

41.1 Introduction

Typically, track positioning in racing games is done by analyzing the vehicles surrounding an AI, choosing the best vehicle to overtake, block, avoid, etc., and then moving the vehicle off the racing line to achieve this behavior. This system works well and has been used in many racing games to excellent effect, but it does have one flaw, namely that it is reacting to a single vehicle at a time. In most racing situations, this works fine but it can lead to some unusual behavior when driving in a pack. An example is when a vehicle pulls out to overtake a vehicle directly in front of it and returns to the racing line, only to then need to pull out again to overtake another vehicle that is a bit further down the track. An intelligent driver would overtake both vehicles in a single maneuver. The purpose of the heat vision system is to solve this problem.

41.2 The Heat Vision System

The heat vision system is based upon the heat map idea used in real-time strategy games. It consists of a one-dimensional "heat line" which spans the width of the track at the car's position. "Heat" is then added to (or removed from) the heat line based upon the position of the racing line, the vehicle's current position, other vehicles, etc. Once all the vehicles have written into the heat line, the vehicle is then directed to move from its current position to a position with lower heat. In this way, the vehicle will find the optimal track position based upon its current circumstances in relation to the other vehicles on track. The heat line is stored in a one-dimensional fixed sized array of floats that is scaled to the width of the track at the vehicle's position.

41.3 Writing into the Heat Line

From here on, the *target vehicle* will refer to the vehicle whose heat line is being written into and the *observed vehicles* are the other vehicles around the target.

Writing into the heat line for each target car is a three-stage process. First, the vehicles are culled to only include the vehicles that the target may be affected by. This would be all the cars within a short distance (e.g., 50 m) of the target, as well as some particular cases (e.g., for gameplay reasons we may always care about any cars approaching from behind the target).

The second stage is to run a series of simple tests that determine details of the observed vehicles. These simple tests will include whether the observed vehicle is on the track, alongside the target, in a good position to block/draft (i.e., not too far away and traveling at a minimum speed), should be overtaken (target is approaching quickly), etc. Note that multiple tests may be true for a given observed vehicle (e.g., a vehicle might be good to draft and also good to overtake).

The final stage is to write into the heat line based upon the results of these tests. This is done by running a number of passes, each writing a different heat signature (shape) into the heat line. It is also important that heat from the ideal racing line is written in at this stage as well. Some examples of these passes include the following:

- *Position:* It is not possible to drive in the same place as an observed vehicle, so write a large amount of heat at this position.
- *Block:* If the observed vehicle is behind the player, it may make a good target to block so remove heat at this position.
- *Draft:* If the observed vehicle is in a good position for drafting, remove heat based upon a drafting cone produced by this vehicle.

Although it is possible to combine the test and write stages into a single stage, keeping them separate has the advantage that they can be used by other systems as well. Furthermore, it is likely that the heat vision system will not be used at all times, so these simple tests can still be used with the more traditional behavior methods. To illustrate this, if the vehicle is off track or facing the wrong way after spinning, it does not make sense to use the heat vision system, but the tests "on track" and "is spun" are still required to aid in the vehicle's recovery to track.

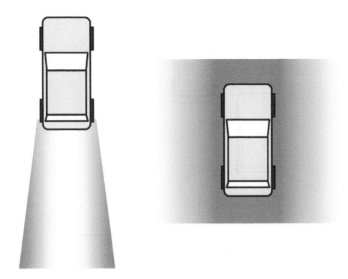

Figure 41.1

An example heat signature used for drafting and for the vehicle's position.

The amount of heat that gets added in or removed is determined by a number of factors. Figure 41.1 shows the heat signatures that a number of different behaviors may add in.

41.4 Smoothing the Output

Once all the observed vehicles have been processed, the resultant heat line may be quite rough with many discontinuities. Since the heat line is a simple array of floating-point values, graphical techniques can be used to smooth it. Smoothing the line is important as it will remove any small discontinuities that may cause "snagging" when determining the desired track position.

41.5 Determining the Desired Track Position

Once the heat line has been created and smoothed, it becomes necessary to determine the desired track position. This is ideally the point on the heat line with the minimal amount of heat. However, it may not be possible to actually move to this point, as there may be a large "heat hill" in the way. This "heat hill" could be caused by a vehicle traveling alongside the target where the large heat acts as a solid boundary to lateral movement. Similarly, the lowest point may be beyond a smaller hill, which would represent a crease between tactical minima that we would want to move past. See Figure 41.2.

In practice, in order to find the ideal track position, the target position should be moved from the vehicle's position along the line with decreasing heat. In order to avoid local minima (i.e., where a small heat hill exists) momentum and friction should be applied to the target point's movement. This is analogous to rolling a ball down the hill, in that the ball will roll downwards and will have enough momentum to overcome any small bumps. Where the ball settles is the target vehicle's ideal track offset position. Once the ideal track

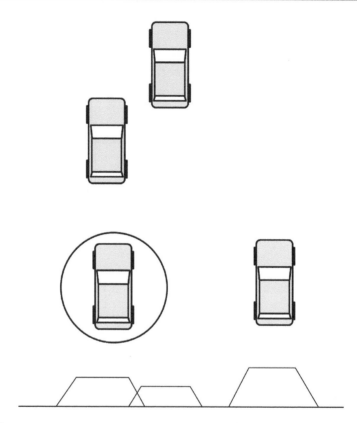

Figure 41.2

The heat line (at the bottom) for the circled car. The heat added is proportional to the distance along the track from the car. Note how the area with lowest heat is closest to the vehicle that the car is alongside.

position has been found, this can be converted into a track offset that can then be passed to the steering controllers.

41.6 Implementation Notes

From the description of how the heat is written, it may appear that it is not necessary to actually retain information of whether an observed vehicle is alongside, good for drafting, etc., since we will write the heat signature for all these tests into the heat line irrespective of what the final behavior is. However, steering is only part of a behavior; it may also be necessary to modify our speed.

A simple example of this would be if the game mode requires the AI to follow another vehicle, such as when doing a parade lap during a Formula 1 race. In this case a modified drafting behavior would be used to add in the heat, but we'd also need to match speed with the vehicle we are drafting/following. Since there are many times when we may need to know which specific observed vehicles are affecting our position, it is useful to maintain an array which maps a point on the heat line to the observed vehicle that has provided the most heat. In this way it is straightforward to quickly identify which vehicle has the most influence on the target vehicle at any one time. Maintaining this list also aids immensely in debugging.

The actual size of the different heat signatures that the vehicles can add is determined by a number of factors that can include relative speed, driver characteristics, and difficulty. As an example, for a vehicle in front, an aggressive driver will add heat with a smaller lateral spread than a less aggressive driver. This will result in the aggressive driver requiring less space to overtake and so he will overtake while leaving a smaller separation between the vehicle, as compared with a less aggressive driver.

For these reasons, as well as game balancing, it is useful to be able to scale the heat signatures in multiple dimensions. For a square-based heat signature, the width across and the distance along the track should be independently scalable, whereas for a drafting cone the length, angle, and fall off should be controllable. By linking these scalable values to a driver characteristic, it becomes possible to give personality to the different drivers. For example, you could have one driver that rarely drafts (short length and small angle) and overtakes giving plenty of space (large width applied to observed vehicle's position heat signature).

41.7 Conclusion

This article has introduced a novel method for determining the optimal track position for a vehicle. Instead of choosing a single vehicle to react to and defining the behavior based upon that vehicle's position (i.e., best target vehicle should be drafted to activate the draft behavior), the heat vision system accounts for all the surrounding vehicles to build up a localized tactical view of the track. Because of this, the vehicle doesn't need different driving behaviors such as alongside, block, or overtake, but instead these actions occur naturally. This system works well when driving on the track, especially when in a pack, but doesn't work in other situations such as recovering back to the track. It is also only suitable for track-style racing games where there is a defined track, so is not suitable for free roaming games like arena-based destruction derby games.

42

A Rubber-Banding System for Gameplay and Race Management

Nic Melder

42.1 Introduction

Rubber-banding is a technique used in racing games to keep the AI drivers near to the players in order to maintain the excitement in races. In simple terms, when an AI-controlled vehicle gets too far in front of the player, it will slow down to allow the player to catch up and, similarly, AI-controlled vehicles behind the player will gain a boost to their speed to help them catch up to the player. In this way, the AI-controlled vehicles will appear to be attached to the player via a rubber band, never getting too far from the player, hence the term *rubber-banding*.

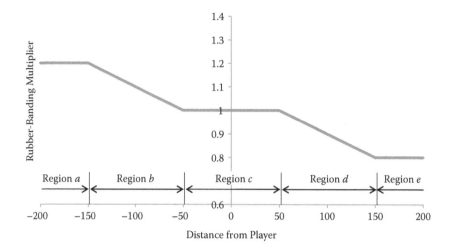

Figure 42.1

Rubber-banding effect versus distance from the player.

When done correctly, this effect can be unnoticeable to the player while keeping the racing feeling close and exciting. However, when done poorly, it can leave the player feeling cheated, especially if the AI, racing in the same car as they, obviously has more speed. This article describes methods to facilitate rubber-banding, discusses some of the special cases that will be encountered, and explains how it can be extended into a fully comprehensive race pace system suitable for longer races.

42.2 Rubber-Banding Implementation

To implement rubber-banding, we want to reduce the speed of the vehicles in front of the player and speed up the vehicles behind the player; the further away from the player, the more we will want to speed up or slow down the vehicles. Figure 42.1 shows a typical graph of what we want to achieve.

Within region c, rubber-banding is disabled. In practice this means any vehicles around the player will behave normally so the player will not see any obvious differences between his vehicle and the AI's vehicle when in close competition. Region d shows a linear negative effect on the cars, causing them to slow down as they get further in front of the player until region e, where the level of negative effect is then maintained. This is referred to as *forward banding*. Similarly, region b shows a linear positive effect on the cars, causing them to speed up until region a is reached. This is referred to as *reverse banding*. It should be noted that a linear relationship is not the only option; the use of a sigmoid or other function would also work.

42.3 Power-Based and Difficulty-Based Rubber-Banding

There are two main methods that can be used for speeding up or slowing down the AI vehicles. Method one modifies the power that the cars have. Cars in front of the player will

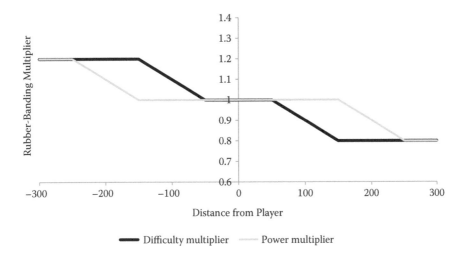

Figure 42.2

Power and difficulty multipliers versus distance from the player. Note how the power multiplier only starts changing once the difficulty multiplier has reached its minimum or maximum value.

have reduced amounts of power, reducing acceleration, and top speed. Similarly, vehicles behind the player will gain power, and so will have better acceleration and will possibly also have a higher top speed.

Method two modifies the driver's skill level. In order to make cars in front of the player slow down, their driver skill is lowered. Depending upon how difficulty is implemented, this can cause the AI to brake earlier than normal, to slow down more for corners, and to accelerate out of corners less vigorously. The overall effect of this lower driver skill is that the AI car will be slower; conversely, increased driver skill will assist in catching up.

In practice, the best approach is to use a combination of the two methods, as they each have distinct advantages and disadvantages. As a rule, it is better to modify the driver skill to slow down or speed up the vehicles, as the drivers are still in the same cars and so no "cheating" is happening. However, the only way to increase the speed of the cars, when the driver skill is already at maximum, is to add extra power to the cars. A similar situation occurs at the lower end where the driver skill is already at a minimum; further slowdown can only be achieved by reducing their power. Figure 42.2 shows how the two methods should be combined to achieve the maximum effect.

42.4 Power-Based Rubber-Banding Issues

Depending on the depth of the underlying physics simulation, power-based application can lead to a number of issues. The severity of these problems is largely a factor of how large the power changes are and include:

1. The AI is unable to control the cars due to the additional power overwhelming the available tire grip, in particular spinning the car when exiting a corner.

This can be countered by setting up the cars to drive with the extra power enabled at all times. Alternatively, extra grip can be added to make it harder to break traction.

2. Underpowered cars are unable to accelerate up hills or change gears.
3. Audio issues if the audio is directly controlled by the car's physics. With extra power, the car will accelerate quicker, which can sound abnormal. Similarly, there is a much greater likelihood that the car will be able to hit the limiter when in the top gear, causing audio to play the limiter effect constantly.

42.5 Disabling Rubber-Banding

There are a number of situations when you do not want power modifiers to be applied to a vehicle. If any of these are present, then all rubber-banding effects should be disabled. These include the following situations:

1. *Race start.* One of the biggest problem areas with racing AI is racing into the first corner, where multiple vehicles need to slow down and navigate the corner simultaneously. Ideally, you want cars to be spread out and be in single file by the time they reach the first corner to avoid pileups, crashes, and blockages. Obviously, forward rubber-banding will cause them to bunch together more, which is the antithesis of what we want to happen. In fact, giving the vehicles in front of the player extra power to help spread them out is actually desirable (i.e., applying reverse banding to the cars in front).
2. *Low speed.* If a vehicle is far in front of the player and its power has been reduced, it will be unable to accelerate effectively. From a standing start (e.g., after a crash) the car may not actually have enough power to get the car to start moving.
3. *Being lapped.* On a circuit, it is possible that an AI may lap the player. In this case the AI will be so far in front of the player (in terms of track distance) that it will be racing with maximum negative rubber-banding being applied (i.e., on lowest driver skill and lowest power). This has the effect that the car will be driving very slowly around the track in a very uncompetitive manner. In this case, it is better to disable rubber-banding on that vehicle so that it is not obvious to the player that rubber-banding is occurring.

42.6 Rubber-Banding in Split-Screen Multiplayer Modes

If there is more than one human vehicle on the track, it is unclear which one should be used as the reference for rubber-banding. A good solution is to treat the rearmost player car as the reference for reverse banding, and the foremost player car as reference for the forward banding, with any AI between the player cars having no rubber-banding applied.

42.7 Improved Rubber-Banding to Reduce Bunching

A side effect of forward banding, especially when using large changes in driver skill/power over short distances, is that the AI vehicles can become bunched together. If the player quickly catches up with them, they will still be in a bunch even though they will have minimal rubber-banding affecting them. This is undesirable as it can enable the player to overtake many vehicles at once. As a player, part of the fun with racing games is battling against the AI to gain position; being able to overtake many opponents at once is detrimental to the player's experience. Two antibunching methods are:

1. *Use the front vehicle distance as the max distance.* As previously described, any vehicle past the maximum distance will have the maximum rubber-banding effect applied. Instead, by using the greater of the maximum defined distance or the distance of the furthest vehicle from the player, the effect of the rubber-banding can be implemented over a greater distance. This does not eliminate the bunching, but slows it down because of the greater distance that the effect is scaled over.

2. *Average positions.* By taking the average position of all the vehicles in front of the player, past a threshold distance, and then affecting all those vehicles the same amount (based upon their average position), the entire pack will reduce their speeds simultaneously. Because multiple vehicles are being affected in the same way simultaneously, they maintain the same spacing while being affected by the rubber-banding.

42.8 Choosing the Parameters

It is important that sensible parameters are chosen when setting up the rubber-banding system, as this can have a large effect on both the difficulty of the game and the perception that the player will have towards the AI. In general, you want to make sure that there is no rubber-banding being applied when close to the player, otherwise power advantages can become visible. It is therefore essential to choose the width of the dead zone in region c so that the AI has no undue, visible advantage, but also so that the AI can still catch up to within the player's rear view.

The rubber-banding system can also be used as part of the difficulty balancing. By having a negative minimum distance for the forward banding, this will allow the player to more easily overtake the AI as, when side by side, the AI will always have less power than the player. Similarly, by adjusting the maximum distance that the rubber-banding operates over, the AI will become more spread out, reducing the number of overtaking opportunities compared with a smaller maximum distance.

42.9 Special Case—First Place Rubber-Banding

The fastest times will always be generated when there is only one vehicle on track, as it is possible to drive the perfect racing line without needing to overtake other vehicles. Essentially, this is the situation that the vehicle in first place is in and so a large gap will normally form between the first vehicle and the rest of the pack. This can be reduced by having additional rubber-banding that only applies to the vehicle in first place. This works in the same way as previously described, but the distance used is between the first and second place instead of the AI and the player.

42.10 Rubber-Banding and Long Races—Race Pace System

The purpose of the rubber-banding system is to slow down or speed up the AI vehicles around the player. Essentially, it makes an AI faster or slower, based upon some predetermined criteria. By adding to these criteria, we can expand the rubber-banding implementation into a system that can adjust the race pace over long races. Across a 50-lap race, a racer will typically race hard for the first 10 laps, then relax (slow down) for the next 30 laps before racing hard for the last 10 laps. If pit stops are involved, then it may be desirable for the AI to race hard on the lap before the pit stop and the lap after, before going back to its relaxed state of driving. These additional rules can be added into the system already described in order to create a much richer AI management tool that can be used to control the pace across the length of an entire race. More ideas on implementing a race pace system can be found in other sources [Jimenez 09].

42.11 Conclusion

This article described a rubber-banding system that works by varying both the driver skill and the vehicle power to keep the AI competitors around the player. Only manipulating the driver skill will allow the AI to stay around the player without appearing to cheat. However, in the situations where the AI just can't go fast or slow enough, power-based rubber-banding can be used. The problems of this approach (in particular, uncontrollability and apparent cheating) have been described, as well as how to avoid them. Improvements to the basic rubber-banding system are also shown (avoiding bunching, the first place lead, working with multiple players) as well as how this system can be further extended into a fully functional race pace system.

References

[Jimenez 09] E. Jimenez. "The Pure Advantage: Advanced Racing Game AI." http://www.gamasutra.com/view/feature/3920/the_pure_advantage_advanced_.php, 2009.

Part VII
Odds and Ends

43

An Architecture for Character-Rich Social Simulation

Michael Mateas and Josh McCoy

43.1 Introduction

More progress has been made creating NPCs that engage in purely autonomous activity or small-group behavior organized around combat (e.g., squad behavior) than creating NPCs that participate in ongoing social activity. Social activity often has no explicit functional goal, but rather involves social actors responding to, displaying, and changing social state. Social action strongly depends on the history of previous social acts. Complex social actions are often best done through dialog, making use of the full richness of natural language to refer to feelings, relationship states, and history. Finally, social action is embedded in a rich social context—actions often have ramifications across multiple social actors. These features of social action are not easily satisfied by NPC architectures that emphasize individual decision making focused on moment-by-moment action selection to accomplish primarily functional goals.

This chapter describes the Comme il Faut (CiF) social simulation architecture. CiF was used to create *Prom Week*,* a social puzzle and storytelling game that was a technical

---

* The design and implementation of *Prom Week*, as well as significant development of CiF, was carried out by a dedicated core team consisting of Josh McCoy, Aaron A. Reed, Ben Samuel, Mike Treanor, Michael Mateas, and Noah Wardrip–Fruin, and by a larger team who provided additional programming, writing, art, music, sound, and animation work. A full credit list is available at http://promweek.soe.ucsc.edu/?page_id=25.

excellence nominee in the Independent Game Festival at GDC 2012 and a nominee for IndieCade 2012. Comme il Faut, which in French roughly translates as "as it should be," satisfies the requirements outlined above. In CiF the concept of a multicharacter social interaction is a first-class AI construct. Characters use many details of the social state, including the history of prior interactions, to decide how to participate in these multicharacter social exchanges. The system automatically retargets dialog within these exchanges to the particularities of specific characters with their detailed personalities and history in specific social situations. The goal of this architecture is to enable casts of characters to engage in rich social interaction, speaking the kind of concrete dialog typically associated with hand-authored dialog trees, but utilizing a level of emergent social simulation typically associated with simulation games.

The rest of this chapter first introduces the released experimental game *Prom Week*, which uses CiF to support a form of interactive storytelling in which the gameplay revolves around solving social puzzles to accomplish story goals. The bulk of the chapter describes CiF's major architectural elements. The chapter then concludes with a description of different interaction styles that a CiF-like architecture can support and a description of related work. The goal of this chapter is to provide enough detail to allow the reader to borrow elements of the CiF architecture in their own work, without drowning the reader in implementation details.

43.2 CiF and *Prom Week*

While an early version of CiF was developed as a stand-alone social simulation system [McCoy and Mateas 09], the architecture and authoring approaches evolved considerably with the development of *Prom Week* [McCoy et al. 10a, McCoy et al. 10b]. Throughout the rest of this chapter, all the examples of different kinds of CiF authoring (knowledge representation) will be from *Prom Week*. Of course, if a CiF-like architecture was used in a different game, different content would be authored, but creating the CiF architecture in the context of creating a complete, playable experience forced us to scale the architecture to the full complexities of authoring and development.

The initial inspiration for developing CiF came from authoring limitations experienced during the creation of the interactive drama *Façade* [Mateas and Stern 02; Mateas and Stern 03]. *Façade* is an interactive drama in which the player, from a first-person perspective, has a short 20-minute interaction with a couple whose marriage is falling apart. *Façade*'s character behaviors are organized around dramatic beats, approximately 1-minute interactions in which the characters work together to convey some aspect of the story or their personality. In *Façade* these behavior clusters were authored for specific characters expressing specific content [Mateas and Stern 07]. Variation in performance was implicitly encoded in behaviors and was not reusable between characters. Our work on CiF started with the goal of generalizing multicharacter exchanges into *reusable* units that support character-specific performance variation *explicitly*. Dynamically retargeting animations allows animation authoring effort to be reused across multiple characters. Similarly, we want to enable dynamically targeted NPC dialog, in which multicharacter dialog performances are authored more generally, and then targeted to specific characters in specific situations. Starting with this initial goal, our final architecture provides the following major features:

- Multicharacter social exchanges are explicitly represented separately from any specific characters. Given a cast of characters, with traits and social state declaratively represented, social exchanges are retargeted for specific characters.
- Characters decide what they want to do and who they want to do it with based on soft decision making (not Boolean flags or rigid preconditions) that can take into account hundreds of considerations.
- Social interactions don't just cause a single change in social state, but have cascading consequences across multiple characters.
- The performance details and outcomes of previous social interactions are stored in an episodic memory and used both during social exchange performances (social exchange dialog can refer to past performances) and to help determine which social exchanges characters want to engage in.

Together, these properties provide the foundation for simulating a *social* world, in which characters are embedded in a constantly evolving sea of social state. After first briefly describing *Prom Week*, we will then walk through the details of these different elements of the architecture.

43.2.1 Prom Week

In *Prom Week*, available for free at promweek.soe.ucsc.edu, the player controls the lives of 18 high school students during the week leading up to the prom. The gameplay consists of the player selecting pairs of characters and choosing a social exchange that the first character initiates with the second. Given a selected pair of characters, CiF determines what actions the first character most wants to initiate, which are presented in a menu to the player, and how the second character responds to a selected interaction. In Figure 43.1, the player is choosing among the five social exchanges CiF most wants to perform between the two selected characters, and is currently highlighting Pick-Up Line, an exchange with the goal of initiating a dating relationship. Once a social exchange is selected, CiF decides how the two characters will perform the social exchange. Figure 43.2 shows an in-progress performance of a Brutal Break-Up, a social exchange with the intention of terminating a dating relationship. The player is trying to accomplish story goals, such as having a character date a specific other character, make a certain number of friends, or have a certain number of good or bad things happen to them. The story goals for one of the *Prom Week* scenarios are shown in Figure 43.3. Because of the underlying social modeling performed by CiF, story goals have multiple emergent, nonprescripted solutions, and different combinations of story goals accomplished by the player open up different endings at the prom. In this way, *Prom Week* combines storytelling and character exploration with simulation-based gameplay.

To help the player master the underlying social system, the *Prom Week* interface allows the player to explore the reasons why characters were motivated to initiate a social exchange, why they responded to a social exchange the way they did, why social exchanges caused the effects they did, and the current social state. Figure 43.4 shows the interface the player can use to explore why a social exchange happened the way it did. The explanations

Figure 43.1

Selecting a social exchange.

Figure 43.2

Social exchange performance.

are generated from an analysis of the most important rules that fired to influence the exchange. Figure 43.5 shows the interface the player can use to explore the current social state, guiding strategic selection of characters and social exchanges. Finding the right amount of complex simulation state to expose to the player in a usable fashion was one of the major design challenges for *Prom Week*.

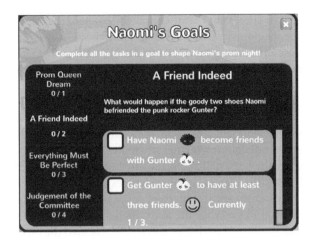

Figure 43.3

Story goals.

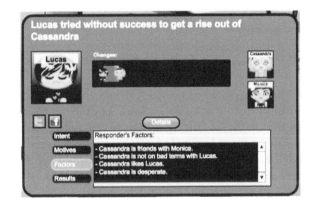

Figure 43.4

Outcome explorer interface.

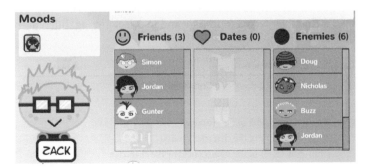

Figure 43.5

Social state explorer interface.

As the player makes successful social exchanges happen, they earn social influence points. Social influence points can be spent to look ahead at the outcome of a social exchange, the factors influencing the social exchange, and/or to override the outcome. Strategic management of social influence points becomes another element of the gameplay.

43.3 CiF Architecture

The primary knowledge representation element in CiF is the social exchange, a collection of patterns of (primarily dialog) interaction where the exact performance and social outcome varies based on the personality-specific attributes of the characters involved and the current social state. The idea of social exchanges was inspired by Erving Goffman's work in sociology on dramaturgical analysis of social interaction [Goffman 59]. Goffman viewed social interaction in everyday life as dramatic performances designed to express properties of one's personality or to change social state. He used the metaphor of theater to analyze how people draft others to perform roles in their performances, organize space and objects into a "stage" and "props" for a performance, and so forth. In CiF, social exchanges comprise a taxonomy of performances organized around what elements of social state they are designed to change or express. Before diving into the details of social exchanges, it is necessary to first understand how characters and social state are represented.

43.3.1 Characters

Characters consist of the elements described in Table 43.1.

Due to the emphasis being placed on social exchanges, the representation of each character is relatively thin, consisting of a small amount of declarative information (that is, information that specifies to the underlying AI system the properties of the character, but leaves it to the system to figure out *how and when* to express these properties). What makes a character rich and unique is their situation in the social world and their history, rather than a bunch of character-specific AI behavior.

Traits and statuses describe the personality and character state of a character. Traits are permanent properties of a character which heavily impact social exchange play. Given a character x, examples include `trait(brainy, x)`, `trait(stubborn, x)`, `trait(attention hog, x)`, and `trait(sex magnet, x)`. Traits only have meaning to the degree that they are referenced in preconditions and influence rules to determine which social exchanges a character wants to initiate and to select among different instantiations of social exchanges.

Table 43.1 Character representation

Character	
Name	The character's name.
Gender	The gender of the character.
Traits	A vector of the character's traits.
Statuses	A vector of the statuses held by the character.
Prospective memory	The character's desires to play social exchanges, represented as a vector of volitions.
Character-specific phrases	Character-specific natural language generation template fill-ins (greetings, pejoratives, exclamations, etc.).

Statuses are temporary, optionally directional, binary social effects that result from social exchange play. Statuses capture transitory states in an agent's mood (e.g., `status(cheerful, x)`), sharp spikes of emotion between agents (e.g., `status(hasACrushOn, x, y)`), and social states (e.g., `status(popular, x)`). They are useful in capturing transitory but potent social situation and character states. When a status is posted by a social exchange, it includes a duration specification of how long the status lasts before it times out.

Prospective memory is a vector of numeric volitions (desires) for characters to engage in specific social exchanges with specific characters. These volitions are computed by initiator influence rules, as described in the *Social Exchanges* section below.

Character-specific phrases are filled into dialog templates in social exchanges. This is one way that the general social exchange dialog is retargeted to specific characters. The character-specific phrases defined in *Prom Week* include `%greeting%` (opening greeting phrase), `%shocked%` (expression of shock), `%positiveAdj%` (positive adjective), `%pejorative%` (a nasty thing to call someone), and `%sweetie%` (a term of endearment). Whenever any of these tags appear in social exchange dialog, they are replaced by the appropriate character-specific phrase. A character definition should include one or more phrases for each of the character-specific tags used in social exchanges.

43.3.2 Social State

The social state of the world is captured by four different representations: social networks, relationships, the cultural knowledge base, and the social facts knowledge base.

Social networks are bidirectional fully connected networks where the edge values measure the feelings between characters. *Prom Week* has three networks: a romance network, which represents how interested characters are in pursuing intimate relationships with each other, a friendship network, which represents how much characters like each other, and a "coolness" network, which represents how much respect characters have for one another. If x has a romance network value of 80 towards y, but y only has a value of 20 towards x, the agents see their situation differently. Social network values are the private feelings characters feel towards each other. Just because two characters have mutually high friendly feelings towards each other does not mean that they automatically have the publicly recognized social state of being friends. Characters with high mutual friendly feelings will be strongly inclined to engage in a social exchange that results in them becoming friends, but a social exchange is necessary to enact the process of turning mutual private friendly feelings into a publicly recognized friendship (and similarly for romance, etc.).

Relationships represent publicly recognized social relationships between characters. In *Prom Week* the three relationships are friends, dating, and enemies. Unlike social network values, which have a numeric range, relationships are binary: two characters either are or aren't friends, are or aren't dating, are or aren't enemies. The distinction between social networks and relationships enables the representation of dramatically interesting (and lamentably true to life) states. For example, given three characters x, y, and z, CiF can represent states such as `relationship(dating, x, y)`, `network(romance, x, y, 20)`, `network(romance, y, x, 95)`, and `network(romance, x, z, 80)`, which translates into x and y are dating, y is head over heels in love with x, while x has fallen out of love with y but has eyes for a third character, z. Given the initiator and responder influence rules we developed for *Prom Week* (see *Social Exchanges* section, below), this state would give x higher volition to want to break up with y but make y more likely not to accept the breakup (to interpret it as a joke or a temporary fight), make x more likely to want to flirt with z to increase romance and possibly to start dating (which would have the consequence of making y angry and lowering y's romance feelings towards x), and make y more likely to want to initiate positive exchanges with x to increase romance but also to initiate negative exchanges with x out of jealousy or anger (e.g., if y sees x flirt with someone else). The relationship representation also allows such complex social relationships as being friends and enemies at the same time (frenemies) – our goal was to support rich and dramatically interesting social states.

The cultural knowledge base (CKB) is a way to further define the world that CiF-driven agents inhabit, providing them with a variety of topics to bond over and squabble about The design intent for creating the CKB is to have a representation of props that is sociologically rich. As props are much more than simple physical objects in dramaturgical analysis, CiF needs a way to understand the cultural importance of items in relationship to the storyworld. The CKB used for *Prom Week* has many items, including zombie movies, chainsaws, and webcomics. Every agent has one or more connections to these items, linked through the uni-directional phrases *likes*, *dislikes*, *wants*, and *has*. Gunter dislikes bobbleheads. Oswald likes web comics. Phoebie likes zombie movies. Additionally, every object in the CKB can be associated with universally agreed-upon properties in the social world (e.g., chainsaws are bad ass, dodgeball is mean). This allows for agents to interact with each other based on their individual opinions of objects in the world. The CKB can be queried to search for patterns of attitudes characters hold for objects. Consider the example query:

```
CKB(item,(x, likes), (y, dislikes), lame)
```

There are four parts (only one has to be specified) to a CKB query: 1) the item to look for, `item`, 2) the first subjective label, e.g., `(x, likes)`, 3) the second subjective label, e.g., `(y, dislikes)`, and 4) the truth label, e.g., `lame`. This query will match an item that x likes, y dislikes, and is universally regarded as `lame`, which could perhaps contribute to y's volition to poke fun at x.

Finally, the social facts knowledge base (SFKB) keeps track of the social history of the story world so that it can be queried for socially relevant information. The SFKB influences what social exchanges characters want to engage in and how they respond, and also affects performances of social exchanges, where the specifics of previous exchanges are brought up in conversation. Typically, games don't record much of the interaction history and use it to make decisions or refer to it in character dialog. By making this history a part of the architecture, CiF provides history-dependence in the social simulation that goes far beyond what can be accomplished with ad hoc techniques such as flags.

The SFKB stores an entry for every social exchange played and for every trigger rule that causes social state change. This entry includes the details of who was involved, as well as any items from the cultural knowledge base mentioned, a natural language generation template that can be used to turn the entry into text for use in performances, and an abstract social exchange label (such as *mean, funny, nice to*) that can be used for querying. For example, if Edward initiates the Bully social exchange with Chloe, engaging in a specific instantiation in which x makes fun of y's SAT score, the following entry is stored in the SFKB.

```
(SocialGameContext exchangeName = "Bully" initiator = "Edward" responder =
"Chloe" initiatorScore = "15" responderScore = "10" time = "5" effectID =
"10" other = "" (SFKBLabel type = "mean"))
```

This entry records the name of the social exchange, the characters involved, the scores computed by the initiator and responder influence rules, a time stamp (for *Prom Week* this is discrete turns, but it could be continuous time as well), an effect ID that indicates which specific instantiation of Bully happened (in this case, making fun of SAT scores), and a label saying that this was a "mean" exchange. SFKB labels are used to support more abstract queries. Rather than querying for specific exchange names or instantiations, often a query only cares about the general tone, finding past events in which one character did something mean, or nice, or lame, etc., to another character. For example, if Chloe later initiates a Backstab exchange with Edward, an instantiation of backstab can query for past mean things Edward did to Chloe: [SFKBLabel(mean, responder, initiator, 0) window(10)], in this case looking through the past 10 social exchanges. The matched entry is then turned into text, resulting in the performance "You know when you made fun of my SAT score?", which the initiator (in this case Chloe) says just before revealing what she's done to get even. In this way, the SFKB supports a compounding effect of history, where the characters refer more and more to past events that have happened, with the past events affecting decision making.

43.3.3 Social Exchanges

Social exchanges are the heart of CiF. The rich social state described in the previous section exists to provide socially interesting reasons for characters to initiate social exchanges; the exchanges then change the social state. Table 43.2 describes the components of a social exchange.

The intent captures the initiator's purpose for initiating the social exchange. These purposes involve changing social state, such as increasing another character's friendship feelings towards the initiator (a social network value change) or initiating or terminating a relationship (such as a dating relationship). If one views social exchanges as complex plan operators, the intent is like the postcondition of the operator. The difference from a

Table 43.2 Social exchange structure.

Social exchange	
Name	The name of the social exchange ("Ask Out," "Text Message Breakup," etc.).
Intent	The intended social change associated with the social exchange.
Precondition	A condition that must be true for the social exchange to be applicable in the current social environment.
Initiator influence rules	The social considerations applicable to the initiator of this social exchange.
Responder influence rules	The social considerations applicable to the responder of this social exchange.
Instantiations	The details of a specific performance including the NLG dialog templates and character animations. Instantiations have a condition that must be true for it to be performed and a specification of how the performance changes the social world.

traditional plan operator is that the social game may be rejected by the responder, which usually has the consequence of causing an almost opposite state change. For example, character x who feels high romance towards y may initiate an "Ask Out" game towards y, with the intent of initiating the dating relationship with y. But just because x initiates "Ask Out", doesn't mean that it somehow magically forces y to start dating; y might have a status of being angry towards x, or have low romance towards x, or have a status of being jealous of x because x has been spending time (engaging in multiple positive social exchanges) with a good friend of y's. There are many factors that may contribute to y rejecting the "Ask Out" exchange, with the reject performance perhaps resulting in y having even lower romance towards x. Additionally, social exchanges can cause cascading effects via trigger rules. In this example, x might gain the status of being embarrassed, and a third party character who wasn't even part of the exchange might gain the status of pitying x. Even if a social exchange is accepted, and the desired intent occurs, there are still often multiple cascading effects of additional social state change, which is a further difference from traditional plan operators. For *Prom Week* there are 12 different intents, 6 for the three social network values and 6 for the three relationships: increase/decrease friendship network, increase/decrease romance network, increase/decrease cool network, initiate/terminate dating relationship, initiate/terminate friendship relationship, and initiate/terminate enemy relationship.

Preconditions are standard predicate conditions that rule a social exchange in or out depending on whether the precondition is satisfied in the current context. One of the goals of CiF is to minimize such hard decision making, relying more on soft decisions that can take many factors into account and that aren't liable to break in unexpected states. Therefore, by convention, preconditions are used very sparingly, only to encode the minimum conditions for a social exchange to make sense. For example, the social exchange "Text Message Breakup," which has the intent of terminating a dating relationship, only makes sense if the initiator and responder are currently dating. Many social exchanges in *Prom Week* have no preconditions (meaning they are always available for consideration).

Initiator influence rules are used to determine the volition (desire) for a character to initiate a social exchange with other characters. Responder influence rules are used to determine whether a responder accepts or rejects the social exchange. Every social exchange has two or three roles: an initiator I, a responder R, and an optional third agent referred to as the other, O. The influence rules refer to these roles in predicate arguments, with CiF appropriately filling in the roles depending on which character a volition is being computed for. Each social exchange has specific initiator and responder rules that combine with a much larger number of inherited general rules called microtheories, to determine volition and accept/reject decisions. The general form of these rules is:

```
<condition> → <increment/decrement volition for an intent>
```

We will first consider examples of initiator influence rules. For the Annoy social exchange in *Prom Week*, whose intent is to decrease the responder's friendship feelings for the initiator, two of the 18 influence rules are:

```
network(romance, I, R) > 66 && trait(I, inarticulate) → +3
[SFKBLabel(cool, R, I) window(10)] → -3
```

The first rule says that if the initiator feels a lot of romance towards the responder (>66) and the initiator has the trait of being inarticulate, add 3 to their tendency to initiate the Annoy social exchange with the responder; characters who can't express themselves well will have a tendency to express being romantically attracted to someone by bothering them. The second rule, which uses a social facts knowledge base query, says that if the responder initiated an exchange with the initiator within the last 10 social exchanges, and the exchange was labeled as cool, subtract 3 from their tendency to initiate the Annoy social exchange; a character is less likely to annoy someone who initiated a cool social exchange with them in the recent past.

While every social exchange has a small number of specific rules, a much larger number of shared rules are stored in microtheories. The purpose of microtheories is to facilitate knowledge reuse; to support writing, just once, rules that might be used across many social exchanges. The microtheory library constitutes a large repository of rules, split between dozens of microtheories. A microtheory consists of a definition and a set of influence rules. The definition of a microtheory is a condition, often times consisting solely of one predicate. For example, `relationship(friends,x,y)` is the definition of the Friends microtheory. Only microtheories whose definitions evaluate to true in the current context are considered when calculating volitions. The microtheory's rule set then provides a general representation of the social "common sense" associated with the condition, for example, in the Friends microtheory, that friends are more likely to get along, and less likely to become enemies, than strangers. So, given the example of the Annoy social exchange, if the initiator and responder happen to be friends, then the Friends microtheory definition will be satisfied, and all the rules in the Friends microtheory will be considered in addition to the Annoy-specific initiator influence rules. In this case, the Friends microtheory contains rules that will subtract from the tendency to engage in behavior with the intent to decrease the buddy network, decreasing the volition to engage in Annoy. Of course, more than one microtheory can be active during volition formation. For example, if in addition to being friends the initiator has the trait of being self-destructive, then the Self-Destructive microtheory will also be active. This microtheory captures general tendencies for a self-destructive character, which in the case of Annoy will actually add to the tendency to engage in friendship decreasing intents.

Forming volitions for a character involves summing the volitions on the right-hand sides of the satisfied initiator influence rules for every potential responder (and other) for every social exchange. At the end of this process is a vector of numbers corresponding to the character's desire to engage in each of the social exchanges with each of the characters. A variety of policies can then be used to decide what action to take, such as weighted random selection from the top N for autonomous action, or placing the top N in a menu for the player to select from as was done in *Prom Week*. The volition calculation process can be made efficient through a combination of rule-caching techniques such as Rete [Forgy 82] and by limiting the set of potential responders (for example to just nearby characters or characters present in a scene) for which volitions are calculated.

Influence rules seek to combine the advantages of utility methods and Boolean predicate representations. Utility methods have well-known advantages including converting disparate decisions into a single comparable basis (numbers), and improving robustness of decision making by avoiding unaccounted-for corners of the state space for which the binary decision making mechanism doesn't have a match [Mark 09]. The predicate calculus, on the other hand, is great at representing complex conjunctions of states, such as "If x feels high romance towards y, and a third party z did something mean to x, followed by y doing something mean to z, then x will have a higher desire to initiate a dating relationship with y." Such complex conjunctive logic is unwieldy to express through combining algebraic functions, especially given the ease with which new conjunctive expressions can be incrementally added. By having predicate calculus expressions on the left-hand side of rules, but having them add weights to a sum on the right-hand side, the rules work together to compute a complex utility surface, combining the benefits of numeric and logic-based decision making.

Responder influence rules are similar to initiator influence rules, except that they are used to score how the responder feels about the exchange that she is included in. In a process very similar to desire formation, the responder gets to determine how they feel about the exchange. If the responder score is too low, the responder will reject the exchange, resulting in a different (and often opposite) social effect than the social exchange intent. In addition to the exchange-specific responder influence rules, microtheories are also used for computing the responder score. For *Prom Week*, the default accept/reject boundary is 0; responder scores higher than 0 result in accepting the social exchange. The responder accept/reject boundary is one of the parameters adjusted by the difficulty settings.

Finally, a social exchange has a set of instantiations, each consisting of effects and natural language generation templates. Instantiations are divided into accept and reject instantiations. Each instantiation is a different possible way a social exchange can play out. Associated with instantiations are conditions that are tested to see if the instantiation is valid in the current context. Every exchange has a generic accept and reject instantiation that places no conditions on the instantiation. More specialized instantiations have additional conditions, and play out the exchange in more specialized ways, in addition to having more effects. For example, one accept instantiation on the Break Up social exchange has the condition `trait(cold,i)`—this instantiation not only leads to terminating the dating relationship, but has additional repercussions, such as terminating the friends' relationship. If multiple instantiations have conditions which evaluate as true, the most salient is chosen, with saliency being computed as a weighted sum of the number of true predicates in each condition (the weight associated with a predicate type indicates how important that predicate is for determining the specificity of a social context).

The instantiation performance consists of lines of dialog, represented using natural language generation templates, to be spoken by the characters during the exchange. In the case of *Prom Week*, the dialog lines are tagged with animations to be performed by the characters. For example, one of the accept instantiations of Reminisce has the condition that the responder has done something recently to embarrass a third party, and the initiator is enemies with the same third party. In this instantiation, the initiator and responder bond (increasing friend feelings) by reminiscing about how the responder embarrassed this disliked third party. The template dialog for this instantiation is:

```
I: Hey%r%. Man, I can't stand%o%...
R: Tell me about it. Hey, remember that time when%SFKB_(embarrassed,r,o)%?
I: Oh god, I totally do!%pronoun(o,he/she)% totally had that coming for
being such a%pejorative%!
```

The bolded elements of the dialog demonstrate some of the natural language generation tags supported by CiF, including an SFKB reference and a character-specific pejorative. In the case of Simon and Monica talking about Oswald, the dialog could turn into:

Simon: Hey **Monica**. Man, I can't stand **Oswald**...

Monica: Tell me about it. Hey, remember that time when **I broke up with Oswald in the middle of his tennis match just to make him lose?**

Simon: Oh god, I totally do! **He** totally had that coming for being such a **n00b!**

The final element of CiF's architecture is the trigger rules. These are effects (and associated conditions) that are shared across all social exchanges. In addition to the social state change caused by the social exchange itself, additional changes may be caused by trigger rules. The trigger rules capture the cascading consequences of social exchanges, as well as state changes crossing multiple social exchanges. Consider the following example trigger rule:

```
~relationship(enemies x, y) && trait(x, cat: nice) &&
[SFKBLabel(cat: negative, z, y) window(7)] &&
~[SFKBLabel(cat: negative, x, y) window(7)] →
status(pities, x, y)
```

This rule says that if x and y aren't enemies, and x has one of the traits that falls into the more general category of "nice" traits, and a third party z has done something that falls into the more general category of negative interactions to y in the last 7 social exchanges, and x hasn't themself done something mean to y in the last 7 exchanges, then x gains the status of pitying y. Or, more succinctly, nice people will pity those who have mean things happen to them as long as they haven't done mean things themselves to the same person. This rule, like all trigger rules, can fire after any social exchange.

43.4 Interaction Approaches

Now that the architecture has been described, this section describes different ways a CiF-like architecture can be integrated into the player interaction loop. The current version of CiF treats social exchanges as discrete dialog units; thus CiF currently supports a discrete-choice model of social interaction.

Prom Week utilizes a god-game interface in which the player doesn't play a specific character, but tells characters what to do. When the player selects two characters, CiF computes the volition for the first character to initiate every social game with the second. The system then displays the top volition actions in a menu, with some intermixing to ensure variety of intentions appearing in the menu. Characters only occasionally take autonomous action. When a character develops an extremely high volition to initiate a social exchange, the player is informed that the action will take place in a small number of moves. This was added to *Prom Week* to create an additional challenge element. For example, the player may be trying to achieve the story goal of having a character date three other characters at the same time. But often, when the player has succeeded in having the character initiate a second dating relationship, the first romantic partner will develop a high volition to play a social exchange terminating the relationship. This autonomously initiated exchange puts a sharp limit on the number of turns the player has left to achieve the goal.

In *Mismanor*, an experimental RPG built using CiF [Sullivan et. al. 10; Sullivan 12], CiF was extended to include information and objects. This version of CiF, dubbed CiF-RPG, supports characters in forming volitions to perform actions related to gaining and sharing information, and gaining, losing, and using objects, in addition to network and relationship intents. Quests often have social, nonprescripted solutions enabled by the CiF model. In *Mismanor* the player plays a specific player character. The player character is modeled like any CiF character, having a collection of traits, statuses, and so forth. Traits are assigned during the character creation process. When the player interacts with an NPC, the menu options presented are determined by the highest volition social exchanges the player character wants to perform with that NPC. In a sense, CiF takes an active, dynamic role in supporting role play. NPCs are also given opportunities to engage in autonomous actions with the player and each other.

Another use of CiF would be as a simulation to create a rich social background around the player. For example, in an RPG, the characters in a village could go about their daily lives engaging each other in social exchanges driven by CiF. The social exchanges could be used to dynamically reveal backstory and frequently reference actions of the player character. In this more autonomous mode, action selection could be performed using any one of a number of well-known utility selection methods (e.g., weighted random based on the volitions, random among the top n, etc.).

Currently, we are working to extend CiF to support moment-by-moment interaction, moving away from the currently atomic social exchanges. In this interaction model, the player controls a real-time character employing individual gestures and limited natural language interaction. To accomplish this, instantiations are represented as collections of ABL behaviors [Mateas and Stern 02], with bottom-up recognition of player-initiated intents.

43.5 Related Work

Here, we briefly describe the most relevant related work. *The Sims 3* employs a social model similar to CiF. Its characters have traits and desires that inform the social practices (social norms and clusters of expectations) they perform [Evans 08]. A Sim can be involved in more than one practice at a time, and a practice can involve more than one Sim at a time. Thus, the *Sims 3* AI represents social practices as nonatomic interactions that can be intermixed, unlike the atomic interactions of CiF. However, the Sims engage in more abstract interactions, and do not use concrete dialog. Further the characters don't have backstories or make complex use of history in decision making. Finally, CiF supports reference to third parties outside of the immediate social exchange, supporting more complex social decision making and cascading social effects.

More recently, Evans has developed *EL*, a deontic logic that "distinguishes between what is in fact the case and what should be the case" [Evans 11]. For example, an *EL* rule can capture inferences such as "if it is the case that x's stomach is empty and that y is food, then it should be the case that x should eat y." While CiF relies upon weight/intent pairs on the right-hand side of a rule to determine character desires, *EL*'s rules infer what a character should be doing as well as what the character thinks other characters should be doing. *L* is a deontic epistemic logic (it can represent what is the case, what should be the case, what has been seen to be communicated, and what is intended to be communicated) [Evans 09] that has been implemented in *EL*. It's a response to Evan's critique of his own earlier work in which social practices are represented as activities that characters unproblematically know how to participate in, versus being activities in which characters actively work to help each other maintain state in the activity (the ethnomethodological approach to human activity). The same critique applies to CiF.

Evans and Short have developed Praxis, a system with many similarities to CiF that lies behind the commercially released game Versu [Evans and Short 12; Evans and Short 13]. In Praxis, social practices are represented as collections of states that provide social affordances for character actions. Unlike CiF social exchanges, which are atomic performances, practices involve multiple state changes with opportunities for player choice. This also supports multiple practices intermixing. Character traits as well as judgements characters make about each other influence the performance of these practices.

43.6 Conclusion

The CiF architecture enables casts of characters to engage in rich social interaction, speaking the kind of concrete dialog typically associated with hand-authored dialog trees but utilizing a level of emergent social simulation typically associated with simulation games.

To accomplish this, multicharacter social exchanges are explicitly represented separately from any specific characters. Given a cast of characters, with traits and social state declaratively represented, social exchanges are retargeted for specific characters. Thus, social exchanges provide both an abstraction layer for reasoning about social exchanges and a mechanism for generalizing reusable dialog.

Characters decide what they want to do and who they want to do it with, based on soft decision making (not Boolean flags or rigid preconditions) that can take into account hundreds of considerations. This allows complex relationship states and history across the entire cast of characters to influence individual decisions.

Social interactions don't just cause a single change in social state, but have cascading consequences across multiple characters. These cascading effects help create a sense of a living world, with the characters enmeshed in a constantly changing social context.

The performance details and outcomes of previous social interactions are stored in an episodic memory and used both during social exchange performances (social exchange dialog can refer to past performances) and to help determine which social exchanges characters want to engage in. This provides a strong sense of history dependency typically missing from NPCs.

Together, these properties provide the foundation for simulating a *social* world, in which characters are embedded in a constantly evolving sea of social state.

Acknowledgments

This material is based upon work supported by the National Science Foundation under Grant No. IIS-0747522.

References

[Evans 08] R. Evans. "Re-expressing normative pragmatism in the medium of computation." *Proceedings of Collective Intentionality VI.* 2008. Available online (http://philpapers.org/rec/EVARNP).

[Evans 09] R. Evans. "The logical form of status-function declarations." *Etica and Politica/ Ethics and Politics*, XI, 2009, 1, pp. 203–259. Available online (http://www2.units.it/etica/2009_1/EVANS.pdf).

[Evans 11] R. Evans. 2011. "Using exclusion logic to model social practices." In *Agents for Games and Simulations II*, pp. 163–178. Springer Lecture Notes in Computer Science, 2011. Available online (http://www.springerlink.com/index/W2675776V4411H58.pdf).

[Evans and Short 12] R. Evans and E. Short. Talk during the AI summit session "Beyond Eliza: Constructing socially engaging AI." *Game Developers Conference*, San Francisco CA. 2012.

[Evans and Short 13] R. Evans and E. Short. "Versu-A Simulationist Storytelling System." IEEF Transactions on Computational Intelligence and Artificial Intelligence in Games, forthcoming 2013.

[Forgy 82] C. Forgy, "Rete: A fast algorithm for the many pattern/many object pattern match problem." *Artificial Intelligence*, 19, pp. 17–37, 1982.

[Goffman 59] E. Goffman. *The Presentation of Self in Everyday Life*. Garden City, NY: Doubleday, 1959.

[Mark 09] D. Mark. *Behavior Mathematics for Game AI*. Boston, MA: Course Technology, 2009.

[Mateas and Stern 02] M. Mateas and A. Stern. "A behavior language for story-based believable agents." *IEEE Intelligent Systems*, Vol. 17, Number 4, 2002, pages 39–47. Available online (http://users.soe.ucsc.edu/~michaelm/publications/mateas-is-2002.pdf).

[Mateas and Stern 03] M. Mateas and A. Stern. "Integrating plot, character and natural language processing in the interactive drama Façade." *Technologies for Interactive Digital Storytelling and Entertainment (TIDSE)*, Darmstadt, Germany. March 24–26, 2003. Available online (http://users.soe.ucsc.edu/~michaelm/publications/mateas-tidse2003.pdf).

[Mateas and Stern 07] M. Mateas and A. Stern. "Procedural authorship: A case-study of the interactive drama Façade." In *Second Person: Role-Playing and Story in Games and Playable Media*, edited by Patrick Harrigan and Noah Wardrip-Fruin, pp. 183–208, Boston, MA: MIT Press. 2007. Available online (http://users.soe.ucsc.edu/~michaelm/publications/mateas-second-person-2007.pdf).

[McCoy and Mateas 09] J. McCoy and M. Mateas. "The Computation of Self in Everyday Life: A Dramaturgical Approach for Socially Competent Agents." Intelligent Narrative Technologies II, Papers from the 2009 AAAI Spring Symposium. AAAI Technical Report, SS-09-06, AAAI Press, Menlo Park, CA, 75–82, 2009. Available online (http://users.soe.ucsc.edu/~mccoyjo/publications/AAAI-INT2-09-McCoy.pdf).

[McCoy et al. 10a] J. McCoy, M. Treanor, B. Samuel, B. Tearse, M. Mateas, and N. Wardrip-Fruin. "Comme il Faut 2 : A fully realized model for socially-oriented gameplay." In *Proceedings of Foundations of Digital Games (FDG 2010) Intelligent Narrative Technologies III Workshop (INT3)*. Monterey, California, 2010. Available online (http://games.soe.ucsc.edu/sites/default/files/CiF-FDG2010-IntelligentNarrativeTechnologies3.pdf).

[McCoy et al. 10b] J. McCoy, M. Treanor, B. Samuel, B. Tearse, M. Mateas, and N. Wardrip-Fruin. 2010. "Authoring game-based interactive narrative using social games and Comme il Faut." In *Proceedings of the 4th International Conference and Festival of the Electronic Literature Organization: Archive and Innovate*, 2010. Providence, Rhode Island, 2010. Available online (http://games.soe.ucsc.edu/sites/default/files/TheProm-ELOAI.pdf).

[Sullivan et al. 10] A. Sullivan, N. Wardrip-Fruin, and M. Mateas. "Rules of engagement: Moving beyond combat-based quests." In *Proceedings of Foundations of Digital Games, Intelligent Narrative Technologies III Workshop*, Monterey, California, June 18, 2010. Available online (http://games.soe.ucsc.edu/sites/default/files/rulesofengagementcameraready.pdf).

[Sullivan 12] A. Sullivan. "The Grail Framework: Making Stories Playable on Three Levels in CRPGs." Ph.D. Dissertation, University of California Santa Cruz, 2012. Available online (http://www.asdesigned.com/dissertation.pdf).

44

A Control-Based Architecture for Animal Behavior

Michael Ramsey

44.1 Introduction

Many games include creatures or animals that exhibit the illusion of life while interacting with the game player and with the world around them. This illusion breaks when a creature does something that seems out of character or unnatural—and these types of breaks in illusion are unfortunately, all too common. Thus, we need to provide the ability for our characters to exhibit *believable behavior* that is purposeful, while being robust enough to appear fully life-like.

For this article, we define *behavior* as the actions an agent performs. *Purposeful behavior* describes actions performed in the context of some objective (for example, going to a food bowl in order to eat, or climbing a tree to sleep in its branches). There are numerous well-known architectures that can generate sets of behaviors and chain them together to be purposeful (for example *behavior trees* (BTs), *finite-state machines* (FSMs), *hierarchical task network planners* (HTNs), and so forth), and many of these are discussed elsewhere in this book. However, if our behavior is going to be *believable* then it needs to be more than just the output from a BT or other AI architecture. It requires a system which can deliver the appropriate interactions regardless of the ever-changing situation in-game.

If purposeful behavior is going to be believable, then it must produce consistent results regardless of varying environmental conditions. This is something that real-world creatures typically handle without much thought, but for an AI character it can be quite hard. Think about the sequence of motions associated with something as simple as walking across a room and hitting a light switch, for example. They vary greatly depending on your starting position and stance, the exact position of the light switch, the types and locations of obstacles between the two, the type of surface being traversed, etc.

Adaptive, purposeful behavior was perhaps best characterized in 1890 by the American psychologist William James [James 90]:

> Romeo wants Juliet as the filings want the magnet; and if no obstacles intervene he moves towards her by as straight a line as they. But Romeo and Juliet, if a wall be built between them, do not remain idiotically pressing their faces against its opposite sides like the magnet and the filings with the card. Romeo soon finds a circuitous way, by scaling the wall or otherwise, of touching Juliet's lips directly.

William James' description of Romeo's behavior provides an intuition of how purposeful behavior could inform our work on virtual characters. Just as Romeo with Juliet, our behavioral modeling solution needs to take into account and handle the variability of the world, and adapt accordingly—so when it is time to kiss, we can make that happen whether it requires crossing a dance floor, climbing a balcony, or simply bending over to pickup a dagger.

World of Zoo is an example of a game that could easily suffer from issues with the believability of its behavior in just this manner. This game is an animal simulator that contains various types of zoo animals in a variety of environments. The player can alter the layout of the zoo, changing the environment around the animals. In the worst case, this can result in massive topological alterations to the animals' game world that directly interferes with an animal's current behavior! This is actually not at all uncommon, since the players rarely plan their changes around the animals' actions, and in some cases will even actively try to "mess with them." As a result, animals need to be able to react believably to shifts in their environment that cannot be predicted when their behavior is being crafted during development, or even when the behavior is being selected by their high-level AI.

The remainder of this chapter provides an introduction to aspects of controller theory that can be used to implement a behavioral system for life-like animals.

44.2 A Control System

Even the simplest observation of the physical world demonstrates that environments do not remain static. No fixed, predetermined behavior will allow an animal to cope with the world, so behavior must somehow take into account an ever-changing and unpredictable world. Clearly then, our animal AI must continually modify its behavior to adjust for disturbances that would cause a predetermined behavior to look incorrect—but how and where do we find the appropriate modifications to make?

One solution can be found in the work of electrical and mechanical engineers in the early 1930s in a discipline known as *control theory*. Where a behavior-centric approach sees the world as being under the control of the animal through its behavior, control theory instead sees the animal as being at the mercy of the world, but able to vary its behavior to compensate for changes in the world through the use of *control systems*. Examples of these systems are found in a variety of electronic devices, such as the thermostat in your home which regulates the heating or cooling system, or even automated antiaircraft guns on naval vessels.

To help us come to grips with what a control system is, we begin with a high-level model of a control system. Fundamentally, there are four things that these systems do:

1. Signals are received.
2. Signals are analyzed.
3. Instructions are made to act on the analyzed signal.
4. These instructions are used to do something in the world or in another control system.

A great example of this kind of control system in practice is the way the cruise control of a vehicle maintains a steady driving speed in the absence of input from the driver. When the cruise control is engaged with a particular desired speed, this speed becomes the control system's *reference signal* (which is also the system's desired goal). If the vehicle's speed varies from the goal, then the control system will increase or decrease the amount of fuel that is delivered to the engine, thus adjusting the speed until it once again matches the goal. Because this system is designed to minimize the variance between the actual value and the goal value, it is referred to as a negative feedback system. We will focus on negative feedback systems throughout the remainder of the chapter.

44.3 Perceptual Control Systems—Negative Feedback

As shown in Figure 44.1, negative feedback can be visualized as a marble in a curved cup. The bottom of the cup represents our reference signal—that is, the value that we want to retain. Much like gravity, the control system constantly pulls the actual value down into the cup, until it matches the goal value that is at the lowest point. When external forces push the actual value away from our desired value (imagine moving the cup from side to side or knocking the marble upward with a finger), the negative feedback brings it back down again.

A more detailed view of how a negative feedback system can be implemented is shown in Figure 44.2. The *input function* converts some variable aspect of the world into a

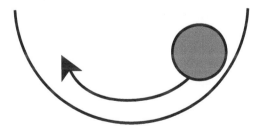

Figure 44.1

Negative feedback in action.

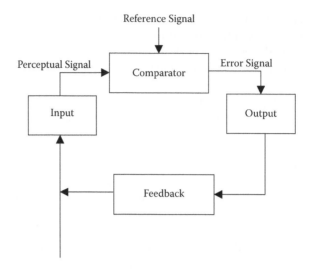

Figure 44.2

A sample negative feedback control system.

perceptual signal. The perceptual signal is then compared with a *reference signal* within the *comparator function*. The difference between these two, called the *error signal*, is then converted within the *output function* into a behavior. A *gain factor* can also be applied to the output. The gain adjusts the magnitude of our output behavior—so in the case of a cruise control, for example, it would change the rate at which we speed up or slow down.

The behavior, as altered by the gain, then acts on the world, changing it in the desired manner. The variable that the system is controlling is not only being influenced by the output from the system, however—it is still being impacted by the ever-changing state of the world. Thus, we continuously reexamine the state of the world, feed that into our control system, and then modify our behavior based on the output of the control system in an attempt to keep the variable as close to the reference signal as possible.

Returning to the cruise control example, we see that a cruise control system has a number of components that allow for the exhibition of purposeful behavior—behavior that is perceived to compensate for disturbances, even when those disturbances are *unknown*. The control system has no understanding of whether the vehicle is proceeding up an incline or descending, if it is hauling a camper, if there is wind resistance, or if the engine is not fully functional. The only aspects of the world that this control system has knowledge of are the vehicle's speed and the rate of fuel delivery to the engine. In this case, the *vehicle's speed* is the *controlled variable*; however, a control system does not directly control its *value*, instead it controls *how that value changes*. The cruise control system senses the speed of the vehicle and the only control it has is by adjusting the flow of fuel. To maintain the goal (set as the reference signal) the control system must continue sensing the vehicle's speed as disturbances attempt to vary the control system's input. Any disturbances are then compensated for and the exhibited behavior changes as the conditions change around the vehicle.

Although we have discussed control systems in the context of automating a process for the user, such as the driver setting the cruise control's desired speed, it's important to highlight that the reference level does not have to be defined as the game is played; the initial value can be specified by a designer during development and then, if necessary, updated as the game progresses.

44.4 Hierarchy of Control Systems

In 1989, William Powers proposed a complex hierarchy with 11 ordered levels of control systems as the foundation for human and animal perception [Powers 89]. The details of this approach are more complex than appropriate for our animal AI, but the general concept is quite useful. The key idea (see Figure 44.3) is that the higher order control systems adjust the lower-order systems' reference signals, and the input that is sensed by the lower-order systems is also made available to the high-order systems. Perceptions in the higher level components of the system are typically composed of combinations of lower-order systems, which are then controlled by the way the high-level system alters their reference level. In this way, we don't create a hierarchy of command; instead we have

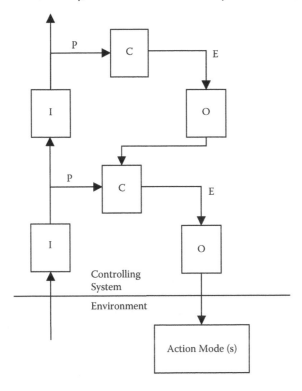

Figure 44.3

A sample hierarchical control system illustrating the input being propagated up to the higher order control system, while the output from the higher order system feeds back as the reference signal. P represents the incoming perceptual signals to a comparator, and E is the applied error amount.

high-level systems adjusting the reference values of the low-level systems, and then those low-level systems directly outputting the appropriate behavior.

Returning once again to the cruise control example, some newer cars have "intelligent cruise controls" that will automatically slow down when following another vehicle. This can be achieved by adding a higher order layer to the system. The new layer takes the input from the existing component (the current speed), but it also considers how closely the car that it's controlling is following the vehicle in front of it. The output for this new component is the reference value for the lower level system—that is, it adjusts the desired speed of the cruise control automatically so as to slow down and avoid a collision.

44.5 Control Systems for Animal Behavior

While many animals appear to exhibit nothing more than a simple stimulus and response mechanic, research into animal psychology has discovered that much of animal behavior is far more complex and intricate than the execution of an if/then/else test. One of the first studies of defensive behavior in an animal's natural environment was conducted by Heini Hediger [Hediger 55]. Hediger provided the initial description of a *flight zone*. The key idea is that an animal will not simply flee at the sight of a predator, but will wait until the predator has approached within a specific distance, at which time the threatened animal will move away in order to recreate the desired space. In Hediger's work we see that defense is not simply a reflexive response to a stimulus, but is instead a constant process of spatial assessment and movement. These constantly executing and assessing systems are, in essence, control systems.

44.6 Customizing a Negative Feedback Controller—Game Extensions

The cruise control system outlined above focused on managing a single floating-point control variable (the speed of the vehicle) using one or at most two controllers. Animals need to be able to do more than travel a linear path at a fixed speed, so they will require more complex inputs, and a greater number of controllers. As a result, we need to provide a custom negative feedback controller implementation that operates on coarse data structures/objects, [Ramsey 09, Ramsey 10]. Examples of controllers appropriate to animal control include the above mentioned flight zone controller, a personal space controller, a biological urge controller (e.g., food, water, or sleep [Toda 82]), and an environmental spatial orientation controller [Ramsey 11].

Perhaps the most important customization is to provide a representation for "spatial semantics." In other words, we need to be able to represent concepts about locations to the control system's input. Examples of these concepts include the location(s) of nearby food sources, nearby obstacles, other entities (friendly or hostile), and so forth. The comparator can then work in much the same way—examining the input signal (perhaps the animal's current location), comparing that to a reference signal (perhaps a position adjacent to a nearby food source), and returning an appropriate action (such as going to the food source and eating it).

Another important modification to the controller model is the addition of a priority value. This is something that will be very dependent on the type of game you are making, but generally speaking, if one control system has relatively low priority its output may be ignored in favor of the output from another control system with a higher priority. The details of this will become more apparent below.

44.7 Gosling Control System

At this point we have all of the building blocks required to create a realistic simulation of a young goose, or "gosling," highlighting some of the interesting ways it can believably interact with a small world.

One approach to tackling the issue of engineering a behavioral system is to attribute a wide variety of drives, needs, or urges to our virtual animal [Toda 82]. These motivations are modifiable by both the designer during development and the game at runtime, and this allows us to influence the current state of our higher order control system. In our example we'll assign two drives to our gosling that are relevant in our example world: security and curiosity.

Konrad Lorenz [Lorenz 81] discovered that a gosling will imprint on the first large animate object that it sees, which is typically its mother. This imprint serves as the initial priming of a control system that requires the gosling to maintain close contact with its mother throughout gosling-hood, by monitoring this distance and moving to compensate for any disturbances that are detected. In nature, these disturbances may be caused by the mother's actions, such as moving away, or by obstacles preventing the gosling from approaching the mother directly.

Of course, goslings do things other than simply stay near their mothers. They also seek out food, avoid predators, and explore the environment around themselves, among other things. Each of those things, taken in isolation, can be modeled fairly simply with a negative feedback control system. So we have one control system responsible for maintaining the distance from the mother; another which tries to move toward (and eat) nearby food; a third that is trying to avoid predators; and a fourth that is trying to seek out things that the gosling hasn't yet examined—trees, rocks, flowers, or areas that it hasn't been to.

Each of those systems takes the gosling's current position, and tries to adjust that position based on an input signal (the position of the nearest food, the position of nearby predators, and so forth). The trick, then, is to decide which of these four controllers should actually control the gosling at any given time—and that is where the priorities come in. Each controller is assigned a priority based on its current urgency. So the controller that seeks out the mother will be lower or higher priority, depending on how far away the mother is. The one that seeks out food will have a priority that depends on how hungry the gosling is. The one that seeks to flee from predators will be very high priority—but only when there is a predator within the flight zone. Finally, the controller that seeks to explore will be relatively low priority, but will always be active.

44.8 Conclusion

This chapter gives an introduction to the use of negative feedback controllers to produce animal behavior that takes into account the dynamic nature of a game world's environment. These control systems use the spatial semantics from the environment to inform its input and compare this with a designer specified reference signal. It is then able to generate an error signal that is used to drive the animal's activity. It's not enough to stitch independent predetermined behaviors together; we need an underlying mechanism that through their interaction with the environment is able to exhibit corrective measures to the animal's desired (reference) state—which then can be viewed as a behavior.

References

[Hediger 55] H. Hediger. *Studies of the Psychology and Behavior of Animals.* New York: Criterion Books, 1955.

[James 90] W. James. *The Principles of Psychology.* New York: Dover Publications, 1890.

[Lorenz 81] K. Lorenz. *The Foundations of Ethology.* New York: Simon and Schuster, 1981.

[Powers 89], W. Powers, *Behavior: The Control of Perception.* New Canaan: Benchmark Publications, 1989.

[Ramsey 09] M. Ramsey. "A unified spatial representation for navigation systems." *Proceedings of the Fifth AAAI Artificial Intelligence and Interactive Digital Conference*, 2009.

[Ramsey 10] M. Ramsey. "A practical spatial architecture for animal and agent navigation." In *Game Programming Gems 8*, edited by Adam Lake. Boston: Charles River Media, 2010.

[Ramsey 11] M. Ramsey, "An egocentric motion management system." In *Game Engine Gems 2*, edited by Eric Lengyel. A K Peters, 2011.

[Toda 82] M. Toda, *Man, Robot and Society: Models and Speculations.* Dordrecht: Martinus Nijhoff Publishing, 1982.

45

Introduction to GPGPU for AI

Conan Bourke and Tomasz Bednarz

45.1 Introduction

Computer hardware has come a long way in the past decade. One core, two core, four core, and now hundreds and thousands of cores! The power in a computer has shifted from the CPU to the GPU, with new APIs allowing programmers to take control of these chips for more than just graphics processing.

With each advance in hardware, game systems have gained more and more processor power, allowing for far more intricate and detailed experiences than previously imagined. For AI this has meant more realistic agents capable of far more complex interactions with each other, the player, and the environment around them.

One of the most important advancements in hardware has been in the GPU and its transition from serving purely as a rendering processor into a general floating-point processor capable of any calculation we wish, within certain limits. The two major hardware vendors, AMD and NVIDIA, both make GPUs that commonly have 512+ processors, with the newest models providing around 3000 processors in consumer models, each able to process data in parallel. That is a lot of processing power, and we don't have to dedicate all of it to high-end graphics. Even the Xbox 360 has a GPU capable of basic general processing techniques, and Sony's PS3 has an architecture similar to the GPU that is capable of the same sort of processing.

One common downside to these processors is the latency and bandwidth between CPU and GPU, but inroads are being made, particularly by AMD, in combining the linear computation models of GPUs with the generic processing models of CPUs, called Accelerated

Processing Units (APUs), that greatly reduce this latency and provide other advantages as will be discussed later in the chapter.

45.2 A History of GPGPU

General-purpose computation on the GPU (GPGPU) is the term given to using the GPU for calculations other than rendering [Harris 02]. With the introduction of early shader models, programmers were able to modify how and what the GPU processed, no longer having to rely on the fixed-function pipelines of OpenGL or Direct3D and not being forced to render out an image for viewing. Instead textures could be used as buffers of data, accessed and processed within a pixel fragment, and the result could be drawn to an output texture. This method had the drawback that buffers were read-only or write-only. In addition, limitations with element independence and the need to represent problems in the context of graphics algorithms and the render pipeline made this technique cumbersome. Nevertheless shaders had evolved from simple assembly language programs into several new C-like languages, and hardware vendors began to acknowledge the growing GPGPU field.

Work was done on exposing the capabilities of the GPU outside of the rendering pipeline, and thus APIs were created that gave programmers access to the power of the GPU without having to treat it as a purely graphics-based device, and with these APIs came buffers that had read-write-modify access and additional mathematical capabilities.

In February 2007 NVIDIA introduced the Compute Unified Device Architecture (CUDA) API with the G80 series of GPUs which heavily accelerated the GPGPU field, and with DirectX11 Microsoft released the DirectCompute API. It shares many similar ideas and methodologies to CUDA but with the advantage of using DirectX's existing resources, allowing easy sharing of data between DirectCompute and Direct3D for visualizations. DirectCompute is also usable on DirectX10 hardware, but is still limited with the rest of DirectX in that it can only run on Windows-based systems.

A competing standard, OpenCL (Open Computing Language), was first released in 2008. OpenCL gives developers easy access to write efficient cross-platform applications for heterogeneous architectures such as multicore CPUs and GPUs, even Sony's PS3, with a single programming interface based on a modern contemporary of the C language. OpenCL's specification is managed by the Khronos Group [Khronos] who also provide a set of C++ bindings we have used for the purpose of this article. These bindings greatly simplify the host API setup and speed of code development.

45.3 OpenCL

OpenCL programs are written as "kernels," functions that execute on single processing units (compute units) in parallel to the other processing units, working independently from each other. Kernel code is very similar to C code, and supports many built-in math functions.

When a host program is running we need to execute the following steps to use OpenCL:

1. OpenCL enumerates the platforms and the compute devices available in the system, i.e., all CPUs and GPUs. Within each device there are one or more compute units, and within these one or more processing units that handle the actual computation.

The number of units corresponds to the number of independent instructions that a device (CPU or GPU) can execute at the same time. Therefore a CPU having 8 units is still considered as a single device, as would be a GPU with 448 units.

2. The most powerful device (usually the GPU) is picked, and its context is set up for further operations.

3. Sharing of data is configured between the host application and OpenCL.

4. An OpenCL program is built for your device using kernel code and an OpenCL context, and then kernel objects are extracted from compiled kernel code.

5. OpenCL makes use of command queues to control synchronization of kernel executions. Reading and writing data to and from the kernel and manipulation of memory objects are also carried out by the command queues.

6. The kernel is invoked and executes across all processing units. The parallel threads share memory and synchronize using barriers. At the end eventually, the output of the work-items is read back into host memory for further manipulation.

45.4 Simple Flocking and OpenCL

What we will cover briefly is the conversion of a classic AI algorithm to run on the GPU using OpenCL. Craig Reynolds [Reynolds 87] introduced the concept of *steering behaviors* for controlling autonomous moving agents and with it the concept of *flocking* and *boids* to simulate crowds and flocks. Many RTS games make use of flocking with beautiful effect—Relic Entertainment's *Homeworld* series being one such example—but these games are usually limited in the number of agents available. Converting this algorithm to run on the GPU, we can increase our agent counts into the thousands quite easily.

We will implement a brute-force approach to flocking, on both the CPU and GPU, to demonstrate the easy gains to be had by simply switching to the GPU without utilizing any partitioning, taking advantage of the GPUs massively parallel architecture. Similar work has been done using the PS3's Cell Architecture [Reynolds 06] utilizing a simple spatial partitioning scheme. Listing 45.1 gives pseudocode for a basic flocking algorithm using a prioritized weighted sum of forces for separation, cohesion, and alignment, and also includes a wander behavior to help randomize the agents. The priority is wander, and then separation, cohesion, and finally alignment. All velocities must be updated before being applied to positions or initial agents will incorrectly influence later agents.

Listing 45.1 Flocking pseudocode.

```
for each agent
    for each neighbor within radius
        calculate agent separation force away from neighbor
        calculate center of mass for agent cohesion force
        calculate average heading for agent alignment force
    calculate wander force
    sum prioritized weighted forces and apply to agent velocity
for each agent
    apply velocity to position
```

On the CPU this algorithm is trivial to implement. Usually an agent will consist of an object containing the relevant agent information (i.e., position, velocity, wander target, and so on). An array of agents would then be looped over twice; first to update the forces and velocity for each agent, and second to apply the new velocity.

When converting this algorithm to the GPU there are a few items that must be considered, but the conversion of CPU code to OpenCL code is straightforward. As seen in the pseudocode above, all neighbors are calculated for each agent, which has $0(n^2)$ complexity. On the CPU this is achieved by double looping through all the agents. On the GPU we are able to parallelize the outer loop and execute sequentially the inner loop interaction for every work item (every agent), greatly reducing the processing time.

Spatial partitioning techniques could be implemented to increase performance, but it must be noted that the GPU works in a very linear fashion, ideal for processing arrays of data which it typically did in the case of vertex arrays for graphics processing. In the case of complex spatial partitioning schemes (such as an octree) the GPU would flail while trying to access nonlinear memory. Craig Reynolds' solution for the PS3 was to use a simple three-dimensional grid of buckets storing neighboring agents [Reynolds 06]. This allows buckets to be processed linearly, with agents only having to have read access to the buckets directly neighboring their own. With this article, however, we are demonstrating a simple conversion from CPU to GPU without this kind of optimization to show the instant gains from converting to GPGPU processing.

One of the first steps when converting to GPGPU is to break up your data into contiguous arrays. GPUs can handle up to three-dimensional arrays, but in our example we will break up our agents into one-dimensional arrays for each element in an agent, that is, positions, velocities, etc.

It is also worth noting that in OpenCL terminology there are two types of memory: local and global. The distinction is that global memory can be accessed by any core, while local memory is unique to a process and is therefore accessed much faster. Think of it like RAM and a CPU's Cache.

45.5 OpenCL Setup

Initializing the compute devices is straightforward using C++ host bindings. At first the host platforms have to be enumerated to access the underlying compute devices. Then a context is created from a platform (note that in this example we initialized the context to specifically use the GPU using CL_DEVICE_TYPE_GPU) along with a command queue in order to execute compute kernels and enqueue memory transfers via the context. Refer to Listing 45.2 for the details.

OpenCL has two types of memory objects: buffers and images. Buffers contain standard 4D floating-point vectors using a Single-Instruction Multiple-Data (SIMD) processing model, while images are defined in terms of texels. For the purposes of this article buffers were chosen as being more appropriate for representing agents located contiguously beside each other.

The buffers can be initialized for read-only, write-only, or read–write, as Listing 45.3 shows. The buffers were created to hold the maximum numbers of agents the simulation will make use of, though we are able to process fewer agents if we desire. In addition to

Listing **45.2.** OpenCL host setup.

```
cl::Platform::get(&m_oclPlatforms);
cl_context_properties aoProperties[] = {
    CL_CONTEXT_PLATFORM,
    (cl_context_properties)(m_oclPlatforms[0])(),
    0};
m_oclContext = cl::Context(CL_DEVICE_TYPE_GPU, aoProperties);
m_oclDevices = m_oclContext.getInfo<CL_CONTEXT_DEVICES>();
std::cout << "OpenCL device count: " << m_oclDevices.size();
m_oclQueue = cl::CommandQueue(m_oclContext, m_oclDevices[0]);
```

Listing **45.3** OpenCL buffer setup.

```
typedef struct Params
{
    float fNeighborRadiusSqr;
    float fMaxSteeringForce;
    float fMaxBoidSpeed;
    float fWanderRadius;
    float fWanderJitter;
    float fWanderDistance;
    float fSeparationWeight;
    float fCohesionWeight;
    float fAlignmentWeight;
    float fDeltaTime;
} Params;
cl::Buffer m_clVPosition;
cl::Buffer m_clVVelocity;
cl::Buffer m_clVParams;
...
m_clVPosition = cl::Buffer(m_oclContext, CL_MEM_READ_WRITE,
uiMaxAgentCount * 4 * sizeof(float));
m_clVParams = cl::Buffer(m_oclContext, CL_MEM_READ_ONLY,
sizeof(Params));
```

agent data we send to the kernel the parameters for the flocking algorithm, along with a time value specifying elapsed time since the last frame for consistent velocities.

In order to create a compute kernel we need to compile the kernel code into a CL program, and then extract the compute kernel. In our example the kernel code is located in a separate file program.cl, loaded to create the program, as shown in Listing 45.4.

Listing 45.5 shows a portion of our example kernel, with the body omitted as it is nearly identical to a CPU implementation. Of note, however, is the last portion of the kernel pertaining to barriers. On the CPU we loop twice to apply the forces to all agents after they have been calculated. We can achieve this in the kernel by placing a barrier, which causes all executed threads to wait at this point until all threads have caught up. Within a kernel

Listing 45.4 Building the OpenCL program.

```
//read source file
std::ifstream sFile("program.cl");
std::string sCode(std::istreambuf_iterator<char>(sFile),
    (std::istreambuf_iterator<char>()));
cl::Program::Sources oSource(1,
    std::make_pair(sCode.c_str(), sCode.length() + 1));
//build the program for the specified devices
m_oclProgram = cl::Program(m_oclContext, oSource);
m_oclProgram.build(m_oclDevices);
m_clKernel = cl::Kernel(m_oclProgram, "Flocking");
```

Listing 45.5. The OpenCL kernel.

```
__kernel void Flocking(
        __global float4* vPosition,
        ...
        __constant struct Params* pp)
{
    //get_global_id(0) accesses the current element index
    unsigned int i = get_global_id(0);
    ...
    barrier(CLK_LOCAL_MEM_FENCE | CLK_GLOBAL_MEM_FENCE);
    vPosition[i] + = vVelocity[i] * pp->fDeltaTime;
    barrier(CLK_LOCAL_MEM_FENCE | CLK_GLOBAL_MEM_FENCE);
}
```

Listing 45.6. Specifying kernel arguments.

```
m_clKernel.setArg(0, sizeof(cl_mem), &m_clVPosition);
m_clKernel.setArg(1, sizeof(cl_mem), &m_clVVelocity);
```

we can access the current index of the input buffers with a call to get_global_id(0) using 0, 1, or 2 depending on the buffer dimensions.

Kernel arguments are passed to OpenCL explicitly once a kernel has been built, shown in listing 45.6. Rather than passing the arguments to the kernel when it is executed, the arguments must be pre-loaded into their corresponding argument index.

Once everything has been initialized and built, we can enqueue our kernel to be computed. Kernels do not execute immediately but are rather queued up to be processed. The kernel must be launched with global work-size equal to the number of elements to be processed. We can also specify an offset into our array range, but we can specify a NullRange to start at the front of the array. Refer to Listing 45.7.

Listing 45.7. Executing the kernel program.

```
m_oclQueue.enqueueNDRangeKernel(
    m_clKernel, cl::NullRange,
    cl::NDRange(uiMaxAgentCount),
    cl::NullRange,
    nullptr, nullptr);
```

45.6 Sharing GPU Processing Between Systems

Initial concerns developers may have when making use of GPGPU, especially for game developers, is that processing time is taken away from graphics processing. Many of today's high-end games make use of GPGPU for graphical pre-processing and post-processing, and also for physics simulations using APIs such as NVidia's PhysX. Adding AI to the mix will reduce the processing time these other systems have available. This is a concern that cannot be avoided. However GPU processing power has increased with massive leaps and bounds, from the core counts in the hundreds for the NVidia 500 series, to thousands in their 600 series. With time more processing power will be available for more systems, and developers will start to find other interesting uses for that power besides graphics, physics, and AI.

In the meantime, at least for OpenCL, there exists interoperability APIs that allow sharing of OpenCL buffers between both OpenGL and Direct3D, reducing the need to constantly transfer information to the GPU and back to the CPU. Positional buffers for AI agents could be both used in flocking computations on the GPU—for instance, rendering buffers for hardware instancing of rendered agents, without the need to return the data to the CPU only for it to be transferred back to the GPU.

45.7 Results

Figure 45.1 displays performance measured in milliseconds to process agents with the brute-force implementation of our example flocking algorithm (lower is better). As clearly shown the GPU offers a massive performance increase with higher agent counts, with minimal work needed to convert the algorithm to OpenCL. However, at lower agent counts the GPU runs slower than the CPU, shown in Figure 45.2, due to the buffer transfers. Also tested is a GPU intended for computation and research, to show the optimized bandwidth and latency in such devices, resulting in faster computations than consumer level GPUs, but also giving an insight into future consumer level performance.

45.8 Conclusion

As our example shows we could easily use GPGPU computing for a game that makes use of extremely high agent counts, such as an RTS game using thousands of entities rather than just the standard dozens to hundreds in most current RTS games. We would still have difficulty moving our agent's decision making to the GPU, but elements such as locomotion

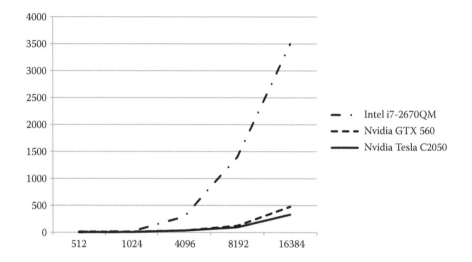

Figure 45.1

Performance in milliseconds to process agent counts of 512, 1024, 4096, 8192, and 16384 with various GPUs and CPUs.

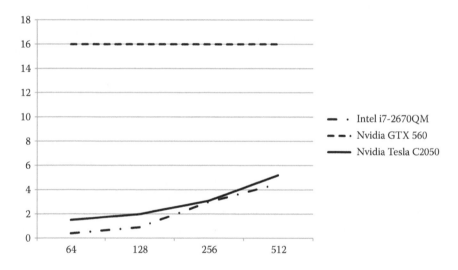

Figure 45.2

Performance in milliseconds with lower agent counts. The consumer GPU stays constant as the processing of the agents takes next to no time at all but buffer transfers to and from the GPU are not optimized. However, the C2050 has a much higher bandwidth and latency.

and even obstacle avoidance can be moved off the CPU. Taking processing time away from other systems, such as graphics, will be another concern, but can be alleviated somewhat with various interoperability APIs.

Other examples of GPGPU for AI exist, and work has been done by groups for neural networks and pathfinding, and the classic Conway's Game of Life can easily be implemented on the GPU [Rumpf 10]. The main limit to the types of AI processing available in GPGPU is the branching nature of most AI decision making.

APUs could allow us to closely couple decision making techniques with GPGPU techniques, but the consumer take-up for such devices will dictate if this style of AI will show up more in games.

As it stands GPGPU is a viable option for mass simulations, with the current most common consumer GPU at the time of writing, according to Valve's Hardware Survey, being the NVidia GTX 560 which packs 336 processors. Plenty for our AI needs.

References

[Harris 02] M. Harris. GPGPU.org. http://www.gpgpu.org, 2002.

[Khronos] The Khronos Group. http://www.khronos.org.

[Reynolds 87] C. Reynolds. "Flocks, herds, and schools: A distributed behavioral model." *SIGGRAPH '87 Conference Proceedings.* Available online (http://www.red3d.com/cwr/papers/1987/SIGGRAPH87.pdf).

[Reynolds 06] C. Reynolds. "Big fast crowds on PS3." *SIGGRAPH '06 Sandbox Symposium.* Available online (http://www.research.scea.com/pscrowd/PSCrowdSandbox2006.pdf).

[Rumpf 10] T. Rumpf. "Conway's game of life accelerated with OpenCL." *CMC11 '10 Conference Proceedings.* Available online (http://cmc11.uni-jena.de/proceedings/rumpf.pdf).

46

Creating Dynamic Soundscapes Using an Artificial Sound Designer

Simon Franco

46.1 Introduction

A game's audio is the end result of the work done by the sound designer. A game's sound designer will typically create audio content (sound effects and music) and then create sound events to trigger that audio content. Sound events are often authored using middleware tools such as Wwise [Wwise 06] or FMOD [FMOD 02] and are triggered by the game.

Game audio is often triggered and managed via a fixed set of conditions—and often these conditions have no connection to each other. For example, sound effects and music can be triggered by a number of different systems, such as the level scripting system, the animation system, and game code reacting to events.

These disconnected methods for triggering audio present us with a number of problems. The player will always have the same audio experience every time they play the game. This is the result of static correlations between in-game triggers and audio events. After playing the game for some time, the soundscape can come across as predictable and boring. You may also have systems competing to play audio cues that serve the same purpose, such as trying to set the game's ambience. In addition, these isolated methods for triggering audio could accidentally inform the player of hidden information. For example, a piece of music starting may accidentally inform the player of a hostile character hidden around a corner. This can lead to scripted sequences of game play being ruined.

In addition to these limited methods for triggering audio, our techniques for mixing audio at runtime are typically very primitive. The sound designer will often create a pool of audio mix snapshots for use in the game [Bridgett 09]. Each audio snapshot will typically hold information on volume settings, volume curves, and various filter settings for each sound category. Categories tend to be groups of similar sound types, such as footsteps. Unfortunately, there are also problems when using audio mix snapshots:

- An appropriate snapshot which complements the game's current state must be chosen and applied. This can be done in a number of ways—for example, having a level designer script when to apply an audio snapshot, or by having some game code monitor for a condition to be met.
- Each snapshot always contains a fixed collection of settings. Typically, these audio snapshots represent a game state, such as a calm moment, being in a safe area, or being in a combat situation. This requires the audio designer to decide ahead of time which game scenarios they would like to create a snapshot for, and author the appropriate snapshots.

This article discusses the idea of developing an Artificial Sound Designer to solve these issues. The Artificial Sound Designer avoids these problems and can make intelligent audio decisions by monitoring the game's current state, as well as retaining knowledge of the game's previous states.

46.2 The Artificial Sound Designer

The purpose of the Artificial Sound Designer (ASD) is to ensure that the player has the richest possible experience by ensuring that they have a varied soundscape and making that soundscape closely match the game's state. The ASD is built around a rule set that represents the knowledge and experience of a human sound designer. At a high level, it is composed of the following pieces:

- An event system to pass information about the game's state to the ASD.
- A database that holds state information on all relevant game objects.
- The rule set, which examines the events raised in this frame, the state of the database, and the audio state, in order to determine which audio actions to execute (if any).

These component pieces are to be used to facilitate the Artificial Sound Designer. Events are posted to the ASD from in-game. We then use those posted events to update the ASD database. Then the ASD examines the events raised plus its database to change the soundscape and play appropriate sounds. Depending on the situation, the ASD may execute one or more of the following actions when a rule is satisfied:

- Play a sound effect or piece of music, and associate that piece of audio with a game object if needed. For example, we may want a piece of audio to track an object in the world.
- Adjust the volume/DSP settings for categories of sounds. This can be used to "duck out" (i.e., reduce the volume of) sounds deemed unimportant to the current in-game situation, or to increase the volume of sounds we want the player to focus on (such as an imminent threat).
- Configure any underlying systems that generate events for the ASD. For example, if you have a system to count the number of hostile characters within proximity to the player—then the ASD must be provided with a way to configure that system's radius.

46.3 Generating Events

The Artificial Sound Designer uses events as a means of being notified of what is happening in game. Events typically have a type in order to help categorize and describe the type of event, such as a footstep, an explosion, or a gun firing. As well as having a type, an event will also have a subject. The subject of the event would typically be a reference to the game object triggering the event. The event will also store any other associated information that was part of that event. For example, a footstep event would typically also store the material that the character stepped on.

We have two basic types of events that can be posted. Information-only events notify the ASD of changes in the game state, which may not be directly related to a sound emitting action. For example, if a game object has been spawned or despawned, or if the game is paused or resumed, then we can use an information-only event to pass this knowledge to the AI. These events may not cause sounds to be played directly, but they can affect the way in which we play other sounds.

The second type of event is the play-request event. These events are used when we want to play a specific type of sound, such as a gunshot. These events replace where previously we would have called directly into the sound system. For example, we now post an event at the point when an explosion occurs, or when the animation system causes feet to strike the ground (so that we can play footstep sounds). By using play-request events, we give the ASD the opportunity to make decisions about which sound sample to play and how loud to play it (e.g., should the volume of gunshot events be reduced so that we can hear enemy speech?). The ASD can evaluate the event and use the player's current context, and the state of the game objects involved, to drive its decisions.

Listing 46.1 shows an example of a general event class that can be inherited from and extended for each type of event. Each event should have a process function which will update the subject game object's database record appropriately for that event type. It can also return whether it is an information-only event or a play-request event.

46.4 Creating and Maintaining the Database

The database contains the Artificial Sound Designer's knowledge. This section will discuss the elements making up that database.

Listing 46.1. An example Event base class.

```
class Event
{
public:
        Event(GameObject * obj) : m_object(obj) {}
        virtual void process(GameObjectRecord &) = 0;
        virtual const GameObject * get_subject_game_object() const
                {return m_object;}
        virtual EVENT_TYPE get_type() const = 0;
        virtual bool is_play_request_event() const
                {return false;}
protected:
        GameObject * m_object;
}
```

46.4.1 The Database Structure

The database contains a number of tables. We will need a table for game objects, a table for sounds previously played, and a table for the ASD to store any additional data it wishes to keep. This last table is used to help the ASD keep track of nonaudio or game object state information. For example, we may want to store the time since the player was last under threat.

Each game object is registered with the ASD's database and, along with a reference to the object, we store a set of flags describing the object's state. This is so the system can query its database of knowledge in order to determine information on a game object, and on the world state.

As well as storing information within a game object's record on the object's actual state, the record should also contain data describing the object's perceived state to the player. For instance, we may wish to store the last position where it was seen by the player. Although the majority of the information about each object is stored in the database, certain information (such as the object's current position) may be queried directly from the engine. This allows us to avoid storing redundant information.

The sound-history table stores a record of each type of sound, along with its category, when it was last played and how many times it was played. This is so the ASD can keep track of what it has previously played. This knowledge is used when selecting which sounds to play back. For example, we may want to avoid playing the same piece of music too often, or perhaps not play a tension piece of music if we had just played a piece of combat music.

This rich body of information allows the Artificial Sound Designer to make informed decisions when selecting audio relating to a particular game object. These decisions take into account not only the object's characteristics, but also its history with the player. For example, if the player is currently engaging in combat with an enemy that had previously dealt damage to the player, or even killed the player, then we could use that information to select appropriate music and dialog (such as playing more intense music, or having the character taunt the player).

Depending on the multithreaded nature of your game and audio engine, it may also be advisable to create a database table to store a record of the audio state (i.e., the sounds that are playing and their settings). By having a separate record of which sounds are playing, we avoid the problem of the sound state changing unexpectedly while we are deciding what audio to play next.

46.5 Defining the Artificial Sound Designer Rule Set

The Artificial Sound Designer has two separate rule sets, which can be thought of in a similar manner to a rule based system [Negnevitsky 11]. One rule set is consulted when making changes to the overall soundscape. Other rule sets can be assigned to the different types of play-request events. These rules are then consulted when processing play-request events in order to select the most appropriate sample to play. The human sound designer needs the facility to easily create and edit these conditional rules for the ASD to process. The rules must be listed in priority order, with the highest priority rules first. When a conditional rule is satisfied, it will perform one or more actions.

To form these rules, the sound designer must have access to typical logical operators such as AND, OR, and NOT. The sound designer will then use these to form the conditions within the rules which the system will process.

The simplest way to implement this is to use an embedded scripting language such as Lua [LUA 93]. This presents an easy way for the sound designer to formulate rules. It also provides easy methods to wrap access to events, the database, and perform sound actions in a Lua interface.

In addition, consideration should be given to adding extra logging functionality to record which rules were fired, and which sound actions were executed. This will help the sound designer and programmer understand how decisions about the game's soundscape were reached.

In Listing 46.2 we show a sample pseudocode snippet to modify the in-game music.

Listing 46.2. A pseudocode sample rule set to control music selection.

```
if (EventRaisedThisFrame(PLAYER_DEATH)) then
        PlayMusic(MUS_GAME_OVER)
elseif (EventRaisedThisFrame(SCRIPTED_MUSIC) and
SoundSystem:PlayingMusic()) then
        StopMusic();
elseif (Database:Objects:NumberOfObjectsInRangeOfPlayer
(GRENADE, NO_FLAGS, 5.0f) > 1) then
        PlayMusic(MUS_WARNING)
elseif (Database:Objects:NumberOfObjectsInRangeOfPlayer
(ENEMIES,SEEN|HEARD,16.0f) > 15) then
        PlayMusic(MUS_BATTLE)
elseif (Database:Objects:NumberOfObjectsInRangeOfPlayer
(ENEMIES,SEEN|HEARD,16.0f) >= 1) then
        PlayMusic(MUS_DANGER)
elseif (not SoundSystem:PlayingMusicInCategory(MUS_CALM)) then
        PlayMusic(Database:Sound:GetLeastPlayedSampleInCategory
(MUS_CALM))
endif
```

46.6 Updating the Artificial Sound Designer

Once per frame, after the other game systems have had a chance to post events, the Artificial Sound Designer will perform its update. This update consists of three phases: updating the database, changing the soundscape, and playing requested audio.

46.6.1 Updating the Database

In the first phase, we process the events raised during the current frame and incorporate them into the database. A simple way to implement this is to give each type of event a `Process()` function, which will handle updating the corresponding database record. We can then simply loop over the events, calling process on each, in order to bring the database up to date.

46.6.2 Changing the Soundscape

Now that the database is up to date, we can perform the main update for the Artificial Sound Designer. During this phase the ASD will process its main rule set in order decide whether to play any new sounds, or change the playback of sounds already in progress (for instance by stopping all sounds of a particular type, or changing the volume of one or more categories).

46.6.3 Playing Requested Audio

In the final phase, we process the play-request events. As discussed in an earlier section, these events are sent from the game in order to request that specific sounds be played. Playing requested audio typically involves processing each event that has requested audio playback. The Artificial Sound Designer can examine the event parameters and use a rule set for that event type (if one has been set) to select the actual audio sample to play. For example, you may have an NPC shout "Who's there?" when they spot an intruder. If the database has information stating that the NPC had seen the player before then we change the speech to "There he is again!" to reflect this. This persistence helps re-enforce the player's interactions with the game world.

46.7 Conclusion

Creating a dynamically changing soundscape that responds closely to the player's actions helps to deliver a rich and varied audio experience. Using an Artificial Sound Designer empowers your sound designers to create a more immersive experience for the player.

Designing the rule set used by your game to shape the soundscape requires careful consideration. Where possible, work should be done to ensure that there is only a short turnaround between changing the rule set and testing it in game.

References

[Bridgett 09] R. Bridgett. "The Future Of Game Audio—Is Interactive Mixing The Key?" http://www.gamasutra.com/view/feature/4025/the_future_of_game_audio__is_.php, 2009.

[FMOD 02] Firelight Technologies. "FMOD." http://www.fmod.org, 2002.

[LUA 93] "Lua." http://www.lua.org, 1993.

[Negnevitsky 11] M. Negnevitsky. *Artificial Intelligence: A Guide to Intelligent Systems*, Addison-Wesley, 2011, pp. 25–54.

[Wwise 06] Audiokinetic "Wwise." http://www.audiokinetic.com, 2006.

47

Tips and Tricks for a Robust Third-Person Camera System

Eric Martel

47.1 Introduction

Working on the camera system for a third-person game is technically challenging, yet critically important to the success of the title. Not only are your teammates relying on you to show off their amazing artwork and level design, but a major part of the player's experience is defined by the way he perceives the environment, which is mostly driven by the camera. At the same time, game development is highly dynamic. Everything from the game design to the art assets themselves can and will change during production. A robust camera system must be easily modifiable and adaptive. It should typically keep the player's character on screen and do its best to make the player aware of dangers in the environment. In this section we explore the tools and techniques that helped us build the camera system for one of the most successful action adventure games.

47.2 Understanding What's Going On

It is often extremely difficult to understand what's going on with the camera, particularly since it is our primary point of view into the game. As a result, effective debug and visualization tools are critical to a good camera system. These tools are going to enable you to investigate problematic situations, tune the system's performance, and make your game's visual artistry shine.

47.2.1 Debug Display

The first feature to implement is a debug display, which includes both 2D and 3D features. The 2D should simply write text to the screen that exposes information such as the active camera set and their state, the selected camera's position, orientation, and FOV (field of view). You can extend the list of rendered information as you see fit with internal data to the system like environmental triggers used, the blending state of the cameras, and so forth. All of these should update in real time, so you can see when and how the information changes.

The 3D debug display draws its information graphically to the screen using a combination of color codes and primitives to easily understand a situation. For example, you could use a pyramid to display the position and the orientation of each camera: blue when the camera is active, black when it is not. When using the debug camera, these will allow you to easily understand what is going on with your gameplay cameras. We will discuss later in this article the different ways you can test the environment surrounding the camera and the player. For each of these tests you should choose different primitive and color combinations to understand the scene at a glance. Collisions are another example of displayable information. Collision geometries are often different from the meshes visible on screen. These two representations for each object can get out of synch—for example, if an artist updates the look of an object but forgets to change the collision geometry to match. Since the collision geometry is not typically displayed, it is often quite difficult to recognize situations where this is the problem—all you see is that the camera is behaving badly. If you display a red cylinder for every collision test that fails, it is much easier to spot situations where these are out of place, allowing you to quickly debug the problem and assign the issue to whoever is best fit to fix it.

You should also consider the lifetime of each piece of information in the debug display. While some text could remain permanently on screen (e.g., the position and orientation of the camera), it is often useful to provide hotkeys for turning on just the information that you need. Additionally, 3D displays tend to clobber the view after a while. Usually, the best options are to either give each debug display object a lifetime—so, for example, the red collision cylinders might stay on screen for 5 seconds—or use some sort of "Etch a Sketch" list of display items that only gets cleared when you send a command to do so. The latter is probably better when trying to find a solution to a problem, as you don't have to think quickly before your display disappears. Implementing both doesn't take much time, and the method can be selected from a command, hotkey, or cheat menu option.

47.2.2 Debug Camera

It is often useful to have the ability to "step outside" of the camera system when debugging, and to watch the behavior of the gameplay camera from an external point of view. In order to do this, you can implement a separate debug camera that is under explicit control of the user. When we implemented our debug camera, we placed the controls for our debug camera on a second controller so as to keep the player and camera movement on the main controller as consistent as possible. We used the left stick to control forward, backward, and strafe left and right movement of the camera, and the right stick to change the orientation. We also used the triggers to pan up and down, the start button to enable/disable the debug camera, and the back button to reset the camera to the gameplay camera's parameters.

We quickly found many other uses for the debug camera. For example, animators would use it to see their animations from a different perspective, level artists would simply go inspect the mesh they wanted without actually having to play the game, and marketing guys would create in-game trailers with one person playing the game and another controlling the camera. The marketing usage required some changes to the system, such as adding controls to roll the camera, modify the field of view, and control its movement speed, but in retrospect it was well worth the time invested.

47.3 Managing Multiple Cameras

If your gameplay changes during the game, you might want to have specific cameras that are built optimally for each situation. For example, when running, the player doesn't care about the same things as when he's using cover; therefore, it's the camera's responsibility to adjust automatically to reflect these changed priorities and provide an optimal view to guide him.

47.3.1 View Manager

The view manager is responsible for providing the renderer with the position, orientation, and field of view to use when drawing the scene. If you decide to implement a debug camera, this would also be a good place to switch to and from it. Finally, this manager is responsible for updating all the active cameras and keeping track of the transitions between the cameras.

47.3.2 Competing Cameras

In addition to a list of available cameras, the camera system can store activation rules to prioritize and pick the most relevant of them. This approach will allow you to add more depth to your gameplay, or even to expose control to your designers. For example, you might give level designers the ability to add triggers in the environment that enable or disable specific cameras, such as cameras introducing the level to the player or a boss fight camera.

47.3.3 Transitions

When a camera change event occurs, there needs to be a transition from the previous camera to the new one. Cutting from one view to the other can feel abrupt, but can be necessary when the orientation between the two views is more than 90 degrees. It can also make sense in some level designs to have camera cuts when the view comes from different discrete point of views, such as another character's point of view or security cameras. Otherwise, it is usually better to blend between the views by linearly interpolating the parameters such as position, orientation, and field of view. More complex interpolation methods can be used if you have specific needs.

It is worth putting some thought into the logic which will drive your transitions. You can begin by giving each camera default transition in and transition out parameters, which specify the transition type and blend time. We settled on using the minimum value of the in and out parameters pair for blend time as our gameplay indicated that when a camera required to blend in or out quickly, this should have precedence over the other camera's slower reaction time. You will probably also want to have the ability to provide specific transition parameters for specific situations or between specific pairs of cameras. For example, you might want to use a very fast blend when switching from the walking camera to the running camera, even though these cameras would normally transition more slowly.

When activating a camera, it's often useful to pass in the state of the previous camera, so that it can update its internal state to match as closely as possible its predecessor. For example, if you change from a standard camera to one farther away with a sharper field of view when a trigger is held, you will want to set the position and orientation of the trigger camera so that the center of view matches that of the previous camera. You could keep them in synch at all times, but it is simpler to just match them up when the transition begins.

47.4 Input Transform

When controlling a character, the player's input will usually be relative to the in-game character he's controlling or to the view. In this article we'll only discuss the latter. Transforming the input into the camera's reference is straightforward—the vector representing the input gets transformed using the view's rotation, but maintaining that transform as the view changes can be quite a bit more challenging. There are two cases: continuous changes over time (such as when the camera is moving or rotating around the player, or when we're blending between cameras) and discrete changes (such as a camera cut).

Our experience has been that when continuously changing the view reference, the player is typically able to adapt and gradually adjusts the input to the new view. In other words, when the player is given visual feedback that is not exactly what he wants, he will automatically move the stick slightly, often without even noticing, to adjust the view appropriately.

Discrete changes are harder to handle. The camera cut entirely changes the reference the player has to the virtual world. As a result, transforming the input using the view after the cut will often result in incorrect input for a short time while the player familiarizes himself with the new view. One solution is to retain the previous view's matrix, and to use this matrix for the transformation as long as the input is held. As soon as the stick is released, the system can switch to using the matrix for the new view. This leaves the player in a comfortable situation where his input will not be drastically changed after a single frame. It also helps avoiding the "ping-pong" effect, when you have two triggers with cameras facing each other. For example, imagine that the player crosses the threshold between two cameras, which face in opposite directions, by pressing up on the stick. If we switched immediately to the matrix of the new camera, and the player did not let go of the stick as soon as the camera changed, then the direction that his character is moving would reverse, causing him to pop right back over the threshold, and back to the first camera. In this way, he could find himself bouncing between the two cameras very rapidly unless he approached the threshold slowly and carefully, with just delicate taps on the stick.

47.5 Configuration

Not specific to cameras, this tip is simply that anything that might change during the production of the game should be an exposed setting. You don't want to waste your time recompiling just to test new configurations.

47.5.1 Data Driven Approach

From the list of default cameras to their settings, everything should be controllable through data. Whether you use .ini files, XML files, objects in the editor, or even an exposed scripting language such as Lua or Python, you need to provide the ability for anyone working with the cameras (including you) to be able to change them efficiently without requiring a new build. Using a factory design pattern, it should be relatively easy to have every part of the configuration settings constructed from a file or object.

47.5.2 Activation Rules

Since you might want to have multiple cameras of the same type with different configurations active at different times, it makes sense to expose the rules of activation in the data as well. Depending on the variety of gameplay you have and the flexibility you want to give to your system, you can create small objects that poll game states internally, like "player is riding a horse at full speed." You can also create a more complex system that exposes the logic to the person configuring the cameras, where a particular camera is activated when the target character "is on a horse" and "is at full speed." That's what we did, and by allowing first level logic operators, it was really easy to test complex combinations of game states. It allowed us to save a lot of time when iterating on the various cameras in the game.

47.5.3 Priorities

Since the activation rules do nothing to prevent more than one camera being active at the same time, we need to find a way to select which one to use. There really is no reason to have something complex here, so having a simple number defining the priority for each camera should be good enough for most projects. To simplify the task of adding new cameras it is often better to bundle the priorities into ranges, giving a hint to new camera creators what sort of priority they should assign to their asset.

47.5.4 Object References

Adding an object wrapper can be a good way to enable you to specify a variety of different objects in data. You might find that you need to support a variety of different types of objects as reference points for your camera, including dynamic objects such as the player or another character, or even pieces of equipment that the player is carrying (such as a weapon), as well as fixed objects (such as security cameras) that can be placed directly in the level. You should provide a mechanism for specifying these objects in data, so with a unique name or by building a tool that lets you specify them from a drop-down. In-game, the cameras will then be able to look up the positions and orientation of their reference objects, and set their own position and orientation accordingly.

47.6 Camera Behaviors

In this section we will discuss various camera behaviors which are common in third-person games. Some of these behaviors are very simple but are really useful to prototype gameplay. By exposing these behaviors in data, we can provide the game designers and level designers with the tools that they need to configure the cameras on their own. This allows us to spend our time developing new features and debugging existing code, and also maximizes their control over the player's experience in the game.

47.6.1 Fixed Camera and Tracking Camera

The simplest camera possible is a fixed one. It's defined by a position and an orientation. Even though it's not doing much, it can still be used for menus or to present a challenge or objective to the player. By adding a target object to the camera, you can easily turn it into a tracking camera; its position remains the same but it reorients to frame the target. For example, a tracking camera with the player as a target might be used to simulate a security camera that has caught the player as he enters a restricted area.

47.6.2 Orbit Camera

Many action adventure games allow the default camera to orbit around the main character, with the player controlling the camera's azimuthal and polar angles using the right stick on the controller. The simplest way to represent this is to use spherical coordinates [Stone 04] relative to the target (i.e., the player), since the camera should always lie on the surrounding sphere.

In order to facilitate navigation, any time that the player is not actively rotating the camera and the character is in motion, it is better to blend the azimuthal angle back to 0 (behind the character) and the polar angle to some default value. This allows the camera to smoothly reset to a position that will allow the player to see where they are going without requiring him to micromanage that control if, for example, he was examining the ceiling or floor when he came under attack and decided to flee.

47.6.3 Over-the-Shoulder Camera

Most third-person shooters will use a camera that is directly behind the main character's shoulder and that always follows the character's facing. This type of camera, even though it's in third-person, mostly reacts like a first-person camera that had been moved behind the character by a couple of meters.

The complexity in this kind of camera is not related to the camera itself, but how you handle the targeting and firing of projectiles. If you're using the center of the screen as the aiming target, you will see that depending on the distance between the character and the aimed position, the direction taken by the projectiles will differ. The closer the target position is, the more the position offset of the character will increase the angle difference between the camera's facing and the character's aiming, as seen in Figure 47.1. For very close targets, it will most likely look pretty stupid. A simple solution is to add a layer of inverse kinematics to dynamically adapt the aiming direction of your character depending on which object is targeted at any moment.

47.6.4 First-Person Camera

Even though your game is in third-person, it is always useful to allow the player to go into first-person, as some players prefer this view to analyze their surroundings. This camera is quite simple to implement; its position can be fixed relative to the character, or attached to the head bone (or a specifically animated bone). The latter approach can provide a more realistic camera movement, including breathing and head bobbing as the character moves.

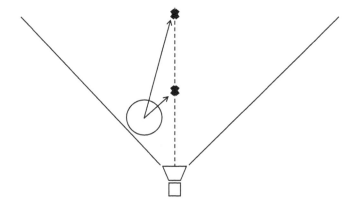

Figure 47.1

Top view showing aiming differences based on distance from the camera.

47.6.5 Camera on Rails

In the movies, they will often mount the camera on a cart that travels on rails in order to create extremely smooth movement. We can take a similar approach procedurally, even using splines to describe the curve of the "rails." This can provide very smooth performance when panning or zooming, and is particularly useful for cut scenes or for the camera in side-scrollers. The usual approach is to define the track that the camera will follow (whether this is a spline or a series of curves and line segments), and then provide a method which takes an input between 0 and 1 and maps that to the corresponding position (and, if appropriate, orientation) along the track. You can then move the camera along the track simply by interpolating the input value smoothly from 0 to 1. An easy way to obtain such a value is to add a box surrounding your play area and calculate the relative position of your target inside that box. Using a single axis, you can divide the relative position on that axis with its length to obtain the mapping you are looking for, giving you continuous values between 0 and 1 when the target moves, for example, from left to right in the level.

47.7 Advanced Features

This section will focus on a collection of features that can be added to your base classes, which can be toggled on or off through your camera settings in order to make your cameras more artistically pleasing. In our implementation, most of these were added late in the project at minimal cost but adding them sooner would allow the artists and level designers to make more widespread use of the advanced features.

47.7.1 Spline for the Vertical Axis

When dealing with high- or low-angle shots on an orbit camera, it is possible that your art director will ask you to tweak the distance of the camera depending on the angle. Usually, a closer shot for a low-angle and moving the camera away for a high-angle shot will give better results. When we introduced the orbit camera, we said the distance should be constant, and we talked about a polar angle. Let's get rid of these concepts and imagine a spline that can rotate around the target on the vertical axis. This curve defines both the

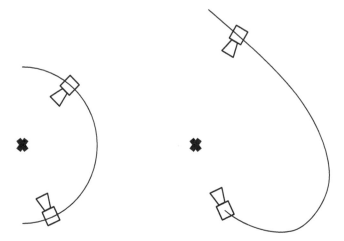

Figure 47.2

Comparison of a standard orbit camera to a camera using a spline as its vertical axis.

distance and the angle the camera should have. The right stick controls remain the same for the horizontal movement, but for the vertical axis we want to control a value between 0 and 1 that maps the position of the camera along the spline (Figure 47.2).

47.7.2 Using Bones

Sometimes, specific actions require some very specific camera movement. For example, you might want the camera to go near the ground when the player performs a duck-and-roll action. Instead of having to program this behavior, you could allow the animators to take control of the position and heading of the camera by animating camera-specific bones. Other settings such as the field of view or the depth of field can be exposed for more cinematographic effects.

Another way to improve the system with bones is to expose a bone property in our object reference system. This way, whenever we're using the object reference to get a position or orientation, it could instead fetch the values from the object's skeleton, if available; otherwise, return a recognizable and valid value that will be helpful in case you need to debug it. You never want to feed the renderer invalid positions or orientations as it will break the view matrix, resulting in undefined behavior.

47.7.3 Sweet Spot

A "sweet spot" is an area on the screen where the target (typically the player character) should be. When enabled, the sweet spot system will only allow the camera to rotate on its own when the target exits this area. This technique helps to stabilize the camera when the target makes subtle movements. The size of the zone can be adjusted to absorb bigger movements, such as crouching or jumping, or focused down to make the camera feel more dynamic. When the player was actively rotating the camera, we would simply recenter the view on its target and disable the sweet spot.

Another use we made of this system is to smoothly frame the enemies around the player during fights, displaying as many as possible while ensuring that the closest enemies (and the player's character, of course!) were always visible. We did this by sorting the closest n enemies by distance and then readjust the camera's heading on each of them, making the smallest change necessary to place each one in the sweet spot. The last heading adjustment was always for the player. As a result, the player would always be on screen, and we would get as many of the enemies as possible while giving preference to the closest ones. This also allowed enemies to join and leave without affecting the view too much.

The area used to define the sweet spot could be anything, but we used a rectangle. This was sufficient to get good-looking performance, and was easy to work with because we can simply convert the screen space rectangle into angles, which can then be used with two simple dot products to determine if the target is in or out of the sweet spot.

47.8 Collision System

The complexity of most camera systems lies in the way the camera interacts with the environment—which is to say, the way that we handle situations where the camera collides with the level's geometry or when objects get in between the camera and the player character, causing occlusion. Games that place the cameras on rails may not need to deal with collisions at all, since the level designer is responsible for creating camera paths that aren't obstructed by the geometry. In many cases over-the-shoulder cameras can simply move closer to the player as needed, but collisions can present a number of challenges for orbit cameras. The remainder of this section will focus on handling those problems.

47.8.1 Collision Flags

We tried to base our collision checks on the collision system that was already in the engine for the physics and AI needs. We found that in some cases the camera's needs were unique, however. As a result, we added collision and occlusion flags that could be used by the modelers to annotate objects appropriately. This made it possible to have the camera ignore small posts, for example, while considering foliage as occluding the view but not blocking camera movement.

47.8.2 Camera Size

Mathematically speaking, your camera is a one-dimensional point; it has no size. Without providing a size, however, graphical issues can arise if you use a very small near clip and the camera is too close to the world geometry. What you might see are large polygons taking up a good portion of the screen. To remedy this problem, one option is to increase the near clip, which should cull the geometry that's too close to the camera. Another approach is to ensure that every movement the camera makes is padded with a virtual size, so that it always keeps a minimum distance from collisions, which could be achieved by moving around a primitive in your physics system. On our project we used the latter but, in retrospect, considering the usage of our camera, it would have been far simpler just to adjust the near clip.

47.8.3 Collision Reaction

When handling collision reactions, we have two cases to worry about: the player driving the camera into a collision and the camera colliding with the environment while autonomously following the player. We describe the approaches that we took for each case below, but you may need to experiment in order to find the solution that best suits your game.

When controlled by the player, our orbit camera would simply reduce its distance to the target in order to avoid colliding with obstacles. Our goal was to keep the player's input intact by keeping the changes in azimuth and position along the spline, but when transforming the camera's position, we would take the point of impact and the camera size to compute a new distance to the target. As the player would walk away from the collision, the camera would therefore keep the same point of view and start following at the original distance once the collision is cleared.

We handled collisions during navigation a bit differently. Since our camera tried to stay behind the player as best as possible, our most common source of collision was when the player was backing towards a wall. The method used was to smoothly modify the azimuth angle of the camera in the direction of the collision's normal vector if it would allow the camera to be closer to its desired distance. This way, we avoided oscillation in corners while moving the camera horizontally along the walls until we were clear of collision.

47.8.4 Occlusion Reaction

For the occlusion reaction, we have the same two cases as for collision, except that when handling user input we decided not to do anything; if the player wanted to occlude his character, it was his choice and we allowed it.

In our case, we only used static geometry for occlusion; therefore, if an occlusion occurred, it had to be because the player moved in a way to insert geometry between his character and the camera's position. We used what seemed to be the simplest way to solve this problem, by compensating to the player's movement by moving the camera in the opposite direction. In the case of vertical movement, we simply moved the camera along the spline. Sometimes, the simplest solutions give the best results, and I believe this is a good example!

47.9 Conclusion

When writing your own camera system, give yourself the proper tools to facilitate your job. Visualization is a very important aspect to understand the interaction between the camera, its targets, and the environment. Make the system as configurable as possible and encourage your designers and animators to play with it. The more they work with it on their own, the more time you have to develop features and debug code, and the more they will feel like they have ownership of the player's experience. When building the actual camera behaviors, try to think what you'd want as a player and make other people test them out before submitting your code. Remember that the camera is a central part of the game, everybody is affected by it, and as such it is critical to get as many people to try it and give you feedback as possible. Always think of the player first and build your cameras accordingly, because the cameras are a vital part of the gameplay!

References

[Stone 04] J. Stone. "Third-person camera navigation." In *Game Programming Gems 4*, edited by Andrew Kirmse. Boston, MA: Charles River Media, 2004, pp. 303–314.

Implementing N-Grams for Player Prediction, Procedural Generation, and Stylized AI

Joseph Vasquez II

48.1 Introduction

AI learning provides exciting possibilities for the next generation of games. As game systems increase in computational power, the fanciest online learning techniques become more feasible for the games of tomorrow. However, until we get there, the AI programmers of today need solid techniques that provide good results with minimal cost. N-grams are a powerful and computationally inexpensive learning technique that can provide adaptive AI in the game you are working on right now [Laramée 02].

N-grams store statistics on behavioral patterns, which simulates learning a style. By exposing an N-gram to a history of player actions, it can predict the player's next move with surprising accuracy—in fact, for certain types of games (such as *Mortal Kombat*-style fighting games) they can work so well that they have to be toned down in order to give the player a chance to win [Millington 06]! This learning can allow your cooperative AI to become more helpful, and your enemy AI to offer a more personalized challenge. By exposing an N-gram to a designer's creation patterns, it can procedurally generate content that mimics the designer's style. The code provided on this book's website (http://www.gameaipro.com) includes a well-optimized N-gram implementation, which you are free to use in your game. Hopefully, this will allow you to easily evaluate just how helpful N-grams can be for you.

This article focuses on getting an N-gram up and running in your game. First we'll go over what N-grams are and how they make predictions. Next we'll cover implementation specifics and optimizations, while aiming for the most accurate predictions possible. Finally, we'll discuss in-game usage of N-grams, and the issues that pop up during integration. At the end, you'll have an N-gram library that you can drop in your game, and you'll know how to use it effectively.

48.2 N-Grams Understood

Before we can use them, we need to know what N-grams are and how they make predictions.

48.2.1 Examining Probability: A Likely Story

Probability can be defined as the likelihood that a given event will occur. Mathematically, we define it as a ratio of the number of ways an event can occur divided by the number of possible outcomes. This ratio is strictly between 0 and 1, so we treat it as a percentage, as shown in Equation 48.1.

$$P(event\ e) = \frac{\#\ of\ ways\ e\ can\ happen}{\#\ of\ all\ possible\ outcomes} \qquad (48.1)$$

Let's assume that a player has three move options: Jump, Attack, and Dodge. Without any other information, the probability of choosing Jump would be P(Jump) = 1/3 = 0.33 = 33%. Informally, we take this to mean that Jump occurs 33% of the time on average. In 100 moves, we expect Jump to occur on average 33 times. Working backwards from this understanding, if we're given a sequence of 100 events in which Jump occurred 33 times, the probability of Jump occurring again is assumed to be 33%, as shown in Equation 48.2.

$$P(event\ e) = \frac{\#\ of\ times\ e\ occurred}{\#\ of\ times\ any\ event\ occurred} \qquad (48.2)$$

This is useful for deriving probability from a sequence of past events. From this history, we can predict that the next event is most likely the event that has occurred most often.

In this sequence: "Jump, Jump, Dodge, Attack, Dodge, Attack, Jump, Jump, Dodge," P(Jump) = 4/9 = 44%, P(Attack) = 2/9 = 22%, and P(Dodge) = 3/9 = 33%. Based on raw probability, the player will jump next. Do you agree with this prediction? Probably not, since you've likely picked up on a pattern. N-grams are used to find patterns in sequences of events. An N-gram could predict that a "Dodge, Attack" pattern was being executed. N-grams provide predictions more accurately than raw probability alone.

48.2.2 Enter N-grams

Each N-gram has an order, which is the *N value*. 1-grams, 2-grams, and 3-grams are called *unigrams*, *bigrams*, and *trigrams*. Above that, we use 4-gram, 5-gram, and so on. The *N* value is the length of patterns that the N-gram will recognize (the N-tuples). N-grams step through event sequences in order and count each pattern of *N* events they find. As new events are added to the sequence, N-grams update their internal pattern counts.

Consider a game where we need to predict the player's next move, Left or Right. So far, the player has moved in the following sequence: "R, R, L, R, R". From this, we can compute the following N-grams:

- A unigram works the same as raw probability; it stores: R: 4, L: 1.
- A bigram finds patterns in twos, "RR, RL, LR, RR", and stores: RR: 2, RL: 1, LR: 1.
- A trigram finds patterns by threes, "RRL, RLR, LRR", and stores each pattern once.
- A 4-gram will store RRLR: 1 and RLRR: 1.
- A 5-gram will store the entire sequence once.
- There isn't enough data yet for an N-gram with order greater than 5.

Notice that we store occurrence counts rather than probabilities, which requires less computation. We can perform the divisions later to calculate probabilities when we need them. With patterns learned, our N-grams can now predict the next event.

48.2.3 Predicting with N-grams

A quick note for your math teacher: Technically, N-grams only store statistics and cannot make predictions. In implementation, however, we usually wrap the storage and functionality together. With this in mind, we'll treat our N-grams as the entire prediction system for convenience.

An N-gram predicts by picking out an observed pattern that it thinks is being executed again. To do so, it considers the most recent events in the sequence, and matches them against previously observed patterns. This set of recent events we'll call the *window*. (See Figure 48.1.)

The length of the window is always *N*-1, so each pattern includes one more event than the window length. Patterns "match" the window if their first *N*-1 events are the same. All matching patterns will have a unique *N*th event. The pattern with the most occurrences has the highest probability, so its *N*th event becomes the prediction. No division is required.

Let's see what our N-grams will predict next in the same sequence, "R, R, L, R, R." (See Table 48.1.)

Using N-gram statistics, we can make the following predictions:

- The unigram predicts Right, since it uses raw probability. Its window size is $N - 1 = 0$.
- The bigram has observed two patterns that match its window, RR and RL. Since RR occurred once more than RL, the bigram chooses RR and predicts Right.

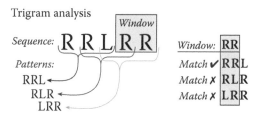

Figure 48.1

The trigram window and observed patterns of the sequence "R, R, L, R, R."

Table 48.1 Assorted N-gram statistics for the sequence,
"R, R, L, R, R"

	Unigram	Bigram	Trigram	4-gram
Window	None	R	RR	LRR
Patterns observed	5	4	3	2
Window matches	R, L	RR, RL	RRL	None
Most occurrences	R: 4	RR: 2	RRL: 1	N/A
Prediction	Right	Right	Left	None

- The trigram finds that only RRL matches its window, so it uses RRL to predict Left.
- The 4-gram has not observed any patterns that start with LRR, so it cannot make a prediction.

In order to make a prediction, N-grams must consider the occurrence counts for all patterns that match the current window. An efficient data structure will facilitate fast pattern lookups. We'll explore good storage options in the implementation section.

48.2.4 Probability of Event Patterns

Equation 48.2 uses occurrence counts of events. N-grams above order 1 count patterns, not events. To calculate pattern probabilities, we need a new formula generalized for any N value.

You don't need to calculate probabilities in order to find the most probable event, as seen previously. However, the probability can be useful in many ways. For example, you might want your AI to ignore a prediction if the probability is too low. As another example, you may want to check the probability of a very meaningful event. Even if the most probable event is Friendly_Handshake with 55%, you might find it useful to know that the probability of a Backstab event is 43%.

Since we are only considering patterns that match the current window, we are now calculating conditional probabilities. This makes the probability of an unmatched pattern equal to 0%. Each matching pattern has a unique Nth event. The probability that an event e will occur next is equal to the probability of the matching pattern containing e as its Nth event, as shown in Equation 48.3.

$$P(event\ e\ is\ next) = P(matching\ pattern\ ending\ in\ e\ is\ next) \qquad (48.3)$$

The probability of a matching pattern is its occurrence count divided by the total occurrences of all matching patterns (all patterns whose first $N–1$ events match the window), as shown in Equation 48.4.

$$P(matching\ pattern\ mp) = \frac{\#\ of\ mp\ occurrences}{Sum\ of\ all\ matching\ pattern\ occurrences} \qquad (48.4)$$

During prediction, you'll likely check the occurrences for all matching patterns to find the max. You can sum them while you're at it, and find the denominator in the same pass.

If needed, you can calculate the probability that an event pattern will occur again anytime in the future, as shown in Equation 48.5. This is a nonconditional probability, as it doesn't use the current window.

$$P\left(event\ pattern\ ep\right)=\frac{\#\ of\ ep\ occurrences}{Sum\ of\ all\ pattern\ occurrences\ so\ far} \qquad (48.5)$$

With the length L of the event sequence, you can calculate the denominator directly:

$$Total\ pattern\ occurrences\ T = L-(N-1) \qquad (48.6)$$

It is simply the sequence length minus the first window. Note that T will be negative when L is less than the window size. If $T < 0$, this means that $|T|+1$ more events are required for a single N length pattern to occur.

48.3 N-Grams Implemented

We now know how N-grams work. Let's cover implementation details to get them ready for a game.

48.3.1 Making a Prediction: I Choose You

You can calculate probabilities for each possible event, but how do you choose one to predict? For example, if a particular N-gram calculated that Right occurred 70% of the time and Left occurred 30% of the time, do you predict Right or Left? You can naively choose the most probable event, in this example Right; however, this isn't your only option. You can tweak your prediction accuracy by varying the selection. There are many ways to do this, such as occasionally choosing a less probable event or choosing an event based on a distribution of probabilities, known as a *weighted random*.

In a weighted random, the percentages calculated by the N-gram for each event give you the percentage chance that you will predict that event. Continuing with the example, to make a prediction, we would roll the dice and predict Right 70% of the time and Left 30% of the time. In this way, the AI prediction doesn't always blindly choose the most probable prediction, and the AI itself becomes less predictable.

48.3.2 Issues with Large Numbers of Events: Show Me Your Moves

Rock-Paper-Scissors only has three possible events. Most games use a lot more than three. Increasing this number has a big effect on an N-gram's storage needs and prediction accuracy.

From combinatorics, each pattern is a permutation of events without repetition. So, with E possible events, E^N total patterns of length N are possible. An N-gram will need to keep counts for E^N different patterns. If $E = 10$ and $N = 6$, $E^N = 1$ million patterns. Some patterns may never occur, especially with large E values. You don't need to store counts for unseen patterns.

Higher order N-grams count longer patterns, so they require longer event sequences to learn from. Larger E values create more pattern possibilities, which raises the sequence length required before an N-gram can make accurate predictions. N-grams learn a style from an event sequence. They need enough exposure to learn the style well. You can't always decrease E, so use the smallest N value possible that still achieves good prediction accuracy.

48.3.3 Adding Robustness

Let's cover a couple situations that will stump an N-gram's predictions in a real game. First we'll describe these two problems, and then we'll offer a solution to address them both. This solution is used in the N-gram library provided with this book.

48.3.3.1 Prediction Failures: Heads or Tails Never Fails

In a simple coin toss, will an N-gram predict heads or tails as the first move? There are no events in the sequence yet, so it will fail to predict anything.

Prediction failures occur when there is no pattern matching the current window. This is always the case when the sequence length L is smaller than N. An N-gram will have to handle this somehow. One method is to report a failure, which nobody likes to check for. A better method is to design the implementation such that it never fails, which we will do below.

48.3.3.2 Unseen Events: Expecting the Unexpected

In a game of *Rock-Paper-Scissors*, a player has made the following moves: "Rock, Paper, Rock, Paper, Rock, Paper." Our N-grams would predict Rock next, and suggest you throw Paper. Assuming a tricky player, what do you think is coming next? Scissors, right?

So far, our N-grams only know of events they've seen. This lowers probability accuracy when the event sequence is too short or unvaried. For more accurate probabilities, you should factor in the possibility that unseen events can occur.

48.3.3.3 Unseen Events: Free Occurrences to the Rescue

With a simple trick, we can provide probabilities for unknown events, and solve the failure problem mentioned previously; we give a single freebie occurrence to each possible pattern.

Let events be represented by an integer ranged $[0, E)$, where E is the number of different event types. Enumerations work well. Give the constraint that E must be provided to our N-gram at initialization. If we need to predict an unseen event, we can simply pick any integer in this range, without caring which game event it even represents.

Actually storing the freebies would be a waste of memory. Instead, we can make them implicit. After looking up an occurrence count, we just add 1 to the count in any calculation. If the pattern is not stored, it's unseen, and we treat the count as $0 + 1$.

We need new probability formulas to account for the implicit freebies. There are always E patterns matching the window, so the probability of the next event becomes:

$$P(matching\ pattern\ mp) = \frac{\#\ of\ mp\ occurrences\ +1}{Sum\ of\ all\ matching\ pattern\ occurrences\ +E} \qquad (48.7)$$

For the probability of an event pattern occurring in the future, remember that there are E^N total patterns possible, and each gets a freebie. Using Equation 48.6, the probability is now:

$$P(event\ pattern\ ep) = \frac{\#\ of\ ep\ occurrences\ +1}{T + E^N} \qquad (48.8)$$

If you really want the probability of an event e occurring in the future, you need the sum of all pattern occurrences that ended in e. However, don't start traversing through all your patterns. Each time an event e occurred, it completed a pattern, right? Yes, aside from in the first $N-1$ events. You can keep a separate list of single event occurrences (a unigram), and a copy of the first window. Don't forget to add in a freebie for all patterns that end in e; there are E^{N-1} of them. The future occurrence probability is now:

$$P(event\ e) = \frac{\#\ of\ e\ occurrences - \#\ of\ e\ in\ first\ window + E^{N-1}}{T + E^N} \qquad (48.9)$$

For the "Rock, Paper, Rock, Paper, Rock, Paper" sequence, our old trigram using Equation 48.4 would have predicted Rock 100%, Paper 0%, and Scissors 0%. Our new trigram using Equation 48.7 will predict Rock 60%, Paper 20%, and Scissors 20%. We've toyed with the probability values by stealing from the rich to give to the poor. This weakens the integrity of the values perhaps, but we can rest assured that they will not change in order from most probable to least. Also, we won't fail if asked to predict the probability of Scissors, which is unseen.

48.3.4 Computation Time: A Need for Speed

At maximum, there will be E matching patterns for a given window. Each time we make a prediction, we need to access the stored occurrence counts for all of them. How expensive are all these searches? Naturally, it depends on your data structure.

The good news is that we can optimize until we only need a single search. If we organize our storage in such a way that *all window matching patterns' counts are stored consecutively in sorted order*, then we'll only need to find the first pattern in a matching set. Afterwards, we can simply increment through the rest for free. A sorted array would perform the search at $O(\log_2 T)$, while a hash table would provide $O(1)$ as usual. A structure such as a prefix tree could provide lookups at $O(N \log_2 E)$ complexity, (where N is the N value), which is pretty good, and is used in the code library provided with this book. Both predictions and Equation 48.7 calculations require the same search, so it is recommended to cache the search result. In practice, probabilities are usually requested with the same window as the prediction (if they are requested at all). If we get a probability request, we can cache the denominator to speed up subsequent requests.

Lookups will also need to be performed whenever a new event is added to the sequence. This will involve incrementing a stored count or inserting a new pattern altogether. As a further optimization, we can keep a max occurrences index and a total count value for each set of matching patterns. Any time we search to add a pattern or increment a pattern's count, we can take the opportunity to update these values. This keeps us from having to walk through all the matching patterns in the set during our next prediction or probability calculation. This has a maximum additional storage requirement of $2E^{N-1}$ values.

In typical usage, you can expect to perform two searches per update: one for updating your N-gram with the latest event, and another for predicting the next event. Any probability requests are free when using the optimizations above.

48.3.5 Ensuring Accurate Predictions: Self-Accountability

On each update, an N-gram is usually provided with an event that occurred since the previous update. This usage allows the N-gram to check if its last prediction was correct

Listing 48.1. A pseudocode algorithm for finding which *N* value provides the highest prediction accuracy for pre-existing event sequences.

```
Instantiate an N-gram for each candidate N value ranged [1,20]
Create accuracy result storage for each N-gram
For each event sequence,
    For each event e ∈ [0,L-1] in the sequence,
        For each N-gram ng,
            store result of e compared to ng.Predict()
            ng.UpdateWithNewEvent(e)
output accuracy results
output N value of most accurate N-gram based on results
```

or not, and provide feedback on its running accuracy for the current sequence. If the accuracy is performing below expectations, your AI can find out about it and switch to plan B. Alternatively, you might ignore predictions until the accuracy reaches an acceptable level.

48.3.6 Which N-Value Provides the Best Prediction?

In practice, choosing the right order for an N-gram is often done by starting with a guess, experimenting, and then adjusting [Millington 06]. With the help of some trustworthy event sequences, we can automate the process of finding which *N* value is right for you. Listing 48.1 shows an example for how to algorithmically find the best *N* value to use based on observed data.

Remember that larger *N* values require increased processing time and memory storage. It's probably best for a human to review the outcomes in order to pick the best compromise of lowest *N* value and good prediction accuracy. You could have each N-gram output its memory usage at the end of each sequence to aid your decision. Upon close inspection, you may find that the most accurate *N* value changed over certain stretches of the sequence. In this case, using multiple N-grams in parallel may offer the best prediction accuracy in your game.

The sequences used must be good representations of real gameplay, so you'll want to write a method to record event sequences from a designer's playthrough. If the new N-gram will alter the next playthrough, you have a feedback loop. Be sure to run through the process again until you're sure your *N* value is well chosen.

The N-gram code provided with this book includes an implementation of the algorithm in Listing 48.1.

48.4 N-Grams in Your Game

Our N-gram is optimized and ready, but there are lots of considerations for integration in a game.

48.4.1 An Event by Any Other Name

N-grams work with events without caring what they really are. Only your game knows what each event actually stands for. They aren't really going to be Rock, Paper, and Scissors.

It's up to you to decide which types of incidents should constitute a unique event in an N-gram. A well picked list will lend itself well to pattern forming, so this is an important task. You may need to play with different approaches to get good results. Consider the different ways you can view events in your game.

For traditional fighting games using complex button combinations, N-grams can use raw controller input to easily predict which combo the player is going to execute. For fighting games without complex button combos, raw controller input may not suffice. It may be better to tokenize these inputs into completed actions, which then become events. Don't lose too much information while tokenizing. A sequence of "Jump, Kick, Land" allows the AI to intervene, while a sequence of only "Jumpkick" does not.

Players often interrupt their course of action in order to respond to the AI. A well-timed kick by the AI may cause the player to perform "Dash, Block" instead of "Dash, Attack." Adding certain AI actions into the event sequence may provide more context to pattern learning. Consider how AI actions affected the sequence.

For RTS games, issued commands can work well as events. Consider grouping commands by type and using separate N-grams for each group. A sequence of "Tease_Oliphaunt, Release_Oliphaunt" should not be separated by several Redundantly_Keep_Miner_Busy commands. Even if the player was spam-clicking on miners, that doesn't need to interrupt the important oliphaunt-angering pattern. You might decide to ignore mining actions altogether. Instead, you could fire an event whenever the player becomes rich enough to build a nontrivial unit. Think about which actions really make a difference.

For uses beyond player prediction, such as procedural generation, only you can know best. Look for branch points and designate events for choices that could define a style. For data using floating-point numbers, try to quantize the data into differentiable thresholds. Turning 2.2, 3.2, 4.2, 6.2 into "Increase1, Increase1, Increase2" creates a pattern you could use.

Your AI needs to determine when an event has occurred. Decide whether to observe state transitions, or rely on messages being received, or some other mechanism.

48.4.2 Predicting the Impossible

In practice, there are event patterns that will never happen. "Sheath_Sword, Draw_Sword" is possible, but "Sheath_Sword, Sheath_Sword" is not. Based on your selection algorithm, your N-gram may predict an impossible pattern. Modifying your N-gram implementation to circumvent this is probably unnecessary. If absolutely needed, your AI can check the prediction returned from the N-gram against a list of invalid patterns before using it.

48.4.3 Dealing with Time Delays

In fighting games like *Street Fighter II*, some special moves require crouching for two seconds before attacking. If the player's last move was crouch, your N-gram must decide between predicting a special move or a normal crouching move. If normal moves are more common, your AI will probably fall victim to the special move every time. Your players will pick up on this very quickly; a golden path is to low-kick twice, then special move once.

This situation might benefit from using time delays as an event. A player doing "Crouch, TimeSecond1, TimeSecond1" will help your N-gram predict that a special attack is forthcoming. Use time events with care, as many time delays can occur unintentionally in normal gameplay. Irrelevant time events sprinkled throughout a sequence will break apart meaningful patterns and wreak havoc on prediction accuracy.

48.4.4 Let's Take This Offline

N-gram learning can take place online or offline. Offline means an event sequence is created during development and the N-gram starts the game with patterns already observed. If you don't allow the N-gram to learn at runtime, it will stick to the style you trained it with during development. The storage requirement will also be fixed, and no update searches are needed.

Online means new events are added to the sequence at runtime. This allows your N-gram to learn new patterns from gameplay. As with any runtime learning technique, this gives your AI the ability to adapt to situations that you haven't anticipated, which should excite you. This includes situations that were never tested, which should scare the crap out of you. Worse still, as shown by the *Street Fighter II* example above, if your players figure out how the AI works then they may be able to find ways to exploit it.

Be sure to keep tight control over the extents of runtime learning. Players are accustomed to outwitting AI; taking advantage of NPCs is a common game mechanic. We want players to do this within the limits we set, so that we can be sure their experience is entertaining. Unearthing a golden path or a crash bug is not the entertainment you want. Your testers should be informed about the learning so they can hammer on it with the appropriate variety. In addition, they should test the learning in very long sessions, to catch problems such as your statistics overflowing, your sequence growing too long, or your pattern storage using too much memory.

48.4.5 Mimicking Style and Procedural Generation

We've mentioned that N-grams can give style to AI, but what does that really mean? Until now, all our examples have been based on recognizing styles in order to predict events, and indeed, this seems to be the most common use in games. N-grams can be trained to control AI according to a consistent style. For example, N-grams can perform procedural generation. Predicting events and choosing actions from a style are functionally equivalent for an N-gram. The real differences are in how and when we use the predictions, event sequence, and window.

We've defined the window to be a set of the last events in the sequence, but this need not be the case. Once an N-gram learns from an event sequence, it can accept any set of $N-1$ events as a window and predict the next event. We can treat the prediction as a creative choice or action. Decoupling the event sequence from the window allows us to separate learning and predicting, like studying a role and then performing it.

We can think of the event sequence as a cookbook that our N-gram memorized, the window as a set of ingredients on hand, and the prediction as the N-gram's completed dish. Present the N-gram with different sets of ingredients, and it will whip up dishes based on how it learned to cook from the event sequence. We could even feed a dish back as an ingredient in the next window, allowing the N-gram to feed off its own output and drive its own patterns.

Say we are building trees for our game using a collection of building blocks, including Start, Trunk, Fork, Branch, Twig, Leaf, and Done. We pick an ordered sequence of: "Start, Trunk, Fork, Branch, Twig, Done, Branch, Twig, Done," and a symmetrical tree appears with a split trunk and a branch and twig on either side. If we were to use this sequence to train a bigram, it would know how to create a tree identical to ours. We could give it the window, "Start," and it would choose, "Trunk." We could return, "Trunk," and it would choose, "Fork." By repeatedly returning its choice as the next window, the bigram would clone our tree. If we built a few different trees with these options, the bigram would create one tree with the most common traits we used. If we added a bit of randomness to its prediction accuracy, it would create a variety of trees in our style, which could populate our game. Accurate and deterministic predictions can work against the N-gram's creativity. There is a time to be creative, and a time to be accurate.

If we restricted prediction of unseen events, the bigram would never create trees with leaves. If unrestricted, it would gently toy with our style by adding a few leaves. It might also try absurd variations such as trunks growing on twigs, so we'd need to watch its output for invalid choices.

Many types of procedural generation can be performed, such as playing music or writing text. You can train an N-gram with the complete text of a book, such as *Green Eggs and Ham*. In this case the text is called the *corpus*. Afterwards, your N-gram can write text to mimic the unique style learned from the corpus. You can play with this in a demo provided on the book's website. You can use N-grams in a game or in a development tool. You can use them here or there. You can use them anywhere.

It's important to note that in the examples in this section, the N-gram is not predicting and learning at the same time. Once your N-gram has learned the style you want, it's time to perform. It can improvise when needed, but it shouldn't be changing its act. Train it up in the way it should behave, and then lock it down so that it won't stray from its style.

48.4.6 Weighting Old versus Recent Events

Thus far our N-grams have remembered each event occurrence equally. For living beings, some actions are more memorable than others. Will it increase prediction accuracy to weight some event occurrences more than others? Applying weights to specific event types will require game-specific information. Weighting events based on time of occurrence could be useful in general.

Applying more weight to older data creates a prediction bias toward the earliest events seen. If an "Approach, Kick" pattern occurred at the beginning of the sequence, an N-gram would still be suspicious of another kick, even if multiple "Approach, Hug" patterns occurred later. This might be utilized as a technique for learning unique styles, such as a puppy whose first impression of someone may forever influence further interaction. If we want accurate predictions, however, then this won't do it. Applying more weight to newer events sounds more promising.

48.4.6.1 Changing with the Times

With longer event sequences, N-grams can better learn the patterns that identify a style. If that style changes, a well-trained N-gram will have difficulty catching up with the times. An N-gram won't predict a new trend until the new patterns obtain higher occurrences than the past patterns. The longer the sequence, the more confident and less flexible an N-gram becomes. This situation arises often when performing player prediction, since players often change their play style. Their style might change upon obtaining a new item, gaining competency in a new ability, or upon simply learning to play the game better. We need a solution that can keep N-grams focused on recent events.

48.4.6.2 Limiting Memory: You Must Unlearn What You Have Learned

If you give your N-gram a limited sequence memory, it will forget old events. This is an all-or-nothing form of weighting recent events, by discarding them once they become stale. You can do this by keeping the event sequence in a queue with a limited size. When the queue is full, each new event will push an old event out. When an old event leaves the queue, you decrement the occurrence counts of matching patterns, thereby forgetting that the event ever occurred. If the entire event sequence is already being stored by another system, your N-gram can keep pointers into it rather than storing its own deep copied queue. This limited memory technique is easy to implement, and can improve prediction accuracy for many games.

When using this technique, picking a good queue size is important. Patterns that occur less frequently than the queue size will not accumulate occurrence counts. This creates a weakness in which uncommon event patterns are never expected. For example, in an RTS, a player might always target the AI's factory with a nuke. Nukes take a long time to build, during which many other events occur. By the time the player's nuke is ready for launch, the N-gram will have forgotten the result of the last nuke, and it won't have a clue where to expect the blast. You might solve this problem by keeping minimum occurrences for all patterns, which would also keep the N-gram from repeatedly adding and removing patterns to and from storage.

48.4.6.3 Focusing on Recent Activity: What's Trending Now

Instead of forgetting old events, another option is to focus on new trends. Your N-gram can keep a small queue of recently completed patterns. This hot-list can be referenced when making predictions, in order to favor the probability of recent activity. When calculating a pattern's probability, a bonus is given if that pattern is currently in the hot-list. This affects caching, since the pattern with the most occurrences may not be the most probable after hot-list bonuses are factored in.

Patterns leave the hot-list over time. If patterns occur when they are already on the hot-list, they are reinserted to remain longer and they get bigger probability bonuses. This helps avoid the problem of forgetting old data altogether, but the extra calculations and hot-list lookups increase processing time during predictions and learning. It's a trade-off you'll only want to explore if needed for your game.

48.4.7 With Great Power Comes Great Responsibility

Memorizing boss patterns and learning their reactions have been the key to victory in many games for over 20 years. N-grams give your AI the power to throw all that back in a player's face. Imagine playing a version of *Punch-Out!!* in which the AI opponents could start predicting your counter-attacks and changing their combos in the middle of the bout. Exciting, yes, but talk about brutal!

N-grams can easily become too powerful [Millington 06]. If your game naturally lends itself well to N-gram prediction, you will probably run into this problem. Rather than trying to hinder the N-gram's prediction prowess, you can have another AI layer intercept the predictions and decide how best to use them. The benefit of the interception layer is that you can still depend on accurate predictions. Rather than being unsure if the player is going to punch or dodge, you can be sure of the punch and have the AI opponent lower its defenses just in time. Accurate predictions are useful for balancing difficulty in either direction.

48.5 Future Research

The following areas are ripe for future research.

48.5.1 Probabilities That Make Sense

We've taken some extreme liberties with probability calculations. Ours will correctly order patterns from least to most probable, but their actual values aren't very meaningful. A good addition would be to factor in error estimation in order to provide meaningful probabilities. Error estimation will likely use the N and E values, sequence length L, and additional information.

48.5.2 Time Exploration

We mentioned the use of a time delay as an event, in order to differentiate patterns that rely on time. The big problem is that unintentional time events occur often, and spamming the sequence with irrelevant time events wreaks havoc on learning. Further exploration on how to use time information would be helpful. A good starting point might be to take a parameter when a new event is added to the sequence, or whenever a prediction is requested. These timestamps might be used in conjunction with feedback to internally discover patterns that rely on a time delay.

48.5.3 What's in an Event?

This article has focused on N-gram implementation and game integration. Event selection is an important consideration that is very game-specific. A survey of various games with real event lists would be a great complement, and would provide more insight on when N-grams are appropriate.

48.5.4 Player Imitation: Jockin' My Style

In the *Forza* series, the Drivatar mode is able to mimic the player's driving style with neural nets. However, for games that can use it, N-grams offer a simpler statistical method to mimic a player's style.

After recording an adequate number of player events, the player's style can be stored as an N-gram's statistics. The N-gram can then be used to control the AI, by using predictions as move choices. This could provide many fun gameplay experiences.

Imagine a game that features cooperative AI. Rather than configure the AI with parameters, a player could perform a playthrough that teaches the AI how to act. If the game allowed sending N-gram statistics to other players, they could play the game with an AI that mimics the experience of playing alongside their friend.

Super Street Fighter IV: 3D Edition allows players to form teams of fighters in the game's Figurine Mode. These teams are sent to other players via the Nintendo 3DS's StreetPass function, after which each player is notified of a battle outcome decided by fighter selection. Such a mode could benefit from N-grams: battles could be decided by actually playing out AI fights using each player's fighting style. In addition, players could then fight the opponent AI directly. Such a feature would allow players a glimpse of how they might fare against someone they'll never get to challenge, such as a game designer, a celebrity, a tournament champion, etc. Of course, N-grams cannot fully copy the experience of playing against a real person, but they are capable of mimicking some of the most easily identifiable patterns. The trick is determining which aspects are most identifiable.

Games particularly suitable for this technique are those in which the move selection itself identifies a style. In *Pokémon Ruby Version* and *Pokémon Sapphire Version*, players can set up their own secret base and send it to their friends. Inside a friend's secret base will be an AI-controlled version of that friend, whom the player can battle against. This AI clone already captures many identifying characteristics of the player, such as a unique avatar, salutation, and Pokémon team selection. The AI version will use the same moves as the player it is personifying, but it does so in unexpected patterns, such as charging up an attack and then not unleashing it. This scenario practically begs for the use of N-grams. By simply repeating the move patterns observed from the original player, the AI's imitation would become drastically more accurate of the player's battling style. In well-matched scenarios like this one, N-grams can provide a social experience that is largely untapped in today's games.

48.6 Conclusion

N-grams find patterns in sequences of events. They are good at learning to predict a player's actions at runtime, enabling your AI to compete or cooperate effectively, and balancing difficulty. Further, N-grams can be taught to act according to a style. They can perform procedural generation with consistency. They require little processing to choose their course of action. Lastly, N-grams are easy to implement. Using them in your game usually requires more work than implementing them alone. Properly designating events is of critical importance to an N-gram's pattern recognition, while identifying new types of events in your game will provide new ways for you to leverage N-grams.

References

[Laramée 02] F. D. Laramée. "Using N-gram statistical models to predict player behavior." In *AI Game Programming Wisdom*, edited by Steve Rabin. Hingham, MA: Charles River Media, 2002.

[Millington 06] I. Millington. *Artificial Intelligence for Games*. San Francisco, CA: Morgan Kaufmann, 2006, pp. 580–591.

Index